The Western Heritage

Since 1648

VOLUME

The Western Heritage

Second Edition

Since 1648

Donald Kagan   YALE UNIVERSITY

Steven Ozment   HARVARD UNIVERSITY

Frank M. Turner   YALE UNIVERSITY

Macmillan Publishing Co., Inc.

NEW YORK

NOTE
The dates cited for monarchs and popes are generally the years of their reign rather than of their
births and deaths.

Macmillan Publishing Co., Inc.
866 Third Avenue, New York, New York 10022

Collier Macmillan Canada, Inc.

Library of Congress Cataloging in Publication Data

Kagan, Donald.
  The Western Heritage.

  Includes bibliographies and indexes.
  Contents: v. 1. To 1715— v. 2. Since 1648.
  1. Civilization, Occidental.   I. Ozment, Steven E.
II. Turner, Frank M. (Frank Miller), Date.
III. Title.
CB245.K28   1983b   909'.09821   82-20365

ISBN   0-02-362390-X

Printing: 2 3 4 5 6 7 8   Year: 3 4 5 6 7 8 9 0

Preface

I
N REVISING *The Western Heritage* we have ben-
efitted from the advice and teaching experience of
fellow historians across the country. Scores of our
professional colleagues sent us or our publisher
suggestions for improvements. More than a dozen
readers drawn from diverse institutions and areas
of historical specialization formally evaluated and
criticized our first edition and early drafts of the
revision. We read and carefully considered all of
these ideas, and we adopted many of them. Consequently, this revision has emerged from a genuinely cooperative effort between authors and
readers.

The result of this cooperation is a new, substantially reshaped edition of *The Western Heritage*.
Readers of our previous volume will note a con-
densation of materials on ancient military history
and the inclusion of a new section on the culture of
the early Roman Republic. We have expanded and
reorganized in a major fashion the coverage of
the Middle Ages, the Renaissance, and the Reformation. The sections on the medieval Catholic

Church, popular religion, Islam, economic life,
and social history have been enlarged. There are
new or expanded treatments of virtually every aspect of the Renaissance. The previous two chapters
on the Reformation have been condensed into one,
and the ideas and events of the Catholic Reformation have received broader coverage. A new section
on medieval Russia provides background for the
reforms of Peter the Great. The discussion of the
industrial revolution is more extensive as is that of
Romanticism. Consideration of Europe since 1945
has been extended to cover the major events of the
last few years. Further revisions in the organization, the prose style, and the section-headings appear in every chapter.

We have also included revised supplementary
materials to aid the teaching and comprehension of
the text itself. Most significantly, we have introduced into every chapter chronological tables of
major events. More than a third of the documents
and illustrations are new, and we have attempted
to integrate them more closely with our general

narrative. We have revised to bring up to date all the bibliographies while attempting to retain many useful older titles.

Our purpose in all of these revisions has been to produce a text that is clear, informative, interesting, and teachable. Just as the revision of a textbook is a joint effort between authors and readers, so the use of a textbook is a joint effort between teachers and students. We hope that this volume will enchance and enliven that latter relationship.

D.K.
S.O.
F.M.T.

New Haven and Cambridge

Contents

Documents

xix

Maps

by Theodore R. Miller

Illustrations in Color

[21] *William Hogarth (1697–1764) did immensely popular paintings and etchings of scenes from the rich variety of English life in the eighteenth century. He was frequently satirical and witty, and his works make up a realistic survey of society from top to bottom. The dissolute party shown here is The Orgy, third in a series called "The Rake's Progress. It dates from approximately 1734 and is in the Sir John Soane's Museum, London. [The Granger Collection.]*

[22] *Even when past the height of its medieval commercial power, Venice in the eighteenth century was a wealthy and unusually picturesque city. One of the numerous painters of its canals, festivals, and buildings was Giovanni Antonio Canaletto (1697–1768), represented here by his Stonemason's Yard, a behind-the-scenes picture of a humbler, seamier side of the city than that usually painted. Painted near 1740, it is in the National Gallery, London. [The Granger Collection.]*

[23] With *A Pilgrimage to Cythera*, Antoine Watteau gained entry to the Paris Royal Academy of Painting and Sculpture in 1717. The painting, which is now in the Louvre, is typical of Watteau's work, which usually shows scenes of upper-class life in outdoor settings. In this painting, a group of young couples has spent the day on Cythera, the island of love (a flower-draped statue of Venus, the goddess of love, is at the far right). We see them as they are about to board the boat back to the mainland after what appears to have been a very pleasant day. [Editorial Photocolor Archives.]

[24] In a painting attributed to Pietro Longhi (1702–1785), *The Banquet at the Palazzo Nani*, we see a self-conscious party of aristocratic Venetian ladies and gentlemen posing at a large formal dinner. The picture is in the Ca' Rezzonico in Venice. [SCALA/Editorial Photocolor Archives.]

[25] *George Stubbs (1724–1806) was an artist with a special—even scientific—interest in animals, a concern that led him to dissect horses in order to get the creatures' anatomy just right. His works have been eagerly collected in this century. Lady and Gentleman in a Carriage (1787), seen here, is in the National Gallery, London. [The Granger Collection.]*

[26] *Venice may have declined as a commercial power, but as a subject for its own artists and for those of other countries it was ever fascinating. In the generation following Canaletto, Francesco Guardi (1712–1793), as in this view of the Piazza San Marco, carried on the tradition of recording the city that was itself rapidly becoming a museum. The painting hangs in the National Gallery, London. [The Granger Collection.]*

[27] *In The Death of Socrates, Jacques Louis David (1748–1825) extolls the values of discipline and idealistic self-sacrifice through his choice of subject and the austere precision with which he depicts it. The ascetic idealism of this painting anticipates David's involvement in the French Revolution. This painting is in the Metropolitan Museum of Art in New York.* [Bettmann Archive.]

[28] *The crucial naval battle of Trafalgar in 1805 between the English and the French fleets quickly caught the imagination of the English artist Joseph Mallard William Turner (1775–1851). He visited Nelson's ship immediately on its return to England with the admiral's body and in 1806 exhibited his first painting of the battle. The picture here (from the National Maritime Museum, London) is a later one (1820). Nelson's flagship,* Victory, *is in the center at the height of the battle.* [The Granger Collection.]

[29]   *The work of the Spanish artist Francisco Goya (1746–1828), like David's, spanned Old Regime, Revolution, Napoleon, and Restoration. In 1814 he painted The Third of May 1808 in continuing revulsion and protest over the gunning down of Spanish hostages by French troops during the Napoleonic invasion of Spain. It remains a powerful indictment of human brutality and the horror of war. The painting is in the Prado, Madrid. [SCALA/Editorial Photocolor Archives.]*

[30] *The painter John Constable (1776–1837) failed to find wide popularity in his lifetime. He kept his attention on the peaceful English countryside that was destined to become the victim of industry, railways, and mines, and today we find his work an important record of a different world. This is his Haywain, painted in 1821. It hangs now in the National Gallery, London. [The Granger Collection.]*

[31] *The Funeral at Ornans (1849) by Gustave Courbet (1819–1877) shows an abandonment of the Romantic traditions of emotion and imagination in favor of a more realistic and naturalistic style. Courbet was born in the village of Ornans, and he often chose rural subjects for his work. This painting beautifully captures the somber dignity of a rural funeral. Note how the clergy and men are grouped on the left and the women on the right. This painting is in the Louvre. [The Granger Collection.]*

[32]   *The hard, never-ending physical labor of the agricultural poor is the subject of* The Gleaners *by the Frenchman Jean François Millet (1814–1875). Millet is often thought over-sentimental, but this 1857 picture is a strong record of the necessary way of life of millions in the nineteenth century. It is in the Louvre, Paris. [The Granger Collection.]*

[33]   *Although classified as a Romantic artist, Honoré Daumier (1808–1879) often depicted the realities of daily life.* The Burden *(1858–1860) is a sympathetic portrayal of an overworked working-class woman and her child. The painting is in the Musee des Beaux-Arts at Dijon. [The Granger Collection.]*

[34] *Nineteenth-century Romanticism reached, literally, a reckless height in the castle of Neuschwanstein, ordered by the unstable King Ludwig II of the south German state of Bavaria. When the castle was built between 1858 and 1886, art and literature had taken on a character of realism; but architecture tended to remain elaborate and ornate— although Neuschwanstein in its spectacular setting was, of course, too extreme to be typical.* [*The Granger Collection.*]

[35] *In The Bar at the Folies-Berberes (1882), Edouard Manet (1832–1883) has created a remarkable sense of stillness in the midst of great activity. The pensive barmaid seems completely withdrawn and remote from the festive crowd reflected in the mirror behind her. This lack of emotion typifies Manet's work; his paintings have been characterized as "pictures of pictures." This painting is in London's Courtauld Institute. [The Granger Collection.]*

[36] *The railway figures also in The Station at Penge (1871) by Camille Pissarro (1831–1903). Railroads caused a transportation revolution in the nineteenth century comparable to that of air travel in our own day, and artists were not long in creating a new kind of landscape that incorporated the new technological development. The machine, artists found, had esthetics of its own. This picture is in the Courtauld Institute, London. [The Granger Collection.]*

[37] *The Moulin de la Galette (1876) is by Pierre Auguste Renoir (1841–1919). One aspect of Parisian bourgeois leisure activity is illustrated in this painting of everyday friends of the artist enjoying the wine and the dancing at an outdoor café. The work is in the Louvre, Paris.* [The Granger Collection.]

[38] *This 1889 painting, The Starry Night by the Dutchman Vincent van Gogh (1853–1890), breaks out of earlier, more staid views of nature and the landscape. To van Gogh the heavens themselves are an exciting theater of colorful and continuing movement.* [The Museum of Modern Art, New York.]

[39] *At the age of thirty-five, Paul Gauguin (1848–1903) abandoned his family and left a successful career as a Parisian stockbroker in order to devote his life to painting. Gauguin believed that the materialism and industrialism of the West thwarted man's innate emotionalism. His search for a more natural, unspoiled way of life led him to Tahiti. He spent the rest of his life in the South Pacific, where he glorified the natives and their way of life in such works as* Two Women of Tahiti *(1889). [The Granger Collection.]*

[40] *Paul Cézanne (1839–1906) painted several pictures called The Card Players. Like the others, this one from about 1890 captures the personalities of its (probably) working-class subjects and is a realistic, unromanticized view of ordinary life. The painting is in the Jeu de Paume, Paris. [The Granger Collection.]*

[41] *Although the subject is too broad for such a narrow definition, "modern art" for many means abstract, nonrepresentational painting and sculpture. This aspect of modern painting is illustrated by the colorful Panel (3) by the Russian-French artist Wassily Kandinsky (1866–1944). Note that "modern" antedates World War I, for this work was painted in 1914. [The Museum of Modern Art, New York.]*

[42] *In contrast to Kandinsky's wild splashes of color, Dutch artist Piet Mondrian (1872–1944) used severe vertical and horizontal lines and precise blocks of primary colors, black, and white in many of his abstract paintings. Composition in Grey, Red, Yellow, and Blue (1920) is an example of a totally nonrepresentational style that Mondrian called Neo-Plasticism. [The Granger Collection.]*

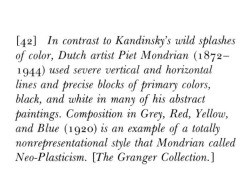

C-28

[43] *Perhaps the best known painter of recent years is the Spaniard Pablo Picasso (1881–1973). His art went through a number of phases. The picture shown here, Three Musicians, comes from 1921 when he was interested in breaking his subjects down into planes, lines, and geometric bodies. [The Museum of Modern Art. New York.]*

C-29

[44] *The dream-like world of Surrealism is seen in Painting (1949) by Joan Miró (born 1893). Surrealism borrowed many concepts from psychoanalytic theory and sought to express the pure process of thought and creativity, unhampered by convention or rationality. Miró's expressive shapes and forms show great energy and fluidity and invite the viewer to make his or her own interpretations of their meaning. [The Granger Collection.]*

[45 OPPOSITE] *Family Group by the Englishman Henry Moore (born 1898) is a large bronze statue from the 1940s by one of the leading sculptors of the last few decades, most of whose pieces are effectively planned for outdoor display. This one is more clearly representational than others. [The Museum of Modern Art, New York.]*

C-31

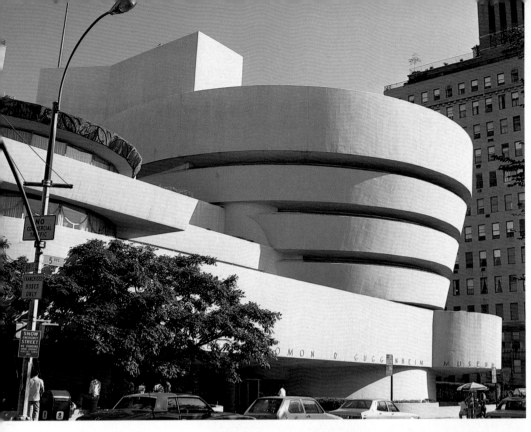

[46 LEFT] *Renowned architect Frank Lloyd Wright (1857–1959) designed the striking Solomon R. Guggenheim Museum of Art in New York City. The museum, which opened on October 21, 1959, is the home of the Solomon R. Guggenheim Foundation of Art, which supports and encourages nonobjective art.* [*Photo © Ann Chwatsky, 1978. Editorial Photocolor Archives.*]

[47 RIGHT] *The Georges Pompidou National Center of Art and Culture in Paris, named for a recent president of France, was built in the 1970s to designs by an Italian-English team of architects, Renzo Piano and Richard Rogers. We spoke earlier of a Gothic structure's "skeleton" being, in a sense, external and visible. Here the designers have managed to make the building appear to be almost all skeleton and in the meantime have achieved a colorful display of its engineering and functional elements.* [*French Government Tourist Office, New York.*]

C-32

The Western Heritage

Since 1648

466

16 England and France in the Seventeenth Century

Constitutional Crisis and Settlement in Stuart England

Between 1603 and 1715 England experienced the most tumultuous years of its long history. In this period Puritan resistance to the Elizabethan religious settlement merged with fierce parliamentary opposition to the aspirations to absolute monarchy of the Stuart kings. During these years no fewer than three foreigners occupied the English throne, and between 1649 and 1660 England was without a king altogether. Yet by the end of this century of crisis England provided a model to Europe of limited monarchy, parliamentary government, and measured religious toleration.

Louis the XIV of France, the dominant political figure in Europe in the second half of the seventeenth century. Known as the Sun King, Louis built his spectacular palace at Versailles as a testament to his glorification of the monarchy. [New York,Public Library Picture Collection.]

James I

The first of England's foreign monarchs was James VI of Scotland (the son of Mary Stuart, Queen of Scots), who in 1603 succeeded the childless Elizabeth as James I of England. This first Stuart king inherited not only the crown but also a royal debt of almost one-half million pounds, a fiercely divided church, and a Parliament already restive over the extent of his predecessor's claims to royal authority. Under James each of these problems worsened. The new king utterly lacked tact, was ignorant of English institutions, and strongly advocated the divine right of kings, a subject on which he had written a book in 1598 entitled *A Trew Law of Free Monarchies*. He rapidly alienated both Parliament and the politically powerful Puritans.

The breach with Parliament was opened by James's seeming usurpation of the power of the purse. Royal debts, his own extravagance, and an inflation he could not control made it necessary for the king to be constantly in quest of additional revenues. These he sought largely by levying—solely on the authority of ill-defined privileges claimed to be attached to the office of king—new custom duties known as "impositions." These were a version of the older such duties known as tonnage and poundage. Parliament resented such independent efforts to raise revenues as an affront to its power, and the result was a long and divisive court struggle between the king and Parliament.

As the distance between king and Parliament widened, the religious problems also worsened. The Puritans, who were prominent among the lesser landed gentry and within Parliament, had hoped that James's experience with the Scottish Presbyterian church and his own Protestant upbringing would incline him to favor their efforts to "purify" the Anglican church. Since the days of Elizabeth the Puritans had sought to eliminate elaborate religious ceremonies and to replace the hierarchical episcopal system of church governance with a more representative presbyterian form like that of the Calvinist churches on the Continent. In January 1604 they had their first direct dealing with the new king. James responded in that month to a statement of Puritan grievances, the so-called Millenary Petition, at a special religious conference at Hampton Court. To the dismay of the Puritans the king firmly declared his intention to maintain and even enhance the Anglican episcopacy. "A Scottish presbytery," he snorted, "agreeth as well with monarchy as God and the devil. No bishops, no king." Nonconformists were clearly forewarned.

Both sides departed the conference with their worst suspicions of one another largely confirmed, and as the years passed, the distrust between them only deepened. It was during James's reign in 1620 that Puritan separatists founded Plymouth Colony in Cape Cod Bay in North America, preferring flight from England to Anglican conformity. The Hampton Court conference did, however, sow one fruitful seed. A commission was appointed to render a new translation of the Bible, a mission fulfilled in 1611 when the eloquent Authorized or King James Version of the Bible was published.

Though he inherited major political and religious difficulties, James also created special problems for himself. His court became a center of scandal and corruption. He governed by favorites, the most influential of whom was the duke of Buckingham, whom rumor made the king's homosexual lover. Buckingham controlled royal patronage and openly sold peerages and titles to the highest bidders—a practice that angered the nobility because it cheapened their rank. James's pro-Spanish foreign policy also displeased the English. In 1604 he concluded a much needed peace with Spain, England's chief adversary during the second half of the sixteenth century. His subjects viewed is as a sign of pro-Catholic sentiment. James further increased suspicions when he attempted unsuccessfully to relax the penal laws against Catholics. The English had not forgotten the brutal reign of Mary Tudor and the acts of treason by Catholics during Elizabeth's reign. In 1618 James hesitated, not unwisely, to rush English troops to the aid of Protestants in Germany at the outbreak of the Thirty Years' War. This hesitation caused his loyalty to the Anglican church to be openly questioned by some. In the king's last years, as his health failed and the reins of government were increasingly given over to his son Charles and Buckingham, parliamentary power and Protestant sentiment combined to undo his pro-Spanish foreign policy, which had also failed to meet the king's own expectations. In 1624 England entered a continental war against Spain.

James I feasting with the Spanish ambassadors, 1624. James's policy of peace with Spain was unpopular with many of his subjects, but the king persevered with it for most of his reign, even negotiating unsuccessfully in 1623 for a marriage between his heir, the future Charles I, and a Spanish princess. [BBC Hulton Picture Library.]

Charles I

Charles I (1625–1649) flew even more brazenly in the face of Parliament and the Puritans than did his father. Unable to gain adequate funds from Parliament for the Spanish war, Charles, like his father, resorted to extraparliamentary measures. He levied new tariffs and duties, attempted to collect discontinued taxes, and even subjected the English people to a so-called forced loan (a tax theoretically to be repaid), imprisoning those who refused to pay. Troops in transit to war zones were quartered in private English homes.

When Parliament met in 1628, its members were furious. Taxes were being illegally collected for a war that was going badly for England and that now, through royal blundering, involved France as well as Spain. Parliament expressed its displeasure by making the king's request for new funds conditional on his recognition of the Petition of Right. This major document of constitutional freedom declared that henceforth there should be no forced loans or taxation without the consent of Parliament, that no freeman should be imprisoned without due cause, and that troops should not be billeted in private homes. Though Charles agreed to the petition, there was little confidence that he would keep his word.

In August 1628 Charles's chief minister, Buckingham, with whom Parliament had been in open dispute since 1626, was assassinated. His death, while sweet to many, did not resolve the hostility between king and Parliament. In January 1629 Parliament further underscored its resolve to limit royal prerogative. It declared that religious innovations leading to "popery"—Charles's high-church policies were meant—and the levying of taxes without parliamentary consent were acts of treason. Perceiving that things were getting out of hand, Charles promptly dissolved Parliament and did not recall it again until 1640, when war with Scotland forced him to do so.

To conserve his limited resources, Charles made peace with France and Spain in 1629 and 1630, respectively. His chief minister, Thomas Wentworth (after 1640 earl of Stafford), instituted a policy known as "thorough," that is, strict efficiency and administrative centralization in government. This policy aimed at absolute royal control of England and required for its success the king's ability to operate independently of Parliament. Every legal fund-raising device was exploited to the full. Neglected laws suddenly were enforced, and existing

Portrait of King Charles I of England hunting, by Anthony van Dyck (1599–1641). Charles was executed by order of Parliament in 1649 following the rise to power of Oliver Cromwell who, among other things, then sold the royal picture collection, so that this portrait is now in France. [Musée du Louvre, Paris. Cliché des Musées Nationaux.]

taxes were extended into new areas. An example of the latter tactic was the inland collection of "ship money." This tax normally was levied only on coastal areas to pay for naval protection, but after 1634 it was gradually applied to the whole of England, interior and coastal towns alike. A great landowner named John Hampden unsuccessfully challenged its extension in a close legal contest. Although the king prevailed, it was a costly victory, for it deepened the animosity toward him among the powerful landowners, who both elected and sat in Parliament.

Charles had neither the royal bureaucracy nor the standing army to rule as an absolute monarch. This became abundantly clear when he and his re-

469

❧ Parliament Attacks Charles I's Royal Abuses of His Subjects ▬▬▬

The tension between King Charles I (1625–1649) and Parliament had very few causes that did not go back to earlier reigns. The Petition of Right can, therefore, be seen as a general catalog of reasons for opposing arbitrary royal power. Specifically, angered by Charles and his levying of new taxes and other revenue-gathering devices, his coercion of freemen, and his quartering of troops in transit in private homes, Parliament refused to grant the king any funds until he rescinded such practices by recognizing the Petition of Right (June 7, 1628). Here is the Petition and the king's reply.

[The Lords Spiritual and Temporal, and Commons in Parliament assembled] do humbly pray your Most Excellent Majesty, that no man hereafter be compelled to make or yield any gift, loan, benevolence, tax, or such like charge, without common consent by Act of Parliament; and that none be called to make answer, or take such oath, or to give attendance, or be confined, or otherwise molested or disquieted concerning the same, or for refusal thereof; and that no freeman, in any such manner as is before-mentioned, be imprisoned or detained; and that your Majesty will be pleased to remove the said soldiers and mariners [who have been quartered in private homes], and that your people may not be so burdened in time to come; and that the foresaid commissions for proceeding by martial law, may be revoked and annulled; and that hereafter no commissions of like

nature may issue forth to any person or persons whatsoever, to be executed as aforesaid, lest by colour of them any of your Majesty's subjects be destroyed or put to death, contrary to the laws and franchise of the land.

All which they most humbly pray of your Most Excellent Majesty, as their rights and liberties according to the laws and statutes of this realm.

[The King's reply: The King willeth that right be done according to the laws and customs of the realm; and that the statutes be put in due execution, that his subjects may have no cause to complain of any wrong or oppressions, contrary to their just rights and liberties, to the preservation whereof he holds himself as well obliged as of his prerogative.]

The Constitutional Documents of the Puritan Revolution, ed. by Samuel R. Gardiner (Oxford, England: Clarendon Press, 1889), pp. 4–5.

---

ligious minister, William Laud (1573–1645; after 1633 the archbishop of Canterbury), provoked a war with Scotland. They tried to impose the English episcopal system and a prayer book almost identical to the Anglican *Book of Common Prayer* on the Scots as they had done throughout England. From his position within the Court of High Commission, Laud had already radicalized the Puritans by denying them the right to publish and preach.

Facing resistance from the Scots, Charles was forced to seek financial assistance from a Parliament that opposed his policies almost as much as the foreign invaders. Led by John Pym (1584–1643), Parliament refused even to consider funds for war until the king agreed to redress a long list of political and religious grievances. The result was the king's immediate dissolution of Parliament—hence its name, the Short Parliament (April–May 1640). When the Presbyterian Scots invaded England and defeated an English army at the battle of Newburn in the summer of 1640, Charles found himself forced to reconvene Parliament. This time it was on the latter's terms and for what would be a long and most fateful duration.

THE LONG PARLIAMENT. The landowners and the merchant classes represented by Parliament had resented the king's financial measures and paternalistic rule for some time. To this resentment was added fervent Puritan opposition. Hence the Long Parliament (1640–1660) acted with widespread support and general unanimity when it convened in November 1640. Both the earl of Stafford and Archbishop Laud were impeached by the House of Commons. Disgraced and convicted by a

The House of Commons in session in 1648 toward the end of the Civil War, as seen in a contemporary engraving. [The Granger Collection.]

Parliamentary bill of attainder (a judgment of treason entailing loss of civil rights), Stafford was executed in 1641. Laud was imprisoned and later executed (1645). The Court of Star Chamber and the Court of High Commission, royal instruments of political and religious "thorough," respectively, were abolished. The levying of new taxes without consent of Parliament and the inland extension of ship money now became illegal. Finally, it was resolved that no more than three years should elapse between meetings of Parliament and that Parliament could not be dissolved without its own consent.

Marxist historians have seen in these measures a major triumph of the "bourgeoisie" over the aristocracy. But lesser aristocratic groups (the gentry) were actually divided between the parliamentary and royal camps, so more was obviously at issue than simple class warfare. The accomplishment of the Long Parliament was to issue a firm and lasting declaration of the political and religious rights of the many English people represented in Parliament, both high and low, against autocratic royal government.

There remained division within Parliament over the precise direction of religious reform. Both moderate Puritans (the Presbyterians) and extreme Puritans (the Independents) wanted the complete abolition of the episcopal system and the *Book of Common Prayer*. The majority Presbyterians sought to reshape England religiously along Calvinist lines, with local congregations subject to higher representative governing bodies (presbyteries). Independents wanted every congregation to be its own final authority. There were also a considerable number of conservatives in both houses who were determined to preserve the English church in its current form, although their numbers fell dramatically after 1642, when those who sympathized with the present Anglican church departed the House of Commons.

The division within Parliament was further intensified in October 1641, when a rebellion erupted in Ireland requiring an army to suppress it. Pym and his followers, loudly reminding the House of Commons of the king's past misdeeds, argued that Charles could not be trusted with an army and that Parliament should become the com-

EUROPE IN 1648

Legend:
- SWEDISH DOMINIONS
- BRANDENBURG-PRUSSIA
- SPANISH MONARCHY
- AUSTRIA HAPSBURGS
- CHURCH LANDS

BOUNDARY OF THE EMPIRE

NORWAY
Bergen
Christiana
Stavanger

KINGDOM OF DENMARK AND NORWAY

SWEDEN
Stockholm
FINLAND

ESTO...
LIVO...
Ri...
COURLAND
Meme...
E... PRUS...

Danzig
Copenhagen
BALTIC SEA

DENMARK
SCHLESWIG
HOLSTEIN

Posen
Warsaw
P...

SCOTLAND
Edinburgh

NORTH SEA

Belfast
IRELAND
Dublin
York
Cork
ENGLAND
WALES
London
Bristol
Plymouth

ATLANTIC

UNITED PROVINCES
SPANISH NETH.
Brussels

BRANDEN-BURG
SAXONY

Breslau
SILESIA
Cracow
G...

MINOR GERMAN STATES
HESSE

BOHEMIA
Prague
MORAVIA

HUNGARY
Pressburg
Buda...

Rouen
Reims
Paris
Orleans
Tours

OCEAN

FRANCE

FRANCHE-COMTÉ

BAVARIA

AUSTRIA HAPSBURG
Vienna

HUNG...

Lyons

SWITZ.

SAVOY
PIED-MONT
AVIGNON
Marseilles

MILAN
PAR.
MOD.
Genoa
LUCCA
Bologna

VENICE
Venice

VEN.
Spalato
(VEN.)

CROATIA
SLAVONIA
SAVA
BOSNIA
SER...

Bordeaux
Toulouse
LANGUEDOC

León
NAVARRE
Burgos
Salamanca
Saragossa
CASTILE
ARAGON
Barcelona

Oporto
PORTUGAL
Lisbon

Madrid
Toledo
SPAIN
Cordova
Seville
Granada
Cadiz

BALEARIC IS.

CORSICA (GEN.)
TUSCANY

PAPAL STATES
ITALY
Rome

BELG...
MONT-NEGRO
REP. RAGUSA
Cattaro (VEN.)
ALBA...

SARDINIA (SP.)

Capua
Naples
Bari

KINGDOM OF THE TWO SICILIES

SICILY

Tangier (PORT.)
Ceuta (SP.)
FEZ & MOROCCO

Algiers
ALGERIA

Tunis (OTT.)

MEDITERRANEAN SEA

mander-in-chief of English armed forces. Parliamentary conservatives, who had winced once at Puritan religious reforms, winced thrice at this bold departure from English practice. On December 1, 1641, Parliament presented Charles with the "Grand Remonstrance," a more-than-200-article summary of popular and parliamentary grievances against the crown.

Charles saw the division within Parliament as a last chance to regain power. In January 1642 he invaded Parliament with his soldiers. He intended to arrest Pym and the other leaders, but they had been forewarned and managed to escape. Shocked by the king's action, a majority of the House of Commons thereafter passed the Militia Ordinance, a measure that gave Parliament control of the army. The die was now cast. For the next four years (1642–1646) civil war engulfed England.

Charles assembled his forces at Nottingham, and in August the civil war began. The main issues were whether England would be ruled by an absolute monarchy or by a parliamentary government and whether English religion would be conformist high Anglican and controlled by the king's bishops or cast into a more decentralized, presbyterian system of church governance. Charles's supporters, known as *Cavaliers*, were located in the northwestern half of England. The parliamentary opposition, known as *Roundheads* because of their close-cropped hair, had its stronghold in the southeastern half of the country. The nobility, identifying the power of their peerage with the preservation of the current form of the monarchy and the church, became prominent supporters of the king, whereas the townspeople supported the Parliamentary army.

Oliver Cromwell and the Puritan Republic

Two factors led finally to Parliament's victory. The first was an alliance with Scotland in 1643 consummated when John Pym persuaded Parliament to accept the terms of the Solemn League and Covenant, an agreement committing Parliament, with the Scots, to a presbyterian system of church government. The second was the reorganization of the parliamentary army under Oliver

MAP 16.1 *At the end of the Thirty Years' War Spain still had extensive possessions, Austria and Brandenburg-Prussia were prominent, the independence of the United Provinces and Switzerland was recognized, and Sweden held important river mouths in north Germany.*

473

A Portrait of Oliver Cromwell

Statesman and historian Edward Hyde, the earl of Clarendon (1609–1674), was an enemy of Oliver Cromwell. However, his portrait of Cromwell, which follows, mixes criticism with grudging admiration for the Puritan leader.

He was one of those men whom his enemies cannot condemn without at the same time also praising. For he could never have done half that mischief without great parts of courage and industry and judgment. And he must have had a wonderful understanding of the natures and humours of men and a great dexterity in applying them . . . [to] raise himself to such a height. . . .

When he first appeared in the Parliament, he seemed to have a person in no degree gracious, no ornament of discourse, none of those talents which reconcile the affections of the standers-by; yet as he grew into his place and authority, his parts seemed to be renewed, as if he concealed faculties til he had occasion to use them. . . .

After he was confirmed and invested Protector . . . he consulted with very few . . . nor communicated any enterprise he resolved upon with more than those who were to have principal parts in the execution of it; nor to them sooner than was absolutely necessary. What he once resolved . . . he would not be dissuaded

from, nor endure any contradiction. . . .

In all other matters which did not concern . . . his jurisdiction, he seemed to have great reverence for the law. . . . And as he proceeded with . . . indignation and haughtiness with those who were refractory and dared to contend with his greatness, so towards those who complied with his good pleasure, and courted his protection, he used a wonderful civility, generosity, and bounty.

To reduce three nations [England, Ireland, and Scotland], which perfectly hated him, to an entire obedience to all his dictates; to awe and govern those nations by an army that was not devoted to him and wished his ruin; this was an instance of a very prodigious address. But his greatness at home was but a shadow of the glory he had abroad. It was hard to discover which feared him most, France, Spain, or the Netherlands. . . . As they did all sacrifice their honour and their interest to his pleasure, so there is nothing he could have demanded that any of them would have denied him.

James Harvey Robinson (Ed.), *Readings in European History*, Vol. 2 (Boston: Ginn and Co., 1906), pp. 248–250.

Cromwell (1599–1658), a middle-aged country squire of iron discipline and strong Independent religious sentiment. Cromwell and his "godly men" favored neither the episcopal system of the king nor the pure presbyterian system of the Solemn League and Covenant. They were willing to tolerate an established majority church, but only if it also permitted Protestant dissenters to worship outside it. The allies won the Battle of Marston Moor in 1644, the largest engagement of the war, and in June 1645 Cromwell's New Model Army, which fought with a disciplined fanaticism, decisively defeated the king at Naseby.

Though defeated militarily, Charles again took advantage of the deep divisions within Parliament, this time seeking to win the Presbyterians and the Scots over to the royalist side. But Cromwell's army firmly imposed its will. In December 1648 Colonel Thomas Pride physically barred the Presbyterians, who made up a majority of Parliament, from taking their seats. After "Pride's Purge," only a "rump" of less than fifty members remained. Though small in numbers, this Independent Rump Parliament had supreme military power within England. It did not hesitate to use this power. On January 30, 1649, after trial by a special court, it executed Charles as a public criminal and thereafter abolished the monarchy, the House of Lords, and the Anglican church. The revolution was consummated by events hardly contemplated at its outset.

From 1649 to 1660 England became officially a Puritan republic. During this period Cromwell's army conquered Ireland and Scotland, creating the single political entity of Great Britain. Cromwell, however, was a military man and no politician.

Oliver Cromwell. Cromwell's New Model Army defeated the royalists in the English Civil War. After the execution of Charles I in 1649, Cromwell dominated the short-lived English republic, conquered Ireland and Scotland and ruled as Lord Protector from 1653 until his death in 1658. This bust was made in 1766 by Joseph Wilton. [Victoria and Albert Museum.]

He was increasingly frustrated by what seemed to him to be pettiness and dawdling on the part of Parliament. When in 1653 the House of Commons entertained a motion to disband the expensive army of fifty thousand men, Cromwell responded by marching in and disbanding Parliament. He ruled thereafter as Lord Protector.

But his military dictatorship proved no more effective than Charles's rule had been and became just as harsh and hated. Cromwell's great army and

The bleeding head of Charles I is exhibited to the crowd after his execution on a cold day in January 1649. The contemporary Dutch artist also professed to see the immediate ascension of Charles's soul to heaven. In fact, to many the king was seen as a martyr. [The Granger Collection.]

🙠 An Account of the Execution of Charles I

Convicted of "high treason and other high crimes," Charles I was beheaded on January 30, 1649. In his last minutes he conversed calmly with the attending bishop and executioner, anxious only that the executioner not strike before he gave the signal.

To the executioner he said, "I shall say but very short prayers, and when I thrust out my hands—"

Then he called to the bishop for his cap, and having put it on, asked the executioner, "Does my hair trouble you?" and the executioner desired him to put it under his cap, which as he was doing by the help of the bishop and the executioner, he turned to the bishop and said, "I have a good cause, and a gracious God on my side."

The bishop said, "There is but one stage more, which, though turbulent and troublesome, yet is a very short one. . . . It will carry you from earth to heaven . . . to a crown of glory. . . ."

Then the king asked the executioner, "Is my hair well?"

And taking off his cloak and George [the Order of the Garter, bearing a figure of Saint George], he delivered his George to the bishop. . . .

Then putting off his doublet and being in his waistcoat, he put on his cloak again, and looking upon the block, said to the executioner, "You must set it fast."

The executioner. "It is fast, sir."

King. "It might have been a little higher."

Executioner. "It can be no higher, sir."

King. "When I put out my hands this way, then—"

Then having said a few words to himself, as he stood with hands and eyes lifted up, immediately stooping down he laid his neck upon the block; and the executioner, again putting his hair under his cap, his Majesty, thinking he had been going to strike, bade him, "Stay for the sign."

Executioner. "Yes, I will, as it please your Majesty."

After a very short pause, his Majesty stretching forth his hands, the executioner at one blow severed his head from his body; which being held up and showed to the people, was with his body put into a coffin covered with black velvet and carried into his lodging.

His blood was taken up by divers persons for different ends: by some as trophies of the villainy; by others as relics of a martyr.

James Harvey Robinson (Ed.), *Readings in European History*, Vol. 2 (Boston: Ginn and Co., 1906), pp. 244–245.

---

foreign adventures inflated his budget to three times that of Charles's. Trade and commerce suffered throughout England, as near chaos reigned in many places. Puritan prohibitions of such pastimes as theaters, dancing, and drunkenness were widely resented. Cromwell's treatment of Anglicans came to be just as intolerant as Charles's treatment of Puritans had been. In the name of religious liberty, political liberty had been lost. And Cromwell was unable to get along even with the new Parliaments that were elected under the auspices of his army. By the time of his death in 1658, a majority of the English were ready to end the Puritan experiment and return to the traditional institutions of government.

Charles II and the Restoration of the Monarchy

The Stuart monarchy was restored in 1660 when Charles II (1660–1685), son of Charles I, returned to England amid great rejoicing. A man of considerable charm and political skill, Charles set a refreshing new tone after eleven years of somber Puritanism. His restoration returned England to the status quo of 1642, as once again a hereditary monarch sat on the throne and the Anglican church was religiously supreme.

Because of his secret Catholic sympathies the king favored a policy of religious toleration. He wanted to allow all persons outside the Church of

England, Catholics as well as Puritans, to worship freely so long as they remained loyal to the throne. But the ultraroyalist Anglicans in Parliament decided otherwise. They did not believe patriotism and religion could be so disjointed. Between 1661 and 1665, through a series of laws known as the Clarendon Code, Parliament excluded Roman Catholics, Presbyterians, and Independents from the religious and political life of the nation. Penalties were imposed for attending non-Anglican worship services, strict adherence to the *Book of Common Prayer* and the Thirty-Nine Articles was required, and all who desired to serve in local government were made to swear oaths of allegiance to the Church of England. This trampling of Puritan sentiments did not go unopposed in Parliament, but the opposition was not strong enough to override the majority.

Under Charles II England stepped up its challenge of the Dutch to become Europe's commercial and business center. Navigation Acts were passed that required all imports into England to be carried either in English ships or in ships registered to the same country as the imports they carried. Because the Dutch were the original suppliers of hardly more than tulips and cheese, these laws struck directly at their lucrative role as Europe's commercial middlemen. A series of naval wars between England and Holland ensued. Charles also undertook at this time to tighten his grasp on the rich English colonies in North America and the Caribbean, many of which had been settled and developed by separatists who desired independence from English rule.

Although Parliament strongly supported the monarchy, Charles, following the habit of his predecessors, required greater revenues than Parliament appropriated. These Charles managed to get in part by increased customs. He also received French aid. In 1670 England and France formally allied against the Dutch in the Treaty of Dover. A secret portion of this treaty pledged Charles to announce his conversion to Catholicism as soon as conditions in England permitted, a declaration for which Louis XIV of France promised to pay 167,000 pounds. (Such a declaration never came to pass.) Charles also received a French war chest of 250,000 pounds per annum.

In an attempt to unite the English people behind the war with Holland, and as a sign of good faith to Louis XIV, Charles issued a Declaration of Indulgence in 1672 suspending all laws against Roman

Charles II of England in a portrait from an unknown hand. [*The Granger Collection.*]

Catholics and Protestant nonconformists. But again the conservative Tory Parliament proved less generous than the king and refused to grant money for the war until Charles rescinded the measure. After Charles withdrew the declaration, Parliament passed the Test Act, which required all officials of the crown, civil and military, to swear an oath against the doctrine of transubstantiation—a requirement that no loyal Roman Catholic could honestly meet.

The Test Act was aimed in large measure at the king's brother, James, duke of York, heir to the throne and a recent, devout convert to Catholicism. In 1678 a notorious liar named Titus Oates swore before a magistrate that Charles's Catholic wife, through her physician, was plotting with Jesuits and Irishmen to kill the king so that James could assume the throne. The matter was taken before Parliament, where it was believed. In the ensuing hysteria, known as the "Popish Plot," several people were tried and executed. In 1680–1681, riding the crest of anti-Catholic sentiment, opposition Whig members of Parliament, led by the earl of

Shaftsbury (1621–1683), made an impressive but unsuccessful effort to enact a bill excluding James from succession to the throne.

More suspicious than ever of Parliament, Charles II turned again to increased customs revenue and the assistance of Louis XIV for extra income and was able to rule from 1681–1685 without recalling Parliament. In these years Charles suppressed much of his opposition, driving the earl of Shaftsbury into exile, executing several Whig leaders for treason, and bullying local corporations into electing members of Parliament submissive to the royal will. When Charles died in 1685 (after a deathbed conversion to Catholicism), he left James the prospect of a Parliament filled with royal friends.

James II and Renewed Fears of a Catholic England

James II (1685–1688) did not know how to make the most of a good thing. He alienated Parliament by insisting upon the repeal of the Test Act. When Parliament balked, he dissolved it and proceeded openly to appoint known Catholics to high positions in both his court and the army. In 1687 James issued a Declaration of Indulgence, which suspended all religious tests and permitted free worship. Local candidates for Parliament who opposed the declaration were removed from their offices by the king's soldiers and were replaced by Catholics. In June 1688 James went so far as to imprison seven Anglican bishops who had refused to publicize his suspension of laws against Catholics.

Under the guise of a policy of enlightened toleration James was actually seeking to subject all English institutions to the power of the monarchy. His goal was absolutism, and even conservative, loyalist Tories could not abide this. The English had reason to fear that James planned to imitate the policy of Louis XIV, who in 1685 had revoked the Edict of Nantes (which had protected French Protestants for almost a century) and had returned France to Catholicism, where necessary, with the aid of dragoons. A national consensus very quickly formed against the monarchy of James II.

The direct stimulus for parliamentary action came when on June 20, 1688, James's second wife, a Catholic, gave birth to a son, a male Catholic heir to the English throne. The English had hoped that James would die without a male heir and that the throne would revert to his Protestant eldest daughter, Mary. Mary was the wife of William III of Orange, *stadholder* of the Netherlands, great-grandson of William the Silent, and the leader of European opposition to Louis XIV's imperial designs. Within days of the birth of a Catholic male heir, Whig and Tory members of Parliament formed a coalition and invited Orange to invade England to preserve "traditional liberties," that is, the Anglican church and parliamentary government.

The "Glorious Revolution."

William of Orange arrived with his army in November 1688 and was received without opposition by the English people. In the face of sure defeat James fled to France and the protection of Louis XIV. With James gone, Parliament declared the throne vacant and on its own authority proclaimed William and Mary the new monarchs in 1689, completing a successful bloodless revolution. William and Mary in turn recognized a Bill of Rights that limited the powers of the monarchy and guaranteed the civil liberties of the English privileged classes. Henceforth, England's monarchs would rule by the consent of Parliament and be subject to law. The Bill of Rights also pointedly prohibited Roman Catholics from occupying the English throne. The Toleration Act of 1689 permitted worship by all Protestants and outlawed Roman Catholics and antitrinitarians (those who denied the Christian doctrine of the Trinity).

The final measure closing the century of strife was the Act of Settlement in 1701. This bill provided for the English crown to go to the Protestant House of Hanover in Germany if Queen Anne (1702–1714), the second daughter of James II and the last of the Stuart monarchs, was not survived by her children. Consequently in 1714 the Elector of Hanover became King George I of England, the third foreign monarch to occupy the English throne in just over a century.

The "Glorious Revolution" of 1688 established a framework of government by and for the governed. It received classic philosophical justification in John Locke's *Second Treatise of Government* (1690), wherein Locke described the relationship of a king and his people in terms of a bilateral contract. If the king broke that contract, the people, by whom Locke meant the privileged and powerful, had the right to depose him. Although it was, neither in fact nor in theory, a "popular" revolution such as would occur in France and America a hundred years later, the Glorious Revolution did estab-

With her husband already in exile and William and Mary about to be proclaimed sovereigns, the ex-queen, wife of James II, is pictured fleeing London in December 1688. [The Granger Collection.]

William of Orange landing at Exmouth Bay in England in 1688. William accepted the English throne primarily to bring England into the continental struggle against the aggression of Louis XIV. [The Mansell Collection.]

The coronation of William III and Mary II, April 11, 1689. This is a detail of a large engraving commemorating the coronation ceremonies. Mary was the daughter of James II. Although closely allied to the Stuarts by birth and marriage—his mother was the daughter of Charles I— William's rule was based on the consent of Parliament, and his powers were limited by law. [The Mansell Collection.]

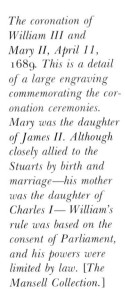

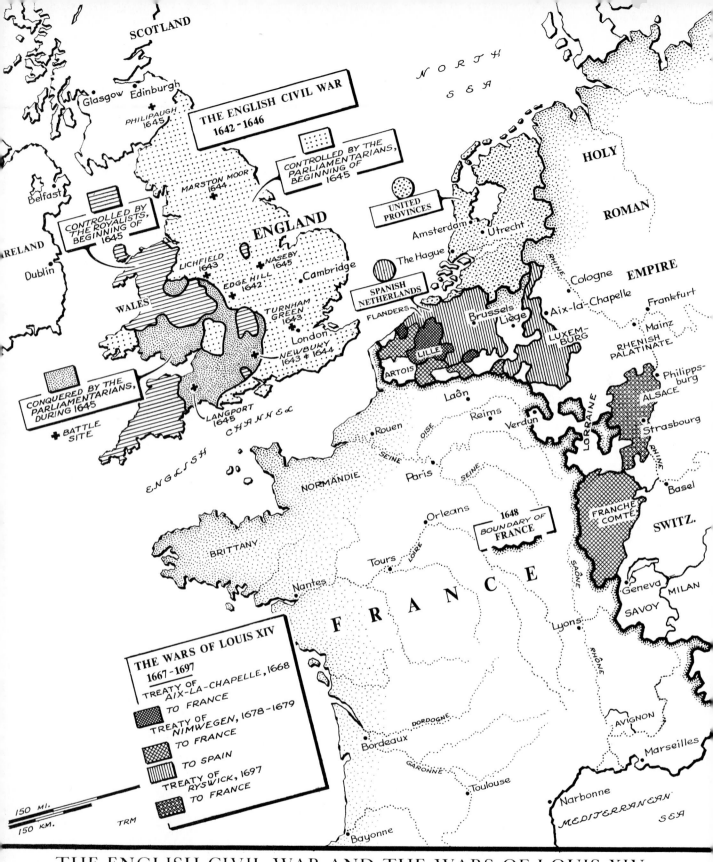

THE ENGLISH CIVIL WAR
1642-1646

CONTROLLED BY THE
PARLIAMENTARIANS,
BEGINNING OF
1645

CONTROLLED BY
THE ROYALISTS,
BEGINNING OF
1645

CONQUERED BY THE
PARLIAMENTARIANS,
DURING 1645

+ BATTLE
SITE

UNITED
PROVINCES

SPANISH
NETHERLANDS

1648
BOUNDARY OF
FRANCE

THE WARS OF LOUIS XIV
1667-1697
TREATY OF
AIX-LA-CHAPELLE, 1668
TO FRANCE
TREATY OF
NIMWEGEN, 1678-1679
TO FRANCE
TO SPAIN
TREATY OF
RYSWICK, 1697
TO FRANCE

150 MI.
150 KM.   TRM

THE ENGLISH CIVIL WAR AND THE WARS OF LOUIS XIV

MAP 16.2   *In the English Civil War, 1645 was a crucial year; here the rapidly deteriorating Royalist position is shown. A bit later in France we see the territorial changes resulting from Louis XIV's first three major wars. The War of the Spanish Succession was yet to come.*

lish in England a permanent check on monarchical power by the classes represented in Parliament.

Rise of Absolutism in France

Regional rights and a degree of religious diversity were recognized within the Holy Roman Empire, England, and the Netherlands during the seventeenth century. The assertion of local autonomy by the numerous member states and cities of the Holy Roman Empire made a strong central government there unthinkable. In England and the Netherlands centuries of parliamentary practice permitted regional freedoms to coexist with a strong central government.

Following the devastation of the Thirty Years' War, the Peace of Westphalia (1648) reaffirmed religious pluralism within the Holy Roman Empire. A degree of religious diversity, long a Netherlands tradition, received final confirmation also in England after decades of dogged Puritan resistance, when the Toleration Act of 1689 granted rights of worship to Protestant nonconformists.

Seventeenth-century France, in contrast, saw both representative government and religious pluralism crushed by the absolute monarchy and the closed Catholic state of Louis XIV (1643–1715). An aggressive ruler who sought glory ("*la gloire*") in foreign wars, Louis subjected his subjects at home to "one king, one law, one faith."

Henry IV and Sully

The foundation was well laid for Louis's grand reign by his predecessors and their exceptional ministers. It was Henry IV (1589–1610) (see Chapter 15) who began in earnest the curtailment of the privileges of the French nobility necessary for the creation of a strong centralized state. His targets were the provincial governors and the regional *parlements*, especially the powerful *Parlement* of Paris, where a divisive spirit lived on. Here were to be found the old privileged groups, tax-exempt magnates whose sole preoccupation was to prevent royal laws from infringing on their self-interests. During Louis XIV's reign their activities came under the strict supervision of royal civil servants known as *intendants*, who implemented the king's will with remarkable success in the provinces.

Also during Henry IV's reign an economy more amenable to governmental regulation emerged as part of the task of reconstruction after the long decades of religious and civil war. Henry and his finance minister, the duke of Sully (1560–1641), prepared the way for the later mercantilist policies of Louis XIV and his minister Colbert by establishing government monopolies on gunpowder, mines, and salt. A canal system was begun to link the Atlantic and the Mediterranean by joining the Saône, the Loire, the Seine, and the Meuse rivers. An involuntary national labor force was created by the introduction of a royal *corvée*, and this drafting of workers provided the labor to improve roads and the conditions of internal travel. Sully even dreamed of the political and commercial organization of the whole of Europe in a kind of common market.

Louis XIII and Richelieu

Henry IV was assassinated in 1610, and the following year Sully retired. Because Henry's successor, Louis XIII (1610–1643), was only nine years old when his father was assassinated, the task of governing fell to the queen mother, Marie de Medicis (d. 1642). Finding herself in a vulnerable position, she sought security abroad by signing a ten-year mutual defense pact with arch-rival Spain in the Treaty of Fontainebleau (1611), an alliance that also arranged for the later marriage of Louis XIII to the Spanish infanta as well as for the marriage of the queen's daughter Elizabeth to the heir to the Spanish throne. The queen sought internal security against the French nobility by promoting the career of Cardinal Richelieu (1585–1642) both as cardinal and as the king's chief adviser, although Richelieu never became her pawn. Richelieu, loyal and shrewd, aspired to make France a supreme European power and he, more than any one person, was the secret of French success in the first half of the seventeenth century.

An apparently devout Catholic who also believed that the church best served both his own ambition and the welfare of France, Richelieu was strongly anti-Hapsburg in politics. On the one hand, he supported the Spanish alliance of the queen and Catholic religious unity within France; on the other, he was determined to contain Spanish power and influence, even when that meant aiding and abetting Protestant Europe. It is an indication both of Richelieu's awkward political situation and of his diplomatic agility that he could pledge funds to the Protestant army of Gustavus Adolphus in the Treaty of Bär Walde, in 1631, while at the same time insisting that Catholic Bavaria be spared from attack and that Catholics in conquered countries be permitted to practice their religion.

At home Richelieu pursued his policies utterly without sentiment. Supported by the king, whose best decision was to let his chief minister make all the decisions of state, Richelieu stepped up the campaign against the separatist provincial governors and *parlements*. He made it clear to all that there was but one law, that of the king, and that none could stand above it. When disobedient noblemen defied his edicts, they were imprisoned and

Cardinal Richelieu, the shrewd mastermind behind French political power in the seventeenth century, in the striking triple portrait by the Flemish-French painter Philippe de Champaigne (1602–1674). [Reproduced by courtesy of the Trustees, The National Gallery, London.]

even executed. Louis XIV had Richelieu to thank for the fact that many of the French nobility became docile beggars at his court. Such treatment of the nobility won Richelieu much enmity, even from the queen mother, who was not always prepared to place the larger interests of the state above the pleasure of favorite princes. But the king let no criticism weaken his chief minister, not even that of his mother. The queen mother had largely ignored Louis during his youth—he was educated mostly at the hands of his falconer—and they remained estranged and ill at ease in each other's presence. This was doubtless a factor in the king's firm support of Richelieu when his mother became Richelieu's accuser.

Richelieu inspired the campaign against the Huguenots that would end in 1685 with Louis XIV's revocation of the Edict of Nantes. Royal armies conquered major Huguenot cities in 1629, and the subsequent Peace of Alais (1629) truncated the Edict of Nantes by denying Protestants the right to maintain garrisoned cities, separate political organizations, and independent law courts. Only Richelieu's foreign policy prevented the earlier implementation of the extreme intolerance of Louis XIV. In the same year that the independent political status of the Huguenots was rescinded,

Richelieu also entered negotiations to make Gustavus Adolphus his counterweight to the expansion of Hapsburg power within the Holy Roman Empire. By 1635 the Catholic soldiers of France fought openly with Swedish Lutherans against the emperor's army in the final phase of the Thirty Years' War.

In the best Machiavellian tradition Richelieu employed the arts and the printing press to defend his actions and to indoctrinate the French in the meaning of *raison d'état* ("reason of state")—again setting a precedent for Louis XIV's elaborate use of royal propaganda and spectacle. It is one measure of Richelieu's success that France made substantial gains in land and political influence when the Treaty of Westphalia (1648) ended hostilities in the Holy Roman Empire and the Treaty of the Pyrenees (1659) sealed peace with Spain.

Young Louis XIV and Mazarin

Richelieu's immediate legacy, however, was strong resentment of the monarchy on the part of the French aristocracy and the privileged bourgeoisie. During the minority of Louis XIV, who was only five years old when Louis XIII died in 1643, the queen mother, Anne of Austria (d. 1666), placed the reins of government in the hands of Cardinal Mazarin (1602–1661), who happened also to be her lover and, some report, her secret husband. Mazarin continued Richelieu's determined policy of centralization. During his regency the long-building backlash occurred when France was shaken to its foundations by the Fronde (1649–1652). Named after the slingshot used by street boys, the Fronde was a series of widespread

Cardinal Mazarin, in whose hands lay the real power in France during the minority of Louis XIV. [The Granger Collection.]

rebellions by segments of the French nobility and townspeople aimed at reversing the drift toward absolute monarchy—a last-ditch effort to preserve their local autonomy. These privileged groups saw their traditional position in French society thoroughly undermined by the crown's steady multipli-

Anne of Austria, the queen mother, surrounded by her court shortly after the death of Louis XIII. On the left are Cardinal Mazarin, in whose hands Anne placed control of the government during Louis XIV's minority, and the five-year-old Louis XIV. This sixteenth-century French engraving was done by Nicolas Picart. [The Granger Collection.]

Jacques-Benigne Bossuet, Bishop of Meaux. Called the "Eagle of Meaux," Bossuet was an eloquent advocate of the "divine right of kings" and a strong defender of the autonomy of the French church against the claims to direct rule by the Pope. This portrait by Hyacinthe Rigaud is in the Louvre. [Giraudon.]

cation of royal offices, the replacement of local with "state" agents, and a reduction of the patronage they received.

The *Parlement* of Paris initiated the revolt in 1649, and the nobility at large soon followed. The latter were urged on by the influential wives of princes who had been imprisoned by Mazarin for treason. The many briefly triumphed over the one when Mazarin released the imprisoned princes in February 1651. He and Louis XIV thereafter entered a short exile (Mazarin leaving France, Louis fleeing Paris) and were unable to return to Paris until October 1652, when the inefficiency and near

anarchy of government by the nobility made them very welcome. The period of the Fronde convinced a majority of the French that being left to the mercy of a strong king was preferable to being subjected to the competing and irreconcilable claims of many regional magnates. After 1652 the French were ready to experiment in earnest with absolute rule.

The World of Louis XIV

Unity at Home

Thanks to the forethought of Mazarin, Louis XIV was well prepared to rule France. The turbulent periods of his youth seem also to have made an indelible impression. Louis wrote in his memoirs that the Fronde caused him to loathe "kings of straw" and made him determined never to become one. Indoctrinated with a strong sense of the grandeur of his crown, he never missed an opportunity to impress it on the French people. When the dauphin (the heir to the French throne) was born in 1662, for example, Louis appeared for the celebration dressed as a Roman emperor. Although his rule became the prototype of the modern centralized state, its inspiration remained a very narrow ideal of personal glory.

King by Divine Right

Reverence for the king and the personification of government in him had been nurtured in France since Capetian times. It was a maxim of French law and popular opinion, evolved during the later Middle Ages through royal efforts to secure the king's domain, that "the king of France is emperor in his realm," that the king's wish is the law of the land.

An important theorist for Louis's even grander concept of royal authority was the Jesuit tutor of the dauphin, Bishop Jacques-Bénigne Bossuet (1627–1704). An ardent champion of the Gallican Liberties—the traditional rights of the French king and church in matters of ecclesiastical appointments and taxation—Bossuet defended what he called the "divine right of kings." He cited the Old Testament example of rulers divinely appointed by and answerable only to God. As medieval popes had insisted that only God could judge a pope, so Bossuet argued that none save God could sit in

484

❧ Bishop Bossuet Defends the Divine Right of Kings

The revolutions of the seventeenth century caused many to fear anarchy far more than tyranny, among them the influential French bishop Jacques Bénigne Bossuet (1627–1704), the leader of French Catholicism in the second half of the seventeenth century. Louis XIV made him court preacher and tutor to his son, for whom Bossuet wrote a celebrated *Universal History*. In the following excerpt Bossuet defended the divine right and absolute power of kings, whom he depicted as embracing in their person the whole body of the state and the will of the people they governed and, as such, as being immune from judgment by any mere mortal.

The royal power is absolute. . . . The prince need render account of his acts to no one. "I counsel thee to keep the king's commandment, and that in regard of the oath of God. Be not hasty to go out of his sight; stand not on an evil thing for he doeth whatsoever pleaseth him. Where the word of a king is, there is power: and who may say unto him, What doest thou? Whoso keepeth the commandment shall feel no evil thing" [Eccles. 8:2–5]. Without this absolute authority the king could neither do good nor repress evil. It is necessary that his power be such that no one can hope to escape him, and finally, the only protection of individuals against the public authority should be their innocence. This confirms the teaching of St. Paul: "Wilt thou then not be afraid of the power? Do that which is good" [Rom. 13–3].

God is infinite, God is all. The prince, as prince, is not regarded as a private person: he is a public personage, all the state is in him; the will of all the people is included in his. As all perfection and all strength are united in God, so all the power of individuals is united in the person of the prince. What grandeur that a single man should embody so much! . . .

Behold an immense people united in a single person; behold this holy power, paternal and absolute; behold the secret cause which governs the whole body of the state, contained in a single head: you see the image of God in the king, and you have the idea of royal majesty. God is holiness itself, goodness itself, and power itself. In these things lies the majesty of God. In the image of these things lies the majesty of the prince.

From *Politics Drawn from the Very Words of Holy Scripture,* in James Harvey Robinson (Ed.), *Readings in European History,* Vol. 2 (Boston: Ginn and Co., 1906), pp. 275–276.

judgment on the king. Although kings remained duty-bound to reflect God's will in their rule—and in this sense Bossuet considered them always subject to a higher authority—as God's regents on earth they could not be bound to the dictates of mere princes and parliaments. Such were among the assumptions that lay behind Louis XIV's alleged declaration: "L'état, c'est moi" ("I am the state").

Versailles

The palace court at Versailles on the outskirts of Paris became Louis's permanent residence after 1682 and was a true temple to royalty, architecturally designed and artistically decorated to proclaim the glory of the Sun King, as Louis was known. A spectacular estate with magnificent fountains and acres of orange groves, it became home to thousands of aristocrats, royal officials, and servants. Although its physical maintenance and new additions, which continued throughout Louis's lifetime, consumed over half his annual revenues—around five million livres a year—Versailles paid political dividends well worth the investment.

Life at court was organized around the king's daily routine.

His rising and dressing were a time of rare intimacy, when nobles, who entered their names on waiting lists to be in attendance, whispered their special requests in Louis's ear.

After the morning Mass, which Louis always observed, there followed long hours in council with the chief ministers, assemblies from which the no-

Versailles as it appeared in 1668 in a painting by Pierre Patel the Elder (1605–1676). The central building is the hunting lodge built for Louis XIII earlier in the century, and some of the first expansion undertaken by Louis XIV appears as wings. The painting is in the Versailles museum. [Cliché des Musées Nationaux, Paris.]

The sumptuous Salon de la Guerre in the Palace of Versailles. It was begun in 1678. Several rooms of the palace were badly damaged by a terrorist's bomb in June 1978. [French Embassy Press and Information Division, New York.]

bility was carefully excluded. Louis's ministers and councilors were hand-picked townsmen, servants who owed everything they had to the king's favor and were for that reason inclined to serve faithfully and without question. There were three main councils: the Council of State, a small group of four or five who met thrice weekly to rule on all matters of state, but especially on foreign affairs and war policy; the Council of Dispatches, which regularly assessed the reports from the *intendants* in the towns and provinces, a boring business that the king often left to his ministers; and finally, the Council of Finances, which handled matters of taxation and commerce.

The afternoons were spent hunting, riding, or strolling about the lush gardens. Evenings were given over to planned entertainment in the large salons (plays, concerts, gambling, and the like), followed by supper at 10:00 P.M.

Even the king's retirement was a part of the day's

A full view of Versailles as it appears today. Louis XIV vastly enlarged his father's hunting lodge into a palace estate beginning in 1661. It became not only the royal residence but the seat of the French government, a symbol of royal and national power, and the frequently imitated model for other seventeenth- and eighteenth-century monarchs. This photograph is from the opposite direction to Patel's painting; the coaches in his picture are arriving on the diagonal road at the top left of the photograph. [French Government Tourist Office, New York.]

Bishop Cornelis Jansen (1585–1638) was the author of the intellectual and theological foundations of what came to be called Jansenism. Several of his key beliefs were eventually declared heretical by the Catholic Church. [The Granger Collection.]

spectacle. Fortunate nobles were permitted briefly to hold his night candle as they accompanied him to his bed.

Although only five feet, four inches in height, the king had presence and was always engaging in conversation. An unabashed ladies' man, he encouraged the belief at court that it was an honor to lie with the king. Married to the Spanish Infanta Marie Thérèse for political reasons in 1660, he kept many mistresses. After Marie's death in 1683 he settled down in secret marriage with one, Madame de Maintenon, and apparently became much less the philanderer.

All this ritual and play served the political purpose of keeping an impoverished nobility, barred by law from high government positions, busy and dependent so that they had little time to plot revolt. The dress codes and the high-stakes gaming at court contributed to the indebtedness and dependency of nobility on the king. Court life was a carefully planned and successfully executed domestication of the nobility.

Suppression of the Jansenists

Like Richelieu before him, Louis believed that political unity required religious conformity. To that end he suppressed two groups of religious dissenters: the Catholic Jansenists, who were opponents of the Jesuits, and the Protestant Huguenots.

Although the king and the French church had always jealously guarded their traditional independence from Rome (the Gallican Liberties), the years following the conversion of Henry IV to Catholicism saw a great influx of Catholic religious orders into France, prominent among which were the Jesuits. Because of their leadership at the Council of Trent and their close Spanish connections, Catherine de Medicis had earlier banned the Jesuits from France. Henry IV lifted the ban in

The abbey of Port Royal near Paris in the seventeenth century, the main center of Jansenist theological activity. Its picture gives a good impression of the layout of a religious community of the time. [The Granger Collection.]

1603, with certain conditions: there was to be a limitation on the number of new colleges they could open; special licenses were required for activities outside their own buildings; and each member of the order was subjected to an oath of allegiance to the king. The Jesuits were not, however, easily harnessed. They rapidly monopolized the education of the upper classes, and their devout students promoted the religious reforms and doctrine of the Council of Trent throughout France. It is a measure of their success that Jesuits served as confessors to Henry IV, Louis XIII, and Louis XIV.

In the 1630s a group that came to be known as *Jansenists* formed an intra-Catholic opposition to both the theology and the political influence of the Jesuits. They were Catholics who adhered to the Augustinian tradition, out of which many Protestant teachings had also come. Serious and uncompromising in their religious doctrine and practice, the Jansenists opposed Jesuit teachings about free will. They believed with Saint Augustine that original sin dominated humankind so completely that individuals could do absolutely nothing good or contributing to their salvation unless they were first specially assisted by the grace of God. The namesake of the Jansenists, Cornelis Jansen (d. 1638), a Flemish theologian and the bishop of Ypres, was the author of a posthumously published book entitled *Augustinus* (1640), which assailed mainly Jesuit teaching on grace and salvation.

Jean du Vergier de Hauranne (1581–1643), the abbot of Saint-Cyran and Jansen's close friend, was instrumental in bringing into the Jansenist fold a Parisian family, the Arnaulds, who were prominent opponents of the Jesuits. The Arnauld family, like many other French people, believed that the Jesuits had been behind the assassination of Henry IV in 1610. Arnauld support added a strong political element to the Jansenists' theological opposition to the Jesuits. Jansenist communities at Port-Royal and Paris were dominated by the Arnaulds during the 1640s. In 1643 Antoine Arnauld published a work entitled *On Frequent Communion* in which he criticized the Jesuits for confessional practices that permitted the easy redress of almost any sin. The Jesuits, in turn, condemned the Jansenists as "crypto-Calvinists" in their theology.

On May 31, 1653, Jansenism was declared a heresy. On that day Pope Innocent X deemed heretical five Jansenist theological propositions on grace and salvation, earlier condemned by the Sorbonne. In 1656 the Pope banned Jansen's *Augustinus*, and

the Sorbonne censured Antoine Arnauld. In this same year Antoine's friend, Blaise Pascal (d. 1662), the most famous of Jansen's followers, published the first of his *Provincial Letters* in defense of Jansenism. A deeply religious man, Pascal tried to reconcile the "reasons of the heart" with growing seventeenth-century reverence for the clear and distinct ideas of the mind. He found Jesuit moral theology to be not only lax and shallow, but also a rationalized approach to religion that did injustice to religious experience.

In 1660 Louis permitted the enforcement of the papal bull *Ad Sacram Sedem* (1656), which banned Jansenism, and he closed down the Port-Royal community. Thereafter Jansenists either capitulated by signing retractions or went underground. At a later date (1710) the French king lent his support to a still more thorough Jesuit purge of Jansenist sentiment. With the fall of the Jansenists went any hope of a Catholicism broad enough to attract the Huguenots.

Revocation of the Edict of Nantes

Since 1598, when the Edict of Nantes was proclaimed, a cold war had existed between the great Catholic majority (nine tenths of the French population remained Catholic) and the Protestant minority. Despite their respectable numbers, about 1.75 million by the 1660s, the Huguenots were in decline in the second half of the seventeenth century. Government harassment had forced the more influential members to withdraw their support. Officially the French Catholic church had long denounced Calvinists as heretical and treasonous and had supported their persecution as both a pious and a patriotic act. Following the Peace of Nijmegen in 1678–1679, which halted for the moment Louis's aggression in Europe, Louis launched a methodical government campaign against the French Huguenots in a determined effort to unify France religiously. He hounded the Huguenots out of public life, banned them from government office, and excluded them from such professions as printing and medicine. Subsidies and selective taxation also became weapons to encourage their conversion to Catholicism. In 1681 Louis further bullied Huguenots by quartering his troops in their towns. The final stage of the persecution came in October 1685, when Louis revoked the Edict of Nantes. In practical terms the revocation meant the closing of Protestant churches and

❧ Louis XIV Revokes the Edict of Nantes

Believing that a country could not be under one king and one law unless it was also under one religious system, Louis XIV stunned much of Europe in October 1685 by revoking the Edict of Nantes, which had protected the religious freedoms and civil rights of French Protestants since 1598.

Art. 1. Know that we . . . with our certain knowledge, full power and royal authority, have by this present, perpetual and irrevocable edict, suppressed and revoked the edict of the aforesaid king our grandfather, given at Nantes in the month of April, 1598, in all its extent . . . together with all the concessions made by [this] and other edicts, declarations, and decrees, to the people of the so-called Reformed religion, of whatever nature they be . . . and in consequence we desire . . . that all the temples of the people of the aforesaid so-called Reformed religion situated in our kingdom . . . should be demolished forthwith.

Art. 2. We forbid our subjects of the so-called Reformed religion to assemble any more for public worship of the above-mentioned religion. . . .

Art. 3. We likewise forbid all lords, of whatever rank they may be, to carry out heretical services in houses and fiefs . . . the penalty for . . . the said worship being confiscation of their body and possessions.

Art. 4. We order all ministers of the aforesaid so-called Reformed religion who do not wish to be converted and to embrace the Catholic, Apostolic, and Roman religion, to depart from our kingdom and the lands subject to us within fifteen days from the publication of our present edict . . . on pain of the galleys.

Art. 5. We desire that those among the said [Reformed] ministers who shall be converted [to the

Catholic religion] shall continue to enjoy during their life, and their wives shall enjoy after their death as long as they remain widows, the same exemptions from taxation and billeting of soldiers, which they enjoyed while they fulfilled the function of ministers. . . .

. . . .

Art. 8. With regard to children who shall be born to those of the aforesaid so-called Reformed religion, we desire that they be baptized by their parish priests. We command the fathers and mothers to send them to the churches for that purpose, on penalty of a fine of 500 livres or more if they fail to do so; and afterwards, the children shall be brought up in the Catholic, Apostolic, and Roman religion. . . .

. . . .

Art. 10. All our subjects of the so-called Reformed religion, with their wives and children, are to be strongly and repeatedly prohibited from leaving our aforesaid kingdom . . . or of taking out . . . their possessions and effects. . . .

. . . .

The members of the so-called Reformed religion, while awaiting God's pleasure to enlighten them like the others, can live in the towns and districts of our kingdom . . . and continue their occupation there, and enjoy their possessions . . . on condition . . . that they do not make public profession of [their religion].

Church and State Through the Centuries: A Collection of Historic Documents, trans. and ed. by S. Z. Ehler and John B. Morrall (New York: Biblo and Tannen, 1967), pp. 209–213.

---

schools, the exile of Protestant ministers, the placement of nonconverting members of the laity in galleys as slaves, and the ceremonial baptism of Protestant children by Catholic priests.

The revocation of the Edict of Nantes became the major blunder of Louis's reign. Thereafter he was viewed throughout Protestant Europe as a new Philip II, intent on a Catholic reconquest of the whole of Europe, who must be resisted at all costs. Internally the revocation of the Edict of Nantes led

to the voluntary emigration of over a quarter million French, who formed new communities and joined the French resistance movement in England, Germany, Holland, and the New World. Thousands of French Huguenots served in the army of Louis's arch foe, William III of the Netherlands, later King William III of England. Those who remained in France became an uncompromising guerrilla force. But despite the many domestic and foreign liabilities created for France by the rev-

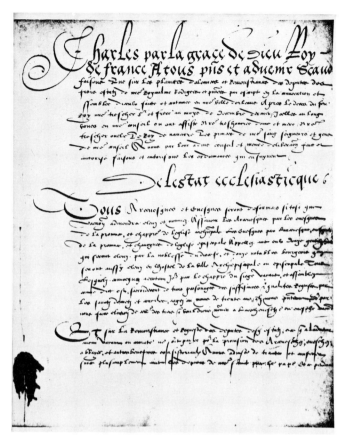

Ever since 1525 the Huguenots suffered harrassment and persecution by the French government. This occurred despite measures of toleration granted temporarily by such documents as the January Edict of 1562, shown here, and the Edict of Nantes. [The Granger Collection.]

A drawing depicting the announcement of the revocation of the Edict of Nantes in 1685. Louis XIV considered the revocation of the policy of religious toleration one of the most important acts of his reign. [The Granger Collection.]

ocation of the Edict of Nantes, Louis to his death, like many other devout Catholics, considered it his most pious act, one that placed God in his debt.

War Abroad

War was the normal state for seventeenth-century rulers and for none more so than for Louis XIV, who would confess on his deathbed that he had "loved war too much." Periods of peace became opportunities for the discontented in town and countryside to plot against the king; war served national unity as well as "glory." By the 1660s France was superior to any other nation in administrative bureaucracy, armed forces, and national unity. It had a population of nineteen million, prosperous farms, vigorous trade, and much taxable wealth. By every external measure Louis was in a position to dominate Europe.

LOUVOIS, VAUBAN, COLBERT. The great French war machine became the work of three ministers: Louvois, Vauban, and Colbert. The army, which maintained a strength of about a quarter of a million men, was the creation of Michel le Tellier and his more famous son, the marquis of Louvois (1641–1691). The latter, who served as Louis's war minister from 1677 to 1691, was a superior military tactician.

Before Louvois the French army had been an amalgam of local recruits and mercenaries, unco-ordinated groups whose loyalty could not always be counted on. Louvois disciplined the French army and made it a respectable profession. He placed a limit on military commissions and intro-

duced a system of promotion by merit, policies that brought dedicated fighting men into the ranks. Enlistment was for four years and was restricted to single men. The pay was good and regular. *Intendants,* those ubiquitous civil servants, carried out regular inspections, monitoring conduct at all levels and reporting to the king.

What Louvois was to military organization Sebastien Vauban (1633–1707) was to military engineering. He perfected the arts of fortifying and besieging towns. He also devised the system of trench warfare and developed the concept of defensive frontiers that remained basic military tactics through World War I.

War cannot be successful without financing, and here Louis had the guidance of his most brilliant minister, Jean-Baptiste Colbert (1619–1683). Colbert worked to centralize the French economy with the same rigor that Louis had worked to centralize the French government. He put the nation to work under state supervision and carefully regulated the flow of imports and exports through tariffs. He created new national industries and organized factories around a tight regimen of work and ideology. Administrative bureaucracy was simplified, unnecessary positions were abolished, and the number of tax-exempt nobles was reduced. Colbert also increased the *taille* on the peasantry, the chief source of royal wealth. Although the French economy continued to be a puppet controlled by many different strings, more of these strings were now in the hand of the king than had been the case in centuries past. This close government control of the economy came to be known as *mercantilism.* Its aim was to maximize foreign exports and the internal reserves of bullion, the gold and silver necessary for making war. Modern scholars argue that Colbert overcontrolled the French economy and cite his "paternalism" as a major reason for French failures in the New World. Be that as it may, Colbert's policies unquestionably transformed France into a major industrial and commercial power, with foreign bases in Africa, India, and the Americas from Canada to the Caribbean.

THE WAR OF DEVOLUTION. Louis's first great foreign adventure was the War of Devolution (1667–1668). It was fought, as still a later and greater war would be, over Louis's claim to a Spanish inheritance through his wife, Marie Thérèse (1638–1683). According to the terms of the Treaty of the Pyrenees (1659), Marie had renounced her claim to the Spanish succession on condition that a 500,000-crown dowry be paid to Louis within eighteen months of the marriage, a condition that was not met. When Philip IV of Spain died in September 1665, he left all his lands to his sickly four-year-old son by a second marriage, Charles II (1665–1700), and explicitly excluded his daughter Marie from any share. Louis had always harbored the hope of turning the marriage to territorial gain and argued even before Philip's death that Marie was entitled to a portion of the inheritance.

Louis had a legal argument on his side, which gave the war its name. He maintained that because in certain regions of Brabant and Flanders, which were part of the Spanish inheritance, property "devolved" to the children of a first marriage rather than to those of a second, Marie had a higher claim than Charles II to these regions. The argument was not accepted—such regional laws could hardly bind the king of Spain—but Louis was not deterred from moving his armies, under the vicomte de Turenne, into Flanders and the Franche-Comté in 1667. In response to this aggression England, Sweden, and the United Provinces of Holland formed the Triple Alliance, a force sufficient to bring Louis to peace terms in the Treaty of Aix-la-Chapelle (1668).

INVASION OF THE NETHERLANDS. In 1670 England and France became allies against the Dutch by signing the Treaty of Dover, a move that set the Stuart monarchy of Charles II on a new international course. With the departure of the English from its membership, the Triple Alliance crumbled. This left Louis in a stronger position to invade the Netherlands for a second time, which he did in 1672. This second invasion was aimed directly at Holland, the organizer of the Triple Alliance in 1667 and the country held accountable by Louis for foiling French designs in Flanders. Louis had been mightily offended by Dutch boasting after the Treaty of Aix-la-Chapelle; cartoons like one depicting the sun (Louis was the "Sun King") eclipsed by a great moon of Dutch cheese cut the French king to the quick. It was also clear that there could be no French acquisition of land in the Spanish Netherlands, nor European hegemony beyond that, until Holland was neutralized.

Louis's successful invasion of the United Provinces in 1672 brought the downfall of Jan and Cornelius De Witt, Dutch statesmen who were blamed for the French success. In their place came the twenty-seven-year-old Prince of Orange, after 1689 King William III of England. Orange was the

great-grandson of William the Silent, who had repulsed Philip II and dashed Spanish hopes of dom-
inating the Netherlands in the sixteenth century.

Orange proved to be Louis's undoing. This un-
pretentious Calvinist, who was in almost every way
Louis's opposite, galvanized the seven provinces
into a fierce fighting unit that did not shrink from
opening the dikes on French armies. In 1673 he
united the Holy Roman Emperor, Spain, Lorraine,
and Brandenburg in an alliance against Louis, who
was now seen by his enemies to be "the Christian
Turk," a menace to the whole of western Europe,
Catholic and Protestant alike. Subsequent battles
saw Louis lose his ablest generals, Turenne and
Condé, in 1675, while the defeat of the Dutch
fleet by Admiral Duquesne established French control of the Mediterranean in 1676. The Peace of
Nimwegen, signed with different parties in succes-
sive years (1678, 1679), ended the hostilities of this
second war. In 1678 France entered agreements
with Holland and Spain and in 1679 with the Holy
Roman Emperor, Brandenburg, and Denmark.

The settlements were not unfavorable to France—
Spain, for example, surrendered the Franche-
Comté—but France still fell far short of the Euro-
pean empire to which Louis aspired.

THE LEAGUE OF AUGSBURG. Between the
Treaty of Nimwegen and the renewal of full-scale
war in 1689, Louis restlessly probed his perimeters.
The army was maintained at full strength. In 1681
it conquered the free city of Strasbourg, setting off
the formation of new defensive coalitions against
Louis. The League of Augsburg, created in 1686 to
resist French expansion into Germany, grew by
1689 to include the Emperor Leopold, Spain, Sweden, the United Provinces, the electorates of Bavaria, Saxony, and the Palatinate, and the England
of William and Mary. That year saw the beginning
of the Nine Years' War (1689–1697) between
France and the League of Augsburg. For the third
time stalemate and exhaustion forced the combatants into an interim settlement. The Peace of
Ryswick in September 1697 became a personal triumph for William, now William III of England,

*The siege of Tournai in 1709 during the War of the Spanish Succession. Tournai, a fortress
city on the border between France and the Spanish Netherlands, had been captured by the
French in 1667. Here it is beseiged by the English and Imperial forces under Marlborough and
Prince Eugene. Under the terms of the Treaty of Utrecht (1713), France ceded Tournai to Austria. This 1709 engraving is by P. Mortier. [BBC Hulton Picture Library.]*

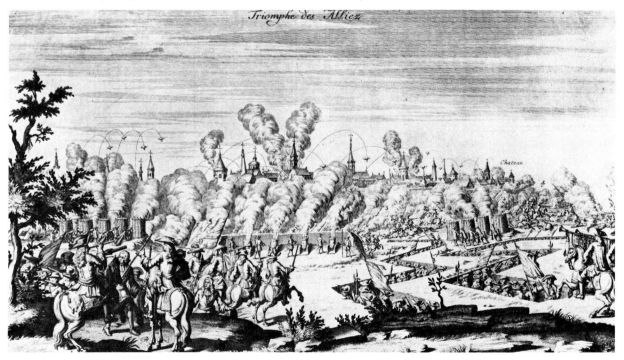

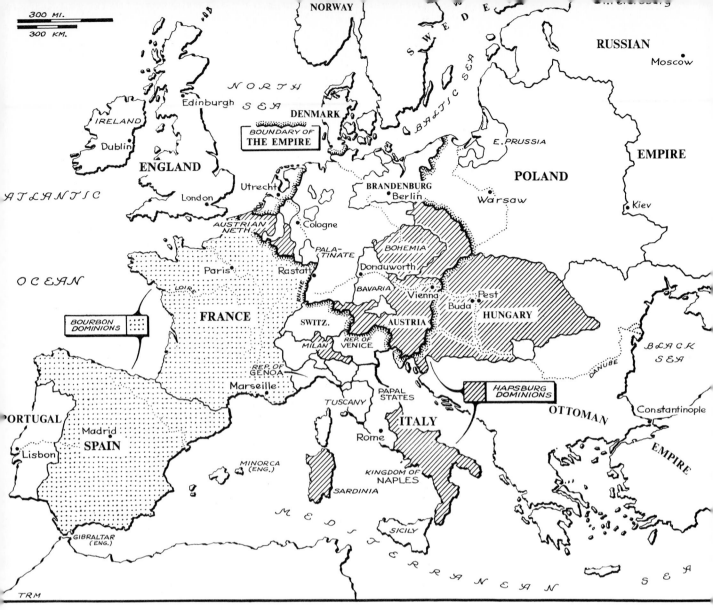

EUROPE IN 1714

MAP 16.3 *The War of the Spanish Succession ended in the year before the death of the aged Louis XIV. By then France and Spain, although not united, were ruled by members of the Bourbon family, and Spain had lost her non-Iberian possessions. Austria had continued to grow.*

and the Emperor Leopold, as it secured Holland's borders and thwarted Louis's expansion into Germany. During this same period England and France fought for control of North America in what came to be known as King William's War (1689–1697).

WAR OF THE SPANISH SUCCESSION: TREATIES OF UTRECHT—RASTADT. After Ryswick, Louis, who seemed to thrive on partial success, made still a fourth attempt to realize his grand design of French European domination, this time assisted by an unforeseen turn of events. On November 1, 1700, Charles II of Spain, known as "the Sufferer" because of his genetic deformities and lingering illnesses, died. Both Louis and the Austrian Emperor Leopold had claims to the Spanish inheritance through their grandsons: Louis by way of his marriage to Marie Thérèse and Leopold through his marriage to her younger sister, Margaret Thérèse.

Although the dauphin had the higher blood claim, it was assumed that the inheritance would go to the grandson of the emperor. The French raised the specter of a belligerent Hapsburg kingdom like that of Charles V in the sixteenth century should Spain come under the imperial crown. Maria Thérèse, however, had renounced any right to the Spanish inheritance in the Treaty of the Pyrenees (1659).

The nations of Europe were far more fearful of a union of the French and Spanish crowns than they were of a union of the imperial and Spanish crowns. Indeed, they were determined that the former alliance should not occur. Hence before Charles's death negotiations began to partition the inheritance in such a way that the current balance of power would be maintained.

Charles II upset all plans by leaving the entire Spanish inheritance to Philip of Anjou, Louis's grandson. At a stroke the Spanish inheritance had fallen to France. Although Louis had been party to the partition agreements in advance of Charles's death, he now saw God's hand in Charles's will and chose to enforce its terms fully rather than abide by those of the partition treaty. Philip of Anjou moved to Madrid and became Philip V of Spain, and Louis, in what was interpreted as naked French aggression, sent his troops once again into Flanders, this time to remove Dutch soldiers from Spanish territory in the name of the new French king of Spain. He also declared Spanish America open to French ships.

In September 1701 the Grand Alliance of England, Holland, and the Holy Roman Emperor formed against Louis in The Hague. Its intent was to preserve the balance of power by once-and-for-all securing Flanders as a neutral barrier between Holland and France and by gaining for the emperor his fair share of the Spanish inheritance. After the formation of the alliance Louis increased the stakes of battle by recognizing the son of James II of England as James III, king of England.

Once again total war enveloped western Europe as the twelve-year War of the Spanish Succession (1702–1714) began. France, for the first time, went to war with inadequate finances, a poorly equipped army, and mediocre military leadership. The English had advanced weaponry (flintlock rifles, paper cartridges, and ring bayonets) and superior tactics (thin, maneuverable troop columns rather than the traditional deep ones). John Churchill, the duke of Marlborough, who succeeded William of Orange as leader of the alliance, bested Louis's soldiers in every major engagement. Marlborough routed

❧ An Appraisal of Louis XIV

In his history of the reigns of the first three Bourbon kings, written in 1746, the Duc de Saint Simon (1675–1755), an army officer and public official during Louis XIV's reign, left the following highly critical portrait of Louis as a king smitten by vanity.

Louis XIV's vanity was without limit or restraint; it colored everything and convinced him that no one even approached him in military talents, in plans and enterprises, and in government. Hence, those pictures and inscriptions in the gallery at Versailles which disgust every foreigner; those opera prologues that he himself tried to sing; that flood of prose and verse in his praise for which his appetite was insatiable; those dedications of statues copied from pagan sculpture, and the insipid and sickening compliments that were continually offered to him in person and which he swallowed with unfailing relish; hence, his distaste for all merit, intelligence, education, and, most of all, independence of character and sentiment in others; his mistakes of judgment in matters of importance; his familiarity and favor reserved entirely for those to whom he felt himself superior in acquirements and ability; and, above everything else, a jealousy of his own authority which determined and took precedence over every other sort of justice, reason, and consideration whatever.

James Harvey Robinson (Ed.), *Readings in European History*, Vol. 2 (Boston: Ginn and Co., 1906), pp. 286—287.

THE REIGN OF LOUIS XIV (1643–1715)

1648	Peace of Westphalia reaffirms religious pluralism in Holy Roman Empire
1649–1652	The Fronde, a revolt of nobility and townsmen against confiscatory policies of the crown
1653	Jansenism declared a heresy by the pope
1659	Treaty of Pyrenees ends hostilities between France and Spain
1660	Louis XIV enforces papal ban on Jansenists
1667–1668	War of Devolution fought over Louis' claims to lands in Brabant and Flanders by virtue of his Spanish inheritance through his wife
1668	The Triple Alliance (England, Sweden, and the United Provinces) repels Louis' army from Flanders and forces the Treaty of Aix-la-Chapelle
1670	Treaty of Dover brings French and English together against the Netherlands
1672	France invades the United Provinces
1678–1679	Peace of Nimwegen ends French wars in United Provinces
1685	Louis XIV revokes Edict of Nantes
1689–1697	Nine Years' War between France and League of Augsburg, a Europe-wide alliance against Louis XIV
1697	Peace of Ryswick ends French expansion into Holland and Germany
1702–1714	England, Holland, and Holy Roman Emperor resist Louis' claim to the Spanish throne in the war of Spanish Succession
1712	Treaty of Utrecht between England and France
1714	Treaty of Rastadt between Spain and France

French armies at Blenheim in August 1704 and on the plain of Ramillies in 1706—two decisive battles of the war. In 1708–1709 famine, revolts, and uncollectable taxes tore France apart internally. Despair pervaded the French court, and Louis wondered aloud how God could forsake one who had done so much for Him.

Though ready to make peace in 1709, Louis could not bring himself to accept the stiff terms of the alliance, which included the demand that he transfer all Spanish possessions to the emperor's grandson Charles and remove Philip V from Madrid. An immediate result of this failure to come to terms was a clash of forces at Malplaquet (September 1709), which left carnage on the battlefield unsurpassed until modern times.

Under the English minister Bolingbroke the allies renewed peace talks in 1711. France signed an armistice with England at Utrecht in July 1712, and hostilities were concluded with Holland and the emperor in the Treaty of Rastadt in March 1714. These agreements confirmed Philip V as king of Spain. They gave England Gibraltar, which made England thereafter a Mediterranean power, and won Louis's recognition of the House of Hanover's right of accession to the English throne.

Politically the eighteenth century would belong to England as the sixteenth had belonged to Spain and the seventeenth to France. The emperor received control of the Spanish Netherlands, which were established as a barrier between France and Holland, with Dutch troops stationed in key towns. France kept the cities of Strasbourg and Lille. Although France remained intact and quite strong, the realization of Louis XIV's ambition had to await the rise of Napoleon Bonaparte. On his deathbed on September 1, 1715, a dying Louis fittingly warned the dauphin not to imitate his love of buildings and his liking for war.

When one looks back on Louis's reign, the grandeur and power of it still remain undimmed by his presumptuous glory-seeking and military ambitions. One remembers not only a king who loved war too much, but also one who built the palace of Versailles and brought a new majesty to France; a king who managed with consummate skill the French aristocracy and bourgeoisie at court and controlled a French peasantry that had all too many just grievances; a king who shrewdly raised up skilled and trustworthy ministers, councillors, and *intendants* from the middle classes; and a king who created a new French empire by the successful expansion of trade into Asia and the colonization of North America.

Suggested Readings

MAURICE ASHLEY, *The Greatness of Oliver Cromwell* (1966). Detailed biography.

TREVOR ASTON (Ed.), *Crisis in Europe 1560–1660* (1965). Essays by major scholars focused on social and economic forces.

WILLIAM F. CHURCH (Ed.), *The Greatness of Louis XIV: Myth or Reality?* (1959). Excerpts from the scholarly debate over Louis's reign.

C. H. FIRTH, *Oliver Cromwell and the Rule of the Puritans in England* (1900). Old but still very authoritative work.

WILLIAM HALLER, *The Rise of Puritanism* (1957). Interesting study based largely on Puritan sermons.

CHRISTOPHER HILL, *The Century of Revolution 1603–1714* (1961). Bold, imaginative synthesis by a controversial master.

W. H. LEWIS, *The Splendid Century* (1953). Focuses on society, especially in the age of Louis XIV.

DAVID OGG, *Europe in the Seventeenth Century* (1925). Among the most authoritative syntheses.

STUART E. PRALL, *The Puritan Revolution: A Documentary History* (1968). Comprehensive document collection.

LAWRENCE STONE, *The Causes of the English Revolution 1529–1642* (1972). Brief survey stressing social history and ruminating over historians and historical method.

G. R. R. TREASURE, *Seventeenth Century France* (1966). Broad, detailed survey of entire century.

MICHAEL WALZER, *The Revolution of the Saints: A Study in the Origins of Radical Politics* (1965). Effort to relate ideas and politics that depicts Puritans as true revolutionaries.

C. V. WEDGWOOD, *Richelieu and the French Monarchy* (1950). Fine biography.

JOHN B. WOLF, *Louis XIV* (1968). Very detailed political biography.

$$\frac{ao}{e} = GF. \quad GF = \frac{nno2}{2e3} + \frac{no3}{2e5}. \quad CF = Voo + aaoo = \frac{no}{e}. \quad 3f = \frac{nnoo}{2e3} + \frac{anno3}{2e5}$$

$$= \frac{nnpp}{2e3} - \frac{annp3}{2e5}. \quad \frac{pp}{2e} - \frac{ap3}{2e} = oo + \frac{ao3}{2e}. \quad o.p:: ee - ap. \quad ee + ao.$$

$$o.p - o:: e. \frac{ao}{e} = BC. 8F:: CF. kf = Cf - CF = 2FH = \frac{naoo}{e}. \quad \frac{naoo}{2e3} = FH. \quad \frac{nnoo}{2e3} = FG:: A. n$$

Ergo $GH \perp FH$ et corpus non acceleratur.

$$\frac{naoo}{2e3} = Cf - CF. \quad \frac{a}{n} = \frac{Cf - CF}{FG} \text{ ut resistentia.} \quad \frac{a}{2ne} \text{ ut densitas.}$$

$$GF = \frac{CF9}{2GD} = \text{dato.} \quad CF\dagger \text{ ut } GD. \quad CF \text{ ut } GD^{\frac{1}{2}}$$

Velocitas ut $GD^{\frac{1}{2}}$. Decrementum $\mathcal{V}$

BD ut $GD^{\frac{3}{2}}$. $4g$ ut $OD, DG^{\frac{1}{2}}$, decrementum $\square^{ti}$ velocitatis.

velocitatis utqs decrementum $\square^{ti}$ velocitatis.

$$\frac{Cf - CF}{2} = HF. \quad \frac{CF9}{2C3} :: \text{resist. Grav.}$$

$$\frac{\sqrt{fg \times fd + dg} - \sqrt{FG} \times \overline{FD + GD}}{2}, FG :: \sqrt{fd + dg} - \sqrt{FD + DG}. \quad 2\sqrt{FG} :: \sqrt{dg} - \sqrt{DG}. \sqrt{2FG}$$

$Ct = CFG. \quad OB = a. \quad BC = e. \quad BD = o = B \bullet i. \quad Bd = p.$

$$2 8o3 \sqrt{oo + RQoo} \text{ io } \quad 4RRo4 \quad \frac{ann}{2e5} \times \frac{n}{e} \text{ ad } \frac{n\dagger}{2e8} \text{ ut } \frac{a}{e} \text{ ad } \frac{n}{2e2}$$

Grav. Resist::

NB 1. The Electors of Brandenburg & Saxony & the House of Lunenburg have agreed for coining their moneys of equal value though not of equal allay.

that the French mark of gold & silver is to y ounce Troy of y Exchequer Tower

2 ounce French for gold & silver equals 7 ounces

59 to 60 26650 (24009 ...

222 . 164 :: 111. 82 :: 325. ...

222 . 16½ :: 178. 18536.

193,536

8 . 1 . 7 . 25.

440 . 1 :: 165.75

6 . 21 . 7½ 21.

27 . 6 . 74

Justin Martyr seems to have read ὁ or ὅς. For so Justin, in his epistle to Diognetus, in saying [Οὗ χάριν ἀπέστειλε Λόγον, ἵνα κόσμω φανῇ ὃς ἀπὸ ἐθνῶν ἐπιστευθη] [For wch διὰ ἀποστόλων κηρυχθεὶς, ὑπὸ ἐθνῶν ἐπιστευθη: ὑπο, being cause A Word that he might appear to the world: was believed on by the Gentiles] he interprets not Θεος God but ὁ or ὅς Λόγος. And had Θεος been in his text it would have needed no interpretation.

For that Photinus held the Word to be the λόγος προφορικός emitted outwardly as it were by speaking before the World began, is signified also by Ambrose in these words. Et Deus erat Verbum. Non ergo in prolatione sermonis hoc Verbum est, sed in illa caelestis designatione virtutis, ut confutatur Photinus. Ambr. l. 1 de fide, c. 4. And Augustin tells us that Photinus

17 New Directions in Science and Thought in the Sixteenth and Seventeenth Centuries

The Scientific Revolution

New Departures

The sixteenth and seventeenth centuries witnessed a sweeping change in the scientific view of the universe. An earth-centered picture of the universe gave way to one in which the earth was only another planet orbiting about the sun. The sun itself became one of millions of stars. This transformation of humankind's perception of its place in the larger scheme of things led to a vast rethinking of moral and religious matters as well as of scientific theory. At the same time the new scientific concepts and the methods of their construction became so impressive that subsequent knowledge in the Western world has been deemed correct

Sir Isaac Newton (1642–1727) was the most illustrious figure of the scientific revolution. This page from his manuscripts shows the variety of his interests: calculations of motion at the top, comparisons of foreign currency in the middle, notes on theology at the bottom. [The University Library, Cambridge.]

only as it has approximated knowledge as defined by science. Perhaps no single intellectual development proved to be more significant for the future of European and Western civilization.

The process by which this new view of the universe and of scientific knowledge came to be established is normally termed the *Scientific Revolution*. However, care must be taken in the use of this metaphor. The word *revolution* normally denotes fairly rapid changes in the political world, involving large numbers of people. The Scientific Revolution was not rapid, nor did it involve more than a few hundred human beings. It was a complex movement with many false starts and many brilliant people with wrong as well as useful ideas. It took place in the studies and the crude laboratories of thinkers in Poland, Italy, Bohemia, France, and Great Britain. It stemmed from two major tendencies. The first, as illustrated by Nicolaus Copernicus, was the imposition of important small changes on existing models of thought. The second, as embodied by Francis Bacon, was the desire to pose new kinds of questions and to use new methods of investigation. In both cases, scientific thought changed the current and traditional opinions in other fields.

Nicolaus Copernicus

Copernicus (1473–1543) was a Polish astronomer who enjoyed a very high reputation throughout his life. He had been educated in Italy and corresponded with other astronomers throughout Europe. However, he had not been known for strikingly original or unorthodox thought. In 1543, the year of his death, Copernicus published *On the Revolutions of the Heavenly Spheres.* Because he died near the time of publication, the fortunes of his work are not the story of one person's crusade for progressive science. Copernicus's book was "a revolution-making rather than a revolutionary text."[1] What Copernicus did was to provide an intellectual springboard for a complete criticism of the then-dominant view of the position of the earth in the universe.

At the time of Copernicus the standard explanation of the earth and the heavens was that associated with Ptolemy and his work entitled the *Almagest* (A.D. 150). There was not just one Ptolemaic system; rather, several versions had been de-

[1] Thomas S. Kuhn, *The Copernican Revolution: Planetary Astronomy in the Development of Western Thought* (New York: Vintage, 1959), p. 135.

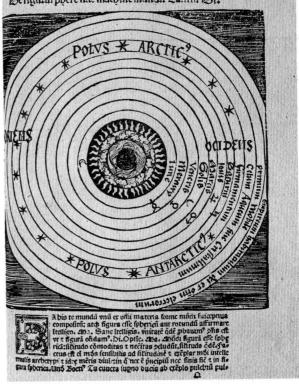

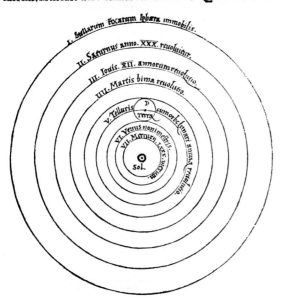

View of the universe as described by Claudius Ptolemy, an astronomer of Alexandria, Egypt, in the second century. Ptolemy's view, which put the earth unmoving in the center with the other heavenly objects circling it (the sun being in the fourth circle), dominated astronomy until the sixteenth century. The illustration is from a book by Gregor Reisch, Margarita Philosophica (1515). [The British Library, London.]

veloped over the centuries by commentators on the original book. Most of these systems assumed that the earth was the center of the universe. Above the earth lay a series of crystalline spheres, one of which contained the moon, another the sun, and still others the planets and the stars. This was the astronomy found in such works as Dante's *Divine Comedy.* At the outer regions of these spheres lay the realm of God and the angels. Aristotelian physics provided the intellectual underpinnings of the Ptolemaic systems. The earth had to be the center

Nicolaus Copernicus's view of the universe with the sun in the center. The basis of the scientific and intellectual revolution initiated by the Polish astronomer (1473–1543) is summarized in this diagram printed in his De Revolutionibus Orbium Coelestium *(On the Revolutions of Heavenly Bodies) of 1543. [The British Library, London.]*

500

because of its heaviness. The stars and the other heavenly bodies had to be enclosed in the crystalline spheres so that they could move. Nothing could move unless something was actually moving it. The state of rest was natural; motion was the condition that required explanation.

Numerous problems were associated with this system, and these had long been recognized. The most important was the observed motions of the planets. Planets could be seen moving in noncircular patterns around the earth. At certain times the planets actually appeared to be going backward. The Ptolemaic systems explained these strange motions primarily through *epicycles*. The planets were said to make a second revolution in an orbit tangent to their primary orbit around the earth. The epicycle was compared with a jewel on a ring. Other intellectual but nonobservational difficulties

❧ Copernicus Ascribes Movement to the Earth

Copernicus published *De Revolutionibus Orbium Caelestium (On the Revolutions of the Heavenly Spheres)* in 1543. In his preface, which was addressed to Pope Paul III, he explained what had led him to think that the earth moved around the sun and what he thought were some of the scientific consequences of the new theory. The reader should note how important Copernicus considered the opinions of ancient writers who had also ascribed motion to the earth. This is a good example of the manner in which familiarity with the ancients gave many Renaissance writers the self-confidence to criticize medieval ideas.

I may well presume, most Holy Father, that certain people, as soon as they hear that in this book about the Revolutions of the Spheres of the Universe I ascribe movement to the earthly globe, will cry out that, holding such views, I should at once be hissed off the stage. . . .

So I should like your Holiness to know that I was induced to think of a method of computing the motions of the spheres by nothing else than the knowledge that the Mathematicians [who had previously considered the problem] are inconsistent in these investigations.

For, first, the mathematicians are so unsure of the movements of the Sun and Moon that they cannot even explain or observe the constant length of the seasonal year. Secondly, in determining the motions of these and of the other five planets, they use neither the same principles and hypotheses nor the same demonstrations of the apparent motions and revolutions. . . . Nor have they been able thereby to discern or deduce the principal thing—namely the shape of the Universe and the unchangeable symmetry of its parts. . . .

I pondered long upon this uncertainty of mathematical tradition in establishing the motions of the system of the spheres. At last I began to chafe that philosophers could by no means agree on any one certain theory of the mechanism of the Universe, wrought for us by a supremely good and orderly Creator. . . . I therefore took pains to read again the works of all the philosophers on whom I could lay hand to seek out whether any of them had ever supposed that the motions of the spheres were other than those demanded by the [Ptolemaic] mathematical schools. I found first in Cicero that Hicetas [of Syracuse, fifth century B.C.] had realized that the Earth moved. Afterwards I found in Plutarch that certain others had held the like opinion. . . .

Thus assuming motions, which in my work I ascribe to the Earth, by long and frequent observations I have at last discovered that, if the motions of the rest of the planets be brought into relation with the circulation of the Earth and be reckoned in proportion to the circles of each planet, not only do their phenomena presently ensue, but the orders and magnitudes of all stars and spheres, nay the heavens themselves, become so bound together that nothing in any part thereof could be moved from its place without producing confusion of all the other parts of the Universe as a whole.

As quoted in Thomas S. Kuhn, *The Copernican Revolution: Planetary Astronomy in the Development of Western Thought* (New York: Vintage Books, 1959), pp. 137–139, 141–142.

related to the immense speed at which the spheres had to move around the earth. To say the least, the Ptolemaic systems were cluttered. However, they were effective explanations as long as one assumed Aristotelian physics and the Christian belief that the earth rested at the center of the created universe.

Copernicus's *On the Revolutions of the Heavenly Spheres* challenged this picture in the most conservative manner possible. It suggested that if the earth were assumed to move about the sun in a circle, many of the difficulties with the Ptolemaic systems would disappear or become simpler. Although not wholly eliminated, the number of epicycles would be somewhat fewer. The motive behind this shift away from an earth-centered universe was to find a solution to the problems of planetary motion. By allowing the earth to move around the sun, Copernicus was able to construct a more mathematically elegant basis for astronomy. He had been discontented with the traditional system because it was mathematically clumsy and inconsistent. The primary appeal of his new system was its mathematical aesthetics: with the sun at the center of the universe, mathematical astronomy would make more sense. A change in the conception of the position of the earth meant that the planets were actually moving in circular orbits and only seemed to be doing otherwise because of the position of the observers on earth.

Except for the modification in the position of the earth, most of the other parts of Copernicus's book were Ptolemaic. The path of the planets remained circular. Genuine epicycles still existed in the heavens. His system was no more accurate than the existing ones for predicting the location of the planets. He had employed no new evidence. The major impact of his work was to provide another way of confronting some of the difficulties inherent in Ptolemaic astronomy. This work did not immediately replace the old astronomy, but it did allow other people who were also discontented with the Ptolemaic systems to think in new directions.

Copernicus's concern about mathematics provided an example of the single most important factor in the developing new science. The key to the future development of the Copernican revolution lay in the fusion of mathematical astronomy with further empirical data and observation, and mathematics became the model to which the new scientific thought would conform. The new empirical evidence helped to persuade the learned public.

Hypothetical reconstruction of the printing press of Johannes Gutenberg of Mainz (in what is not West Germany). Between about 1435 and 1455, Gutenberg worked out the complete technology of making individual rectangular metal types, composing the type into pages held together by pressure, and printing from those on an adaptation of the wooden standing press with ink of lampblack mixed with oil varnish. This new technology for the first time made it possible to manufacture numerous identical copies of written works and was basic to the intellectual development of the West. [Gutenberg-Museum, Mainz.]

Tycho Brahe and Johannes Kepler

The next major step toward the conception of a sun-centered system was taken by Tycho Brahe (1546–1601). He actually spent most of his life opposing Copernicus and advocating a different kind of earth-centered system. He suggested that the moon and the sun revolved around the earth and that the other planets revolved around the sun. However, in attacking Copernicus, he gave the latter's ideas more publicity. More importantly, this Danish astronomer's major weapon against Copernican astronomy was a series of new naked-eye astronomical observations. Brahe constructed the most accurate tables of observations that had been drawn up for centuries.

When Brahe died, these tables came into the possession of Johannes Kepler (1571–1630), a German astronomer. Kepler was a convinced Copernican, but his reasons for taking that position were not scientific. Kepler was deeply influenced by Renaissance Neoplatonism and its honoring of the sun. These Neoplatonists were also determined to discover mathematical harmonies in those numbers that would support a sun-centered universe. After much work Kepler discovered that to keep the sun at the center of things, he must abandon the Copernican concept of circular orbits. The mathematical relationships that emerged from a consideration of Brahe's observations suggested that the orbits of the planets were elliptical. Kepler published his findings in 1609 in a book entitled *On the Motion of Mars*. He had solved the problem of planetary orbits by using Copernicus's sun-centered universe and Brahe's empirical data.

Kepler had, however, also defined a new problem. None of the available theories could explain why the planetary orbits were elliptical. That solution awaited the work of Sir Isaac Newton.

Galileo Galilei

From Copernicus to Brahe to Kepler there had been little new information about the heavens that might not have been known to Ptolemy. However, in the same year that Kepler published his volume on Mars, an Italian scientist named Galileo Galilei (1564–1642) first turned a telescope on the heavens. Through that recently invented instrument he saw stars where none had been known to exist, mountains on the moon, spots moving across the sun, and moons orbiting Jupiter. The heavens were far more complex than anyone had formerly suspected. None of these discoveries proved that the earth orbited the sun, but they did suggest the complete inadequacy of the Ptolemaic system. It simply could not accommodate itself to all of these new phenomena. Some of Galileo's colleagues at the university of Padua were so unnerved that they refused to look through the telescope. Galileo publicized his findings and arguments for the Copernican system in numerous works, the most famous of which was his *Dialogues on the Two Chief Systems of the World* (1632). This book brought down on him the condemnation of the Roman Catholic church. He was compelled to recant his opinions. However, he is reputed to have muttered after the recantation, "E pur si muove" ("It [the earth] still moves").

Galileo's discoveries and his popularization of the Copernican system were of secondary importance in his life work. His most important achievement was to articulate the concept of a universe totally subject to mathematical laws. More than any other writer of the century he argued that nature in its most minute details displayed mathematical regularity. He once wrote:

Galileo Galilei, the Florentine whose observations through a telescope helped confirm Copernicus' theories. Galileo's revolutionary findings showed the inaccuracy of the Ptolemaic assumption that the earth was the center of the universe and laid the foundations of modern astronomy. [New York Public Library Picture Collection.]

❧ Galileo Discusses the Relationship of Science and the Bible

The religious authorities were often critical of the discoveries and theories of six-teenth- and seventeenth-century science. For many years religious and scientific writers debated the implications of the Copernican theory in the reading of the Bible. For years before his condemnation by the Roman Catholic Church in 1633, Galileo had contended that scientific theory and religious piety were compatible. In his *Letter to the Grand Duchess Christiana* (of Tuscany) written in 1615, Galileo argued that God had revealed truth in both the Bible and physical nature and that the truth of physical nature did not contradict the Bible if the latter were properly under-stood.

The reason produced for condemning the opinion that the earth moves and the sun stands still is that in many places in the Bible one may read that the sun moves and the earth stands still. . . .

With regard to this argument, I think in the first place that it is very pious to say and prudent to affirm that the holy Bible can never speak untruth—whenever its true meaning is understood. But I be-lieve nobody will deny that it is often very abstruse, and may say things which are quite different from what its bare words signify. . . .

This being granted, I think that in discussions of physical problems we ought to begin not from the au-thority of scriptural passages, but from sense-experi-ences and necessary demonstrations; for the holy Bible and the phenomena of nature proceed alike from the divine Word, the former as the dictate of the Holy Ghost and the latter as the observant executrix of God's commands. It is necessary for the Bible, in order to be accommodated to the understanding of every man, to speak many things which appear to differ from the absolute truth so far as the bare mean-ing of the words is concerned. But Nature, on the other hand, is inexorable and immutable; she never transgresses the laws imposed upon her, or cares a whit whether her abstruse reasons and methods of operation are understandable to men. For that rea-son it appears that nothing physical which sense-

experience sets before our eyes, or which necessary demonstrations prove to us, ought to be called in question (much less condemned) upon the testimony of biblical passages which may have some different meaning beneath their words. For the Bible is not chained in every expression to conditions as strict as those which govern all physical effects; nor is God any less excellently revealed in Nature's actions than in the sacred statements of the Bible. . . .

From this I do not mean to infer that we need not have an extraordinary esteem for the passages of holy Scripture. On the contrary, having arrived at any certainties in physics, we ought to utilize these as the most appropriate aids in the true exposition of the Bible and in the investigation of those meanings which are necessarily contained therein for these must be concordant with demonstrated truths. I should judge the authority of the Bible was designed to per-suade men of those articles and propositions which, surpassing all human reasoning, could not be made credible by science, or by any other means than through the very mouth of the Holy Spirit. . . .

But I do not feel obliged to believe that the same God who has endowed us with senses, reason, and intellect has intended to forgo their use and by some other means to give us knowledge which we can at-tain by them.

Discoveries and Opinions of Galileo, trans. and ed. by Stillman Drake (Garden City, N.Y.: Double-day Anchor Books, 1957), pp. 181–183.

Philosophy is written in that great book which ever lies before our eyes—I mean the universe—but we cannot understand it if we do not first learn the language and grasp the symbols in which it is written. This book is writ-ten in the mathematical language, and the symbols are triangles, circles, and other geometrical figures, without whose help it is impossible to comprehend a single word of it; without which one wanders through a dark laby-rinth.[2]

[2] Quoted in E. A. Burtt, *The Metaphysical Foundations of Modern Physical Science* (Garden City, N.Y.: Anchor-Doubleday, 1954), p. 75.

ABOVE: *Galileo, working at first from others' suggestion, effectively invented the telescope. This is his 1609 instrument. His observations of the physical features on earth's moon and of the cyclical phases of the planet Venus and his discovery of the most prominent moons of the planet Jupiter were the first major astronomical observations since antiquity and had revolutionary intellectual and theological implications. [Istituto e Museo de Storia della Scienza, Florence.]*

BELOW: *A page from Galileo's notebook showing his notations about his observations of Jupiter and its satellites. [Dr. G.B. Pineider, Florence.]*

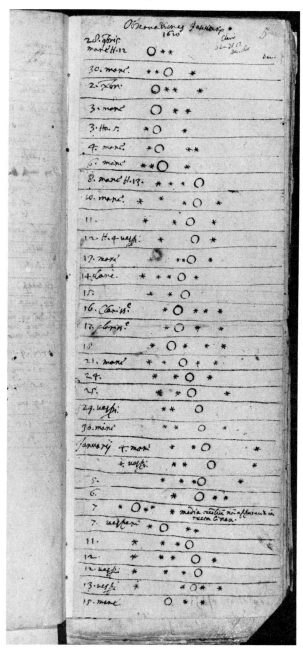

The microscope was the telescope's companion as a major optical invention of the seventeenth century. Several people, including Galileo, had a hand in its development, but the greatest progress—and the most amazing results—came from the Hollander Anton van Leeuwenhoek (1632–1723) who, using only primitive simple instruments made by himself, was the first person actually to see protozoa and bacteria, and from the Englishman Robert Hooke (1635–1703). Hooke's fairly elaborate microscope is shown here. [Courtesy Bausch and Lomb, Inc.]

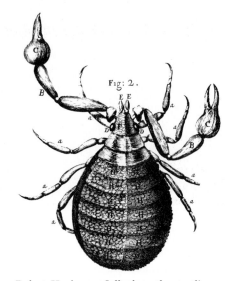

ABOVE: *Robert Hooke carefully drew the startling results of his microscopic explorations. From his book* Micrographia *(1665) comes this rendering of the body louse; even such familiar small creatures had not been seen before in this detail.*

AT LEFT: *Spectacles were an earlier optical aid. They were known at least as early as the fourteenth century, and by the sixteenth they appear fairly frequently in portraits. Here the sixteenth-century German painter Hermann Tom Ring imagines the classical Roman author Vergil reading with spectacles. [Bettmann Archive.]*

The universe was rational; however, its rationality was not that of Scholastic logic but of mathematics. Copernicus had thought that the heavens conformed to mathematical regularity; Galileo saw this regularity throughout all physical nature. He believed that the smallest atom behaved with the same mathematical precision as the largest heavenly sphere.

Galileo's thought meant that a world of quantity was replacing one of qualities. Mathematical quantities and relationships would henceforth increasingly be used to describe nature. Color, beauty, taste, and the like would be reduced to numerical relationships. And eventually social relationships would be envisioned in a mathematical model. Nature was cold, rational, mathematical, and mechanistic. What was real and lasting in the world was what was mathematically measurable. Few intellectual shifts have wrought such momentous changes for Western civilization.

René Descartes

No writer of the seventeenth century more fully adopted the geometric spirit of contemporary mathematics than René Descartes (1596–1650). He was a gifted mathematician who invented analytic geometry, and he was the author of major works on numerous scientific topics. However, his most important contribution was to scientific method. He wanted to proceed by deduction rather than by empirical observation and induction.

In 1637 Descartes published a *Discourse on Method* in which he attempted to provide a basis for all thinking founded on a mathematical model. He published the work in French rather than in Latin because he wanted it to have wide circulation and application. He began by saying that he would doubt everything except those propositions about which he could have clear and distinct ideas. This approach rejected all forms of intellectual authority except the conviction of his own reason. He concluded that he could not doubt his own act of thinking and his own existence. From this base he proceeded to deduce the existence of God. The presence of God was important to Descartes because God was the guarantor of the correctness of clear and distinct ideas. Because God was not a deceiver, the ideas of God-given reason could not be false.

Descartes believed that this powerful human rea-

Rene Descartes, the reputed father of modern philosophy. He was famed for his declaration "Cogito, ergo sum" ("I think, therefore I am"). This engraving was made from a picture by Francis Hals in the Louvre. [New York Public Library Picture Collection.]

son could fully comprehend the world. He divided existing things into mind and body. Thinking was the characteristic of the mind, extension of the body. Within the material world, mathematical laws reigned supreme. These could be grasped by the human reason. Because the laws were mathematical, they could be deduced from each other and constituted a complete system. The world of extension was the world of the scientist, whereas the mind was related to theology and philosophy. In the material world there was no room for spirits, divinity, or anything nonmaterial. Descartes had separated mind from body in order to banish the former from the realm of scientific speculation. He wanted to resurrect the speculative use of reason, but in a limited manner. It was to be applied only to the mechanical and mathematical realm of matter.

Descartes's emphasis on deduction and rational speculation exercised broad influence. Well into the eighteenth century European thinkers ap-

MAJOR WORKS OF THE SCIENTIFIC REVOLUTION

1543	*On the Revolutions of the Heavenly Spheres* (Copernicus)
1605	*The Advancement of Learning* (Bacon)
1609	*On the Motion of Mars* (Kepler)
1620	*Novum Organum* (Bacon)
1632	*Dialogues on the Two Chief Systems of the World* (Galileo)
1637	*Discourse on Method* (Descartes)
1687	*Principia Mathematica* (Newton)

An 1827 engraving of Sir Francis Bacon by J. Thompson. Bacon's beliefs that knowledge should produce useful results and that one must observe phenomena before trying to explain them challenged Scholastic modes of thinking and learning. [New York Public Library Picture Collection.]

pealed to Descartes's method, which moved from broad intellectual generalizations to specific phenomena. The method then attempted to see how the phenomena could be interpreted so as to mesh with the generalization. However, that method was eventually overcome by the force of scientific induction, whereby the observer or scientist began with observations of empirical data and then attempted to draw generalizations from those observations. The major champion of the inductive method during the early seventeenth century had been Francis Bacon.

Francis Bacon

Bacon (1561–1626) was an Englishman of almost universal accomplishment. He was a lawyer, a high royal official, and the author of histories, moral essays, and philosophical discourses. Traditionally he has been regarded as the father of empiricism and of experimentation in science. Much of this reputation is unearned. Bacon was not a scientist except in the most amateur fashion. His accomplishment was setting a tone and helping to create a climate in which other scientists worked. In books such as *The Advancement of Learning* (1605), the *Novum Organum* (1620), and the *New Atlantis* (1627), Bacon attacked the Scholastic belief that most truth had already been discovered and only required explanation, as well as the Scholastic reverence for intellectual authority in general. He believed that Scholastic thinkers paid too much attention to tradition and to knowledge achieved by the ancients. He urged contemporaries to strike out on their own in search of a new understanding of nature. He wanted seventeenth-century Europeans

to have confidence in themselves and their own abilities rather than in the people and methods of the past. Bacon was one of the first major European writers to champion the desirability of innovation and change.

Bacon believed that human knowledge should produce useful results. In particular, knowledge of nature should be brought to the aid of the human condition. Those goals required the modification or abandonment of Scholastic modes of learning and thinking. Bacon contended, "The [Scholastic] logic now in use serves more to fix and give stability to the errors which have their foundation in commonly received notions than to help the search after truth."[3] Scholastic philosophers could not escape from their syllogisms to examine the foundations of their thought and intellectual presuppositions. Bacon urged that philosophers and investi-

[3] Quoted in Franklin Baumer, *Main Currents of Western Thought*, 4th ed. (New Haven, Conn.: Yale, 1978), p. 281.

gators of nature examine the evidence of their senses before constructing logical speculations. In a famous passage he divided all philosophers into "men of experiment and men of dogmas." He observed:

The men of experiment are like the ant, they only collect and use; the reasoners resemble spiders, who make cobwebs out of their own substance. But the bee takes a middle course: it gathers its material from the flowers of the garden and of the field, but transforms and digests it by a power of its own. Not unlike this is the true business of philosophy.[4]

By directing scientists toward an examination of empirical evidence, Bacon hoped that they would achieve new knowledge and thus new capabilities for humankind.

[4]Quoted in ibid., p. 288.

❧ Bacon Attacks the Idols That Harm Human Understanding

Francis Bacon wanted the men and women of his era to have the courage to change the way in which they thought about physical nature. In this famous passage from the *Novum Organum* (1620) Bacon attempted to explain why people had such difficulty in asking new questions and seeking new answers. His observations may still be relevant to the manner in which people form and hold their opinions in our own day.

The idols and false notions which are now in possession of the human understanding, and have taken deep root therein, not only so beset men's minds that truth can hardly find entrance, but even after entrance is obtained, they will again in the very instauration of the sciences meet and trouble us, unless men being forewarned of the danger fortify themselves as far as may be against their assaults.

There are four classes of Idols which beset men's minds. To these for distinction's sake I have assigned names,—calling the first class Idols of the Tribe; *the second,* Idols of the Cave; *the third,* Idols of the Marketplace; *the fourth,* Idols of the Theatre.

. . . .

The Idols of the Tribe have their foundation in human nature itself; and in the tribe or race of men. For it is a false assertion that the sense of man is the measure of things. On the contrary, all perceptions as well as the sense as of the mind are according to the measure of the individual and not according to the measure of the universe. And the human understanding is like a false mirror, which, receiving rays irregularly, distorts and discolours the nature of things by mingling its own nature with it.

The Idols of the Cave are the idols of the individual man. For every one (besides the errors common to human nature in general) has a cave or den of his own, which refracts and discolours the light of nature; owing either to his own proper and peculiar nature; or to his education and conversation with others; or to the reading of books, and the authority of those whom he esteems and admires. . . .

There are also Idols formed by the intercourse and association of men with each other, which I call Idols of the Marketplace, on account of the commerce and consort of men there. For it is by discourse that men associate; and words are imposed according to the apprehension of the vulgar. And therefore the ill and unfit choice of words wonderfully obstructs the understanding. . . .

Lastly, there are Idols which have immigrated into men's minds from the various dogmas of philosophies, and also from wrong laws of demonstration. These I call Idols of the Theatre; because in my judgment all the received systems are but so many stageplays, representing worlds of their own creation after an unreal and scenic fashion.

Francis Bacon, *Essays, Advancement of Learning, New Atlantis, and Other Pieces,* ed. by Richard Foster Jones (New York: Odyssey, 1937), pp. 278–280.

Bacon compared himself with Columbus plotting a new route to intellectual discovery. The comparison is significant, because it displays the consciousness of a changing world that appears so often in writers of the late sixteenth and early seventeenth centuries. They were rejecting the past not from simple hatred but rather from a firm understanding that the world was much more complicated than their medieval forebears had thought.

Neither Europe nor European thought could remain self-contained. There were not only new worlds on the globe but also new worlds of the mind. Most of the people in Bacon's day, including the intellectuals, thought that the best era of human history lay in antiquity. Bacon dissented vigorously from that point of view. He looked to a future of material improvement achieved through the empirical examination of nature. His own theory of induction from empirical evidence was quite unsystematic, but his insistence on appeal to experience influenced others whose methods were more productive. His great achievement was persuading increasing numbers of thinkers that scientific thought must conform to empirical experience.

Bacon gave science a progressionist bias. Science was to have a practical purpose and the goal of human improvement. Some scientific investigation does possess this character. Much pure research does not. However, Bacon linked in the public mind the concepts of science and material progress. This was a powerful idea and has continued to influence Western civilization to the present day. It has made science and those who can appeal to the authority of science major forces for change and innovation. Thus, though not making any major scientific contribution himself, Bacon directed investigators of nature to a new method and a new purpose.

Isaac Newton

Isaac Newton (1642–1727) drew on the work of his predecessors and his own brilliance to solve the major remaining problem of planetary motion and to establish a basis for physics that endured more than two centuries. The question that continued to perplex seventeenth-century scientists who accepted the theories of Copernicus, Kepler, and Galileo was how the planets and other heavenly bodies moved in an orderly fashion. The Ptolemaic

and Aristotelian answer had been the crystalline spheres and a universe arranged in the order of the heaviness of its parts. Numerous unsatisfactory theories had been set forth to deal with the question.

In 1687 Newton published *The Mathematical Principles of Natural Philosophy*, better known by its Latin title of *Principia Mathematica*. Much of the research and thinking for this great work had taken place more than fifteen years earlier. Newton was heavily indebted to the work of Galileo and particularly to the latter's view that inertia could exist in either a state of motion or a state of rest. Galileo's mathematical bias permeated Newton's thought. Newton reasoned that the planets and all other physical objects in the universe moved through mutual attraction. Every object in the uni-

Sir Isaac Newton, discoverer of the mathematical and physical laws governing the force of gravity. Newton believed that religion and science were compatible and mutually supportive. To study nature was to gain a better understanding of the Creator. [New York Public Library Picture Collection.]

*William Blake's Newton is, of course, not a portrait of an individual. Instead, it dramatizes
and glorifies the detached, almost God-like scientist who can solve the mysteries of the universe
and display the results with mathematical precision. [The Tate Gallery, London.]*

verse affected every other object through gravity. The attraction of gravity explained why the planets moved in an orderly rather than a chaotic manner. He had found that "the force of gravity towards the whole planet did arise from and was compounded of the forces of gravity towards all its parts, and towards every one part was in the inverse proportion of the squares of the distances from the part."[5] Newton demonstrated this relationship mathematically. He made no attempt to explain the nature of gravity itself.

Newton was a great mathematical genius, but he also upheld the importance of empirical data and observation. He believed, in good Baconian fashion, that one must observe phenomena before attempting to explain them. The final test of any theory or hypothesis for him was whether it described what could actually be observed. He was a great opponent of Descartes's rationalism, which he believed included insufficient guards against error. As Newton's own theory of universal gravitation became increasingly accepted, the Baconian bias also became more fully popularized.

With the work of Newton the natural universe became a realm of law and regularity. Spirits and

[5] Quoted in A. Rupert Hall, *From Galileo to Newton,* 1630–1720 (London: Fontana, 1970), p. 300.

❧ Newton Sets Forth Rules of Reasoning in Philosophy

Philosophy was the term that seventeenth-century writers used to describe the new science. In this passage from his *Principia Mathematica* (1687) Isaac Newton laid down what he regarded as the fundamental rules for scientific reasoning. The reader should notice the importance he placed on experimental evidence and his desire to find rules or regularities that exist throughout the natural order.

Rule I. We are to admit no more causes of natural things than such as are both true and sufficient to explain their appearances.

To this purpose the philosophers say that Nature does nothing in vain, and more is in vain when less will serve; for Nature is pleased with simplicity, and affects not the pomp of superfluous causes.

Rule II. Therefore to the same natural effects we must, as far as possible, assign the same causes.

As to respiration in a man and in a beast; the descent of stones in Europe and in America; the light of our culinary fire and of the sun; the reflection of light in the earth, and in the planets.

Rule III. The qualities of bodies, which admit neither intension nor remission of degrees, and which are found to belong to all bodies within the reach of our experiments, are to be esteemed the universal qualities of all bodies whatsoever.

For since the qualities of bodies are only known to us by experiments, we are to hold for universal all such as universally agree with experiments and such as are not liable to diminution can never be quite taken away. We are certainly not to relinquish the evidence of experiments for the sake of dreams and vain fictions of our own devising. . . . We no other way know the extension of bodies than by our senses,

nor do these reach it in all bodies; but because we perceive extension in all that are sensible, therefore we ascribe it universally to all others also. That abundance of bodies are hard, we learn by experience; and because the hardness of the whole arises from the hardness of the parts, we therefore justly infer the hardness of the undivided particles not only of the bodies we feel but of all others. That bodies are impenetrable, we gather not from reason, but from sensation. . . .

Lastly, if it universally appears, by experiments and astronomical observations, that all bodies about the earth gravitate towards the earth, and that in proportion to the quantity of matter which they severally contain; . . . we must, in consequence of this rule, universally allow that all bodies whatsoever are endowed with a principle of universal gravitation. . . .

Rule IV. In experimental philosophy we are to look upon propositions collected by general induction from phaenomena as accurately or very nearly true, notwithstanding any contrary hypotheses that may be imagined, till such time as other phaenomena occur, by which they may either be made more accurate, or liable to exceptions.

This rule must follow, that the argument of induction may not be evaded by hypotheses.

Introduction to Contemporary Civilization in the West, 3rd ed., Vol. 1 (New York: Columbia University Press, 1960), pp. 850–852.

---

divinities were no longer necessary to explain its operation. Thus the Scientific Revolution liberated human beings from the fear of a chaotic or haphazard universe. Most of the scientists were very devout people. They saw the new picture of physical nature as suggesting a new picture of God. The Creator of this rational, lawful nature must also be rational. To study nature was to come to a better understanding of that Creator. Science and religious faith were not only compatible but mutually supporting. As Newton wrote, "The main Business of Natural Philosophy is to argue from Phaenomena without feigning Hypothesis, and to deduce Causes from Effects, till we come to the very first Cause, which certainly is not mechanical."[6]

This reconciliation of faith and science allowed

[6] Quoted in Baumer, p. 323.

the new physics and astronomy to spread rapidly. At the very time when Europeans were finally tiring of the wars of religion, the new science provided the basis for a view of God that might lead away from irrational disputes and wars over religious doctrine. Faith in a rational God encouraged faith in the rationality of human beings and in their capacity to improve their lot once liberated from the traditions of the past. The Scientific Revolution provided the great model for the desirability of change and of criticism of inherited views. Yet at the same time the new science caused some people to feel that the mystery had been driven from the universe and that the rational Creator was less loving and less near to humankind than the God of earlier ages.

Writers and Philosophers

The end of the sixteenth century saw weariness with religious strife and incipient unbelief as many could no longer embrace either old Catholic or new Protestant absolutes. Intellectually as well as politically the seventeenth century was a period of transition, one already well prepared for by the thinkers of the Renaissance, who had reacted strongly against medieval intellectual traditions, especially those informed by Aristotle and Scholasticism.

Even as they sought to find a purer culture before the Middle Ages in pagan and Christian antiquity, however, Humanists and Protestants continued to share much of the medieval vision of a unified Christendom. Few were prepared to embrace the secular values and preoccupations of the growing scientific movement, which found its models in mathematics and the natural sciences, rather than in the example and authority of antiquity. Some strongly condemned the work of Copernicus, Kepler, and Galileo, whose theories seemed to fly in the face of commonsense experience as well as to question hallowed tradition.

The thinkers of the Renaissance and the Reformation nonetheless paved the way for the new science and philosophy, both by their attacks on tradition and by their own failure to implement radical reforms. The Humanist revival of interest in ancient skepticism proved an effective foundation for attacks on traditional views of authority and rationality in both religion and science. Already such thinkers as the Italian Pico della Mirandola (1463–1494), the German Agrippa of Nettisheim

(1486–1535), and the Frenchman François Rabelais (1494–1553) had questioned the ability of reason to obtain certitude. Sebastian Castellio (1515–1563), Michel de Montaigne (1533–1592), and Pierre Charron (1541–1603) had been as much repulsed by the new Calvinist religion as John Calvin had been by medieval religion. It was in the wake of such criticism that René Descartes developed a more modest, yet surer, definition of rationality as the tool of the new scientific philosophy.

The writers and philosophers of the seventeenth century were aware that they lived in a period of transition. Some embraced the new science wholeheartedly (Hobbes and Locke), some tried to straddle the two ages (Cervantes, Shakespeare, and Milton), and still others ignored or opposed the new developments that seemed mortally to threaten traditional values (Pascal and Bunyan).

Miguel de Cervantes Saavedra (1547–1616)

Spanish literature of the sixteenth and seventeenth centuries was influenced by the peculiar religious and political history of Spain in this period. Spain was dominated by the Catholic church. Since the joint reign of Ferdinand and Isabella (1479–1504) the church had received the unqualified support of reigning political power. Although there was religious reform in Spain, a Protestant Reformation never occurred, thanks largely to the abiding power of the church and the Inquisition.

The second influence was the aggressive piety of the Spanish rulers Charles I—who became the Holy Roman Emperor as Charles V (1516–1556)—and his son, Philip II (1556–1598). The intertwining of Catholic piety and Spanish political power underlay the third major influence on Spanish literature: preoccupation with medieval chivalric virtues—in particular, questions of honor and loyalty. The novels and plays of the period almost invariably focus on a special decision involving a character's reputation as his honor or loyalty is tested. In this regard Spanish literature may be said to have remained more Catholic and medieval than that of England and France, where major Protestant movements had occurred. Two of the most important Spanish writers in this period became priests (Lope de Vega and Pedro Calderón de la Barca), and the one generally acknowledged to be the greatest Spanish writer of all time, Cervantes, was preoccupied in his work with the strengths and weaknesses of religious idealism.

Cervantes was born in Alcalá, the son of a nomadic physician. Having received only a smattering of formal education, he educated himself by insatiable reading in vernacular literature and immersion in the "school of life." As a young man he worked in Rome for a Spanish cardinal. In 1570 he became a soldier and was even decorated for gallantry in the Battle of Lepanto (1571), an engagement that maimed his left hand. While he was returning to Spain in 1575, his ship was captured by pirates, and Cervantes spent five years as a slave in Algiers. On his release and return to Spain he held many odd jobs, among them that of a tax collector. He was several times imprisoned for padding his accounts. He conceived and began to write his most famous work, *Don Quixote,* in 1603, while languishing in prison.

Don Quixote and Sancho Panza, from a nineteenth-century French edition of Cervantes's Don Quixote *illustrated by the French artist Doré.* Don Quixote *is perhaps the supreme literary work of its age.* [*New York Public Library Picture Collection.*]

The first part of *Don Quixote* appeared in 1605 and a second part followed in 1615. If, as many argue, the intent of this work was to satirize the chivalric romances so popular in Spain, Cervantes nonetheless failed to conceal his deep affection for the character he created as an object of ridicule, Don Quixote. The work is satire only on the surface and has remained as much an object of study by philosophers and theologians as by students of Spanish literature. Don Quixote, a none-too-stable middle-aged man, is presented by Cervantes as one driven mad by reading too many chivalric romances. He finally comes to believe that he is an aspirant to knighthood and must prove by brave deeds his worthiness of knightly rank. To this end he acquires a rusty suit of armor, mounts an aged steed (named Rozinante), and chooses for his inspiration a quite unworthy peasant girl, Dulcinea, whom he fancies to be a noble lady to whom he can, with honor, dedicate his life.

Don Quixote's foil in the story—Sancho Panza, a clever, worldly wise peasant who serves as Don Quixote's squire—is an equally fascinating character. Sancho Panza watches with bemused skepticism, but also with genuine sympathy, as his lord does battle with a windmill (which he mistakes for a dragon) and repeatedly makes a fool of himself as he gallops across the countryside. The story ends tragically with Don Quixote's humiliating defeat by a well-meaning friend, who, disguised as a knight, bests Don Quixote in combat and forces him to renounce his quest for knighthood. The humiliated Don Quixote does not, however, come to his senses as a result. He returns sadly to his village to die a shamed and broken-hearted old man.

Throughout *Don Quixote* Cervantes juxtaposed the down-to-earth realism of Sancho Panza with the old-fashioned religious idealism of Don Quixote. The reader perceives that Cervantes really admired the one as much as the other and meant to portray both as representing attitudes necessary for a happy life. Like his English counterpart, William Shakespeare, Cervantes understood the complexity of human nature. He wanted his readers to remember that if they are to be truly happy, men and women need dreams, even impossible ones, just as much as they need a sense of reality.

The other major Spanish writers of the period had a far less universal vision than Cervantes. Lope Felix de Vega Carpio (1562–1635), the author of an incredible number of epics, romances, novels, lyrics, and plays, pandered to popular Spanish tastes and remained content to meet the contemporary demand for entertainment rather than venturing on profound and lasting works. He never wanted for variety in his work, however, and almost singlehandedly created the Spanish national theater. Pedro Calderón de la Barca (1600–1681) wrote court dramas, comedies, and highly sentimental "point of honor" plays that spoke to current national interests and became favorites among later Romantic writers.

William Shakespeare (1564–1616)

Shakespeare, the greatest playwright in the English language, was born in Stratford-on-Avon, where he lived almost all of his life except for the years when he wrote in London. There is much less factual knowledge about him than one would expect of such an important figure. Shakespeare married in 1582 at the early age of eighteen, and he and his wife, Anne Hathaway, had three children (two were twins) by 1585. He apparently worked as a schoolteacher for a time and in this capacity acquired his broad knowledge of Renaissance learning and literature. The argument of some scholars that he was an untutored natural genius is highly questionable. His own learning and his enthusiasm for the education of his day are manifest in the many learned allusions that appear in his plays.

Shakespeare was a man of the country as well as of the town and manifestly enjoyed the life of a country gentleman. There is none of the Puritan distress over worldliness in his work. He took the new commercialism and the bawdy pleasures of the Elizabethan Age in stride and with amusement. The few allusions to the Puritans that exist in his works appear to be more critical than complimentary. In matters of politics, as in those of religion, he was very much a man of his time and not inclined to offend his queen.

That Shakespeare was interested in politics is apparent from his history plays and the references to contemporary political events that fill all his plays. He seems to have viewed government simply, however, through the character of the individual ruler, whether Richard III or Elizabeth Tudor, not in terms of ideal systems or social goals. By modern standards he was a political conservative, accepting the social rankings and the power structure of his day and demonstrating unquestioned patriotism.

The English dramatist and poet, William Shakespeare. This engraving by Martin Droeshout appears on the title page of the collected edition of his plays published in 1623 and is probably as close as we shall come to knowing what he looked like.

Shakespeare knew the theatre as one who participated in every phase of its life—as a playwright, an actor, and a part owner of a theater. He was a member and principal dramatist of a famous company of actors known as the King's Men. During the tenure of Edmund Tilney, who was Queen Elizabeth's Master of Revels during the greater part of Shakespeare's active period (1590–1610), many of Shakespeare's plays were performed at court. The queen was herself a most enthusiastic patron of plays and pageants.

Elizabethan drama was already a distinctive form when Shakespeare began writing. Unlike French drama of the seventeenth century, which was dominated by the court and classical models, English drama developed in the sixteenth and seventeenth centuries as a blending of many extant forms, ranging from classical comedies and tragedies to the medieval morality play and contemporary Italian short stories. In Shakespeare's own library were

This 1596 sketch of the interior of the Swan Theater in London by Johannis de Witt, a Dutch visitor, is the only known contemporary view of an Elizabethan playhouse. In this kind of setting the plays of Marlowe, Shakespeare, Jonson, and their fellows were first seen. [The Granger Collection.]

to be found Holinshed's and other English chronicles; the works of Plutarch, Ovid, and Vergil, among other Latin authors; Arthurian romances and popular songs and fables; the writings of Montaigne and Rabelais; and the major English poets and prose writers.

Shakespeare's tragedies were especially influenced by the work of two of his contemporaries: Thomas Kyd and Christopher Marlowe. Kyd (1558–1594) was the author of the first dramatic version of *Hamlet* and a master at weaving together motive, plot, and tragic intensity. The tragedies of Marlowe (1564–1593) set a model for character, poetry, and style that only Shakespeare among the English playwrights of the period surpassed.

Shakespeare's work was an original synthesis of the best past and current achievements.

Shakespeare mastered the psychology of human motivation and passion. He had a unique talent for psychological penetration, one rivaled only by the French Jansenist dramatist Jean Racine (1639–1699), who, however, remained confined to classical forms and rules. Later Romantic writers claimed Shakespeare as one of their own and contrasted his work sharply with the neoclassicism of Pierre Corneille and Racine, whom they found by comparison to be narrow and mechanical.

Shakespeare wrote histories, comedies, and tragedies. *Richard III* (1593), a very early play, stands out among the examples of the first genre, although some historians have criticized as historically inaccurate his patriotic depiction of Richard, the foe of Henry Tudor, as an unprincipled villain. Shakespeare's comedies, while not attaining the heights of his tragedies, surpass in originality his history plays. Save for *The Tempest* (1611), his last play, the comedies most familiar to modern readers were written between 1598–1602: *Much Ado About Nothing* (1598–1599), *As You Like It* (1598–1600), and *Twelfth Night* (1602).

The tragedies are considered his unique achievement. Four of these were written within a three-year period: *Hamlet* (1603), *Othello* (1604), *King Lear* (1605), and *Macbeth* (1606). The most original of the tragedies, *Romeo and Juliet* (1597), transformed an old popular story into a moving drama of "star-cross'd lovers." Both Romeo and Juliet, denied a marriage by their factious families, die tragic deaths. Romeo, finding Juliet and thinking her dead after she has taken a sleeping potion, poisons himself. Juliet, awakening to find Romeo dead, stabs herself to death with his dagger.

Throughout his lifetime and ever since, Shakespeare has been immensely popular with both the playgoer and the play reader. As Ben Jonson, a contemporary classical dramatist who created his own school of poets, aptly put it in a tribute affixed to the First Folio edition of Shakespeare's plays (1623): "He was not of an age, but for all time."

John Milton (1608–1674)

John Milton was the son of a devout Puritan father. Educated at Saint Paul's School and then at Christ's College of Cambridge University, he became a careful student of Christian and pagan classics. In 1638 he traveled to Italy, where he found in the lingering Renaissance a very congenial intellectual atmosphere. The Phlegraean Fields near Naples, a volcanic region, later became the model for hell in *Paradise Lost,* and it is suspected by some scholars that the Villa d'Este provided the model for paradise in *Paradise Regained.* Milton remained throughout his life a man more at home in the Italian Renaissance, with its high ideals and universal vision, than in the strife-torn England of the seventeenth century.

A man of deep inner conviction and principle, Milton believed that standing a test of character was the most important thing in an individual's life. This belief informed his own personal life and is the subject of much of his literary work. An early poem, *Lycidas,* was a pastoral elegy dealing with one who lived well but not long, Edward King, a close college friend who tragically drowned. In

The English writer and poet John Milton in an engraving by William Faithorne—one of the few authentic contemporary likenesses of him. [The Granger Collection.]

Gul. Faithorne ad Vivum   Delin. et sculpsit.

Joannis Miltoni Effigies Ætat: 62.
1670.

1639 Milton joined the Puritan struggle against Charles I and Archbishop Laud. Employing his literary talents as a pamphleteer, he defended the presbyterian form of church government against the episcopacy and supported other Puritan reforms. After a month-long unsuccessful marriage in 1642 (a marriage later reconciled), he wrote several tracts in defense of the right to divorce. These writings became a factor in Parliament's passage of a censorship law in 1643, against which Milton wrote an eloquent defense of the freedom of the press, *Areopagitica* (1644).

Until the upheavals of the civil war moderated his views, Milton believed that government should have the least possible control over the private lives of individuals. When Parliament divided into Presbyterians and Independents, he took the side of the latter, who wanted to dissolve the national church altogether in favor of the local autonomy of individual congregations. He also defended the execution of Charles I in a tract on the *Tenure of Kings and Magistrates* and later served as secretary to the executive committee of Parliament during Cromwell's protectorate. It was after his intense labor on this tract that his eyesight failed. Milton was totally blind when he wrote his acclaimed masterpieces.

Paradise Lost, Milton's masterpiece of English blank verse, was completed in 1665 and published in 1667. A study of the destructive qualities of pride and the redeeming possibilities of humility, it elaborates in traditional Christian language and concept the revolt of Satan in heaven and the fall of Adam on earth. Milton was throughout preoccupied with the motives of Satan and all who rebel against God. His proud but tragic Satan, one of the great figures of all literature, represents the absolute corruption of potential greatness.

In *Paradise Lost* Milton aspired to give England a lasting epic like that given Greece in Homer's *Iliad* and ancient Rome in Vergil's *Aeneid.* In choosing biblical subject matter, he revealed the influence of contemporary theology on his work. Milton tended to agree with the Arminians, who, unlike the extreme Calvinists, did not believe that all worldly events, including the Fall of Man, were immutably fixed in the eternal decree of God. Milton shared the Arminian belief that human beings must take responsibility for their fate and that human efforts to improve character could, with God's grace, bring salvation.

Perhaps his own blindness, joined with the hope

of making the best of a failed religious revolution, inclined Milton to sympathize with those who urged people to make the most of what they had, even in the face of seemingly sure defeat. That is a manifest concern of his last works, *Samson Agonistes,* which recounts the biblical story of Samson, and *Paradise Regained,* the story of Christ's temptation in the wilderness, both published in 1671.

John Bunyan (1628–1688)

Bunyan was the English author of two classics of sectarian Puritan spirituality: *Grace Abounding* (1666) and *The Pilgrim's Progress* (1678). A Bedford tinker, his works speak especially for the seventeenth-century working people and popular religious culture. Bunyan received only the most basic education before taking up his father's craft. He was drafted into Oliver Cromwell's revolutionary army in 1644 and served for two years, although without seeing actual combat. The visionary fervor of the New Model Army and the imagery of warfare abound in Bunyan's work.

After the restoration of the monarchy in 1660 Bunyan was arrested for his fiery preaching and remained in prison for twelve years. Had he been willing to agree to give up preaching, he might have been released much sooner. But Puritans considered the compromise of one's beliefs a tragic flaw, and Bunyan steadfastly refused all such suggestions.

It was during this period of imprisonment that Bunyan wrote his famous autobiography, *Grace Abounding.* It is both a very personal statement and a model for the faithful. Like *The Pilgrim's Progress,* Bunyan's later masterpiece, *Grace Abounding* expresses Puritan piety at its most fervent. Puritans believed that individuals could do absolutely nothing to save themselves, and this made them extremely restless and introspective. The individual believer could only trust that God had placed her or him among the elect and try each day to live a life that reflected such a favored status. So long as men and women struggled successfully against the flesh and the world, they had presumptive evidence that they were among God's elect. To falter or to become complacent in the face of temptation was to cast doubt on one's faith and salvation and even to raise the specter of eternal damnation.

This anxious questing for salvation came to classic expression in *The Pilgrim's Progress,* a work unique in its contribution to Western religious sym-

A seventeenth-Century illustration from The Pilgrim's Progress. *Bunyan's chief purpose in writing the work was to illustrate the manner in which a Christian could, with faith, successfully confront the temptations of life.* [*The Fotomas Index, London.*]

bolism and imagery. The story of the journey of Christian and his friends Hopeful and Faithful to the Celestial City, it teaches that one must deny spouse, children, and all earthly security and go in search of "Life, life, eternal life." During the long journey, the travelers must resist the temptations of Worldly-Wiseman and Vanity Fair, pass through the Slough of Despond, and endure a long dark night in Doubting Castle, their faith being tested at every turn. Bunyan later wrote a work tracing the progress of Christian's opposite, entitled *The Life*

MAJOR WORKS OF SEVENTEENTH-CENTURY
LITERATURE AND PHILOSOPHY

1605	*King Lear* (Shakespeare)
	Don Quixote, Part I (Cervantes)
1651	*Leviathan* (Hobbes)
1656–1657	*Provincial Letters* (Pascal)
1667	*Paradise Lost* (Milton)
1677	*Ethics* (Spinoza)
1678	*Pilgrim's Progress* (Bunyan)
1690	*Two Treatises of Government* (Locke)
	An Essay Concerning Human Understanding (Locke)

and Death of Mr. Badman (1680), the story of a man so addicted to the bad habits of Restoration society, of which Bunyan strongly disapproved, that he journeyed steadfastly not to heaven but to hell.

The loss of national unity during the Puritan struggle against the Stuart monarchy and the Anglican church took its toll on English literature and drama during the seventeenth century. In 1642 the Puritans had closed the theaters of London. They were reopened after the Restoration of Charles II in 1660, and drama revived following the long Puritan interregnum.

Literary thought thereafter became less experimental and adopted proven classical forms, as a new movement to subject reality to the strict rules of reason began. During the so-called Augustan Age, from John Dryden (1631–1700) to Alexander Pope (1688–1744), classicism was the literary rule.

There was a preoccupation with the world of mundane facts, rather than with universal ideals, and a waning of the transcendental concerns of the Elizabethans and the Puritan divines. As in France, where the French comedy writer Molière (1622–1673) is the outstanding example, English writers tried to please the royal court and aristocracy by turning to more earthy and entertaining popular topics.

Blaise Pascal (1623–1662)

Pascal was a French mathematician and a physical scientist widely acclaimed by his contemporaries. He was also a most devout man, who surrendered all his wealth so that he might more easily pursue an austere, self-disciplined life. Torn between the continuing dogmatism and the new skepticism of the seventeenth century, he aspired to write a work that would refute both the Jesuits, whose casuistry (i.e., confessional tactics designed to minimize and even excuse sinful acts) he considered a distortion of Christian teaching, and the skeptics of his age, who either denied religion altogether (atheists) or accepted it only as it conformed to reason (deists). Such a definitive work was never realized, and his views on these matters exist only in piecemeal form. He wrote against the Jesuits in his *Provincial Letters* (1656–1657), and he left behind a provocative collection of reflections on humankind and religion that was published posthumously under the title *Pensées.*

Pascal was early influenced by the Jansenists, seventeenth-century Catholic opponents of the Jesuits. His sister was a member of the Jansenist

The arithmetical machine invented in 1642 by Blaise Pascal, the French philosopher and mathematician. Its main feature was the automatic carry-forward. The wheels, each divided into nine sections, were connected in such a way that the complete rotation of one of them caused the wheel on the left of it to move forward by one digit. The foundations of adding machines and other mechanical calculators were thus laid by this device. [Culver Pictures.]

❧ Pascal Meditates on Human Beings As Thinking Creatures

Pascal was both a great religious and a great scientific writer. Unlike other scientific thinkers of the seventeenth century, he was not overly optimistic about the ability of science to improve the human condition. Pascal believed that science and philosophy would instead help human beings to understand their situation better. In these passages from his *Pensées (Thoughts)*, he discussed the uniqueness of human beings as the creatures who alone in all the universe are capable of thinking.

339

I can well conceive a man without hands, feet, head (for it is only experience which teaches us that the head is more necessary than feet). But I cannot conceive man without thought; he would be a stone or a brute.

344

Reason commands us far more imperiously than a master; for in disobeying the one we are unfortunate, and in disobeying the other we are fools.

346

Thought constitutes the greatness of man.

347

Man is but a reed, the most feeble thing in nature; but he is a thinking reed. The entire universe need not arm itself to crush him. A vapour, a drop of water suffices to kill him. But, if the universe were to crush him, man would still be more noble than that which killed him, because he knows that he dies and the advantage which the universe has over him; the universe knows nothing of this.

All our dignity consists, then, in thought. By it we must elevate ourselves, and not by space and time which we cannot fill. Let us endeavour, then, to think well; this is the principle of morality.

348

A thinking reed—It is not from space that I must seek my dignity, but from the government of my thought. I shall have no more if I possess worlds. By space the universe encompasses and swallows me up like an atom; by thought I comprehend the world.

Blaise Pascal, *Pensées and The Provincial Letters* (New York: Modern Library, 1941), pp. 115–116.

community of Port Royal near Paris, and after 1654 Pascal himself closely identified with this community. The Jansenists shared with the Calvinists St. Augustine's belief in man's total sinfulness, his eternal predestination by God, and his complete dependence on faith and grace for knowledge of God and salvation.

Pascal believed that reason and science, although attesting to human dignity, remained of no avail in matters of religion. Here only the reasons of the heart and a "leap of faith" could prevail. Pascal saw two essential truths in the Christian religion: that a loving God, worthy of human attainment, exists, and that human beings, because they are corrupted in nature, are utterly unworthy of God. Pascal believed that the atheists and the deists of the age had spurned the lesson of reason. For him rational analysis of the human condition attested humankind's utter mortality and corruption and exposed the weakness of reason itself in resolving the problems of human nature and destiny. Reason should rather drive those who truly heed it to faith and dependence on divine grace.

Pascal made a famous wager with the skeptics. It

is a better bet, he argued, to believe that God exists and to stake everything on his promised mercy than not to do so, because if God does exist, everything will be gained by the believer, whereas the loss incurred by having believed in him should he prove not to exist is by comparison very slight.

Pascal was convinced that belief in God measurably improved earthly life psychologically and disciplined it morally, regardless of whether or not God proved in the end to exist. He thought that great danger lay in the surrender of traditional religious belief. Pascal urged his contemporaries to seek self-understanding by "learned ignorance" and to discover humankind's greatness by recognizing its misery. Thereby Pascal hoped to counter what he believed to be the false optimism of the new rationalism and science.

The Glockenspiel, or clock performance, occurring hourly at the Munich city hall, is another ingenious time-keeping device. [German Information Center, New York.]

Even before Pascal's day, of course, there was a tradition of elaborate mechanical devices throughout Europe. For example, by 1500 there were public clocks in practically every town. One of the most famous is the astronomical clock of Strasbourg's cathedral in France, which presents a parade of allegorical figures every day at noon. [French Government Tourist Office, New York.]

Baruch Spinoza (1632–1677)

The most controversial thinker of the seventeenth century was Baruch Spinoza, the son of a Jewish merchant of Amsterdam. Spinoza's philosophy caused his excommunication by his own synagogue in 1656. In 1670 he published his *Treatise on Religious and Political Philosophy*, a work that criticized the dogmatism of Dutch Calvinists and championed freedom of thought. During his lifetime both Jews and Protestants attacked him as an atheist.

Spinoza's most influential writing, the *Ethics*, was published after his death in 1677. Religious leaders universally condemned it for its apparent espousal of pantheism. God and nature were so closely identified by Spinoza that little room seemed left either for divine revelation in scripture or for the personal immortality of the soul, denials equally repugnant to Jews and to Christians. The *Ethics* was a very complicated work, written in the spirit of the new science as a geometrical system of definitions, axioms, and propositions. It was divided into five parts, which dealt with God, the mind, emotions, human bondage, and human freedom.

The most controversial part of the *Ethics* deals with the nature of substance and of God. According to Spinoza, there is but one substance, which is self-caused, free, and infinite, and God is that substance. From this definition it follows that everything that exists is in God and cannot even be conceived of apart from him. Such a doctrine is not literally pantheistic because God is still seen to be more than the created world that he, as primal substance, embraces. It may perhaps best be described as *panentheism:* the teaching that all that is is within God, yet God remains more than and beyond the natural world. Nonetheless, in Spinoza's view, statements about the natural world are also statements about divine nature. Mind and matter are seen to be extensions of the infinite substance of God; what transpires in the world of humankind and nature is a necessary outpouring of the divine.

Such teaching clearly ran the danger of portraying the world as eternal and human actions as unfree and inevitable, the expression of a divine fatalism. Such points of view have been considered heresies by Jews and Christians because they deny the creation of the world by God in time and destroy any voluntary basis for personal reward and punishment.

Spinoza found enthusiastic supporters in the nineteenth-century German philosopher Georg Wilhelm Friedrich Hegel and in romantic writers of the same century, especially Johann Wolfgang von Goethe and Percy Bysshe Shelley. Modern thinkers who are unable to accept traditional religious language and doctrines have continued to find in Spinoza a congenial rational religion.

Thomas Hobbes (1588–1679)

Thomas Hobbes was incontestably the most original political philosopher of the seventeenth century. The son of a clergyman, he was educated at Magdalen College of Oxford University during a period when Puritanism was dominant there. Although he never broke with the Church of England, he came to share basic Calvinist beliefs, especially the low view of human nature and the ideal of a commonwealth based on a covenant, both of which find eloquent expression in Hobbes's political philosophy.

Hobbes was an urbane and much-traveled man and one of the most enthusiastic supporters of the new scientific movement. He worked as tutor and secretary to three earls of Devonshire over a fifty-year period. During the 1630s he visited Paris, where he came to know Descartes, and after the outbreak of the Puritan Revolution in 1640, he lived as an exile in Paris until 1651. In 1646 Hobbes became the tutor of the Prince of Wales, the future Charles II, and remained on good terms with him after the restoration of the Stuart monarchy. Hobbes also spent time with Galileo in Italy and took a special interest in the works of William Harvey (1578–1657). Harvey was a physiologist famed for the discovery of how blood circulated through the body; his scientific writings influenced Hobbes's own tracts on bodily motions. Hobbes became an expert in geometry and optics. Also highly trained in classical languages, his first published work was a translation of Thucydides' *History of the Peloponnesian War,* the first English translation of this work and one that is still reprinted today.

Hobbes was driven to the vocation of political philosophy by the English Civil War. In 1651 his *Leviathan* appeared. Written as the concluding part of a broad philosophical system that analyzed physical bodies and human nature, the work established Hobbes as a major European thinker. Its subject was the political consequences of human passions and its originality lay in (1) its making natural law, rather than common law (i.e., custom or precedent), the basis of all positive law, and (2) its defense of a representative theory of absolute authority against the theory of the divine right of kings. Hobbes maintained that statute law found its justification only as an expression of the law of nature and that political authority came to rulers by way of the consent of the people.

Hobbes viewed humankind and society in a thoroughly materialistic and mechanical way. Human beings are defined as a collection of material particles in motion. All their psychological processes begin with and are derived from bare sensation, and all their motivations are egoistical, intended to increase pleasure and minimize pain. The human power of reasoning, which Hobbes defined unspectacularly as a process of adding and subtracting the consequences of agreed-upon general names of things, develops only after years of concentrated industry. Human will Hobbes defined as simply "the last appetite before choice."

Despite this seemingly low estimate of human beings, Hobbes believed much could be accomplished by the reasoned use of science. All was contingent, however, on the correct use of that

Non est potestas Super Terram quæ Comparetur ei Iob. 41. 24.

The famous title-page illustration for Hobbes's Leviathan. *The ruler is pictured as absolute lord of his lands, but note that the ruler incorporates the mass of individuals whose self-interests are best served by their willing consent to accept him and cooperate with him.*

greatest of all human powers, one compounded of the powers of most people: the commonwealth, in which people are united by their consent in one all-powerful person.

The key to Hobbes's political philosophy is a brilliant myth of the original state of humankind. According to this myth, human beings in the natural state are generally inclined to a "perpetual and restless desire of power after power that ceases only in death."[7] As all people desire and in the state of nature have a natural right to everything, their equality breeds enmity, competition, diffidence, and the desire for glory beget perpetual quarreling—"a war of every man against every man."[8] As Hobbes put it in a famous summary:

In such condition there is no place for industry, because the fruit thereof is uncertain; and consequently no culture of the earth; no navigation nor use of the commodities that may be imported by sea; no commodious building; no instruments of moving and removing such things

[7]*Leviathan Parts I and II,* ed. by H. W. Schneider (Indianapolis: Bobbs-Merrill, 1958), p. 86.

[8]Ibid., p. 106.

as require much force; no knowledge of the face of the earth; no account of time; no arts; no letters; no society; and, which is worst of all, continual fear and danger of violent death; and the life of man solitary, poor, nasty, brutish, and short.[9]

Whereas earlier and later philosophers saw the original human state as a paradise from which humankind had fallen, Hobbes saw it as a corruption from which only society had delivered people. Contrary to the views of Aristotle and Christian thinkers like Thomas Aquinas, in the view of Hobbes human beings are not by nature sociable, political animals; they are self-centered beasts, law unto themselves, utterly without a master unless one is imposed by force.

According to Hobbes, people escape the impossible state of nature only by entering a social contract that creates a commonwealth tightly ruled by law and order. They are driven to this solution by their fear of death and their desire for "commodious living." The social contract obliges every person, for the sake of peace and self-defense, to agree to set aside personal rights to all things and to be content with as much liberty against others as he or she would allow others against himself or herself. All agree to live according to a secularized version of the golden rule: "Do not that to another which you would not have done to yourself."[10]

Because words and promises are insufficient to guarantee this state, the social contract also establishes the coercive force necessary to compel compliance with the covenant. Hobbes believed that the dangers of anarchy were far greater than those of tyranny and conceived of the ruler as absolute and unlimited in power, once established in office. There is no room in Hobbes's political philosophy for political protest in the name of individual conscience, nor for resistance to legitimate authority by private individuals—features of the *Leviathan* criticized by contemporary Catholics and Puritans alike. To his critics, who lamented the loss of their individual liberty in such a government, Hobbes pointed out the alternative:

The greatest that in any form of government can possibly happen to the people in general is scarce sensible in respect of the miseries and horrible calamities that accompany a civil war or that dissolute condition of masterless men, without subjection to laws and a coercive power to tie their hands from rapine and revenge.[11]

It is puzzling why Hobbes believed that absolute rulers would be more benevolent and less egoistic than all other people. He simply placed the highest possible value on a strong, efficient ruler who could save human beings from the chaos attendant on the state of nature. In the end it mattered little to Hobbes whether this ruler was Charles I, Oliver Cromwell, or Charles II, each of whom received Hobbes's enthusiastic support, once he was established in power.

John Locke (1632–1704)

Locke has proved to be the most influential political thinker of the seventeenth century. His political philosophy came to be embodied in the Glorious Revolution of 1688–1689. Although he was not as original as Hobbes, his political writings were a major source of the later Enlightenment criticism of absolutism, and they gave inspiration to both the American and the French revolutions.

Locke was reared in a family whose sympathies lay with the Puritans and the Parliamentary forces that challenged the Stuart monarchy. His father fought with the Parliamentary army during the English Civil War. Locke read deeply in the works of Francis Bacon, René Descartes, and Isaac Newton and was a close friend of the English physicist and chemist Robert Boyle (1627–1691). Some argue that Locke was the first philosopher to be successful in synthesizing the rationalism of Descartes and the experimental science of Bacon, Newton, and Boyle.

Locke was for a brief period strongly influenced by the conservative political views of Hobbes. This influence changed, however, after his association with Anthony Ashley Cooper, the earl of Shaftesbury. In 1667 Locke moved into Shaftesbury's London home, where he served as physician, secretary, and traveling companion. A zealous Protestant, Shaftesbury was considered by his contemporaries a radical in both religion and politics. He organized an unsuccessful rebellion against Charles II in 1682 in the hope of excluding Charles's Catholic brother, James, from the English throne and putting the king's bastard son, the earl

[9] Ibid., p. 107.
[10] Ibid., p. 130.

[11] Ibid., p. 152.

of Monmouth, in James's place. Although Locke had no part in the plot, both he and Shaftesbury were forced to flee to Holland after its failure.

Locke's two most famous works are the *Essay Concerning Human Understanding* (1690), completed during his exile in Holland, and the *Two Treatises of Government* (1690). In the *Essay Concerning Human Understanding* Locke stressed the creative function of the human mind. He believed that the mind at birth was a blank tablet. In Locke's view, contrary to that of much medieval philosophy, there are no innate ideas; all knowledge is derived from actual sensual experience. Human ideas are either simple (that is, passive receptions from daily experience) or complex (that is, products of sustained mental exercise). What people know is not the external world in itself but the results of the interaction of the mind with the outside world. Locke also denied the existence of innate moral norms. Moral ideals are the product of humankind's subjection of their

❧ John Locke Explains the Sources of Human Knowledge

An Essay Concerning Human Understanding (1690) was probably the most influential philosophical work ever written in English. Locke's most fundamental idea, which is explicated in the passage below, was that human knowledge is grounded in the experiences of the senses and in the reflection of the mind on those experiences. He rejected any belief in innate ideas. His emphasis on experience led to the wider belief that human beings are creatures of their environment. After Locke, numerous writers argued that human beings could be improved if the environment in which they lived were reformed.

Let us then suppose the mind to be, as we say, white paper void of all characters, without any ideas. *How comes it to be furnished? Whence comes it by that vast store which the busy and boundless fancy of man has painted on it with an almost endless variety? Whence has it all the materials of reason and knowledge? To this I answer, in one word, from* experience; *in that all our knowledge is founded, and from that it ultimately derives itself. Our observation, employed either about* external sensible objects, *or about the* internal operations *of our minds perceived and reflected on by ourselves, is that which supplies our understanding with all the materials of thinking.* These two are the fountains of knowledge, *from whence all the ideas we have, or can naturally have, do spring.*

First, our senses, *conversant about particular sensible objects, do* convey into the mind *several distinct* perceptions *of things, according to those various ways wherein those objects do affect them. And thus we come by those* ideas *we have of* yellow, white, heat, cold, soft, hard, bitter, sweet, *and* all those which we call sensible qualities. . . . *This great source of most of the* ideas *we have, depending wholly upon our senses, and derived by them to the understanding, I call* SENSATION.

Secondly, the other fountain from which experience furnisheth the understanding with ideas *is the* perception of the operations of our own minds *within us, as it is employed about the* ideas *it has got. . . . And such are* perception, thinking, doubting, believing, reasoning, knowing, willing, *and all the different actings of our own minds. . . . I call this* REFLECTION, *the ideas it affords being such only as the mind gets by reflecting on its own operations within itself. . . . These two, I say, viz. external material things as the objects of* SENSATION, *and the operations of our own minds within as the objects of* REFLECTION, *are to me the only originals from whence all our* ideas *take their beginnings. . . .*

The understanding seems to me not to have the least glimmering of any ideas *which it doth not receive from one of these two.*

John Locke, *An Essay Concerning Human Understanding,* Vol. 1 (London: Everyman's Library, 1961), pp. 77–78.

self-love to their reason—a freely chosen self-disciplining of natural desires so that conflict in conscience may be avoided and happiness attained. Locke also believed that the teachings of Christianity were identical to what uncorrupted reason taught about the good life. A rational person would therefore always live according to simple Christian precepts. Although Locke firmly denied toleration to Catholics and atheists—both were considered subversive in England—he otherwise sanctioned a variety of Protestant religious practice.

Locke wrote *Two Treatises of Government* during the reign of Charles II. They are directed against the argument that rulers were absolute in their power. According to the preface of the published edition, which appeared after the Glorious Revolution, the treatises were written "to justify to the world the people of England, whose love of their just and natural rights, with their resolution to preserve them, saved the nation when it was on the brink of slavery and ruin."[12] Locke opposed particularly the views of Sir Robert Filmer and Thomas Hobbes.

Filmer had written a work entitled *Patriarcha, or the Natural Power of Kings* (published in 1680), in which the rights of kings over their subjects were compared with the rights of fathers over their children. Locke devoted the entire first treatise to a refutation of Filmer's argument, maintaining not only that the analogy was inappropriate, but that even the right of a father over his children could not be construed as absolute and was subject to a higher natural law. Both fathers and rulers, Locke argued, remain bound to the law of nature, which is the voice of reason, teaching that "all mankind [are] equal and independent, [and] no one ought to harm another in his life, health, liberty, or possessions,"[13] inasmuch as all human beings are the images and property of God. According to Locke, people enter into social contracts, empowering legislatures and monarchs to "umpire" their disputes, precisely in order to preserve their natural rights, and not to give rulers an absolute power over them. Rulers are rather "entrusted" with the preservation of the law of nature and transgress it at their peril:

Whenever that end [namely, the preservation of life, liberty, and property for which power is given to rulers by a commonwealth] is manifestly neglected or opposed, the trust must necessarily be forfeited and the power devolve into the hands of those that gave it, who may place it anew where they think best for their safety and security.[14]

From Locke's point of view absolute monarchy was "inconsistent" with civil society and could be "no form of civil government at all."

Locke's main differences with Hobbes stemmed from the latter's well-known views on the state of nature. Locke believed that the natural human state was one of perfect freedom and equality. Here the natural rights of life, liberty, and property were enjoyed, in unregulated fashion, by all. The only thing lacking in the state of nature was a single authority to give judgment when disputes inevitably arose because of the natural freedom and equality possessed by all. Contrary to the view of Hobbes, human beings in their natural state were not creatures of monomaniacal passion but were possessed of extreme goodwill and rationality. They did not surrender their natural rights unconditionally when they entered the social contract; rather, they established a means whereby these rights could be better preserved. The state of warfare that Hobbes believed characterized the state of nature emerged for Locke only when rulers failed in their responsibility to preserve the freedoms of the state of nature and attempted to enslave people by absolute rule, that is, to remove them from their "natural" condition. Only then were the peace, goodwill, mutual assistance, and preservation in which human beings naturally live and socially ought to live undermined, and a state of war was created.

Suggested Readings

V. M. BRITTAIN, *Valiant Pilgrim: The Story of John Bunyan and Puritan England* (1950). Illustrated historical biography.

K. C. BROWN, *Hobbes Studies* (1965). A collection of important essays.

HERBERT BUTTERFIELD, *The Origins of Modern Science 1300–1800* (1949). An authoritative survey.

---

[12] *The Second Treatise of Government*, ed. by T. P. Peardon (Indianapolis: Bobbs-Merrill, 1952), Preface.

[13] Ibid., Ch. 2, sects. 4–6, pp. 4–6.

[14] Ibid., Ch. 13, sect. 149, p. 84.

JOHN CAIRD, *Spinoza* (1971). Intellectual biography by a philosopher.

NORMAN F. CANTOR, (Ed.), *Seventeenth Century Rationalism: Bacon and Descartes* (1969).

CERVANTES, *The Portable Cervantes*, ed. and trans. by Samuel Putnam (1969).

HARDIN CRAIG, *Shakespeare: A Historical and Critical Study with Annotated Texts of Twenty-one Plays* (1958).

MAURICE CRANSTON, *Locke* (1961). Brief biographical sketch.

J. DUNN, *The Political Thought of John Locke; An Historical Account of the "Two Treatises of Government"* (1969). An excellent introduction.

MANUEL DURAN, *Cervantes* (1974). Detailed biography.

GALILEO GALILEI, *Discoveries and Opinions of Galileo*, ed. and trans. by Stillman Drake (1957).

A. R. HALL, *The Scientific Revolution 1500–1800: The Formation of the Modern Scientific Attitude* (1966). Traces undermining of traditional science and rise of new sciences.

THOMAS HOBBES, *Leviathan. Parts I and II*, ed. by H. W. Schneider (1958).

MARGARET JACOB, *The Newtonians and The English Revolution* (1976). A controversial book that attempts to relate science and politics.

T. E. JESSOP, *Thomas Hobbes* (1960). Brief biographical sketch.

H. KEARNEY, *Science and Change 1500–1700* (1971). Broad survey.

ALEXANDER KOYRE, *From the Closed World to the Infinite Universe* (1957). Treated from perspective of the historian of ideas.

THOMAS S. KUHN, *The Copernican Revolution* (1957). A scholarly treatment.

PETER LASLETT, *Locke's Two Treatises of Government*, 2nd ed. (1970). Definitive texts with very important introductions.

JOHN D. NORTH, *Isaac Newton* (1967). Brief biography.

ALAN G. R. SMITH, *Science and Society* (1973). A readable, well-illustrated history of the Scientific Revolution.

E. M. W. TILLYARD, *Milton* (1952). Brief biographical sketch.

RICHARD S. WESTFALL, *Never at Rest: A Biography of Isaac Newton* (1981). A new and very important major study.

528

18 The Waxing and Waning of States (1686-1740)

HE LATE seventeenth and early eighteenth centuries witnessed significant shifts of power and influence among the states of Europe. Nations that had been strong lost their status as significant military and economic units. Other countries, which had in some cases figured only marginally in international relations, came to the fore. Great Britain, France, Austria, Russia, and Prussia emerged during this period as the powers that would dominate Europe until at least World War I. The establishment of their political and economic dominance occurred at the expense of Spain, the United Netherlands, Poland, Sweden, and the Ottoman Empire. Equally essential to their rise was the weakness of the Holy Roman Empire after the Treaty of Westphalia (1648).

Peter the Great, who epitomized the state-building monarchs of the late seventeenth and early eighteenth centuries. This portrait, which was done by Kneller in 1698, is in Kensington Palace in London. [*New York Public Library Picture Collection.*]

The successful competitors for international power were those states that in differing fashions created strong central political authorities. Far-sighted observers in the late seventeenth century already understood that in the future those domains that would become or remain great powers must imitate the political and military organization of Louis XIV. Monarchy alone could impose unity of purpose on the state. The turmoil of seventeenth-century civil wars and aristocratic revolts had impressed people with the value of the monarch as a guarantor of minimum domestic tranquillity. Imitation of French absolutism involved other factors besides belief in a strong monarchy. It usually required building a standing army, organizing an efficient tax structure to support the army, and establishing a bureaucracy to collect the taxes. Moreover the political classes of the country, especially the nobles, had to be converted to a sense of duty and loyalty to the central government that was more intense than their loyalty to other competing political and social institutions.

The waning powers of Europe were those whose leaders failed to achieve such effective organization. They were unable to employ their political, economic, and human resources to resist external aggression or to overcome the forces of domestic dissolution. The internal and external failures were closely related. If a state failed to maintain or establish a central political authority with sufficient power over the nobility, the cities, the guilds, and the church, it could not raise a strong army to defend its borders or its economic interests. More often than not the key element leading to success or failure was the character, personality, and energy of the monarch.

The Maritime Powers

In western Europe, Britain and France emerged as the dominant powers. This development represented a shift of influence away from Spain and the United Netherlands. Both the latter countries had been quite strong and important during the sixteenth and seventeenth centuries, but they became negligible during the course of the eighteenth century. However, neither disappeared from the map. Both retained considerable economic vitality and influence. The difference was that France and Britain attained so much more power and economic strength.

Spain

Spanish power had depended on the influx of wealth from the Americas and on the capacity of the Spanish monarchs to rule the still largely autonomous provinces of the Iberian peninsula. The economic life of the nation was never healthy. Except for wool Spain had virtually no exports with which to pay for its imports. Instead of promoting domestic industries, the Spanish government financed imports by using the gold and silver mined in its New World empire. This external source of wealth was not certain because the treasure fleets from the New World could be and sometimes were captured by pirates or the navies of other nations. The political life of Spain was also weak. Within Castile, Aragon, Navarre, the Basque provinces, and other districts, the royal government could not operate without the close cooperation of strong local nobles and the church. From the defeat of the Spanish Armada in 1588 to the Treaty of the Pyrenees in 1659, Spain experienced a series of foreign policy reverses that harmed the domestic

The reign of Charles II of Spain (1665–1700) saw the power of the crown greatly weaken. He was the last Hapsburg king of the country, for in him the line at last failed; deformed (the Hapsburg jaw carried to parody made it almost impossible for him to eat), dull, and impotent, he left no heir. Louis XIV's successful determination to have his grandson succeed Charles led to the War of the Spanish Succession. [The Granger Collection.]

prestige of the monarchy. Furthermore, between 1665 and 1700 the physically malformed, dull-witted, and sexually impotent Charles II was monarch. Throughout his reign the local provincial estates and the nobility increased their power. On his death the War of the Spanish Succession saw the other powers of Europe contesting the issue of the next ruler of Spain.

The Treaty of Utrecht (1713) gave the Spanish crown to Philip V (1770–1746), who was a Bourbon and the grandson of Louis XIV. The new king should have attempted to consolidate his internal power and to protect Spanish overseas trade. However, his second wife, Elizabeth Farnese, wanted to use Spanish power to carve out interests for her sons on the Italian peninsula. Such machinations diverted government resources and allowed the nobility and the provinces to continue to assert their privileges against the authority of the monarchy. Not until the reign of Charles III (1759–1788) did Spain possess a monarch concerned with efficient administration and internal improvement. By the third quarter of the century the country was better governed, but it could no longer compete effectively in power politics.

The Netherlands

The demise of the United Netherlands occurred wholly within the eighteenth century. After the death of William III in 1702, the various local provinces successfully prevented the emergence of another strong *stadtholder*. Unified political leadership therefore vanished. During the earlier long wars of the Netherlands with Louis XIV and England, naval supremacy slowly but steadily had passed to the British. The fishing industry declined, and the Dutch lost their technological superiority in shipbuilding. Countries between which Dutch ships had once carried goods now came to trade directly with each other. For example, the British began to use more and more of their own vessels in the Baltic traffic with Russia. Similar stag-

Dutch shipbuilding remained important throughout the seventeenth and eighteenth centuries, although not as prosperous as in the sixteenth. Ships, such as this one being constructed at Amsterdam in 1694, were the sinews of trade during the period. The building in the background is the headquarters of the Dutch West Indies Company, which settled New Amsterdam (subsequently New York). [The Granger Collection.]

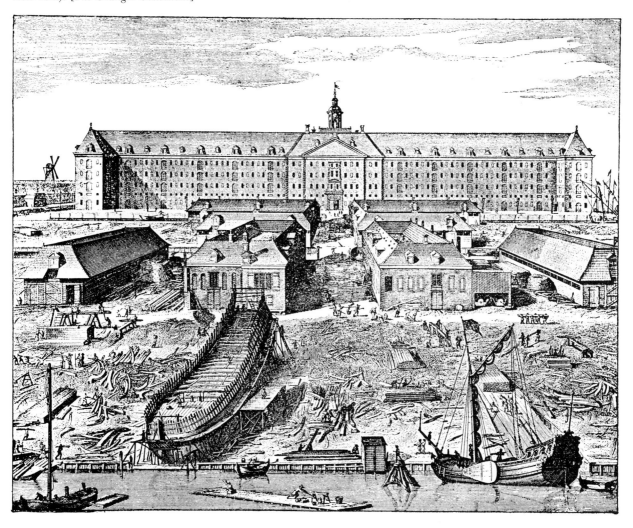

nation overtook the Dutch domestic industries, such as textile finishing, paper making, and glass blowing. The disunity of the provinces and the absence of vigorous leadership hastened this economic decline and prevented action that might have slowed or halted it. What saved the United Netherlands from becoming completely insignificant in European matters was their continued dominance of the financial community. Well past the middle of the century their banks continued to provide loans and financing for European trade.

France After Louis XIV

Despite its military losses in the War of the Spanish Succession, France remained a great power. It was less strong in 1715 than in 1680, but it still possessed a large population, an advanced if troubled economy, and the administrative structure bequeathed it by Louis XIV. Moreover, even if France and its resources had been badly drained by the last of Louis's wars, the other major states of Europe emerged from the conflict similarly debilitated. What the country required was a period of economic recovery and consolidation, wiser political leadership, and a less ambitious foreign policy. It did enjoy a period of recovery, but the quality of its leadership was at best indifferent. Louis XIV was succeeded by his five-year-old great-grandson Louis XV (1715–1774). The young boy's uncle, the duke of Orléans, became regent and remained so until 1720. The regency further undermined the already faltering prestige of the monarchy.

The duke of Orléans was a gambler, and for a time he turned over the financial management of the kingdom to John Law (1671–1729), a Scottish mathematician and fellow gambler. Law believed that an increase in the paper money supply would stimulate the postwar economic recovery of the country. With the permission of the regent he established a bank in Paris that issued paper money. Law then organized the Mississippi Company, which was to possess a monopoly on trading privileges with the French colony of Louisiana in North America.

The Mississippi Company also assumed the management of the French national debt. The company issued shares of its own stock in exchange for government bonds, which had fallen sharply in value. In order to redeem large quantities of bonds, Law encouraged speculation in Mississippi

Company stock. In 1719 the price of the stock rose handsomely. However, smart investors took their profits by selling their stock in exchange for money from Law's bank. Then they sought to exchange the currency for gold. To make the second transaction, they went to Law's bank, but that institution lacked sufficient gold to redeem all the money brought to it.

In February 1720 all gold payments were halted in France. Soon thereafter Law himself fled the country. The Mississippi Bubble, as the affair was called, had burst. The fiasco brought disgrace on the government that had made Law its controller general. The Mississippi Company was later reorganized and functioned quite profitably, but fear of paper money and speculation marked French economic life for the rest of the century.

The duke of Orléans made a second departure that also lessened the power of the monarchy. He attempted to draw the French nobility once again

The Duke of Orleans was regent of France during the minority of Louis XV, years marked by financial scandal and weak administration. [The Granger Collection.]

❧ Saint-Simon Shows the French Nobility's Incapacity to Govern

The regent under the young Louis XV hoped that France's nobility might assume an active role in government in place of the passive role assigned to them by Louis XIV. This plan involved displacing many nonnoble bureaucrats and others who were regarded as noble by virtue of holding office rather than by virtue of noble birth ("nobles of the robe"). As described by the duke of Saint-Simon (1675–1755), the plan failed because the real nobles proved unequal to their new duties.

The design was to begin to put the nobility into the ministry, with the dignity and authority befitting them, at the expense of the high civil servants and nobles of the robe, and by degree and according to events to guide affairs wisely so that little by little those commoners would lose all those administrative duties that are not purely judicial . . . in order to submit to the nobility all modes of administration. The difficulty was the ignorance, the frivolity, and the lack of diligence of the nobility who were accus-

tomed to being good for nothing except getting killed, succeeding at war only by seniority, and romping around for the rest of the time in the most mortal uselessness. As a result they were devoted to idleness and disgusted with all knowledge outside war by their conditioned incapacity for being able to provide themselves with anything useful to do. It was impossible to make the first step in this direction without overturning the monster that had devoured the nobility, the controller general and the secretaries of state.

Duc de Saint-Simon, *Memoires*, trans. by Frank M. Turner, cited in John Lough, *An Introduction to Eighteenth Century France* (New York: David MacKay, 1964), pp. 135–136.

---

into the decision-making processes of the government. Louis XIV had downgraded the nobility and had filled his ministries and bureaucracies with persons of nonnoble families. The regent was seeking to restore a balance. He adopted a system of councils on which the nobles were to serve along with the bureaucrats. However, the years of noble domestication at Versailles had worked too well, and the nobility seemed to lack both the talent and the desire to govern. The experiment failed.

The failure of the great French nobles to function as satisfactory councilors did not mean that they had surrendered their ancient ambition to assert their rights, privileges, and local influence over those of the monarchy. The chief feature of the French political life from this time until the French Revolution was the attempt of the nobility to impose its power on the monarchy. The most effective instrument in this process was the *parlements,* or courts dominated by the nobility. The French *parlements* were very different institutions from the English Parliament. These French courts, the most important of which was the *Parlement* of Paris, did not have the power to legislate. Rather, they had

the power to recognize or not to recognize the legality of an act or law promulgated by the monarch. By long tradition their formal approval had been required to make a royal law valid. Louis XIV had often overridden stubborn, uncooperative *parlements.* However, in another of his many major political blunders, the duke of Orléans had formally approved the reinstitution of the *parlements'* power to allow or disallow laws. Thereafter the growing financial and moral weakness of the eighteenth-century monarchy allowed these aristocratic judicial institutions to reassert their authority. This situation meant that for the rest of the century until the revolution the *parlements* became natural centers for aristocratic resistance to royal authority.

By 1726 the chief minister of the French court was Cardinal Fleury (1653–1743). He was the last of those great churchmen who had so loyally and effectively served the French monarchy. Like his seventeenth-century predecessors, the cardinals Richelieu and Mazarin, Fleury was a realist. He understood the political ambition and incapacity of the nobility and worked quietly to block their undue influence. Fleury was also aware of the pre-

In 1722 the young great-grandson of Louis XIV was crowned the new King of France as Louis XV in the Cathedral of Rheims. He was then twelve years old and had already been king for seven years. This painting by J. B. Martin shows the moment in the darkened cathedral when the young king was anointed. It is now in the museum at Versailles. [Cliché des Musées Nationaux.]

carious financial situation in which the wars of Louis XIV had left the royal treasury.

The cardinal, who was seventy-three years old when he came to office, was determined to give the country a period of peace. He surrounded himself with generally able assistants who attempted to solve the financial problems. Part of the national debt was repudiated. New industries enjoying special privileges were established, and new roads and bridges were built. On the whole the nation prospered, but Fleury was never able to draw from the nobles or the church sufficient tax revenues to put the state on a stable financial footing.

Fleury died in 1743, having unsuccessfully attempted to prevent France from intervening in the war then raging between Austria and Prussia. All of his financial pruning and planning had come to nought. Another failure must also be credited to this elderly churchman. Despite his best efforts he had not trained Louis XV to become an effective monarch. Louis XV possessed most of the vices and almost none of the virtues of his great-grandfather. He wanted to hold on to absolute power but was unwilling to work the long hours required. He did not choose many wise advisers after Fleury. He was tossed about by the gossip and intrigues of the court nobles. His personal life was scandalous. His reign became more famous for his mistress, Madame de Pompadour, than for anything else. Louis

Louis XV in coronation robes, painted by Hyacinthe Rigaud in 1730. Although by no means unintelligent, Louis was lazy and pleasure-loving. His scandalous private life lessened respect for the French monarchy. [Photographie Bulloz, Paris.]

Cardinal Fleury, tutor and chief minister of Louis XV from 1726 until 1743. He strove to bring peace and financial stability to France but was finally unsuccessful on both counts. This portrait by Hyacinthe Rigaud is at Versailles. [Photographie Bulloz, Paris.]

XV was not an evil person but a mediocre one. And in a monarch mediocrity was unfortunately often a greater fault than vice.

Despite this political drift France remained a great power. Its army at mid-century was still the largest and strongest military force on the Continent. Its commerce and production expanded. Its colonies produced wealth and spurred domestic industries. Its cities grew and prospered. The wealth of the nation waxed as the absolutism of the monarchy waned. France did not lack sources of power and strength, but it did lack the political leadership that could organize, direct, and inspire its people.

Madame de Pompadour (1721–1764) was the first official mistress of Louis XV and a person of beauty, cultivation, and ambition. After her death the king had an increasing number of mistresses, both unofficial and official, but none were as cultured as she, and inevitably, the increasingly low moral tone of the French court did much to undermine the loyalty of the general public for the throne. This lovely portrait of his patroness is by one of the eighteenth century's masters, François Boucher (1703–1770). It is now in the National Gallery of Scotland in Edinburgh. [The Granger Collection.]

Great Britain: The Age of Walpole

In 1713 Britain had emerged as a victor over Louis XIV, but the nation required a period of recovery. As an institution the British monarchy was not in the degraded state of the French monarchy, but its stability was not certain. In 1714 the Hanoverian dynasty, designated by the Act of Settlement (1701), came to the throne. Almost immediately George I (1714–1727) confronted a challenge to his new title. The Stuart pretender James Edward (1688–1766), the son of James II, landed in Scotland in December 1715. His forces marched southward but met defeat less than two months later.

Although militarily successful against the pretender, the new dynasty and its supporters saw the need for consolidation. During the seventeenth

FRANCE AND GREAT BRITAIN IN THE EARLY EIGHTEENTH CENTURY

1713	Treaty of Utrecht ends the War of the Spanish Succession
1714	George I becomes king of Great Britain and thus establishes the Hanoverian dynasty
1715	Louis XV becomes King of France
1715–1720	Regency of the duke of Orléans in France
1720	Mississippi Bubble bursts in France and South Sea Bubble bursts in Great Britain
1720–1742	Robert Walpole dominates British politics
1726–1743	Cardinal Fleury serves as Louis XV's chief minister
1727	George II becomes king of Great Britain
1733	Excise bill crisis in Britain
1739	War of Jenkins's Ear commences between England and Spain

George I of Great Britain was originally the Elector of Hanover in Germany. He succeeded to the British throne in 1714. This painting is from Godfrey Kneller's studio. [*The Granger Collection.*]

century England had been one of the most politically restive countries in Europe. The closing years of Queen Anne's reign (1702–1714) had seen sharp clashes between the political factions of Whigs and Tories over the coming Treaty of Utrecht. The Tories had urged a rapid peace settlement and after 1710 had opened negotiations with France. During the same period the Whigs were seeking favor from the Elector of Hanover, who would soon be their monarch. His concern for his domains in Hanover made him unsympathetic to the Tory peace policy. In the final months of Anne's reign some Tories, fearing loss of power under the waiting Hanoverian dynasty, opened channels of communication with the Stuart pretender; and a few even rallied to his losing cause.

Under these circumstances it was little wonder that George I, on his arrival in Britain, clearly favored the Whigs and proceeded with caution. Previously the differences between the Whigs and the Tories had been vaguely related to principle. The Tories emphasized a strong monarchy, low taxes for landowners, and firm support of the Anglican church. The Whigs supported monarchy but wanted Parliament to retain final sovereignty.

They tended to favor urban commercial interests as well as the prosperity of the landowners. They encouraged a policy of religious toleration toward the Protestant nonconformists in England. Socially both groups supported the status quo. Neither was organized like a modern political party. Organizationally, outside of Parliament, each party consisted of political networks based on local political connections and local economic influence. Each group acknowledged a few spokesmen on the national level who articulated positions and principles. However, after the Hanoverian accession and the eventual Whig success in achieving the firm confidence of George I, the chief difference for almost forty years between the Whigs and the Tories was that one group did have access to public office and patronage and the other did not. This early Hanoverian proscription of Tories from public life was one of the most prominent features of the age.

The political situation after 1715 had at first remained in a state of flux until Robert Walpole (1676–1745) took over the helm of government. This Norfolk squire had been active in the House of Commons since the reign of Queen Anne, and he had served as a cabinet minister. What gave him special prominence under the new dynasty was a British financial scandal similar to the French Mississippi Bubble.

Management of the British national debt had been assigned to the South Sea Company, which

A series of four Hogarth etchings satirizing an English parliamentary election. In a savage indictment of the notoriously corrupt English electoral system, Hogarth shows the voters going to the polls after having been bribed and intoxicated with free gin. (Note that voting was in public. The secret ballot was not introduced in England until 1872.) The fourth etching, Chairing the Member, shows the triumphal procession of the victorious candidate, which is clearly turning into a brawl. [Metropolitan Museum of Art.]

Sir Robert Walpole (1676–1745) dominated the British government under George I and George II from 1721 to 1742. He brought political stability to eighteenth-century Britain by winning the king's trust and by his skillful, if sometimes ruthless, use of government patronage. [National Portrait Gallery, London.]

exchanged government bonds for company stock. As in the French case, the price of the stock flew high, only to crash in 1720 when prudent investors sold their holdings and took their speculative profits. Parliament intervened and under Walpole's leadership adopted measures to honor the national debt. To most contemporaries Walpole had saved the financial integrity of the country and, in so doing, had proved himself a person of immense administrative capacity and political ability.

George I gave Walpole his full confidence. For this reason Walpole has often been regarded as the first prime minister of Great Britain and the originator of the cabinet system of government. However, unlike a modern prime minister he was not chosen by the majority of the House of Commons.

His power largely depended on the good will of George I and later of George II (1727–1760). Walpole generally demanded that all of the ministers in the cabinet agree on policy, but he could not prevent frequent public differences on policy. The real source of Walpole's power was the combination of the personal support of the king, his ability to handle the House of Commons, and his iron-fisted control of government patronage. To oppose Walpole on either minor or more substantial matters was to risk the almost certain loss of government patronage for oneself, one's family, or one's friends. Through the skillful use of patronage Walpole bought support for himself and his policies from people who wanted to receive jobs, appointments, favors, and government contracts. Such corruption supplied the glue of political loyalty.

Walpole's favorite slogan was *quieta non movere* (roughly, "let sleeping dogs lie"). To that end he pursued a policy of peace abroad and promotion of the status quo at home. In this regard he and Cardinal Fleury were much alike. The structure of the eighteenth-century British House of Commons aided Walpole in his pacific policies. It was neither a democratic nor a representative body. Each of the counties elected two members. But if the more powerful landed families in a county agreed on the candidates, there was no contest. Other members were elected from units called *boroughs*, of which there were a considerable variety. There were many more borough seats than county seats. A few were large enough for elections to be relatively democratic. However, most boroughs had a very small number of electors. For example, a local municipal corporation or council of only a dozen members might have the legal right to elect a member of Parliament. In Old Sarum, one of the most famous corrupt or "rotten" boroughs, the Pitt family for many years simply bought up those pieces of property to which a vote was attached and thus in effect owned a seat in the House of Commons. Through proper electoral management, which involved favors to the electors, the House of Commons could be controlled.

The structure of Parliament and the manner in which it was elected meant that the government of England was dominated by the owners of property and by especially wealthy nobles. They did not pretend to represent people and districts or to be responsive to what would later be called public opinion. They regarded themselves as representing various economic and social interests, such as the West Indian interest, the merchant interest, or the landed interest. These owners of property were suspicious of an administrative bureaucracy controlled by the crown or its ministers. For this reason they or their agents served as local government administrators, judges, militia commanders, and tax collectors. In this sense the British nobility and other substantial landowners actually did govern the nation. And because they regarded the Parliament as the political sovereign, there was no absence of central political authority and direction. Consequently the supremacy of Parliament provided Britain with the kind of unity that elsewhere in Europe was sought through the institutions of absolutism.

British political life was genuinely more free than that on the Continent. There were real limits to the power of Robert Walpole. Parliament could not be wholly unresponsive to popular political pressure. Even with the extensive use of patronage many members of Parliament maintained independent views. Newspapers and public debate flourished. Free speech could be exercised, as could freedom of association. There was no large standing army. Tories barred from political office and Whig enemies of Walpole could and did voice their opposition to his policies, as would not have been possible on the Continent.

For example, in 1733 Walpole presented to the House of Commons a scheme for an excise tax that would have raised revenue somewhat in the fash-

❧ Lady Mary Wortley Montagu Gives Advice on Election to Parliament

In this letter of 1714 Lady Mary Wortley Montagu discussed with her husband the various paths that he might follow to gain election to the British House of Commons. Note the emphasis she placed on knowing the right people and on having large amounts of money to spend on voters. Eventually her husband was elected to Parliament in a borough that was controlled through government patronage.

You seem not to have received my letters, or not to have understood them: you had been chose undoubtedly at York, if you had declared in time; but there is not any gentleman or tradesman disengaged at this time; they are treating every night. Lord Carlisle and the Thompsons have given their interest to Mr Jenkins. I agree with you of the necessity of your standing this Parliament, which, perhaps, may be more considerable than any that are to follow it; but, as you proceed, 'tis my opinion, you will spend your money and not be chose. I believe there is hardly a borough unengaged. I expect every letter should tell me you are sure of some place; and, as far as I can perceive you are sure of none. As it has been managed, perhaps it will be the best way to deposit a certain sum in some friend's hands, and buy some little Cornish borough: it would, undoubtedly, look better to be chose for a considerable town; but I take it to be now too late. If you have any thoughts of Newark, it

will be absolutely necessary for you to enquire after Lord Lexington's interest; and your best way to apply yourself to Lord Holdernesse, who is both a Whig and an honest man. He is now in town, and you may enquire of him if Brigadier Sutton stands there; and if not, try to engage him for you. Lord Lexington is so ill at the Bath, that it is a doubt if he will live 'till the elections; and if he dies, one of his heiresses, and the whole interest of his estate, will probably fall on Lord Holdernesse.

'Tis a surprize to me, that you cannot make sure of some borough, when a number of your friends bring in so many Parliament-men without trouble or expense. 'Tis too late to mention it now, but you might have applied to Lady Winchester, as Sir Joseph Jekyl did last year, and by her interest the Duke of Bolton brought him in, for nothing; I am sure she would be more zealous to serve me, than Lady Jekyl.

Lord Wharncliffe (ed.), *Letters and Works of Lady Mary Wortley Montagu*, 3rd ed., Vol. 1 (London, 1861), p. 211.

ion of a modern sales tax. The public outcry in the press, on the public platform, and in the streets was so great that he eventually withdrew the measure. What the English regarded as their traditional political rights raised a real and potent barrier to the power of the government. Again in 1739, the public outcry over the Spanish treatment of British merchants in the Caribbean pushed Britain into the War of Jenkins's Ear, which Walpole opposed and deplored.

Walpole's ascendancy, which lasted until 1742, did little to raise the level of British political morality, but it brought the nation a kind of stability that it had not enjoyed for well over a century. Its foreign trade grew steadily and spread from New England to India. Agriculture improved its productivity. All forms of economic enterprise seemed to prosper. The navy became stronger. As a result of this political stability and economic growth, Great Britain became a European power of the first order and stood at the beginning of its era as a world power. Its government and economy during the next generation became a model for all progressive Europeans.

Central and Eastern Europe

The major factors in the shift of political influence among the maritime nations were naval strength, economic progress, foreign trade, and sound domestic administration. The conflicts among them occurred less in Europe than on the high seas and in their empires. These nations already existed in well-defined geographical areas with established borders. Their populations generally accepted the authority of the central government.

The situation in central and eastern Europe was rather different. Except for the cities on the Baltic, the economy was agrarian. There were fewer cities and many more large estates populated by serfs. The states in this region did not possess overseas empires. Changes in the power structure normally involved changes in borders, or at least in the prince who ruled a particular area. Military conflicts took place at home rather than overseas. The political structure of this region, which lay largely east of the Elbe River, was very "soft." The almost constant warfare of the seventeenth century had led to a habit of temporary and shifting political loyalties. The princes and aristocracies of small states and principalities were unwilling to subordinate themselves voluntarily to a central monarchical authority. Consequently the political life of the region and the kind of state that emerged there were different from those of western Europe.

Beginning in the last half of the seventeenth century, eastern and central Europe began to assume the political and social contours that would characterize it for the next two hundred years. After the Peace of Westphalia the Austrian Hapsburgs recognized the basic weakness of the position of Holy Roman Emperor and began a new consolidation of their power. At the same time the state of Prussia began to emerge as a factor in north German politics and as a major challenger to Hapsburg domination of Germany. Most importantly, Russia at the opening of the eighteenth century rose to the status of a military power of the first order. These three states (Austria, Prussia, and Russia) achieved their new status largely as a result of the political decay or military defeat of Sweden, Poland, and the Ottoman Empire.

Sweden: The Ambitions of Charles XII

Under Gustavus Adolphus II (1611–1632) Sweden had played an important role as a Protestant combatant in the Thirty Years' War. During the rest of the seventeenth century Sweden had consolidated its control of the Baltic, preventing Russian possession of a Baltic port and permitting Polish and German access to the sea only on Swedish terms. The Swedes also possessed one of the better armies in Europe. However, Sweden's economy, based primarily on the export of iron, was not strong enough to ensure continued political success.

In 1697 Charles XII (1697–1718) came to the throne. He was headstrong, to say the least, and perhaps insane. In 1700 Russia began a drive to the west against Swedish territory. The Russian goal was a foothold on the Baltic. In the resulting Great Northern War (1700–1721) Charles XII led a vigorous and often brilliant campaign, but one that eventually resulted in the defeat of Sweden. In 1700 he defeated the Russians at the battle of Narva, but then he turned south to invade Poland. The conflict dragged on, and the Russians were able to strengthen their forces. In 1708 the Swedish monarch began a major invasion of Russia but became bogged down in the harsh Russian winter. The next year his army was decisively defeated at

Charles XII of Sweden (1697–1718). Although a brave and sometimes brilliant general, Charles overreached himself. After his death, Sweden was never again the dominant Northern Power. [Svenska Portrattarkivet, Nationalmuseum, Stockholm.]

the battle of Poltava. Thereafter the Swedes could maintain only a holding action. Charles himself sought refuge with the Ottoman army and then eventually returned to Sweden in 1714. He was shot four years later while fighting the Norwegians.

The Great Northern War came to a close in 1721. Sweden had exhausted its military and economic resources and had lost its monopoly on the Baltic coast. Russia had conquered a large section of the eastern Baltic, and Prussia had gained a portion of Pomerania. Internally, after the death of Charles XII, the Swedish nobles were determined to reassert their power over that of the monarchy. They did so but then fell into quarrels among themselves. Sweden played a very minor role in European affairs thereafter.

The Ottoman Empire

At the southeastern extreme of Europe the Ottoman Empire lay as a barrier to the territorial ambitions of the Austrian Hapsburgs and of Poland and Russia. The empire in the late seventeenth century still controlled most of the Balkan peninsula and the entire coastline of the Black Sea. It was an aggressive power that had for two centuries attempted to press its control further westward in Europe. The Ottoman Empire had probably made its greatest military impression on Europe in 1683, when it laid siege to the city of Vienna.

However, the Ottomans had overextended themselves politically, economically, and militarily. The major domestic political groups resisted any substantial strengthening of the central government in Constantinople. Rivalries for power among army leaders and nobles weakened the effectiveness of the government. In the outer provinces, such as Transylvania, Wallachia, and Moldavia (all parts of modern Romania), the empire depended on the goodwill of local rulers, who never submitted themselves fully to the imperial power. The empire's economy was weak, and its exports were primarily raw materials. Moreover the actual conduct of most of its trade had been turned over to representatives of other nations.

By the early eighteenth century the weakness of the Ottoman Empire meant that on the southeastern perimeter of Europe there existed an immense political vacuum. In 1699 the Turks concluded a treaty with their longtime Hapsburg enemy and surrendered all pretensions of control over Hungary, Transylvania, Croatia, and Slavonia. From this time onward Russia also attempted to extend its territory and influence at the expense of the empire. For almost two hundred years the decay of the Ottoman Empire constituted a major factor in European international relations. The area always proved tempting to the major powers, but their distrust of each other and their conflicting rivalries, as well as a considerable residual strength on the part of the Turks, prevented the dismemberment of the empire.

Poland

In no other part of Europe was the failure to maintain a competitive political position so complete as in Poland. In 1683 King John III Sobieski (1673–1696) had led a Polish army to rescue Vi-

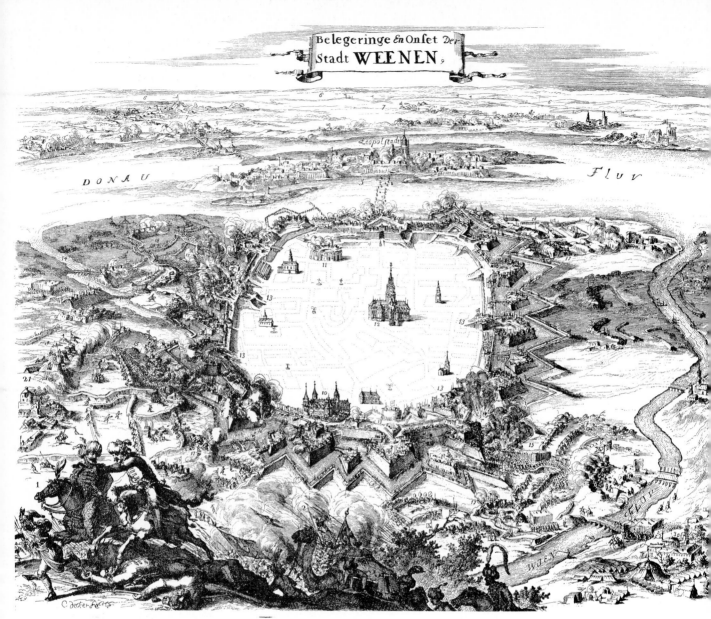

Belegeringe En Onſet Der Stadt WEENEN

A contemporary Dutch print views the 1683 *Turkish siege of Vienna from a remarkably reveal-ing position in the hills west of the city. We are fortunate to capture the scene on the point of the Turkish forces deciding to give up the summer-long attack; their commanders, the Ottoman Grand Vizier and the Pasha of Adrianople, lower left, are just beginning their flight back toward the Ottoman homelands. Polish and other Christian aid for the beleaguered Hapsburg forces had arrived, and the battle was clearly going against the Turks. Vienna was not cap-tured, and never again did the progressively weakening Muslim Ottoman Empire penetrate so far west.*

In the picture, note the Danube River toward the top, the elaborate zig-zag fortifications out-side the walls, and bursts of artillery fire at several points. Most details inside the walled city are omitted, but the central cathedral and the imperial palace, toward the bottom, are shown. The walls themselves, when later torn down, made space for the Ring, the famous boulevard still encircling central Vienna.

One unforeseen lasting social result of the siege was the further boost given to coffee drinking by the Viennese discovery of the beverage in the deserted Turkish camps around the city. [The Granger Collection.]

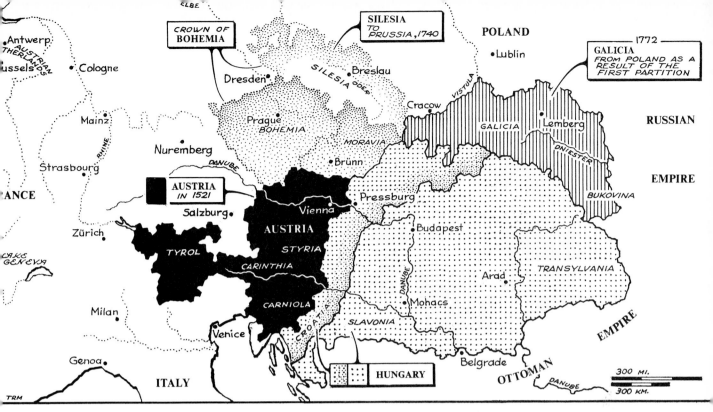

THE AUSTRIAN HAPSBURG EMPIRE, 1521–1772

MAP 18.1   *The Empire had three main units—Austria, Bohemia, Hungary. Expansion was mainly eastward: east Hungary from the Ottomans (17th century) and Galicia from Poland (1772). Meantime, Silesia was lost, but Hapsburgs retained German influence as Holy Roman Emperors.*

enna from the Turkish siege. But following that spectacular effort, Poland became little more than a byword for the dangers of aristocratic independence. In Poland as nowhere else on the Continent the nobility became the single most powerful political factor in the country. Unlike the British nobility and landowners, the Polish nobility would not even submit to a central authority of their own making. There was no effective central authority in the form of either a king or a parliament.

The Polish monarchy was elective, but the deep distrust and divisions among the nobility prevented their electing a king from among their own numbers. Sobieski was a notable exception. Most of the Polish monarchs came from outside the borders of the kingdom and were the tools of foreign powers. The Polish nobles did have a central legislative body called the *Diet*. It included only the nobles and specifically excluded representatives from corporate bodies, such as the towns. In the Diet, however, there existed a practice known as the *liberum veto*, whereby the staunch opposition of any single member could require the body to disband. Such opposition was termed *exploding the Diet*.

Government as it was developing elsewhere in Europe simply was not tolerated in Poland. Localism reminiscent of the Middle Ages continued to hold sway as the nobles used all their energy to maintain their traditional "Polish liberties." There was no way to collect sufficient taxes to build up an army. The price of this noble liberty was eventually the disappearance of Poland from the map of Europe during the last half of the eighteenth century.

The Hapsburg Empire and the Pragmatic Sanction

The close of the Thirty Years' War marked a fundamental turning point in the history of the Austrian Hapsburgs. Previously, in alliance with the Spanish branch of the family, they had hoped to dominate all of Germany politically and to bring it back to the Catholic fold. They had failed to achieve either goal, and the decline of Spanish power meant that in future diplomatic relations the Austrian

545

Hapsburgs were very much on their own. The Treaty of Westphalia permitted Protestantism within the Holy Roman Empire, and the treaty also recognized the political autonomy of more than three hundred corporate German political entities within the empire. These included large units (such as Saxony, Hanover, Bavaria, and Brandenburg) and also scores of small cities, bishoprics, principalities, and territories of independent knights.

After 1648 the Hapsburg family retained firm hold on the title of Holy Roman Emperor, but the effectiveness of the title depended less on force of arms than on the cooperation that the emperor could elicit from the various political bodies in the empire. The Diet of the empire sat at Regensburg from 1663 until its dissolution in 1806. The Diet and the emperor generally regulated the daily economic and political life of Germany. The post-Westphalian

Holy Roman Empire in many ways resembled Poland with its lack of central authority. However, unlike its Polish neighbor, the Holy Roman Empire was reorganized from within as the Hapsburgs attempted to regain their authority and, as will be seen shortly, as Prussia set out on its course toward European power.

While establishing a new kind of position among the German states, the Hapsburgs began to consolidate their power and influence within their hereditary possessions. These included, first, the kingdom of Bohemia (in modern Czechoslovakia), which encompassed Silesia and Moravia, and second, the Crown of Saint Stephen, which ruled Hungary, Croatia, and Transylvania. The Hapsburgs also possessed stretches of northern Italy, as well as the Austrian Netherlands, which is present-day Belgium. In the next two centuries Haps-

Schönbrunn Palace of the Austrian Hapsburgs stands outside Vienna. Like many royal palaces of the eighteenth century, it was modeled after Louis XIV's palace of Versailles. [Austrian Information Service, New York.]

CENTRAL AND EASTERN EUROPE

burg power and influence in Europe would be based primarily on these territories rather than on their position in Germany.

In the second half of the seventeenth century and later the Hapsburgs confronted immense problems in these hereditary territories. In each they ruled by virtue of a different title and had to gain the cooperation of the local nobility. The most difficult province was Hungary, where the Magyar nobility seemed ever ready to rebel. There was almost no common basis for political unity among peoples of such diverse languages, customs, and geography. Even the Hapsburg zeal for Roman Catholicism no longer proved a bond for unity as they continued to confront the equally zealous Calvinism of the Magyar nobles. The Hapsburgs established various central councils to chart common policies for their far-flung domains. None of these proved effective because the dynasty repeatedly had to bargain with nobles in one part of Europe in order to maintain their position in another. Consequently, for all practical purposes, not until well into the nineteenth century did the Vienna government directly affect the lives of any social group below the nobility.

Despite all these internal difficulties Leopold I (1657–1705) rallied his domains to resist the advances of the Turks and to resist the aggression of Louis XIV. He achieved Ottoman recognition of his sovereignty over Hungary in 1699 and suppressed the long rebellion of his new Magyar subjects between 1703 and 1711. He also extended his territorial holdings over much of what is today Yugoslavia and western Romania. These southeastward extensions allowed the Hapsburgs to hope to develop Mediterranean trade through the port of Trieste. The expansion at the cost of the Ottoman Empire also helped the Hapsburgs to compensate for their loss of domination over the Holy Roman Empire. Strength in the east gave them greater political leverage in Germany. Leopold was succeeded by Joseph I (1705–1711), who continued his policies.

When Charles VI (1711–1740) succeeded Joseph, he added a new problem to the old chronic one of territorial diversity. He had no male heir, and there was only the weakest of precedents for a female ruler of the Hapsburg domains. Charles feared that on his death the Austrian Hapsburg lands might fall prey to the surrounding powers, as had those of the Spanish Hapsburgs in 1700. He was determined to prevent that disaster and to provide his domains with the semblance of legal unity. To those ends, he devoted most of his reign to seeking the approval of his family, the estates of his realms, and the major foreign powers for a curious document called the *Pragmatic Sanction*.

This instrument provided the legal basis for a single line of inheritance within the Hapsburg dynasty through Charles VI's daughter Maria Theresa (1740–1780). Other members of the Hapsburg family recognized her as the rightful heir. The nobles of the various Hapsburg domains did likewise after extracting various concessions from Charles. The major states of Europe followed a similar course. Consequently, when Charles VI died in October 1740, he believed that he had secured legal unity for the Hapsburg Empire and a safe succession for his daughter. Less than two months after his death the fragility of such a paper agreement became all too apparent. In December 1740 Frederick II of Prussia invaded the Hapsburg province of Silesia. Maria Theresa would have to fight to defend her inheritance.

Prussia and the Hohenzollerns

The Hapsburg achievement was to draw together into an uncertain legal unity a collection of domains possessed by dint of separate feudal titles. The achievement of the Hohenzollerns of Brandenburg–Prussia was to acquire a similar collection of titular holdings and then to forge them into a cen-

---

AUSTRIA AND PRUSSIA IN THE LATE SEVENTEENTH AND EARLY EIGHTEENTH CENTURIES

1640–1688	Reign of Frederick William, the Great Elector
1657–1705	Leopold I rules Austria and resists the Turkish invasions
1683	Turkish siege of Vienna
1688–1713	Reign of Frederick I of Prussia
1699	Peace Treaty between Turks and Hapsburgs
1711–1740	Charles VI rules Austria and secures agreement to the Pragmatic Sanction
1713–1740	Frederick William I builds up the military power of Prussia
1740	Maria Theresa succeeds to the Hapsburg throne
	Frederick II violates the Pragmatic Sanction by invading Silesia

❧ Maria Theresa Discusses One Weakness of Her Throne ═══

Scattered subjects of the multilanguage Austrian Empire (Germans, Hungarians, Czechs, Slovaks, Slovenes, Croatians, Poles, and Romanians, for example) made impossible the unifying of the empire into a strong centralized monarchy. Maria Theresa, writing in 1745, explained how previous Hapsburg rulers had impoverished themselves by attempting with little success to purchase the political and military support of the nobles in different provinces. The more privileges they gave the nobles, the more they were expected to give.

To return once again to my ancestors, these individuals not only gave away most of the crown estates, but absorbed also the debts of those properties confiscated in time of rebellion, and these debts are still in arrears. Emperor Leopold [1658–1705] found little left to give away, but the terrible wars he fought no doubt forced him to mortgage or pawn additional crown estates. His successors did not relieve these burdens, and when I became sovereign, the crown revenues barely reached eighty thousand gulden. Also in the time of my forebears, the ministers received enormous payments from the crown and from the local Estates because they knew not only how to exploit selfishly the good will, grace, and munificence of the Austrian house by convincing each ruler that his predecessor had won fame by giving freely but also how to win the ears of the provincial lords and

clergy so that these ministers acquired all that they wished. In fact they spread their influence so wide that in the provinces they were more feared and respected than the ruler himself. And when they had finally taken everything from the sovereign, these same ministers turned for additional compensation to their provinces, where their great authority continuously increased. Even though complaints reached the monarch, out of grace and forebearance toward the ministers, he simply allowed the exploitations to continue. . . .

This system gave the ministers such authority that the sovereign himself found it convenient for his own interests to support them because he learned by experience that the more prestige enjoyed by the heads of the provinces, the more of the sovereign's demands these heads could extract from their Estates.

Maria Theresa, *Political Testament*, cited in Karl A. Roider (ed. and trans.), *Maria Theresa* (Englewood Cliffs, N.J.: Prentice-Hall, 1973), pp. 32–33.

---

trally administered unit. In spite of the geographical separation of their territories and the paucity of their natural economic resources, they transformed feudal ties and structures into bureaucratic ones. They subordinated every social class and most economic pursuits to the strengthening of the one institution that united their far-flung realms: the army. In so doing they made the term *Prussian* synonymous with administrative rigor and military discipline.

The rise of Prussia occurred within the German power vacuum created by the Peace of Westphalia. It is the story of the extraordinary Hohenzollern family, which had ruled the German territory of Brandenburg since 1417. Through inheritance the family had acquired the Duchy of Cleves and the counties of Mark and Ravensburg in 1609, the Duchy of East Prussia in 1618, and the Duchy of

Pomerania in 1637. Except for Pomerania, none of these lands was contiguous with Brandenburg. East Prussia lay inside Poland and outside the authority of the Holy Roman Emperor. All of the territories lacked good natural resources, and many of them were devastated during the Thirty Years' War. At Westphalia the Hohenzollerns lost part of Pomerania to Sweden but were compensated by receiving three more bishoprics and the promise of the archbishopric of Magdeburg when it became vacant, as it did in 1680. By the late seventeenth century the scattered Hohenzollern holdings represented a block of territory within the Holy Roman Empire second in size only to that of the Hapsburgs.

Despite its size the Hohenzollern conglomerate was weak. The areas were geographically separate, and there was no mutual sympathy or common con-

The Brandenburg Gate in Berlin, 1764. Berlin had become the principal seat of the Hohenzollerns in the fifteenth century. In the 1760s it had about 70,000 inhabitants. [Landesbildstelle Berlin.]

cern among them. In each there existed some form of local noble estates that limited the power of the Hohenzollern prince. The various areas were exposed to foreign aggression.

The person who began to forge these areas and nobles into a modern state was Frederick William (1640–1688), who became known as the Great Elector. He established himself and his successors as the central uniting power by breaking the estates, organizing a royal bureaucracy, and establishing a strong army.

Between 1655 and 1660 Sweden and Poland engaged in a war that endangered the Great Elector's holdings in Pomerania and East Prussia. Frederick William had neither an adequate army nor the tax revenues to confront this foreign threat. In 1655 the Brandenburg estates refused to grant him new taxes; however, he proceeded to collect the required taxes by military force. In 1659 a different grant of taxes, originally made in 1653, elapsed; Frederick William continued to collect them as well as those he had imposed by his own authority. He used the money to build up an army, which allowed him to continue to enforce his will without the approval of the nobility. Similar processes of threats and coercion took place against the nobles in his other territories.

However, there was a political and social trade-off between the elector and his various nobles. These *Junkers,* or German noble landlords, were allowed almost complete control over the serfs on their estates. In exchange for their obedience to the Hohenzollerns the *Junkers* received the right to demand obedience from their serfs. Frederick William also tended to choose as the local administrators of the tax structure men who would normally have been members of the noble estates. In this fashion, he coopted potential opponents into his service. The taxes fell most heavily on the backs of the peasants and the urban classes. As the years passed, sons

of *Junkers* increasingly dominated the army officer corps, and this practice became even more pronounced during the eighteenth century. All officials and army officers took an oath of loyalty directly to the elector. The army and the elector thus came to embody the otherwise absent unity of the state. The existence of the army made Prussia a valuable potential ally and a state with which other powers needed to curry favor.

Yet even with the considerable accomplishments of the Great Elector, the house of Hohenzollern did not possess a crown. The achievement of a royal title was one of the few state-building accomplishments of Frederick I (1688–1713). This son of the Great Elector was the least "Prussian" of his family during these crucial years. He built palaces, founded Halle University (1694), patronized the arts, and lived luxuriously. However, in 1700, at the outbreak of the War of the Spanish Succession, he put his army at

Frederick William I of Prussia ruthlessly forged the Prussian army into a major instrument of state. But he also attempted to avoid committing his valuable troops to warfare. [The Granger Collection.]

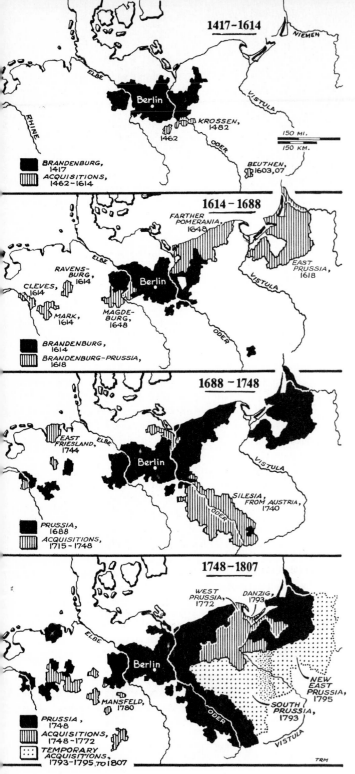

1417-1614

BRANDENBURG, 1417
ACQUISITIONS, 1462-1614

1614-1688

BRANDENBURG, 1614
BRANDENBURG-PRUSSIA, 1618

1688-1748

PRUSSIA, 1688
ACQUISITIONS, 1715-1748

1748-1807

PRUSSIA, 1748
ACQUISITIONS, 1748-1772
TEMPORARY ACQUISITIONS, 1793-1795,70 1807

EXPANSION OF BRANDENBURG–PRUSSIA

the disposal of the Hapsburg Holy Roman Emperor. In exchange for this loyal service the emperor permitted Frederick to assume the title of "King in Prussia." Thereafter Frederick became Frederick I, and he passed the much-desired royal title to his son Frederick William I in 1713.

Frederick William I (1713–1740) was both the most eccentric personality to rule the Hohenzollern domains and one of its most effective monarchs. After giving his father a funeral that matched the luxury of his life, Frederick William I immediately imposed policies of strict austerity. In some cases jobs were abolished, and in others salaries were lowered. His political aims seem to have been nothing else than the consolidation of an obedient, compliant bureaucracy and the expansion of the army. He initiated a policy of *Kabinett* government, which meant that lower officials submitted all relevant documents to him in his office or *Kabinett*. Then he alone examined the papers, made his decision, and issued his orders. Frederick William I thus skirted the influence of ministers and ruled alone.

Frederick William organized the bureaucracy along the lines of military discipline. He united all departments under the *General-Ober-Finanz-Kriegs-und-Domänen-Direktorium*, which is more happily known to us as the *General Directory*. He imposed taxes on the nobility and changed most remaining feudal dues into money payments. He sought to transform feudal and administrative loyalties into a sense of duty to the monarch as a political institution rather than as a person. He once described the perfect royal servant as

an intelligent, assiduous, and alert person who after God values nothing higher than his king's pleasure and serves him out of love and for the sake of honor rather than money and who in his conduct solely seeks and constantly bears in mind his king's service and interests, who, moreover, abhors all intrigues and emotional deterrents.[1]

Service to the state and the monarch was to become

[1] Quoted in Hans Rosenberg, *Bureaucracy, Aristocracy, and Autocracy* (Boston: Beacon Press 1958), p. 93.

MAP 18.2 *Seventeenth-century Brandenburg-Prussia expanded mainly by acquiring dynastic titles in geographically separated lands. Eighteenth-century expansion occurred through aggression to the east: Silesia seized in 1740 and various parts of Poland in 1772, 1793, and 1795.*

impersonal, mechanical, and, in effect, unquestioning.

The discipline that Frederick William applied to the army was little less than fanatical. During his reign the size of the military force grew from about thirty-nine thousand in 1713 to over eighty thousand in 1740. It was the third or fourth largest army in Europe, whereas Prussia ranked thirteenth in size of population. Rather than using recruiters, the king made each canton or local district responsible for supplying a certain number of soldiers.

After 1725 Frederick William always wore an officer's uniform. He built one regiment from the tallest soldiers he could find in Europe. Separate laws applied to the army and to civilians. Laws, customs, and royal attention made the officer corps the highest social class of the state. Military service attracted the sons of *Junkers*. In this fashion the army, the *Junker* nobility, and the monarchy became forged into a single political entity. Military priorities and values dominated Prussian government, society, and daily life as in no other state of Europe. It has often been

❧ Instructions for the Education of a Prussian Prince

Frederick William I directed toward the rearing of his son, who became Frederick the Great, the same kind of rigor he applied to the running of the army and the government of Prussia. In this letter to the royal tutors he emphasized the importance of practical subjects and voiced his contempt for the arts and the teaching of Latin. Frederick rebelled against his father and became quite accomplished in music.

. . . Above all else, it is important that his character—and it is character which governs all human action—should be, from earliest youth, so formed that he will love and delight in virtue and feel horror and disgust for vice. Nothing can so greatly contribute to this end as to implant the true fear of God so early in the young heart that it shall take root and bear fruit in the time when there is no longer any guidance or oversight. For other men are guided toward virtue and away from evil by the rewards and punishments dealt out by those who are set above them, but the prince must rely on the fear of God alone, since he is subject to no human law, punishment, or reward.

My son and all his attendants shall say their prayers on their knees both morning and evening, and after prayers shall read a chapter from the Bible.

He shall be kept away from operas, comedies, and other worldly amusements and, as far as possible, be given a distaste for them. He must be taught to pay proper respect and submission to his parents, but without slavishness.

His tutors must use every means they can devise to restrain him from puffed-up pride and insolence and train him in good management, economy, and modesty. . . .

As for the Latin language, he is not to learn it, and I desire that no one shall even speak to me on this subject; but his tutors shall see to it that he acquires a terse and elegant style in writing French as well as German. Arithmetic, mathematics, artillery, and agriculture he must be taught thoroughly, ancient history only superficially, but that of our own time and of the last one hundred and fifty years as accurately as possible. He must have a thorough knowledge of law, of international law, of geography, and of what is most remarkable in each country; and, above all, my son must be carefully taught the history of his own house.

His tutors must take the greatest pains to imbue my son with a sincere love for the soldier's profession and to impress upon him that nothing else in the world can confer upon a prince such fame and honor as the sword; . . . and his chief tutor shall provide for his being taught the practice of arms as play in his recreation hours.

James Harvey Robinson (Ed.), *Readings in European History*, Vol. 2 (Boston: Ginn and Co., 1906), pp. 319-321.

said that whereas other nations possessed armies, the Prussian army possessed its nation.

Although Frederick William I built the best army in Europe, he followed a policy of avoiding conflict. He wanted to drill his soldiers but not to order them into battle. Although Frederick William terrorized his family and associates and on occasion knocked out teeth with his walking stick, he was not a militarily aggressive monarch. The army was for him a symbol of Prussian power and unity, not an instrument to be used for foreign adventures or aggression. At his death in 1740 he passed to his son Frederick II (1740–1786; Frederick the Great) this superb military machine, but he could not pass to his son the wisdom to refrain from using it. Almost immediately on coming to the throne, Frederick II upset the Pragmatic Sanction and invaded Silesia. He thus crystallized the Austrian–Prussian rivalry for control of Germany that would dominate central European affairs for over a century.

The Entry of Russia into the European Political Arena

Though ripe with consequences for the future, the rise of Prussia and the new consolidation of the Austrian Hapsburg domains seemed to many at the time only one more shift in the long-troubled German scene. However, the emergence of Russia as an active European power constituted a wholly new factor in European politics. Previously Russia had been considered a part of Europe only by courtesy. Geographically and politically it lay on the periphery of Europe. Hemmed in by Sweden on the Baltic and by the Ottoman Empire on the Black Sea, the country had no warm-water ports. Its chief outlet to the west was Archangel on the White Sea, which was open to ships during only part of the year. There was little trade. What Russia did possess was a vast reserve of largely undeveloped natural and human resources.

The Medieval Russian Background

Several factors besides geography had accounted for this isolation of Russia prior to the eighteenth century. Early in the ninth century missionaries from Byzantium had converted Russia to the Christianity of the Eastern Orthodox Church.

This development meant that Russia would remain culturally separated from the Latin Christianity of western Europe. Between the late ninth century and the mid-thirteenth century the city of Kiev had been the center of Russian political life. Although the city enjoyed fairly extensive trade relations with its neighbors, it failed to develop a political system that provided effective resistance to foreign domination. The external threat to Kievan Russia came from the east when the Mongols moved across the vast Eurasian plains and into Russia as Genghis Khan built his empire. By 1240 the Mongols had conquered most of Russia and had turned its various cities and their surrounding countryside into dependent principalities from which tribute could be exacted. The portion of the Mongol empire to which Russia thus stood in the relationship of a vassal was called the *Golden Horde*. It included the steppe in what is now south Russia with its largely nomadic population. This vassal relationship encouraged an eastern orientation on the part of the Russians for over two centuries, although the connection of the Russian church to the Byzantine Empire remained important. During this period there was no single central political authority in Russia. The land was divided into numerous appanages or feudal principalities, each of which was militarily weak and subject in one degree or another to the Golden Horde.

The rise of Moscow as a relatively strong power eventually brought the appanage age of Russian history to an end. In the fourteenth century, under Grand Prince Ivan I, the city began to cooperate with its Mongol—or as the Russians called them, Tatar—overlords in the collection of tribute. Ivan kept much of this tribute for himself and was soon called Ivan Kalita, or John of the Moneybag. When Mongol authority began to weaken, the princes of Moscow, who had become increasingly wealthy, filled the political power vacuum in the territory near the city. The princes extended their authority and that of the city by purchasing some territory, colonizing other areas, and conquering new lands. This slow extension of the appanage, or principality, of Moscow is usually known as *gathering the Russian land*.

In 1380 Grand Prince Dmitrii of Moscow defeated the Mongols in battle. The result was not militarily decisive, but Moscow had demonstrated that the Mongol armies were not invincible. Conflict with the Mongols continued for another cen-

mongols 1240–1340

tury before they were driven out. During these years the princes of Moscow asserted their right to be regarded as the successors of the earlier Kievan rulers, and they also made Moscow the religious center of Russia.

The person who most benefited from the accomplishments of these early Moscow princes and who transformed the principality into a new kind of state was Ivan IV (1533–1584), who is better known as Ivan the Terrible. His reign displayed a pattern that would be repeated frequently, and often tragically, in later Russian history: early years of reform and solid accomplishment followed by a period of almost inexplicable tyranny.

Ivan came into his political inheritance at the age of three. Consequently, there was a long regency that witnessed numerous clashes among the *boyars* or Russian nobles. The first key moment in his personal reign occurred in 1547, when at the age of sixteen he had himself crowned czar (the Russian equivalent of *Caesar* or *Kaiser*) rather than prince of Moscow.

During the opening years of his personal reign Ivan IV consulted with the great *boyars* and other able advisers in a relationship of mutual trust. He worked toward formulating a revised law code and a mode of local government that would be responsive to the needs of the areas governed. He reorganized the army, and he established direct economic contact with western Europe. During the 1550s Ivan undertook successful military campaigns against the Ottomans in the south, the Tatars in the south and east, and for a time the Livonians in the northwest. It appeared that his reign would be well regarded at home and abroad.

Beginning in about 1560, however, a profound change took place in his personality. He began to mistrust his most honest advisers and believed that they were plotting against him. When his first wife died in 1560, he thought she had been poisoned by a conspiracy. In the late 1560s he created a set of *boyars* and officials who were personally loyal to him and an army also loyal to him alone. He loosed these troops, who always dressed in black and who were called the *oprichniki*, against anyone he regarded as an enemy. He imprisoned, tortured, and executed *boyars* without cause and without trial. In 1581 Ivan killed his own son. He himself died in 1584. While he had pursued this utterly irrational behavior at home, his military forces in Livonia had been defeated by both Sweden and Poland. His reign ended in domestic political turmoil and foreign military defeat.

The reign of Ivan the Terrible, which had begun so well and closed so frighteningly, was followed by a period of anarchy and civil war known as the *Time of Troubles*. In 1613, hoping to resolve the tension and end the uncertainty, an assembly of nobles elected as czar a seventeen-year-old boy named Mikhail Romanov (1613–1654). Thus began the dynasty that in spite of palace revolutions, military conspiracies, assassinations, and family strife ruled Russia until 1917.

Mikhail Romanov and his two successors, Alexis I (1654–1676) and Theodore III (1676–1682), brought stability and bureaucratic centralization to Russia. However, Russia remained militarily weak

---

RISE OF RUSSIAN POWER

1533–1584	Reign of Ivan the Terrible
1584–1613	Time of Troubles
1613	Mikhail Romanov becomes czar
1682	Peter the Great becomes czar as a boy
1689	Peter assumes personal rule
1696	Russia captures Azov on the Black Sea from the Turks
1697	European tour of Peter the Great
1698	Peter returns to Russia to put down the revolt of the *streltsi*
1700	The Great Northern War opens between Russia and Sweden; Russia defeated at Narva by Swedish Army of Charles XII
1703	Saint Petersburg founded
1709	Russia defeats Sweden at the Battle of Poltava
1718	Charles XII of Sweden dies
	Son of Peter the Great dies under mysterious circumstances in prison
1721	Peace of Nystad ends the Great Northern War
	Peter establishes a synod for the Russian church
1722	Peter issues the Table of Ranks
1725	Peter dies leaving an uncertain succession

and financially impoverished. The bureaucracy after these years of turmoil still remained largely controlled by the *boyars*. This administrative apparatus was only barely capable of putting down a revolt of peasants and cossacks under Stepan Razin in 1670–1671. Furthermore, the government and the czars faced the danger of mutiny from the *streltsi*, or guards of the Moscow garrison.

Peter the Great

In 1682 another boy—ten years old at the time—ascended the fragile Russian throne as coruler with his half brother. His name was Peter (1682–1725), and Russia would never be the same after him. He and his ill half-brother, Ivan V, had come to power on the shoulders of the *streltsi*, who expected rewards from the persons they favored. Much violence and bloodshed had surrounded the disputed succession. Matters became even more confused when their sister, Sophia, was named regent. Peter's followers overthrew her in 1689. From that

date onward Peter ruled personally, although in theory he shared the crown with Ivan, who died in 1696. The dangers and turmoil of his youth convinced Peter of two things. First, the power of the czar must be made secure from the jealousy of the *boyars* and the greed of the *streltsi*. Second, the military power of Russia must be increased.

Peter I, who became Peter the Great, was fascinated by western Europe, particularly its military resources. He was an imitator of the first order. The products and workmen from the West who had filtered into Russia impressed and intrigued him. In 1697 he made a famous visit in rather weak disguises throughout western Europe. There he dined and talked with the great and the powerful, who considered this almost seven-foot-tall ruler both crude and rude. His happiest moments on the trip were spent inspecting shipyards, docks, and the manufacture of military hardware. He returned to Moscow determined by whatever means necessary to copy what he had seen abroad, for he knew that warfare would be necessary to make

❧ Bishop Burnet Looks Over a Foreign Visitor

In 1697 and 1698 Peter the Great of Russia toured western Europe to discover how Russia must change its society and economy in order to become a great power. As this description by Bishop Gilbert Burnet in England indicates, the west Europeans found the czar a curious person in his own right.

He came this winter over to England, and stayed some months among us. . . . I had good interpreters, so I had much free discourse with him; he is a man of a very hot temper, soon inflamed, and very brutal in his passion; he raises his natural heat, by drinking much brandy, . . . he is subject to convulsive motions all over his body, and his head seems to be affected with these; he wants not capacity, and has a larger measure of knowledge, than might be expected from his education, which was very indifferent; a want of judgment, with an instability of temper, appear in him too often and too evidently; he is mechanically turned, and seems designed by nature rather to be a ship-carpenter, than a great prince. This was his chief study and exercise, while he stayed here: he wrought much with his own hands, and made all about him work at the models of ships. . . . He was . . . resolved to encourage learning, and to polish his people, by sending some of them to travel in other countries, and to draw strangers to come and live among them. . . . After I had seen him often, and had conversed much with him, I could not but adore the depth of the providence of God, that had raised up such a furious man to so absolute an authority over so great a part of the world.

Bishop Burnet's History of His Own Time, Vol. 4 (Oxford, England: Clarendon Press, 1823), pp. 396–397.

Russia a great power. The czar's drive toward westernization, though unsystematic, had four general areas of concern: taming the *boyars* and the *streltsi*, achieving secular control of the church, reorganizing the internal administration, and developing the economy. Peter pursued each of these goals with violence and ruthlessness.

He made a sustained attack on the Russian *boyars*. In 1698, immediately on his return from abroad, he personally shaved the long beards of the court *boyars* and sheared off the customary long, hand-covering sleeves of their shirts and coats, which had made them the butt of jokes throughout Europe. More importantly, he demanded that the nobles provide his state with their services.

In 1722 Peter published a Table of Ranks, which henceforth equated a person's social position and privileges with his rank in the bureaucracy or the army rather than with his position in the nobility. However, unlike the case in Prussia, the Russian nobility never became perfectly loyal to the state. They repeatedly sought to reassert their independence and their control of the Russian imperial court.

After Peter the Great of Russia returned from his journey to western Europe, he personally cut off the traditional and highly prized long sleeves and beards of the Russian nobles. His action symbolized his desire to see Russia become more powerful and more modern. [SLEEVES: *Culver Pictures;* BEARDS: *The Granger Collection.*]

The *streltsi* fared less well than the *boyars*. In 1698 they had rebelled while Peter was on his European tour. When he returned and put down the revolt of these Moscow troops, he directed massive violence and brutality against both leaders and followers. There were private tortures and public executions, in which Peter's own ministers took part. Almost twelve hundred of the rebels were put to death, and their corpses long remained on public display to discourage future disloyalty.

Peter dealt with the potential political independence of the Russian Orthodox Church with similar ruthlessness. Here again Peter had to confront a problem that had arisen in the turbulent decades that had preceded his reign. The Russian church had long opposed the scientific as well as the theological thought of the West. In the mid-seventeenth century a reformist movement led by Patriarch Nikon arose in the church. In 1667 certain changes had been introduced into the texts and the ritual of the church. These reforms caused great unrest because the Russian church had always claimed to be the protector of true ritual. The Old Believers, a group of Russian Christians who strongly opposed these changes, were condemned by the hierarchy, but they persisted in their opposition. Late in the century thousands of them committed suicide rather than submit to the new rituals. The Old Believers' movement represented a rejection of change and innovation; its presence discouraged the church hierarchy from making any further substantial moves toward modern thought.

In the future Peter wanted to avoid two kinds of difficulties with the Russian church. First, the clergy must not constitute a group within the state who would oppose change and westernization. Second, the hierarchy of the church must not be permitted to reform liturgy, ritual, or doctrine in a way that might again give rise to discontent such as that of the Old Believers. Consequently in 1721 Peter simply abolished the position of patriarch of the Russian church. In its place he established a synod headed by a layman to rule the church in accordance with secular requirements. So far as transforming a traditional institution was concerned, this action toward the church was the most radical policy of Peter's reign. It produced still further futile opposition from the Old Believers, who saw the czar as leading the church into new heresy.

In his reorganization of domestic administration, Peter looked to institutions then used in Sweden. These were "colleges," or bureaus, composed of several persons rather than departments headed by a single minister. These colleges, which he imposed on Russia, were to look after matters such as the collection of taxes, foreign affairs, war, and economic matters. This new organization was an attempt to breathe life into the generally stagnant and inefficient administration of the country. In 1711 he created a central senate of nine members who were to direct the Moscow government when the czar was away with the army. The purpose of these and other local administrative reforms was to establish a bureaucracy that could collect and spend tax revenues to support an efficient army.

The economic development advocated by Peter the Great was closely related to his military needs. He encouraged the establishment of an iron industry in the Ural Mountains, and by mid-century Russia had become the largest iron producer in Europe. He sent prominent young Russians abroad to acquire technical and organizational skills. He attempted to attract west European craftsmen to live and work in Russia. Except for the striking growth of the iron industry, which later languished, all these efforts had only marginal success.

The goal of these internal reforms and political departures was to support a policy of warfare. Peter was determined to secure warm-water ports that would allow Russia to trade with the West and to have a greater impact on European affairs. This policy led him into wars with the Ottoman Empire and with Sweden. His armies commenced fighting the Turks in 1695 and captured Azov on the Black Sea in 1696. It was a temporary victory, for in 1711 he was compelled to return the port.

Peter had more success against Sweden, where the inconsistency and irrationality of Charles XII were no small aid. In 1700 Russia moved against the Swedish territory on the Baltic. The Swedish king's failure to follow up his victory at Narva in 1700 allowed Peter to regroup his forces and hoard his resources. In 1709, when Charles XII returned to fight Russia again, Peter was ready, and the Battle of Poltava sealed the fate of Sweden. In 1721, at the Peace of Nystad, which ended the Great Northern War, the Russian conquest of Estonia, Livonia, and part of Finland was confirmed. Henceforth Russia possessed warm-water ports and a permanent influence on European affairs.

At one point the domestic and foreign policies of Peter the Great literally intersected. This was at the spot on the Gulf of Finland where Peter founded his new capital city of Saint Petersburg (now Leningrad). There he built government structures and compelled his *boyars* to construct town houses. In this fashion he imitated those west European monarchs who had copied Louis XIV by constructing smaller versions of Versailles. However, the founding of Saint Petersburg went beyond the construction of a central court. It symbolized a new western orientation of Russia and Peter's determination to hold his position on the Baltic coast. He had commenced the construction of the city and had moved the capital there in 1703, even before his victory over Sweden was assured.

Despite his notable success on the Baltic, Peter's reign ended with a great question mark. He had long quarreled with his only son, Alexis. Peter was jealous of the young man and fearful that he might undertake sedition. In 1718 Peter had his son imprisoned, and during this imprisonment the presumed successor to the throne died mysteriously. Thereafter Peter claimed for himself the right of naming a successor, but he could never bring himself to designate the person either orally or in writing. Consequently, when he died in 1725, there was no firmer policy on the succession to the

Peter the Great built St. Petersburg on the Gulf of Finland to prove his intention of maintaining recently conquered territory and to provide Russia with better contact with Western Europe. This is an eighteenth-century view of the city. [John R. Freeman.]

throne than when he had acceded to the title. For over thirty years, once again soldiers and nobles would determine who ruled Russia. Peter had laid the foundations of a modern Russia, but he had failed to lay the foundations of a stable state.

Eighteenth-Century European States

By the second quarter of the eighteenth century the major European powers were not yet nation-states in which the citizens felt themselves united by a shared sense of community, culture, language, and history. They were still monarchies in which the personality of the ruler and the personal relationships of the great noble families exercised considerable influence over public affairs. The monarchs, except in Great Britain, had generally succeeded in making their power greater than the nobility's. However, the power of the aristocracy and its capacity to resist or obstruct the policies of the monarchs were not destroyed. In Britain, of course, the nobility had tamed the monarchy, but even there tension between nobles and monarchs would continue through the rest of the century.

In foreign affairs the new arrangement of military and diplomatic power established during the early years of the century prepared the way for two long-term conflicts. The first was a commercial rivalry for trade and overseas empire between France and Great Britain. During the reign of Louis XIV these two nations had collided over the French bid for dominance in Europe. During the eighteenth century they dueled for control of commerce on other continents. The second arena of warfare was central Europe, where Austria and Prussia fought for the leadership of the states of Germany.

However, behind these international conflicts and the domestic rivalry of monarchs and nobles, the society of eighteenth-century Europe began to experience momentous change. The character and the structures of the society over which the monarchs ruled were beginning to take on some features associated with the modern age. These economic and social developments would in the long run produce transformations in the life of Europe beside which the state building of the early eighteenth-century monarchs paled.

Suggested Readings

M. S. ANDERSON, *Europe in the Eighteenth Century, 1713–1783* (1961). The best one-volume introduction.

F. L. CARSTEN, *The Origins of Prussia* (1954). Discusses the groundwork laid by the Great Elector in the seventeenth century.

A. COBBAN, *A History of Modern France*, Vol. 1, 2nd ed. (1961). A lively and opinionated survey.

L. COLLEY, *In Defiance of Oligarchy: The Tory Party, 1714–60.* (1982) An important study that challenges much conventional opinion about eighteenth-century British politics.

R. R. ERGANG, *The Potsdam Führer* (1941). The biography of Frederick William I.

S. B. FAY AND K. EPSTEIN, *The Rise of Brandenburg–Prussia to 1786* (1937, rev. 1964). A brief outline.

M. T. FLORINSKY, *Russia: A History and an Interpretation*, 2 vols. (1953). A useful and far-ranging work.

FRANKLIN FORD, *Robe and Sword: The Regrouping of the French Aristocracy After Louis XIV* (1953). An important book for political, social, and intellectual history.

G. P. GOOCH, *Maria Theresa and Other Studies* (1951). A sound introduction to the problems of the Hapsburgs.

G. P. GOOCH, *Louis XV, The Monarchy in Decline* (1956). A discussion of the problems of France after the death of Louis XIV.

H. HOLBORN, *A History of Modern Germany, 1648–1840* (1966). The best and most comprehensive survey in English.

HUBERT C. JOHNSON, *Frederick the Great and His Officials* (1975). An excellent recent examination of the Prussian administration.

V. K. KLYUCHEVSKY, *Peter the Great*, tr. by Liliana Archibald (1958). A standard biography.

DORTHY MARSHALL, *Eighteenth-Century England* (1962). Emphasizes social and economic background.

ROBERT K. MASSIE, *Peter the Great: His Life and His World* (1980). A good popular biography.

L. B. NAMIER AND J. BROOKE, *The History of Parliament: The House of Commons, 1754–1790*, 3 vols. (1964). A detailed examination of the unreformed British House of Commons and electoral system.

L. J. OLIVA (Ed.), *Russia and the West from Peter the Great to Khrushchev* (1965). An anthology of articles tracing an important and ambiguous subject.

J. B. OWEN, *The Eighteenth Century* (1974). An excellent introduction to England in the period.

J. H. PLUMB, *Sir Robert Walpole*, 2 vols. (1956, 1961). A masterful biography ranging across the sweep of European politics.

J. H. PLUMB, *The Growth of Political Stability in England, 1675–1725* (1969). An important interpretive work.

NICHOLAS V. RIASANOVSKY, *A History of Russia*, 3rd ed. (1977). The best one-volume introduction.

P. ROBERTS, *The Quest for Security, 1715–1740* (1947). Very good on the diplomatic problems of the period.

H. ROSENBERG, *Bureaucracy, Aristocracy, and Autocracy: The Prussian Experience, 1660–1815* (1960). Emphasizes the organization of Prussian administration.

B. H. SUMMER, *Peter the Great and the Emergence of Russia* (1950). A brief, but well-organized discussion.

E. N. WILLIAMS, *The Ancien Régime in Europe* (1972). A state by state survey of very high quality.

A. M. WILSON, *French Foreign Policy During the Administration of Cardinal Fleury, 1726–1743* (1936). The standard account.

J. B. WOLF, *The Emergence of the Great Powers, 1685–1715* (1951). A comprehensive survey.

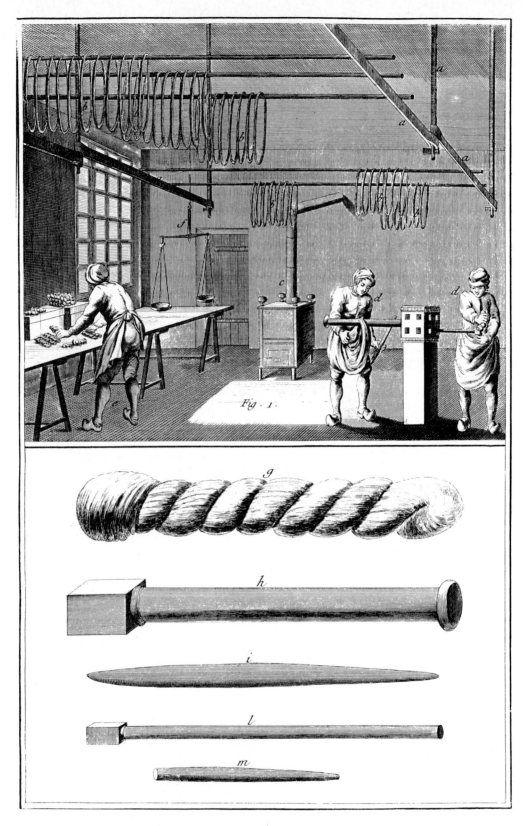

Fig. 1.

19 Society Under the Old Regime in the Eighteenth Century

During the French Revolution (1789) and the turmoil spawned by that upheaval it became customary to refer to the patterns of social, political, and economic relationships that had existed in France before 1789 as the *ancien régime,* or the "old regime." The term has come to be applied generally to the life and institutions of prerevolutionary Europe. Politically the term indicated the rule of theoretically absolute monarchies with growing bureaucracies and aristocratically led armies. Economically the old regime was characterized by scarcity of food, the predominance of agriculture, slow transport, a low level of iron production, rather unsophisticated financial institutions, and in some cases competitive commercial overseas empires. Socially prerevolutionary Europe was based

This drawing is from the mid-eighteenth-century French Encyclopedie, ou Dictionnaire Raisonné des Sciences, des Arts et des Métiers *(hereafter known as the* Encyclopedia*). It shows part of the dyeworks that supplied thread and yarn for the renowned Gobelin tapestries. It also shows enlargements of various components of the dyeing process.* [The New York Public Library Picture Collection.]

on aristocratic elites possessing a wide variety of inherited legal privileges, established Roman Catholic and Protestant churches intimately related to the state and the aristocracy, an urban labor force usually organized into guilds, and a rural peasantry subject to high taxes and feudal dues. It should be remembered that the men and women living during this period did not know it was the *old* regime. In most cases they earned their livelihoods and went through the various stages of life as their forebears had done for generations before them and as they expected their children to do after them.

Probably the most striking feature of the old regime was the marked contrasts in the lives and experiences of people in different social ranks, different countries, and even different regions of the same country. The bonds created by rapid transport and communication that have today led to similar patterns of life throughout the Western world simply did not yet exist.

Within the major monarchies there was usually no single standard of uniform law, money, or weights and measures. Except in Britain there were

561

Castle Howard in Yorkshire, England, designed by the architect and playwright, Sir John Vanbrugh (1665–1726), was one of the grandest of the homes of the aristocracy from the time of its completion in 1714. From such great houses the aristocrats looked after their estates and their local political interests. [British Tourist Authority, New York.]

internal tolls that hampered the passage of goods. The nobility of Great Britain lived in the most magnificent luxury the order had ever known. On the Continent some groups of nobles were also very wealthy, but other members of the continental nobility were little better off than the wealthier peasants. So far as the peasantry was concerned, it tended to prosper in western Europe while reaching new depths of social and economic degradation east of the Elbe River.

In Britain, Holland, and parts of France there was a healthy and growing middle class, but such an order hardly existed in the German principalities, the Austrian Empire, or Russia. Finally, there was a stark contrast between the refinement of taste, fashion, and manners of the upper levels of society and the simultaneous presence of public whipping, torture, and executions inflicted on the lower classes. Historians often point to the difficulties of life and the differences in wealth in our in-

dustrial society, but these were far more extreme in the society of the old regime.

Eighteenth-century society was traditional. The past weighed more heavily on people's minds than did the future. Few persons outside the government bureaucracies and the movement for reform called the *Enlightenment* considered change or innovation desirable. This was especially true of social relationships. Both nobles and peasants, for very different reasons, repeatedly called for the restoration of traditional or customary rights. The nobles asserted what they considered their ancient rights against the intrusion of the expanding monarchical bureaucracies. The peasants, in petitions and revolts, called for the revival or the maintenance of the customary manorial rights that provided them access to particular lands, courts, or grievance procedures.

With the exception of the early industrial development in Britain, the eighteenth-century econ-

At the opposite end of the social scale from Castle Howard is the mid-eighteenth-century rural laborer's hut far to the east in Austria. However proper a subject for the artist, Franz Edmund Weirotter (1730–1771), the scene is probably a realistic one of the wretched housing endured by many. [Charles Farrell Collection.]

omy was also quite traditional. The quality and quantity of the harvest remained the single most important fact of life for the overwhelming majority of the population and the gravest concern of the governments.

Closely related to this traditional social and economic outlook was the hierarchical structure of the society. The medieval sense of rank and degree not only persisted but became more rigid in the course of the century. In several continental cities "sumptuary laws" regulating the dress of the different classes remained on the books. These laws forbade persons in one class or occupation to wear clothes like those worn by people in a socially higher position. The point of such laws, which were largely ineffective in the eighteenth century, was to make the social hierarchy actually visible. Rather than by such legislation, the hierarchy was really enforced through the corporate nature of social relationships. Each state or society was considered a community of numerous smaller communities. People in eighteenth-century Europe did not enjoy what Americans regard as individual rights. A person enjoyed such rights and privileges as were guaranteed to the particular communities or groups of which he was a part. The "community" might include the village, the municipality, the nobility, the church, the guild, or the parish. In turn, each of these bodies enjoyed certain privileges, some of which were great and some small. The privileges might involve exemption from taxation or from some especially humiliating punishment, the right to practice a trade or craft, the right of one's children to pursue a particular occupation, or in the case of the church the right to collect the tithe.

Tradition, hierarchy, corporateness, and privilege were the chief social characteristics of the old regime. Yet it was by no means a static society. Factors of change and innovation were fermenting in its midst. There was a strong demand from the colonies in the Americas for European goods and manufactures. Merchants in seaports and other cities were expanding their businesses. By preparing their states for war, the various governments put new demands on the resources and the economic organizations of their nations. The spirit of rationality that had been so important to the Scientific Revolution of the seventeenth century continued to manifest itself in the economic life of the eighteenth century. Perhaps most importantly, the population of Europe grew rapidly. The old regime itself fostered the changes that eventually transformed it into a very different kind of society.

The Land and Its Tillers

Land constituted the economic basis of eighteenth-century life. Well over three fourths of all Europeans lived in the country, and few of these people ever traveled beyond a ten-mile radius of their birthplace. Male children tended to follow the occupation of their fathers. Village families tended to intermarry; there were only occasional marriages between men and women from neighboring villages. The lot of women continued to be circumscribed by family duties, the family economy, and the burden of childbearing and child rearing. With the exception of the nobility and the wealthier nonaristocratic landowners, the dwellers on the land were poor, and by any modern standard their lives were difficult. They lived in various modes of economic and social dependency, exploitation, and vulnerability.

Peasants and Serfs

The major forms of rural social dependency related directly to the land. Those who worked the land were subject to immense influence and in some cases direct control by the landowners. This situation prevailed in differing degrees for free peasants, such as English tenants and most French cultivators, and for the serfs of Germany, Austria, and Russia, who were legally bound to a particular plot of land and a particular lord. In all cases the class that owned most of the land also controlled the local government and the courts. For example, in Great Britain all farmers and smaller tenants had the legal rights of English citizens. But the justices of the peace who presided over the county courts and who could call out the local militia were

Agriculture, basic to society, is illustrated in this plate from the mid-eighteenth-century French Encyclopédie, ou Dictionnaire Raisonné des Sciences, des Arts et des Métiers *(hereafter the* Encyclopedia). *New machinery, such as the plows shown at the bottom, helped to increase yield from the land and thus the food supply for Europe.*

always substantial landowners, as were also the members of Parliament, who made the laws.

The intensity of landlord power increased as one moved from west to east. In France the situation differed somewhat from province to province. Most French peasants owned some land, but there were a few serfs. However, practically all peasants were subject to certain feudal dues, called *banalités*, that included required use-for-payment of the lord or seigneur's mill to grind grain and his oven to bake bread. The seigneur could also require a certain number of days each year of the peasant's labor. This practice of forced labor was termed the *corvée*. Because even landowning French peasants rarely possessed enough land to support their fam-

Lunchtime on an eighteenth-century French farm. The softened style of drawing gives a somewhat romanticized cast to the scene, but farm workers did usually work in the kind of group shown here. [The Granger Collection.]

J. J. De Boissieu's 1780 etching of the interior of a French dairy barn associates the life of the land with the life of the family. [Charles Farrell Collection.]

Eighteenth-century France had some of the best roads in the world, but they were often built with forced labor. French peasants were required to work for part of each year on such projects. This system, called the corvée, was not abolished until the French Revolution in 1789. This painting, Construction of a Major Road by Joseph Vernet, is in the Louvre. [Giraudon.]

A drawing from the Encyclopédie of French peasants threshing grain with flails. This method of separating the edible part of the grain from the inedible chaff had been practiced since Biblical times. [New York Public Library.]

William Coxe Describes Serfdom in Eighteenth-Century Russia

William Coxe was an Englishman who traveled widely in eastern Europe. His description of Russian serfdom portrays the brutality of the institution. It also illustrates his amazement at the absence in Russia of civil liberties such as he and more humble citizens enjoyed in England.

Peasants belonging to individuals are the private property of the landholders, as much as implements of agriculture, or herds of cattle; and the value of an estate is estimated, as in Poland, by the number of boors [serfs], and not by the number of acres. . . . If the Polish boor is oppressed, and he escapes to another master, the latter is liable to no pecuniary penalty for harbouring him; but in Russia the person who receives another's vassal is subject to an heavy fine. With respect to his own demands upon his peasants, the lord is restrained by no law, either in the exaction of any sum, or in the mode of employing them. He is absolute master of their time and labour: some he employs in agriculture: a few he makes his menial servants, and perhaps without wages; and from others he exacts an annual payment.

Each vassal, therefore, is rated according to the arbitrary will of his master. Some contribute four or five shillings a year; others, who are engaged in traffic or trade, are assessed in proportion to their supposed profits. . . . With regard to any capital which they may have acquired by their industry, it may be seized, and there can be no redress. . . .

. . . [S]ome of the Russian nobility send their vassals to Moscow or Petersburg for the purpose of learning various handcraft trades: they either employ them on their own estates; let them out for hire; sell them at an advanced price; or receive from them an annual compensation for the permission of exercising trade for their own advantage.

William Coxe, *Travels into Poland, Russia, Sweden, and Denmark,* 4th ed., Vol. 3 (London: T. Cadell 1972, first printed 1784), pp. 174–181.

ilies, they were also subject to feudal dues attached to the plots of land they rented. In Prussia and Austria, despite attempts by the monarchies late in the century to improve the lot of the serfs, the landlords continued to exercise almost complete control over them. In Austria law and custom required the serfs to provide service or *robot* to the lords. Moreover, throughout continental Europe in addition to these feudal services, the burden of state taxation fell on the tillers of the soil. Many peasants, serfs, and other agricultural laborers were forced to undertake supplemental work to raise the cash required to pay the tax collector. Through various legal privileges and the ability to demand further concessions from the monarchs, the landlords escaped the payment of numerous taxes. They also presided over the manorial courts.

The condition of the serfs was the worst in Russia. The Russian custom of enumerating the number of "souls" (that is, male serfs) owned rather than the acreage possessed reveals the contrast.

The serfs were, in effect, regarded merely as economic commodities. Russian landlords could demand as many as six days a week of labor, and like Prussian and Austrian landlords they enjoyed the right to punish their serfs. On their own authority alone they could even exile a serf to Siberia. The serfs had no legal recourse against the orders and whims of their lords. There was actually little difference between Russian serfdom and slavery.

The Russian monarchy itself contributed to the degradation of the serfs. Peter the Great gave whole villages to favored nobles. Later in the century Catherine the Great (1762–1796) confirmed the authority of the nobles over their serfs in exchange for the political cooperation of the landowners. The situation in Russia led to considerable unrest. There were well over fifty peasant revolts between 1762 and 1769. These culminated between 1771 and 1775 in Pugachev's rebellion, during which all of southern Russia experienced intense unrest. Emelyan Pugachev (1726–1775)

Catherine the Great Issues a Proclamation Against Pugachev

> Against a background of long-standing human degradation, and ever increasing landowner authority, the greatest serf rebellion in Russian history was led from 1773 to 1775 by a Don Cossack named Emelyan Pugachev. Empress Catherine the Great's proclamation of 1773 argues that he was alienating the serfs from their natural and proper allegiance to her and their masters.

By the grace of God, we Catherine II . . . make known to our faithful subjects, that we have learnt, with the utmost indignation and extreme affliction, that a certain Cossack, a deserter and fugitive from the Don, named Emelyan Pugachev, after having traversed Poland, has been collecting, for some time past, in the districts that border on the river Irghis, in the government of Orenburg, a troop of vagabonds like himself; that he continues to commit in those parts all kinds of excesses, by inhumanly depriving the inhabitants of their possessions, and even of their lives. . . .

In a word, there is not a man deserving of the Russian name, who does not hold in abomination the odious and insolent lie by which Pugachev fancies himself able to seduce and to deceive persons of a simple and credulous disposition, by promising to free them from the bonds of submission, and obedience to their sovereign, as if the Creation of the universe had established human societies in such a manner as that they can subsist without an intermediate authority between the sovereign and the people.

Nevertheless, as the insolence of this vile refuse of the human race is attended with consequences pernicious to the provinces adjacent to that district; as the report of the flagrant enormities which he has committed, may affright those persons who are accustomed to imagine the misfortunes of others as ready to fall upon them, and as we watch with indefatigable care over the tranquility of our faithful subjects, we inform them . . . that we have taken . . . such measures as are the best adapted to stifle the sedition. . . .

We trust . . . that every true son of the country will unremittedly fulfill his duty, of the contributing to the maintenance of good order and of public tranquility, by preserving himself from the snares of seduction, and by discharging his obedience to his lawful sovereign.

William Tooke, *Life of Catherine II, Empress of Russia*, 4th ed., Vol. 2 (London: T. N. Longman and O. Rees, 1800), pp. 460–461 (spelling modernized).

Emelyan Pugachev (1726–1775) led the largest peasant revolt in Russian history. Here in a contemporary propaganda picture he is shown in chains. An inscription in Russian and German was printed below the picture discussing the evil of revolution and insurrection. [Bildarchiv Preussischer Kulturbesitz.]

promised the serfs land of their own and freedom from their lords. The rebellion was brutally suppressed. Thereafter any thought of liberalizing or improving the condition of the serfs was set aside for a generation.

Pugachev's was the greatest rebellion in Russian history and the largest peasant uprising of the eighteenth century. Smaller peasant revolts or disturbances occurred outside of Russia. Rebellions took place in Bohemia in 1775, in Transylvania in 1784, in Moravia in 1786, and in Austria in 1789. Revolts in western Europe were almost nonexistent, but England experienced numerous local enclosure riots. Rural rebellions were violent, but the peasants and serfs normally directed their wrath against property rather than persons. The rebels usually sought to reassert traditional or customary rights against practices they perceived as innovations. Their targets were carefully chosen and included unfair pricing, onerous new or increased feudal dues, changes in methods of payment or land use, unjust officials, or extraordinarily brutal overseers and landlords. In this respect the peasant revolts were quite conservative in nature.

The main goal of peasant society was a stability that would ensure the local food supply. In western Europe most rural society was organized into villages, and on about half of the land the owners of individual plots or strips would decide communally what crops would be planted. In eastern Europe, with its great estates of hundreds or thousands of acres, the landlords decided how to use the land. But in either case the tillers resisted changes that might endanger the sure supply of food, which they generally believed to be promised by traditional cultivation. However, throughout the eighteenth century landlords across the Continent began to search for higher profits from their holdings. They embraced innovation in order to increase their own prosperity. They commercialized agriculture and thereby challenged the traditional peasant ways of production. Peasant revolts and disturbances often resulted. The governments of Europe, hungry for new taxes and dependent on the goodwill of the nobility, used their armies and militias to smash the peasants who defended the past. In certain areas, such as the Low Countries and parts of Germany, the peasants themselves began to innovate so that they could more easily raise the cash they needed for tax payments.

The Revolution in Agriculture

Even more basic than the social dependency of peasants and small tenant farmers was their dependency on the productiveness of nature. The quantity and quality of the annual grain harvest was the most fundamental fact in their lives. On

---

❧ Turgot Describes the Results of Poor Harvests in France

Failure of the grain crop and other plantings could bring both hunger and social disruption during the eighteenth century. Anne Robert Jacques Turgot (1727–1781), who later became finance minister of France, emphasized the role of private charity and government policy in relieving the suffering. His description, written in 1769, also provides a brief survey of the diet of the French peasant.

Everyone has heard of the terrible dearth that has just afflicted this generality [a local administrative district]. The harvest of 1769 in every respect proved to be one of the worst in the memory of man. The dearths of 1709 and 1739 were incomparably less cruel. To the loss of the greatest part of the rye was added the total loss of the chestnuts, of the buckwheat, and of the Spanish wheat—cheap food stuffs with which the peasant sustained himself habitually a great part of the year, reserving as much as he could of his corn [grain], in order to sell it to the inhabitants of the towns. . . . The people could exist only by exhausting their resources, by selling at a miserable price their articles of furniture and even their clothes. Many of the inhabitants have been obliged to disperse *themselves through other provinces to seek work or to beg, leaving their wives and children to the charity of the parishes. It has been necessary for the public authority to require the proprietors and inhabitants in better circumstances in each parish to assess themselves for the relief of the poor people; nearly a fourth of the population is dependent upon charitable contributions. After these melancholy sufferings which the province has already undergone, and with the reduced condition in which it was left by the dearth of last year, even had the harvest of the present year been a good one, the poverty of the inhabitants would have necessitated the greatest efforts to be made for their relief. But we have now to add the dismal fact of our harvest being again deficient. . . .*

W. W. Stephens (Ed.), *The Life and Writings of Turgot* (London: Longmans, Green, and Co., 1895), p. 50.

the Continent bread was the primary component of the diet of the lower classes. The food supply was never certain, and the farther east one traveled, the more uncertain it became. Failure of the harvest meant not only hardship but actual death from either outright starvation or protracted debility. Quite often people living in the countryside encountered more difficulty finding food than did city dwellers, whose local government usually stored reserve supplies of grain.

Poor harvests also played havoc with prices. Smaller supplies or larger demand raised grain prices. Even small increases in the cost of food could exert heavy pressure on peasant or artisan families. If prices increased sharply, many of those families fell back on poor relief from their local municipality or county or the church. What made the situation of food supply and prices so difficult was the peasants' sense of helplessness before the whims of nature and the marketplace.

Over the course of the century, historians now believe, there occurred a slow but steady inflation of bread prices, spurred largely by population growth. This inflation put pressure on all of the poor. The prices rose faster than urban wages and brought no appreciable advantage to the very small peasant producer. On the other hand, the rise in grain prices benefited landowners and those wealthier peasants who had surplus grain to sell.

The increasing price of grain presented landlords with an opportunity to improve their incomes and lifestyle. To those ends they began a series of innovations in farm production that are known as the *agricultural revolution*. This movement commenced during the sixteenth and seventeenth centuries in the Low Countries, where the pressures of the growing population and the shortage of land required changes in cultivation. Dutch landlords and farmers devised better ways to build dykes and to drain land so that they could farm more extensive areas. They also experimented with new crops, such as clover and turnips, that would increase the supply of animal fodder and restore the soil. These improvements became so famous that early in the seventeenth century Cornelius Vermuyden, a Dutch drainage engineer, was hired in England to drain thousands of acres of land around Cambridge.

The methods that the Dutch farmers had pioneered were extensively adopted in England during the early eighteenth century. The major agricultural innovations undertaken by the English included new methods of farming, new crops, and new modes of land holding, all of which eventually led to greater productivity. This advance in food production was necessary for the development of an industrial society. It assured food to people living in cities and freed agricultural labor for industrial production. The changing modes of agriculture sponsored by the landlords undermined the assumptions of traditional peasant production. Farming now took place not only for the local food supply but also to assure the landlord a handsome profit. The latter goal meant that the landlords began to exert new pressures on their tenants and serfs.

Landlords in Great Britain during the eighteenth century provided the most striking examples of the agricultural improvement. They originated almost no genuinely new methods of farming, but they provided leadership in popularizing ideas developed in the previous century either in the Low Countries or in England. Some of these landlords and agricultural innovators became very famous. For example, Jethro Tull (1674–1741) contributed a willingness to experiment and to finance the experiments of others. Many of his ideas, such as the refusal to use manure as fertilizer, were wrong. Others, however, such as using iron plows to overturn earth more deeply and planting wheat by a drill rather than by casting, were excellent. His methods permitted land to be cultivated for longer periods without having to be left fallow.

Charles "Turnip" Townsend (1674–1738) encouraged even more important innovations. He learned from the Dutch how to cultivate sandy soil with fertilizers. He also instituted crop rotation, using wheat, turnips, barley, and clover. This new system of rotation abolished the fallow field and replaced it with a field sown in a crop that both replaced soil nutrients and supplied animal fodder. The additional fodder meant that more livestock could be raised. The larger number of animals increased the quantity of manure available as fertilizer for the grain crops. Consequently, in the long run there was more food for both animals and human beings.

A third British agricultural improver was Robert Bakewell (1725–1795), who pioneered new methods of animal breeding that produced more and better animals and more milk and meat.

These and other innovations received widespread discussion in the works of Arthur Young (1741–1820), who edited the *Annals of Agriculture* and who in 1793 became secretary of the British

Board of Agriculture. Young traveled widely across Europe, and his books are among the most important documents of life during the second half of the eighteenth century.

Many of the agricultural innovations, which were adopted only very slowly, were incompatible with the existing organization of land in Britain. Small cultivators who lived in village communities still farmed most of the soil. Each farmer tilled an assortment of unconnected strips. The two- or three-field systems of rotation left large portions of land annually fallow and unproductive. Animals grazed on the common land in the summer and on the stubble of the harvest in the winter. Until at least the middle of the eighteenth century the decisions about what crops would be planted were made communally. The entire system discouraged improvement and favored the poorer farmers, who needed the common land and stubble fields for their animals. The village method provided little possibility of expanding the pasture land to raise more animals, that would in turn produce more manure, which could be used for fertilizer. Thus, the methods of traditional production aimed at a steady but not a growing supply of food.

In 1700 approximately half the arable land in Britain was farmed by this open-field method. By the second half of the century the rising price of wheat encouraged landlords to consolidate or enclose their lands to increase production. The enclosures were intended to use land more rationally and to achieve greater commercial profits. The process involved the fencing of common lands, the reclamation of previously untilled waste, and the transformation of strips into block fields. These procedures brought turmoil to the economic and social life of the countryside. Riots often ensued. Because many British farmers either owned their strips or rented them in a manner that amounted to ownership, the larger landlords had usually to resort to parliamentary acts to legalize the enclosure of the land, which they owned but rented to the farmers. Because the large landowners controlled Parliament, there was little difficulty in passing such measures. Between 1761 and 1792 almost 500,000 acres were enclosed through parliamentary act, as compared with 75,000 acres between 1727 and 1760. In 1801 a general enclosure act streamlined the process.

The enclosures were at the time and have remained among historians a very controversial topic. They permitted the extension of both farming and innovation. In that regard they increased food production on larger agricultural units. At the same time they disrupted the small traditional communities. They forced off the land some independent farmers, who had needed the common pasturage, and very poor cottagers, who had lived on the reclaimed waste land. However, the enclosures did not depopulate the countryside. In some counties where the enclosures took place, the population increased. New soil had come into production, and services subsidiary to farming also expanded.

The enclosures did not create the labor force for the British Industrial Revolution. What the enclosures most conspicuously displayed was the introduction of the entrepreneurial or capitalistic attitude of the urban merchant into the countryside. This commercialization of agriculture, which spread from Britain very slowly across the Continent during the next century, strained the paternal relationship between the governing and governed classes. Previously the landlords had somewhat looked after the welfare of the lower orders through price controls or alleviation of rents during depressed periods. However, as the landlords became increasingly concerned about profits, they began to leave the peasants to the mercy of the marketplace.

Improving agriculture tended to characterize farm production west of the Elbe. Dutch farming was quite efficient. In France, despite the efforts of the government to improve agriculture, enclosures were restricted. Yet there was much discussion in France about improving agricultural methods. These new procedures benefited the ruling classes because better agriculture increased their incomes and assured a larger food supply, which tended to discourage social unrest.

In Prussia, Austria, Poland, and Russia only very limited agricultural improvement took place. Nothing in the relationship of the serfs to their lords encouraged innovation. In eastern Europe the chief method of increasing production was to extend farming to previously untilled lands. The management of farms was usually under the direction of the landlords or their agents rather than of the villages. By extending tillage, the great landlords sought to squeeze more labor from their serfs rather than greater productivity from the soil. As in the West, the goal was increased profits for the landlords. But on the whole east European landlords were much less ambitious and successful. The only significant nutritional gain achieved through their efforts was the introduction of maize and the potato. Livestock production did not increase significantly.

Population Expansion

The assault on human dependence on nature through improved farming was both a cause and a result of an immense expansion in the population of Europe. The population explosion with which the entire world must today contend seems to have had its origins in the eighteenth century. Before this time Europe's population had experienced dramatic increases, but plagues, wars, or harvest failures had in time decimated the increase. Beginning in the second quarter of the eighteenth century, the population began to grow without decimation.

Exact figures are lacking, but the best estimates suggest that in 1700 Europe's population, excluding the European provinces of the Ottoman Empire, stood between 100 million and 120 million people. By 1800 the figures had risen to almost 190 million, and by 1850 to 260 million. The population of England and Wales rose from 6 million in 1750 to over 10 million in 1800. France grew from 18 million in 1715 to approximately 26 million in 1789. Russia's population increased from 19 million in 1722 to 29 million in 1766. Such extraordi-

---

❧ Parliament Legislates Against the Consumption of Gin (1751)

The excessive drinking of gin in the middle of the eighteenth century raised much concern in England. Physicians believed that it led to the premature death of the poor. Magistrates believed that such drinking contributed to rioting and other public disorders. Under much public pressure the English Parliament passed an act in 1751 designed to limit the consumption of gin. The law placed a tax on the beverage and also regulated the licensing of establishments that sold gin.

Whereas the immoderate drinking of distilled spirituous liquors by persons of the meanest and lowest sort, hath of late years increased, to the great detriment of the health and morals of the common people; and the same hath in great measure been owing to the number of persons who have obtained licences to retail the same, under pretence of being distillers, and of those who have presumed to retail the same without licence . . . ; and whereas we your Majesty's dutiful and loyal subjects the commons of Great Britain in parliament assembled, ever attentive to the preservation and health of your Majesty's subjects, have taken this great evil into our serious consideration, and proposed such laws and provisions as appear to us to be most likely to put a stop to the same. . . . we do most humbly beseech your Majesty that it may be enacted . . . that from and after the first day of July, one thousand seven hundred and fifty one, there shall be raised, levied, collected and paid unto his Majesty, his heirs and successors, for the several kinds of spirituous liquors herein after mentioned, specified and enumerated (. . .) the several rates and duties

herein after-mentioned and expressed. . . .

[XIII] And be it further enacted by the authority aforesaid, That no license shall be granted for the retailing of spirituous liquors within any gaol, prison, house of correction, workhouse, or house of entertainment for any parish poor, and that all licenses granted or to be granted, contrary to this provision shall be void and of no effect from and after the said first day of July one thousand seven hundred and fifty one. . . .

[XXVIII] And it is further enacted by the authority aforesaid, That if any persons, to the number of five or more, shall . . . , in a tumultuous and riotous manner assemble themselves to rescue any offenders against this or any other act, relating to spirituous liquors or strong waters . . . or to assault, beat or wound any person or persons who shall have given or be about to give any information against . . . any person or persons offending against this or any of the said former acts . . . [they] shall be, and be adjudged to be guilty of felony. . . .

The Gin Act, 1751, Statutes at Large, XX, pp. 234–250. 24 Geo. II, c. 40, in D. B. Horn and Mary Ransome, *English Historical Documents, 1714–1783* (London: Eyre and Spottiswoode, 1957), pp. 552–555.

nary, sustained growth put new demands on all resources and considerable pressure on existing social organization.

The population expansion occurred across the Continent in both the country and the cities. Only a limited consensus exists about the causes of this growth. There was a clear decline in the death rate. There were fewer wars and somewhat fewer epidemics in the eighteenth century. Hygiene and sanitation also improved. Better medical knowledge and techniques were once thought to have contributed to the decline in deaths. This factor is now discounted because the more important medical advances came after the initial population explosion or would not have contributed directly to it. Rather, changes in the food supply itself may have provided the chief factor that allowed the population growth to be sustained. The improved and expanding grain production made one contribution. Another and even more important modification was the cultivation of the potato. This tuber was a product of the New World and came into widespread European production during the eighteenth century. On a single acre a peasant could raise enough potatoes to feed his family for an entire year. With this more certain food supply, more children could be reared, and more could survive.

The impact of the population explosion can hardly be overestimated. It created new demands for food, goods, jobs, and services. It provided a new pool of labor. Traditional modes of production and living had to be revised. More people came to live in the countryside than could find employment there. Migration increased. There were also more people who might become socially and politically discontent. And because the population growth fed on itself, all of these pressures and demands continued to increase. The society and the social practices of the old regime literally outgrew their traditional bounds.

The Industrial Revolution of the Eighteenth Century

The second half of the eighteenth century witnessed the beginning of the industrialization of the European economy. The Industrial Revolution constituted the achievement of sustained economic growth. Previously production had been limited.

The economy of a province or a country might grow, but it soon reached a plateau. However, since the late eighteenth century the economy of Europe has managed to expand relatively uninterrupted. Depressions and recessions have been of a temporary nature, and even during such economic downturns the Western economy has continued to grow.

Industrialism at considerable social cost made possible more goods and more services than ever before in human history. Industrialism in Europe eventually overcame the economy of scarcity. The new means of production demanded new kinds of skills, new discipline in work, and a large labor force. The goods produced both met immediate consumer demand and created new demands. In the long run, industrialism clearly raised the standard of living and overcame the poverty that had been experienced by the overwhelming majority of Europeans who lived during the eighteenth century and earlier. Industrialization provided human beings greater control over the forces of nature than they had ever known before. The wealth produced by industrialism upset the political structures of the old regime and led to reforms. The economic elite of the emerging industrial society would eventually challenge the political dominance of the aristocracy.

Industrial Leadership of Great Britain

Great Britain was the home of the Industrial Revolution and, until the middle of the nineteenth century, maintained the industrial leadership of Europe. Several factors contributed to the early start in Britain. The nation constituted the single largest free-trade area in Europe. The British possessed good roads and waterways without internal tolls or other internal trade barriers. The country was endowed with rich deposits of coal and iron ore. The political structure was stable, and property was absolutely secure. Taxation was not especially heavy. In addition to the existing domestic consumer demand, the British economy also benefited from demand from the colonies in North America.

Finally, British society was relatively mobile by the standards of the time. Persons who had money or could earn money could rise socially. The British aristocracy would receive into its midst people who had amassed very large fortunes. No one of these factors preordained the British advance toward industrialism. However, the combination of them plus the progressive state of British agriculture provided the nation with the marginal advantage in the creation of a new mode of economic production.

While this economic development was occurring, people did not call it a *revolution*. That term came to be applied to the British economic phenomena only after the French Revolution. Then continental writers observed that what had taken place in Britain was the economic equivalent of the political events in France; hence the concept of an *industrial* revolution. It was revolutionary less in its speed, which was on the whole rather slow, than in its implications for the future of European society.

NEW METHODS OF TEXTILE PRODUCTION. Although eighteenth-century society was primarily devoted to agriculture, manufacturing permeated the countryside. The same peasants who tilled the land in spring and summer often spun thread or wove textiles in the winter. Under what is termed the *domestic* or *putting-out system,* agents of urban textile merchants took wool or other unfinished fibers to the homes of peasants, who spun it into thread. The agent then transported the thread to other peasants, who wove it into the finished product. The merchant sold the wares. In literally thousands of peasant cottages from Ireland to Austria, there stood either a spinning wheel or a handloom. Sometimes the spinners or weavers owned their own equipment, but more often than not by the middle of the century the merchant capitalist owned the machinery as well as the raw material.

What must be kept constantly in mind is the rather surprising fact that eighteenth-century industrial development took place within a rural setting. The peasant family living in a one- or two-room cottage was the basic unit of production rather than the factory. The family economy, rather than the industrial factory economy, characterized the century.

The married small farmer or peasant, burdened by taxes and feudal dues, could not support himself and his family by his own labor alone. It was necessary not merely for comfort but for economic survival that his wife spin or weave or knit and that his children be set to work as soon as they were physically able. The subsistence of these families depended on their capacity to find makeshift ways of earning income beyond what they received from farming. Certain members of the family, including the women, might migrate with the harvest. The

children might ultimately go to the city to seek employment. If any of these sources of income failed, the entire family might fall into dependence on some form of charity or crime. As Olwen Hufton has written, it was a life in which "one lived daily from hand to mouth without provision for old age, sickness, incapacity to work, or disasters such as harvest failure or even the arrival of a baby."[1]

The domestic system of textile production was a basic feature of this family economy. However, by mid-century a series of production bottlenecks had developed within the domestic system. The demand for cotton textiles was growing more rapidly than production. This demand arose particularly in Great Britain, where there existed a large domestic demand for cotton textiles from the growing population. There was a similar foreign demand on British production from its colonies in North America. It was in response to this consumer demand for cotton textiles that the most famous inventions of the Industrial Revolution were devised.

Cotton textile weavers had the technical capacity to produce the quantity of fabric that was in demand. However, the spinners did not possess the equipment to produce as much thread as the weavers needed and could use. This imbalance had been created during the 1730s by James Kay's invention of the flying shuttle, which increased the productivity of the weavers. Thereafter various groups of manufacturers and merchants offered prizes for the invention of a machine to eliminate this bottleneck. About 1765 James Hargreaves (d. 1778) invented the spinning jenny. Initially this machine allowed 16 spindles of thread to be spun, but by the close of the century its capacity had been increased to as many as 120 spindles.

The spinning jenny broke the bottleneck between the productive capacity of the spinners and the weavers, but it was still a piece of machinery that was used in the cottage. The invention that took cotton textile manufacture out of the home and put it into the factory was Richard Arkwright's (1732–1792) water frame, patented in 1769. It was a water-powered device designed to permit the production of a purely cotton fabric rather than a cotton fabric containing linen fiber for durability.

[1] Alan Mitchell and Istvan Deak (Eds.), *Everyman in Europe: Essays in Social History* Vol. 2 (Englewood Cliffs, N.J.: Prentice-Hall, 1974), p. 82.

❧ Josiah Tucker Praises the New Use of Machinery in England

The extensive use of recently invented machines made the Industrial Revolution possible in England. This passage from a 1757 travel guide illustrates how contemporaries regarded the application of machines to various manufacturing processes as new and exciting.

Few countries are equal, perhaps none excel, the English in the number of contrivances of their Machines to abridge labour. Indeed the Dutch are superior to them in the use and application of Wind Mills for sawing Timber, expressing Oil, making Paper and the like. But in regard to Mines and Metals of all sorts, the English are uncommonly dexterous in their contrivance of the mechanic Powers; some being calculated for landing the Ores out of the Pits, such as Cranes and Horse Engines; others for draining off superfluous Water, such as Water Wheels and Steam Engines; others again for easing the Expense of Carriage such as Machines to run on inclined Planes or Roads downhill with wooden frames, in order to carry many Tons of Material at a Time. And

to these must be added the various sorts of Levers used in different processes; also the Brass Battery works, the Slitting Mills, Plate and Flatting Mills, and those for making Wire of different Fineness. Yet all these, curious as they may seem, are little more than Preparations or Introductions for further Operations. Therefore, when we still consider that at Birmingham, Wolverhampton, Sheffield and other manufacturing Places, almost every Master Manufacturer hath a new Invention of his own, and is daily improving on those of others; we may aver with some confidence that those parts of England in which these things are seen exhibit a specimen of practical mechanics scarce to be paralleled in any part of the world.

Josiah Tucker, *Instructions to Travellers* (London: Privately Printed, 1757), p. 20.

Eventually Arkwright lost his patent rights, and other manufacturers were able to use his invention freely. As a result, numerous factories sprang up in the countryside near streams that provided the necessary waterpower. From the 1780s onward the cotton industry could meet an ever-expanding demand. In the last two decades of the century cotton output increased by 800 per cent over the production of 1780. By 1815 cotton composed 40 per cent of the value of British domestic exports, and by 1830 just over 50 per cent.

The Industrial Revolution had commenced in earnest by the 1780s, but the full economic and social ramifications of this unleashing of human productive capacity were not really felt until the early nineteenth century. The expansion of industry and the incorporation of new inventions often occurred rather slowly. For example, Edmund Cartwright (1743–1822) invented the power loom for machine weaving in the late 1780s. Yet not until the 1830s were there more power-loom weavers than hand-loom weavers in Britain. Nor did all of the social ramifications of industrialism appear

immediately. The first cotton mills used waterpower, were located in the country, and rarely employed more than two dozen workers. Not until the late-century application of the steam engine, perfected by James Watt (1736–1819) in 1769, to the running of textile machinery could factories easily be located in or near existing urban centers. The steam engine not only vastly increased and regularized the available energy but also made possible the combination of urbanization and industrialization.

MAJOR INVENTIONS IN THE TEXTILE-MANUFACTURING REVOLUTION

1733	James Kay's flying shuttle
1765	James Hargreaves's spinning jenny (patent 1770)
1769	James Watt's steam engine patent
	Richard Arkwright's water-frame patent
1787	Edmund Cartwright's power loom

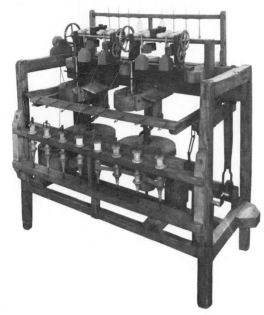

Richard Arkwright's water-frame spinning machine, so named because it ran by water power. Cotton spinning and weaving were major classic industries of the early industrial era. [Science Museum, London. Copyright Crown.]

THE STEAM ENGINE. The new technology in textile manufacture vastly increased cotton production and revolutionized a major consumer industry. But the invention that more than any other permitted industrialization to grow on itself and to expand into one area of production after another was the steam engine. This machine provided for the first time in human history a steady and essentially unlimited source of inanimate power. Unlike engines powered by water or the wind, the steam engine, driven by the burning of coal, was a portable source of industrial power that did not fail or falter as the seasons of the year changed. Unlike human power or animal power the steam engine depended on mineral energy that did not tire over the course of a day. Finally, the steam engine could be applied to a very large number of industrial and, eventually, transportation uses.

The first practical engine using steam power had been the invention of Thomas Newcomen in the early eighteenth century. The piston of this device was moved when the steam that had been induced into the cylinder condensed, causing the piston to fall. The Newcomen machine was very large. It was inefficient in its use of energy because both the condenser and the cylinder were heated, and it was practically untransportable. Despite these problems English mine operators employed the Newcomen machines to pump water out of coal and tin mines. By the third quarter of the eighteenth century almost a hundred Newcomen machines were operating in the mining districts of England.

During the 1760s James Watt, a Scottish engineer and machine maker, began to experiment with a model of a Newcomen machine at the University of Glasgow. He gradually understood that if the condenser were separated from the piston and the cylinder, much greater energy efficiency would result. In 1769 he patented his new invention, but transforming his idea into application presented difficulties. His design required exceedingly precise metalwork. Watt soon found a partner in Matthew Boulton, a toy manufacturer in Birmingham, the city with the most skilled metalworkers in Britain. Watt and Boulton, in turn, consulted with John Wilkinson, a cannon manufacturer, to find ways to drill the precise metal cylinders required by Watt's design. In 1776 the Watt steam engine found its first commercial application pumping water from mines in Cornwall.

An eighteenth-century Newcomen engine used for pumping water from coal and tin mines. Thomas Newcomen's invention was the first engine to make practical use of steam power. [Science Museum, London. Copyright Crown.]

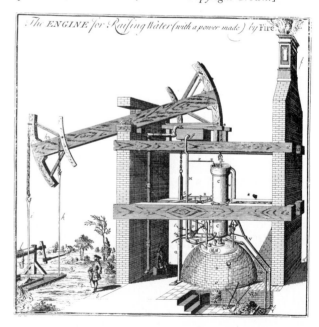

This landscape painting by an unknown contemporary British artist portrays the pithead of an eighteenth-century coal mine in England. The machinery on the left included a steam engine that powered equipment either to bring the mined coal to the surface or to pump water from the mine. [*Walker Art Gallery, Liverpool.*]

The use of the steam engine spread slowly because until 1800 Watt retained the exclusive patent rights. He was also reluctant to make further changes in his invention that would permit the engine to operate more rapidly. Boulton eventually persuaded him to make modifications and improvements. These allowed the engines to be used not only for pumping but also for running cotton mills. By the early nineteenth century the steam engine had become the prime mover for all industry. With its application to ships and then to wagons on iron rails, the steam engine also revolutionized transportation.

IRON PRODUCTION. The manufacture of high-quality iron has been basic to modern industrial development. It constitutes the chief element of all heavy industry and land or sea transport. Iron has also been the material out of which most productive machinery itself has been manufactured. During the early eighteenth century British ironmak-

ers produced somewhat less than twenty-five thousand tons annually. Three factors held back the production of the metal. Charcoal rather than coke was used to smelt the ore. Charcoal, which is derived from wood, was becoming a scarce commodity, and it did not burn at as high a temperature as coke, which is derived from coal. Until the perfection of the steam engine, insufficient blasts could be achieved in the furnaces. Finally, the demand for iron was limited. The elimination of the first two problems eliminated the third.

In the course of the century British ironmakers began to use coke, and the steam engine provided new power for the blast furnaces. Coke was an abundant fuel because of Britain's large coal deposits. The existence of the steam engine both improved iron production and increased the demand for iron.

In 1784 Henry Cort (1740–1800) introduced a new puddling process, that is, a new method for

Throughout most of the eighteenth century nearly all industrial manufacture took place in relatively small workshops such as the lead-casting shop illustrated in this print from the French Encyclopedia. Very large factories became established only quite late in the eighteenth century and early in the nineteenth.

melting and stirring the molten ore. Cort's process allowed more slag (the impurities that bubbled to the top of the molten metal) to be removed and a purer iron to be produced. Cort also developed a rolling mill that continuously shaped the still-molten metal into bars, rails, or other forms. Previously the metal had been pounded into these forms.

All of these innovations achieved a better, more versatile product at a lower cost. The demand for iron grew as its price became lower. By the early years of the nineteenth century British iron production amounted to over a million tons annually. The lower cost of iron, in turn, lowered the cost of steam engines and allowed them to be used more widely.

The Aristocracy

Despite the emerging Industrial Revolution, the eighteenth century remained the age of the aristocracy. The nobility of every country was the single wealthiest sector of the population; possessed the widest degree of social, political, and economic power; and set the tone of polite society. Land continued to provide the aristocracy with its largest source of income, but the role of the aristocrat was not limited to the estate. The influence of aristocrats was felt in every area of life. To be an aristocrat was a matter of birth and legal privilege. This much they had in common across the Continent. In almost every other respect they differed markedly from country to country.

The smallest, wealthiest, best-defined, and most socially responsible aristocracy resided in Great Britain. It consisted of about four hundred families, whose eldest male member sat in the House of Lords. Through the corruptions of the electoral system these families also controlled a large number of seats in the House of Commons. The estates of the British nobility ranged from a few thousand to fifty thousand acres, from which they received rents. The nobles owned approximately one fourth of all the arable land in the country. Increasingly the money of the aristocracy was being invested in commerce, canals, urban real estate, mines, and sometimes industrial ventures. Because only the eldest son inherited the title and the land, younger sons moved into commerce, the army, the professions, and the church. The British landowners in the House of Commons levied taxes in Parliament and also paid taxes. They had almost no significant legal privileges, but their direct or indirect control of local government gave them immense political power and social influence. The aristocracy quite simply dominated the society and the politics of the English counties.

The openness of the English aristocracy and its acceptance of social and political responsibility as well as of power brought a degree of social mobility to English social life that was generally absent from other countries during the old regime. This factor may in large measure account for both the eco-

nomic and the political advancement of Britain during the period.

The situation of the continental nobilities was less clear-cut. In France the nobility was divided between nobles of the sword and those of the robe. The former families enjoyed privileges deriving from military service; the latter had either gained their titles by serving in the bureaucracy or had purchased them. The two groups had frequently quarreled in the past but tended to cooperate during the eighteenth century to defend their common privileges.

The French nobility were also divided between those who held office or favor with the royal court

This famous portrait painting, Robert Andrews and His Wife, by the British artist Thomas Gainsborough (1728–1788) illustrates the peaceful and prosperous life of an English landowner. As the gun and dog indicate, he enjoyed considerable leisure time for sports such as hunting. [Reproduced by courtesy of the Trustees, The National Gallery, London.]

The Scots brothers Adam dominated British decorative taste in the late eighteenth century. About 1770, Robert, the more important, planned this elegant drawing room for Home House in London. [The Courtauld Institute of Art and Country Life, London.]

at Versailles and those who did not. The court nobility reaped the immense wealth that could be gained from holding high offices. The noble hold on such offices intensified over the course of the century. By the late 1780s appointments to the church, the army, and the bureaucracy, as well as other profitable positions tended to go to the nobles already established in court circles. Whereas these well-connected aristocrats were quite rich, other nobles who lived in the provinces were often rather poor. These *hobereaux*, as the poverty-stricken nobles were called, were sometimes little or no better off than wealthy peasants.

Despite differences in rank, origin, and wealth, all French aristocrats enjoyed certain hereditary privileges that set them apart from the rest of society. They were exempt from many taxes. For example, most French nobles did not pay the *taille*, which was the basic tax of the old regime. The nobles were technically liable for payment of the *vingtième*, or the "twentieth," which resembled an income tax. However, by virtue of protests and legal procedures, the nobility rarely felt the entire weight of this tax. The nobles were not liable for the royal *corvées*, or labor donations, which fell on the peasants. In addition to these exemptions, the approximately 400,000 French nobles could collect feudal dues from their tenants and enjoyed hunting and fishing privileges denied their tenants.

East of the Elbe River the character of the nobility became even more complicated and repressive. In Poland there were thousands of nobles, or *szlachta,* who after 1741 were entirely exempt from taxes. Until 1768 these Polish aristocrats possessed the right of life and death over their serfs. Most of the Polish nobility were relatively poor. The political power of the fragile Polish state resided in the few very rich nobles.

In Austria and Hungary the nobility continued to possess broad judicial powers over the peasantry through manorial courts.

In Prussia, after the accession of Frederick the Great in 1740, the position of the *Junker* nobles became much stronger. Frederick's various wars required the support of his nobles. He drew his officers almost wholly from the *Junker* class. The bureaucracy was also increasingly composed of nobles. As in other parts of eastern Europe, the Prussian nobles enjoyed extensive judicial authority over the serfs.

In Russia the eighteenth century saw what amounted to the creation of the nobility. Peter the Great's linking of state service and noble social status through the Table of Ranks (1722) established among Russian nobles a self-conscious class identity that had not previously existed. Thereafter they stood united in their determination to resist compulsory state service. In 1736 Empress Ann reduced such service to a period of twenty-five years. In 1762 Peter III removed the liability for compulsory service entirely from the greatest nobles. In 1785, in the Charter of the Nobility, Catherine the Great granted an explicit legal definition of noble rights and privileges in exchange for assurances of voluntary state service from the nobility. The noble privileges included the right of transmitting noble status to one's wife and children, the judicial protection of noble rights and property, considerable power over the serfs, and exemption from personal taxes.

The Russian Charter of the Nobility constituted one aspect of the broader European-wide development termed the *aristocratic resurgence.* Throughout the century the various nobilities felt their social position and privileges threatened by the expanding power of the monarchies and the growing wealth of merchants, bankers, and other commercial groups. All nobilities attempted to preserve their exclusiveness by making entry into their

ranks and institutions more difficult. They also pushed for exclusively noble appointments to the officer corps of the armies, the bureaucracies, the government ministries, and the church. In that manner the nobles hoped to control the power of the monarchies.

On a third level the nobles attempted to use the authority of existing aristocratically controlled institutions against the power of the monarchies. These institutions included the British Parliament and on the Continent the French courts or *parlements,* the local aristocratic estates, and the provincial diets. Economically the aristocratic resurgence took the form of pressing the peasantry for higher rents or collecting long-forgotten feudal dues. There was a general tendency for the nobility to shore up its position by various appeals to traditional and often ancient privileges that had lapsed over the course of time. To contemporaries this aristocratic challenge to the monarchies and to the rising commercial classes constituted one of the most fundamental political facts of the day.

Cities

The Urban Setting

The influence of land and the landed society extended to the cities of the old regime. The cities of the eighteenth century, like those of today, depended on the countryside for their food supply. The specter of famine or food shortages haunted the cities. The governments took great care to ensure adequate supplies of grain by building granaries and by paying careful attention to the fluctuation of bread prices. The nobility were not absent from the cities. They owned homes in the urban centers and often possessed large blocks of city real estate, which they developed as sources of new rents. Frequently nobles controlled the municipal government and sat as judges in the municipal courts.

A two-way migration of people took place between the country and the city. In many cities, especially of central and eastern Europe, rural day laborers lived in the towns and traveled outward to find their work. Other cities witnessed what has become a common modern phenomenon: the migration of people from the countryside into the town to find work, better wages, and possibly a more exciting life. Thousands of men and women

London in 1711. St. James Place is in the right foreground, and the church of St. James in Picadilly is at the center left. This engraving by Johannes Kip is in the British Museum. [The Fotomas Index, London.]

born in the country moved to the city to become domestic servants or artisans.

Fernand Braudel has rightly described cities as "so many electric transformers," which "increase tension, accelerate the rhythm of exchange and ceaselessly stir up men's lives."[2] The eighteenth century witnessed a considerable growth of towns. The tumult of the day and the revolutions with which the century closed had a strong relationship to that urban expansion. London grew from about 700,000 inhabitants in 1700 to almost 1 million in 1800. By the time of the French Revolution the population of Paris stood over 500,000. Berlin's population tripled over the course of the century, reaching 170,000 in 1800. Saint Petersburg, founded in 1703, numbered over 250,000 inhabitants a century later. In addition to the growth of these capitals, the number of smaller urban units of 20,000–50,000 people increased considerably. However, this urban growth must be kept in per-

spective. Even in France and Great Britain probably somewhat less than 20 percent of the population lived in cities. And the town of 10,000 inhabitants was much more common than the giant urban center.

Practically all of these urban conglomerates were nonindustrial cities. They grew and expanded for reasons other than being the location of factories or other large manufacturing establishments. Only Manchester in England had experienced such industrial growth, and even its most spectacular expansion occurred after 1800.

Eighteenth-century cities fall into three broad and rather imperfect categories. The first and most common were market centers for the exchange of goods, most of which were produced locally. These relatively small provincial centers might also be the sites of local courts and state administration. The second category consisted of commercial, trading, shipping, and financial centers. These included the major sea and river ports. Finally, there were the great capital cities, which were also frequently commercial centers. In a sense both of the latter kinds of cities were the creation of the expanding bureaucratic states, whose rulers wished to see trade and commerce prosper. The great taxing power of those monarchies meant that vast wealth flowed into the capitals.

With the exception of Saint Petersburg, the cities of the eighteenth century were largely unplanned. A few urban developers might create elegant squares for the wealthy merchants or urban-dwelling aristocrats, but most cities simply expanded on the base of their medieval precursors. London had burned in 1666. Its reconstruction benefited from the planning and architecture of Sir Christopher Wren (1632–1723), but expansion was still quite haphazard. On the Continent many cities retained their medieval walls, within which and beyond which growth occurred. There was usually a central square with civic buildings or a cathedral or a fortress nearby. Quite often urban expansion pressed beyond the original city border and onto the territory of nonurban landlords. The authority of the latter would then extend over that part of the city. Consequently some urban areas found themselves governed by manorial courts and other institutions of the countryside.

Visible segregation often existed between the urban rich and the urban poor. The former, including the nobles and the upper middle class, lived in fashionable town-houses, often con-

---

[2] Fernand Braudel, *Capitalism and Material Life, 1400–1800* (New York: Harper Torchbooks, 1973), p. 373.

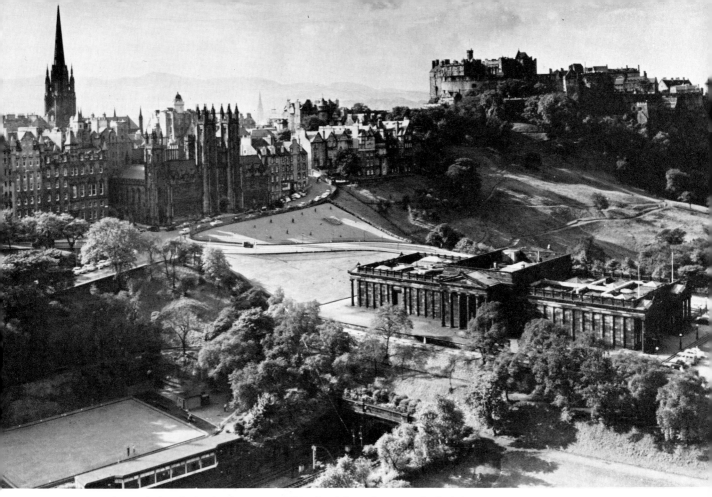

The great park in Edinburgh, Scotland, was created in the eighteenth century by draining a lake that had previously existed in its place. The mid-nineteenth-century building in the center of the picture is the National Gallery of Scotland. [British Tourist Authority, New York.]

structed around newly laid-out green squares. The poorest town dwellers usually congregated along the rivers. Small merchants and craftsmen lived above their shops. Whole families might live in a single room. Sanitary facilities such as now exist were still unknown. There was little pure water. Cattle, pigs, goats, and other animals walked the streets with the people. All reports on the cities of Europe during this period emphasize both the striking grace and beauty of the dwellings of the wealthy and the dirt, filth, and stench that filled the streets.

Despite the more obvious drawbacks, it was still in the cities that men and women from all walks and stations of life found entertainment and excitement. More modes of recreation were available in cities than in the countryside. The cities provided more opportunities for theater, gambling,

The Royal Crescent in Bath, England, is an example of fashionable eighteenth-century town planning. The elliptical crescent contained luxury housing for wealthy families who vacationed in Bath, which is on the site of a Roman town of the first century B.C. [British Tourist Authority, New York.]

A hospital in Hamburg, 1746. The patients are crowded together in one large room, regardless of the type of their illness or state of health. Note the wigged doctor performing an amputation in the foreground. [Germanisches National-museum, Nuremberg.]

In late eighteenth-century Vienna, apprehended prostitutes had to appear before courts, as in this print, where they were ordered to have their hair shorn and then sent out to sweep the streets. [Österreichische Nationalbibliothek, Vienna]

GIN LANE.

S.GRIPE PAWN BROKER

GIN ROYAL

Designd by W.Hogarth

Gin cursed Fiend, with Fury fraught,
    Makes human Race a Prey;
It enters by a deadly Draught,
    And steals our Life away.

Virtue and Truth driv'n to Despair,
    It's Rage compells to fly,
But cherishes with hellish Care,
    Theft, Murder, Perjury.

Publish'd according to Act of Parliam! Feb.1751.

Damn'd Cup! that on the Vitals preys,
    That liquid Fire contains,
Which Madness to the Heart conveys,
    And rolls it thro' the Veins.

Price 1.s

womanizing, and husband hunting. The season of parties in London drew noble and upper-gentry families from all over England. Here marriages were sought, and friendships were renewed. The French nobility had learned to enjoy Paris after Louis XIV had initially forced them to come to his court at nearby Versailles. And many Russian nobles came to crave life in Saint Petersburg after having first arrived under the compulsion of Peter the Great. The eighteenth-century town-house as much as the country house provided the aristocracy with its public stage.

There was, however, another side to urban life. This was the lot of the poor, who often depended on charity in the city. Poverty was not a city problem; it was usually worse in the countryside. But in the city poverty more visibly manifested itself in terms of crime, prostitution, vagrancy, begging, and alcoholism. Many a young man or woman from the countryside migrated to the nearest city to seek a better life, only to discover poor housing, little food, disease, degradation, and finally death. It did not require the Industrial Revolution and the urban factory to make the cities into hellholes for the poor and the dispossessed. The full darkness of London life during the mid-century "gin age," when consumption of that liquor blinded and killed many poor people, is evident in the engravings of William Hogarth (1697–1764). Also contrasting with the serenity of the aristocratic and upper-commercial-class lifestyle were the public executions that took place all over Europe, the breaking of men and women on the wheel in Paris, and the public floggings in Russia. Brutality condoned and carried out by the ruling classes was quite simply a fact of everyday life.

Urban Classes

Social divisions were as marked in the cities of the eighteenth century as they were in the industrial centers of the nineteenth. At the top of the urban social structure stood a generally small group of nobles, large merchants, bankers, financiers, clergy, and government officials. These men (and they were always men) controlled the political and economic affairs of the town. Normally they constituted a self-appointed and self-electing oligarchy who governed the city through its corporation or city council. These rights of self-government had normally been granted by some form of royal charter that gave the city corporation its authority and the power to select its own members. In a few cities on the Continent, artisan guilds controlled the corporations, but more generally the councils were under the influence of the local nobility and the wealthiest commercial people.

THE MIDDLE CLASS. Another group in the city were the prosperous but not immensely wealthy merchants, tradesmen, bankers, and professional people. These were the most dynamic element of the urban population and constituted the persons traditionally regarded as the middle class, or *bourgeoisie.* The concept of the middle class was much less clear-cut than that of the nobility. They had less wealth than most nobles but more than urban artisans. The middle-class people lived in the cities and towns, and their sources of income had little or nothing to do with the land. The middle class normally stood on the side of reform, change, and economic growth. The middle-class commercial figures—traders, bankers, manufacturers, and lawyers—often found their pursuit of both profit and prestige blocked by the privileges of the nobility and its social exclusiveness. The bourgeoisie also wanted more rational regulations for trade and commerce, as did some of the more progressive aristocrats.

During the eighteenth century the middle class and the aristocracy were on a collision course. The former often imitated the lifestyle of the latter, and the nobles were increasingly embracing the commercial spirit of the middle class. The bourgeoisie was not rising to challenge the nobility; both were seeking to add new dimensions to their existing power and prestige. However, tradition and political connection gave the advantage to the nobility. Consequently, as the century passed, members of the middle class felt and voiced increasing resentment of the aristocracy. That resentment became more bitter as the wealth and the numbers of the *bourgeoisie* increased and the aristocratic control of political and ecclesiastical power became tighter. The growing influence of the nobility seemed to mean that the middle class would continue to be excluded from the political decisions of the day.

On the other hand, the middle class in the cities tended to fear the lower urban classes as much as they resented the nobility. The lower orders constituted a potentially violent element in the society, a potential threat to property, and, in their poverty, a drain on national resources. However, the lower orders were much more varied than either the city aristocracy or the middle class cared to admit.

French wines and silks arriving in London in 1757. French luxury goods were prized through-out Europe. The rising prosperity of the middle and upper-middle classes created an increasing market for such goods in Britain. This anti-French cartoon is by L. Boitard. It shows porters staggering under a chest full of imported cloth, emaciated Englishmen gratefully welcoming a French cook, a "lady of quality" offering the tuition of her children to a cringing French abbé as the English chaplain who has been instructing them looks on with sorrow, another "lady of quality" greeting a French dancing girl, a load of French cheese spilling from a cask as a small boy holds his nose against the stench, and dozens of imported luxury goods in chests and casks. [Guildhall Library, London.]

ARTISANS. The segment of the urban population that suffered from both the grasping of the middle class and the local nobility was that made up of the shopkeepers, the artisans, and the wage earners. These people constituted the single largest group in any city. The lives and experience of this class were very diverse. They included grocers, butchers, fishmongers, carpenters, cabinetmakers, smiths, printers, hand-loom weavers, and tailors, to give but a few examples. They had their own culture, values, and institutions. Like the peasants of the countryside they were in many respects very conservative. Their economic position was highly vulnerable. If a poor harvest raised the price of food, their own businesses suffered.

The entire life of these artisans and shopkeepers centered on their work. They usually lived near or at their place of employment. Most of them worked in shops with fewer than a half dozen other craftsmen. Their primary institution had historically been the guild, but by the eighteenth century the guilds rarely possessed the influence of their predecessors in medieval or early modern Europe.

Nevertheless the guilds were not to be ignored. They played a conservative role. They did not seek economic growth or innovation. They attempted to preserve the jobs and the skills of their members. The guilds still were able in many countries to determine who might and might not pursue a particular craft. They attempted to prevent too many people from learning a particular skill. The guilds also provided a framework for social and economic advancement. A boy might at an early age become an apprentice to learn a craft or trade. After several years he would be made a journeyman. Still later, if successful and sufficiently competent, he

Several examples of non-agricultural working-class skills can be shown. Printing shops produced the flood of eighteenth-century publications. Type was set and presses operated by hand, and the workmen were among the most highly skilled urban craftsmen. The picture is from the Encyclopedia. [*Charles Farrell Collection.*]

might become a master. The artisan could also receive certain social benefits from the guilds. These might include aid for his family during sickness or the promise of admission for his son. The guilds constituted the chief protection for artisans against the operation of the commercial market. They were particularly strong in central Europe.

The artisan class, with its generally conservative outlook, maintained a rather fine sense of social and economic justice. These ideals were based largely on traditional practices. If the collective sense of what was economically "just" was offended, artisans frequently manifested their displeasure through the instrument of the riot. The

OPPOSITE: *The skills of the blacksmith were required in both city and countryside. It is noteworthy that when Joseph Moxon, an English publisher and map-maker, wrote a series of* Mechanick Exercises: Or, the Doctrine of Handy-works, *published in parts between* 1677 *and* 1683 *and the first textbooks in any language on several of the major crafts, he began with the smith's trade because, as he said, "without the Invention of* Smithing *primarily, most other Mechanick Inventions would be at a stand: The Instruments or Tools that are used in them being either made of Iron, or of some other matter form'd by the help of Iron. But pray take notice, that by Iron I also mean Steel, it being originally Iron . . . . Some perhaps would have thought it more Policy to have introduced these* Exercises *with a more curious and less Vulgar Art than that of* Smithing; *but I am not of their opinion; for* Smithing *is (in all its parts) as curious a Handy-craft as any is . . ." This striking painting is by Joseph Wright of Derby (*1734–1797*). [*Yale Center for British Art, New Haven.*]

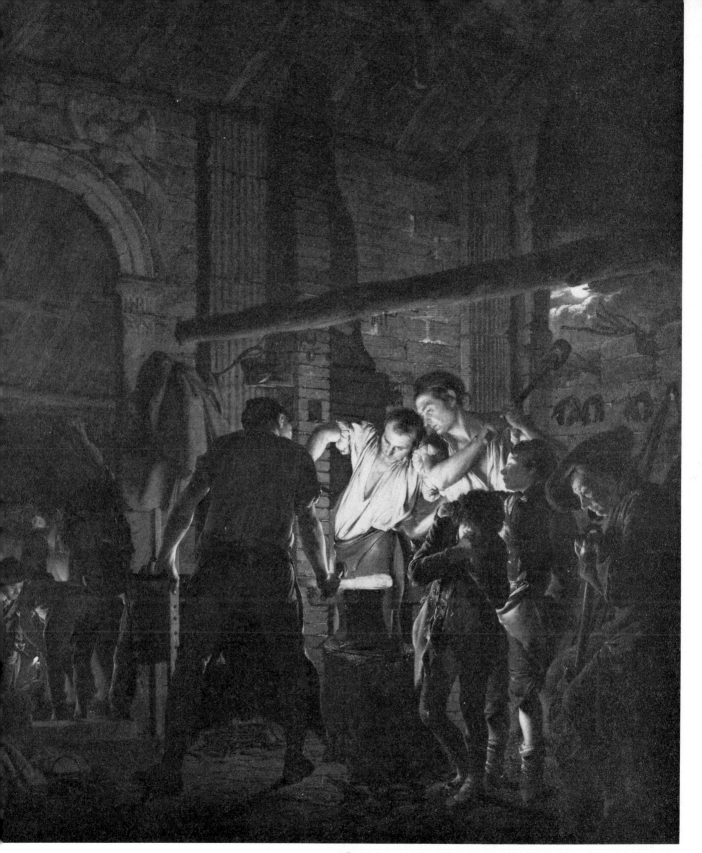

589

Bread was the single most important foodstuff in the eighteenth century, and its relative availability and price were constant social, economic, and political problems. This etching of an urban bakery from the Encyclopedia *illustrates, from right to left, the kneading of the dough, the weighing of the loaves, the shaping of the loaves, and the baking of the bread. [The Granger Collection.]*

most sensitive area was the price of bread. If a baker or a grain merchant announced a price that was considered unjustly high, a bread riot might well ensue. Artisan leaders would confiscate the bread or grain and sell it for what the urban crowd considered a "just price." They would then give the money paid for the bread or grain to the baker or merchant. The possibility of bread riots acted as a restraint on the greed of merchants. Such disturbances represented a collective method of imposing the "just price" in place of the price set by the commercial marketplace. In other words, bread and food riots, which occurred throughout Europe, were not irrational acts of screaming hungry people but highly ritualized social phenomena of the old regime and its economy of scarcity.

Torture and public executions were still quite common during the eighteenth century. In some places, weights, as shown here, were used as a torture to extract information. Pressing was also a mode of execution for prisoners who refused to plead to the charges. [Bettmann Archive.]

The burning of Newgate Prison, London, in June 1780 during the anti-Catholic Gordon riots, which raged for several days. It is said that some three hundred prisoners were released and the unfortunate warden, Mr. Akerman, lost all his furniture in the fire. [The Granger Collection.]

Other kinds of riots were also a basic characteristic of eighteenth-century society and politics. The riot was a way in which people excluded in every other way from the political processes could make their will known. Sometimes urban rioters were incited by religious bigotry. For example, in 1753 London Protestant mobs compelled the government ministry to withdraw an act meant to legalize Jewish naturalization. In 1780 the same rabidly Protestant spirit manifested itself in the Gordon riots, named after Lord George Gordon, who had raised the specter of an imaginary Catholic plot after the government relieved military recruits from having to take specifically anti-Catholic oaths. In these riots and in food riots, violence was normally directed against property rather than against people. The rioters themselves were not "riffraff" but usually small shopkeepers, freeholders, craftsmen, and wage earners. They usually had no other purpose than to restore a traditional right or practice that seemed endangered. Nevertheless considerable turmoil and destruction could result from their actions.

During the last half of the century urban riots increasingly involved political ends. Though often simultaneous with economic disturbances, the political riot always had nonartisan leadership or instigators. In fact, the "crowd" of the eighteenth century was often the tool of the upper classes. In Paris the aristocratic *Parlement* often urged crowd action in their disputes with the monarchy. In Geneva middle-class citizens supported artisan riots against the local urban oligarchy. In Great Britain in 1792 the government turned out mobs to attack English sympathizers of the French Revolution. All of these and other various outbursts of popular unrest suggest that the crowd or mob first entered the European political and social arena well before the Revolution in France.

A Society on the Edge of Modern Times

This chapter opened by describing eighteenth-century society as traditional, hierarchical, corporate, and privileged. These features had characterized Europe for hundreds of years. However, by the close of the eighteenth century each of these facets of European life stood undermined or challenged in a fundamental fashion by developments within the society itself. Europe was on the brink of a new era in which the social, economic, and political relationships of centuries would be destroyed.

Society had remained traditional and corporate largely because of the economy of scarcity. The agricultural and industrial revolutions would eventually overcome most scarcity in Europe and the West generally. The commercial spirit and values of the marketplace clashed with the traditional values and practices of the peasants and the guilds. The desire to make money and accumulate profits was hardly new, but beginning in the eighteenth century, it was permitted fuller play than ever before in European history. The commercial spirit was a major vehicle of social change and, by the early nineteenth century, led increasingly to a conception of human beings as individuals rather than as members of communities.

The expansion of population provided a further stimulus for change and a challenge to tradition, hierarchy, and corporateness. The traditional economic and social organization had presupposed a stable or declining population. The additional numbers of people meant that new ways had to be devised to solve old problems. More people also meant more labor, more energy, and more minds contributing to the creation and solution of social difficulties. The improvements in health and the longer life span may have given that larger population a new sense of confidence. The social hierarchy had to accommodate itself to more people. Corporate groups, such as the guilds, had to confront the existence of an expanded labor force. Moreover the products and industries arising from the Industrial Revolution made the society and the economy much more complicated. Class structure and social hierarchy remained, but the boundaries became blurred. New wealth meant that birth would eventually become less and less a determining factor in social relationships except in regard to the social role assigned to the two sexes.

Finally, the conflicting political ambitions of the monarchs, the nobilities, and the middle class generated innovation. The monarchs wanted to make their nations rich enough to wage war. As will be seen, this goal led them to attempt to interfere further with the privileges of the nobles. In the name of ancient rights the nobles attempted to secure and expand their existing social privileges by achieving further political power in the state. By making their privileges so exclusive, they helped to undermine the principle of privilege itself. The middle class, in all of its diversity, was growing wealthier from trade, commerce, and the practice of the professions. Its members wanted social prestige and political influence equal to their wealth. And they wanted the government to function in an efficient and businesslike manner. They resented privileges, frowned at hierarchy, and rejected tradition.

All of these factors meant that the society of the eighteenth century stood at the close of one era in European history and at the opening of another. What began to make contemporaries aware of that fact were the great wars of mid-century, the revolt of the British colonies in North America, and the intellectual currents of the Enlightenment.

Suggested Readings

C. B. A. BEHRENS, *The Ancien Régime* (1967). A brief account of life in France with excellent illustrations.

J. BLUM, *Lord and Peasant in Russia from the Ninth to the Nineteenth Century* (1961). A thorough and wide-ranging discussion.

J. BLUM, *The End of the Old Order in Rural Europe* (1978). The most comprehensive treatment of life in rural Europe, especially central and eastern, from the early eighteenth through the mid-nineteenth centuries.

F. BRAUDEL, *Capitalism and Material Life, 1400–1800* (1974). An investigation of the physical resources and human organization of preindustrial Europe.

F. BRAUDEL, *The Structures of Everyday Life: The Limits of the Possible,* trans. by M. Kochan (1982). A magisterial survey by the most important social historian of our time.

P. DEANE, *The First Industrial Revolution,* 2nd ed. (1979). A well-balanced and systematic treatment.

J. DEVRIES, *The Economy of Europe in an Age of Crisis, 1600–1750* (1976). An excellent overview that sets forth the main issues.

P. EARLE (Ed.), *Essays in European Economic History, 1500–1800* (1974). A useful collection of articles that cover most of the major states of western Europe.

F. FORD, *Robe and Sword: The Regrouping of the French Aristocracy After Louis XIV* (1953). An important treatment of the growing social tensions within the French nobility during the eighteenth century.

R. FORSTER, *The Nobility of Toulouse in the Eighteenth Century* (1960). A local study that displays the variety of noble economic activity.

R. FORSTER AND E. FORSTER, *European Society in the Eighteenth Century* (1969). An excellent collection of documents.

D. GEORGE, *London Life in the Eighteenth Century* (1925). A lively account.

D. V. GLASS AND D. E. C. EVERSLEY (Eds.), *Population in History: Essays in Historical Demography* (1965). Fundamental for an understanding of the eighteenth-century increase in population.

A. GOODWIN (Ed.), *The European Nobility in the Eighteenth Century* (1953). Essays on the nobility in each state.

P. GOUBERT, *The Ancien Régime: French Society, 1600–1750,* trans. by Steve Cox (1974). A superb account of the peasant social order.

H. J. HABAKKUK AND M. POSTAN (Eds.), *The Cambridge Economic History of Europe* (1965). Separate chapters by different authors on major topics.

D. HAY et al., *Albion's Fatal Tree: Crime and Society in Eighteenth-Century England* (1976). Separate essays on a previously little explored subject.

O. H. HUFTON, *The Poor of Eighteenth-Century France, 1750–1789* (1975). A brilliant study of poverty and the family economy.

E. L. JONES, *Agriculture and Economic Growth in England, 1650–1815* (1968). A good introduction to an important subject.

P. LASLETT, *The World We Have Lost* (1965). Examination of English life and society before the coming of industrialism.

J. LOUGH, *An Introduction to Eighteenth-Century France* (1960). A systematic survey with good quotations (in French) from contemporaries.

S. POLLARD AND C. HOLMES, *Documents of European Economic History: The Process of Industrialization, 1750–1870* (1968). A very useful collection.

G. RUDÉ, *The Crowd in History, 1730–1848* (1964). This and the following work were pioneering studies.

G. RUDÉ, *Paris and London in the Eighteenth Century* (1973).

G. RUDÉ, *Europe in the Eighteenth Century* (1972). A survey with emphasis on social history.

L. STONE, *The Family, Sex and Marriage in England 1500–1800* (1977). A pioneering study of a subject receiving new interest from historians.

T. TACKETT, *Priest and Parish in Eighteenth-Century France: A Social and Political Study of the Curés in a Diocese of Dauphiné, 1750–1791* (1977). A very important local study that displays the role of the church in the fabric of social life in the old regime.

C. WILSON, *England's Apprenticeship, 1603–1763* (1965). A broad survey of English economic life on the eve of industrialism.

The BLOODY MASSACRE perpetuated in King — Street BOSTON on March 5th 1770, by a party of the 29th REGT.

BUTCHER'S HALL

Engrav'd Printed & Sold by PAUL REVERE BOSTON

Unhappy Boston! see thy Sons deplore,
Thy hallow'd Walks besmear'd with guiltless Gore,
While faithless P—n and his savage Bands,
With murd'rous Rancour stretch their bloody Hands;
Like fierce Barbarians grinning o'er their Prey,
Approve the Carnage, and enjoy the Day.

If scalding drops from Rage from Anguish Wrung,
If speechless Sorrows lab'ring for a Tongue,
Or if a weeping World can ought appease
The plaintive Ghosts of Victims such as these;
The Patriot's copious Tears for each are shed,
A glorious Tribute which embalms the Dead.

But know Fate summons to that awful Goal,
Where Justice strips the Murd'rer of his Soul:
Should venal C—ts the scandal of the Land,
Snatch the relentless Villain from her Hand,
Keen Execrations on this Plate inscrib'd,
Shall reach a Judge who never can be brib'd.

The unhappy Sufferers were Messrs SamL GRAY, SamL MAVERICK, JamS CALDWELL, CRISPUS ATTUCKS & PatK CARR
Killed. Six wounded; two of them (CHRISTR MONK & JOHN CLARK) Mortally

20 Empire, War, and Colonial Rebellion

THE MIDDLE of the eighteenth century witnessed a renewal of European warfare on a worldwide scale. The conflict involved two separate but interrelated rivalries. Austria and Prussia fought for dominance in central Europe while Great Britain and France dueled for commercial and colonial supremacy. The wars were long, extensive, and very costly in both men and money. They resulted in a new balance of power on the Continent and on the high seas. Great Britain gained a world empire, and Prussia was recognized as a great power. Moreover the expense of these wars led every major European government after the Peace of Paris of 1763 to reconstruct their policies of taxation and finance. Those revised fiscal programs produced internal conditions for the monarchies of Europe that had most significant results for the rest of the century. These included the American Revolution, enlightened absolutism on the Continent, and a continuing financial crisis for the French monarchy.

The "Boston Massacre" of March 5, 1770 was depicted in an engraving quickly made and put on sale by Paul Revere. [The Granger Collection.]

Eighteenth-Century Empires

Periods of European Overseas Empires

Since the Renaissance, European contacts with the rest of the world have gone through four distinct stages. The first was that of the discovery, exploration, and initial conquest and settlement of the New World. This period had closed by the end of the seventeenth century. The second era, which is largely the concern of this chapter, was one of colonial trade rivalry among Spain, France, and Great Britain. The Anglo-French side of the contest has often been compared to a second hundred years' war. During this second period, which may be said to have closed during the 1820s, both the British colonies of the North American seaboard and the Spanish colonies of Central and South America emancipated themselves from European control. The third stage of European contact with

595

the non-European world occurred in the nineteenth century, when new formal empires involving the European administration of indigenous peoples were carved out in Africa and Asia. Those nineteenth-century empires also included new areas of European settlement, such as Australia, New Zealand, and South Africa. The bases of these empires were trade, national honor, and military strategy. The last period of European empire came in the present century, with the decolonization of peoples previously under European colonial rule.

During the four and a half centuries before decolonization, Europeans exerted political dominance over much of the rest of the world. They frequently treated other peoples as social, intellectual, and economic inferiors. They ravaged existing cultures because of greed, religious zeal, or political ambition. These actions are major facts of European history and significant factors in the contemporary relationship of Europe and its former colonies. What allowed the Europeans to exert such influence and domination for so long over so much of the world was not any innate cultural superiority but a technological supremacy closely related to naval power and gunpowder. Ships and guns allowed the Europeans to exercise their will almost wherever they chose.

Mercantile Empires

Navies and merchant shipping were the keystones of the mercantile empires of the eighteenth century. These empires were meant to bring profit to a nation rather than to provide areas for settlement. The Treaty of Utrecht (1713) established the boundaries of empire during the first half of the century. Except for Brazil, which was governed by Portugal, Spain controlled all of mainland South America, and in North America it controlled Florida, Mexico, and California. The Spanish also governed the island of Cuba and half of Hispaniola. The British Empire consisted of the colonies along the North Atlantic seaboard, Nova Scotia, Newfoundland, Jamaica, and Barbados. Britain also possessed a few trading stations on the Indian subcontinent. The French domains covered the Saint Lawrence River valley; the Ohio and Mississippi river valleys; the West Indian islands of Saint Domingue, Guadeloupe, and Martinique; and stations in India. The Dutch controlled Surinam, or Dutch Guiana, in South America; various trading stations in Ceylon and Bengal; and, most impor-

tantly, the trade with Java in what is now Indonesia. All of these powers also possessed numerous smaller islands in the Caribbean. So far as eighteenth-century developments were concerned, the major rivalries existed among the Spanish, the French, and the British.

To the extent that any formal economic theory lay behind the conduct of these empires, it was mercantilism, that practical creed of hardheaded businessmen. Initially, the fundamental point of this outlook was the necessity of acquiring a favorable trade balance of gold and silver bullion. Such bullion was regarded as the measure of a country's wealth, and a nation was truly wealthy only if it amassed more bullion than its rivals. By the late seventeenth century mercantilist thinking, as developed by writers such as Thomas Mun in *England's Treasure by Forraign Trade* (1664), had come to regard general foreign trade and the level of domestic industry as the true indications of a nation's prosperity. But from beginning to end the economic well-being of the home country was the first concern of mercantilist writers. Colonies were to provide markets and natural resources for the industries of the home country. In turn, the home country was to furnish military security and political administration for the colonies. For decades both sides assumed that the colonies were the inferior partner in the relationship. The mercantilist statesmen and traders regarded the world as an arena of scarce resources and economic limitation. They assumed that one national economy could grow only at the expense of others. The home country and its colonies were to trade only with each other. To that end they attempted to forge trade-tight systems of national commerce through navigation laws, tariffs, bounties to encourage production, and prohibitions against trading with the subjects of other monarchs. National monopoly was the ruling principle.

Mercantilist ideas had always been neater on paper than in practice. By the early eighteenth century mercantilist assumptions were held only in the vaguest manner. They stood too far removed from the economic realities of the colonies and perhaps from human nature. The colonial and home markets simply failed to mesh. Spain could not produce sufficient goods for South America. Economic production in the British North American colonies challenged English manufacturing and led to British attempts to limit certain colonial industries, such as iron and hat making. Colonists of

*The Custom House in Dublin, Ireland, is one of the most elegant political buildings of Europe.
Its fine architecture suggests the importance that eighteenth-century governments attached to
trade and the regulation of trade. [Irish Tourist Board, New York.]*

different countries wished to trade with each other.
English colonists could buy sugar more cheaply
from the French West Indies than from English
suppliers. The traders and merchants of one nation always hoped to break the monopoly of another. For all these reasons the eighteenth century
became the "golden age of smugglers."[1] The governments could not control the activities of all their
subjects. Clashes among colonists could and did
bring about conflict between governments.

Areas of Rivalry and Conflict

The Spanish Empire stood on the defensive
throughout the century. It was a sprawling expanse of territory over which the Spanish government wished to maintain a commercial monopoly
without possessing the capacity to do so. Spanish
colonists looked to illegal imports from French and
British traders to supply needed goods. Both

[1] Walter Dorn, *Competition for Empire*, 1740–1763 (New York:
Harper, 1940), p. 266.

France and Britain assumed a very aggressive
stance toward the Spanish Empire because they
viewed it as a vast potential market and a major
source of gold. Their rivalry for intrusion into the
mainland Spanish markets was duplicated by their
other conflicts in North America, India, and the
West Indies.

Neither the French nor the British colonies of
North America fit particularly well into the mercantile pattern of empire. Trade with these areas
during the early part of the century was smaller
than with the West Indies. These mainland colonies were settlements rather than arenas for economic exploitation. The French lands of Canada
were quite sparsely populated. Relations with the
Indians were troublesome. The economic interests
and the development of the colonies were not
wholly compatible with those of the home countries. Major flash points existed between France
and Britain on the North American continent.
Their colonists quarreled endlessly with each
other. Both groups of settlers were jealous over
rights to the lower Saint Lawrence River valley,

❧ The Mercantilist Position Stated

One of the earliest discussions of the economic theory of mercantilism appeared in *England's Treasure by Forraign Trade* (1664) by Thomas Mun. In this passage from that work Mun explained why it was necessary to the prosperity of the nation for more goods to be exported than imported. Although later mercantilist theory became somewhat more sophisticated, all writers in the eighteenth century emphasized the necessity of a favorable balance of trade.

The ordinary means therefore to increase our wealth and treasure is by Forraign Trade *wherein wee must ever observe this rule; to sell more to strangers yearly than wee consume of theirs in value. For suppose that when this Kingdom is plentifully served with the Cloth, Lead, Tinn, Iron, Fish and other native commodities, we doe yearly export the overplus to forraign countries to the value of twenty two hundred thousand pounds; by which means we are enabled beyond the Seas to buy and bring in forraign wares for our use and Consumptions, to the value of twenty hundred thousand pounds; By this order duly kept in our trading, we may rest assured that the Kingdom shall be enriched yearly two hundred thousand pounds, which must be brought to us in so much Treasure; because that part of our stock which is not returned to us in wares must necessarily be brought home in treasure [i.e., gold or silver bullion].*

Thomas Mun, *England's Treasure by Forraign Trade,* as quoted in Charles Wilson, *England's Apprenticeship, 1603–1763* (London: Longman, 1965), p. 60.

upper New England, and later the Ohio River valley. There were other rivalries over fishing rights, fur trade, and relationships with the Indians.

Unlike North America or the West Indies, India was neither the home of migrating Europeans nor an integral part of their imperial schemes. The Indian subcontinent was an area where both France and Britain traded through privileged, chartered companies that enjoyed a legal monopoly. The East India Company was the English institution; the French equivalent was the Compagnie des Indes. The trade of India and Asia figured only marginally in the economics of empire. Some bullion gained by trade or piracy in the West Indies was shipped to India, where it was used to purchase cotton cloth that was shipped to England and then used to purchase slaves in Africa for the West Indies. The commercial problem with the states of India was that the European countries produced little or nothing wanted in the region.

Nevertheless throughout the century trade and involvement on the subcontinent continued. Enterprising Europeans always hoped that in some fashion profitable commerce with India might develop. Others regarded India as a springboard into the even larger potential market of China. The original European footholds in India were trading posts called *factories.* They existed through privileges granted by the various Indian governments. Two circumstances arose during the middle of the eighteenth century to change this situation. First, in several of the Indian states decay occurred in the indigenous administration and government. Second, Joseph Dupleix (1697–1763) for the French and Robert Clive (1725–1774) for the British saw these developments as opportunities for expanding the control of their respective companies (the Compaigne des Indes and the East India Company). To maintain their own security and to expand their privileges, the companies began to fill the power vacuum and in effect took over the government of some regions. Each group of Europeans hoped to checkmate the other.

Struggle for the West Indies. The heart of the eighteenth-century colonial rivalry was the West Indies. These islands, close to the American continents, constituted the jewels of empire. Here the colonial powers pursued their greedy ambitions in close proximity to each other. The West Indies raised tobacco, cotton, indigo, coffee, and sugar, for which there existed strong markets in Europe. Sugar in particular had become a product of standard consumption rather than a luxury. It was used in coffee, tea, and cocoa, for making candy and preserving fruits, and in the brewing industry. There seemed no limit to its uses. Sugar was also important to the domestic economy of Europe. Sugar refining had become a major industry in France. Sugar and tobacco figured prominently in the reexport industry. For example, large quantities of tobacco were shipped from Scotland to the Continent.

Basic to the economy of the West Indies as well as to that of South America and the British colonies on the south Atlantic seaboard of North America was the institution of slavery. Hundreds of thousands of slaves were imported into the Americas during the eighteenth century. Planters could not attract sufficient quantities of free labor to these areas. They became wholly dependent on slaves. Slavery and the slave trade touched most of the economy of the transatlantic world. Cities such as Newport, Rhode Island; Liverpool, England; and Nantes, France, enjoyed prosperity that rested almost entirely on the slave trade. All of the shippers who handled cotton, tobacco, and sugar depended on slavery, though they might have no direct contact with the institution. There was a general triangle of trade that consisted of carrying goods to Africa to be exchanged for slaves, who were then taken to the West Indies, where they were traded for sugar and other tropical produce, which were then shipped to Europe. Not all ships necessarily covered all three legs of the triangle.

Another major trade pattern existed between New England and the West Indies. New England fish or ship stores were traded for sugar.

Within the rich commerce and agriculture of the West Indies there existed three varieties of colonial rivalry. Producers of different nations were intensely jealous of each other. The quantity of sugar produced had expanded so as to depress the price in Europe. Consequently one group of planters hoped not to conquer the lands of their competitors but rather to destroy the productive capacity of those islands. There was a second form of rivalry among shippers in the Caribbean. Every captain hoped to transport as much sugar as possible to Europe. Finally, the West Indies possessions of France and Britain provided excellent bases for penetration of the trade of the Spanish Empire. Many French and British ship captains in the West Indies were admitted smugglers, and some were little better than pirates.

The close interrelationship of the West Indies and the European economies meant that significant numbers of British, French, and Spanish subjects had an interest in the area. This West India Interest, as it was called in England, consisted of absentee plantation owners, shippers, insurers, merchants, bankers, owners of domestic industries dependent on West Indian products, and all of those involved in the slave trade. In Great Britain it was an articulate and well-organized pressure

An eighteenth-century sugar press in Cuba. At this period it was tended by slaves. Most of the sugar would eventually end up in Europe, where there was a growing market for the product. [Bettmann Archive.]

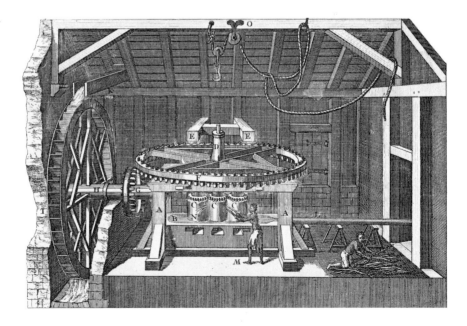

On a French West Indian plantation slaves pick cotton on the right while other slaves on the left remove the seeds from the fiber. The particular variety of cotton shown in this engraving grew on shrubs rather than on the bushes grown in the American south. [The Granger Collection.]

group. In 1739 the West India Interest along with the political enemies of Robert Walpole succeeded in driving Britain into a war with Spain, the War of Jenkins's Ear.

The Treaty of Utrecht (1713) included two special privileges for Great Britain in regard to the Spanish Empire. The British received a thirty-year *asiento,* or contract, to furnish slaves to the Spanish. Britain also gained the right to send one ship each year to the trading fair at Portobello, a major Caribbean seaport on the Panamanian coast. These two privileges allowed British traders and smugglers potential inroads into the Spanish market. Little but friction arose from these rights. The annual ship to Portobello was often supplied with additional goods during the night as it lay in port. Much to the chagrin of the British, the Spanish

government took its own alleged trading monopoly seriously and maintained coastal patrols, which boarded and searched English vessels to look for contraband.

In 1731 during one such boarding operation there was a fight, and an English captain named Robert Jenkins had his ear cut off by the Spaniards. Thereafter he carried about his severed ear preserved in a jar of brandy. This incident was of little importance until 1738, when Jenkins appeared before the British Parliament, reportedly brandishing his ear as an example of Spanish atrocities to British merchants in the West Indies. The British merchant and West Indies interests put great pressure on Parliament to do something about Spanish intervention in their trade. Robert Walpole attempted to reach a solution through negotiations. However, Parliament—and especially the members who believed that the war would drive Walpole from office—refused all accommodation. In late 1739 Great Britain went to war with Spain.

At the outbreak of hostilities, the French, under the administation of Cardinal Fleury, stood ready to profit from the British–Spanish conflict. They expected to see British trade harmed and eventually to receive Spanish commercial favors for aid. None of the major European powers except Britain had any standing grudge against France. The years of Fleury's cautious policy were about to pay off. Then, quite literally overnight, the situation on the Continent changed.

Mid-Century Wars

The War of the Austrian Succession (1740–1748)

In December 1740, after possessing the throne of Prussia for less than seven months, Frederick II ordered his troops to occupy the Austrian province of Silesia. The invasion shattered the provisions of the Pragmatic Sanction and upset the continental balance of power as established by the Treaty of Utrecht. The young king of Prussia had treated the House of Hapsburg simply as another German state rather than as the leading state in the region. The province of Silesia itself rounded out Prussia's

---

CONFLICTS OF THE MID-EIGHTEENTH CENTURY

1713	Treaty of Utrecht
1739	Outbreak of War of Jenkins's Ear between England and Spain
1740	War of the Austrian Succession commences
1748	Treaty of Aix-la-Chapelle
1756	Convention of Westminster between England and Prussia Seven Years' War opens
1757	Battle of Plassey
1759	British forces capture Quebec
1763	Treaty of Hubertusburg Treaty of Paris

---

possessions, and Frederick was determined to keep his ill-gotten prize. In 1740 the other European states were not sure whether to consider the Prussian invasion the act of a great power or that of a mere aggressive upstart. The wars of the next quarter century affirmed the former judgment.

Maria Theresa was twenty-three years old and had succeeded to the Austrian crown only two months before Frederick's move. Her army was weak, her bureaucracy inefficient, and the loyalty of her subjects uncertain. She herself was inexperienced and was more usually guided by the values of piety than by hardheaded statecraft. Yet she succeeded in rallying to her side the Magyars of Hungary and the aristocratic leaders of her other domains. They were genuinely sympathetic to her plight and inspired by her courage. Maria Theresa's great achievement was not the reconquest of Silesia, which eluded her, but the preservation of the Hapsburg Empire as a major political power.

The seizure of Silesia could have marked the opening of a general hunting season on Hapsburg holdings and the beginning of revolts by Hapsburg subjects. Instead it proved the occasion for new political allegiances. Maria Theresa achieved these new loyalties, especially between herself and the Magyars, not merely through heroism but more specifically by granting new privileges to the nobles of the various Hapsburg realms. The empress recognized Hungary as the most important of her crowns and promised the Magyars considerable local autonomy. In this fashion she preserved the Hapsburg state, but at great cost to the power of the central monarchy. As a result, the Hapsburg holdings would never become a centrally unified modern political entity.

The war over the Austrian succession and the British–Spanish commercial conflict could have remained separate disputes. They were neither logically nor necessarily politically related. What ultimately united them was the role of France. Cardinal Fleury understood that the long-range interests of France lay in the direction of commercial growth. However, just as British merchant interests had pushed Robert Walpole into war, a group of court aristocrats led by the Comte de Belle Isle compelled the elderly Fleury to abandon his planned naval attack on British trade and to support the Prussian aggression against Austria. This proved to be one of the most fateful decisions in French history.

❧ Prince Frederick Discusses Statecraft and European Affairs

King Frederick William I of Prussia thought at times that he had reason for concern about the qualities of his flute-playing, philosophizing son, Prince Frederick. He need not have worried. The young prince was already able to write this hard-nosed essay in 1738, two years before he became King Frederick II. He stated the view common at the time that a monarch normally seeks to increase the power of his state. He also suggested that the major states of Europe were not in a healthy balance. Two years later he followed up these thoughts by invading Silesia.

It is an unshaken principle among kings to aggrandize themselves as much as their power will permit; and, though such aggrandizement must be subject to different modifications, and infinitely varied according to the situation of princes, the power of neighboring states, or fortunate opportunities, the principle is not the less unchangeable, and is never abandoned by monarchs. Their pretended fame is part of this system. In a word, it is necessary they should increase in greatness.

From what has been said, it will be easy to perceive that the political body of Europe is in a perilous situation. It is deprived of its due equilibrium, and is in a state in which it cannot long remain, without great risk. The political body resembles the human body, which can only subsist by a mixture of equal quantities of the acid and the alkali. Whenever one of these *two substances predominates, the body is made sensible of it, and the health is considerably injured: should that substance continue to increase, it may finally cause the destruction of the machine. Thus, whenever the policy and prudence of the princes of Europe lose sight of the maintenance of a just balance, between the principal powers, it is felt by the constitution of the whole body-politic. Violence on the one side, weakness on the other; the desire of invading on the one, and on the other the inability to prevent invasion. The most puissant [powerful] gives law, and the feeble are under the necessity of adding their signature. All finally concur in augmenting disorder and confusion. Force acts like an impetuous torrent, passes its bounds, carries everything with it, and exposes this unfortunate body-politic to the most fatal revolutions.*

Frederick the Great, "Considerations on the Present State of the Body-Politic of Europe" (1738), in *Posthumous Works of Frederic II, King of Prussia*, vol. 4 trans. by Thomas Holcroft (London: G. G. J. and J. Robinson 1789), pp. 364–365, 381–382.

Even though the Hapsburgs had been the historic enemy of France, a war against Austria was not in the French interest in 1741. In the first place, aid to Prussia had the effect of consolidating a new and powerful state in Germany. That new power could, and indeed later did, endanger France. Second, the French move against Austria brought Great Britain into the continental war. The British, as usual, wanted to see the Low Countries remain in friendly hands. In the eighteenth century that policy required continued Hapsburg control of the Austrian Netherlands. In 1744 the British–French conflict expanded beyond the Continent, as France decided to support Spain against Britain in the New World. As a result, French military and economic resources became badly divided. France could not bring sufficient strength to the colonial struggle. Having chosen to continue a struggle from the past with Austria, France lost the struggle for the future against Great Britain.

By 1748 the war had become a military stalemate for all concerned. Austria had not been able to regain Silesia, but it had fended off further aggression from other German states. The French army, led by Marshal Maurice de Saxe (1696–1750), won a series of splendid victories over the British and the Austrians in the Netherlands during 1747 and 1748. Britain, for its part, had pursued a very successful colonial campaign. Its forces in America captured the fortress of Louisburg at the mouth of the Saint Lawrence River, and the British more than held their own on the Indian subcontinent.

Maria Theresa of Austria (seated right) and her husband, Emperor Frances I (seated left), with their very large family. Her son and successor, Joseph II, is the tall adolescent near her. The artist was Martin Meytens (1695–1770), court painter in Vienna. [*Kunsthistorisches Museum, Vienna.*]

Warfare on French commerce had been highly effective. These victories overseas compensated for the poor showing on the Continent. Consequently the war was brought to a close by the Treaty of Aix-la-Chapelle (1748). In effect the treaty restored the conditions that had existed prior to the war, with the exception that Prussia retained Silesia. Spain renewed the *asiento* agreement with Great Britain. All observers believed that the treaty constituted a truce rather than a permanent peace.

*The Battle of Fontenoy, 1745, during the War of the Austrian Succession. The French under
Marechal de Saxe defeated an English army that was defending the territory of Maria Theresa
in the Austrian Netherlands. [Giraudon.]*

The "Diplomatic Revolution" of 1756

Before the rivalries again erupted into war, a
dramatic shift of alliances took place. In 1756 Prussia and Great Britain signed the Convention of
Westminster. It was a defensive alliance aimed at
preventing the entry of foreign troops into the
Germanies. Frederick II feared invasions by both
Russia and France. The convention meant that
Great Britain, the ally of Austria since the wars of
Louis XIV, had now joined forces with Austria's
major eighteenth-century enemy.

Maria Theresa was despondent over this development. However, her foreign minister, Count
Wenzel Anton Kaunitz (1711–1794), was delighted. This brilliant diplomat and servant of the
Hapsburg dynasty had long hoped for an alliance
between Austria and France for the dismemberment of Prussia. The Convention of Westminster
made this alliance, unthinkable a few years earlier,
possible. France was agreeable because Frederick
had not consulted it before coming to his understanding with Britain. Consequently, later in 1756,
France and Austria signed a defensive alliance.
Kaunitz had succeeded in completely reversing the
direction of French foreign policy from Richelieu
through Fleury. France would now fight to restore
Austrian supremacy in central Europe. But the

In August 1756 Frederick II invaded the kingdom of Saxony. He regarded this invasion as a continuation of the defensive strategy of which the Convention of Westminster had been a part. Frederick believed that there existed an international conspiracy on the part of Saxony, Austria, and France to undermine and destroy Prussian power. The attack on Saxony was in Frederick's mind a preemptive strike. The invasion itself created the very destructive alliance that Frederick feared. In the spring of 1757 France and Austria made a new alliance dedicated to the destruction of Prussia. They were eventually joined by Sweden, Russia, and the smaller German states.

Count Kaunitz. As foreign minister of the Hapsburg Monarchy, Kaunitz negotiated the famous reversal of alliances (1756) by which France later entered the Seven Years' War allied with Austria against Prussia and Britain. [Bildarchivs der Osterreichischen Nationalbibliothek, Vienna.]

French monarchy, though having changed its German ally, would remain diverted from its commercial interests on the high seas.

The Seven Years' War (1756–1763)

The Treaty of Aix-la-Chapelle had brought peace in Europe, but the conflict between France and Great Britain continued unofficially on the colonial front. There were continuous clashes between American and French settlers in the Ohio River valley and in upper New England. These were the prelude to what is known in American history as the French and Indian War. These colonial skirmishes would certainly have led in time to a broader conflict. However, once again the factor that opened a general European war that extended into a colonial theater was the action of the king of Prussia.

Frederick the Great of Prussia in his later years displayed in his face the burden of personal hardship that his ambitious wars had brought to him and to his nation. Yet he did succeed in making Prussia a major power. [Culver Pictures.]

❧ Prussia and Great Britain Agree to the Convention of Westminster ══

> The Diplomatic Revolution of 1756 saw a reversal of the alliances that had existed during the War of the Austrian Succession. France and Austria became allies against Prussia and Great Britain. The Convention of Westminster was the agreement that created the Prussian–British alliance. That alliance allowed Prussia to receive the financial backing of Britain in case of war and provided Britain with a continental ally that would divert the resources of France from the war for overseas empire. Prussia hoped that the treaty would provide protection from Russia, Austria, and France.

As the differences which had arisen in America between the King of Great Britain and the most Christian King [i.e., the king of France], and the consequences of which become every day more alarming, give room to fear for the public tranquillity of Europe; H.M. the King of Great Britain, etc., and H.M. the King of Prussia, etc., attentive to an object so very interesting, and equally desirous of preserving the peace of Europe in general and that of Germany in particular, have resolved to enter into such measures as may the most effectually contribute to so desirable an end. . . .

I. There shall be, between the said most Serene Kings, a perfect peace and mutual amity, notwithstanding the troubles that may arise in Europe, in consequence of the above-mentioned differences; so

that neither of the contracting parties shall attack, or invade, directly or indirectly, the territories of the other; but, on the contrary, shall exert their utmost efforts to prevent their respective allies from undertaking anything against the said territories in any manner whatever.

II. If contrary to all expectation, and in violation of the peace which the high contracting parties propose to maintain by this treaty in Germany, any foreign power should cause troops to enter into the said Germany, under any pretext whatsoever; the two high contracting parties shall unite their forces to punish this infraction of the peace, and maintain the tranquillity of Germany, according to the purport of the present treaty.

H. Butterfield (Ed.), *Select Documents of European History, 1715–1920* (London: Methuen, 1931), pp. 20–21.

Prussia was surrounded by enemies, and Frederick II confronted the gravest crisis of his career. It was after these struggles that he came to be called Frederick the Great. He won several initial battles, the most famous of which was Rossbach on November 5, 1757. Thereafter, however, the Prussians experienced a long series of defeats that might have destroyed the state. Two factors in addition to Frederick's stubborn leadership saved Prussia. The first was major financial aid from Great Britain. The British contributed as much to the Prussian war effort as did the Prussian treasury itself. Second, in 1762 Empress Elizabeth of Russia died. Her successor was Czar Peter III (he also died in the same year), whose admiration for Frederick knew almost no bounds. He immediately made peace with Prussia, thus relieving the country of one enemy and allowing it to hold its own

against Austria and France. The treaty of Hubertusburg of 1763 closed the continental conflict with no significant changes in prewar borders. Silesia remained Prussia's province, and Prussia clearly stood in the ranks of the great powers.

The survival of Prussia was less impressive to the rest of Europe than the victories of Great Britain over France in every theater of conflict. The architect of this victory was William Pitt the Elder (1708–1778). He came from a family that had made its fortune from commerce. His grandfather, "Diamond" Pitt, had laid the foundations of the family's wealth by commercial ventures in India. The grandson was no less dedicated to the growth of British trade and economic interests. Pitt was a person of colossal ego and administrative genius. From the time of the War of Jenkins's Ear he had criticized the government as being too timid in its

William Pitt the Elder guided the armies and navies of Great Britain to a stunning victory in the Seven Years' War. His portrait is from the studio of the artist Richard Brompton. [The Granger Collection.]

colonial policy. He had been strongly critical of all continental involvement, including the Convention of Westminster. During the 1750s he had gained the favor of the London merchant interest. Once war had commenced again, these groups clamored for his appointment to the cabinet. In 1757 he was named the secretary of state in charge of the war. He soon drew into his own hands all the power he could grasp. A person of supreme confidence, he

George II (1727–1760) was the British monarch during the great wars of the mid-century. The painting is by Thomas Worlidge. [The Granger Collection.]

once told his friends, "I am sure that I can save the country, and that no one else can."

Once in office Pitt changed his attitude toward British involvement on the Continent. He came to regard the German conflict as a way to divert French resources and attention from the colonial struggle. He pumped huge financial subsidies to Frederick the Great and later boasted of having won America on the plains of Germany. North America was the center of Pitt's real concern. Put quite simply, he wanted all of North America east of the Mississippi for Great Britain, and that was exactly what he won. He turned more than forty thousand regular English and colonial troops against the French in Canada. Never had so many soldiers been devoted to a colonial field of warfare. He achieved unprecedented cooperation with the American colonies, whose leaders realized that they might finally defeat their French neighbors. The French government was unwilling and unable to direct similar resources against the English in America. Their military administration was corrupt; the military and political command in Canada was divided; and the food supply to the French army failed. In September 1759, on the Plains of Abraham overlooking the valley of the Saint Lawrence River at Quebec City, the British army under General James Wolfe defeated the French under Lieutenant General Louis Joseph Montcalm. The French empire in Canada was coming to an end.

However, Pitt's colonial vision extended beyond the Saint Lawrence valley and the Great Lakes basin. The major islands of the French West Indies fell to the British fleets. Income from the sale of captured sugar helped finance the British war effort. British slave interests captured the bulk of the French slave trade. Between 1755 and 1760 the value of the French colonial trade fell by over 80 per cent. On the Indian subcontinent the British forces under the command of Robert Clive defeated the French in 1757 at the Battle of Plassey. This victory opened the way for the eventual conquest of Bengal and later all of India by the British East India Company. Never had Great Britain or any other European power experienced such a complete worldwide military victory.

The Treaty of Paris of 1763 reflected somewhat less of a victory than Britain had won on the battlefield. Pitt was no longer in office. George III (1760–1820) had succeeded to the British throne in 1760. He and Pitt had quarreled over policy, and the minister had departed. His replacement

Both the British general James Wolfe and the French general Montcalm died at the Battle of Quebec in September 1759, in which the British forces won the crucial encounter and thus drove the French out of their North American empire. The picture of the death of Wolfe is an engraving from a famous painting by the American artist Benjamin West (1738–1820). [Culver Pictures.]

was the earl of Bute, a favorite of the new monarch. The new minister was responsible for the peace settlement. Britain received all of Canada, the Ohio River valley, and the eastern half of the Mississippi River valley. Britain partially surrendered the conquest in India by giving France footholds at Pondicherry and Chandernagore. The sugar islands of Guadeloupe and Martinique were restored to the French. Britain could have gained more territory only with further war involving more taxation, against which the country was already complaining.

The Seven Years' War had been a vast conflict. Tens of thousands of soldiers had been killed or wounded. Major battles had been fought around the globe. At great internal sacrifice Prussia had permanently wrested Silesia from Austria and had turned the Holy Roman Empire into an empty shell. Hapsburg power now depended largely on the Hungarian domains. France, though still possessing sources of colonial income, was no longer a great colonial power. The Spanish Empire remained largely intact, but the British were still determined to penetrate its markets. On the Indian

The Battle of the Plains of Abraham, 1759. The British victory at Quebec meant the end of French rule in Canada. This engraving is by P. C. Cariot, after a work by Captain Hervey Smith. [Courtesy of the Trustees, National Maritime Museum, Greenwich, England.]

subcontinent the British East India Company was in a position to continue to press against the decaying indigenous governments and to impose its own authority. The results of that situation would be felt until the middle of the twentieth century. In North America the British government faced the task of organizing its new territories. From this time until World War II Great Britain assumed the status not simply of a European but also of a world power.

The quarter century of warfare also caused a long series of domestic crises among the European powers. The French defeat convinced many people in the nation of the necessity of political and administrative reform. The financial burdens of the wars had astounded all contemporaries. Every power had to begin to find ways to increase revenues to pay its war debt and to finance its preparation for the next combat. Nowhere did this search for revenue lead to more far-ranging consequences than in the British colonies in North America.

The American Revolution and Europe

Events in the British Colonies

The revolt of the British colonies in North America was an event in transatlantic and European history. It erupted from problems of revenue collection common to all the major powers after the Seven Years' War. The War of the American Revolution was a continuation of the conflict between France and Great Britain. The French support of the Americans deepened the existing financial and administrative difficulties of the monarchy.

The political ideals of the Americans had roots in the thought of John Locke and other English political theorists. The colonists raised questions of the most profound nature about monarchy, political authority, and constitutionalism. These questions had ramifications for all European states. Part of

❧ France Turns Over French Canada to Great Britain

The Treaty of Paris (1763) concluded the French and English portion of the Seven Years' War. In this particular clause the previously French portion of Canada was turned over to Great Britain.

His Most Christian Majesty [the King of France] renounces all pretensions which he has heretofore formed or might have formed to Nova Scotia or Acadia in all its parts, and guarantees the whole of it, and with all its dependencies, to the King of Great Britain: Moreover, His Most Christian Majesty cedes and guarantees to his said Britannic Majesty, in full right, Canada, with all its dependencies, as well as the island of Cape Breton, and all the other islands and coasts in the gulf and river of St. Laurence, and in general, everything that depends on the said countries, land, islands, and coasts, with the sovereignty, property, possession, and all rights acquired by treaty, or otherwise, which the Most Christian King and the Crown of France have had till

now over the said countries, lands, islands, places, coasts, and their inhabitants, so that the Most Christian King cedes and makes over the whole to the said King, and to the Crown of Great Britain, and that in the most ample manner and form, without restriction, and without any liberty to depart from the said cession and guarantee under any pretence, or to disturb Great Britain in the possessions above mentioned. His Britannic Majesty, on his side, agrees to grant the liberty of the Catholic Religion, to the inhabitants of Canada: he will, in consequence, give the most precise and effectual orders, that his new Roman Catholic subjects may profess the worship of their religion according to the rights of the Romish Church, as far as the laws of Great Britain permit.

H. Butterfield (Ed.), *Select Documents of European History*, 1715–1920 (London: Methuen, 1931), pp. 29–30.

the difficulties from the British side arose because of the characteristic European political friction between the monarch and the aristocracy. Finally, many Europeans saw the Americans as inaugurating a new era in the history of European peoples and indeed of the world.

After the Treaty of Paris of 1763 the British government faced three imperial problems. The first was the sheer cost of empire, which the British felt they could no longer carry alone. The national debt had risen considerably, as had taxation. The American colonies had been the chief beneficiaries of the conflict. It made rational sense that they should henceforth bear part of the cost of their protection and administration. The second problem was the vast expanse of new territory in North America that the British had to organize. This included all the land from the mouth of the Saint Lawrence River to the Mississippi River with its French settlers and, more importantly, its Indian possessors.

As the British ministers pursued solutions to these difficulties, a third and more serious issue arose. The British colonists in North America resisted taxation and were suspicious of the imperial policies toward the western lands. Consequently the British had to search for new ways to exert their authority over the colonies. The Americans became increasingly resistant because their economy had outgrown the framework of mercantilism, because the removal of the French relieved them of dependence on the British army, and because they believed that their liberty was in danger.

The British drive for revenue commenced in 1764 with the passage of the Sugar Act under the ministry of George Grenville (1712–1770). The measure attempted to produce more revenue from imports into the colonies by the rigorous collection of what was actually a lower tax. Smugglers who violated the law were to be tried in admiralty courts without juries. The next year Parliament passed the Stamp Act, which put a tax on legal documents and certain other items such as newspapers. The British considered these taxes legal because they had been passed by Parliament. The taxes seemed just because the money was to be spent in the colonies. The Americans responded that they had the right to tax themselves and that they were not represented in Parliament. The colonists quite simply argued there should be no taxation without representation. Moreover, because the king had granted most of the colonial charters, the Americans claimed that their legal connection to Britain was

through the monarch rather than through the Parliament. The expenditure in the colonies of the revenue levied by Parliament did not reassure the colonists. They feared that if colonial government were financed from outside, they would lose control over their government. In October 1765 the Stamp Act Congress met in America and drew up a protest to the crown. There was much disorder in the colonies, particularly in Massachusetts. The colonists agreed to refuse to import British goods. In 1766 Parliament repealed the Stamp Act, but through the Declaratory Act it said that Parliament had the power to legislate for the colonies.

The Stamp Act crisis set the pattern for the next ten years. Parliament, under the leadership of a royal minister, would approve a piece of revenue or administrative legislation. The Americans would then resist by reasoned argument, economic pressure, and violence. Then the British would repeal the legislation, and the process would begin again. Each time, tempers on both sides became more frayed and positions more irreconcilable. In 1767 Charles Townshend (1725–1767), as Chancellor of the Exchequer, led Parliament to pass a series of revenue acts relating to colonial imports. The colonists again resisted. The ministry sent over its own customs agents to administer the laws. To protect these new officers, the British sent troops to Boston in 1768. The obvious tensions resulted, and in March 1770 the Boston Massacre, in which British troops killed five citizens, took place. That same year Parliament repealed all of the Townshend duties except for the one on tea.

In May 1773 Parliament passed a new law relating to the sale of tea by the East India Company. The measure permitted the direct importation of tea into the American colonies. It actually lowered the price of tea while retaining the tax imposed without the colonists' consent. In some cities the colonists refused to permit the unloading of the tea; in Boston a shipload of tea was thrown into the harbor. The British ministry of Lord North (1732–1792) was determined to assert the authority of Parliament over the resistant colonies. During 1774 Parliament passed a series of laws known in American history as the Intolerable Acts. These measures closed the port of Boston, reorganized the government of Massachusetts, allowed troops to be quartered in private homes, and removed the trials of royal customs officials to England. The same year Parliament approved the Quebec Act for the future administration of that province. It extended the boundaries of Quebec to include the

Ohio River valley. The Americans regarded the Quebec Act as an attempt to prevent the extension of their mode of self-government westward beyond the Appalachian Mountains.

During these years committees of correspondence composed of citizens critical of Britain had been established throughout the colonies. They made the various sections of the eastern seaboard aware of common problems and aided united action. In September 1774 these committees organized the gathering of the First Continental Congress in Philadelphia. This body hoped to persuade Parliament to restore self-government in the colonies and to abandon its attempt at direct supervision of colonial affairs. However, conciliation was not forthcoming. By April 1775 the battles of Lexington and Concord were fought. In June the colonists suffered defeat at the Battle of Bunker Hill. Despite the defeat, the colonial assemblies soon began to meet under their own authority rather than under that of the king.

The Second Continental Congress gathered in May 1775. It still sought conciliation with Britain, but the pressure of events led that assembly to begin to conduct the government of the colonies. By August 1775 George III had declared the colonies in rebellion. During the winter Thomas Paine's pamphlet *Common Sense* galvanized public opinion in favor of separation from Great Britain. A colonial army and navy were organized. In April 1776 the Continental Congress opened American ports to the trade of all nations. And on July 4, 1776, the Continental Congress adopted the Declaration of Independence. Thereafter the War of the American Revolution continued until 1781, when the forces of George Washington defeated those of Lord Cornwallis at Yorktown. However, early in 1778 the war had widened into a European conflict when Benjamin Franklin persuaded the French government to support the rebellion. In 1779 the Spanish also came to the aid of the colonies. The 1783 Treaty of Paris concluded the conflict, and the thirteen American colonies had established their independence.

This series of events is generally familiar to American readers. The relationship of the American Revolution to European affairs and the European roots of the American revolutionary ideals are less familiar.

The political theory of the American Declaration of Independence derived from the writings of seventeenth-century English Whig theorists, such as John Locke, and eighteenth-century Scottish moral

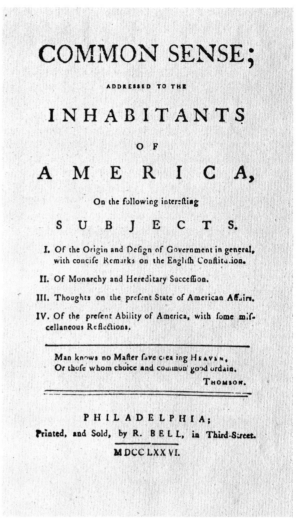

Common Sense, *written by Tom Paine, was the most important political pamphlet published during* 1776 *when the American colonies were deciding to make a final break with Great Britain.* [The Granger Collection.]

philosophers, such as Francis Hutcheson. Their political ideas had in large measure arisen out of the struggle of seventeenth-century English aristocrats and gentry against the absolutism of the Stuarts. The American colonists looked to the English Revolution of 1688 as having established many of their own fundamental political liberties as well as those of the English. The colonists claimed that through the measures imposed from 1763 to 1776 George III and the British Parliament had attacked those liberties and dissolved the bonds of moral and political allegiance that had formerly united the two peoples. Consequently the colonists employed a theory that had developed to justify an aristocratic rebellion in order to support their own popular revolution.

These Whig political ideas were only a part of the English ideological heritage that affected the Americans. Throughout the eighteenth century they had become familiar with a series of British political writers called the *Commonwealthmen*. They held republican political ideas and had their intellectual roots in the most radical thought of the Puritan revolution. During the early eighteenth century these writers had relentlessly criticized the government patronage and parliamentary management of Robert Walpole and his successors. They argued that such government was corrupt and that it undermined liberty. They regarded much parliamentary taxation as simply a means of financing political corruption. They also attacked standing armies, which they considered instruments of tyranny. In Great Britain this political tradition had only a marginal impact. The writers were largely ignored because most British subjects regarded themselves as the freest people in the world. However, over three thousand miles away in the colonies, these radical books and pamphlets were read widely and were often accepted at face value. The events in Great Britain following the accession of King George III made many colonists believe that the worst fears of the Commonwealth writers were coming true.

Events in Great Britain

George III (1760–1820) believed that his two immediate royal predecessors had been improperly bullied and controlled by their ministers. Royal power had in effect amounted to little more than the policies carried out by a few powerful Whig families. The new king intended to rule through Parliament, but he was determined to have ministers of his own choice. Moreover George III believed that Parliament should function under royal rather than aristocratic management. When William Pitt resigned after a disagreement with George over war policy, the king appointed the earl of Bute as his first minister. In doing so, he ignored the great Whig families that had run the country since 1715. The king sought the aid of politicians whom the Whigs hated. Moreover he attempted to use the same kind of patronage techniques developed by Walpole to achieve royal control of the House of Commons.

Between 1761 and 1770 George tried one minister after another, but each in turn failed to gain sufficient support from the various factions in the House of Commons. Finally, in 1770 he turned to Lord North (1732–1792), who remained the king's

THE HORSE AMERICA, *throwing his Master.*

"The Horse America throwing his Master," an eighteenth-century cartoon mocking George III about the rebellion of the American colonies. [Library of Congress.]

George III (1760–1820). Although he never sought to make himself a tyrant as his critics charged, George did try to reassert the political influence of the monarchy which had been eroded under the first two Hanoverian kings, George I and George II. [New York Public Library Picture Collection.]

first minister until 1782. The Whig families and other political spokesmen claimed that George III was attempting to impose a tyranny. What they meant was that the king was attempting to curb the power of a particular group of the aristocracy. George III certainly was seeking to restore more royal influence to the government of Great Britain, but he was not attempting to make himself a tyrant.

THE CHALLENGE OF JOHN WILKES. Then in 1763 began the affair of John Wilkes (1725–1797). This London political radical and member of Parliament published a newspaper called *The North Briton*. In issue Number 45 of this paper Wilkes strongly criticized Lord Bute's handling of the peace negotiations with France. Wilkes was arrested under the authority of a general warrant issued by the secretary of state. He pled the privileges of a member of Parliament and was released. The courts also later ruled that the vague kind of general warrant by which he had been arrested was illegal. However, the House of Commons ruled that issue Number 45 of *The North Briton* was a libel and expelled Wilkes from the Commons. He soon fled the country and was outlawed. Throughout these procedures there was very widespread support for Wilkes, and many demonstrations were held in his cause.

In 1768 Wilkes returned to England and again stood for election to Parliament. He won the election, but the House of Commons, under the influence of George III's friends, refused to seat him. He was elected three more times. After the fourth

John Wilkes Esqr
Drawn from the Life and Etch'd in Aquafortis by Willm Hogarth.

This satirical portrait etching of John Wilkes was made by William Hogarth. It suggests the unattractive personal character of Wilkes and also tends to question the sincerity of his calls for liberty. [Charles Farrell Collection.]

The American colonists followed all of these developments of the 1760s very closely. The contemporary events in Britain confirmed their fears about a monarchical and parliamentary conspiracy against liberty. The king, as their Whig friends told them, was behaving like a tyrant. The Wilkes affair displayed the arbitrary power of the monarch, the corruption of the House of Commons, and the contempt of both for popular electors. That same monarch and Parliament were attempting to overturn the traditional relationship of Great Britain to its colonies by imposing parliamentary taxes. The same government had then landed troops in Boston, changed the government of Massachusetts, and undermined the traditional right of jury trial. All of these events fulfilled too exactly the portrait of political tyranny that had developed over the years in the minds of articulate colonists.

MOVEMENT FOR PARLIAMENTARY REFORM IN BRITAIN. The political influences between America and Britain operated both ways. The colonial demand for no taxation without representation and the criticism of the adequacy of the British sys-

Major John Cartwright (1740–1824) was the first English political reformer to call for universal manhood suffrage in parliamentary elections. [The Granger Collection.]

election the House of Commons simply ignored the election results and seated the government-supported candidate. As earlier in the decade, large popular demonstrations of shopkeepers, artisans, and small property owners supported Wilkes. He also received aid from some aristocratic politicians who wished to humiliate George III. Wilkes himself contended during all of his troubles that his cause was the cause of English liberty. "Wilkes and Liberty" became the slogan of all political radicals and many noble opponents of the monarch. Wilkes was finally seated in 1774, after having become the lord mayor of London.

❧ Major Cartwright Calls for the Reform of Parliament

During the years of the American Revolution there were many demands in England itself for a major reform of Parliament. In this pamphlet of 1777 Major John Cartwright demanded that a much larger number of English citizens be allowed to vote for members of the House of Commons. He also heaped contempt on the opponents of reform.

Suffering as we do, from a deep parliamentary corruption, it is no time to tamper with silly correctives, and trifle away the life of public freedom: but we must go to the bottom of the stinking sore and cleanse it thoroughly: we must once more infuse into the constitution the vivifying spirit of liberty and expel the very last dregs of this poison. Annual parliaments *with an* equal representation of the commons are the only specifics in this case: and they would effect a radical cure. That a house of commons, formed as ours is, should maintain septennial elections, and laugh at every other idea is no wonder. The wonder is, that the British nation which, but the other day, was the greatest nation on earth, should be so easily laughed out of its liberties. . . .

Those who now claim the exclusive *right of send-* *ing to parliament the* 513 *representatives for about six millions souls (amongst whom are one million five hundred thousand males,* competent as electors) *consist of about two hundred and fourteen thousand persons; and* 254 *of these representatives are elected by* 5,723. . . . *Their pretended rights are many of them, derived from* royal favour; *some from antient usage and presciption; and some indeed from act of parliament; but neither the most authentic acts of royalty, nor precedent, nor prescription, nor even parliament can establish any flagrant injustice; much less can they strip one million two hundred and eighty six thousand of an inalienable right, to vest it in a number amounting to only one seventh of that multitude. . . .*

John Cartwright, *Legislative Rights of the Commonality Vindicated,* cited in S. Maccoby, *The English Radical Tradition, 1763–1914* (London: Adam and Charles Black, 1966), pp. 32–33.

tem of representation struck at the core of the eighteenth-century British political structure. Colonial arguments could be adopted by British subjects at home who were no more directly represented in the House of Commons than were the Americans. The colonial questioning of the taxing authority of the House of Commons was related to the protest of John Wilkes. Both the Americans and Wilkes were challenging the power of the monarch and the authority of Parliament. Moreover both the colonial leaders and Wilkes appealed over the head of legally constituted political authorities to popular opinion and popular demonstrations. Both were protesting the power of a largely self-selected aristocratic political body. The British ministry was fully aware of these broader implications of the American troubles.

The American colonists also demonstrated to Europe how a politically restive people in the old regime could fight tyranny and protect political liberty. They established revolutionary but orderly political bodies that could function outside the existing political framework. These revolutionary political institutions were the congress and the convention. These began with the Stamp Act Congress of 1765 and culminated in the Constitutional Convention of 1787. The legitimacy of those congresses and conventions lay not in existing law but in the alleged consent of the governed. This approach represented a new way to found a government.

Toward the end of the War of the American Revolution, calls for parliamentary reform were voiced in Britain itself. The method proposed for changing the system was the extralegal Association Movement.

By the close of the 1770s there was much resentment in Britain about the mismanagement of the war, the high taxes, and Lord North's ministry. In northern England in 1778 Christopher Wyvil (1740–1822), a landowner and retired clergyman, organized the Yorkshire Association Movement.

Property owners or freeholders of Yorkshire met in a mass meeting to demand rather moderate changes in the corrupt system of parliamentary elections. They organized corresponding societies elsewhere. They intended that the association examine, and suggest reforms for, the entire government. The Association Movement was thus a popular attempt to establish an extralegal institution to reform the government. The movement collapsed during the early 1780s because its supporters, unlike Wilkes and the American rebels, were not willing to appeal for broad popular support. Nonetheless the agitation of the Association Movement provided many people with experience in political protest. Several of its younger figures lived to raise the issue of parliamentary reform after 1815.

Parliament was not insensitive to the demands of the Association Movement. In April 1780 the Commons passed a resolution that called for lessening the power of the crown. In 1782 Parliament adopted a measure for "economical" reform, which abolished some patronage at the disposal of the monarch. However, these actions did not prevent George III from appointing a minister of his own choice. In 1783 Lord North had to form a ministry with Charles James Fox (1749–1806), a long-time critic of George III. The monarch was most unhappy with the arrangement. In 1783 he approached William Pitt the Younger (1759–1806), son of the victorious war minister, to manage the House of Commons. During the election of 1784 Pitt received immense patronage support from the crown and constructed a House of Commons favorable to the king. Thereafter Pitt sought to formulate trade policies that would give his ministry broad popularity. He attempted in 1785 one measure of modest parliamentary reform. When it failed, the young prime minister, who had been only twenty-four at the time of his appointment, abandoned the cause of reform.

By the mid-1780s George III had achieved a part of what he had sought beginning in 1761. He had reasserted the influence of the monarchy in political affairs. It proved a temporary victory because his own mental illness, which would finally require a regency, weakened the royal power. The cost of his years of dominance had been very high. On both sides of the Atlantic the issue of popular sovereignty had been raised and widely discussed. The American colonies had been lost. Economically this loss did not prove disastrous. British trade with America after independence actually increased. However, the Americans—through the state constitutions, the Articles of Confederation, and the federal Constitution—had demonstrated to Europe the possibility of government without kings and without aristocracies. They had established the example of a nation in which written documents based on popular consent and popular sovereignty—rather than on divine law, natural law, tradition, or the will of kings—stood as the highest political and legal authority. Writers throughout western Europe sensed that a new kind of political era was dawning. It was to be an age of constituent assemblies, constitutions, and declarations of rights.

Colonies founded to serve the economic requirements of Britain and Europe repaid the debt by serving as laboratories for new political ideals and institutions. The ideas had generally been developed in Europe, but America was the place where most of them were initially put into practice. America for a time served as an experiment station for the advanced political ideas of Europe. Soon the ideas would find their way back to the lands of their origins.

Suggested Readings

B. BAILYN, *The Ideological Origins of the American Revolution* (1967). An important work illustrating the role of English radical thought in the perceptions of the American colonists.

C. BECKER, *The Declaration of Independence: A Study in the History of Political Ideas* (1922). An examination of the political and imperial theory of the Declaration.

J. BREWER, *Party Ideology and Popular Politics at the Accession of George III* (1976). An important series of essays on popular radicalism.

J. BROOKE, *King George III* (1972). The best recent biography.

H. BUTTERFIELD, *George III, Lord North, and the People, 1779–1780* (1949). Explores the domestic unrest in Britain during the American Revolution.

D. B. DAVIS, *The Problem of Slavery in Western Culture* (1966). A brilliant and far-ranging discussion.

D. B. DAVIS, *The Problem of Slavery in the Age of Revolution, 1770–1823* (1975). A major work for both European and American history.

WALTER DORN, *Competition for Empire, 1740–1763* (1940). Still one of the best accounts of the mid-century struggle.

L. H. GIPSON, *The British Empire Before the American Rev-*

olution, 13 vols. (1936–1967). A magisterial account of the mid-century wars from an imperial viewpoint.

R. LODGE, *Great Britain and Prussia in the Eighteenth Century* (1923). The standard account.

E. MORGAN AND H. MORGAN, *The Stamp Act Crisis* (1953). A lively account of the incident from the viewpoint of both the colonies and England.

J. B. OWEN, *The Eighteenth Century* (1974). A recent survey of British politics.

R. PARES, *War and Trade in the West Indies* (1936). Relates the West Indies to Britain's larger commercial and naval concerns.

R. PARES, *King George III and the Politicians* (1953). An important analysis of the constitutional and political structures.

J. H. PARRY, *Trade and Dominion: The European Overseas Empires in the Eighteenth Century* (1971). A comprehensive account with attention to the European impact on the rest of the world.

C. D. RICE, *The Rise and Fall of Black Slavery* (1975). An excellent survey of the subject with careful attention to the numerous historiographical controversies.

C. G. ROBERTSON, *Chatham and the British Empire* (1948). A brief study.

G. RUDÉ, *Wilkes and Political Liberty* (1962). A close analysis of popular political behavior.

P. D. G. THOMAS, *British Politics and the Stamp Act Crisis: The First Phase of the American Revolution, 1763–1767* (1975). An interesting work from the British point of view.

J. S. WATSON, *The Reign of George III, 1760–1815* (1960). Covers the British domestic political scene in a traditional manner.

G. WILLS, *Inventing America: Jefferson's Declaration of Independence* (1978). An important new study that challenges much of the analysis in the Becker volume noted above.

G. S. WOOD, *The Creation of the American Republic, 1776–1787* (1969). A far-ranging work dealing with Anglo-American political thought.

618

21 The Age of Enlightenment: Eighteenth-Century Thought

URING the eighteenth century the conviction began to spread throughout the literate sectors of European society that change and reform were both possible and desirable. This attitude is now commonplace, but it came into its own only after 1700. It represents one of the primary intellectual inheritances from that age. The movement of people and ideas that fostered such thinking is called the *Enlightenment*. Its leading voices combined confidence in the human mind inspired by the Scientific Revolution and faith in the power of rational criticism to challenge the intellectual authority of tradition and the Christian past. These writers stood convinced that human beings could comprehend the operation of physical nature and mold it to the ends of material and moral improvement. The rationality of the physical universe became a standard against which the customs and tra-

The young Voltaire. Philosopher, dramatist, poet, historian, novelist, scientist—Voltaire was the most famous and influential of the eighteenth-century French philosophes. This painting by Quentin Latour is at Versailles. [Bulloz.]

ditions of society could be measured and criticized. Such criticism penetrated every corner of contemporary society, politics, and religious opinion. As a result the spirit of innovation and improvement came to characterize modern European and Western society.

The *Philosophes*

The writers and critics who forged this new attitude and who championed change and reform were the *philosophes*. They were not usually philosophers in a formal sense; rather, they were people who sought to apply the rules of reason and common sense to nearly all the major institutions and social practices of the day. The most famous of their number included Voltaire, Montesquieu, Diderot, Rousseau, Hume, Gibbon, Smith, Bentham, Lessing, and Kant. A few of them occupied professorships in universities, but most were free agents who might be found in London coffeehouses, Edinburgh drinking spots, the salons of fashionable Parisian ladies, the country houses of reform-minded nobles, or the courts of the most powerful monarchs on the Continent. They were not an organized group; they disagreed on many issues. Their relationship with each other and with lesser figures of the same turn of mind has quite appropriately been compared with that of a family, in which despite quarrels and tensions a basic unity still remains.[1]

The chief unity of the *philosophes* lay in their desire to reform thought, society, and government for the sake of human liberty. As Peter Gay has suggested, this goal included "freedom from arbitrary power, freedom of speech, freedom of trade, freedom to realize one's talents, freedom of aesthetic response, freedom, in a word, of moral man to make his way in the world."[2] No other single set of ideas has done so much to shape the modern world. The literary vehicles through which the *philosophes* delivered their message included books, pamphlets, plays, novels, philosophical treatises, encyclopedias, newspapers, and magazines. During the Reformation and the religious wars writers had used the printed word to debate the proper mode of faith in God. The *philosophes* of the Enlightenment employed the printed word to proclaim a new faith in the capacity of humankind to improve itself without the aid of God.

Many of the *philosophes* were middle class in their social origins. The bulk of their readership were also drawn from the prosperous commercial and professional people of the eighteenth-century towns and cities. These people discussed the reformers' writings and ideas in local philosophical societies, Freemason lodges, and clubs. They had sufficient income and leisure time to buy and read the *philosophes'* works. Although the writers of the Enlightenment did not consciously champion the goals or causes of the middle class, they did provide an intellectual ferment and a major source of ideas that could be used to undermine existing social practices and political structures. They taught their contemporaries how to pose pointed, critical questions. Moreover the *philosophes* generally supported the economic growth, the expansion of trade, and the improvement of transport that were transforming the society and the economy of the eighteenth century and that were enlarging the middle class.

[1] Peter Gay, *The Enlightenment: An Interpretation*, Vol. 1 (New York: Knopf, 1967), p. 4.
[2] Ibid, p. 3.

Edward Jenner (1749–1823), an English physician, discovered that by inoculating human beings with the relatively mild disease of cowpox he could make them immune to the dread disease of smallpox. That discovery eventually led to the practically complete removal of the danger of smallpox. [Culver Pictures.]

Formative Influences

The Newtonian world view, the stability and prosperity of Great Britain after 1688, and the degradation that the wars of Louis XIV had brought to France were the chief factors that fostered the discussion of reform throughout Europe.

Isaac Newton (1642–1727) and John Locke (1632–1704) were the major intellectual forerunners of the Enlightenment. Newton's formulation of the laws of universal gravitation exemplified the power of the human mind. His example and his writing encouraged Europeans to approach the study of nature directly and to avoid metaphysics and supernaturalism. Newton had formulated general laws but had always insisted on a foundation of specific empirical evidence for those laws. Empirical experience had provided a constant check on his rational speculation. This emphasis on concrete experience became a keystone for Enlightenment thought. Moreover Newton had discerned a pattern of rationality in natural physical phenomena. During the eighteenth century the ancient idea of following nature became trans-

This elaborate eighteenth-century engraving pays homage to Isaac Newton. Newton was a major intellectual influence on the Enlightenment. This engraving is in the collection of the British Museum. [British Museum.]

formed under the Newtonian influence into the idea of following reason. Because nature was rational, society should be organized in a rational manner.

As explained in Chapter 17, Newton's scientific achievement had inspired his fellow countryman John Locke to seek a human psychology based on experience. In *An Essay Concerning Human Understanding* (1690), Locke argued that each human being enters the world as a *tabula rasa*, or blank page. His or her personality is consequently the product of the sensations that impinge from the external world throughout the course of life. The significant conclusion that followed from this psychology was that human nature is changeable and can be molded by modification of the surrounding physical and social environment. Locke's was a reformer's psychology. It suggested that improve-

ment in the human situation was possible. Locke also, in effect, rejected the Christian view of humankind as creatures permanently flawed by sin. Human beings need not wait for the grace of God or other divine aid to better their lives. They could take charge of their own destiny.

Newton's physics and Locke's psychology provided the theoretical basis for reform. The domestic stability of Great Britain after the Revolution of 1688 furnished a living example of a society in which enlightened reforms functioned for the benefit of all concerned. England permitted religious

This handsome portrait (1788) of the eighteenth-century French chemist Antoine Lavoisier and his wife is by Jacques Louis David (1748–1825). Unlike Lavoisier, guillotined by the ungrateful French Revolutionists, the artist David lived to portray many events of the Revolution and the Napoleonic period. [The Metropolitan Museum of Art. Purchase, Mr. and Mrs. Charles Wrightsman Gift, 1977.]

toleration to all creeds except Unitarianism and Roman Catholicism, whose believers were not actually persecuted. Relative freedom of the press and free speech prevailed. The monarchy was limited in its authority, and political sovereignty resided in the Parliament. The courts protected citizens from arbitrary government action. The army was quite small. These liberal policies had produced not disorder and instability but economic prosperity and loyalty to the political system. The continental view of England was somewhat idealized; nevertheless the country was sufficiently freer than any other nation to make the point that the reformers sought.

If the example of Great Britain suggested that change need not be disastrous to a nation and society, France exhibited many of the practices and customs of European politics and society that most demanded reform. Louis XIV had built his power on the bases of absolute monarchy, a large standing army, heavy taxation, and a religious unity requiring persecution. However, the enemies of France had defeated that nation in war. Its people were miserable, and celebrations had marked the death of the great king. His successors had been unable to reform the state. Critics of the monarchy were subject to arbitrary arrest. There was no freedom of worship. Political and religious censors interfered with the press and other literary productions. Offending authors could be imprisoned, although some achieved cooperative relations with the authorities. State regulations hampered economic growth. Many aristocrats regarded themselves as a military class and upheld militaristic values. Yet throughout the French social structure there existed people who wanted to see changes brought about. These people read and supported the *philosophes* of their nation and of other countries. Consequently France became the major center for the Enlightenment, for there, more than in any other state, the demand for reform daily confronted writers and political thinkers.

Stages of the Enlightenment

The movement that came to be known as the Enlightenment evolved over the course of the century and involved a number of writers living at different times in various countries. Its early exponents popularized the rationalism and scientific ideas of the seventeenth century. They worked to expose contemporary social and political abuses and argued that reform was necessary and possible. The advancement of their cause and ideas was anything but steady. They confronted the obstacles of vested interests, political oppression, and religious condemnation. Yet by the mid-century they had brought enlightened ideas to the European public in a variety of formats. The *philosophes'* "family" had come into being. They corresponded with each other, wrote for each other as well as for the general public, and defended each other against the political and religious authorities.

By the second half of the century they were sufficiently safe to quarrel among themselves on occasion. They had stopped talking in generalities, and their major advocates were addressing themselves to specific abuses. Their books and articles had become more specialized and more practical. They had become more concerned with politics than with religion. Having convinced the Europeans that change was a good idea, they began to suggest exactly what changes were most desirable. They had become honored figures.

Voltaire

One of the earliest and by far the most influential of the *philosophes* was François Marie Arouet, known to posterity as Voltaire (1694–1778). During the 1720s Voltaire had offended the French authorities by certain of his writings, and he was arrested and put in prison for a brief time.

Later Voltaire went to England, where he visited in the best literary circles, observed the tolerant intellectual and religious climate, felt free in the atmosphere of moderate politics, and admired the science and economic prosperity. In 1733 he published *Letters on the English,* which appeared in French the next year. The book praised the virtues of the English and indirectly criticized the abuses of French society. In 1738 he published *Elements of the Philosophy of Newton,* which popularized the thought of the great scientist. Both works were well received and gave Voltaire a reputation as an important writer.

Thereafter Voltaire lived part of the time in France and part near Geneva, just across the French border, where the royal authorities could not bother him. He wrote essays, history, plays, stories, and letters that made him the literary dictator of Europe. He brought the bitter venom of his satire and sarcasm against one evil after another in

French and European life. His most famous satire is *Candide* (1759), in which he attacked war, religious persecution, and unthinking optimism about the human condition. Like most *philosophes*, Voltaire believed that improvement of human society was necessary and possible. But he was never certain that reform, if achieved, would be permanent. The optimism of the Enlightenment constituted a tempered hopefulness rather than a glib certainty. Pessimism provided an undercurrent to most of the works of the period.

Montesquieu

Among the other pioneers of the early Enlightenment, Charles Louis de Secondat, Baron de Montesquieu (1689–1755), was outstanding. He was a lawyer, a noble of the robe, and a member of a provincial *parlement.* He also belonged to the Bordeaux Academy of Science, before which he presented papers on scientific topics. Although living comfortably within the bosom of French society, he saw the need for reform. In 1721 he published *The Persian Letters* to satirize contemporary institutions. The book consisted of letters purportedly written by two Persians visiting Europe. They explained to friends at home how European behavior contrasted with Persian life and customs. Behind the humor lay the cutting edge of criticism and an exposition of the cruelty and irrationality of much contemporary European life. In his most enduring work, *The Spirit of the Laws* (1748), Montesquieu held up the example of the British constitution as the wisest model for regulating the power of government. (We shall examine *The Spirit of the Laws* more closely later in this chapter.)

The Encyclopedia

The mid-century witnessed the publication of one of the greatest monuments of the Enlightenment. Under the heroic leadership of Denis Diderot (1713–1784), and Jean le Rond d'Alembert (1717–1783), the first volume of the *Encyclopedia* appeared in 1751. The project reached completion in 1772, numbering seventeen volumes of text and eleven of plates. The *Encyclopedia* was the product of the collective effort of more than one hundred authors, and its editors had at one time or another solicited articles from all the major French *philosophes.* The project reached fruition only after numerous attempts to censor it and halt its publica-

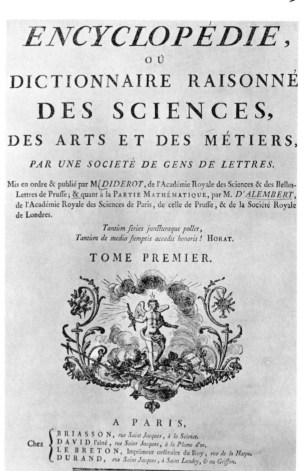

The title page of the first volume of the Encylcopedia. *The early volumes of the text received the approval of the royal censor, as noted on the last line, but when it became evident that the work challenged many widely held religious and political views, its opponents obtained withholding of approval for later volumes which were eventually published.* [*The Mansell Collection.*]

tion. The *Encyclopedia* set forth the most advanced critical ideas in religion, government, and philosophy. This criticism often had to be hidden in obscure articles or under the cover of irony. The articles represented a collective plea for freedom of expression. However, the large volumes also provided important information on manufacturing, canal building, ship construction, and improved agriculture.

Between fourteen and sixteen thousand copies

Denis Diderot, the principal editor of the Encyclopedia *who saw it through to the end; d'Alembert withdrew when the opposition turned nasty. [The Granger Collection.]*

of various editions of the *Encyclopedia* were sold before 1789. The project had been designed to secularize learning and to undermine the intellectual assumptions remaining from the Middle Ages and the Reformation. The articles on politics, ethics, and society ignored concerns about divine law and concentrated on humanity and its immediate well-being. The encyclopedists looked to antiquity rather than to the Christian centuries for their intellectual and ethical models. The future welfare of humankind lay not in pleasing God or following divine commandments but rather in harnessing the power of the earth and its resources and in living at peace with one's fellow human beings. The good life lay here and now and was to be achieved through the application of reason to human relationships.

With the publication of the *Encyclopedia,* enlightened thought became more fully diffused over the Continent. Enlightened ideas penetrated German and Russian intellectual and political circles. The *philosophes* of the latter part of the century turned from championing the general cause of reform and discussed specific areas of practical application. Gotthold Lessing (1729–1781) wrote plays to plead for religious toleration. Adam Smith (1723–1790) attacked the mercantile system. Cesare Beccaria (1738–1794) and Jeremy Bentham (1748–1832) called for penal and legal reforms. By this time the concepts of reform and the rationalization of existing institutions had become deeply impressed on European thinking and soci-

A dinner party of philosophes, *from an eighteenth-century engraving by Hubert. In the center is Voltaire with his hand raised. In a circle beginning to his right are Diderot, Adam, Condorcet, d'Alembert, the Abbe Maure, and La Harpe. [The Mansell Collection.]*

ety. The issue then became, and would remain for over a century, how best to implement those reforms.

The Enlightenment and Religion

Throughout the century, in the eyes of the *philosophes* the chief enemy of the improvement of humankind and the enjoyment of happiness was the existence and influence of ecclesiastical institutions. The hatred of the *philosophes* for the church and Christianity was summed up in Voltaire's cry of "Crush the Infamous Thing." Almost all varieties of Christianity, but especially Roman Catholicism, invited the criticism of the *philosophes*. Intellectually the churches perpetuated a religious rather than a scientific view of humankind and physical nature. The clergy taught that human beings were basically depraved and that they required divine grace to become worthy creatures. The doctrine of original sin in either its Catholic or its Protestant formulation suggested that meaningful improvement in human nature on earth was impossible. Religious concerns turned human interest away from this world to the world to come. In the view of the *philosophes* the concept of predestination suggested that the condition of the human soul after death had little or no relationship to virtuous living during this life. Through disagreements over obscure doctrines the various churches favored the politics of intolerance and bigotry that in the past had caused human suffering, torture, and war.

To attack the Christian churches in this manner was to raise major questions about the life and society of the old regime. Politically and socially the churches were deeply enmeshed in the power structure. They owned large amounts of land and collected tithes from peasants before any other taxes were collected. Most of the clergy were legally exempt from taxation and made only annual voluntary grants to the government. The upper clergy in most countries were relatives of aristocrats. Churchmen were actively involved in politics, serving in the British House of Lords and advising princes on the Continent. In Protestant countries the local clergyman of a particular parish was usually appointed by the local major landowner. Across the Continent membership in the predominant denomination of the kingdom gave certain subjects political advantages. Nonmembership often excluded other subjects from political participation. Clergymen of all faiths preached the sinfulness of political disobedience, and they provided the intellectual justification for the social and political status quo. They were active where possible in exerting religious and literary censorship. The churches were thus privileged and powerful corporate bodies of the old regime. The *philosophes* chose to attack both their ideas and their power.

Deism

The *philosophes* believed that religion should be reasonable and should lead to moral behavior. The Newtonian world view had convinced many writers that nature was rational. Therefore the God who had created nature must also be rational, and the religion through which that God was worshiped should be rational. Moreover Lockean psychology, which limited human knowledge to empirical experience, raised the question whether such a thing as divine revelation to humankind was, after all, possible. These considerations gave rise to a movement for enlightened religion known as *deism*. The title of one of its earliest expositions, *Christianity Not Mysterious* (1696) by John Toland, indicates the general tenor of this religious outlook. Toland and later writers wished to consider religion a natural and rational, rather than a supernatural and mystical, phenomenon. In this respect the deists made a departure from the general piety of Newton and Locke, both of whom regarded themselves as distinctly Christian. Newton had believed that God might interfere with the natural order, whereas the deists regarded God as resembling a divine watchmaker who had set the mechanism of nature to work and had then departed from the scene.

There were two major points in the deists' creed. The first was the belief in the existence of God. They thought that this belief could be empirically deduced from the contemplation of nature. Joseph Addison's poem on the spacious firmament (1712), illustrates this idea:

> The spacious firmament on high,
> With all the blue ethereal sky,
> And spangled heav'n, a shining frame,
> Their great Original proclaim:
> Th' unwearied Sun, from day to day,
> Does his Creator's power display,
> And publishes to every land
> The work of an Almighty hand.

Because nature provided evidence of a rational God, that deity must also favor rational morality. Consequently the second point in the deists' creed was the belief in life after death, when rewards and punishments would be meted out according to the virtue of the life a person led on this earth.

Deism was empirical, tolerant, reasonable, and capable of encouraging virtuous living. It was the major positive religious component of the Enlightenment. Voltaire declared:

The great name of Deist, which is not sufficiently revered, is the only name one ought to take. The only gospel one ought to read is the great book of Nature, written by the hand of God and sealed with his seal. The only religion that ought to be professed is the religion of worshiping God and being a good man.[3]

If such a faith became widely accepted, the fanaticism and rivalry of the various Christian sects might be overcome. Religious conflict and persecutions encouraged by that fulsome zeal would end. There would also be little or no necessity for a priestly class to foment fanaticism, denominational hatred, and bigotry.

The *philosophes* did not rest with the formulation of a rational religious alternative to Christianity. They also attacked the churches and the clergy with great vehemence. Voltaire repeatedly questioned the truthfulness of priests and the morality of the Bible. In his *Philosophical Dictionary* (1764) he humorously pointed out inconsistencies in biblical narratives and immoral acts of the biblical heroes. In the chapter "Of Miracles" published in 1748 as part of his *Inquiry into Human Nature*, the Scottish *philosophe* David Hume (1771–1776) argued that divine miracles, in which the churches put great store, were not grounded in rational belief or empirical evidence. For Hume, the greatest miracle was to believe in miracles. In *The Decline and Fall of the Roman Empire* (1776) Edward Gibbon (1737–1794), the English historian, examined the early history of Christianity and explained the rise of that faith in terms of natural causes rather than the influence of miracles and piety. A few *philosophes* went further. Baron d'Holbach (1723–1789) and Julien Offray de La Mettrie (1709–1751) embraced positions very near to atheism and materialism. Theirs was distinctly a minority position, however. Most of the *philosophes* sought not the

---

[3] Quoted in J. H. Randall, *The Making of the Modern Mind*, rev. ed. (New York: Houghton Mifflin, 1940), p. 292.

MAJOR PUBLICATION DATES OF THE ENLIGHTENMENT

1687	Newton's *Principia Mathematica*
1690	Locke's *Essay Concerning Human Understanding*
1696	Toland's *Christianity Not Mysterious*
1721	Montesquieu's *Persian Letters*
1733	Voltaire's *Letters on the English*
1738	Voltaire's *Elements of the Philosophy of Newton*
1748	Montesquieu's *Spirit of the Laws*
	Hume's *Inquiry into Human Nature* with the chapter "Of Miracles"
1750	Rousseau's *Discourse on the Moral Effects of the Arts and Sciences*
1751	First volume of *The Encyclopedia* edited by Diderot
1755	Rousseau's *Discourse on the Origin of Inequality*
1762	Rousseau's *Social Contract*
1763	Voltaire's *Treatise on Toleration*
1764	Voltaire's *Philosophical Dictionary*
	Beccaria's *On Crimes and Punishments*
1776	Gibbon's *Decline and Fall of the Roman Empire*
	Bentham's *Fragment on Government*
	Smith's *Wealth of Nations*
1779	Lessing's *Nathan the Wise*

---

abolition of religion but its transformation into a humane force that would encourage virtuous living.

Toleration

A primary social condition for such a life was the establishment of religious toleration. Again Voltaire took the lead in championing this cause. In 1762 the Roman Catholic political authorities in Toulouse ordered the execution of a Huguenot named Jean Calas. He stood accused of having murdered his son to prevent him from converting to Roman Catholicism. Calas had been viciously tortured and publicly strangled without ever having confessed his guilt. The confession would not have saved his life, but it would have given the Catholics good propaganda to use against Protestants.

Voltaire learned of the case only after Calas's death. He made the dead man's cause his own. In 1763 he published a *Treatise on Tolerance* and hounded the authorities for a new investigation. Finally, in 1765, the judicial decision against the unfortunate man was reversed. For Voltaire the case illustrated the fruits of religious fanaticism and the need for rational reform of judicial processes. Somewhat later in the century the German playwright and critic Gotthold Lessing (1729–1781) wrote *Nathan the Wise* (1779) as a plea for toleration not only of different Christian sects but also of religious faiths other than Christianity. All of these calls for toleration stated in effect that life on earth and human relationships should not be subordinated to religion. Secular values and considerations were more important than religious ones.

❧ Voltaire Attacks Religious Fanaticism

The chief complaint of the *philosophes* against Christianity was that it bred a fanaticism that led people to commit crimes in the name of religion. In this passage from his *Philosophical Dictionary* (1764) Voltaire directly reminded his readers of the intolerance of the Reformation era and indirectly referred to examples of contemporary religious excesses. He argued that the philosophical spirit can overcome fanaticism and foster toleration and more humane religious behavior. In a manner that shocked many of his contemporaries, he praised the virtues of Confucianism over those of Christianity.

Fanaticism is to superstition what delirium is to fever and rage to anger. The man visited by ecstasies and visions, who takes dreams for realities and his fancies for prophecies, is an enthusiast; the man who supports his madness with murder is a fanatic. . . .

The most detestable example of fanaticism was that of the burghers of Paris who on St. Bartholomew's Night [1572] went about assassinating and butchering all their fellow citizens who did not go to mass, throwing them out of windows, cutting them in pieces.

Once fanaticism has corrupted a mind, the malady is almost incurable. . . .

The only remedy for this epidemic malady is the philosophical spirit which, spread gradually, at last tames men's habits and prevents the disease from starting; for once the disease has made any progress, one must flee and wait for the air to clear itself. Laws and religion are not strong enough against the spiritual pest; religion, far from being healthy food for infected brains, turn to poison in them. . . .

Even the law is impotent against these attacks of rage; it is like reading a court decree to a raving maniac. These fellows are certain that the holy spirit with which they are filled is above the law, that their enthusiasm is the only law they must obey.

What can we say to a man who tells you that he would rather obey God than men, and that therefore he is sure to go to heaven for butchering you?

Ordinarily fanatics are guided by rascals, who put the dagger into their hands; these latter resemble that Old Man of the Mountain who is supposed to have made imbeciles taste the joys of paradise and who promised them an eternity of the pleasures of which he had given them a foretaste, on condition that they assassinated all those he would name to them. There is only one religion in the world that has never been sullied by fanaticism, that of the Chinese men of letters. The schools of philosophy were not only free from this pest, they were its remedy; for the effect of philosophy is to make the soul tranquil, and fanaticism is incompatible with tranquility. If our holy religion has so often been corrupted by this infernal delirium, it is the madness of men which is at fault.

Voltaire, *Philosophical Dictionary*, trans. by P. Gay (New York: Harcourt, Brace, and World, 1962), pp. 267–269.

The Enlightenment and Society

Although the *philosophes* wrote much on religion, humanity was the center of their interest. As one writer in the *Encyclopedia* observed, "Man is the unique point to which we must refer everything, if we wish to interest and please amongst considerations the most arid and details the most dry."[4] The *philosophes* believed that the application of human reason to society would reveal laws in human relationships similar to those found in physical nature. Although the term did not appear until later, the idea of social science originated with the Enlighten-

[4]Quoted in F. L. Baumer, *Main Currents of Western Thought*, 4th ed. (New Haven, Conn.: Yale University Press, 1978), p. 374.

ment. The purpose of discovering social laws was the removal of the inhumanity that existed through ignorance of them. These concerns became especially evident in the work of the *philosophes* on law and prison procedures.

Beccaria

In 1764 Cesare Beccaria (1738–1794), an Italian *philosophe*, published *On Crimes and Punishments*, in which he applied critical analysis to the problem of making punishments both effective and just. He wanted the laws of monarchs and legislatures—that is, positive law—to conform with the rational laws of nature. He rigorously and eloquently attacked both torture and capital punishment. He

❧ Beccaria Objects to Capital Punishment as Unenlightened

In the eighteenth century the death penalty was commonly applied throughout Europe for small as well as great crimes. The young north Italian nobleman Cesare Beccaria thought the penalty was unproductive of law and order and was also unenlightened. *On Crimes and Punishments* appeared when he was only twenty-six, and Voltaire, Bentham, and Catherine the Great professed to admire the work. His 1764 comments are a good example of the Enlightenment application of the criteria of reason and utility to social problems.

Is the death penalty really useful *and* necessary *for the security and good order of society? Are torture and torments* just, *and do they attain the* end *for which laws are instituted? What is the best way to prevent crimes? Are the same punishments equally effective for all times? What influence have they on customary behavior? These problems deserve to be analyzed with that geometric precision which the mist of sophisms, seductive eloquence, and timorous doubt cannot withstand. . . . If, by defending the rights of man and of unconquerable truth, I should help to save from the spasm and agonies of death some wretched victim of tyranny or of no less fatal ignorance, the thanks and tears of one innocent mortal in his transports of joy would console me for the contempt of all mankind.*

.   .   .   .

If one were to cite against me the example of all the

ages and of almost all the nations that have applied the death penalty to certain crimes, my reply would be that the example reduced itself to nothing in the face of truth, against which there is no prescription; that the history of men leaves us with the impression of a vast sea of errors; among which, at great intervals, some rare and hardly intelligible truths appear to float on the surface. Human sacrifices were once common to almost all nations, yet who will dare to defend them? That only a few societies, and for a short time only, have abstained from applying the death penalty, stands in my favor rather than against me, for that conforms with the usual lot of great truths, which are about as long-lasting as a lightning flash in comparison with the long dark night that envelops mankind. The happy time has not yet arrived in which truth shall be the portion of the greatest number, as error has heretofore been.

Cesare Beccaria, *On Crimes and Punishments*, trans. by Henry M. Paolucci (Indianapolis: Bobbs Merrill, 1963), pp. 10, 51.

thought that the criminal justice system should ensure speedy trial, sure punishment, and punishment intended to deter further crime. The purpose of law was not to impose the will of God or some other ideal of perfection; its purpose was to secure the greatest good or happiness for the greatest number of human beings. This utilitarian philosophy based on happiness in this life permeated most of the Enlightenment writing on practical reforms.

Bentham

Although utilitarianism did not originate with him, it is particularly associated with the English legal reformer Jeremy Bentham (1748–1832). He sought to create codes of scientific law that were founded on the principle of utility, that is, the greatest happiness for the greatest number. In the *Fragment on Government* (1776) and *The Principles of Morals and Legislation* (1789), Bentham explained that the application of the principle of utility would overcome the special interests of privileged groups who prevented rational government. Bentham regarded the existing legal and judicial systems as burdened by traditional practices that harmed the very people whom the law should serve. The application of reason and utility would remove the legal clutter that prevented justice from being realized.

The Physiocrats

Another area of social relationships where the *philosophes* saw existing legislation and administration preventing the operation of natural social laws was the field of economic policy. They believed that mercantilist legislation and the labor regulations established by various governments and guilds actually hampered the expansion of trade, manufacture, and agriculture. In France these economic reformers were called the *physiocrats*. Their leading spokesmen were François Quesnay (1694–1774) and Pierre Dupont de Nemours (1739–1817). They believed that the primary role of government was to protect property and to permit freedom in the use of property. They particularly felt that all economic production was dependent on sound agriculture, and they favored the consolidation of small peasant holdings into larger, more efficient farms. Here as elsewhere there was a close relationship between the rationalism of the Enlightenment and the spirt of improvement at

work in eighteenth-century European economic life.

Adam Smith

The most important Enlightenment exposition of economics was Adam Smith's (1723–1790) *Inquiry into the Nature and Causes of the Wealth of Na-*

Adam Smith was one of the most important members of what may be called the Class of 1776—the astonishing outburst of British historical writing that centered on that year. In addition to Smith's Inquiry into the Nature and Causes of the Wealth of Nations, *Gibbon published the first volume of* The Decline and Fall, *Dr. Charles Burney (1726–1814) published the first volume of* A General History of Music *(completed in 1789), and Sir John Hawkins (1719–1789) managed to publish the entire five volumes of his* A General History of the Science and Practice of Music. *Moreover, in 1774, Thomas Warton (1728–1790) published the first volume of* The History of English Poetry *(third volume, 1781; never completed), while in 1777 the Scottish historian William Robertson (1721–1793) finished his career with the publication of his* History of America. *[Culver Pictures.]*

❧ Adam Smith Argues for Individual Industry and Wealth

Adam Smith (1723–1790) wanted to see a general, though not complete, application of individual self-interest to economic activity in place of existing mercantilist policies of state regulation. As he explained in this famous passage from *The Wealth of Nations* (1776), he thought that basically unregulated individual economic actions would produce more goods and services than mercantilist policy.

The annual revenue of every society is always precisely equal to the exchangeable value of the whole annual produce of its industry, or rather is precisely the same thing with that exchangeable value. As every individual, therefore, endeavours as much as he can both to employ his capital in the support of domestic industry, and so to direct that industry that its produce may be of the greatest value; every individual necessarily labours to render the annual revenue of the society as great as he can. He generally, indeed, neither intends to promote the public interest, nor knows how much he is promoting it. By prefer-ring the support of domestic to that of foreign industry, he intends only his own security; and by directing that industry in such a manner as its produce may be of the greatest value, he intends only his own gain, and he is in this, as in many other cases, led by an invisible hand to promote an end which was no part of his intention. Nor is it always the worse for the society that it was no part of it. By pursuing his own interest he frequently promotes that of the society more effectually than when he really intends to promote it. I have never known much good done by those who affected to trade for the public good.

Adam Smith, *The Wealth of Nations* (New York: Modern Library, 1965), p. 423.

---

tions (1776). Smith, who was for a time a professor at Glasgow, urged that the mercantile system of England—including the navigation acts, the bounties, most tariffs, special trading monopolies, and the domestic regulation of labor and manufacture—be abolished. Smith believed that these modes of economic regulation by the state interfered with the natural system of economic liberty. They were intended to preserve the wealth of the nation, to capture wealth from other nations, and to assure a maximum amount of work for the laborers of the country. However, Smith regarded such regulations as preventing the wealth and production of the country from expanding. He wanted to encourage economic growth and a consumer-oriented economy. The means to those ends was the unleashing of individuals to pursue their own selfish economic interest. The free pursuit of economic self-interest would ensure economic expansion as each person sought enrichment by meeting the demands of the marketplace. Consumers would find their wants met as manufacturers and merchants sought their business.

Smith's book challenged the concept of scarce goods and resources that lay behind mercantilism and the policies of the guilds. Smith saw the realm of nature as a boundless expanse of water, air, soil, and minerals. The physical resources of the earth seemed to demand exploitation for the enrichment and comfort of humankind. In effect, Smith was saying that the nations and peoples of Europe need not be poor. The idea of the infinite use of nature's goods for the material benefit of humankind—a concept that has dominated Western life until recent years—stemmed directly from the Enlightenment. When Smith wrote, the population of the world was smaller, its people were poorer, and the quantity of undeveloped resources per capita was much greater. For people of the eighteenth century it was in the uninhibited exploitation of natural resources that the true improvement of the human condition seemed to lie.

Smith is usually regarded as the founder of *laissez-faire* economic thought and policy, which has argued in favor of a very limited role for the government in economic life and regulation. However, *The Wealth of Nations* was a very complex book. Smith was no simple dogmatist. For example, he was not opposed to all government activity touching on the economy. The state should provide schools, armies, navies, and roads. It should also undertake certain commercial ventures, such as the opening of dangerous new trade routes, that were economically desirable but the expense or risk of which discouraged private enterprise. His reasonable tone and recognition of the complexity of social and economic life displayed a very important point about the *philosophes*. Most of them were much less rigid and doctrinaire than any brief summary of their thought may tend to suggest. They recognized the passions of humanity as well as its reason. They adopted reason and nature as tools of criticism through which they might create a climate of opinion that would allow the fully developed human personality to flourish.

Political Thought of the *Philosophes*

Nowhere did the appreciation of the complexity of the problems of contemporary society become more evident than in the *philosophes'* political thought. Nor did any other area of their reformist enterprise so clearly illustrate the tension and conflict within the "family" of the Enlightenment. Most *philosophes* were discontented with certain political features of their countries, but they were especially discontent in France. There the corruptness of the royal court, the blundering of the

Charles de Secondat Baron de Montesquieu (1689–1744) was the author of The Spirit of the Laws, *which may well have been the most influential work of political thought of the eighteenth century. [Bulloz.]*

bureaucracy, the less than glorious mid-century wars, and the power of the church compounded all problems. Consequently it was in France that the most important political thought of the Enlightenment occurred. However, the French *philosophes* stood quite divided as to the proper solution. Their attitudes spanned the whole spectrum from aristocratic reform to democracy to absolute monarchy.

The Spirit of the Laws

Montesquieu's *The Spirit of the Laws* (1748) may well have been the single most influential book of the century. It is a work that exhibits the internal tensions of the Enlightenment. Montesquieu pursued an empirical method, taking illustrative examples from the political experience of both ancient and modern nations. From these he concluded that there could be no single set of political laws that applied to all peoples at all times and in all places. Rather, there existed a large number of political variables, and the good political life depended on the relationship of those variables. Whether a monarchy or a republic was the best form of government was a matter of the size of the political unit and its population, its social and religious customs, its economic structure, its traditions, and its climate. Only a careful examination and evaluation of these elements could reveal what mode of government would prove most beneficial to a particular people. A century later such speculations would have been classified as sociology.

So far as France was concerned, Montesquieu had some rather definite ideas. He believed in monarchical government, but with a monarchy whose power was tempered and limited by various sets of intermediary institutions. The latter included the aristocracy, the towns, and the other corporate bodies that enjoyed particular liberties that the monarch must respect. These corporate bodies might be said to represent various segments of the general population and thus of public opinion. In France he regarded the aristocratic courts, or *parlements*, as the major example of an intermediary association. Their role was to limit the power of the monarchy and thus preserve the liberty of the subjects. In championing these aristocratic bodies and the general role of the aristocracy, Montesquieu was a political conservative. However, he adopted that stance in the hope of achieving reform, for in his opinion it was the oppressive and inefficient absolutism of the monarchy that accounted for the degradation of French life.

Montesquieu Defends the Separation of Powers

The Spirit of the Laws (1748) was probably the most influential political work of the Enlightenment. In this passage Montesquieu explained how the division of powers within a government would make that government more moderate and would protect the liberty of its subjects. This idea was adopted by the writers of the United States Constitution when they devised the checks and balances of the three branches of government.

Democratic and aristocratic states are not in their own nature free. Political liberty is to be found only in moderate governments; and even in these it is not always found. It is there only when there is no abuse of power. But constant experience shows us that every man invested with power is apt to abuse it, and to carry his authority as far as it will go. . . .

To prevent this abuse, it is necessary from the very nature of things that power should be a check to power. . . .

In every government there are three sorts of power: the legislative; the executive in respect to things dependent on the law of nations; and the executive in regard to matters that depend on the civil law [the realm of the judiciary]. . . .

The political liberty of the subject is a tranquillity of mind arising from the opinion each person has of his safety. In order to have this liberty, it is requisite that government be so constituted as one man need not be afraid of another.

When the legislative and executive powers are united in the same person, or in the same body of magistrates, there can be no liberty; because apprehensions may arise, lest the same monarch or senate should enact tyrannical laws, to execute them in a tyrannical manner.

Again, there is no liberty, if the judiciary power be not separated from the legislative and executive. Were it joined with the legislative, the life and liberty of the subject would be exposed to arbitrary control; for the judge would be then the legislator. Were it joined to the executive power, the judge might behave with violence and oppression.

There would be an end of everything, were the same man or the same body, whether of the nobles or of the people, to exercise those three powers, that of enacting laws, that of executing the public resolutions, and that of trying the causes of individuals.

Baron de Montesquieu, *The Spirit of the Laws,* trans. by Thomas Nugent (New York: Hafner Press, 1949), pp. 150–152.

One of Montesquieu's most influential ideas was that of division of power within any government. For his model of a government with power wisely separated among different branches, he took contemporary Great Britain. There he believed he had found a system in which executive power resided in the king, legislative power in the Parliament, and judicial power in the courts. He thought any two branches could check and balance the power of the other. His perception of the eighteenth-century British constitution was incorrect because he failed to see how patronage and electoral corruption allowed a handful of powerful aristocrats to dominate the government. Moreover he was also unaware of the emerging cabinet system, which meant that the executive power was slowly becoming a creature of the Parliament. Nevertheless the analysis illustrated Montesquieu's strong sense of the need to limit the exercise of power through constitutionalism and the formation of law by legislatures rather than by monarchs. In this manner, although Montesquieu set out to defend the political privileges of the French aristocracy, his ideas had a profound and still-lasting effect on the liberal democracies of the next two centuries.

Rousseau

Jean Jacques Rousseau (1712–1778) held a view of the exercise and reform of political power quite different from Montesquieu's.

Rousseau was a strange, isolated genius who never felt particularly comfortable with the other *philosophes.* Yet perhaps more than any other writer of the mid-eighteenth century he transcended the thought and values of his own time. Rousseau had a deep antipathy toward the world and the society in which he lived. It seemed impossible for human beings living according to contemporary commercial values to achieve moral, virtuous, or sincere lives. In 1750, in his *Discourse on the Moral Effects of the Arts and Sciences,* he contended that the process of civilization and enlightenment had corrupted human nature. Human beings in the state of nature had been more dignified. In 1755, in a *Discourse on the Origin of Inequality,* Rousseau blamed much of the evil in the world on maldistribution of property.

In both works Rousseau brilliantly and directly challenged the social fabric of the day. He drew into question the concepts of material and intellectual progress and the morality of a society in which commerce and industry were regarded as the most important of human activites. He felt that the real purpose of society was to nurture better people. In this respect Rousseau's vision of reform was much more radical than that of other contemporary writers. The other *philosophes* believed that human life would be improved if people could enjoy more of the fruits of the earth or could produce more

Jean-Jaques Rousseau (1712–1778). His writings raised some of the most profound social and ethical questions of the Enlightenment. This bust by Houdon is at Orleans. [Bulloz.]

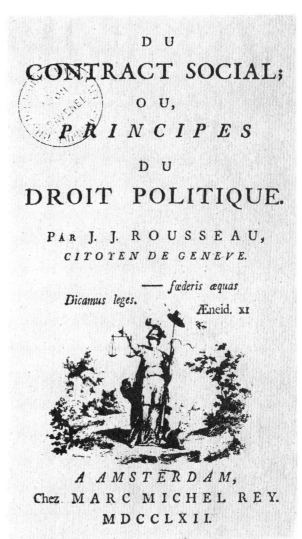

Rousseau's Social Contract *(1762) challenged the political thought of an aristocratic age by calling for radical political equality. Note that, like many other unorthodox works, it was published in relatively free Amsterdam. [The Granger Collection.]*

goods. Rousseau raised the more fundamental question of what the good life is. This question has haunted European social thought ever since the eighteenth century. Much of the criticism of Europe's post-World War II society is rooted in this Rousseauean approach.

Rousseau carried these same concerns into his political thought. His most extensive discussion of politics appeared in *The Social Contract* (1762). Although the book attracted rather little immediate

❧ Rousseau Argues that Inequality Is Not Natural

Jean Jacques Rousseau was one of the first writers to assert the social equality of human beings. He argued, as in this 1755 passage, that inequality had developed through the ages and was not "natural." He directly questioned the sanctity of property based on the assumed natural inequality of human beings.

I have endeavoured to trace the origin and progress of inequality, and the institution and abuse of political societies, as far as these are capable of being deduced from the nature of man merely by the light of reason, and independently of those sacred dogmas which give the sanction of divine right to sovereign authority. It follows from this survey that, as there is hardly any inequality in the state of nature, all the inequality which now prevails owes its strength and growth to the development of our faculties and the advance of the human mind, and becomes at last permanent and legitimate by the establishment of property and laws. Secondly, it follows that moral inequality, authorized by positive right alone, clashes with natural right, whenever it is not proportionate to physical inequality—a distinction which sufficiently determines what we think of that species of inequality which prevails in all civilized countries; since it is plainly contrary to the law of nature, however defined, that children should command old men, fools wise men, and that the privileged few should gorge themselves with superfluities while the starving multitude are in want of the bare necessities of life.

Jean Jacques Rousseau, *The Social Contract and Discourses,* trans. by G. D. H. Cole (New York: Dutton, 1950), pp. 271–272.

---

attention, by the end of the century it was widely read in France. *The Social Contract,* as compared to Montesquieu's *Spirit of the Laws,* was a very abstract book. It did not propose specific reforms but outlined the kind of political structure that Rousseau believed would overcome the evils of contemporary politics and society.

In the tradition of Thomas Hobbes and John Locke, most eighteenth-century political thinkers, regarded human beings as individuals and society as a collection of such independent individuals pursuing personal, selfish goals. These writers wished to liberate these individuals from the undue bonds of government. Rousseau picked up the stick from the other end. His book opens with the declaration, "All men are born free, but everywhere they are in chains."[5] The rest of the volume constitutes a *defense* of the chains of a properly organized society over its members. Rousseau suggested that society is more important than its individual members, because they are what they are only because of their relationship to the larger community. Independent human beings living

---

[5] Jean Jacques Rousseau, *The Social Contract and Discourses,* trans. by G. D. H. Cole (New York: Dutton, 1950), p. 3.

alone can achieve very little. Through their relationship to the larger community, they become moral creatures capable of significant action. The question then becomes what kind of community allows people to behave morally. In his two previous discourses Rousseau had explained that contemporary European society was not such a community. It was merely an aggregate of competing individuals whose chief social goal was to preserve selfish independence in spite of all potential social bonds and obligations.

Rousseau sought to project the vision of a society in which each person could maintain personal freedom while at the same time behaving as a loyal member of the larger community. To that end Rousseau drew on the traditions of Plato and Calvin to define freedom as obedience to law. In his case the law to be obeyed was that created by the general will. This concept normally indicated the will of the majority of voting citizens who acted with adequate information and under the influence of virtuous customs and morals. Such democratic participation in decision making would bind the individual citizen to the community. Rousseau believed that the general will must always be right and that to obey the general will was to be free.

This argument led him to the notorious conclusion that under certain circumstances some people must be forced to be free. Rousseau's politics thus constituted a justification for radical direct democracy and for collective action against individual citizens.

Rousseau had in effect launched an assault on the eighteenth-century cult of the individual and the fruits of selfishness. He stood at odds with the commercial spirit that was transforming the society in which he lived. Rousseau would have disapproved of the main thrust of Adam Smith's *Wealth of Nations,* which he may or may not have read, and would no doubt have preferred a study on the virtue of nations. Smith wanted people to be prosperous; Rousseau wanted them to be good even if being good meant that they might remain economically poor. He saw human beings not as independent individuals but as creatures enmeshed in necessary social relationships. He believed that loyalty to the community should be encouraged. As one device to that end he suggested a civic religion based on the creed of deism. Such a shared tolerant religious faith would provide unity for the society. Rousseau's chief intellectual inspiration arose from his study of Plato and the ancient Greek *polis.* Especially in Sparta he thought he had discovered human beings dwelling in a moral society inspired by a common purpose. He hoped that modern human beings might also create such a moral commonwealth in which virtuous living would become subordinate to commercial profit.

Rousseau's thought had only a marginal impact on his own time. The other *philosophes* questioned his critique of material improvement. Aristocrats and royal ministers could hardly be expected to welcome his proposal for radical democracy. Too many people were either making or hoping to make money to pay attention to his criticism of commercial values. However, he proved to be a figure to whom later generations returned. Many leaders in the French Revolution were familiar with his writing. Thereafter his ideas were important to most writers who felt called on to criticize the general tenor and direction of Western culture. Rousseau hated much about the emerging modern society in Europe, but he contributed much to modernity by exemplifying for later generations the critic who dared to call into question the very foundations of social thought and action. Whatever our opinions of Rousseau, we have not yet escaped him.

Enlightened Absolutism

Most of the *philosophes* favored neither Montesquieu's reformed and revived aristocracy nor Rousseau's democracy as a solution to contemporary political problems. Like other thoughtful people of the day in other stations and occupations, they looked to the existing monarchies. The *philosophes* hoped in particular that the French monarchy might assert really effective power over the aristocracy and the church to bring about significant reform. Voltaire was a very strong monarchist. He and others—such as Diderot, who visited Catherine II of Russia, and physiocrats who were ministers to the French kings—did not wish to limit the power of monarchs but sought to redirect that power toward the rationalization of economic and political structures and the liberation of intellectual life. Most *philosophes* were not opposed to power if they could find a way of using it for their own purposes.

During the last third of the century it seemed to some observers that several European rulers had actually embraced many of the reforms set forth by the *philosophes. Enlightened absolutism* is the term used to describe this phenomenon. The phrase indicates monarchical government dedicated to the rational strengthening of the central absolutist administration at the cost of other lesser centers of political power. However, the monarchs most closely associated with it—Frederick II of Prussia, Joseph II of Austria, and Catherine II of Russia—were neither genuinely enlightened nor truly absolute in the exercise of royal power. Their enlightenment was a veneer, and the realities of political and economic life limited their absolutism. Frederick II corresponded with the *philosophes,* for a time provided Voltaire with a place at his court, and even wrote history and political tracts. Catherine II, who was a master of what would later be called public relations, consciously sought to create the image of being enlightened. She read the works of the *philosophes,* became a friend of Diderot and Voltaire, and made frequent references to their ideas, all in the hope that her nation might seem more modern and Western. Joseph II undertook a series of religious, legal, and social reforms that contemporaries believed he had derived from suggestions of the *philosophes.*

Despite such appearances the requirements of state security and political ambition rather than the humanitarian and liberating zeal of the Enlightenment directed the policies of these monarchs. They sought the rational economic and social integration of their realms so that they could wage more efficient future wars—a policy profoundly hateful to the *philosophes*. All of the states of Europe had emerged from the Seven Years' War understanding that they would require stronger armed forces for the next conflict and looking for new sources of taxation to finance those armies. The search for new revenues and further internal political support for their rule led these eastern European monarchs to make "enlightened" reforms. They and their advisers used rationality to further what the *philosophes* considered irrational militarism.

Frederick the Great of Prussia

After the mid-century wars, during which Prussia had suffered badly and had almost been defeated, Frederick II (1740–1786) hoped to achieve recovery and consolidation. At grave military and financial cost he had succeeded in retaining Silesia, which he had seized from Austria in 1740. He worked to stimulate its potential as a manufacturing district. Like his Hohenzollern forebears he continued to import workers from outside Prussia. He directed new attention to Prussian agriculture. Under state supervision, swamps were drained, new crops introduced, and peasants encouraged and sometimes compelled to migrate. For the first time in Prussia potatoes and turnips came into general production. Frederick also established a Land-Mortgage Credit Association to aid landowners in raising money for agricultural improvements.

Throughout this process, the impetus for development came from the state. The monarchy and its bureaucracy were the engine for change. Despite new policies and personal exhortations the general populace of Prussia did not prosper under Frederick's reign. The burden of taxation still fell disproportionally on peasants and townspeople.

In less material areas Frederick pursued enlightened policies with somewhat more success. He allowed Catholics and Jews to settle in his predominately Lutheran country, and he protected the Catholics residing in Silesia. He ordered a new codification of Prussian law, which was completed after his death. The policy of toleration allowed foreign workers to contribute to the economic growth of the state. The new legal code was to rationalize the existing system, to make it more efficient, to eliminate regional peculiarities, and to eliminate excessive aristocratic influence. The enlightened monarchs were very concerned about legal reforms, primarily as a means of extending and strengthening royal power.

Frederick liked to describe himself as "the first servant of the State." That image represented an important change in the European conception of monarchy. The idea of an impersonal state was beginning to replace the concept of a personal monarchy. Kings might come and go, but the impersonal apparatus of government—the bureaucracy, the armies, the laws, the courts, and the citizens' loyalty arising from fear and from appreciation of state services and protection—remained. The state as an entity separate from the personality of the ruler came into its own after the French Revolution, but it was born in the monarchies of the old regime.

Joseph II of Austria

No eighteenth-century ruler so embodied rational, impersonal force as the emperor Joseph II of Austria. He was the son of Maria Theresa and co-ruler with her from 1765 to 1780. During the next ten years he ruled alone. He has been aptly described as "an imperial puritan and a good deal of a prig."[6] During much of his life he slept on straw and ate little but beef. He prided himself on a narrow, passionless rationality, which he sought to impose by his own will on the various Hapsburg domains. Despite his eccentricities and the coldness of his personality Joseph II genuinely and sincerely wished to improve the lot of his people. He was much less a political opportunist and cynic than either Frederick the Great of Prussia or Catherine the Great of Russia. The ultimate result of his well-intentioned efforts was a series of aristocratic and peasant rebellions extending from Hungary to the Austrian Netherlands.

As explained in Chapter 20, of all the rising states of the eighteenth century, Austria was the most diverse in its people and problems. Robert Palmer has likened it to "a vast holding company."[7] The Hapsburgs never succeeded in creat-

[6] R. J. White, *Europe in the Eighteenth Century* (New York: St. Martin's, 1965), p. 214.
[7] Robert R. Palmer, *The Age of the Democratic Revolution*, Vol. 1 (Princeton N.J.: Princeton University Press, 1959), p. 103.

ing either a unified administrative structure or a strong aristocratic loyalty. The price of the preservation of the monarchy during the War of the Austrian Succession (1740–1748) had been guarantees of considerable aristocratic independence. Joseph sought to overcome the pluralism of his holdings by increasing the power of the central monarchy. He also wished to expand the borders of his territory in the direction of Poland and the Ottoman Empire.

The first target of Joseph's reassertion of royal absolutism was the church. From the reign of Charles V in the sixteenth century to that of Maria Theresa, the Hapsburgs had been the single most important dynastic champion of Roman Catholicism. Maria Theresa had surrounded herself with pious and sometimes very superstitious advisers. Joseph changed these policies. He was a practicing and perhaps even a believing Catholic, but he rid himself of priestly advisers. He extended genuine toleration to all Christians and relieved the Jews living in Austria of many special taxes and signs of degradation. He sought to undermine in every possible way the influence of the papacy in his lands. He drove monks and nuns from monasteries and reduced the number of religious holidays. While encouraging the construction of churches, he confiscated ecclesiastical lands. He considered church use of that property unproductive. Revenues tradi-

tionally going to the church were redirected to the state. Priests, in effect, became the employees of the state. The influence of the Roman Catholic Church as an independent institution came to a close. Joseph was willing to have religious faith and practice flourish, but religious institutions and the people they employed must stand subordinate to the power of the government. In many respects the ecclesiastical policies of Joseph II prefigured those of the French Revolution.

Like Frederick of Prussia, Joseph sought to improve the economic life of his domains. He abolished many internal tariffs and encouraged road building and the improvement of river transport. He went on personal inspection tours of farms and manufacturing districts. Joseph also reconstructed the judicial system to make laws more uniform and rational and to lessen the influence of local landlords. National courts with power over the landlord courts were established. All of these improvements were expected to bring new unity to the state and more taxes into the coffers at Vienna.

The most revolutionary of Joseph's departures was his attitude toward serfdom and the land. The emperor believed that if the peasantry were legally free and to some extent liberated from special feudal payments to their landlords, they would become more productive and industrious. However, to interfere with the landlord–serf relation-

Emperor Joseph II of Austria encouraged improved farming and industry in his domains. This propaganda painting portrayed him plowing a field and providing a good example to his subjects. [Austrian Information Service, New York.]

❧ Joseph II of Austria Promotes Toleration in His Realm ━━━

Toleration was frequently an important policy of enlightened absolutism and the area of political action that most directly reflected the influence of the *philosophes*. As shown in this 1787 passage, Joseph II of Austria believed that toleration would remove religious fanaticism from his realms, lead to greater human knowledge, and at the same time make his subjects more loyal. The reader may wish to compare this statement with Voltaire's attack on religious fanaticism that appears earlier in this chapter.

Till now the Protestant religion has been opposed in my states; its adherents have been treated like foreigners; civil rights, possession of estates, titles, and appointments, all were refused them.

I determined from the very commencement of my reign to adorn my diadem with the love of my people, to act in the administration of affairs according to just, impartial, and liberal principles; consequently, I granted toleration, and removed the yoke which had oppressed the protestants for centuries.

Fanaticism shall in future be known in my states only by the contempt I have for it; nobody shall any longer be exposed to hardships on account of his creed; no man shall be compelled in future to profess the religion of the state, if it be contrary to his persuasion, and if he have other ideas of the right way of insuring blessedness. . . .

Tolerance is an effect of that beneficent increase of knowledge which now enlightens Europe, and which is owing to philosophy and the efforts of great men; it is a convincing proof of the improvement of the human mind, which has boldly reopened a road through the dominions of superstition, which was trodden centuries ago by Zoroaster and Confucius, and which, fortunately for mankind, has now become the highway of monarchs.

"Letters of Joseph II," *The Pamphleteer*, Vol. 19 (1822), pp. 289–290.

ship was to breach what had been one of the foundation stones of eastern European absolutism: the trade-off of aristocratic support for the monarchy in exchange for a free hand with the serfs.

In 1781, 1783, and 1785 Joseph issued a series of decrees giving legal freedom to the serfs in Bohemia, Austria, Transylvania, and Hungary. They could marry and migrate without the permission of their landlords and could appeal decisions from manorial courts to the civil courts of the state. Between 1783 and 1789 Joseph went even further and drew up a tax list on which all occupiers of land were enumerated. Henceforth all proprietors of the land were to be taxed regardless of social status. In 1789 by royal decree the emperor abolished *robot*, or the services due landlords from their serfs. The service was commuted to a tax, only part of which went to the landlord, while the remainder reverted to the state. These measures brought turmoil to the Hapsburg domains. Peasants revolted against their landlords over the interpretation of their newly granted rights. Then the nobles of the various realms also rose up in rebellion over the emperor's decrees.

Having sowed the wind, Joseph died in 1790. His brother and successor, Leopold II (1790–1792), reaped the noble whirlwind. Although quite sympathetic with Joseph's goals, Leopold repealed most of the reformist decrees to shore up the stability of his own rule. Serfdom or feudal obligations persisted in most of the Hapsburg lands until 1848. Joseph II had possessed a narrow vision attached to an unbending will. For all his intellectual brilliance and hard work he had failed to understand that his policies enjoyed no supporters except for a few royal bureaucrats. He had ruled without consulting any political constituency. The nobles, the church, the towns with their chartered liberties, and the absence of a strong bureaucracy or army stood as barriers to his absolutism. His was a mind of classical rationalism in conflict with political and social realities of baroque complexity.

Catherine the Great of Russia

Joseph II never grasped the practical necessity of cultivating political support for his policies. Catherine II (1762–1796), who had been born a

German princess but who became empress of Russia, understood only too well the fragility of the Romanov dynasty's base of power.

After the death of Peter the Great in 1725 the court nobles and the army had repeatedly determined the Russian succession. As a result, the crown fell primarily into the hands of people with little talent. Peter's wife, Catherine I, ruled for two years (1725–1727) and was succeeded for three years by Peter's grandson Peter II. In 1730 the crown devolved on Anna, who was a niece of Peter the Great. During 1740 and 1741 a child named Ivan VI, who was less than a year old, was the nominal ruler. Finally in 1741 Peter the Great's daughter Elizabeth came to the throne. She held the title of empress until 1762, but she did not rule. Her court was a shambles of political and romantic intrigue. Needless to say, much of the power possessed by the czar at the opening of the century had vanished.

At her death in 1762 Elizabeth was succeeded by Peter III, one of her nephews. He was a weak ruler whom many contemporaries considered mad. He immediately exempted the nobles from compulsory military service and then made rapid peace with Frederick the Great, for whom he held unbounded admiration. That decision probably saved Prussia from military defeat. The one positive feature of this unbalanced creature's life was his marriage in 1745 to a young German princess born in Pomerania. This was the future Catherine the Great, who for almost twenty years lived in misery and frequent danger at the court of Elizabeth. During that time she befriended important nobles and read widely in the books of the *philosophes*. She was a shrewd person whose experience in a court crawling with rumors, intrigue, and conspiracy had taught her how to survive. She had neither love nor loyalty for her demented husband. After a few months of rule Peter III was deposed and murdered with the approval, if not the aid, of Catherine. On his deposition she was immediately proclaimed empress.

Catherine's familiarity with the Enlightenment and the general culture of western Europe convinced her that Russia was very backward and that it must make major reforms if it were to remain a great power. She understood that any major reform must have a wide base of political and social support. In 1767 she summoned a Legislative Commission to revise the law and government of Russia. There were over five hundred delegates from all sectors of Russian life. Prior to the conven-

EXPANSION OF RUSSIA,
1689–1796

MAP 21.1 *The overriding territorial aim of Peter the Great in the first quarter and of Catherine the Great in the last half of the eighteenth century was the securing of northern and southern navigable-water outlets for the vast Russian Empire. Hence Peter's push to the Baltic Sea and Catherine's to the Black Sea. Catherine also managed to acquire large areas of Poland through the partitions of that country.*

639

Empress Catherine the Great of Russia, born Sophia Augusta Frederica in the tiny German state of Anhalt-Zerbst, cultivated the friendship of the philosophes *but pursued many policies of which they disapproved, including warfare and censorship. The artist represented here is Boroviloosky.* [*John R. Freeman.*]

ing of the commission she issued a set of *Instructions* partly written by herself. They contained numerous ideas drawn from the political writings of the *philosophes.* The commission considered the *Instructions* as well as other ideas and complaints raised by its members. The revision of Russian law, however, did not occur for more than a half-century. In 1768 Catherine simply dismissed the commission, which had reached few concrete decisions. Yet the meeting had not been useless, for considerable information had been gathered about the condition of the realm. The inconclusive debates and the absence of programs from the delegates themselves suggested that most Russians saw no alternative to an autocratic monarchy.

Catherine proceeded to carry out limited reforms on her own authority. She gave strong support to the rights and local power of the nobility. In 1775 she reorganized local government to solve problems brought to light by the Legislative Commission. She put most local offices into the hands of nobles rather than creating a royal bureaucracy. In 1785 Catherine issued the Charter of the Nobil-

RUSSIA FROM PETER THE GREAT THROUGH CATHERINE THE GREAT

1725	Death of Peter the Great
1725–1727	Catherine I
1727–1730	Peter II
1730–1741	Anna
1740–1741	Ivan VI
1741–1762	Elizabeth
1762	Peter III
1762	Catherine II (the Great) becomes empress
1767	Legislative Commission summoned
1769	War with Turkey
1771–1775	Pugachev's Rebellion
1772	First Partition of Poland
1774	Treaty of Kuchuk-Kainardji ends war with Turkey
1775	Reorganization of local government
1783	Russia annexes the Crimea
1785	Catherine issues the Charter of the Nobility
1793	Second Partition of Poland
1795	Third Partition of Poland
1796	Death of Catherine the Great

ity, which guaranteed many noble rights and privileges. In part the empress had no choice but to favor the nobles. They had the capacity to topple her from the throne. There were too few educated subjects in her realm to establish an independent bureaucracy, and the treasury could not afford an army strictly loyal to the crown. So Catherine wisely made a virtue of necessity. She strengthened the stability of her crown by making convenient friends with her nobles.

Part and parcel of Catherine's program was a continuation of the economic development begun under Peter the Great. She attempted to suppress internal barriers to trade. Exports of grain, flax, furs, and naval stores grew dramatically. She also favored the expansion of the small Russian middle class. Russian trade required such a vital urban class. And through all of these departures Catherine attempted to maintain ties of friendship and correspondence with the *philosophes*. She knew that if she treated them kindly, they would be sufficiently flattered and would give her a progressive reputation throughout Europe.

The limited administrative reforms and the policy of economic growth had a counterpart in the diplomatic sphere. The Russian drive for warm-water ports continued. This goal required warfare with the Turks. In 1769, as a result of a minor Russian incursion, the Ottoman empire declared war on Russia. The Russians responded in a series of strikingly successful military moves. During 1769 and 1770 the Russian fleet sailed all the way from the Baltic Sea into the eastern Mediterranean. The Russian army won several major victories that by 1771 gave Russia control of Ottoman provinces on the Danube River and the Crimean coast of the Black Sea. The conflict dragged on until 1774, when it was closed by the Treaty of Kuchuk-Kainardji. The treaty gave Russia a direct outlet on the Black Sea, free navigation rights in its waters, and free access through the Bosporus. Moreover, the province of the Crimea became an independent state, which Catherine painlessly annexed in 1783.

The Partition of Poland

These military successes obviously brought the empress much domestic political support. However, they made the other states of eastern Europe uneasy. These anxieties were overcome by an extraordinary division of Polish territory known as the First Partition of Poland. The Russian victories

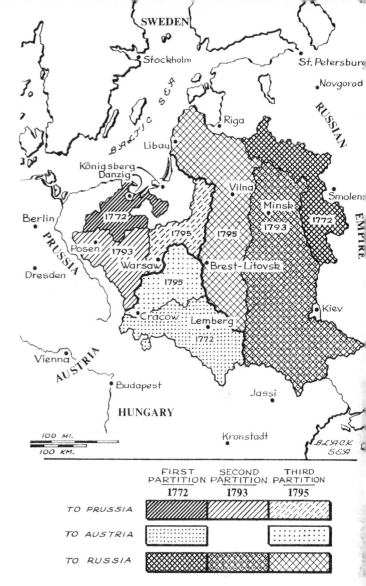

	FIRST PARTITION 1772	SECOND PARTITION 1793	THIRD PARTITION 1795
TO PRUSSIA			
TO AUSTRIA			
TO RUSSIA			

PARTITIONS OF POLAND, 1772–1793–1795

MAP 21.2 *The callous eradication of Poland from the map displayed eighteenth-century power politics at its most extreme. Poland, without strong central governmental institutions, fell victim to those states in central and eastern Europe that had developed such institutions.*

along the Danube River were most unwelcome to Austria, which also harbored ambitions of territorial expansion in that direction. At the same time, the Ottoman Empire was pressing Prussia for aid against Russia. Frederick the Great made a proposal to Russia and Austria that would give each something it wanted, prevent conflict among the

This French engraving is a satirical comment on the first partition of Poland (1772) by Russia, Austria, and Prussia. The distressed monarch attempting to retain his crown is Stanislaus of Poland. Catherine of Russia, Joseph of Austria, and Frederick of Prussia point out their respective shares of the loot.

powers, and save appearances. After long, complicated, secret negotiations the three powers agreed that Russia would abandon the conquered Danubian provinces. In compensation Russia received a large portion of Polish territory with almost two million inhabitants. As a reward for remaining neutral Prussia annexed most of the territory between East Prussia and Prussia proper. This land allowed Frederick to unite two previously separate sections of his realm. Finally, Austria took Galicia, with its important salt mines, and other Polish territory with over two and one-half million inhabitants. In September 1772 the helpless Polish aristocracy, paying the price for the maintenance of their internal liberties, ratified this seizure of their territory. The Polish state had lost approximately one third of its territory.

There were two additional partitions of Poland by Russia and Prussia, and one more by Austria. These occurred in 1793 and 1795 and removed Poland from the map of Europe. Each time the great powers contended that they were saving themselves and by implication the rest of Europe from Polish anarchy. The fact of the matter was that the political weakness of Poland made the country and its resources a rich field for plunderous aggression. The last two partitions took place during the French Revolution. The three eastern European absolute monarchies objected to certain reforms undertaken by the Polish nobles for fear that even minor Polish reform might endanger the stability of their own societies.

The End of the Eighteenth Century in Eastern Europe

During the last quarter of the eighteenth century all three regimes based on enlightened absolutism had become more repressive. Frederick lived much removed from his people during his old age. The aristocracy, looking out for its own self-interest, filled the major Prussian military and administrative posts. As Joseph II confronted growing frustration and political unrest over his plans for restructuring the society of his realms, he used more and more censorship and secret police. Catherine the Great never fully recovered from the fears raised by Pugachev's rebellion. Once the French Revolution broke out in 1789, the Russian empress censored books based on Enlightenment thought and sent offensive authors into Siberian exile.

By the close of the century all three states were characterized by autocracy, censorship, increasingly downtrodden serf populations, grasping nobilities, and fear of change permeating all the ruling classes. These attitudes had come into existence prior to 1789, but the events in France froze those points of view for almost half a century. Paradoxically nowhere did the humanity and liberalism of the Enlightenment ultimately have a more difficult time surviving and entering the mainstream of life and thought than in those states that had had "enlightened" rulers.

Although the enlightened absolute monarchs lacked the humanity of the *philosophes*, they had embraced the Enlightenment spirit of innovation. They wanted to change the political, social, and economic structures of their realms. From the close of the Seven Years' War (1763) until the opening of the French Revolution in 1789, the monarchies of both western and eastern Europe had been the major forces working for significant institutional change. In every case they had stirred up considerable aristocratic and some popular resistance and resentment. George III of Britain fought for years with Parliament and lost the colonies of North America in the process. Frederick II of Prussia carried out his program of reform only because he accepted new aristocratic influence over the bureaucracy and the army. Catherine II of Russia had had to come to terms with her nobility. Joseph II had left his domains in turmoil by imposing changes without consulting the nobility.

These monarchs pushed for innovations because of their desires for increased revenue. The same problem existed in France. There the royal drive for adequate fiscal resources also led to aristocratic rebellion. However, in France neither the monarchy nor the aristocracy could control the social and political forces unleashed by their quarrel.

Suggested Readings

C. BECKER, *The Heavenly City of the Eighteenth Century Philosophers* (1932). An influential, but very controversial discussion.

P. P. BERNARD, *Joseph II* (1968). A brief biography.

T. BESTERMANN, *Voltaire* (1969). A recent biography by the editor of Voltaire's letters.

E. CASSIRER, *The Philosophy of the Enlightenment* (1951). A brilliant but difficult work by one of the great philosophers of the twentieth century.

G. R. CRAGG, *The Church and the Age of Reason* (1961). A general survey of eighteenth-century religious life.

R. DARNTON, *The Business of Enlightenment: A Publishing History of the Encyclopedia*, 1775–1800 (1979). A wide-ranging examination of the printing and dispersion of the *Encyclopedia*.

P. FUSSELL, *The Rhetorical World of Augustan Humanism* (1969). Examines English writers during the Enlightenment.

J. GAGLIARDO, *Enlightened Despotism* (1967). A discussion of the subject in its European context.

P. GAY, *The Enlightenment: An Interpretation*, 2 vols. (1966, 1969). The most important and far-reaching recent treatment.

P. GAY, *The Enlightenment: A Comprehensive Anthology* (1973). A large, well-edited set of documents.

L. GERSHOY, *From Despotism to Revolution*, 1763–1793 (1944). A sound treatment of the political background.

N. HAMPSON, *A Cultural History of the Enlightenment* (1969). A useful introduction.

P. HAZARD, *The European Mind: The Critical Years*, 1680–1715 (1935), and *European Thought in the Eighteenth Century from Montesquieu to Lessing* (1946). The two volumes portray the century as the turning point for the emergence of the modern mind in Europe.

H. C. JOHNSON, *Frederick the Great and His Officials* (1975). An examination of the administrative apparatus of enlightened absolutism.

R. KREISER, *Miracles, Convulsions, and Ecclesiastical Politics in Early Eighteenth-Century Paris* (1978). An important study of the kind of religious life that the *philosophes* opposed.

L. KRIEGER, *Kings and Philosophers*, 1689–1789 (1970). A survey that relates the social and political thought of the Enlightenment writers to their immediate political setting.

I. DE MADARIAGE, *Russia in the Age of Catherine the Great* (1981). The best discussion in English.

F. MANUEL, *The Eighteenth Century Confronts the Gods* (1959). A broad examination of the *philosophes'* treatment of Christian and pagan religion.

R. R. PALMER, *Catholics and Unbelievers in Eighteenth Century France* (1939). A discussion of the opponents of the *philosophes*.

G. RITTER, *Frederick the Great* (trans. 1968). A useful biography.

R. O. ROCKWOOD (Ed.), *Carl Becker's Heavenly City Revisited* (1958). Important essays qualifying Becker's thesis.

J. N. SHKLAR, *Men and Citizens, a Study of Rousseau's Social Theory* (1969). A thoughtful and provocative overview of Rousseau's political thought.

A. M. WILSON, *Diderot* (1972). A splendid biography of the person behind the project for the *Encyclopedia* and other major Enlightenment publications.

L'ABOLITION DES TITRES DE NOBLESSE
par le Decret de l'Assemblée Nationale en juin 1790.

Des Aristocrates l'engeance est allarmée
Grands titres, vains honneurs, vous n'êtes que fumée
Qui se seroit douté d'un tel evenement.
C'est ainsi que chez nous la pluïe abat le vent.

644

22 The French Revolution

I N THE spring of 1789 the long-festering conflict between the French monarchy and aristocracy erupted into a new political crisis. This dispute, unlike earlier ones, quickly outgrew the issues of its origins and produced the wider disruption of the French Revolution. The quarrel that began as a struggle between the most exclusive elements of the political nation soon involved all sectors of French society and eventually every major state in Europe. Before the turmoil settled, small-town provincial lawyers and Parisian street orators exercised more influence over the fate of the Continent than did aristocrats, royal ministers, or monarchs. Armies commanded by persons of low birth and filled by conscripted village youths emerged victorious over forces composed of professional soldiers and directed by officers of noble birth. The very

In this French cartoon of 1790, rats and flames consume the symbols of aristocratic privilege. The abolition of titles of nobility and of feudal dues was a major step toward the Revolution's goal of establishing the equality of all Frenchmen before the law. [Editorial Photocolor Archives.]

existence of the Roman Catholic faith in France was challenged. Politically and socially neither France nor Europe would ever be quite the same after these events.

The Crisis of the French Monarchy

Although the French Revolution constituted one of the central turning points in modern European history, it originated from the basic tensions and problems that characterized practically all late eighteenth-century states. From the Seven Years' War (1756–1763) onward, the French monarchy was unable to handle its finances on a sound basis. It emerged from the conflict both defeated and in debt. The French support of the American revolt against Great Britain further deepened the financial difficulties of the government. On the eve of the revolution the interest and payments on the royal debt amounted to just over one half of the entire budget. The annual deficit was in the vicinity of 126 million livres. Given the economic vitality of the nation, this debt was neither overly large nor disproportionate to the debts of other European powers. The problem lay with the inability of the royal government to tap the wealth of the French nation through taxes to service and repay the debt. Paradoxically France was a rich nation with an impoverished government.

The debt was symptomatic of the failure of the eighteenth-century French monarchy to come to terms with the resurgent social and political power of the aristocracy. For twenty-five years after the Seven Years' War there was a standoff between them. The monarchy attempted to pursue a program somewhat resembling that associated with enlightened absolutism in eastern Europe. However, both Louis XV (1715–1774) and Louis XVI (1774–1792) lacked the character and the resolution for such a departure. The moral corruption of the former and the indecision of the latter meant that the monarchy could not rally the French public to its side.

In place of a consistent policy to deal with the growing debt, the monarchy gave way to hesitancy, retreat, and even duplicity. In 1763 the monarchy issued a new set of tax decrees that would have extended the collection of certain taxes that were supposed to have been discontinued at the close of the war. There were also new tax assessments. This search for revenue was not unlike the one that led the British government to attempt to tax the American colonies. Several of the provincial *parlements* and finally the *Parlement* of Paris—all controlled by nobles—declared the taxes illegal. During the ensuing dispute the aristocratic *parlements* set themselves up as the spokesmen of the nation and as the protectors of French liberty against the illegal assertion of monarchical power. This was one of the political functions of the nobility that Montesquieu had outlined in *The Spirit of the Laws* (1748).

In 1770 Louis XV appointed René Maupeou (1714–1792) as chancellor. The new minister was determined to break the *parlements* and impose a greater part of the tax burden on the nobility. He abolished the *parlements* and exiled their members to different parts of the country. He then commenced an ambitious program of reform and efficiency. What ultimately doomed Maupeou's policy was less the resistance of the nobility than the death of Louis XV in 1774. His successor, Louis XVI, in an attempt to regain what he conceived to be popu-

lar support, restored all the *parlements* and confirmed their old powers. This action, in conjunction with the later aid to the American colonies, locked the monarchy into a continuing financial bind. Thereafter meaningful fiscal or political reform through existing institutions was probably doomed.

Louis XVI's first minister was the physiocrat Jacques Turgot (1727–1781), who attempted various economic reforms, including the removal of restrictions on the grain trade and the elimination of the guilds. He transformed the *corvée*, or road-working obligation of peasants, into money payments. Turgot also intended to restructure the taxation system in order to tap the wealth of the nobility. These and other ideas represented a program of bold new departures for the monarchy. They proved too bold for the tremulous young king, who dismissed Turgot in 1776. By 1781 the debt, as a result of the aid to America, was larger and the sources of revenues were unchanged. However, the new director-general of finances, Jacques Necker (1732–1804), a Swiss banker, produced a public report that suggested that the situation was not so bad as had been feared. He argued that if the expenditures for the American war were removed, the budget was in surplus. However, Necker's report also revealed that a large portion of the royal expenditure went to pensions for aristocrats and other royal court favorites. This infor-

Louis XVI of France (1774–1792) was unable to regain control of the political situation in France after the summer of 1789. The drawing is by Ducreux. [French Cultural Services, New York.]

Queen Marie Antoinette (1755–1793) was the daughter of Empress Maria Theresa of Austria and the wife of Louis XVI. Around her gathered many of the popularly believed unfavorable stories of the French court. The painting is by Elisabeth Vigée-Lebrun (1755–1842). [The Granger Collection.]

mation aroused the anger of court aristocratic circles against the banker, who soon left office. His financial sleight of hand, nonetheless, made it more difficult for later government officials to claim a real need to raise new taxes.

The monarchy hobbled along until 1786. By this time Charles Alexandre de Calonne (1734–1802) was the minister of finance. He was probably the most able administrator to serve Louis XVI. More carefully than previous ministers he charted the size of the debt and the deficit. He submitted a program for reform quite similar to that presented by Turgot a decade earlier. Calonne proposed to encourage internal trade, to lower some taxes such as the *gabelle* on salt, and to transform peasants' services to money payments.

More important, Calonne urged the introduction of a new land tax that would require payments from all landowners regardless of their social status. If this tax could have been imposed, the monarchy would have been able to abandon other indirect taxes. The government would also rarely have had to seek approval for further new taxes from the aristocratically dominated *parlements*. Calonne also intended to establish new local assemblies to approve land taxes; in these assemblies the voting

power would depend on the amount of land owned rather than on the social status of the owner. All these proposals would have undermined both the political and the social power of the French aristocracy.

A new clash with the nobility was unavoidable, and the monarchy had very little room for maneuver. The creditors were at the door; the treasury was nearly empty. Consequently, in 1787 Calonne met with an Assembly of Notables drawn from the upper ranks of the aristocracy and the church to seek support and approval for his plan. The assembly adamantly refused any such action; rather, it demanded that the aristocracy be allowed a greater share in the direct government of the kingdom. The notables called for the reappointment of Necker, who they believed had left the country in sound fiscal condition. Finally, they claimed that they had no right to consent to new taxes and that such a right was vested only in the medieval institution of the Estates General of France, which had not met since 1614. The notables believed that the calling of the Estates General, which was traditionally organized to allow aristocratic and church dominance, would produce a victory for the nobility over the monarchy.

Again Louis XVI backed off. He dismissed Calonne and replaced him with Étienne Charles Loménie de Brienne (1727–1794), who was archbishop of Toulouse and the chief opponent of Calonne at the Assembly of Notables. Once in office Brienne found to his astonishment that the situation was as bad as his predecessor had asserted. Brienne himself now sought to impose the land tax. However, the *Parlement* of Paris took the new position that it lacked authority to authorize the tax and said that only the Estates General could do so. Shortly thereafter Brienne appealed to the Assembly of the Clergy to approve a large subsidy to allow funding of that part of the debt then coming due for payment. The clergy, like the *Parlement* dominated by aristocrats, not only refused the subsidy but also reduced their existing contribution or *don gratuit* to the government. As these unfruitful negotiations were transpiring at the center of political life, local aristocratic *parlements* and estates in the provinces were demanding a restoration of the privileges they had enjoyed during the early seventeenth century before Richelieu and Louis XIV had crushed their independent power. Consequently, in July 1788 the king, through Brienne, agreed to convoke the Estates General the next year. Brienne resigned and was replaced by Necker. The institutions of the aristocracy—and to a lesser degree, of the church—had brought the French monarchy to its knees. In the country of its origin, royal absolutism had been defeated.

The Revolutions of 1789

The Estates General Becomes the National Assembly

The aristocratic triumph proved to be quite brief. It unloosed social and political forces that neither the nobles nor the monarchy could control. The new difficulties arose from clashes among the groups represented in the Estates General. The body was composed of three divisions: the First Estate of the clergy, the Second Estate of the nobility, and the Third Estate, which represented everyone else in the kingdom. During the widespread public discussions preceding the meeting of the Estates General, it became clear that the Third Estate, which included all the professional, commercial, and the middle-class groups of the country, would not permit the monarchy and the aristocracy to decide the future course of the nation. Their spirit was best displayed in a pamphlet published during 1789 in which the Abbé Sieyès (1748–1836) declared, "What is the Third Estate? Everything. What has it been in the political order up to the present? Nothing. What does it ask? To become something."[1]

The split between the aristocracy and the Third Estate occurred before the Estates General gathered. Debate over the proper organization of the body drew the lines of basic disagreement. Members of the aristocracy demanded an equal number of representatives for each estate. In September 1788 the *Parlement* of Paris ruled that voting in the Estates General should be conducted by order rather than by head, that is, that each estate, or order, should have one vote, rather than that each member should have one vote. That procedure would ensure that the aristocratic First and Second Estates could always outvote the Third. Both moves on the part of the aristocracy unmasked its alleged concern for French liberty and exposed it

as a group determined to maintain its privileges. Spokesmen for the Third Estate denounced the arrogant claims of the aristocracy. The royal council eventually decided that the cause of the monarchy and fiscal reform would best be served by a strengthening of the Third Estate, and in December 1788 the council announced that the Third Estate would elect twice as many representatives as either the nobles or the clergy. This so-called doubling of the Third Estate meant that it could easily dominate the Estates General if voting were allowed by head rather than by order. It was properly assumed that some liberal nobles and clergy would support the Third Estate. The method of voting was settled by the king only after the Estates General had gathered at Versailles in May 1789.

When the representatives came to the royal palace, they brought with them *cahiers de doléances,* or lists of grievances, registered by the local electors, to be presented to the king. Large numbers of these have survived and provide considerable information about the state of the country on the eve of the revolution. These documents recorded criticisms of government waste, indirect taxes, church taxes and corruption, and the hunting rights of the aristocracy. They included calls for periodic meetings of the Estates General, more equitable taxes, more local control of administration, unified weights and measures, and a free press. The overwhelming demand of the *cahiers* was for equality of rights among the king's subjects.

These complaints and demands could not be discussed until the questions of organization and voting had been decided. From the beginning, the Third Estate, whose members consisted largely of local officials, professional men, and lawyers, refused to sit as a separate order as the king desired. For several weeks there was a standoff. Then on June 1 the Third Estate invited the clergy and the nobles to join them in organizing a new legislative body. A few members of the lower clergy did so. On June 17 that body declared itself the National Assembly.

Three days later, finding themselves accidentally locked out of their usual meeting place, the National Assembly moved to a nearby tennis court, where its members took an oath to continue to sit until they had given France a constitution. This was the famous Tennis Court Oath. Louis XVI ordered the National Assembly to desist from their actions, but shortly afterward a majority of the clergy and a

---

[1] Quoted in Leo Gershoy, *The French Revolution and Napoleon* (New York: Appleton-Century-Crofts, 1964), p. 102.

THE FRENCH REVOLUTION

1789

May 5	The Estates General opens at Versailles
June 17	The Third Estate declares itself the National Assembly
June 20	The National Assembly takes the Tennis Court Oath
July 14	Fall of the Bastille in the city of Paris
Late July	The Great Fear spreads in the countryside
August 4	The nobles surrender their feudal rights in a meeting of the National Constituent Assembly
August 27	Declaration of the Rights of Man and Citizen
October 5–6	Parisian women march to Versailles and force Louis XVI and his family to return to Paris

1790

July 12	Civil Constitution of the Clergy adopted
July 14	A new constitution is accepted by the king

1791

June 20–24	Louis XVI and his family attempt to flee France and are stopped at Varennes
August 27	The Declaration of Pillnitz
October 1	The Legislative Assembly meets

1792

April 20	France declares war on Austria
August 10	The Tuileries palace is stormed, and Louis XVI takes refuge with the Legislative Assembly
September 2–7	The September Massacres
September 20	France wins the battle of Valmy
September 21	The Convention meets, and the monarchy is abolished

1793

January 21	Louis XVI is executed
February 1	France declares war on Great Britain
March	Counterrevolution breaks out in the Vendée
April	The Committee of Public Safety is formed
June 22	The Constitution of 1793 is adopted but not put into operation
July	Robespierre enters the Committee of Public Safety
August 23	*Levée en masse* proclaimed
September 17	Maximum prices set on food and other commodities
October 16	Queen Marie Antoinette is executed
November 10	The Cult of Reason is proclaimed. The revolutionary calendar beginning on September 22, 1792, is adopted

1794

March 24	Execution of the Hébertist leaders of the *sans-culottes*
April 6	Execution of Danton
May 7	Cult of the Supreme Being proclaimed
June 8	Robespierre leads the celebration of the Festival of the Supreme Being.
June 10	The Law of 22 Prairial is adopted
July 27	The Ninth of Thermidor and the fall of Robespierre
July 28	Robespierre is executed

1795

August 22	The Constitution of the Year III is adopted, establishing the Directory

❧ The Third Estate of a French City Petitions the King

The *cahiers de doléances* were the lists of grievances brought to Versailles in 1789 by members of the Estates General. This particular *cahier* originated in Dourdan, a city of central France, and reflects the complaints of the Third Estate. The first two articles refer to the organization of the Estates General. The other articles ask that the king grant various forms of equality before the law and in matters of taxation. These demands for equality appeared in practically all the *cahiers* of the Third Estate.

The order of the third estate of the City . . . of Dourdan . . . supplicates [the king] to accept the grievances, complaints, and remonstrances which it is permitted to bring to the foot of the throne, and to see therein only the expression of its zeal and the homage of its obedience.

It wishes:

1. *That his subjects of the third estate, equal by such status to all other citizens, present themselves before the common father without other distinction which might degrade them.*

2. *That all the orders, already united by duty and a common desire to contribute equally to the needs of the State, also deliberate in common concerning its needs.*

3. *That no citizen lose his liberty except according to law; that, consequently, no one be arrested by virtue of special orders, or, if imperative circumstances necessitate such orders, that the prisoner be handed over to regular courts of justice within forty-eight hours at the latest.*

12. *That every tax, direct or indirect, be granted only for a limited time, and that every collection beyond such term be regarded as peculation, and punished as such.*

15. *That every personal tax be abolished; that thus the* capitation *[a poll tax] and the* taille *[tax from which nobility and clergy were exempt] and its accessories be merged with the* vingtièmes *[an income tax] in a tax on land and real or nominal property.*

16. *That such tax be borne equally, without distinction, by all classes of citizens and by all kinds of property, even feudal . . . rights.*

17. *That the tax substituted for the* corvée *be borne by all classes of citizens equally and without distinction. That said tax, at present beyond the capacity of those who pay it and the needs to which it is destined, be reduced by at least one-half.*

John Hall Stewart, *A Documentary Survey of the French Revolution* (New York: Macmillan, 1951), pp. 76–77.

---

large group of nobles joined the assembly. On June 27 the king capitulated and formally requested the First and Second Estates to meet with the National Assembly where voting would occur by head rather than by order. Had nothing further occurred, the government of France would have been transformed. Government by privileged orders had come to an end, for the National Assembly, which renamed itself the National Constituent Assembly, was composed of persons from all three orders who possessed shared liberal goals for the administrative, constitutional, and economic re-

form of the country. The revolution in the governing of France had commenced.

Fall of the Bastille

Two new forces soon intruded on the scene. The first was Louis XVI himself, who attempted to regain the initiative by mustering royal troops in the vicinity of Versailles and Paris. It appeared that he might be contemplating the disruption of the National Constituent Assembly. Such was the advice of Queen Marie Antoinette, his brothers, and the

The Estates-General opened at Versailles in 1789 with much pomp and splendor. In the old French print shown here, Louis XVI is on the throne. The First Estate, the clergy, is at the left; the Second Estate, the nobility, sits at the upper right; and the more numerous Third Estate, dressed in black suits and capes, sits at the lower right. [Culver Pictures.]

This well-known painting by Jacques Louis David (1748–1825) portrays the Tennis Court Oath, June 20. The emotion of the scene should be compared with the calm shown in the previous picture of the opening of the Estates-General. In the center foreground are members of different Estates joining hands in cooperation as equals. The presiding officer leading the oath is Jean Sylvain Bailly, soon to become mayor in a reorganized government of the city of Paris. The painting is in the Musée Carnavalet in Paris. [French Embassy Press and Information Division, New York.]

most conservative nobles, with whom he had begun to consult. On July 11, without consultation with the assembly leaders, Louis abruptly dismissed Necker. These actions marked the beginning of a steady, but consistently poorly executed, royal attempt to undermine the assembly and halt the revolution. Most of the National Constituent Assembly wished to create some form of constitutional monarchy, but from the start Louis's refusal to cooperate thwarted that effort. The king fatally decided to throw his lot in with the aristocracy against the nation.

The second new factor to impose itself on the events at Versailles was the populace of Paris. The mustering of royal troops created anxiety in the city, where throughout the winter and spring of 1789 there had been several bread riots. The Parisians who had elected their representatives to the Third Estate had continued to meet after the elections. By June they were organizing a citizen militia and collecting arms. They regarded the dismissal of Necker as the opening of a royal offensive against the National Constituent Assembly and the city. On July 14 somewhat over eight hundred people, most of whom were small shopkeepers, trades-

people, artisans, and wage earners, marched to the Bastille in search of weapons for the militia. This great fortress, with ten-foot-thick walls, had once held political prisoners. Through miscalculations and ineptitude on the part of the governor of the fortress, the troops in the Bastille fired into the crowd, killing ninety-eight people and wounding many others. Thereafter the crowd stormed the fortress and eventually gained entrance. They released the seven prisoners, none of whom were there for political reasons, and killed several troops and the governor. They found no weapons.

On July 15 the militia of Paris, by then called the National Guard, offered its command to Lafayette. The hero of the American Revolution gave the guard a new insignia in the design of the red and blue stripes of the city of Paris separated by the white stripe of the king. This emblem became the revolutionary cockade worn by the soldiers and eventually the flag of revolutionary France.

The attack on the Bastille marked the first of many crucial *journées,* or days when the populace of Paris would redirect the course of the revolution. The fall of the fortress signaled that the political future of the nation would not be decided solely

The capture of the Bastille on July 14, 1789, by the people of Paris, portrayed too much like a battle in this eighteenth-century engraving, was a major turning point during the early weeks of the French Revolution. [The Mansell Collection.]

by the National Constituent Assembly. As the news of the taking of the Bastille spread, similar disturbances took place in the provincial cities. A few days later Louis XVI again bowed to the force of events and personally visited Paris, where he wore the revolutionary cockade and recognized the organized electors as the legitimate government of the city. The king also recognized the National Guard. The citizens of Paris were for the time being satisfied.

The Great Fear and the Surrender of Feudal Privileges

Simultaneously with the popular urban disturbances a movement known as the *Great Fear* swept across much of the French countryside. Rumors had spread that royal troops would be sent into the rural districts. The result was an intensification of the peasant disturbances that had begun during the spring. The Great Fear witnessed the burning of chateaux, the destruction of records and documents, and the refusal to pay feudal dues. The peasants were determined to take possession of food supplies and land that they considered rightfully theirs. They were reclaiming rights and property that they had lost through the aristocratic resurgence of the last quarter-century, as well as venting their general anger against the injustices of rural life.

On the night of August 4, 1789, aristocrats in the National Constituent Assembly attempted to halt the spreading disorder in the countryside. By prearrangement a number of liberal nobles and churchmen rose in the assembly and renounced their feudal rights, dues, and tithes. In a scene of great emotion, hunting and fishing rights, judicial authority, and special exemptions were surrendered. In a sense these nobles gave up what they had already lost and what they could not have regained without civil war in the rural areas. Later they would also, in many cases, receive compensation for their losses. Nonetheless, after the night of August 4 all French citizens were subject to the same and equal laws. That dramatic session of the assembly paved the way for the legal and social reconstruction of the nation. Without those renunciations the constructive work of the National Constituent Assembly would have been much more difficult.

Both the attack on the Bastille and the Great Fear displayed varieties of the rural and urban riots that had characterized much of eighteenth-century political and social life. Louis XVI first thought that the turmoil over the Bastille was simply another bread riot. The popular disturbances also were only partly related to the events at Versailles. A deep economic downturn had struck France during 1787 and had continued into 1788. The harvests for both years had been poor, and food prices in 1789 stood higher than at any time since 1703. Wages had not kept up with the rise in prices. Throughout the winter of 1788–1789, an unusually cold one, many people suffered from hunger. Several cities had experienced wage and food riots. These economic difficulties helped the revolution reach such vast proportions. The political, social, and economic grievances of numerous sections of the country became combined. The National Constituent Assembly could look to the popular forces as a source of strength against the king and the conservative aristocrats. When the various elements of the assembly later fell into quarrels among themselves, their factions succumbed to the temptation of appealing to the politically sophisticated and well-organized shopkeeping and artisan classes for support. When this turn of events came to pass, the popular classes could demand a price for their cooperation.

The Declaration of the Rights of Man and Citizen

In late August 1789 the National Constituent Assembly decided that before writing a new constitution, it should set forth a statement of broad political principles. On August 27 the assembly issued the Declaration of the Rights of Man and Citizen. This declaration drew together much of the political language of the Enlightenment and was also influenced by the Declaration of Rights adopted by Virginia in America in June 1776. The French declaration proclaimed that all men were "born and remain free and equal in rights." The natural rights so proclaimed were "liberty, property, security, and resistance to oppression." Governments existed to protect those rights. All political sovereignty resided in the nation and its representatives. All citizens were to be equal before the law and were to be "equally admissible to all public dignities, offices and employments, according to their capacity, and with no other distinction than that of

❧ The National Assembly Decrees Civic Equality in France

These famous decrees of August 4, 1789, in effect created civic equality in France. The special privileges previously possessed or controlled by the nobility were removed.

1. *The National Assembly completely abolishes the feudal regime. It decrees that, among the rights and dues . . . all those originating in real or personal serfdom, personal servitude, and those which represent them, are abolished without indemnification; all others are declared redeemable, and that the price and mode of redemption shall be fixed by the National Assembly. . . .*

2. *The exclusive right to maintain pigeon-houses and dove-cotes is abolished. . . .*

3. *The exclusive right to hunt and to maintain unenclosed warrens is likewise abolished. . . .*

4. *All manorial courts are suppressed without indemnification.*

5. *Tithes of every description and the dues which have been substituted for them . . . are abolished, on condition, however, that some other method be de-*

vised to provide for the expenses of divine worship, the support of the officiating clergy, the relief of the poor, repairs and rebuilding of churches and parsonages, and for all establishments, seminaries, schools, academies, asylums, communities, and other institutions, for the maintenance of which they are actually devoted. . . .

7. *The sale of judicial and municipal offices shall be suppressed forthwith. . . .*

8. *Pecuniary privileges, personal or real, in the payment of taxes are abolished forever. . . .*

11. *All citizens, without distinction of birth, are eligible to any office or dignity, whether ecclesiastical, civil or military. . . .*

Frank Maloy Anderson (Ed. and Trans.), *The Constitutions and Other Select Documents Illustrative of the History of France,* 1789–1907, 2nd ed., rev. and enlarged (Minneapolis: H. W. Wilson, 1908), pp. 11–13.

their virtues and talents." There were to be due process of law and presumption of innocence until proof of guilt. Freedom of religion was affirmed. Taxation was to be apportioned equally according to capacity to pay. Property constituted "an inviolable and sacred right."[2] Although these statements were rather abstract, practically all of them were directed against specific abuses of the old aristocratic and absolutist regime. If any two principles of the future governed the declaration, they were civic equality and protection of property. The Declaration of the Rights of Man and Citizen has often been considered the death certificate of the old regime.

Louis XVI stalled before ratifying both the declaration and the aristocratic renunciation of feudalism. The longer he hesitated, the larger existing

suspicions grew that he might again try to resort to the use of troops. Moreover bread continued to be in short supply. On October 5 a large crowd of Parisian women marched to Versailles demanding more bread. They milled about the palace, and many stayed the night. Under this pressure the king agreed to sanction the decrees of the assembly. The next day he and his family appeared on a balcony before the crowd. The Parisians were deeply suspicious of the monarch and believed that he must be kept under the watchful eye of the people. Consequently they demanded that Louis and his family return to Paris. The monarch had no real choice in the matter. On October 6, 1789, his carriage followed the crowd into the city, where he and his family settled in the palace of the Tuileries. The National Constituent Assembly soon followed. Thereafter both Paris and France remained relatively stable and peaceful until the summer of 1792.

[2]Quoted in Georges Lefebvre, *The Coming of the French Revolution,* trans. by R. R. Palmer (Princeton, N.J.: Princeton University Press, 1967), pp. 221–223.

An unknown contemporary German depicted the march of the women of Paris on the palace of Versailles in October 1789. On their return to the city they were accompanied by Louis XVI and his family. [The Granger Collection.]

The Reconstruction of France

Once established in Paris, the National Constituent Assembly set about reorganizing France. In government it pursued a policy of constitutional monarchy; in administration, rationalism; in economics, unregulated freedom; and in religion, anticlericalism. Throughout its proceedings the assembly was determined to protect property and to limit the impact on national life of the unpropertied elements of the nation and even of possessors of small amounts of property. While championing civic equality before the law, the assembly spurned social equality and extensive democracy. In all these areas the assembly charted a general course that to a greater or lesser degree nineteenth-century liberals across Europe would follow.

Political Reorganization

The Constitution of 1791, which was the product of the National Constituent Assembly's deliberations, established a constitutional monarchy. There was to be a unicameral Legislative Assembly in which all laws would originate and in which the major political authority of the nation would reside. The monarch was allowed a suspensive veto that could delay but not halt legislation. Powers of war and peace were vested in the assembly. The constitution provided for an elaborate system of indirect elections intended to thwart direct popular pressure on the government. The citizens of France were divided into active and passive categories. Only active citizens—that is, men paying annual taxes equal to three days of local labor wages—could vote. They chose electors who then in turn voted for the members of the legislature. At the levels of electors, or members, still further property qualifications were imposed. Only about fifty thousand citizens of a population of about twenty-five million could qualify as electors or members of the Legislative Assembly.

In reconstructing the local and judicial administration, the National Constituent Assembly applied

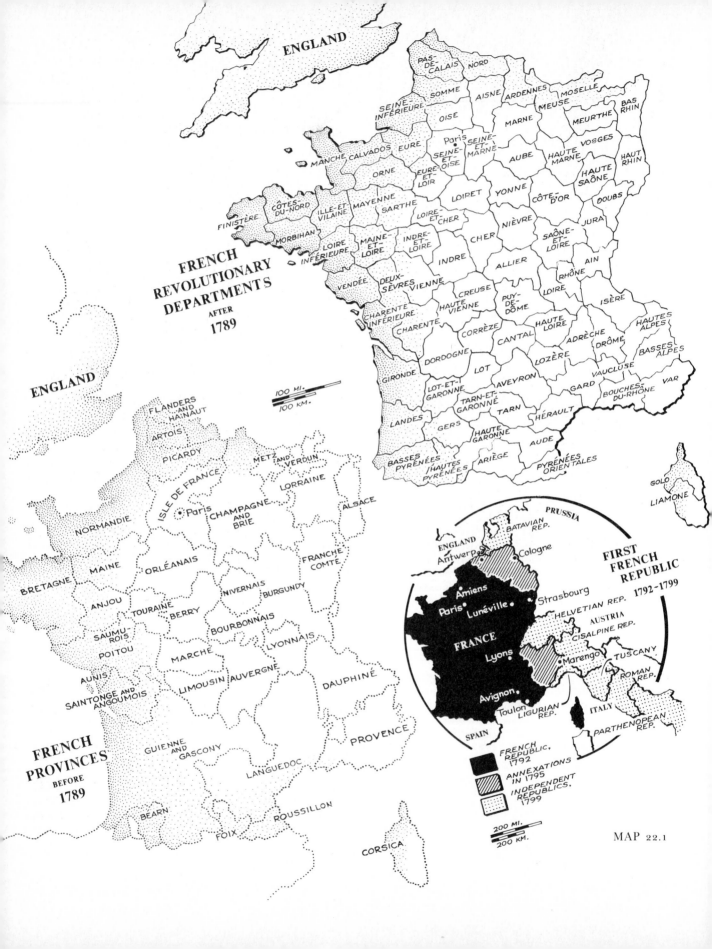

ENGLAND

PAS-DE-CALAIS | NORD
SOMME | AISNE | ARDENNES | MOSELLE
SEINE-INFÉRIEURE | OISE | MARNE | MEUSE | MEURTHE | BAS-RHIN
MANCHE | CALVADOS | EURE | SEINE-ET-OISE | SEINE-ET-MARNE | AUBE | HAUTE-MARNE | VOSGES | HAUT-RHIN
ORNE | EURE-ET-LOIR | | | | HAUTE-SAÔNE
Paris
CÔTES-DU-NORD | ILLE-ET-VILAINE | MAYENNE | SARTHE | LOIRET | YONNE | CÔTE-D'OR | DOUBS
FINISTÈRE | | | LOIR-ET-CHER | | NIÈVRE | | JURA
MORBIHAN | LOIRE-INFÉRIEURE | MAINE-ET-LOIRE | INDRE-ET-LOIRE | CHER | | SAÔNE-ET-LOIRE
VENDÉE | DEUX-SÈVRES | VIENNE | INDRE | ALLIER | AIN
| | | CREUSE | | RHÔNE
CHARENTE-INFÉRIEURE | HAUTE-VIENNE | PUY-DE-DÔME | LOIRE | ISÈRE
CHARENTE | | | HAUTE-LOIRE | HAUTES-ALPES
| CORRÈZE | CANTAL | ADRÈCHE | DRÔME | BASSES-ALPES
DORDOGNE | LOT | LOZÈRE | VAUCLUSE
GIRONDE | LOT-ET-GARONNE | AVEYRON | GARD | BOUCHES-DU-RHÔNE | VAR
LANDES | TARN-ET-GARONNE | TARN | HÉRAULT
GERS | HAUTE-GARONNE | AUDE
BASSES-PYRÉNÉES | HAUTES-PYRÉNÉES | ARIÈGE | PYRÉNÉES-ORIENTALES

FRENCH REVOLUTIONARY DEPARTMENTS AFTER 1789

100 MI.
100 KM.

GOLO
LIAMONE

ENGLAND

FLANDERS AND HAINAUT
ARTOIS
PICARDY
METZ AND VERDUN
ISLE DE FRANCE
LORRAINE
NORMANDIE
Paris
CHAMPAGNE AND BRIE
ALSACE
MAINE
ORLÉANAIS
FRANCHE COMTÉ
BRETAGNE
ANJOU
NIVERNAIS
BURGUNDY
TOURAINE
BERRY
SAUMU-ROIS
BOURBONNAIS
POITOU
MARCHE
LYONNAIS
AUNIS
LIMOUSIN
AUVERGNE
DAUPHINÉ
SAINTONGE AND ANGOUMOIS
PROVENCE
GUIENNE AND GASCONY
LANGUEDOC
BÉARN
ROUSSILLON
FOIX
CORSICA

FRENCH PROVINCES BEFORE 1789

PRUSSIA
BATAVIAN REP.
ENGLAND
Antwerp
Cologne
FIRST FRENCH REPUBLIC
1792-1799
Amiens
Paris
Lunéville
Strasbourg
HELVETIAN REP.
AUSTRIA
CISALPINE REP.
FRANCE
Lyons
Marengo
TUSCANY
ROMAN REP.
Avignon
ITALY
LIGURIAN REP.
Toulon
SPAIN
PARTHENOPEAN REP.

FRENCH REPUBLIC, 1792
ANNEXATIONS IN 1795
INDEPENDENT REPUBLICS, 1799

200 MI.
200 KM.

MAP 22.1

the rational spirit of the Enlightenment. It abolished the ancient French provinces, such as Burgundy and Brittany, and established in their place eighty-three departments (*départements*) of generally equal size named after rivers, mountains, and other geographical features. The departments in turn were subdivided into districts, cantons, and communes. Most local elections were also indirect. The departmental reconstruction proved to be one of the most permanent achievements of the assembly. The departments exist to the present day. All of the ancient judicial courts, including the seigneurial courts and the *parlements,* were also abolished. In their place were organized uniform courts with elected judges and prosecutors. Procedures were simplified, and the most degrading punishments were removed from the books.

Economic Policy

In economic matters the National Constituent Assembly continued the policies formerly advocated by Louis XVI's reformist ministers. It suppressed the guilds and liberated the grain trade. The assembly established the metric system to provide the nation with uniform weights and measures. These policies of economic freedom and uniformity disappointed both peasants and urban workers caught in the cycle of inflation. By decrees of 1790 the assembly placed the burden of proof on the peasants to rid themselves of the residual feudal dues for which compensation was to be paid. On June 14, 1791, the assembly crushed the attempts of urban workers to protect their wages by enacting the Chapelier Law, which forbade worker associations. Peasants and workers were henceforth to be left to the freedom and mercy of the marketplace.

While these various reforms were being put into effect, the original financial crisis that had occasioned the calling of the Estates General persisted. The royal debt was not repudiated, because it was owed to the bankers, the merchants, and the commercial traders of the Third Estate. The National Constituent Assembly had suppressed many of the old, hated indirect taxes and had substituted new land taxes, but these proved insufficient. Moreover there were not enough officials to collect them. The continuing financial problem led the assembly to take what may well have been, for the future of French life and society, its most decisive action. The assembly decided to finance the debt by confiscating and then selling the land and property of the Roman Catholic Church in France. The results were further inflation, religious schism, and civil war. In effect, the National Constituent Assembly had opened a new chapter in the relations of church and state in Europe.

Having chosen to plunder the land of the church, in December 1790 the assembly authorized the issuance of *assignats,* or government bonds, the value of which was guaranteed by the revenue to be generated from the sale of church property. Initially a limit was set on the quantity of *assignats* to be issued. However, the bonds proved so acceptable to the public that they began to circulate as currency. The assembly decided to issue an ever larger

The assignats *were government bonds that were backed by confiscated church lands. They circulated as money. When the government printed too many of them, inflation resulted and their value fell.* [Bettmann Archive.]

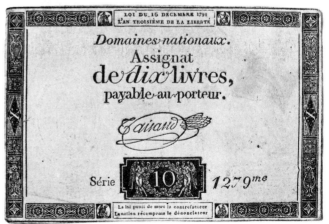

number of them to liquidate the national debt and to create a large body of new property owners with a direct stake in the revolution. However, within a few months the value of the *assignats* began to fall. Inflation increased and put new stress on the lives of the urban poor.

The Civil Constitution of the Clergy

The confiscation of church lands required an ecclesiastical reconstruction. In July 1790 the National Constituent Assembly issued the Civil Constitution of the Clergy, which transformed the Roman Catholic Church in France into a branch of the secular state. This legislation reduced the number of bishoprics from 135 to 83 and brought the borders of the dioceses into conformity with those of the new departments. It also provided for the election of priests and bishops, who henceforth became salaried employees of the state. The assembly consulted neither the pope nor the French clergy about these broad changes. The king approved the measure only with the greatest reluctance.

The Civil Constitution of the Clergy was the major blunder of the National Constituent Assembly. The measure created immense opposition within the French church even from bishops who had long championed Gallican liberties over papal domination. In the face of this resistance the assembly unwisely ruled that all clergy must take an oath to support the Civil Constitution. Only seven bishops and about half the clergy did so. In reprisal the assembly designated the clergy who had not taken the oath as "refractory" and removed them from their clerical functions.

Further reaction was swift. Refractory priests attempted to celebrate Mass. In February 1791 the pope condemned not only the Civil Constitution of the Clergy but also the Declaration of the Rights of Man and Citizen. That condemnation marked the opening of a Roman Catholic offensive against liberalism and the revolution that continued throughout the nineteenth century. Within France itself the pope's action created a crisis of conscience and political loyalty for all sincere Catholics. Religious devotion and revolutionary loyalty became incompatible for many people. French citizens were divided between those who supported the constitutional priests and those who resorted to the refractory clergy. Louis XVI and his family favored the latter.

Counterrevolutionary Activity

The revolution had other enemies besides the pope and the devout Catholics. As it became clear that the old political and social order was undergoing fundamental and probably permanent change, considerable numbers of aristocrats left France. Known as the *émigrés,* they settled in countries near the French border, where they sought to foment counterrevolution. Among the most important of their number was the king's younger brother, the Count of Artois (1757–1836). In the summer of 1791 his agents and the queen persuaded Louis XVI to attempt to flee the country. On the night of June 20, 1791, Louis and his immediate family, disguised as servants, left Paris. They traveled as far as Varennes on their way to Metz. At Varennes the king was recognized, and his flight was halted. On June 24 a company of soldiers escorted the royal family back to Paris. The leaders of the National Constituent Assembly, determined to save the constitutional monarchy, announced that the king had been abducted from the capital. However, such a convenient public fiction could not cloak the reality that the chief counterrevolutionary in France now sat on the throne.

Two months later, on August 27, 1791, under pressure from a group of *émigrés,* Emperor Leopold II of Austria, who was the brother of Marie Antoinette, and Frederick William II, the king of Prussia, issued the Declaration of Pillnitz. The two monarchs promised to intervene in France to protect the royal family and to preserve the monarchy *if* the other major European powers agreed. The latter provision rendered the statement meaningless because at the time Great Britain would not have given its consent. However, the declaration was not so read in France, where the revolutionaries saw the nation surrounded by aristocratic and monarchical foes.

The National Constituent Assembly drew to a close in September 1791. Its task of reconstructing the government and the administration of France had been completed. One of its last acts was the passage of a measure that forbade any of its own members to sit in the Legislative Assembly then being elected. The new body met on October 1 and had to confront the immense problems that had emerged during the earlier part of the year. Within the Legislative Assembly major political divisions also soon developed over the future course of the nation and the revolution.

Here, as seen by a contemporary Dutchman, Louis XVI and his family are being led back to Paris by armed escort after their attempt to flee France in June 1791 was foiled near Varennes. [The Granger Collection.]

A Second Revolution

End of the Monarchy

The issues of the Civil Constitution of the Clergy and the trustworthiness of Louis XVI undermined the unity of the revolution. Much factionalism displayed itself throughout the short life of the Legislative Assembly (1791–1792). Ever since the original gathering of the Estates General, deputies from the Third Estate had organized themselves into clubs composed of politically like-minded persons. The most famous and best organized of these were the Jacobins, whose name derived from the fact that Dominican friars were called *Jacobins,* and the group met in a Dominican monastery in Paris. The Jacobins had also established a network of local clubs throughout the provinces. They had constituted the most advanced political group in the National Constituent Assembly and had pressed for a republic rather than a constitutional monarchy. The events of the summer of 1791 led them to renew those demands.

In the Legislative Assembly a group of Jacobins known as the *Girondists* (because many of them came from the department of the Gironde) assumed leadership.[3] They were determined to oppose the forces of counterrevolution. They passed a measure ordering the *émigrés* to return or suffer loss of property and another requiring the refractory clergy to support the Civil Constitution or lose their state pensions. The king vetoed both acts. On April 20, 1792, the Girondists led the Legislative Assembly to declare war on Austria, by this time governed by Francis II (1768–1835) and allied to Prussia. The Girondists believed that the war would preserve the revolution from domestic enemies and bring the most advanced revolutionaries to power. Paradoxically Louis XVI and other monarchists also favored the war. They thought that the conflict would strengthen the executive power (i.e., the monarchy). The king also entertained the

[3] The Girondists are also frequently called the *Brissotins* after Jacques-Pierre Brissot (1754–1793), who was their chief spokesman in early 1792.

659

Louis XVI and the royal family fled on August 10, 1792, from the mobs attacking their palace. The royal family (behind the screened reporter's box at the right) took refuge with the Legislative Assembly. [New York Public Library Picture Collection.]

hope that French forces might be defeated and the old regime restored. Both sides were playing dangerously foolish politics.

The war radicalized the revolution and led to what is usually called the second revolution, which overthrew the constitutional monarchy and established a republic. Initially the war effort went quite poorly. Both the country and the revolution seemed in danger. In July 1792 the Duke of Brunswick, commander of the Prussian forces, issued a manifesto promising the destruction of Paris if harm came to the French royal family. This statement stiffened support for the war and increased the already significant distrust of the king.

Late in July, under radical working-class pressure, the government of the city of Paris passed from the elected council to a committee, or commune, of representatives from the sections (municipal wards) of Paris. On August 10, 1792, a very large Parisian crowd invaded the Tuileries palace and forced Louis XVI and Marie Antoinette to take refuge in the Legislative Assembly itself. The crowd fought with the royal Swiss guards. When Louis was finally able to call off the troops, several hundred of them and a large number of Parisian citizens lay dead. The monarchy itself was also a casualty of that melee: thereafter the royal family was imprisoned in comfortable quarters, but the king was allowed to perform none of his political functions.

The Convention and the Role of the Sans-culottes

Early in September the Parisian crowd again made its will felt. During the first week of the month, in what are known as the *September Massacres,* the Paris Commune summarily executed or murdered about twelve hundred people who were in the city jails. Many of these people were aristocrats or priests, but the majority were simply common criminals. The crowd had assumed that the prisoners were all counterrevolutionaries. The Paris Commune then compelled the Legislative Assembly to call for the election by universal manhood suffrage of a new assembly to write a democratic constitution. That body, called the *Convention* after its American counterpart of 1787, met on September 21, 1792. The previous day the French army had halted the Prussian advance at the battle of Valmy in eastern France. The victory of democratic forces at home had been confirmed by victory on the battlefield.

As its first act, the Convention declared France a republic, that is, a nation governed by an elected assembly without a king. The second revolution had been the work of Jacobins more radical than the Girondists and of the people of Paris known as the *sans-culottes.* The name of the latter means "without breeches" and derived from the long trousers that as working people they wore instead of aristocratic knee breeches. The sans-culottes were shopkeepers, artisans, wage earners, and, in a few cases, factory workers. The persistent food shortages and the revolutionary inflation had made their generally difficult lives even more burdensome. The politics of the old regime had ignored them, and the policies of the National Constituent Assembly had left them victims of unregulated economic liberty. However, the nation required their labor and their lives if the war was to succeed. From the summer of 1792 until the summer of 1794 their attitudes, desires, and ideals were the primary factors in the internal development of the revolution.

The sans-culottes generally knew what they wanted. The Parisian tradespeople and artisans sought immediate relief from food shortages and rising prices through the vehicle of price controls. They believed that all people had a right to subsistence and profoundly resented most forms of social inequality. This attitude led them to intense hostility toward the aristocracy and toward the original leaders of the revolution, who they believed simply wanted to take over the social privileges of the aristocracy. Their hatred of inequality did not go so far as to demand the abolition of property. Rather, they advocated a community of relatively small property owners. In politics they were antimonarchical, strongly republican, and suspicious even of representative government. They believed that the people should make the decisions of government to as great an extent as possible. In Paris, where their influence was most important, the sans-culottes' political experience had been gained in meetings of the Paris sections. Those gatherings exemplified direct community democracy and were not unlike a New England town meeting. The economic hardship of their lives made them impatient to see their demands met.

The goals of the sans-culottes were not wholly compatible with those of the Jacobins. The latter were republicans who sought representative gov-

❧ A *Pamphleteer* Describes a *Sans-culotte*

This pamphlet is a 1793 description of a sans-culotte written either by one or by a sympathizer. It describes the sans-culotte as a hardworking, useful, patriotic citizen who bravely sacrifices himself to the war effort. It contrasts those virtues to the lazy and unproductive luxury of the noble and the personally self-interested plottings of the politician.

A sans-culotte *you rogues? He is someone who always goes on foot, who has no millions as you would all like to have, no* chateaux, *no valets to serve him, and who lives simply with his wife and children, if he has any, on a fourth or fifth storey.*

He is useful, because he knows how to work in the field, to forge iron, to use a saw, to use a file, to roof a house, to make shoes, and to shed his last drop of blood for the safety of the Republic.

And because he works, you are sure not to meet his person in the Café de Chartres, or in the gaming houses where others conspire and game; nor at the National theatre . . . nor in the literary clubs. . . .

In the evening he goes to his section, not powdered or perfumed, or smartly booted in the hope of catching the eye of the citizenesses in the galleries, but ready to support good proposals with all his might, and to crush those which come from the abominable faction of politicians.

Finally, a sans-culotte *always has his sabre sharp, to cut off the ears of all enemies of the Revolution; sometimes he even goes out with his pike; but at the first sound of the drum he is ready to leave for the Vendée, for the army of the Alps or for the army of the North. . . .*

"Reply to an Impertinent Question: What Is a *Sans-culotte?*" April 1793. Reprinted in Walter Markov and Albert Soboul (Eds.), *Die Sansculotten von Paris,* and republished translated by Clive Emsley in Merryn Williams (Ed.), *Revolutions: 1775–1830* (Baltimore: Penguin Books, in association with The Open University, 1971), pp. 100–101.

Although many of the victims of the Reign of Terror were executed by other methods, the guillotine became the symbol of those frightening months in 1793 and 1794. Here prisoners are being prepared for decapitation, as the heads of those already executed are displayed to the crowd. [Bettmann Archive.]

The execution of Louis XVI on January 21, 1793. [New York Public Library Picture Collection.]

ernment. Jacobin hatred of the aristocracy did not extend to a general suspicion of wealth. Basically the Jacobins favored an unregulated economy. However, from the time of Louis XVI's flight to Varennes onward, the more extreme Jacobins began to cooperate with leaders of the Parisian sans-culottes and the Paris Commune for the overthrow of the monarchy. Once the Convention began its deliberations, these advanced Jacobins, known as the *Mountain* because of their seats high in the assembly hall, worked with the sans-culottes to carry the revolution forward and to win the war. This willingness to cooperate with the forces of the popular revolution separated the Mountain from the Girondists, who were also members of the Jacobin Club.

By the spring of 1793 several issues had brought the Mountain and its sans-culottes allies to domination of the Convention and the revolution. In December 1792 Louis XVI was put on trial as mere "Citizen Capet," the family name of extremely distant forebears of the royal family. The Girondists looked for some way to spare his life, but the Mountain defeated the effort. Louis was convicted, by a very narrow majority, of conspiring against the liberty of the people and the security of the state. He was condemned to death and was beheaded on January 21, 1793. The next month the Convention declared war on Great Britain, Holland, and Spain. Soon thereafter the Prussians renewed their offensive and drove the French out of Belgium. To make matters worse, General Dumouriez, the Girondist victor of Valmy, deserted to the enemy. Finally, in March 1793 a royalist revolt led by aristocratic officers and priests erupted in the Vendée in western France and roused much popular support. Consequently the revolution found itself at war with most of Europe and much of the French nation. The Girondists had led the country into the war but had proved themselves incapable either of winning it or of suppressing the enemies of the revolution at home. The Mountain stood ready to take up the task.

Every major European power was now hostile to the revolution.

The Revolution and Europe at War

Initially the attitude of the rest of Europe toward the revolutionary events in France had been am-

bivalent. Those people who favored political reform regarded the revolution as wisely and rationally reorganizing a corrupt and inefficient government. The major foreign governments thought that the revolution meant that France would cease to be an important factor in European affairs for several years. In 1790, however, the Irish-born writer and British statesman Edmund Burke (1729–1797) argued a different position in *Reflections on the Revolution in France*. Burke regarded the reconstruction of French administration as the application of a blind rationalism that ignored the historical realities of political development and the complexities of social relations. He also forecast further turmoil as persons without political experience attempted to govern France. As the revolutionaries proceeded to attack the church, the monarchy, and finally the rest of Europe, Burke's ideas came to have many admirers, and his *Reflections* became the handbook of European conservatives for decades.

By the time of the commencement of the war with Austria in April 1792, the other European monarchies recognized the danger of both the ideas and the aggression of revolutionary France. The ideals of the Rights of Man and Citizen were highly exportable and applicable to the rest of Europe. One government after another turned to repressive domestic policies. In Great Britain William Pitt the Younger (1759–1806), the prime minister, who had unsuccessfully supported moderate

Edmund Burke. The portrait is from the studio of Joshua Reynolds. [National Portrait Gallery, London.]

❧ Burke Condemns the Work of the French National Assembly

Burke was undoubtedly the most important and articulate foreign critic of the French Revolution. He believed that governments could not be quickly created or organized, as seemed to have occurred in France. He was also deeply opposed to democracy, which he thought would lead to unwise, extreme actions on the part of government. Burke left a legacy of brilliantly argued conservative thought that remained a comfort to many followers, a serious challenge to liberals in nineteenth-century Europe, and an important statement in political theory. This passage is from his 1790 *Reflections on the Revolution in France*.

To make a government requires no great prudence. Settle the seat of power; teach obedience: and the work is done. To give Freedom is still more easy. It is not necessary to guide; it only requires to let go the rein. But to form a free government; *that is, to temper together these opposite elements of liberty and restraint in one consistent work, requires much thought, deep reflection, a sagacious, powerful, and combining mind. This I do not find in those who take the lead in the National Assembly. Perhaps they are not so miserably deficient as they appear. I rather believe it. It would put them below the common level of human understanding. But when the leaders choose to make themselves bidders at an auction of popularity, their talents, in the construction of the state, will be of no service. They will become flatterers instead of legislators; the instruments, not the guides, of the people. If any of them should happen to propose a scheme of liberty, soberly limited, and defined with proper qualifications, he will be immediately outbid by his competitors, who will produce something more splendidly popular. Suspicions will be raised of his fidelity to his cause. Moderation will be stigmatized as the virtue of cowards; and compromise as the prudence of traitors; until, in hopes of preserving the credit which may enable him to temper, and moderate, on some occasions, the popular leader is obliged to become active in propagating doctrines, and establishing powers, that will afterwards defeat any sober purpose at which he ultimately might have aimed.*

. . . The improvements of the National Assembly are superficial, their errors fundamental.

Edmund Burke, *Reflections on the Revolution in France*, in *The Works of the Right Honourable Edmund Burke*, Vol. 2 (London: Henry G. Bohn, 1864), pp. 515–516.

---

reform of Parliament during the 1780s, turned against both reform and popular movements. The government suppressed the London Corresponding Society founded in 1792 as a working-class reform group. In Birmingham the government sponsored mob action to drive Joseph Priestley (1733–1804), a chemist and a radical political thinker, out of the country. In early 1793 Pitt secured parliamentary approval for acts suspending habeas corpus and making it possible to commit treason in writing. With less success Pitt attempted to curb freedom of the press. All political groups who dared to oppose the action of the government were in danger of becoming associated with revolutionary sedition.

In eastern Europe the revolution brought to a close the life of enlightened absolutism. The aristocratic resistance to the reforms of Joseph II in the Hapsburg lands led his brother, Leopold II, to come to terms with the landowners. Leopold's successor, Francis II (1792–1835), became a major leader of the counterrevolution. In Prussia Frederick William II (1786–1797), the nephew of Frederick the Great, looked to the leaders of the Lutheran church and the aristocracy to discourage any potential popular uprisings, such as those of the downtrodden Silesian weavers. In Russia Catherine the Great burned the works of her onetime friend Voltaire and exiled Alexander Radishchev (1749–1802) to Siberia for publishing *Journey from Saint Petersburg to Moscow*, a work critical of Russian social conditions.

In 1793 and 1795 the eastern powers once again combined against Poland. In that unhappy land aristocratic reformers had finally achieved the abolition of the *liberum veto* and had organized a new constitutional monarchy in 1791. Russia and Prussia, which already had designs on Polish territory, saw or pretended to see a threat of revolution in the new Polish constitution. In 1793 they annexed large sections of the country; in 1795 Austria joined the two other powers in a final partition that removed Poland from the map of Europe until after World War I. The governments of eastern Europe had used the widely shared fear of further revolutionary disorder to justify old-fashioned eighteenth-century aggression.

Consequently, in a paradoxical fashion the very success of the revolution in France brought to a rapid close reform movements in the rest of Europe. The French invasion of the Austrian Netherlands and the revolutionary reorganization of that territory roused the rest of Europe to the point of active hostility. In November 1792 the Convention declared that it would aid all peoples who wished to cast off the burdens of aristocratic and monarchical oppression. The Convention had also proclaimed the Scheldt River in the Netherlands open to the commerce of all nations and thus had broken a treaty that Great Britain had made with Austria and Holland. The British were on the point of declaring war on France over this issue when the Convention issued its own declaration of hostilities. By April 1793, when the Mountain began to direct the French government, the nation stood at war with Austria, Prussia, Great Britain, Spain, Sardinia, and Holland. The governments of those nations were attempting to protect their social structures, political systems, and economic interests against the aggression of the revolution.

The Reign of Terror

The Republic Defended

In April 1793 the Convention established a Committee of General Security and a Committee of Public Safety to perform the executive duties of the government. The latter committee became more important and eventually enjoyed almost dictatorial power. The most prominent leaders of the Committee of Public Safety were Jacques Danton (1759–1794), who had provided heroic leadership in September 1792; Maximilien Robespierre (1758–1794), who became for a time the single most powerful member of the committee; and Lazare Carnot (1753–1823), who was in charge of the military. All of these men and the other figures on the committee were strong republicans and had opposed the weak policies of the Girondists. They

conceived of their task as saving the revolution from mortal enemies at home and abroad. They generally enjoyed a working political relationship with the sans-culottes of Paris, but this was an alliance of expediency on the part of the committee.

The major problem was to wage the war and to secure domestic support for the effort. In early June 1793 the Parisian sans-culottes invaded the Convention and successfully demanded the expulsion of the Girondist members. That action further radicalized the Convention and gave the Mountain complete control. On June 22 the Convention approved a fully democratic constitution but suspended its operation until the conclusion of the war emergency. On August 23 Carnot began a mobilization for victory by issuing a *levée en masse,* or general military requisition of the population, which conscripted males into the army and directed economic production for military purposes. On September 17 a maximum on prices was established in accord with sans-culotte demands. During these same months the armies of the revolution also successfully crushed many of the counterrevolutionary disturbances in the provinces.

Never before had Europe seen a nation organized in this way nor one defended by a citizen army. Other events within France astounded Europeans even more. The Reign of Terror had begun. Those months of quasi-judicial executions and murders stretching from the autumn of 1793 to the midsummer of 1794 are probably the most famous or infamous period of the revolution. They can be understood only in the context of the war on the one hand and the revolutionary expectations of the Convention and the sans-culottes on the other.

The Republic of Virtue

The presence of armies closing in on the nation created a situation in which it was relatively easy to dispense with legal due process. However, the people who sat in the Convention and composed the Committee of Public Safety also believed that they had made a new departure in world history. They had established a republic in which civic virtue rather than aristocratic and monarchical corruption might flourish. The republic of virtue manifested itself in the renaming of streets from the egalitarian vocabulary of the revolution, in republican dress copied from that of the sansculottes or the Roman Republic, in the absence of powdered wigs, in the suppression of plays that were insuffi-

❧ The French Convention Calls Up the Entire Nation

This proclamation for the levée en masse, *August 23, 1793, marked the first time in European history that all citizens of a nation were called to contribute to a war effort. The decree set the entire nation on a wartime footing under the centralized direction of the Committee of Public Safety.*

1. From this moment until that in which the enemy shall have been driven from the soil of the Republic, all Frenchmen are in permanent requisition for the service of the armies.

The young men shall go to battle; the married men shall forge arms and transport provisions; the women shall make tents and clothing and shall serve in the hospitals; the children shall turn old linen into lint; the aged shall betake themselves to the public places in order to arouse the courage of the warriors and preach the hatred of kings and the unity of the Republic.

2. The national buildings shall be converted into barracks, the public places into workshops for arms, the soil of the cellars shall be washed in order to extract therefrom the saltpetre.

3. The arms of the regulation calibre shall be reserved exclusively for those who shall march against the enemy; the service of the interior shall be performed with hunting pieces and side arms.

4. The saddle horses are put in requisition to complete the cavalry corps; the draught-horses, other than those employed in agriculture, shall convey the artillery and the provisions.

5. The Committee of Public Safety is charged to take all the necessary measures to set up without delay an extraordinary manufacture of arms of every sort which corresponds with the ardor and energy of the French people. . . .

. . . .

8. The levy shall be general. . . .

Frank Maloy Anderson (Ed. and Trans.), *The Constitutions and Other Select Documents Illustrative of the History of France,* 1789–1907, 2nd ed., rev. and enlarged (Minneapolis: H. W. Wilson, 1908), pp. 184–185.

ciently republican, and in a general attack against crimes, such as prostitution, that were supposedly characteristic of aristocratic society.

The most dramatic departure of the republic of virtue, and one that illustrates the imposition of political values that would justify the Terror, was an attempt by the Convention to dechristianize France. In October 1793 the Convention proclaimed a new calendar dating from the first day of the French Republic. There were twelve months of thirty days with names associated with the seasons and climate. Every tenth day rather than every seventh was a holiday. Many of the most important events of the next few years became known by their dates on the revolutionary calendar.[4] In November 1793 the convention decreed the Cathedral of Notre Dame to be a Temple of Reason. The legislature then sent trusted members, known as

[4] From summer to spring the months on the revolutionary calendar were Messidor, Thermidor, Fructidor, Vendémiaire, Brumaire, Frimaire, Nivôse, Pluviôse, Ventôse, Germinal, Floréal, and Prairial.

deputies on mission, into the provinces to enforce dechristianization by closing churches, persecuting clergy and believers, and occasionally forcing priests to marry. Needless to say, this religious policy roused much opposition and deeply separated the French provinces from the revolutionary government in Paris.

During the crucial months of late 1793 and early 1794 the person who emerged as the chief figure on the Committee of Public Safety was Robespierre. He was a complex person who has remained controversial to the present day. He was utterly selfless and from the earliest days of the revolution had favored a republic. The Jacobin Club provided his primary forum and base of power. A shrewd and sensitive politician, he had opposed the war in 1792 as a measure that might aid the monarchy. He largely depended on the support of the sans-culottes of Paris, but he continued to dress as he had prior to the revolution and opposed dechristianization as a political blunder. For him the republic of virtue meant wholehearted

An engraving by M. Bovi of the trial of Queen Marie Antoinette, who was executed on October 16, 1793. Note the contrast between her simple dress and veil here and her elaborate appearance in the portrait earlier in this chapter. [The Mansell Collection.]

support of republican government and the renunciation of selfish gains from political life. He once told the Convention, "If the mainspring of popular government in peacetime is virtue, amid revolution it is at the same time virtue and *terror:* virtue, without which terror is fatal; terror, without which virtue is impotent. Terror is nothing but prompt, severe, inflexible justice; it is therefore an emanation of virtue."[5] He and those who supported his policies were among the first apostles of secular ideologies who in the name of humanity would bring so much suffering to European politics of the left and the right in the next two centuries.

Progress of the Terror

The Reign of Terror manifested itself through a series of revolutionary tribunals established by the Convention during the summer of 1793. They were to try the enemies of the republic, but the definition of *enemy* remained uncertain and shifted as the months passed. The enemies included those who might aid other European powers, those who

[5] Quoted in Richard T. Bienvenu, *The Ninth of Thermidor: The Fall of Robespierre* (New York: Oxford University Press, 1968), p. 38.

Marie Antoinette on the way to her execution, sketched from life by David, as her tumbril passed his window. [Bettmann Archive.]

endangered republican virtue, and finally good republicans who opposed the policies of the dominant faction of the government. In a very real sense the terror of the revolutionary tribunals systematized and channeled the popular resentment that had manifested itself in the September Massacres of 1792. The first victims were Marie Antoinette, other members of the royal family, and some aristocrats, who were executed in October 1793. They were followed by certain Girondist politicians who had been prominent in the Legislative Assembly.

By the early months of 1794 the Terror had moved to the provinces, where the deputies on mission presided over the summary execution of thousands of people who had allegedly supported internal opposition to the revolution. One of the most infamous incidents occurred in Nantes, where several hundred people were simply tied to rafts and drowned in the river. By early 1794 the victims of the Terror were coming from every social class, including the sans-culottes.

In Paris during the late winter Robespierre began to orchestrate the Terror against republican political figures of the left and right. On March 24 he secured the execution of certain extreme sans-

❧ The Convention Establishes the Worship of the Supreme Being

On May 7, 1794, the Convention passed one of the most extraordinary pieces of revolutionary legislation. It established the worship of the Supreme Being as a state cult. Although the law drew on the religious ideas of deism, the point of the legislation was to provide a religious basis for the new secular French state, which had repeatedly attacked traditional French Catholicism. The reader should pay particular attention to Article 7, which outlines the political and civic values that the cult of the Supreme Being was supposed to nurture.

1. *The French people recognize the existence of the Supreme Being and the immortality of the soul.*

2. *They recognize that the worship worthy of the Supreme Being is the observance of the duties of man.*

3. *They place in the forefront of such duties detestation of bad faith and tyranny, punishment of tyrants and traitors, succoring of unfortunates, respect of weak persons, defence of the oppressed, doing to others all the good that one can, and being just towards everyone.*

4. *Festivals shall be instituted to remind man of the concept of the Divinity and of the dignity of his being.*

5. *They shall take their names from the glorious events of our Revolution, or from the virtues most dear and most useful to man, or from the greatest benefits of nature.*

. . . .

7. *On the days of décade [the name given to a particular day in each month of the revolutionary calendar] it shall celebrate the following festivals:*

To the Supreme Being and to nature; to the human race; to the French people; to the benefactors of humanity; to the martyrs of liberty; to liberty and equality; to the Republic; to the liberty of the world; to the love of the Patrie; *to the hatred of tyrants and traitors; to truth; to justice; to modesty; to glory and immortality; to friendship; to frugality; to courage; to good faith; to heroism; to disinterestedness; to stoicism; to love; to conjugal love; to paternal love; to maternal tenderness; to filial piety; to infancy; to youth; to manhood; to old age; to misfortune; to agriculture; to industry; to our forefathers; to posterity; to happiness.*

8. *The Committees of Public Safety and Public Instruction are responsible for presenting a plan of organization for said festivals.*

9. *The National Convention summons all talents worthy of serving the cause of humanity to the honor of concurring in their establishment by hymns and civic songs, and by every means which may contribute to their embellishment and utility.*

John Hall Stewart, *A Documentary Survey of the French Revolution* (New York: Macmillan, 1951), pp. 526–527.

The Festival of the Supreme Being took place in Paris in June 1794. It was one of the chief displays of the civic religion of the French Revolution. The painting is by P. A. de Machy. [*Musée Carnavalet, Paris. Giraudon.*]

culottes leaders known as the *enragés*. They had wanted further measures regulating prices, securing social equality, and pressing dechristianization. Robespierre then turned against more conservative republicans, including Danton. They were insufficiently militant on the war, had profited monetarily from the revolution, and had rejected any link between politics and moral virtue. Danton was executed during the first week in April. In this fashion Robespierre exterminated the leadership from both groups that might have threatened his position. Finally, on June 10, he secured passage of the Law of 22 Prairial, which permitted the revolutionary tribunal to convict suspects without hearing substantial evidence. The number of executions was growing steadily.

In May 1794, at the height of his power, Robespierre, considering the worship of Reason too ab-

stract for most citizens, abolished it and established the Cult of the Supreme Being. This deistic cult was in line with Rousseau's idea of a civic religion that would induce morality among citizens. However, Robespierre did not long preside over his new religion. On July 26 he made an ill-tempered speech in the Convention declaring that there existed among other leaders of the government a conspiracy against himself and the revolution. Such accusations against unnamed persons had usually preceded his earlier attacks. On July 27—the Ninth of Thermidor—by prearrangement, members of the Convention shouted him down when he rose to make another speech. That night Robespierre was arrested, and the next day he was executed. The revolutionary sans-culottes of Paris would not save him because he had deprived them of their chief leaders. The other Jacobins turned against him because after Danton's death they feared becoming the next victims. Robespierre had destroyed rivals for leadership without creating supporters for himself. In that regard he was the selfless creator of his own destruction.

The fall of Robespierre might simply have been one more shift in the turbulent politics of the revolution. Those who brought about his demise were motivated by instincts of self-preservation rather than by major policy differences. They had generally supported the Terror and the executions. Yet within a short time the Reign of Terror, which ultimately claimed over twenty-five thousand victims,

In this cartoon, the government of Robespierre is attacked for having killed everyone: clergy, nobility, legislators, the people. [Editorial Photocolor Archives.]

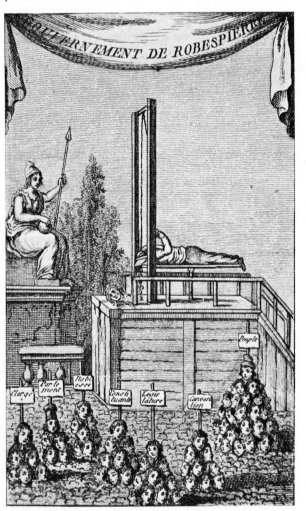

did come to a close. The largest number of executions had involved peasants and sans-culottes who had joined rebellions against the revolutionary government. By the late summer of 1794 those provincial uprisings had been crushed, and the war against foreign enemies was also going well. Those factors, combined with the feeling in Paris that the revolution had consumed enough of its own children, brought the Terror to an end.

The Thermidorian Reaction

The End of the Terror and Establishment of the Directory

A tempering of the revolution called the *Thermidorian Reaction* began in July 1794. It consisted of the destruction of the machinery of terror and the institution of a new constitutional regime. The influence of generally wealthy middle-class and professional people replaced that of the sans-culottes. Within days and weeks of Robespierre's execution the Convention allowed the Girondists who had been in prison or hiding to return to their seats. There was a general amnesty for political prisoners. The Convention restructured the Committee of Public Safety and gave it much less power. The Convention also repealed the notorious Law of 22 Prairial. Some, though by no means all, of the people responsible for the Terror were removed from public life. Leaders of the Paris Commune and certain deputies on mission were executed. The Paris Commune itself was outlawed. The Paris Jacobin Club was closed, and Jacobin clubs in the provinces were forbidden to correspond with each other.

The executions of former terrorists marked the beginning of "the white terror." Throughout the country people who had been involved in the Reign of Terror were attacked and often murdered. Jacobins were executed with little more due process than they had extended to their victims a few months earlier. The Convention itself approved some of these trials. In other cases gangs of youths who had aristocratic connections or who had avoided serving in the army roamed the streets beating known Jacobins. In Lyons, Toulon, and Marseilles these "bands of Jesus" dragged suspected terrorists from prisons and murdered them much as alleged royalists had been murdered during the September Massacres of 1792.

The republic of virtue gave way, if not to one of

One of the major events during the Thermidorian Reaction was the closing in November 1794 of the Jacobin Club in Paris. The structure was part of a former convent in the center of the city. [*The Granger Collection.*]

vice, at least to one of frivolous pleasures. The dress of the sans-culottes and the Roman Republic disappeared among the middle class and the aristocracy. New plays appeared in the theaters, and prostitutes again roamed the streets of Paris. Families of victims of the Reign of Terror gave parties in which they appeared with shaved necks like the victims of the guillotine and red ribbons tied about them. Although the Convention continued to favor the Cult of the Supreme Being, it allowed Catholic services to be held. Many refractory priests returned to the country. One of the unanticipated results of the Thermidorian Reaction was a genuine revival of Catholic worship.

The Thermidorian Reaction also involved still further political reconstruction. The fully democratic constitution of 1793, which had never gone into effect, was abandoned. The Convention issued in its place the Constitution of the Year III, which reflected the Thermidorian determination to reject both constitutional monarchy and democracy. The new document provided for a legislature of two houses. Members of the upper body, or Council of Elders, were to be men over forty years of age who were either husbands or widowers. The lower Council of Five Hundred was to consist of married or single men at least thirty years old. The executive body was to be a five-person Directory chosen by the Elders from a list submitted by the Council of Five Hundred. Property qualifications limited the franchise except for soldiers, who even without property were permitted to vote.

Thermidor became a term associated with political reaction. However, if the French Revolution had originated in political conflicts characteristic of the eighteenth century, it had by 1795 become something very different. A society and a political structure based on rank and birth had given way to one based on civic equality and social status stemming from the ownership or nonownership of property. People who had never been allowed direct, formal access to political power had to differing degrees been admitted to those activities. Their entrance had given rise to questions of property distribution and economic regulations that could not again be totally ignored. Representation had been established as a principle of practical politics. Henceforth the question before France and eventually before all of Europe would be which new groups would be admitted to representation. In the *levée en masse* the French had demonstrated to Europe the power of the secular ideal of nationhood.

All of these stunning changes in the political and social contours of Europe are not to be forgotten in a consideration of the post-Thermidorian course of the French Revolution. What triumphed in the Constitution of the Year III was the revolution of the holders of property. For this reason the French Revolution has usually been considered the victory of the bourgeoisie, or middle class. However, the property that won the day was not industrial wealth but the wealth stemming from commerce and the professions. Moreover the largest new propertied class to emerge from the revolutionary turmoil was the peasantry, who as a result of the destruction of feudal privileges had achieved personal ownership of the land. Unlike peasants liberated from feudalism in other parts of Europe during the next century, French peasants had to pay no monetary compensation.

The most decisively reactionary element in the Thermidorian Reaction and the new constitution was the removal of the sans-culottes from political life. With the war effort succeeding, the Convention severed its ties with the sans-culottes. True to their belief in an unregulated economy, the Thermidorians repealed the ceiling on prices. As a result, the winter of 1794–1795 brought the worst food shortages of the period. There were numerous food riots, which the Convention put down with force to prove that the era of the sans-culottes

journées had come to a close. On October 5, 1795—13 Vendémiaire—the sections of Paris rose up against the Convention. For the first time in the history of the revolution, artillery was turned against the people of Paris. A general named Napoleon Bonaparte (1769–1821) commanded the cannon, and with a "whiff of grapeshot" he dispersed the crowd.

By the Treaty of Basel in March 1795, the Convention concluded peace with Prussia and Spain. However, the legislators feared a resurgence of both radical democrats and royalists in the upcoming elections for the Council of Five Hundred. Consequently the Convention ruled that at least two thirds of the new legislature must have been members of the older body. The Thermidorians did not even trust the property owners as voters. The next year the newly established Directory again faced social unrest. In Paris Gracchus Babeuf (1760–1797) led the Conspiracy of Equals. He and his followers called for more radical democracy and for more equality of property. Babeuf was arrested, tried, and executed. This quite minor plot became famous many decades later when European socialists attempted to find their historical roots in the French Revolution.

The suppression of the sans-culottes, the narrow franchise of the constitution, the rule of the two thirds, and the Catholic royalist revival presented the Directory with problems that it never succeeded in overcoming. It lacked any broad base of meaningful political support. It particularly required active loyalty because France remained at war with Austria and Great Britain. Consequently the Directory came to depend on the power of the army rather than on constitutional processes for governing the country. All of the soldiers could vote. Moreover, within the army, created and sustained by the revolution, stood officers who were eager for power and ambitious for political conquest. The results of the instability of the Directory and the growing role of the army held profound consequences not only for France but for the entire Western world.

Suggested Readings

C. BRINTON, *The Jacobins: An Essay in the New History* (1930). An examination of the social background of these revolutionaries.

C. BRINTON, *A Decade of Revolution*, 1789–1799 (1934).

A general survey of Europe during the revolutionary years.

R. COBB, *The Police and the People: French Popular Protest, 1789–1820* (1970). An interesting and imaginative treatment of the question of social control during the revolution.

A. COBBAN, *Edmund Burke and the Revolt Against the Eighteenth Century* (1929). Sets Burke's thought in a broader intellectual context.

A. COBBAN, *Aspects of the French Revolution* (1970). Essays on numerous subjects.

C. CONE, *The English Jacobins: Reformers in Late Eighteenth Century England* (1968). The fortunes of English radicals during the repression following the outbreak of war with France.

K. EPSTEIN, *The Genesis of German Conservatism* (1966). A major study of antiliberal forces in Germany before and during the revolution.

J. GODECHOT, *The Taking of the Bastille, July 14, 1789* (1970). The best modern discussion of the subject and one that places the fall of the Bastille in the context of crowd behavior in the eighteenth century.

J. GODECHOT, *The Counter-Revolution: Doctrine and Action, 1789–1804* (1971). An examination of opposition to the revolution.

A. GOODWIN, *The Friends of Liberty: The English Democratic Movement in the Age of the French Revolution* (1979). A major new work that explores the impact of the French Revolution on English radicalism.

D. M. GREER, *The Incidence of the Terror During the French Revolution: A Statistical Interpretation* (1935). A study of what people in which regions became the victims of the Terror.

N. HAMPSON, *A Social History of the French Revolution* (1963). A clear account with much interesting detail.

D. JOHNSON (Ed.), *French Society and the Revolution* (1976). A useful collection of important essays on the social history of the revolution.

G. LEFEBVRE, *The Coming of the French Revolution* (trans., 1947). An examination of the crisis of the French monarchy and the events of 1789.

G. LEFEBVRE, *The French Revolution*, 2 vols. (1962–1964). A major study by one of the most important modern writers on the subject.

R. R. PALMER, *Twelve Who Ruled: The Committee of Public Safety During the Terror* (1941). A clear narrative and analysis of the policies and problems of the committee.

R. R. PALMER, *The Age of the Democratic Revolution: A Political History of Europe and America, 1760–1800*, 2 vols. (1959, 1964). An impressive survey of the political turmoil in the transatlantic world.

G. RUDÉ, *The Crowd in the French Revolution* (1959). Examines who composed the revolutionary crowds and why.

A. SOBOUL, *The Parisian Sans-Culottes and the French Revolution, 1793–94* (1964). The best work on the subject.

A. SOBOUL, *The French Revolution* (trans., 1975). An important work by a Marxist scholar.

J. H. STEWART, *A Documentary Survey of the French Revolution* (1951). Major sources in translation.

J. M. THOMPSON, *Robespierre*, 2 vols. (1935). The best biography.

C. TILLY, *The Vendée* (1964). A significant sociological investigation.

M. WALZER (Ed.), *Regicide and Revolution: Speeches at the Trial of Louis XVI* (1974). An important and exceedingly interesting collection of documents with a useful introduction.

In this French allegory of 1799, Napoleon is portrayed as the First Consul saving France from discord and ignorance. [Bibliotheque Nationale.]

23 The Age of Napoleon and the Triumph of Romanticism

THE GOVERNMENT of the Directory represented a new class made up of politicians, merchants, bankers, war speculators, and profiteers sprung from the nonaristocratic order of the old regime, as well as a few undistinguished nobles. Together they formed a society of recently enriched and powerful people whose chief goal was to halt the revolutionary movement without rolling it back. They wanted to perpetuate their own rule. They sought to achieve peace and quiet in order to gain more wealth and to establish a society in which money would become the only requirement for eminence and power. They and their goals confronted a host of enemies.

The Rise of Napoleon Bonaparte

The chief danger to the Directory came from the royalists, who hoped to restore the Bourbon monarchy by legal means. Many of the *émigrés* had drifted back into France. Their plans for a restoration drew support from devout Catholics and from those citizens whom the excesses of the revolution had disgusted. Monarchy seemed to hold the promise of stability. The spring elections of 1797 turned out most of the incumbents and replaced them with a majority of constitutional monarchists and their sympathizers. To prevent an end to the republic and a peaceful restoration of monarchy, the antimonarchist Directory staged a *coup d'état* on 18 Fructidor (September 4, 1797). They put their own supporters into the legislative seats won by their opponents. They then imposed censorship and exiled some of their enemies. Napoleon Bonaparte, the general in charge of the Italian military campaign, had made these political actions possible. At the request of the Directors, he had sent one of his subordinates to Paris to guarantee the success of the *coup*. In 1797, as in 1795, the army and Bonaparte had saved the day for the government installed in the wake of the Thermidorian Reaction.

Napoleon Bonaparte was born in 1769 to a poor family of lesser nobles at Ajaccio, Corsica. Because France had annexed Corsica in the previous year, he went to French schools, pursued a military career, and in 1785 obtained a commission as a French artillery officer. He strongly favored the revolution and was a fiery Jacobin. In 1793 he played a leading role in recovering the port of Toulon from the British. In reward for his service the government appointed him a brigadier general. His radical associations threatened his career during the Thermidorian Reaction, but his defense of the new regime on 13 Vendémiaire restored him to favor and won him another promotion and a command in Italy.

By 1795 French arms and diplomacy had shattered the enemy coalition, but France's annexation of Belgium guaranteed continued fighting with Britain and Austria. The attack on Italy aimed at depriving Austria of the provinces of Lombardy and Venetia. In a series of lightning victories Bonaparte crushed the Austrian and Sardinian armies. On his own initiative, and in many ways contrary to the wishes of the government in Paris, he concluded the Treaty of Campo Formio in October 1797. The treaty took Austria out of the war and crowned Napoleon's campaign and independent policy with success. Before long all of Italy and Switzerland had fallen under French domination.

In November 1797 the triumphant Bonaparte returned to Paris to be hailed as a hero and to confront France's only remaining enemy, Britain. He judged it impossible to cross the channel and invade England at that time. Instead he chose to capture Egypt from the Ottoman Empire. By this strategy he hoped to drive the British fleet from the Mediterranean, cut off British communication with India, damage British trade, and threaten the British empire. The invasion of Egypt was a failure. Admiral Horatio Nelson (1758–1805) destroyed the French fleet at Abukir on August 1, 1798. The French army could then neither accomplish anything of importance in the Near East nor get home. To make matters worse, the situation in Europe was deteriorating. The French invasion of Egypt had alarmed Russia, which had its own ambitions in the Near East. The Russians, the Austrians, and the Ottomans soon joined Britain to form the Second Coalition. In 1799 the Russian and Austrian armies defeated the French in Italy and Switzerland and threatened to invade France.

Economic troubles and the dangerous international situation eroded the already fragile support of the Directory. One of the Directors, the Abbé Sieyès, proposed a new constitution. The author of the pamphlet *What Is the Third Estate?* (1789) wanted to establish a vigorous executive body independent of the whims of electoral politics, a government based on the principle of "confidence from below, power from above." The change would require another *coup d'état* with military support. News of France's diplomatic misfortunes had reached Napoleon in Egypt. Without orders and leaving his doomed army behind, he returned to France in October 1799. He received much popular acclaim, although some people thought that he deserved a court-martial for desertion. He soon joined Sieyès. On 19 Brumaire (November 10, 1799) his troops drove out the legislators and permitted the success of the *coup*.

Sieyès appears to have thought Napoleon could be used and then dismissed, but if so he badly misjudged his man. The proposed constitution divided executive authority among three consuls. Bonaparte quickly pushed it aside, as he did Sieyès, and in December 1799 he issued the Constitution of the Year VIII. Behind a screen of universal manhood suffrage that suggested democratic principles, a complicated system of checks and balances that appealed to republican theory, and a Council of State that evoked memories of Louis XIV, the constitution in fact established the rule of one man, the First Consul, Bonaparte. To find a reasonably close historical analogy one must go back to Caesar and Augustus and the earlier Greek tyrants. The career of Bonaparte, however, pointed forward to the dictators of the twentieth century. He was the first modern political figure to employ the rhetoric of revolution and nationalism, to back it with military force, and to combine those elements into a mighty weapon of imperial expansion in the service of his own power and ambition.

The Consulate in France (1799–1804)

The establishment of the Consulate, in effect, closed the revolution in France. The leading elements of the Third Estate—that is, officials, landowners, doctors, lawyers, and financiers—had achieved most of their goals by 1799. They had abolished hereditary privilege, and the careers thus opened to talent allowed them to achieve the wealth and status they sought. The peasants were also satisfied. They had acquired the land they had

In this cartoon supporting Napoleon's coup of 18 Brunaire (November 9, 1799) the toppled sphinx represents the downfall of the incompetent, disordered, and corrupt government of the Directory. [Library of Congress.]

always wanted and had destroyed oppressive feudal privileges as well. The newly established dominant classes were profoundly conservative. They had little or no desire to share their recently won privileges with the lower social orders. Bonaparte seemed just the person to give them security. When he submitted his constitution to the voters in a plebiscite, they approved it by 3,011,077 votes to 1,567.

Bonaparte quickly justified the public's confidence by setting about achieving peace with France's enemies. Russia had already quarreled with its allies and left the Second Coalition. A campaign in Italy brought another victory over Austria at Marengo in 1800. The Treaty of Lunéville early in 1801 took Austria out of the war and confirmed the earlier settlement of Campo Formio. Britain was now alone and, in 1802, concluded the Treaty of Amiens, which brought peace to Europe. Bona-

parte was equally effective in restoring peace and order at home. He employed generosity, flattery, and bribery to win over some of his enemies. He issued a general amnesty and employed in his own service persons from all political factions. He required only that they be loyal to him. Some of the highest offices were occupied by persons who had been extreme radicals during the Reign of Terror, others by persons who had fled the Terror and favored constitutional monarchy, and still others by former high officials of the old regime.

On the other hand, Bonaparte was ruthless and efficient in suppressing opposition. He established a highly centralized administration in which all departments were managed by prefects directly responsible to the central government in Paris. He employed secret police. He stamped out once and for all the royalist rebellion in the west and made the rule of Paris effective in Brittany and the

❧ Napoleon Describes Conditions Leading to the Consulate

In this passage from his memoirs Napoleon described the manner in which the Directory came to an end in 1799 and the Consulate began. In reading of his supposed concern about the army, one should remember that he had abandoned his troops in Egypt to return to Paris to undertake this *coup*.

On my return to Paris I found division among all authorities, and agreement upon only one point, namely, that the Constitution was half destroyed and was unable to save liberty.

All parties came to me, confided to me their designs, disclosed their secrets, and requested my support; I refused to be the man of a party.

The Council of Elders summoned me; I answered its appeal. A plan of general restoration had been devised by men whom the nation has been accustomed to regard as the defenders of liberty, equality, and property; this plan required an examination, calm, free, exempt from all influence and all fear. Accordingly, the Council of Elders resolved upon the removal of the Legislative Body to Saint-Cloud; it gave me the responsibility of disposing the force necessary for its independence. I believed it my duty to my fellow citizens, to the soldiers perishing in our armies, to the national glory acquired at the cost of their blood, to accept the command. . . .

I presented myself at the Council of Five Hundred, alone, unarmed, my head uncovered, just as the Elders had received and applauded me; I came to remind the majority of its wishes, and to assure it of its power.

*The stilettos which menaced the deputies were in-*stantly raised against their liberator; twenty assassins threw themselves upon me and aimed at my breast. The grenadiers of the Legislative Body whom I had left at the door of the hall ran forward, placed themselves between the assassins and myself. One of these brave grenadiers had his clothes pierced by a stiletto. They bore me out.*

At the same moment cries of "Outlaw" were raised against the defender of the law. It was the fierce cry of assassins against the power destined to repress them.

They crowded around the president, uttering threats, arms in their hands; they commanded him to outlaw me; I was informed of this; I ordered him to be rescued from their fury, and six grenadiers of the Legislative Body secured him. Immediately afterwards some grenadiers of the Legislative Body charged into the hall and cleared it.

The factions, intimidated, dispersed and fled. . . .

Frenchmen, you will doubtless recognize in this conduct the zeal of a soldier of liberty, a citizen devoted to the Republic. Conservative, tutelary, and liberal ideas have been restored to their rights through the dispersal of the rebels who oppressed the Councils. . . .

John Hall Stewart, *A Documentary Survey of the French Revolution* (New York: Macmillan, 1951), pp. 763–765.

Vendée for the first time in many years. Nor was he above using or even inventing opportunities to destroy his enemies. When a plot on his life surfaced in 1804, he used the event as an excuse to attack the Jacobins, even though the bombing was the work of royalists. In 1804 his forces invaded the sovereignty of Baden to seize the Bourbon Duke of Enghien. The duke was accused of participation in a royalist plot and put to death, even though Bonaparte knew him to be innocent. The action was a flagrant violation of international law and of due process. Charles Maurice de Talleyrand-Périgord (1754–1838), Bonaparte's foreign minister, later termed the act "worse than a crime—a blunder," because it helped to provoke foreign opposition. On the other hand, it was popular with the former Jacobins, for it seemed to preclude the possibility of a Bourbon restoration. The person who killed a Bourbon was hardly likely to restore the royal family. The execution seems to have put an end to royalist plots.

A major obstacle to internal peace was the steady hostility of French Catholics. Refractory clergy continued to advocate counterrevolution. The religious revival that dated from the Thermidorian Reaction increased discontent with the secular state created by the revolution. Bonaparte regarded religion as a political matter. He approved its role in preserving an orderly society but was suspicious of any such power independent of the state.

In 1801 Napoleon concluded a concordat with Pope Pius VII, to the shock and dismay of his anticlerical supporters. The settlement gave Napoleon what he most wanted. Both the refractory clergy and those who had accepted the revolution were forced to resign. Their replacements received their spiritual investiture from the pope, but the state named the bishops and paid their salaries and the salary of one priest in each parish. In return the church gave up its claims on its confiscated property. The concordat declared that "Catholicism is the religion of the great majority of French citizens." This was merely a statement of fact and fell far short of what the pope had wanted, religious dominance for the Roman Catholic Church. The clergy had to swear an oath of loyalty to the state, and the Organic Articles of 1802, which were actually distinct from the concordat, established the supremacy of State over Church. Similar laws were applied to the Protestant and Jewish religious communities as well, reducing still further the privileged position of the Catholic church.

Peace and efficient administration brought pros-

Charles Maurice de Talleyrand-Périgord, known to history as Talleyrand, was one of the most talented—or adaptable—political survivors of the Revolution. Before 1789 he had been a Roman Catholic bishop. Later he became a major diplomat, first for the revolutionary government, and then for Napoleon. Finally, in 1815, he represented the restored Bourbon government at the Congress of Vienna. The portrait is by Pierre-Paul Prud'hon. [The Granger Collection.]

perity and security to the French and gratitude and popularity to Bonaparte. In 1802 a plebiscite appointed him consul for life, and he soon produced still another new constitution, which granted him what amounted to full power. The years of the Consulate were employed in reforming and estab-

❧ The Consuls Proclaim the End of the French Revolution

In this proclamation of December 15, 1799, the three new consuls, of whom Napoleon was one, presented the Constitution of the Year VIII to the French people and ceremoniously declared the end of the French Revolution.

Frenchmen!

A Constitution is presented to you.

It terminates the uncertainties which the provisional government introduced into external relations, into the internal and military situation of the Republic.

It places in the institutions which it establishes first magistrates whose devotion has appeared necessary for its success.

The Constitution is founded on the true principles of representative government, on the sacred rights of property, equality, and liberty.

The powers which it institutes will be strong and stable, as they must be in order to guarantee the rights of citizens and the interests of the State.

Citizens, the Revolution is established upon the principles which began it: It is ended.

John Hall Stewart, *A Documentary Survey of the French Revolution* (New York: Macmillan, 1951), p. 780.

lishing the basic laws and institutions of France. The settlement imposed by Napoleon was an ambiguous combination of liberal principles derived from the Enlightenment and the early years of the revolution and conservative principles and practices going back to the old regime or adapted to the conservative spirit that had triumphed at Thermidor.

The abolition of all privileges based on birth, the establishment of equality before the law, the disappearance of all authority except that of the national state and all legal distinctions based on class or locality, and the end of all purchased offices and the substitution of salaried officials chosen for merit represented the application of rationality and the achievement of goals sought by the people who had made the revolution. Most of these were embodied in the general codification of laws carried out under Bonaparte's direction. This was especially true of the Civil Code of 1804, usually called the Napoleonic Code. However, these laws stopped far short of the full equality advocated by liberal rationalists. Fathers were granted extensive control over their children and men over their wives. Labor unions were still forbidden, and the rights of workers were inferior to those of their employers.

In the political arena and in administration Napoleonic institutions ran contrary to the tendencies of the revolution. They aimed at a kind of enlightened absolutism that was similar to but more effective than what had existed in the old regime. Rep-

❧ Napoleon Makes Peace with the Papacy

In 1801 Napoleon concluded a concordat with Pope Pius VII. This document was the cornerstone of Napoleonic religious policy. The concordat which was announced on April 8, 1802, allowed the Roman Catholic Church to function freely in France only within the limits of church support for the government as indicated in the oath included in Article 6.

The government of the French Republic recognizes that the Roman, catholic and apostolic religion is the religion of the great majority of French citizens.

His Holiness likewise recognizes that this same religion has derived and in this moment again expects the greatest benefit and grandeur from the establishment of the catholic worship in France and from the personal profession of it which the consuls of the Republic make.

In consequence, after this mutual recognition, as well for the benefit of religion as for the maintenance of internal tranquility, they have agreed as follows:

1. The catholic, apostolic and Roman religion shall be freely exercised in France: its worship shall be public, and in conformity with the police regulations which the government shall deem necessary for the public tranquility.

. . . .

4. The First Consul of the Republic shall make appointments, within the three months which shall follow the publication of the bull of His Holiness, to *the archbishoprics and bishoprics of the new circumscription. His Holiness shall confer the canonical institution, following the forms established in relation to France before the change of government.*

. . . .

6. Before entering upon their functions, the bishops shall take directly, at the hands of the First Consul, the oath of fidelity which was in use before the change of government, expressed in the following terms:

"I swear and promise to God, upon the holy scriptures, to remain in obedience and fidelity to the government established by the constitution of the French Republic. I also promise not to have any intercourse, nor to assist by any counsel, nor to support any league, either within or without, which is inimical to the public tranquility; and if, within my diocese or elsewhere, I learn that anything to the prejudice of the state is being contrived, I will make it known to the government."

F. M. Anderson, *The Constitutions and Other Select Documents Illustrative of the History of France 1789–1907*, 2nd ed. (Minneapolis: H. W. Wilson, 1908), pp. 296–297.

resentative government, local autonomy, and personal freedom were rejected in favor of the centralization of all power and the subordination of personal rights and political freedom to the needs of the state as interpreted by the First Consul. All of this was acceptable to the dominant bourgeoisie and the peasantry. They accepted censorship, the arbitrary and sometimes brutal suppression of dissent, and even the restoration of a new quasi nobility in the Legion of Honor as long as order, prosperity, and security of property were preserved.

In 1804 Bonaparte seized on the bomb attack on his life to make himself emperor. He argued that the establishment of a dynasty would make the new regime secure and make further attempts on his life useless. Another new constitution was promulgated in which Napoleon Bonaparte was called Emperor of the French, instead of First Consul of the Republic. This constitution was also overwhelmingly ratified in a plebiscite.

To conclude the drama, Napoleon invited the pope to Notre Dame to take part in the coronation. But at the last minute the pope agreed that Napoleon should place the crown on his own head. The emperor had no intention of allowing anyone to think that his power and authority depended on the approval of the church. Henceforth, he was called Napoleon I. This act was the natural goal of his career. His aims had always been profoundly selfish: power and glory for himself and his family. There was, moreover, a romantic streak in Napoleon. He thought of himself as a rival of Alexander the Great and Caesar, a conqueror as well as a ruler. Had Napoleon wished it, Europe might well have had peace; but his ambition would not permit it.

Napoleon's Empire (1804-1814)

In the decade between his coronation as emperor and his final defeat at Waterloo (1815), Napoleon conquered most of Europe in a series of military campaigns that astonished the world. France's victories changed the map of Europe, put an end to the old regime and its feudal trappings in western Europe, and forced the eastern European states to reorganize themselves to resist Napoleon's armies. Everywhere Napoleon's advance unleashed the powerful force of nationalism. The militarily mobilized French nation, one of the achievements of the revolution, was Napoleon's weapon. He could put as many as 700,000 men under arms at one time, risk as many as 100,000 troops in a single battle, endure heavy losses, and come back to fight again. He could conscript citizen soldiers in unprecedented numbers, thanks to their loyalty to the nation and to their remarkable leader. No single enemy could match such resources, and even coalitions were unsuccessful until Napoleon at last overreached himself and made mistakes that led to his own defeat.

Napoleon deserves his reputation as one of the great commanders of all time. His genius lay not in strategic or tactical invention, in which he had many eighteenth-century French forerunners, but in execution and leadership. His strategy depended on mobility and timing. He liked to divide his forces into units of moderate size, disperse them across the country, and then use their superior speed and his own planning skill to unite them at the critical point at the right time. All of this emphasis on speed of maneuver had a single goal: to bring the hostile armies together for a swift major battle. Napoleon departed from the usual eighteenth-century tactics, which emphasized maneuver and strategic position and the fighting of a battle only as a last resort. His aim was not to control territory nor to gain strong points but to destroy the enemy army. After that, rest for his army might follow. As long as conditions permitted such warfare, Napoleon was unbeatable.

Self-sufficiency was another important Napoleonic military principle that related to his emphasis on swiftness of maneuver. It was this self-sufficiency that allowed him to disperse and reunite his armies so rapidly. The whole army traveled light, with few supplies. By living off the country in which it fought, the army was free of the need to establish and follow a chain of supply depots. This was a great advantage in fertile areas like western and central Europe but proved a problem later against the guerrilla fighters in Spain and in the vast expanse of Russia during the winter. Under those conditions Napoleon's brilliant tactics could not be carried out, and he was eventually defeated. But those events lay many years ahead.

The Peace of Amiens (1802) was doomed to be merely a truce. Napoleon's unlimited ambitions shattered any hope that it might last. He sent an army to restore the rebellious island of Haiti to French rule. This move aroused British fears that he was planning the renewal of a French empire in

OPPOSITE: *This formal portrait of Napoleon by Jean A. D. Ingres (1780–1867) reveals and glorifies the repressive emperor. He is clothed in the splendor of a monarch and seems to represent the total power of the state. The painting is in the Musée de la Légion d'Honneur, Paris. [French Cultural Services, New York.]*

America, because Spain had restored Louisiana to France in 1800. More serious were his interventions in the Dutch Republic, Italy, and Switzerland and his role in the reorganization of Germany. The Treaty of Campo Formio had required a redistribution of territories along the Rhine River, and the petty princes of the region engaged in a shameful scramble to enlarge their holdings. Among the results were the reduction of Austrian influence in Germany and the emergence of a smaller number of larger German states in the west, all dependent on Napoleon.

The British found all of these developments alarming enough to justify an ultimatum. When Napoleon ignored it, Britain declared war in May 1803. William Pitt the Younger returned to office as prime minister in 1804 and began to construct the Third Coalition. By August 1805 he had persuaded Russia and Austria to move once again against French aggression. A great naval victory soon raised the fortunes of the allies. On October 21, 1805, the British admiral Horatio, Lord Nelson destroyed the combined French and Spanish fleets at the Battle of Trafalgar just off the Spanish coast. Nelson died in the battle, but the British lost no ships. The victory of Trafalgar put an end to all French hope of an invasion of Britain and guaranteed British control of the sea for the rest of the war.

On land the story was very different. Even before Trafalgar Napoleon had marched to the Danube River to attack his continental enemies. In mid-October he forced a large Austrian army to surrender at Ulm and soon occupied Vienna. On December 2, 1805, in perhaps his greatest victory, Napoleon defeated the combined Austrian and Russian forces at Austerlitz. The Treaty of Pressburg, which followed, won major concessions from Austria. The Austrians withdrew from Italy and left Napoleon in control of everything north of Rome. He was recognized as king of Italy.

Extensive changes also came about in Germany. In July 1806 Napoleon organized the Confederation of the Rhine, which included most of the western German princes. The withdrawal of these princes from the Holy Roman Empire led Francis II of Austria to dissolve that ancient political body and henceforce to call himself only emperor of Austria.

Prussia, which had carefully remained neutral up to this point, was now provoked into war against France. The famous Prussian army was quickly crushed at the battles of Jena and Auerstädt on October 14, 1806. Two weeks later Napoleon was in Berlin. There, on November 21, he issued the Berlin Decrees forbidding his allies to import British goods. On June 13, 1807, Napoleon defeated the Russians at Friedland and was able to occupy

British Admiral Horatio Nelson (1758–1805) was the brilliant naval strategist in the wars against Napoleonic France—wars in which he lost an eye, an arm, and finally his life. His last battle, in which he was killed, was a stunning victory over the combined French and Spanish fleets off Trafalgar on the coast of Spain, October 21, 1805, and ended any possible sea threat to England. The painting is by Lemuel Francis Abbott and is in the National Portrait Gallery, London. [The Granger Collection.]

This painting of Napoleon and his officers at the battle of Eylau in 1807 clearly shows the vast number of troops that he customarily used in combat—although in this picture the troops are included only as a backdrop for a romantic rendering of the emperor and his aides on the field of battle. The artist was Antoine Jean Gros (1771–1835). [The Granger Collection.]

In 1807 Czar Alexander I of Russia (center left) and Napoleon (center right) met on a raft in the Niemen River near Tilsit (on the Lithuanian border). At that conference they signed a treaty in which they divided Europe into spheres of French and Russian influence. The scene is imagined here by the artist Ludwig Wolf. [Bildarchiv Preussischer Kulturbesitz.]

Königsberg, the capital of East Prussia. The French emperor was master of all Germany.

Unable to fight another battle and unwilling to retreat into Russia, Czar Alexander I (1801–1825) was ready to make peace. He and Napoleon met on a raft in the middle of the Niemen River while the two armies and the nervous king of Prussia watched from the bank. On July 7, 1807, they signed the Treaty of Tilsit, which confirmed France's gains. Moreover the Prussian state was reduced to half its size and was saved from extinction only by the support of Alexander. Prussia openly and Russia secretly became allies of Napoleon in his war against Britain.

Napoleon organized conquered Europe much like the domain of a great Corsican family. The great French Empire was ruled directly by the head of the clan, Napoleon. On its borders lay a number of satellite states carved out as the portions of the several family members. His stepson ruled Italy for him, while three of his brothers and his brother-in-law were made kings of other conquered states. Napoleon denied a kingdom to his brother Lucien, of whose wife he disapproved. The French emperor expected his relatives to take orders without question. When they failed to do so, he rebuked and even punished them. This establishment of the Napoleonic family as the collective sovereign of Europe was offensive to the growing national feeling in many states and helped to create nationalism in others. The rule of puppet kings was unpopular and provoked political opposition that needed only encouragement and assistance to flare up into serious resistance.

After the Treaty of Tilsit such assistance could come only from Britain, and Napoleon knew that he must defeat the British before he could feel safe. Unable to compete with the British navy, he continued the economic warfare begun by the Berlin Decree. His plan was to cut off all British trade with the European continent. In this manner he hoped to cripple the commercial and financial power on which Britain depended, to cause domestic unrest and revolution, and thus to drive the British from the war. The Milan Decree of 1807 attempted to stop neutral nations from trading with Britain. For a time it appeared that this Continental System might work. British exports dropped, and riots broke out in England. But in the end the system failed and may even have contributed significantly to Napoleon's defeat.

The British economy survived because of its access to the growing markets of North and South

---

NAPOLEONIC EUROPE

1797	Napoleon concludes the Treaty of Campo Formio
1798	Nelson defeats the French navy in the harbor of Abukir
1799	Consulate established
1801	Concordat between France and the papacy
1802	Treaty of Amiens
1803	War renewed between France and Britain
1804	Execution of Duke of Enghien
	Napoleonic Civil Code issued
	Napoleon crowned as Emperor
1805	Nelson defeats French fleet at Trafalgar (October 21)
	Austerlitz (December 2)
1806	Jena
	Continental System established by Berlin Decree
1807	Friedland
	Treaty of Tilsit
1808	Beginning of Spanish resistance to Napoleonic domination
1809	Wagram
	Napoleon marries Archduchess Marie Louise of Austria
1812	Invasion of Russia and French defeat at Borodino
1813	Leipzig (Battle of the Nations)
1814	Treaty of Chaumont (March) establishes Quadruple Alliance
	Congress of Vienna convenes (September)
1815	Napoleon returns from Elba (March 1)
	Waterloo (June 18)
	Holy Alliance formed at Congress of Vienna (September 26)
	Quadruple Alliance renewed at Congress of Vienna (November 20)
1821	Napoleon dies on Saint Helena

America and of the eastern Mediterranean, all assured by the British control of the seas. At the same time, the Continental System did great harm to the European economies. The system was meant not only to hurt Britain but also to help France economically. Napoleon resisted advice to turn his empire into a free-trade area. Such a policy would have been both popular and helpful. Instead, his tariff policies favored France, increased the resentment of foreign merchants, and made them less willing to enforce the system and more ready to engage in smuggling. It was in part to prevent smuggling that Napoleon invaded Spain in 1808, and the resulting peninsular campaign in Spain and Portugal helped to bring on his ruin.

European Response to the Empire

Napoleon's conquests stimulated the two most powerful political forces in nineteenth-century Europe: liberalism and nationalism. The export of his version of the French Revolution directly and indirectly spread the ideas and values of the Enlightenment and the principles of 1789. Wherever Napoleon ruled, the Napoleonic Code was imposed and class distinction was abolished. Feudal dues disappeared and the peasants were freed from serfdom and manorial dues. In the towns the guilds and the local oligarchies that had been dominant for centuries were dissolved or deprived of their power. New freedom thus came to serfs, artisans, workers, and entrepreneurs outside the privileged circles. The established churches were deprived of their traditional independence and were made subordinate to the state. Church monopoly of religion was replaced by general toleration.

These reforms were not undone by the fall of Napoleon, and along with the demand for representative, constitutional government, they remained the basis of later liberal reforms. However, at the same time it became increasingly clear that Napoleon's policies were intended first and foremost for his own glory and that of France. The Continental System demonstrated that France rather than Europe generally was to be enriched by Napoleon's rule. Consequently, before long the conquered states and peoples became restive.

German Nationalism and Prussian Reform

The German response to Napoleon's success was particularly interesting and important. There had never been a unified German state. The great German writers of the Enlightenment, such as Kant, Schiller, and Lessing, were neither political nor nationalistic.

At the beginning of the nineteenth century the Romantic movement had begun to take hold. One of its basic features in Germany was the emergence of nationalism. This movement went through two distinct stages. Initially, nationalistic writers emphasized the unique and admirable qualities of German culture, which, they argued, arose from

The king and queen of Prussia are portrayed as birds to be plucked in this French cartoon of 1806. The French victories at Jena and Auerstadt on October 14, 1806 destroyed the Prussian army in one day. The battle showed beyond all doubt that a citizen army led by officers chosen on merit was far superior to an army of serfs and mercenaries led by incompetent noblemen. The Prussians learned their lesson, and their defeat led to a thorough reform of army and state. This print is in the Musee Carnavalet. [Bulloz.]

the peculiar history of the German people. Such cultural nationalism prevailed until Napoleon's humiliation of Prussia at Jena in 1806. At that point many German intellectuals began to urge resistance to Napoleon on the basis of German nationalism. The French conquest endangered the independence and achievements of the German people. Many nationalists were also critical of the German princes, who ruled selfishly and inefficiently and who seemed ever ready to lick the boots of Napoleon. No less important in forging a German national sentiment was the example of France, which had attained greatness by enlisting the active support of the entire people in the patriotic cause. Henceforth many Germans sought to solve their internal political problems by establishing a unified German state, reformed to harness the energies of the entire people.

After Tilsit only Prussia could arouse such patriotic feelings. Elsewhere German rulers were either under Napoleon's thumb or actively collaborating with him. Defeated, humiliated, and shrunk in size, Prussia continued to resist, however feebly. To Prussia fled German nationalists from other states, calling for reforms and unification that were, in fact, feared and hated by Frederick William III and the *Junker* nobility. Reforms came about in spite of such opposition because the defeat at Jena had made clear the necessity of new departures for the Prussian state.

The Prussian administrative and social reforms were the work of Baron vom Stein (1757–1831) and Count von Hardenberg (1750–1822). The architects of military reform were General Gerhard von Scharnhorst (1755–1813) and Count von Gneisenau (1760–1831). None of these reformers intended to reduce the autocratic power of the Prussian monarch or to put an end to the dominance of the *Junkers,* who formed the bulwark of the state and of the army officer corps. Rather, they aimed at fighting the revolution and French power with their own version of the French weapons. As Hardenberg declared:

Our objective, our guiding principle, must be a revolution in the better sense, a revolution leading directly to the great goal, the elevation of humanity through the wisdom of those in authority. . . . Democratic rules of conduct in a monarchical administration, such is the formula . . . which will conform most comfortably with the spirit of the age.[1]

[1] Quoted in Geoffrey Bruun, *Europe and the French Imperium* (New York: Harper & Row, 1938), p. 174.

Although the reforms came from the top, they brought important changes in Prussian society.

Stein's reforms put an end to the existing system of Prussian landownership. The *Junker* monopoly of landholding was broken. Serfdom was generally abolished. However, the power of the *Junkers* did not permit the total end of the system, as in the western principalities of Germany. Peasants remaining on the land were forced to continue manorial labor, although they were free to leave the land if they chose. They could obtain the ownership of the land they worked only at the price of forfeiting a third of it to the lord. The result was that *Junker* holdings grew larger. Some peasants went to the cities to find work; others became agricultural laborers; and some did actually become small freeholding farmers. Serfdom had come to an end, but new social problems that would fester for another half-century had been created as a landless labor force, enlarged by the population explosion, emerged.

The military reforms sought to increase the supply of soldiers and to improve their quality. Jena had shown that an army of free patriots commanded by officers chosen on merit rather than by birth could defeat an army of serfs and mercenaries commanded by incompetent nobles. To remedy the situation, the Prussian reformers abolished inhumane punishments, sought to inspire patriotic feelings in the soldiers, opened the officer corps to commoners, gave promotions on the basis of merit, and organized war colleges that developed new theories of strategy and tactics. These reforms soon put Prussia in a condition to regain its former power. However, because Napoleon had put a strict limit on the size of the Prussian army, universal conscription could not be introduced until 1813. Before that date the Prussians got around the limit of 42,000 men in arms by training one group each year, putting them into the reserves, and then training a new group the same size. In this manner Prussia could boast an army of 270,000 by 1814.

The Wars of Liberation

In Spain more than elsewhere in Europe national resistance to France had deep social roots. Spain had achieved political unity as early as the sixteenth century. The Spanish peasants were devoted to the ruling dynasty and especially to the Roman Catholic Church. France and Spain had been allies since 1796. In 1807, however, a French army came into the Iberian Peninsula to force Por-

Arthur Wellesley, the duke of Wellington, first led troops against Napoleon in Spain and later defeated him at the battle of Waterloo, June 18, 1815. Unlike his great naval contemporary, Nelson, he lived to become an elder statesman of Britain. The portrait is by the celebrated Spanish painter Francisco Goya (1746–1828). [The Granger Collection.]

Goya's "Barbarians" portrays the brutality of the guerrilla warfare waged against Napoleon's armies in Spain. [Metropolitan Museum of Art.]

tugal to abandon its traditional alliance with Britain. The army stayed in Spain to protect lines of supply and communication. When a revolt broke out in Madrid in 1808, Napoleon used it as a pretext to depose the Spanish Bourbon dynasty and to place his brother Joseph on the Spanish throne. Attacks on the privileges of the church increased public outrage. Many members of the upper classes were prepared to collaborate with Napoleon, but the peasants, urged on by the lower clergy and the monks, rose in a general rebellion.

Napoleon faced a new kind of warfare not vulnerable to his usual tactics. Guerrilla bands cut lines of communication, killed stragglers, destroyed isolated units, and then disappeared into the mountains. The British landed an army under Sir Arthur Wellesley (1769–1852), later the duke of Wellington, to support the Spanish insurgents. Thus began the long peninsular campaign that would drain French strength from elsewhere in Europe and play a critical role in Napoleon's eventual defeat.

The French troubles in Spain encouraged the Austrians to renew the war in 1809. Since their defeat at Austerlitz they had sought a war of revenge. The Austrians counted on Napoleon's distraction in Spain, French war weariness, and aid from other German princes. However, Napoleon was fully in command in France; and the German princes did not move. The French army marched swiftly into Austria and won the battle of Wagram. The resulting Peace of Schönbrunn deprived Austria of much territory and three and a half million subjects. Another spoil of victory was the Austrian Archduchess Marie Louise, daughter of the emperor. Napoleon's wife, Josephine de Beauharnais, was forty-six and had borne him no children. His dynastic ambitions, as well as the desire for a marriage matching his new position as master of Europe, led him to divorce his wife and to marry the eighteen-year-old Austrian princess. Napoleon had also considered the sister of Czar Alexander but had received a polite rebuff.

The failure of Napoleon's marriage negotiations

When their marriage failed to produce a male heir, Napoleon divorced his first wife, Joséphine de Beauharnais (1763–1814), [LEFT]. Many considered the action one aspect of Napoleon's betrayal of the Revolution, especially because he then married a daughter of the Hapsburg emperor. This portrait is by F. P. Gerard. [The Granger Collection.]

[RIGHT]: Napoleon's second wife, Marie Louise (1791–1814), bore him a son. It was clear that Napoleon hoped to establish a new imperial dynasty in France. This portrait is by J. B. Isabey. [The Granger Collection.]

THE
CONTINENTAL
SYSTEM
1806 · 1810

NORWAY
SWEDEN
DENMARK
ENGLAND
PRUSSIA
POLAND
RHINE CONF.
RUSSIA
FRANCE
AUSTRIA
PORT.
ITALY
SPAIN

AREAS IN WHICH
BRITISH EXPORTS
WERE PROHIBITED

THE
FRENCH EMPIRE

THE
GRAND EMPIRE

ALLIED WITH
NAPOLEON

300 MI.

300 KM.

BATTLE
SITES

DENMARK
Christiana

SWEDEN
Stockholm

KINGDOM OF
DENMARK
AND
NORWAY

GOTHLAND

Gothenburg

DENMARK · Copenhagen

BALTIC S.

SCOTLAND
Edinburgh

NORTH

SEA

HELIGO-
LAND
(U.K.)

Lübeck

SWEDISH
POMERANIA

PRUSSIA

MECK.

THORN
GRAN.

Posen

York

UNITED
KINGDOM

Hamburg

HOLLAND
OLDEN-
BURG

BERLIN

Breslau

London
Dover

WALES

WEST-
PHALIA

HESSE

SAXONY

LEIPZIG
DRESDEN

BAUTZEN

Boulogne

Brussels
WATERLOO

BERG
Cologne

JENA

Brest

Amiens

Reims

Mainz

CONFEDERATION
OF THE
RHINE

Prague
BOHEMIA

AUSTERLITZ

QUIBERON

Paris

Versailles

VALMY
Strasbourg

BADEN

RATISBON

ULM

Munich

WAGRAM

ASPERN

Fontainebleau

Nantes

Orléans

VENDÉE

FRANCE

SWITZ.
ST. GOTTHARD

HOHENLINDEN

BAVARIA
INNSBRUCK

Vienna

EMPIRE

BAY OF

BISCAY

Rochefort

Lyons

SAVOY

Turin
MARENGO
Genoa

LOMBARDY
Milan
LODI

VENETIA
SACILE

Trieste

ILLYRIAN PROVIN.

Bordeaux

Avignon

Marseilles

Nice

LUCCA

Leghorn

ITALY

K. OF
SARDINIA

BO

CAPE
FINISTERRE

Corunna

TOULOUSE

Toulon

ELBA

Rome

Urbino

Oporto

ALMEIDA

VITORIA

Burgos

SARAGOSSA

GERONA

CORSICA

Bari

PORTUGAL

CIUDAD
RODRIGO

SALAMANCA

Barcelona

TARRAGONA

Naples

VIMEIRO
CINTRA

Lisbon

ELVAS

TALAVERA

Madrid

SPAIN

OCAÑA

CIUDAD
REAL

VALENCIA

VALENCIA

K. OF
NAPLES

BADAJOZ

BAYLEN

BALEARIC IS.

Cordova

Seville

MURCIA

ANDALUCIA

Cagliari

K. OF
SICILY

Cadiz

TRAFALGAR

GIBALTAR
(U.K.)

Algiers

M E D I T E R R A N E A N   S E A

Tunis

690

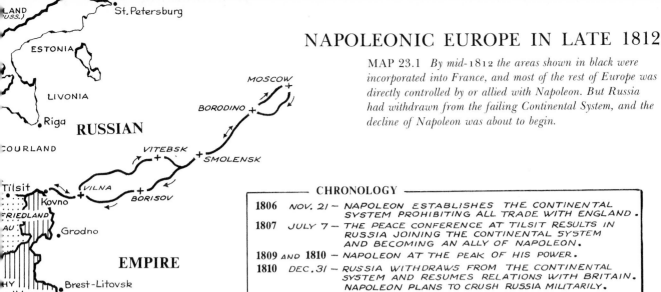

NAPOLEONIC EUROPE IN LATE 1812

MAP 23.1 By mid-1812 the areas shown in black were incorporated into France, and most of the rest of Europe was directly controlled by or allied with Napoleon. But Russia had withdrawn from the failing Continental System, and the decline of Napoleon was about to begin.

with Russia emphasized the shakiness of the Franco-Russian alliance concluded at Tilsit. The alliance was unpopular with Russian nobles because of the liberal politics of France and because of the prohibition of the Continental System on timber sales to Britain. Only French aid in gaining Constantinople could justify the alliance in their eyes, but Napoleon gave them no help against the Ottoman Empire. The organization of the Grand Duchy of Warsaw as a Napoleonic satellite on the Russian doorstep and its enlargement in 1809 after the battle of Wagram angered Alexander I. Napoleon's annexation of Holland in violation of the Treaty of Tilsit, his recognition of the French Marshal Bernadotte as King Charles XIV of Sweden, and his marriage to an Austrian princess further disturbed the czar. At the end of 1810 Russia withdrew from the Continental System and began to prepare for war.

Napoleon was determined to put an end to the Russian military threat. He amassed an army of over 600,000 men, including a core of Frenchmen and over 400,000 other soldiers drawn from the rest of his empire. He intended the usual short campaign crowned by a decisive battle, but the Russians disappointed him by retreating before his advance. His vast superiority in numbers—the Russians had only about 160,000 troops—made it foolish for them to risk a battle. Instead they followed a "scorched-earth" policy, destroying all food and supplies as they retreated. The so-called Grand Army of Napoleon could not live off the country, and the expanse of Russia made supply lines too long to maintain. Terrible rains, fierce heat, shortages of food and water, and the courage of the Russian rear guard defending their country against the invader eroded the morale of Napoleon's army. Napoleon's advisers urged him to abandon the venture, but he feared that an unsuccessful campaign would undermine his position in the empire and in France. He pinned his faith on the Russians' unwillingness to abandon Moscow without a fight.

In September 1812 Russian public opinion forced the army to give Napoleon the battle he wanted in spite of the canny Russian General Kutuzov's wish to avoid the fight and to let the Russian winter defeat the invader. At Borodino, not far west of Moscow, the bloodiest battle of the Napoleonic era cost the French thirty thousand casualties and the Russians almost twice as many. Yet the Russian army was not destroyed. Napoleon had won nothing substantial, and the battle was regarded as a defeat for him. Fires, set by the Russians, soon engulfed Moscow and left Napoleon far from home with a badly diminished army lacking adequate supplies as winter came to a vast country whose people hated the invader. Napoleon, after capturing the burned city, addressed several peace offers to Alexander, but the czar ignored them. By October what was left of the Grand Army was forced to retreat. By December Napoleon realized that the Russian fiasco would encourage plots against him at home and returned to Paris, leaving the remnants of his army to struggle westward. Perhaps only as many as 100,000 lived to tell the tale of their terrible ordeal.

Even as the news of the disaster reached the west, the total defeat of Napoleon was far from certain. He was able to put down his opponents in Paris and to raise another army of 350,000 men. Neither the Prussians nor the Austrians were eager to risk another bout with Napoleon, and even the Russians hesitated. The Austrian foreign minister, Prince Klemens von Metternich (1773–1859), would have been glad to make a negotiated peace that would leave Napoleon on the throne of a shrunk and chastened France rather than see Europe dominated by Russia. Napoleon might have won a reasonable settlement by negotiation had he been willing to make concessions that would have split his jealous opponents, but he would not consider that solution. As he explained to Metternich, "Your sovereigns born on the throne can let them-

selves be beaten twenty times and return to their capitals. I cannot do this because I am an upstart soldier. My domination will not survive the day when I cease to be strong, and therefore feared."[2]

In 1813 patriotic pressure and national ambition brought together the last and most powerful coalition against Napoleon. The Russians drove westward and were joined by Prussia and then Austria. All were assisted by vast amounts of British money. From the west Wellington marched his peninsular army into France. Napoleon's new army was inexperienced and poorly equipped. His generals had lost confidence and were tired. The emperor himself was worn out and sick. Still he was able to wage a skillful campaign in central Europe and to defeat the allies at Dresden. In October, however, he met the combined armies of the enemy at Leipzig in what the Germans called the Battle of the Nations and was decisively defeated. At the end of March 1814 the allied army marched into Paris, and a few days later Napoleon abdicated and went into exile on the island of Elba off the coast of northern Italy.

The Congress of Vienna and the European Settlement

Fear of Napoleon and hostility to his ambitions had held the victorious coalition together. As soon as he was removed, the allies began to pursue their own separate ambitions. The key person in achieving eventual agreement among the allies was Robert Stewart Viscount Castlereagh (1769–1822), the British foreign secretary. Even before the victorious armies had entered Paris, he brought about the signing of the Treaty of Chaumont on March 9, 1814. It provided for the restoration of the Bourbon dynasty to the French throne and the contraction of France to its frontiers of 1792. Even more important was the agreement by Britain, Austria, Russia, and Prussia to form a Quadruple Alliance for twenty years to guarantee the peace terms and to act together to preserve whatever settlement they later agreed on. Remaining problems—and they were many—and final details were left for a conference to be held at Vienna.

[2] Quoted in Felix Markham, *Napoleon and the Awakening of Europe* (New York: Macmillan, 1965), pp. 115–116.

The leading figures of the Congress of Vienna are here portrayed in a single group. Talleyrand has his arm on the table at right, and Metternich, in white breeches, stands toward the left. The actual work of the Congress took place in small meetings, with only a few of these statesmen present. The artist was Isabey. [Austrian Information Service, New York.]

The Congress of Vienna assembled in September 1814 but did not conclude its work until November 1815. Although a glittering array of heads of state attended the gathering, the four great powers conducted the important work of the conference. The only full session of the congress met to ratify the arrangements made by the big four. The easiest problem facing the great powers was France. All the victors agreed that no single state should be allowed to dominate Europe, and all were determined to see that France should be prevented from doing so again. The restoration of the French Bourbon monarchy, which was again popular, and a nonvindictive boundary settlement kept France calm and satisfied. In addition the powers constructed a series of states to serve as barriers to any new French expansion. They established the kingdom of the Netherlands, including Belgium, in the north and added Genoa to Piedmont in the south. Prussia, whose power was increased by accessions in eastern Europe, was given important new territories in the west along the Rhine River to

deter French aggression in that area. Austria was given full control of northern Italy to prevent a repetition of Napoleon's conquests there. As for the rest of Germany, most of Napoleon's arrangements were left untouched. The venerable Holy Roman Empire, which had been dissolved in 1806, was not revived. In all these areas the congress established the rule of legitimate monarchs and rejected any hint of the republican and democratic politics that had flowed from the French Revolution.

On these matters agreement was not difficult, but the settlement of eastern Europe sharply divided the victors. Alexander I of Russia wanted all Poland under his rule. Prussia was willing if it received all of Saxony. But Austria was unwilling to surrender its share of Poland or to see the growth of Prussian power and the penetration of Russia deeper into central Europe. The Polish–Saxon question brought the congress to a standstill and almost brought on a new war among the victors, but defeated France provided a way out. The wily

EUROPE, 1815
AFTER THE
CONGRESS OF VIENNA

N O R T H

S E A

NORWAY
AND
SWEDEN
1814

FINLAND
RUSS. 18

Bergen

Christiania

Stockholm

SCOTLAND

Edinburgh

Belfast

IRELAND

DENMARK

Dublin

Liver-
pool

Manchester

London

UNITED
KINGDOM

A T L A N T I C

O C E A N

Brest

Rennes

Nantes

Paris

Orléans

Rouen

FRANCE

Lyons

Bordeaux

Montpelier

Marseilles

SCHLESWIG

HOLSTEIN

BOUNDARY OF THE
GERMAN
CONFEDERATION

(FORMER
DUTCH
REP.)

(FORMER
AUSTR.
NETHS.)

K. OF THE
NETHERLANDS

Brussels

Reims

Strassburg

LORRAINE

ALSACE

Berne

SWITZ.

SAVOY

PIEDMONT

NICE

ANDORRA

HANOVER

Cologne

BAVARIA

Munich

TYROL

LOM-
BARDY

VENETIA

PRUSSIA

Berlin

Breslau

Prague

BOHEMIA

MORAVIA

AUSTRIA

Vienna

Trieste

PAR. MOD.

Bologna

LUCCA

TUSCANY

Danzig

EAST
PRUSSIA

Warsaw

K. OF
POLAND
(RUSS.)

Cracow

AUSTRIAN

HUNGARY

Budapest

EMPIRE

Agram

CROATS

BOSNIA

Belgrade

Sarajevo

SERBIA

MONTE-
NEGRO

A D R I A T I C   S E A

PORTUGAL

Lisbon

Oviedo

Burgos

Madrid

SPAIN

Valencia

Cordova

Seville

Barcelona

BALEARIC IS.
(SP.)

KINGDOM OF
SARDINIA

ELBA

CORSICA
(FR.)

SARDINIA

STATES
OF THE
CHURCH

ITALY

Rome

Naples

KINGDOM OF THE
TWO SICILIES

Cosenza

M E D I T E R

SICILY

R A N E A N

Tangier

GIBRALTAR (U.K.)

Ceuta
(SP.)

Fez

MOROCCO

THE BARBARY STATES

Algiers

ALGERIA
TURK TO 1830

Tunis

TUNISIA
(TURK.)

MALTA
(U.K.)

Och

Ja

B A L T I C   S E A

T R MILLER

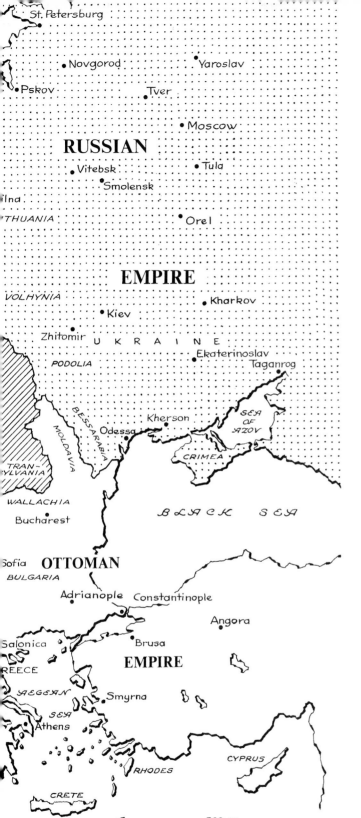

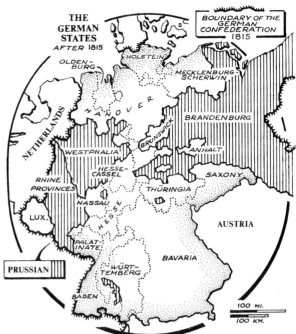

MAP 23.2 *The Congress of Vienna achieved the post-Napoleonic territorial adjustments shown on the map. The most notable arrangements dealt with areas along France's borders (Netherlands, Prussia, Switzerland, and Piedmont) and in Poland and northern Italy.*

Talleyrand, now representing France at Vienna, suggested that the weight of France added to that of Britain and Austria might bring Alexander to his senses. When news of a secret treaty among the three leaked out, the czar agreed to become ruler of a smaller Poland, and Frederick William III of Prussia agreed to accept only part of Saxony. Thereafter France was included as a fifth great power in all deliberations.

Unity among the victors was further restored by Napoleon's return from Elba on March 1, 1815. The French army was still loyal to the former emperor, and many Frenchmen thought that their fortunes might be safer under his rule than under that of the restored Bourbons. The coalition seemed to be dissolving in Vienna. Napoleon seized the opportunity, escaped to France, and was soon restored to power. He promised a liberal constitution and a peaceful foreign policy. The allies were not convinced. They declared Napoleon an outlaw (a new device under international law) and sent their armies to crush him. Wellington, with the crucial help of the Prussians under Field Marshal von Blücher, defeated Napoleon at Waterloo in Belgium on June 18, 1815. Napoleon again abdicated and was sent into exile on Saint Helena, a tiny Atlantic island off the coast of Africa, where he died in 1821.

The Hundred Days, as the period of Napoleon's return is called, frightened the great powers and made the peace settlement harsher for France. In addition to some minor territorial adjustments, the victors imposed a war indemnity and an army of occupation on France. Alexander proposed a Holy Alliance, whereby the monarchs promised to act in accordance with Christian principles. Austria and Prussia signed; but Castlereagh thought it absurd, and England abstained. The czar, who was then embracing mysticism, believed his proposal a valuable tool for international relations. The Holy Alliance soon became a symbol of extreme political reaction. The Quadruple Alliance between England, Austria, Prussia, and Russia was renewed on November 20, 1815.

The chief aims of the Congress of Vienna were to prevent a recurrence of the Napoleonic nightmare and to arrange an acceptable settlement for Europe that might produce lasting peace. It was remarkably successful in achieving these goals. France accepted the new situation without undue resentment. The victorious powers settled difficult problems in a reasonable way. They established a legalistic balance of power and methods for adjusting to change. The work of the congress has been criticized for failing to recognize and provide for the great forces that would stir the nineteenth century—nationalism and democracy—but such criticism is inappropriate. The settlement, like all such agreements, was aimed at solving past ills, and in that it succeeded. If the powers failed to anticipate future problems or to yield to forces of which they disapproved, they were more than human to have done so. Perhaps it was unusual enough to produce a settlement that remained essentially intact for almost half a century and that allowed Europe to suffer no general war for one hundred years.

The Romantic Movement

The years of the French Revolution and the conquests of Napoleon saw the emergence of a new and very important intellectual movement throughout Europe. Romanticism in its various manifestations was a reaction against much of the thought of the Enlightenment. Romantic writers opposed what they considered the excessive scientific narrowness of the eighteenth-century *philosophes*. The latter stood accused of subjecting everything to geometrical and mathematical models and thereby demeaning feelings and imagination. Romantic thinkers refused to conceive of human nature as primarily rational. They wanted to interpret both physical nature and human society in organic rather than in mechanical terms and categories. Where the Enlightenment *philosophes* had often criticized religion and faith, the Romantics saw religion as basic to human nature and faith as a means to knowledge. Expressing this reaction to the rationalism of the previous century, the German Romantic composer Franz Schubert (1797–1828) called the Enlightenment "that ugly skeleton without flesh or blood."

Some historians, most notably Arthur O. Lovejoy, have warned against speaking of a single European-wide Romantic movement. They have pointed out that a variety of such movements—occurring almost simultaneously in Germany, England, and France—arose independently and had their own particular courses of development. Such considerations have not, however, prevented the designation of a specific historical period, dated roughly from 1780 to 1830, as the Age of Romanticism or of the Romantic movement. Despite national differences a shared reaction to the Enlightenment marked all of these writers and artists. They generally saw the imagination or some such intuitive intellectual faculty supplementing the reason as a means of perceiving and understanding the world. Many of these writers urged a revival of Christianity such as had permeated Europe during the Middle Ages. And unlike the *philosophes*, the Romantics liked the art, the literature, and the architecture of medieval times. They were also deeply interested in folklore, folk songs, and fairy tales. The Romantics were also fascinated by dreams, hallucinations, sleepwalking, and other phenomena that suggested the existence of a world beyond that of empirical observation, sensory data, and discursive reasoning.

Romantic Questioning of the Supremacy of Reason

Several historical streams fed the Romantic movement. These included the individualism of the Renaissance and the Reformation and the Pietism of the seventeenth century and the eighteenth-century English Methodist movement, which encouraged a heartfelt, practical religion in place of dogmatism, rationalism, and deism. The sentimental novels of the eighteenth century, such as Samuel Richardson's *Clarissa,* also paved the way for thinkers who would emphasize feeling and emotion. The so-called *Sturm und Drang* ("storm and stress") period of German literature and German idealist philosophy were important to the Romantics. However, two writers who were also closely related to the Enlightenment provided the immediate intellectual foundations for Romanticism. They were Rousseau and Immanuel Kant, both of whom raised questions about the sufficiency of the rationalism so dear to the *philosophes.*

It has already been pointed out in Chapter 21 that Jean Jacques Rousseau, though sharing in some of the reformist spirit of the Enlightenment, opposed many of its other facets. What Romantic writers especially drew from Rousseau was his conviction that society had corrupted human nature. In the two *Discourses* and others of his works Rousseau had portrayed humankind as created happy and innocent by nature and originally living in a state of equilibrium, able to do what it desired and desiring only what it was able to do. For humankind to become happy again, it must remain true to its natural being, while still attempting to realize the new moral possibilities of life in society. In the *Social Contract* (1762) Rousseau had provided his prescription for the reorganization of political life that would achieve that goal.

Rousseau set forth his view on the individual's development toward the good and happy life in a novel entitled *Émile* (1762). Initially this treatise on education was far more influential than the *Social Contract.* In *Émile* Rousseau stressed the difference between children and adults. He distinguished the stages of human maturation and urged that in rearing children, one must give them maximum individual freedom. Each child should be allowed to grow freely, like a plant, and to learn by trial and error what reality is and how best to deal with it. The parent or teacher would help most by providing the basic necessities of life and warding off what was manifestly harmful. Otherwise the adult should stay completely out of the way, like a gardener who waters and weeds a garden but otherwise lets nature take its course.

This was a revolutionary concept of education in an age accustomed to narrow, bookish, and highly regimented vocational education and learning.

Rousseau thought that the child's sentiments as well as its reason should be permitted to flourish. To Romantic writers this concept of human development vindicated the rights of nature over those of artificial society, and they thought that such a form of education would eventually lead to a natural society. In its fully developed form this view of life led the Romantics to place a high value on the uniqueness of each individual person and to explore in great detail the experiences of childhood. Like Rousseau the Romantics saw humankind, nature, and society as organically related to each other.

Immanuel Kant (1724–1804) wrote the two greatest philosophical works of the late eighteenth century: *The Critique of Pure Reason* (1781) and *The Critique of Practical Reason* (1788). He sought to accept the rationalism of the Enlightenment and still to preserve a belief in human freedom, immortality, and the existence of God. Against Locke and other philosophers who saw knowledge rooted in sensory experience alone, Kant argued for the subjective character of human knowledge. For Kant the human mind did not simply reflect the world around it like a passive mirror; rather, it actively imposed on the world of sensory experience "forms of sensibility" and "categories of understanding." These categories were generated by the mind itself. In other words, the human mind perceives the world as it does because of its own internal mental categories. What this meant was that

Immanuel Kant was the most important German philosopher of the late eighteenth century. His thought was the capstone of the philosophy of the Enlightenment and paved the way for Romanticism. [Bettmann Archive.]

human perceptions were as much the product of the mind's own activity as of sensory experience.

Kant found the sphere of reality that was accessible to pure reason to be quite limited. However, he believed that beyond the phenomenal world of sensory experience, over which "pure reason" was master, there existed what he called the "noumenal" world, a sphere of moral and aesthetic reality known by "practical reason" and conscience. Kant thought that all human beings possessed an innate sense of moral duty or an awareness of what he called a "categorical imperative." This term referred to an inner command to act in every situation as one would have all other people always act in the same situation. Kant regarded the existence of this imperative of conscience as incontrovertible proof of humankind's natural freedom. On the basis of humankind's moral sense Kant went on to postulate the existence of God, eternal life, and future rewards and punishments. He believed that these transcendental truths could not be proved by discursive reasoning. Still he was convinced that they were realities to which every reasonable person could attest.

To many Romantic writers Kantian philosophy was a decisive refutation of the narrow rationality of the Enlightenment. Whether they called it "practical reason," "fancy," "imagination," "intuition," or simply "feeling," the Romantics believed in the presence of a special power in the human mind that could penetrate beyond the limits of human understanding as set forth by Hobbes, Locke, and Hume. Most of them also believed that poets and artists generally possessed these powers in particular abundance. Other Romantic writers appealed to the limits of human reason in order to set forth new religious ideas or political thought that was often at odds with that of Enlightenment writers.

Romantic Literature

The term *romantic* appeared in English and French literature as early as the seventeenth century. Neoclassical writers then used the word to describe literature that they considered unreal, sentimental, or excessively fanciful. In the eighteenth century the English writer Thomas Warton associated *romantic* with medieval romances. In Germany, a major center of the Romantic literary movement, Johann Gottfried Herder used the terms *romantic* and *Gothic* interchangeably. In both England and Germany the term came to be ap-

plied to all literature that failed to observe classical forms and rules and that gave free play to the imagination. English Romantic poets and essayists looked on the period of literature from John Dryden to Alexander Pope, roughly 1670–1750, as a classical "dark age." For both English and German Romantics the French Neoclassicists of the seventeenth century, such as Pierre Corneille and Jean Racine, were slavish imitators of the classics and represented all that literature should not be.

As an alternative to such dependence on the ancients August Wilhelm von Schlegel (1767–1845) praised the "romantic" literature of Dante, Petrarch, Boccaccio, Shakespeare, the Arthurian legends, Cervantes, and Calderón. According to Schlegel, Romantic literature was to classical literature what the organic and living were to the merely mechanical. He set forth his views in *Lectures on Dramatic Art and Literature* (1809–1811).

The Romantic Movement had peaked in Germany and England before it became a major force in France under the leadership of Madame de Staël (1766–1817) and Victor Hugo (1802–1885). So influential was the classical tradition in France that not until 1816 did a French writer openly declare himself a Romantic. That was Henri Beyle, who wrote under the pseudonym Stendhal (1783–1842). He praised Shakespeare and Lord Byron and criticized his own countryman, the seventeenth-century classical dramatist Racine.

The English Romantics believed that poetry was enhanced by freely following the creative impulses of the mind. In this belief they directly opposed Lockean psychology, which regarded the mind as a passive receptor and poetry as a mechanical exercise of "wit" following prescribed rules. For William Blake and Samuel Taylor Coleridge the artist's imagination was God at work in the mind. As Coleridge expressed his views, the imagination was "a repetition in the finite mind of the eternal act of creation in the infinite I AM." Percy Bysshe Shelley believed that "A poet participates in the eternal, the infinite, and the One." So conceived of, poetry could not be considered idle play. It was the highest of human acts, humankind's self-fulfillment in a transcendental world.

William Blake (1757–1827) considered the poet a seer and poetry translated vision. He thought it a great tragedy that so many people understood the world only rationally and could perceive no innocence or beauty in it. In the 1790s he experienced a period of deep personal depression, which seems to have been related to his own inability to perceive

An illustration made in 1825 for the Biblical book of Job by the English Romantic poet and engraver William Blake. [The Granger Collection.]

the world as he believed it to be. The better one got to know the world, the more the life of the imagination and its spiritual values seemed to recede. Blake saw this problem as evidence of the materialism and injustice of English society. He was deeply impressed by the strong sense of contradiction between a true childlike vision of the world and conceptions of it based on actual experience. Through his own poetry he sought to bring childlike innocence and experience together and to transform experience by imagination. The conflict of which he was so much aware can be seen in *Songs of Innocence* (1789) and *Songs of Experience* (1794). In "The Tyger," published in the latter, he asked:

> Tyger, Tyger, burning bright
> In the forests of the night,
> . . . .
> When the stars threw down their spears
> And watered heaven with their tears,
> Did He smile His work to see?
> Did He who made the lamb make thee?

Samuel Taylor Coleridge (1772–1834) was the master of Gothic poems of the supernatural. His three poems, "Christabel," "The Ancient Mariner," and "Kubla Khan," are of this character. "The Ancient Mariner" relates the story of a sailor cursed for killing an albatross. The poem treats the subject as a crime against nature and God and raises the issues of guilt, punishment, and the redemptive possibilities of humility and penance. At the end of the poem the mariner discovers the unity and beauty of all things and, having repented, is delivered from his awful curse, which has been symbolized by the dead albatross hung around his neck.

> O happy living things! no tongue
> Their beauty might declare:
> A spring of love gushed from my heart,
> And I blessed them unaware . . .
> The self-same moment I could pray;
> And from my neck so free
> The Albatross fell off, and sank
> Like lead into the sea.

Coleridge also made major contributions to Romantic literary criticism in his lectures on Shakespeare and in *Biographia Literaria* (1817), which presents his theories of poetry.

William Wordsworth (1770–1850) was Coleridge's closest friend. Together they published *Lyrical Ballads* in 1798 as a manifesto of a new poetry that rejected the rules of eighteenth-century criticism. Among Wordsworth's most important later poems

William Wordsworth was among the earliest and most influential of the English Romantic poets. He was particularly noted for his nature poetry. [Culver Pictures.]

is his "Ode on Intimations of Immortality" (1803), written in part to console Coleridge, who was in the midst of a deep personal crisis. Its subject is the loss of poetic vision, something Wordsworth also keenly felt at this time in himself. Nature, which he had worshiped, no longer spoke freely to him, and he feared that it might never speak to him again:

> There was a time when meadow, grove, and stream,
> The earth, and every common sight,
>   To me did seem
>   Appareled in celestial light,
> The glory and the freshness of a dream.
> It is not now as it hath been of yore—
>   Turn whereso'er I may,
>   By night or day,
> The things which I have seen I now can see no more.

What he had lost was the vision that he believed all human beings lose in the necessary process of maturation: their childlike vision and closeness to spiritual reality. For both Wordsworth and Coleridge childhood was the bright period of creative imagination. Wordsworth held a theory of the soul's preexistence in a celestial state prior to its creation. The child, being closer in time to its eternal origin and undistracted by much worldly experience, recollects the supernatural world much more easily. Aging and urban living corrupt and deaden the imagination and make one's inner feelings and the beauty of nature less important. Yet Wordsworth took consolation in the occasional moments of later life when he still found in nature "intimations of immortality," a brief glimpse of humankind's eternal origin and destiny:

> O joy! that in our embers
> Is something that doth live,
> That Nature yet remembers
> What was so fugitive!

In his book-length poem *The Prelude* (1850) Wordsworth presented a long autobiographical account of the growth of the poet's mind.

Percy Bysshe Shelley (1792–1822), a very philosophical poet, lived in a Platonic world of ideas more real to him than anything in the sensible world. One of his greatest poetic works, *Prometheus Unbound* (1820), was written in Rome when he was twenty-seven years old. It was stimulated by Aeschylus's *Prometheus Bound,* the story of a defiant Titan who stole fire from the gods and paid for his crime by being eternally bound to a rock and at-

tacked by savage birds. For Shelley, Prometheus was a symbol of all that was good in life, the principle of life itself. He was the friend of humanity, who, like Christ, suffered because he tried to improve humankind. He was the soul's unconquerable desire to create harmony in the world through reasonableness and love. In the poem Prometheus struggles against Jupiter, who represents tyranny and the power of evil in the world. He receives assistance in his struggle from Asia, a symbol of unspoiled nature, and from Mother Earth. In the end Jupiter is overthrown by his own son, Demogorgon, who rewards Prometheus's patience and endurance by setting him free. Demogorgon summarizes the poem's Romantic message:

> To suffer woes which Hope thinks infinite;
> To forgive wrongs darker than death or night;
>   To defy Power, which seems omnipotent;
> To live, and bear; to hope til Hope creates
> From its own wreck the thing it contemplates;
>   Neither to change, nor falter, nor repent;
> This, like thy glory, Titan, is to be
> Good, great and joyous, beautiful and free;
> This alone Life, Joy, Empire, and Victory.

A true rebel among the Romantic poets was Lord Byron (1788–1824). At home even the other Romantic writers distrusted and generally disliked

George Gordon, Lord Byron not only wrote important Romantic poetry but also became a romantic hero in his own right by his death in the Greek revolution in 1824. The portrait by Richard Westall is itself a bit of Romanticism. [The Granger Collection.]

him. He had little sympathy for their views of the imagination. However, outside England Byron was regarded as the embodiment of the new person of the French Revolution. He rejected the old traditions (he was divorced and famous for his amours) and championed the cause of personal liberty. Byron was outrageously skeptical and mocking, even of his own beliefs. In *Childe Harold's Pilgrimage* (1812) he created the figure of a brooding, melancholy romantic hero. In *Don Juan* (1819) he wrote with ribald humor, acknowledged nature's cruelty as well as its beauty, and even expressed admiration for urban life. Byron tended to be content with the world as he directly knew it. He found his own experience of nature and love, objectively described and reported without embellishment, sufficient for poetic inspiration. He had the rare ability to encompass in his work the whole of his age and to write on subjects that other Romantics considered unworthy of poetry.

The major figures of the early Romantic movement in Germany are August Wilhelm Schlegel and his brother Friedrich (1772–1829); Friedrich von Hardenberg, known under the pseudonym Novalis (1772–1801); Ludwig Tieck (1773–1853), famous for the story *Puss-in-Boots;* and Heinrich Wackenroder (1773–1798). In 1798 this group, under the leadership of the Schlegels, founded the principal organ of German Romanticism, the journal *Athenäum*. Their principles were derived from Shakespeare, Calderón, Johann Wolfgang von Goethe (1749–1832), Johann Christoph Friedrich von Schiller (1759–1805), and Friedrich Gottlieb Klopstock (1724–1803). *Athenäum* featured the most definitive Romantic views on art, literature, philosophy, and life, with contributions that were original, provocative, and seminal.

Much Romantic poetry was also written on the Continent, but almost all major German Romantics wrote at least one novel. Romantic novels tended to be highly sentimental and often borrowed material from medieval romances. Novalis's *Heinrich von Ofterdingen* (1802), for example, was the story of a brooding poetical knight in search of a blue flower, symbolic of truth. The characters of Romantic novels were treated as symbols of the larger truth of life. Purely realistic description was avoided. The first German Romantic novel, Ludwig Tieck's *William Lovell* (1793–1795), contrasts the young Lovell, whose life is built on love and imagination, with those who live by cold reason alone and who thus become an easy prey to unbelief, misanthrophy, and egoism. As the novel rambles to its con-

The poetry of the German Johann Wolfgang von Goethe illustrated humankind striving with physical nature and attempting to discover the possibility of moral life on earth. The picture is a detail of a 1786 painting by Tischbein. [Bettmann Archive.]

clusion, Lovell is ruined by a mixture of philosophy, materialism, and skepticism, which are administered to him by two women whom he naively loves.

Friedrich Schlegel wrote a very progressive early Romantic novel, *Lucinde* (1799), which attacked contemporary prejudices against women as capable of being little more than lovers and domestics. Schlegel's novel reveals the ability of the Romantics to become involved in the social issues of their day. He depicted Lucinde as the perfect friend and companion, as well as the unsurpassed lover, of the hero. Like other early Romantic novels the work shocked contemporary morals by frankly discussing sexual activity and by describing Lucinde as equal in all ways to the male hero.

Another important early Romantic novelist, E. T. A. Hoffmann (1776–1822), in *The Devil's Elixir* (1815–1816), traced in psychological detail the moral downfall of a monk aroused by sexuality. In these and other similiar works the Romantics attempted to repudiate many of the more widespread social values of their day. Their writings often reflect the world of dissolving certainties brought about by the continentwide turmoil of the French Revolution and Napoleonic wars. What began as a movement in rebellion against literary norms became a movement in rebellion against social prejudices.

Towering above all of these German writers stood the figure of Johann Wolfgang von Goethe

(1749–1832). Perhaps the greatest German literary figure of modern times, Goethe defies any easy classification. Part of his literary production fits into the Romantic mold, and part of it was a condemnation of Romantic excesses. The book that made his early reputation was *The Sorrows of Young Werther* published in 1774. This novel, like many of the eighteenth century, is composed of a series of letters. The hero falls in love with Lotte, another man's wife. The letters explore this relationship and display the kind of emotional sentimentalism that was characteristic of the age. Eventually Werther and Lotte part, but in his grief over his abandoned love Werther takes his own life. This novel became very popular throughout Europe. Virtually all later Romantic authors, and especially those in Germany, admired it because of its emphasis on feeling and on living outside the bounds of polite society. Much of Goethe's early poetry was also erotic in nature. However, as he became older, Goethe became much more serious and self-consciously moral. He published numerous other works, including *Wilhelm Meister's Apprenticeship* and *Iphigenia at Tauris,* that explored the manner in which human beings come to live moral lives while still acknowledging the life of the senses.

Goethe's greatest masterpiece was *Faust,* a long dramatic work of poetry in two parts. Part I was published in 1808. It tells the story of Faust who, weary of life, makes a pact with the Devil: he will exchange his soul for greater knowledge than other human beings. As the story progresses, Faust seduces a young woman named Gretchen. She dies but is received into heaven as the grief-stricken Faust realizes that he must continue to live. In Part II, completed in the year of Goethe's death (1832), Faust is taken through a series of strange adventures involving witches and various mythological characters. This portion of the work has never been admired as much as Part I. However, at the conclusion Faust dedicates his life, or what remains of it, to the improvement of humankind. In this dedication he feels that he has found a goal that will allow him to overcome the restless striving that first made him make the pact with the Devil. That new knowledge breaks the pact. Faust then dies and is received by angels. In this great work Goethe obviously was criticizing much of his earlier thought and that of contemporary Romantic writers, but he was also attempting to portray the deep spiritual problems that Europeans would encounter as the traditional moral and religious values of Christianity were abandoned. Yet Goethe himself could not reaffirm those values. In that respect both he and his characters symbolized the spiritual struggle of the nineteenth century.

Religion in the Romantic Period

During the Middle Ages the foundation of religion had been the church. The Reformation leaders had appealed to the authority of the Bible. Then, later Enlightenment writers had attempted to derive religion from the rational nature revealed

John Wesley was the founder of the Methodist movement in Great Britain. His preaching, teaching, and revivals constituted—and expressed—one of the major impulses toward Romantic religion. [The Granger Collection.]

❧ Chateaubriand Describes the Appeal of a Gothic Church

Throughout most of the eighteenth century writers had harshly criticized virtually all aspects of the Middle Ages, which were then considered an unenlightened time. One of the key elements of Romanticism was a new appreciation of all things medieval. In this passage from *The Genius of Christianity* Chateaubriand praised the beauty of the Middle Ages and the strong religious feelings produced by stepping into a Gothic church. The description exemplifies the typically Romantic emphasis on feelings as the chief foundation of religion.

You could not enter a Gothic church without feeling a kind of awe and a vague sentiment of the Divinity. You were all at once carried back to those times when a fraternity of cenobites [a particular order of monks], after having meditated in the woods of their monasteries, met to prostrate themselves before the altar and to chant the praises of the Lord, amid the tranquility and the silence of the night. . . .

Every thing in a Gothic church reminds you of the labyrinths of a wood; every thing excites a feeling of religious awe, of mystery, and of the Divinity.

The two lofty towers erected at the entrance of the edifice overtop the elms and yew trees of the church yard, and produce the most picturesque effect on the azure of heaven. Sometimes their twin heads are illumined by the first rays of dawn; at others they appear crowned with a capital of clouds or magnified in a foggy atmosphere. The birds themselves seem to make a mistake in regard to them, and to take them for the trees of the forests; they hover over their summits, and perch upon their pinnacles. But, lo! confused noises suddenly issue from the tops of these towers and scare away the affrighted birds. The Christian architect, not content with building forests, has been desirous to retain their murmurs; and, by means of the organ and of bells, he has attached to the Gothic temple the very winds and thunders that roar in the recesses of the woods. Past ages, conjured up by these religious sounds, raise their venerable voices from the bosom of the stones, and are heard in every corner of the vast cathedral. The sanctuary re-echoes like the cavern of the ancient Sibyl; loud-tongued bells swing over your head, while the vaults of death under your feet are profoundly silent.

Vicomte François René de Chateaubriand, *The Genius of Christianity,* trans. by C. I. White (Baltimore: J. Murphy, 1862), as quoted in Howard E. Hugo (Ed.), *The Romantic Reader* (New York: Viking, 1957), pp. 341–342.

by Newtonian physics. Romantic religious thinkers, on the other hand, appealed to the inner emotions of humankind for the foundation of religion. Their forerunners were the mystics of Western Christianity. One of the first great examples of a religion characterized by Romantic impulses—Methodism—occurred in England.

Methodism originated in the middle of the eighteenth century as a revolt against deism and rationalism in the Church of England. The Methodist revival formed an important part of the background of English Romanticism. The leader of the Methodist movement was John Wesley (1703–1791). His education and religious development had been carefully supervised by a remarkable mother, Susannah Wesley, who bore eighteen children in addition to John.

While at Oxford, Wesley organized a religious group known as the "Holy Club." He soon left England to give himself to missionary work in Georgia in America, where he arrived in 1735. While crossing the Atlantic, he had been deeply impressed by a group of German Moravians on the ship. These German pietists exhibited unshakable faith and confidence during a violent storm at sea while Wesley despaired of his life. Wesley concluded that they knew far better than he the meaning of justification by faith. When he returned to England in 1738 after an unhappy missionary career, Wesley began to worship with Moravians in London. There, in 1739, he underwent a conversion experience that he described in the words, "My heart felt strangely warmed." From that point on he felt assured of his own salvation.

Wesley discovered that he could not preach his version of Christian conversion and practical piety in Anglican church pulpits. Therefore, late in 1739, he began to preach in the open fields about the cities and towns of western England. Literally thousands of humble people responded to his message of repentance and good works. Soon he and his brother Charles, who became famous for his hymns, began to organize Methodist societies. By the late eighteenth century the Methodists had become a separate church. They ordained their own clergy and sent missionaries to America, where the Methodists eventually achieved their greatest success and most widespread influence.

The essence of Methodist teaching lay in its stress on inward, heartfelt religion and the possibility of Christian perfection in this life. John Wesley described Christianity as "an inward principle . . . the image of God impressed on a created spirit, a fountain of peace and love springing up into everlasting life." True Christians were those who were "saved in this world from all sin, from all unrighteousness . . . and now in such a sense perfect as not to commit sin and . . . freed from evil thoughts and evil tempers."[3] Many people, weary of the dry rationalism that derived from deism, found Wesley's ideal relevant to their own lives. The Methodist preachers emphasized the role of enthusiastic emotional experience as part of Christian conversion. After Wesley, religious revivals became highly emotional in style and content.

Similar religious developments based on feeling appeared on the Continent. After the Thermidorian Reaction a strong Roman Catholic revival took place in France. Its followers were people who had disapproved of both the religious policy of the revolution and the anticlericalism of the Enlightenment. The most important book to express these sentiments was *The Genius of Christianity* (1802) by Vicomte François René de Chateaubriand (1768–1848). In this work, which became known as the "Bible of Romanticism," Chateaubriand argued that the essence of religion was "passion." The foundation of faith in the church was the emotion that its teachings and sacraments inspired in the heart of the Christian.

Against the Newtonian view of the world and of a rational God, the Romantics found God immanent in nature. No one stated the Romantic religious ideal more eloquently or with greater impact on the modern world than Friedrich Schleiermacher (1768–1834). In 1799 he published *Speeches on Religion to Its Cultured Despisers*. It was a response to Lutheran orthodoxy, on the one hand, and to Enlightenment rationalism, on the other. The advocates of both were the "cultured despisers" of real or heartfelt religion. According to Schleiermacher, religion was neither dogma nor a system of ethics. It was an intuition or feeling of absolute dependence on an infinite reality. Religious institutions, doctrines, and moral activity expressed that primal religious feeling only in a secondary or indirect way.

Although Schleiermacher considered Christianity the "religion of religions," he also believed that every world religion was unique in its expression of the primal intuition of the infinite in the finite. He thus turned against the universal natural religion of the Enlightenment, which he termed "a name applied to loose, unconnected impulses," and defended the meaningfulness of the numerous world religions. Every such religion was seen to be a unique version of the emotional experience of de-

---

MAJOR PUBLICATION DATES IN THE ROMANTIC MOVEMENT

1762	Rousseau's *Émile*
1774	Goethe's *Sorrows of Young Werther*
1781	Kant's *Critique of Pure Reason**
1788	Kant's *Critique of Practical Reason**
1789	Blake's *Songs of Innocence*
1794	Blake's *Songs of Experience*
1798	Wordsworth and Coleridge's *Lyrical Ballads*
1799	F. Schlegel's *Lucinde*
	Schleiermacher's *Speeches on Religion to Its Cultured Despisers*
1802	Chateaubriand's *Genius of Christianity*
1806	Hegel's *Phenomenology of Mind*
1808	Goethe's *Faust*, Part I
1812	Byron's *Childe Harold's Pilgrimage*
1819	Byron's *Don Juan*
1820	Shelley's *Prometheus Unbound*

* Kant's books were not themselves part of the Romantic movement, but they were fundamental to later Romantic writers.

---

[3] Quoted in Albert C. Outler (Ed.), *John Wesley: A Representative Collection of His Writings* (New York: Oxford University Press, 1964), p. 220.

François René de Chateaubriand was the author of The Genius of Christianity, *one of the key documents of the Roman Catholic revival of the Romantic period. The portrait is by the Marquise de Custine.* [The Granger Collection.]

Johann Gottfried von Herder was one of the founders of nationalism in Europe. He thought that each nationality had a particular contribution to offer to the cultural life of the human race. [Bettmann Archive.]

pendence on an infinite being. In so arguing, Schleiermacher interpreted the religions of the world in the same way that other Romantic writers interpreted the variety of unique peoples and cultures.

Romantic Views of Nationalism and History

One of the most distinctive features of Romanticism, especially in Germany, was its glorification of both the individual person and individual cultures. Behind these views lay the philosophy of German idealism, which understood the world as the creation of subjective egos. J. G. Fichte (1762–1814), an important German philosopher and nationalist, identified the individual ego with the Absolute that underlies all existing things. According to him and other similar philosophers, the world is truly the creation of humankind. The world is as it is because especially strong persons conceive of it in a particular way and impose their wills on the world and other people. Napoleon served as the contemporary example of such a great person. This philosophy has ever since served to justify the glorification of great persons and their actions in overriding all opposition to their will and desires.

In addition to this philosophy the influence of new historical studies lay behind the German glorification of individual cultures. German Romantic writers went in search of their own past in reaction to the copying of French manners in eighteenth-century Germany, the impact of the French Revolution, and the imperialism of Napoleon. An early leader in this effort was Johann Gottfried Herder (1744–1803). Herder had early resented the French cultural preponderance in Germany. In 1778 Herder published an influential essay entitled "On the Knowing and Feelings of the Human Soul." In it he vigorously rejected the mechanical explanation of nature so popular with Enlightenment writers. He saw human beings and societies as developing organically, like plants, over time. Human beings were different at different times and places.

Herder revived German folk culture by urging the collection and preservation of distinctive German songs and sayings. His most important followers in this regard were the Grimm brothers, Jakob (1785–1863) and Wilhelm (1786–1859), famous for their collection of fairy tales. Believing that each language and culture was the unique expression of a people, Herder opposed both the concept and the use of a "common" language, such as French, and "universal" institutions, such as those imposed on Europe by Napoleon. These, he believed, were forms of tyranny over the individuality of a people. Herder's writings led to a broad revival of interest in history and philosophy. Although initially directed toward the identification of German origins, such work soon expanded to embrace other world cultures as well. Eventually the ability of the Romantic imagination to be at home in any age or culture spurred the study of non-Western religion, comparative literature, and philology.

Perhaps the most important person to write about history during the Romantic period was the German Georg Wilhelm Friedrich Hegel (1770–1831). He is one of the most difficult philos-ophers in the history of Western civilization. He is also one of the most important.

Hegel believed that ideas develop in an evolutionary fashion that involves conflict. At any given time a predominant set of ideas, which he termed the *thesis*, holds sway. They are challenged by other conflicting ideas, which he termed the *antithesis*. As these patterns of thought clash, there emerges a *synthesis*, which eventually becomes the new thesis. Then the process begins all over again. Periods of world history receive their character from the patterns of thought predominating during them. A number of important philosophical conclusions followed from this analysis. One of the most significant was the belief that all periods of history have been of almost equal value because each was by

❧ Fichte Calls for the Regeneration of Germany

Johann Gottlieb Fichte (1762–1814) began to deliver his famous *Addresses to the German Nation* late in 1807 as a series of Sunday lectures in Berlin. Earlier that year Prussia had been crushed by Napoleon's armies. In this passage from his concluding lecture, presented in early 1808, Fichte challenged the younger generation of Germans to recognize the national duty that historical circumstances had placed on their shoulders. They might either accept their defeat and the consequent slavery or revive the German nation and receive the praise and gratitude of later generations. It is important to note that Fichte saw himself speaking to all Germans as citizens of a single cultural nation rather than as the subjects of various monarchs and princes.

Review in your own minds the various conditions between which you now have to make a choice. If you continue in your dullness and helplessness, all the evils of serfdom are awaiting you; deprivations, humiliations, the scorn and arrogance of the conqueror; you will be driven and harried in every corner, because you are in the wrong and in the way everywhere; until, by the sacrifice of your nationality and your language, you have purchased for yourselves some subordinate and petty place, and until in this way you gradually die out as a people. If, on the other hand, you bestir yourselves and play the man, you will continue in a tolerable and honorable existence, and you will see growing up among and around you a generation that will be the promise for you and for the Germans of most illustrious renown.

You will see in spirit the German name rising by means of this generation to be the most glorious among all peoples; you will see this nation the regenerator and re-creator of the world.

It depends on you whether you want to be the end, and to be the last of a generation unworthy of respect and certain to be despised by posterity even beyond its due—a generation of whose history . . . your descendants will read the end with gladness, saying its fate was just; or whether you want to be the beginning and the point of development for a new age glorious beyond all your conceptions, and the generation from whom posterity will reckon the year of their salvation. Reflect that you are the last in whose power this great alteration lies.

Johann Gottlieb Fichte, *Addresses to the German Nation,* ed. by George Armstrong Kelly (New York: Harper Torchbooks, 1968), pp. 215–216.

A lithograph of G. W. F. Hegel in the robes of a university professor. Hegel was the most important philosopher of history in the Romantic period. [Bildarchiv Perussischer Kulturbesitz.]

definition necessary to the achievement of the civilization that came later. Also all cultures are valuable because each contributes to the necessary clash of values and ideas that allows humankind to develop. Hegel discussed these concepts in *The Phenomenology of Mind* (1806), *Lectures on the Philosophy of History* (1822–1831), and numerous other works, many of which were published only after his death. During his lifetime his ideas became widely known through his university lectures at Berlin.

These various Romantic ideas made a major contribution to the emergence of nationalism, which proved to be one of the strongest motivating forces of the nineteenth and twentieth centuries. The writers of the Enlightenment had generally championed a cosmopolitan outlook on the world. But the emphasis of the Romantic thinkers was on the individuality and worth of each separate people and culture. The factors that helped to define a people or a nation were common language, common history, a homeland that possessed historical associations, and common customs. This cultural nationalism gradually became transformed into a political creed. It came to be widely believed that every people, ethnic group, or nation should constitute a separate political entity and that only when it so existed could the nation be secure in its own character.

The example of France under the revolutionary government and then Napoleon had demonstrated the power of nationhood. Other peoples came to desire similar strength and confidence. Napoleon's toppling of ancient political structures, such as the Holy Roman Empire, demonstrated

❧ Hegel Explains the Role of Great Men in History

Hegel believed that behind the development of human history from one period to the next lay the mind and purpose of what he termed the "World Spirit," a concept somewhat resembling the Christian God. Hegel thought particular heroes from the past (such as Caesar) and in the present (such as Napoleon) were the unconscious instruments of that Spirit. In this passage from his lectures on the philosophy of history Hegel explained how these heroes could change the course of history. All of these concepts are characteristic of the Romantic belief that human beings and human history are always intimately connected with larger, spiritual forces at work in the world.

Such are all great historical men—whose own particular aims involve those large issues which are the will of the World-Spirit. They may be called Heroes, inasmuch as they have derived their purposes and their vocation, not from the calm, regular course of things, sanctioned by the existing order; but from a concealed fount—one which has not attained to phenomenal, present existence—from that inner Spirit, still hidden beneath the surface, which, impinging on the outer world as on a shell, bursts it in pieces, because it is another kernel than that which belonged to the shell in question. They are men, therefore, who appear to draw the impulse of their life from themselves; and whose deeds have produced a condition of things and a complex of historical relations which appear to be only their interest, *and their* work.

Such individuals had no consciousness of the general Idea they were unfolding, while prosecuting those aims of theirs; on the contrary, they were practical, political men. But at the same time they were thinking men, who had an insight into the requirements of the time—what was ripe for development. This was the very Truth for their age, for their world; the species next in order, so to speak, and which was already formed in the womb of time. It was theirs to know this nascent principle; the necessary, directly sequent step in progress, which their world was to take; to make this their aim, and to expend their energy in promoting it. World-historical men— the Heroes of an epoch—must, therefore, be recognized as its clear-sighted ones; their deeds, their words are the best of that time.

G. W. F. Hegel, *The Philosophy of History,* trans. by J. Sibree (New York: Dover, 1956), pp. 30–31.

---

the need for new political organization in Europe. By 1815 these were the aspirations of only a few Europeans, but as time passed, such yearnings came to be shared by scores of peoples from Ireland to the Ukraine. The Congress of Vienna could ignore such feelings, but for the rest of the nineteenth century, statesmen had to confront the growing reality of their power.

Suggested Readings

M. H. ABRAMS, *The Mirror and the Lamp: Romantic Theory and the Critical Tradition* (1958). A standard text on Romantic literary theory that looks at English Romanticism in the context of German Romantic idealism.

M. H. ABRAMS, *Natural Supernaturalism: Tradition and Revolution in Romantic Literature* (1971). A brilliant survey of Romanticism across West European literature.

J. F. BERNARD, *Talleyrand: A Biography* (1973). A recent useful account.

H. BLOOM, *The Visionary Company,* rev. ed. (1971). A standard reading of the major English Romantic poetic texts.

G. BRUUN, *Europe and the French Imperium, 1799–1814* (New York, 1938). A good survey.

E. CASSIRER, *Kant's Life and Thought* (1981). A brilliant work by one of the major philosophers of this century

D. G. CHANDLER, *The Campaigns of Napoleon* (New York, 1966). A good military study.

K. CLARK, *The Romantic Rebellion* (1973). A useful discussion that combines both art and literature.

O. CONNELLY, *Napoleon's Satellite Kingdoms* (1965): The rule of Napoleon and his family in Europe.

H. C. DEUTSCH, *The Genesis of Napoleon's Imperialism, 1801–1805* (1938). Basic for foreign policy.

Dictionary of the History of Ideas, Vol. 4 (1973), pp. 198–208. Contributions by Rene Wellek, "Romanticism in Literature"; Franklin L. Baumer, "Romanticism (ca. 1780–ca. 1830)"; and Jacques Droz, "Political Romanticism in Germany." Excellent and succinct.

J. ENGELL, *The Creative Imagination: Enlightenment to Romanticism* (1981). An important book on the role of the imagination in Romantic literary theory.

P. GEYL, *Napoleon: For and Against* (1949). A fine survey of the historical debate.

M. GLOVER, *The Peninsular War, 1807–1814: A Concise Military History* (1974). An interesting account of the military campaign that so drained Napoleon's resources in Western Europe.

E. HECKSCHER, *The Continental System: An Economic Interpretation* (1922). Napoleon's commercial policy.

J. C. HEROLD, *The Age of Napoleon* (1968). A lively, readable account.

R. HOLTMAN, *The Napoleonic Revolution* (1950). Good on domestic policy.

H. KISSINGER, *A World Restored: Metternich, Castlereagh and the Problems of Peace, 1812–1822* (1957). A provocative study by an author who became an American Secretary of State.

S. KÖRNER, *Kant* (1955). A very clear introduction to a difficult thinker.

M. LeBRIS, *Romantics and Romanticism* (1981). A recent work, lavishly illustrated, that relates politics and romantic art.

G. LEFEBVRE, *Napoleon,* 2 vols., trans. by H. Stockhold, (1969). The fullest and finest biography.

A. O. LOVEJOY, "The Meaning of Romanticism for the Historian of Ideas," in Franklin L. Baumer, (Ed.), *Intellectual Movements in Modern European History* (1965). A very influential summary of the basic characteristics of Romanticism.

F. MARKHAM, *Napoleon and the Awakening of Europe* (1954). Emphasizes the growth of nationalism.

F. MARKHAM, *Napoleon* (1963). A good biography strong on military questions.

H. NICOLSON, *The Congress of Vienna* (1946). A good, readable account.

S. PRAWER (Ed.), *The Romantic Period in Germany* (1970). Contributions covering all facets of the movement.

J. L. TALMON, *Romanticism and Revolt: Europe, 1815–1848* (1967). An effort to sketch the Romantic movements and relate them to one another and to the larger political history of the period.

C. TAYLOR, *Hegel* (1975). The best one-volume introduction.

J. M. THOMPSON, *Napoleon Bonaparte: His Rise and Fall* (1952). A sound biography.

L. A. WILLOUGHBY, *The Romantic Movement in Germany* (1930). An older but still very useful treatment.

710

24 Restoration, Reaction, and Reform (1815-1832)

THE DEFEAT of Napoleon and the diplomatic settlement of the Congress of Vienna restored a conservative political and social order in Europe. Legitimate monarchies, landed aristocracies, and established churches constituted the major pillars of conservatism. The institutions themselves were ancient, but the self-conscious alliance of throne, land, and altar was new. Throughout the eighteenth century these groups had been in frequent conflict. Only the upheavals of the French Revolution and the Napoleonic era transformed them into natural, if sometimes reluctant, allies. They retained their former arrogance but neither their former privileges nor their old confidence. They knew they could be toppled by the political groups who hated them. They understood

Czar Alexander I (1801–1825) pictured by Kruger at the height of his influence in 1815. A mild reformer at the time of his accession to the throne, Alexander became increasingly conservative after 1812. The victory of Russia's armies in the war against Napoleon spread the influence of the czar's conservatism far beyond Russia's borders. [The Bettmann Archive.]

that revolution in one country could spill over into another. The conservatives regarded themselves as surrounded by enemies and as standing permanently on the defensive against the forces of liberalism, nationalism, and popular sovereignty. These potential sources of unrest had to be confronted both at home and abroad.

Conservative Governments on the Domestic Scene

The course of nineteenth-century history is frequently associated with the emergence of the liberal, national state and industrial society. But the staying power of the restored conservative institutions, especially in Great Britain and eastern Europe, is an equally and perhaps even more striking feature of the century. Actually not until World War I did their power and pervasive influence come to an end. One need not admire these institutions or the policies and personalities associated with them, yet one must admit that their persistence constituted one of the most important features of nineteenth-century political and social life. To ignore or to disparage their relatively successful attempts at self-preservation is to underestimate the grave obstacles that confronted liberals and nationalists.

The more theoretical political and religious ideas of the conservative classes were associated with Romantic thinkers, such as Burke and Hegel. Conservatives shared other, less formal attitudes forged by the revolutionary experience. The fate of Louis XVI convinced most monarchs that they could trust only aristocratic governments or governments of aristocrats in alliance with the very wealthiest middle-class and professional people. The European aristocracies believed that their property and influence would rarely be safe under any form of genuinely representative government. All conservatives spurned the idea of a written constitution unless they were permitted to promulgate the document themselves. Even then some could not be reconciled to the concept.

The churches were equally apprehensive of popular movements except their own revivals. The ecclesiastical leaders throughout the Continent regarded themselves as entrusted with the educational task of supporting the social and political status quo. They also feared and hated most of the ideas associated with the Enlightenment because those rational concepts and reformist writings enshrined the critical spirit and undermined revealed religion. Conservative Europeans came to regard as *liberal* any idea or institution that they opposed. However, as will be seen, that word actually had rather different meanings in different countries.

Russia and Alexander I

The pursuit of Napoleon's army across Europe after the burning of Moscow created a new image of vast Russian power. The image remained until the Russian defeat in the Crimean War (1854–1856). In Vienna Czar Alexander I had played a more important personal role than any other participating monarch. Both in those negotiations and in his governance of Russia, Alexander was and has remained a puzzling figure. He was torn between an intellectual attraction to the doctrines of the Enlightenment and reform and a very pragmatic adherence to traditional autocracy. His own development as a person and as a ruler reflected the turn of eastern European states from

enlightened absolutism to rigid conservatism and defense of the status quo.

Alexander I came to the Russian throne in 1801 after the murder of his father, Czar Paul. The son had condoned the palace revolution. Paul had been an unstable person who ruled in an arbitrary and unpredictable manner. Paul had attempted to reverse the policies of his mother, Catherine the Great, whom he loathed. He attacked the privileges of the nobility. The result was a *coup d'état* led by court nobles and the army. Alexander I intended to return to the policies of his grandmother and to consider at least the possibility of political and administrative change in Russia. He confirmed the privileges of the nobles and abolished the security police. He was well educated in the ideas of the Enlightenment. In 1801 he appointed a government reform committee composed of liberal friends. Little came from the reformist plans submitted by this group, and by 1803 Alexander had declared that no group had a right to challenge the legality of the decrees of the czar.

Once Alexander had led Russia into war against Napoleon, even the mild reformist tendencies began to wane. In 1807 the security police were, in effect, reestablished. Yet the military reverses of the campaign and his personal admiration of Napoleon's administrative genius convinced the czar that a reconstruction of the Russian government was necessary. In 1808 he turned to Michael Speransky (1772–1839) to guide his thinking on matters of administrative reform. This enlightened minister, who held a series of government appointments, drew up a plan for constitutional government that included an elected legislative body. He even dared talk about an eventual, gradual abolition of serfdom. The czar could not support such bold departures. Speransky had to be satisfied with a restructuring of the ministries and the bureaucracy. In 1812 he introduced new, progressive taxes on landed income. Each of these policies alienated the nobility. In March 1812 Alexander, fearing the discontent among the nobles, dismissed his once-trusted minister. Again reform came to a close almost without having begun.

Thereafter Alexander, though occasionally using liberal rhetoric, became an increasingly hardened conservative. For the renewed struggle against Napoleon he needed the support of his nobility and the army. Also during this post-Speransky period he was deeply drawn to those mystical religious feelings that lay behind his project for forming the Holy Alliance in 1815. The czar came to regard the Enlightenment, the French Revolution, and Napoleon as one vast attack on Christianity. His new chief adviser was Alexis Arakcheiev (1769–1834), a general and a political opponent of Speransky. This reactionary military figure became the most powerful person in the country except for Alexander himself. Together they pursued a consistently conservative policy. Censorship and religiously dominated education became the order of the day. They also established "military farms." These institutions transformed whole districts of the country into military establishments where the army farmed and supported itself when not fighting. There was little or no toleration of political opposition or criticism of the regime. By the early 1820s the czar, whose early years had seemed to hold out the promise of possible reform, had become a leading symbol of conservative reaction.

Austria and the Germanies

The early nineteenth-century statesman who more than any other epitomized conservatism was the Austrian Prince Metternich, whom we have already met at the Congress of Vienna. This devoted servant of the Hapsburg emperor had been, along with Castlereagh, the chief architect of the Vienna settlement. It was he who seemed to exercise chief control over the forces of the European reaction. The conservative foreign and domestic policy that he forged for Austria stemmed from the pragmatic needs of that peculiar state rather than from ideology. The Austrian government could make no serious compromises with the new political forces in Europe. To no other country were the programs of liberalism and nationalism potentially more dangerous. The Hapsburg domains were peopled with Germans and Hungarians, as well as Poles and other nationalities or ethnic groups. Through puppet governments Austria also dominated the Italian peninsula. Pursuit of dynastic integrity required Austrian domination of the newly formed German Confederation to prevent the formation of a German national state that might absorb the heart of the empire and exclude the other realms governed by the Hapsburgs. So far as Metternich and other officials were concerned, the recognition of the political rights and aspirations of any of the various national groups would mean the probable dissolution of the empire. If Austria permitted representative government, Metternich feared that the national groups would fight their battles inter-

Prince Klemens von Metternich (1773–1859). Foreign Minister, then Chancellor, of Austria, was the chief architect of reactionary politics in Europe between 1815 and 1848. [Culver Pictures.]

nally at the probable cost of Austrian international influence.

During the immediate postwar years Metternich's primary concern lay with Germany. The Congress of Vienna had created the German Confederation to replace the defunct Holy Roman Empire. It consisted of thirty-nine states under Austrian leadership. Each state remained more-or-less autonomous, but Austria was determined to prevent any movement toward constitutionalism in as many of them as possible.

The majory victory for this holding policy came in Prussia. In 1815 Frederick William III (1797–1840), during the exhilaration after the War of Liberation, as Germans termed the last part of their conflict with Napoleon, had promised some mode of constitutional government. However, he immediately stalled on keeping his pledge. In 1817 he formally reneged and created a new Council of State, which did bring about more efficient administration but which was not a constitutional mode of government. In 1819 the king moved further away from thoughts of reform. After a major disagreement over the organization of the army, his chief reform-minded ministers resigned. The monarch replaced them with hardened conservatives. On their advice in 1823 Frederick William III established eight provincial estates, or diets, which were dominated by the *Junkers* and which exercised only an advisory function. The old alliance between the

Prussian monarchy, the army, and the landholders stood reestablished. This conservative alliance opposed German nationalist aspirations that seemed to threaten the social and political order.

Three south German states—Baden, Bavaria, and Württemberg—had received constitutions after 1815 as their monarchs attempted to secure wider political support. Each of these constitutions was a very limited document that refused to recognize popular sovereignty and that defined political rights as the gift of the monarch. But the nationalist and liberal aspirations raised by the collective national experience of defeating the French armies remained alive in the hearts and minds of many young Germans. The most important of these groups was the university students. They had grown up during the days of the reforms of Stein and Hardenburg and the initial circulation of the writings of Fichte and other German nationalists. Many of them had fought Napoleon. When they went to the universities, they continued to dream their dream of a united Germany. They formed *Burschenschaften,* or student associations. Like student groups today, these clubs served numerous social functions, but one of them was severing old provincial loyalties and replacing them with loyalty to the concept of a united German state.

In 1817 in Jena one such student club organized a large celebration of the fourth anniversary of the battle of Leipzig and of the tercentenary of Luther's Ninety-five Theses. There were bonfires, songs, and processions as more than five hundred people gathered for the festivities. The event made German rulers uneasy, for it was known that some republicans were involved with the student clubs. Two years later, in March 1819, a young man named Karl Sand, who was a *Burschenschaft* member, assassinated the conservative dramatist August von Kotzebue. Sand, who was tried, condemned, and publicly executed, became a martyr in the eyes of some nationalists. Although the assassin had acted alone, Metternich decided to use the incident to suppress the student clubs and other potential institutions of liberalism.

In July 1819 Metternich persuaded representatives of the major German states to issue the Carlsbad Decrees, which dissolved the *Burschenschaften.* The decrees also provided for university inspectors and press censors. The next year the German Confederation promulgated the Final Act, which limited the subjects that might be discussed in the constitutional chambers of Bavaria, Württemberg, and Baden. The measure also asserted the right of the monarchs to resist demands of constitutionalists.

In 1817 on the fourth anniversary of the defeat of Napoleon by Prussians, Austrians, and Russians at Leipzig, German students held a nationalist festival near the Wartburg Castle. Such meetings were considered very dangerous by conservative statesmen who opposed nationalism in Germany. [Bildarchiv Preussischer Kulturbesitz.]

❧ Metternich Criticizes the Political Activity of the Middle Class ══

In 1820 the emperor of Austria asked Prince Klemens von Metternich to compose a political "confession of faith" to be sent to Alexander I of Russia. In the course of that document Metternich described what he regarded as the political evil of middle-class liberals. He argued that liberals sought to undermine the natural loyalty of subjects to monarchs. This action stemmed from the intellectual pride or presumption of these liberals, who had adopted many of the ideas of the Enlightenment. Metternich also pointed to the role of a free press in causing political unrest. Metternich himself did much to foster extensive press censorship in eastern Europe.

The evil exists and it is enormous. We do not think we can better define it and its cause at all times and in all places than we have already done by the word "presumption," that inseparable companion of the half-educated, that spring of an unmeasured ambition, and yet easy to satisfy in times of trouble and confusion.

It is principally the middle classes of society which this moral gangrene has affected, and it is only among them that the heads of the party [working for liberal reform] are found. . . .

Europe thus presents itself to the impartial observer under an aspect at the same time deplorable and peculiar. We find everywhere the people praying for the maintenance of peace and tranquillity, faithful to God and their Princes, remaining proof against the efforts and seductions of the factious who call themselves friends of the people and wish to lead them to an agitation which the people themselves do not desire!

The Governments, having lost their balance, are frightened, intimidated, and thrown into confusion by the cries of the intermediary class of society, which placed between Kings and their subjects, breaks the

sceptre of the monarch, and usurps the cry of the people. . . .

We see this intermediary class abandon itself with a blind fury and animosity which proves much more its own fears than any confidence in the success of its enterprises, to all the means which seem proper to assuage its thirst for power, applying itself to the task of persuading Kings that their rights are confined to sitting upon a throne, while those of the people are to govern, and to attack all that centuries have bequeathed as holy and worthy of man's respect—denying, in fact, the value of the past, and declaring themselves the masters of the future. . . . It takes possession of the press, and employs it to promote impiety, disobedience to the laws of religion and the State, and goes so far as to preach murder as a duty for those who desire what is good. . . .

If the same elements of destruction which are now throwing society into convulsion have existed in all ages . . . yet ours, by the single fact of the liberty of the press, possesses more than any preceding age the means of contact, seduction, and attraction whereby to act on these different classes of men.

Prince Richard Metternich (Ed.), *Memoirs of Prince Metternich*, 1815–1829, Vol. 5 (New York: Charles Scribner's 1881), pp. 465–466, 468, 472–473.

Thereafter, for many years the secret police of the various German states harassed potential dissidents. In the opinion of the princes these included almost anyone who sought even moderate social or political change.

Great Britain

The years 1819 and 1820 marked a high tide for conservative influence and repression in western as

well as eastern Europe. After 1815 Great Britain experienced two years of poor harvests. There was also considerable industrial unemployment, to which discharged sailors and soldiers added their numbers.

The Tory ministry of Lord Liverpool (1770–1828) was unprepared to deal with these problems of postwar dislocation. Instead, it sought to protect the interests of the landed and other wealthy classes. In 1815 the Parliament passed a

Corn Law to maintain high prices for domestically produced grain through import duties on foreign grain. The next year Parliament abolished the income tax paid by the wealthy and replaced it with excise or sales taxes on consumer goods paid by both the wealthy and the poor. These laws represented a continuation of previous legislation through which the British ruling class had abandoned much of its traditional role of paternalistic protector of the poor. In 1799 Parliament had passed the Combination Acts forbidding workers' organizations or unions. During the war, wage protection had been removed. The taxpaying classes grumbled about supporting the poor law that provided public relief for those destitute or without work; many people called for its abolition.

In light of these policies and the postwar economic downturn, it is hardly surprising that the lower social orders began to doubt the wisdom of their rulers and to call for a reform of the political system. Mass meetings calling for the reform of Parliament were held. Reform clubs were organized. Radical newspapers, such as William Cobbett's *Political Registrar*, demanded political change. In the hungry, restive agricultural and industrial workers the government could see only images of continental sans-culotte crowds ready to hang aristocrats from the nearest lamppost. Government ministers regarded radical leaders, such as Cobbett (1763–1835), Major John Cartwright (1740–1824), and Henry "Orator" Hunt (1773–1835), as demagogues who were seducing the people away from allegiance to their natural leaders. The answer of the government to the discontent was repression. In December 1816 a very unruly mass meeting took place at Spa Fields near London. This disturbance provided an excuse to pass the Coercion Acts of March 1817. These measures temporarily suspended habeas corpus and extended existing laws against seditious gatherings.

This initial repression, accompanied by improved harvests, brought calm for a time to the political landscape. However, by 1819 the people were restive again. Throughout the industrial north a large number of well-organized mass meetings were held to demand the reform of Parliament. Major radical leaders gave speeches to thousands of people. The radical reform campaign culminated on August 16, 1819, with a meeting in Manchester at St. Peter's Fields. Royal troops and the local militia were on hand to ensure order. Just as the speeches were about to begin, a local magistrate ordered the militia to move into the audience. The result was panic and death. At least eleven people in the crowd were killed; scores were injured. The event became known as the "Peterloo" Massacre through a contemptuous comparison with the victory at Waterloo.

Peterloo had been the act of the local Manchester officials. However, the Liverpool ministry felt that those officials must be supported. The Cabinet also decided to act once and for all to end these troubles. Most of the radical leaders were arrested and thus taken out of circulation. In December

George IV, king of Great Britain from 1820 to 1830. Although an intelligent patron of the arts, George was very unpopular with the British aristocracy and people, who considered him a debauched spendthrift. [New York Public Library Picture Collection.]

GEORGE·IV

TO HENRY HUNT, ESQᴿ

As CHAIRMAN of the Meeting assembled on St. Peter's Field, Manchester on the 16ᵀᴴ or AUGUST, 1819.
and to the **Female Reformers** of MANCHESTER and the adjacent TOWNS who were exposed to and suffered from
THE WANTON and FURIOUS ATTACK MADE ON THEM BY THAT BRUTAL ARMED FORCE THE MANCHESTER and CHESHIRE YEOMANRY CAVALRY

This contemporary print depicting the "Peterloo" Massacre of 1819 in Manchester, England, was intended to evoke sympathy for political radicalism. Note that in addition to being dedicated to Henry "Orator" Hunt, it is also dedicated to women who supported political reform. A large number of women and children had been present at the political rally the authorities turned into a massacre. [The Mansell Collection.]

1819, a few months after the German Carlsbad Decrees, Parliament passed a series of laws called the Six Acts. These forbade large meetings, raised the fines for seditious libel, speeded up the trials of political agitators, increased newspaper taxes, prohibited the training of armed groups, and allowed local officials to search homes in certain disturbed counties. In effect the Six Acts attempted to re-

move the instruments of agitation from the hands of radical leaders and to provide the authorities with new powers.

Two months after the passage of the Six Acts, the Cato Street Conspiracy was unearthed. Under the guidance of a possibly demented figure named Thistlewood, a group of extreme radicals plotted to blow up the entire British Cabinet. The plot was

❧ Shelley Deplores the Condition of England in 1819

Percy Bysshe Shelley, one of the greatest of the Romantic poets, was a political radical. In 1819 he was living in Italy. On hearing the news of the Peterloo Massacre, he wrote the most famous of his political poems, "Sonnet: England in 1819." In it he attacked George III, who had long been mentally unstable; the Church of England, which was insensitive the plight of the common people; and Parliament, which had passed repressive laws after Peterloo.

An old, mad, blind, despised, and dying king,—
Princes, the dregs of their dull race, who flow
Through public scorn,—mud from a muddy
    spring,—
Rulers who neither see, nor feel, nor know,
But leech-like to their fainting country cling,
Till they drop, blind in blood, without a blow,—
A people starved and stabled in the untilled
    field,—

An army, which liberticide and prey
Makes as a two-edged sword to all who wield,—
Golden and sanguine laws which tempt and slay;
Religion Christless, Godless—a book sealed;
A Senate,—Time's worst statute unrepealed,—
Are graves, from which a glorious Phantom may
Burst, to illumine our tempestuous day.

The Complete Poetical Works of Percy Bysshe Shelley, ed. by Thomas Hutchinson (London: Oxford University Press, 1929), p. 570.

foiled. The leaders were arrested and tried, and four of them were executed. The conspiracy was little more than a half-baked plot, but it provided new support for the repression of the government. More importantly, the conspiracy helped further to discredit the movement for parliamentary reform.

Bourbon Restoration in France

The abdication of Napoleon in 1814 opened the way for a restoration of Bourbon rule in the homeland of the great revolution. The new king was the former count of Provence, and brother of Louis XVI. The son of the executed monarch had died in prison. Royalists had regarded the dead boy as Louis XVII, and so his uncle became Louis XVIII (1814–1824). This fat, awkward man had become a political realist during his more than twenty years of exile. He understood that he could not govern if he attempted to turn back the clock. France had undergone too many irreversible changes. Consequently Louis XVIII agreed to become a constitutional monarch, but under a constitution of his own making.

The constitution of the French restoration was the Charter. It provided for a hereditary monarchy and a bicameral legislature. The monarch appointed the upper house; the lower house, the Chamber of Deputies, was elected according to a very narrow franchise that upheld a high property qualification. The Charter guaranteed most of the rights enumerated by the Declaration of the Rights of Man and Citizen. There was to be religious toleration, but Roman Catholicism was designated as the official religion of the nation. Most importantly for thousands of Frenchmen at various stations of life who had profited from the revolution, the Charter promised not to disturb the property changes brought about by the confiscation and sale of aristocratic and church land. In this manner Louis XVIII attempted to reconcile to his restored regime those classes who had benefited from the revolution.

This moderate spirit did not penetrate deeply into the ranks of royalist supporters. Their families had suffered much at the hands of the revolution. They now demanded their revenge. The king's brother, the count of Artois (1757–1836), served as a rallying point for those people who were more royalist than the monarch. In the months after Napoleon's final defeat at Waterloo, royalists in the south and west carried out a White Terror against former revolutionaries and supporters of the de-

Louis XVIII of France. After his elevation to the throne of his executed brother, Louis XVI, he attempted to rule with moderation. [Bettmann Archive.]

posed emperor. The king could do little or nothing to halt this bloodbath of royalist revenge. Similar extreme royalist sentiment existed in the Chamber of Deputies. The ultraroyalist majority elected in 1816 proved so dangerously reactionary that the king soon dissolved the chamber. The majority returned by the second election were more moderate. Under the ministry of the duke of Richelieu the country paid off the war indemnity to the allies, and the occupation troops withdrew in 1818. Yet royalist discontent remained. Louis XVIII attempted to pursue a policy of mild accommodation with liberals through his minister Decazes, who took office in 1818 but the king's younger brother, the count of Artois, pushed for reactionary departures.

This give and take might have continued for some time. However, in February 1820 the duke of Berri, son of Artois and heir to the throne after his father, was murdered by a lone assassin. The ultraroyalists persuaded Louis XVIII that the murder was the result of Decazes's cooperation with liberal politicians. The duke of Richelieu was recalled. The electoral laws were revised to give wealthy electors two votes. Press censorship was imposed. Persons suspected of dangerous political activity could be easily arrested. By 1821 the direction of secondary education in France was put under the control of the Roman Catholic bishops. All of these actions revealed the basic contradiction of the French restoration. There had been no intention of creating a genuinely parliamentary system. The king rather than the Chamber of Deputies chose the ministers. The government constantly tinkered with the electoral apparatus to disqualify opponents from voting. By the early 1820s the veneer of constitutionalism had worn away. Liberals were

being driven out of legal political life and into near-illegal activity.

The Conservative International Order

The Congress System

At the Congress of Vienna the major powers—Russia, Austria, Prussia, and Great Britain—had agreed to consult with each other from time to time on matters affecting Europe as a whole. The vehicle for this consultation was a series of postwar congresses. Later, as differences arose among the powers, the consultations became more informal. This mode of working out issues of foreign policy was known as the Concert of Europe. It meant that no one nation could take a major action in international affairs without the assent of the others. The major goal of the Concert of Europe was to maintain the balance of power against new French aggression and against the military might of Russia. The Concert of Europe continued to function on large and small issues until the third quarter of the century.

The years that witnessed the domestic conservative consolidation of power also saw a generally successful functioning of the congress system. The first congress occurred in 1818 at Aix-la-Chapelle. As a result of this congress the four major powers removed their troops from France, which had paid its war reparations, and readmitted that nation to good standing among European nations. Despite unanimity on these decisions, problems did arise during the conference. Czar Alexander I, displaying his full reactionary colors, suggested that the Quadruple Alliance agree to uphold the borders and existing governments of all European countries. Castlereagh, representing Britain, flatly rejected the proposal. He contended that the Quadruple Alliance was intended only to prevent future French aggression.

THE SPANISH REVOLUTION OF 1820. These disagreements appeared somewhat academic in 1818. But two years later a series of revolutions commenced in southern Europe. The Spanish rebelled against Ferdinand VII (1814–1833). When placed on his throne at the time of Napoleon's downfall, this Bourbon monarch had promised to govern according to a written constitution. Once securely in power Ferdinand simply ignored that pledge. He dissolved the parliament (the *Cortes*) and ruled alone. In 1820 a group of army officers about to be sent to suppress revolution in Spain's Latin American colonies rebelled. In March Ferdinand once again announced that he would abide by the provisions of the constitution. For the time being the revolution had succeeded. Almost at the same time, in July 1820, the revolutionary spirit erupted in Naples, where the King of the Two Sicilies very quickly accepted a constitution. There were other, lesser revolts in Italy, but none of them succeeded.

These events frightened the ever-nervous Metternich. Italian disturbances were especially troubling to him. Austria hoped to dominate the peninsula to provide a buffer against the spread of revolution on its own southern flank. The other powers were divided on the best course of action. Britain opposed joint intervention in either Italy or Spain. Metternich turned to Prussia and Russia for support. The three eastern powers, along with unofficial delegations from Britain and France, met at the Congress of Troppau in late October 1820. The members of the Holy Alliance, led by Alexander of Russia, issued the Protocol of Troppau. This declaration asserted that stable governments might intervene to restore order in countries experiencing revolution. Yet even Russia hesitated to authorize Austrian intervention in Italian affairs. That decision was finally reached in January 1821 at the Congress of Laibach. Shortly thereafter Austrian troops marched into Naples and restored the King of the Two Sicilies to unconstitutional government.

The final postwar congress took place in October 1822 at Verona. Its primary purpose was to resolve the situation in Spain. Once again Britain balked at joint action. Shortly before the meeting Castlereagh had committed suicide. George Canning (1770–1827), the new foreign minister, was much less sympathetic to Metternich's goals. At Verona Britain, in effect, withdrew from continental affairs. Austria, Prussia, and Russia agreed to support French intervention in Spain. In April 1823 the French army crossed the Pyrenees and within a few months suppressed the Spanish revolution. Liberals and revolutionaries were tortured, executed, and driven from the country. The intervention in Spain in 1823 was one of the most bloody examples of reactionary politics during the entire century.

There was a second diplomatic result of the Congress of Verona and the Spanish intervention. George Canning was much more interested in the fate of British commerce and trade than Castlereagh had been. Consequently Canning sought to prevent the politics of European reaction from being extended to the Spanish colonies then revolting in Latin America. He intended to use those South American revolutions as the occasion for British penetration of the old Spanish trading monopoly in that area. To that end the British foreign minister supported the American Monroe Doctrine in 1823, prohibiting further colonization and intervention by European powers in the Americas. Britain soon recognized the Spanish colonies as independent states. Through the rest of the century British commercial interests dominated Latin America. In this fashion Canning may be said to have brought to a successful conclusion the War of Jenkins's Ear (1739).

The Greek Revolution of 1821

While the powers were plotting the new restorations in Italy and Spain, a third Mediterranean revolt had erupted in Greece. The Greek revolution became one of the most famous of the century because it attracted the support and participation of many illustrious literary figures. Liberals throughout Europe, who were seeing their own hopes crushed at home, imagined that the ancient Greek democracy was being reborn. "The world's great age begins anew," wrote Shelley. Lord Byron went to fight and in 1824 died in the cause of Greek liberty. Philhellenic societies were founded in practically every major country.

The Greeks were rebelling against the Ottoman

Greece Expiring on the Ruins of Missolonghi, by Eugène Delacroix (1799–1863) illustrates the manner in which small nationalities were idealized in sentimental liberal art in Western Europe. Greece is pictured as a beautiful, defenseless woman appealing for help against the dangers surrounding her. [Musée des Beaux-Arts, Bordeaux, A. Danvers.]

THE PERIOD OF REACTION AND REFORM

1812	Alexander I of Russia dismisses Speransky
1814	Louis XVIII restored in France under the Charter
1815	Holy Alliance formed among Russia, Austria, and Prussia
	Quadruple Alliance renewed among Russia, Austria, Prussia, and Britain
1817	Wartburg Festival at Jena
1818	Congress of Aix-la-Chapelle
1819	March 23 Assassination of Kotzebue
	July Carlsbad Decrees
	August 16 Peterloo Massacre
	December Six Acts passed in Great Britain
1820	January Spanish revolution
	February 13 Assassination of the Duke of Berri
	October Congress of Troppau
1821	January Congress of Laibach
	February Greek revolution
1822	Congress of Verona
1823	Frances intervenes to crush the Spanish revolution
1824	Charles X becomes king of France
1825	Decembrist Revolt in Russia
1829	Catholic Emancipation Act in Great Britain
1830	July 9 News of French victory in Algeria reaches Paris
	July 25 Charles X issues the Four Ordinances
	August 2 Charles X abdicates; Louis Philippe proclaimed king
	August 25 Belgian revolution
	November 29 Polish revolution
1832	Great Reform Bill passed in Great Britain

Empire. The weakness of that empire troubled Europe for the entire century and raised what was known as the *eastern question*. The residue of the problem remains alive today in the tensions between Greece and Turkey and in the instability in the Middle East. Most of the major powers were interested in what happened to the Ottoman holdings for reasons less idealistic than the poets'. Russia and Austria coveted land in the Balkans. France and Britain were concerned with the empire's commerce and with control of key naval positions in the eastern Mediterranean. There was also the issue of protection of Christian access to the shrines in the Holy Land.

These conflicting interests, as well as mutual distrust, prevented any direct intervention in Greek affairs for several years. In 1827 a joint British, French, and Russian fleet supported the Greek revolt. The fleet was enforcing the Treaty of London of 1827, in which those powers demanded Turkish recognition of Greek independence. They had decided that their domestic security would not be endangered by an independent Greek state and that their several foreign policy concerns in the area would prosper from such a new nation. In 1828 Russia sent troops against the Ottoman holdings in what is today Rumania. By the treaty of Adrianople of 1829 Russia gained effective control of that territory. The treaty further stipulated that the Turks would allow Britain, France, and Russia to decide the future of Greece.

In 1830 Greece was declared an independent kingdom by a second Treaty of London. Two years later Otto I (1832–1862), the son of the king of Bavaria, was chosen as the first king of the new Greek royal dynasty. The Greek revolt was the only successful national revolution of the first quarter of the century. Elsewhere the conservative powers had defeated the attempts at revolution.

Liberalism in the Early Nineteenth Century

The nineteenth century is frequently considered the great age of *isms*. Throughout the Western world secular ideologies began to take hold of the popular and learned imagination in opposition to the political and social status quo. These included liberalism, nationalism, socialism, republicanism, and communism. One noted historian has called all such words "trouble-breeding and usually thought-obscuring terms."[1] They are just that if one uses them as an excuse to avoid thinking or if one fails to see the variety of opinions concealed beneath each word.

It was just such intellectual laziness that characterized European conservatives as they faced their political opposition after the Napoleonic wars.

[1] Arthur O. Lovejoy, *The Great Chain of Being: A Study in the History of an Idea* (New York: Harper Torchbook, 1936), p. 6.

They tended to call "liberal" almost anything or anyone who drew into question their own political, social, or religious values. Moreover, the word *liberal* for twentieth-century Americans carries with it meanings and connotations that have little or nothing to do with its significance to nineteenth-century Europeans. European conservatives of the last century saw liberals as more radical than they actually were; present-day Americans think of them as being more conservative than they were.

Liberal Goals and Their Circumstances

POLITICS. Liberals derived their political ideas from the writers of the Enlightenment, the example of English liberties, and the so-called principles of 1789 as embodied in the French Declaration of the Rights of Man and Citizen. Liberal political figures sought to establish a framework of legal equality, religious toleration, and freedom of the press. Their general goal was a political structure that would limit the arbitrary power of the government against the persons and property of individual citizens. They generally believed that the legitimacy of government emanated from the freely given consent of the governed. The popular basis of such government was to be expressed through elected, representative or parliamentary bodies. Most importantly, free government required that state or crown ministers must be responsible to the representatives rather than to the monarch.

These goals may seem very limited, and they were. However, such responsible government existed in none of the major European countries in 1815. Even in Great Britain the Cabinet ministers were at least as responsible to the monarch as to the House of Commons. The kinds of people who espoused these changes in government tended to be those who were excluded from the existing political processes but whose wealth and education made them feel that such exclusion was unjustified. Liberals were often academics, members of the learned professions, and people involved in the rapidly expanding commercial and manufacturing segments of the economy. They believed in and were products of the career open to talent. The existing monarchical and aristocratic regimes often failed to recognize sufficiently their new status and to provide for their economic and professional interests.

Although the liberals wanted broader political participation, they were *not* advocates of democracy. Second only to their hostility to the privileged aristocracies was their general contempt for the lower, unpropertied classes. Liberals transformed the eighteenth-century concept of aristocratic liberty into a new concept of privilege based on wealth and property instead of on birth. As the French liberal theorist Benjamin Constant (1767–1830) wrote in 1814:

Those whom poverty keeps in eternal dependence are no more enlightened on public affairs than children, nor are they more interested than foreigners in national prosperity, of which they do not understand the basis and of which they enjoy the advantages only indirectly. Property alone, by giving sufficient leisure, renders a man capable of exercising his political rights.[2]

By the middle of the century this widely shared attitude meant that throughout Europe liberals had separated themselves from both the rural and the urban working class.

ECONOMICS. The economic goals of the liberals also furthered that important future split in European politics and society. Here the Enlightenment and the economic thought deriving from Adam Smith set the pattern. The manufacturers of Great Britain, the landed and manufacturing middle class of France, and the commercial interests of Germany and Italy sought the removal of the economic restraints associated with mercantilism. They wanted to be able to manufacture and sell goods freely. To that end they favored the general removal of internal barriers to trade and of international tariffs. Economic liberals opposed the old paternalistic legislation that established wages and labor practices by government regulation or by guild privileges. Labor was simply one more commodity to be bought and sold freely. Liberals sought an economic structure in which people were at liberty to use whatever talents and property they possessed to enrich themselves. By this means, the liberals contended, there would be more goods and more services for everyone at lower prices. Such a system of economic liberty was to provide the basis for material progress.

NATIONALISM. Another major ingredient of liberalism, as it developed in Germany, Italy, and the Austrian Empire, was nationalism. The idea of nationhood was not necessarily or logically linked to liberalism. There were conservative nationalists.

[2] Quoted in Frederick B. Artz, *Reaction and Revolution, 1814–1832* (New York: Harper, 1934), p. 94.

Protection

FOR THE

INDUSTRIOUS

Weavers.

INFORMATION having been received that a great number of industrious Weavers have been deterred by threats and acts of violence from the pursuit of their lawful occupations, and that in many instances their Shuttles have been taken, and their Materials damaged by persons acting under the existing Combinations :

Notice is hereby Given,

That every Protection will be afforded to persons so injured, upon giving Information to the Constables of Stockport : And a Reward of

FIFTY GUINEAS

Will be paid, on conviction, to the person who will come forward with such evidence as may be the means of convicting any one or more of the offences mentioned in the Act of Parliament, of which an Extract is subjoined : And a Reward of

TWENTY GUINEAS

Will be paid, on conviction, to the person who will come forward and inform of any person being guilty of assaulting or molesting industrious and honest Weavers, so as to prevent them from taking out or bringing in their Work peaceably.

PETER BROWN,
Stockport, June 17th, 1808.   T. CARTWRIGHT, } CONSTABLES.

By the 22nd, Geo. 3, C. 40, S. 3.

It is enacted, " *That if any person enter, by force, into any House or Shop, with intent to Cut and Destroy any Linen or Cotton, or Linen and Cotton mixed with any other Materials, in the Loom, or any Warp or Shute, Tools, Tackle, and Utensils, or shall Cut or Destroy the same, or shall Break and Destroy any Tools, Tackle, or Utensils, for Weaving, Preparing, or Making any such Manufactures, every such Offender shall be guilty of FELONY, without Benefit of Clergy*".

This poster is evidence of the industrial discontent that spread in some parts of Britain during the Napoleonic wars. That discontent became even sharper during the years of unemployment that followed Waterloo. [The Granger Collection.]

However, liberalism and nationalism were often complementary. Behind the concept of a people joined naturally together by the bonds of common language, customs, culture, and history lurked the idea of popular sovereignty. The idea of the career open to talent could be applied to suppressed national groups who were not permitted to realize their cultural or political potential. The efficient government and administration required by commerce and industry would mean the replacement of the petty dynasties of the small German and Italian states with larger political units. Moreover nationalist groups in one country could gain the sympathy of liberals in other nations by espousing the cause of representative government and political liberty.

Because the social and political circumstances of various countries differed, the specific programs of their liberals also differed. Great Britain already possessed institutions, such as Parliament, that could be reformed to provide more nearly representative government. The monarchy was already limited, and most individual liberties had been secured. Links between land, commerce, and industry existed. French liberals possessed a code of modern law in the Napoleonic Code. They could appeal to the widely accepted "principles of 1789." As in England, representatives of the different economic interests had worked together. Their problem was to protect the civil liberties by law, to define the respective powers of the monarch and the elected representative body, and to expand the electorate moderately while avoiding democracy.

The situation in Germany was quite different and very complex. Distinct social divisions existed between the aristocratic landowning classes, who filled the bureaucracies and officer corps, and the small middle-class commercial and industrial interests. There was little or no precedent for the latter groups' participating in the government or the army. There was no strong tradition of civil or individual liberty. From the time of Martin Luther through Kant and Hegel, freedom in Germany had meant conformity to a higher moral law rather than participation in politics. Consequently the mainstream of German liberalism differed from its British and French counterparts. There was much greater opposition from both the monarchs and the aristocracies. German liberals had little direct access to political influence. Most of them favored a united Germany that was to be created through the instrument of either the Austrian or the Prussian monarchy. This policy meant that they tended to stress the power of the state and the monarchy rather more than did other liberals. Once unification had been achieved, a freer social and political order might be established. The great difficulty for German liberals was the refusal of the Austrian or the Prussian monarchy to cooperate. Thus in Germany liberals were generally frustrated and had to remain satisfied with the lowering of internal trade barriers.

Between 1819 and 1822 the institutions of the restored conservative order had held back the forces of liberalism. In the Germanies, Austria, and Italy the liberal challenge was smothered for at least another twenty-five years. However, during the 1820s the conservative governments of Russia, France, and Great Britain faced new stirrings of political discontent. In Russia the result was suppression; in France, revolution; and in Britain, accommodation.

Russia: The Decembrist Revolt of 1825 and the Autocracy of Nicholas I

During the mid-1820s Russia took the lead in suppressing both liberal and nationalistic tendencies within its domains. In the process of driving Napoleon's army across Europe and then of occupying defeated France, many officers in the Russian army were introduced to the ideas of the French Revolution and the Enlightenment. They realized how economically backward and politically stifled their own nation remained. The domestic repression in Russia hardened as Alexander I became more conservative. Under these conditions groups within the army officer corps formed secret societies. One such reformist coterie was the Southern Society. Led by an officer named Pestel, these men sought a representative government and the abolition of serfdom. Pestel himself favored democracy and a moderately independent Poland. The Northern Society was a second, more moderate group. It favored constitutional monarchy and the abolition of serfdom but protection for the interests of the aristocracy. Both societies were very small; there was much friction between them. They agreed only that there must be a change in the government of Russia. Sometime during 1825 they seem to have decided to carry out a *coup d'état* in 1826.

Other events intervened. In late November 1825 Czar Alexander I suddenly and unexpectedly died. His death created two crises. The first was a dynastic one. Alexander had no direct heir. His brother Constantine stood next in line to the throne. However, Constantine, who was then the commander of Russian forces in occupied Poland, had married a woman who was not of royal blood. He had thus excluded himself from the throne and was more than willing to renounce any claim.

ПОЛЯРНАЯ ЗВѢЗДА

25 Іюля 1826 года.

The five Decembrists who were executed by Czar Nicholas I. Although a total failure, the Decembrist revolt came to symbolize the yearnings of all Russian liberals in the nineteenth century for a constitutional government. [Fotomas Index. John R. Freeman & Co., Ltd.]

Through a series of secret instructions made public only after his death, Alexander had named his younger brother, Nicholas (1825–1855), as the new czar. Once Alexander was dead, the legality of these instructions became uncertain. Constantine acknowledged Nicholas as czar, and Nicholas acknowledged Constantine. This family muddle continued for about three weeks, during which Russia actually had no ruler to the astonishment of all Europe. Then, during the early days of December, the army command reported to Nicholas the existence of a conspiracy among certain officers. Able to wait no longer for the working out of legal niceties, Nicholas had himself declared czar, much to the delight of the by-now-exasperated Constantine.

The second crisis now proceeded to unfold. There was a plot devised by a number of junior officers intent on rallying the troops under their command to the cause of reform. On December 26, 1825, the army was to take the oath of allegiance to Nicholas, who was less popular than Constantine and was regarded as more conservative. Nearly all of the regiments did so. But the Moscow regiment, whose chief officers, surprisingly, were not secret society members, marched into the Senate Square in Saint Petersburg and refused to swear allegiance. Rather, they called for Constantine and a constitution. Attempts to settle the situation peacefully failed. Late in the afternoon Nicholas ordered the cavalry and the artillery to attack the insurgents. Over sixty people were killed. Early in 1826 Nicholas himself presided over the commission that investigated the Decembrist Revolt and the secret army societies. Five of the plotters were executed and over one hundred other officers were exiled to Siberia.

Although the Decembrist Revolt completely failed, it was the first rebellion in modern Russian history whose instigators had specific political goals. They wanted constitutional government and the abolition of serfdom. As the century passed, the Decembrists, in their political martyrdom, came to symbolize the yearnings of all Russian liberals, whose numbers were always quite small. The more immediate result of the revolt was the crushing of liberalism as even a moderate political influence in Russia. Nicholas I was determined that never again would his power come under question. He eventually epitomized the most extreme form of nineteenth-century autocracy.

Nicholas was neither an ignorant nor a bigoted reactionary. He was quite simply afraid of change. He knew that Russia required reforms for economic growth and social improvement. In 1842 he told his State Council, "There is no doubt that serfdom, in its present form, is a flagrant evil which everyone realizes, yet to attempt to remedy it now would be, of course, an evil more disastrous."[3] To remove serfdom would necessarily, in his view, have undermined the nobles' support of the czar. Consequently Nicholas turned his back on this and practically all other reforms. Literary and political censorship and a widespread system of secret police flourished throughout his reign. There was lit-

---

[3] Quoted in Michael T. Florinsky, *Russia: A History and an Interpretation*, Vol. 2 (New York: Macmillan, 1953), p. 755.

Czar Nicholas I of Russia was the most conservative major ruler of the early nineteenth century. He resisted practically all attempts to reform Russia and offered the use of Russian troops to other European nations endangered by revolutionary disturbances. [*Culver Pictures.*]

tle attempt to forge even an efficient and honest administration. The only significant reform of his rule was a codification of Russian law published in 1833.

In place of reform Nicholas and his closest advisers embraced a program called *Official Nationality.* Its slogan, published repeatedly in government documents, newspapers, journals, and schoolbooks, was "Orthodoxy, Autocracy, and Nationalism." The Russian Orthodox faith was to provide the basis for morality, education, and intellectual life. The church, which since the days of Peter the Great had been an arm of the secular government, controlled the schools and universities. Young Russians were taught to accept their place in life and to spurn rising in the social structure. The program of autocracy championed the unrestrained power of the czar as the only authority that could hold the vast expanse of Russia and its peoples together in an orderly fashion. Political writers stressed that only under the autocracy of Peter the Great, Catherine the Great, and Alexander I had Russia prospered and exerted a major influence on world affairs. Through the glorification of Russian nationality, the country was urged to see its religion, language, and customs as a source of perennial wisdom that separated the nation from the moral corruption and political turmoil of the West. The person who presided over the program of Official Nationality was Count S. S. Uvarov, minister of education from 1833 to 1849. The result of his efforts and those of the czar was the profound alienation of serious Russian intellectual life from the czarist government.

Nicholas I also manifested extreme conservatism in foreign affairs. After the Congress of Vienna, Poland had been given a constitutional government, but within the limits of the Russian domination that dated back to the eighteenth-century partitions of Poland. Grand Duke Constantine, the brother of Alexander I and Nicholas I, was in charge of the Polish government by authority delegated by the czars. Although both czars frequently infringed on the constitutional arrangement and quarreled with the Polish Diet, the constitution itself remained. Nevertheless Polish nationalists continued to agitate for change.

In late November 1830, after the news of the French and Belgian revolutions of that summer had penetrated Poland, a small military insurrection broke out in Warsaw. Disturbances soon spread throughout the rest of the country. On December 18 the Polish Diet declared the revolution to be a nationalist movement. In early January 1831 the Diet voted to depose Nicholas as ruler of Poland. The czar reacted by sending troops into the country. After several months the revolt was thoroughly suppressed. In February 1832 Nicholas issued the Organic Statute, which declared Poland to be an integral part of the Russian empire. The statute guaranteed certain Polish liberties, but they were systematically ignored. The Polish uprising had confirmed all the czar's worst fears. Henceforth Russia and Nicholas became the gendarme of Europe, ever ready to provide troops to suppress liberal and nationalist movements.

❧ Uvarov Praises the Policy of Official Nationality

Uvarov was the Russian minister of education under Nicholas I. In that capacity he was largely responsible for the policy of Official Nationality and its program of orthodoxy, autocracy, and nationality. In 1843 he explained that this ideology was to prevent Russia from experiencing the political turmoil that had occurred in western Europe.

In the midst of rapid collapse in Europe of religious and civil institutions, at the time of a general spread of destructive ideas, at the sight of grievous phenomena surrounding us on all sides, it was necessary to establish our fatherland on firm foundations upon which is based the well-being, strength, and life of a people; it was necessary to find the principles which form the distinctive character of Russia, and which belong only to Russia; it was necessary to gather into one whole the sacred remnants of Russian nationality and to fasten to them the anchor of our salvation. Fortunately, Russia had retained a warm faith in the sacred principles without which she cannot prosper, gain in strength, live. Sincerely and deeply attached to the church of his fathers, the Russian has of old considered it the guarantee of social and family happiness. Without a love for the faith of its ancestors a people, *as well as an individual must perish. A Russian devoted to his fatherland, will agree as little to the loss of a single dogma of our* Orthodoxy *as to the theft of a single pearl from the tsar's crown.* Autocracy *constitutes the main condition of the political existence of Russia. The Russian giant stands on it as on the cornerstone of his greatness. An innumerable majority of the subjects of* Your Majesty *feel this truth; they feel it in full measure although they are placed on different rungs of civil life and although they vary in education and in their relations to the government. The saving conviction that Russia lives and is protected by the spirit of a strong, humane, and enlightened autocracy must permeate popular education and must develop with it. Together with these two national principles there is a third, no less important, no less powerful:* nationality.

Cited in Nicholas Riasanovsky, *Nicholas I and Official Nationality in Russia, 1825–1855* (Berkeley: University of California Press, 1959), pp. 74–75.

Revolution in France (1830)

The Polish revolt was the most distant of several disturbances that flowed from the overthrow of the Bourbon dynasty in France during July 1830. In 1824 Louis XVIII had died. He was succeeded by his brother, the count of Artois, who became Charles X (1824–1830). The new king, who had been the chief leader of the ultraroyalists at the time of the restoration, considered himself a monarch by divine right. He was crowned with elaborate ceremony and ritual at the Cathedral of Reims. At long last in power, he intended to roll back as much of the revolution as possible and to repay the loyalty of the French royalists.

His first action was to have the Chamber of Deputies in 1824 and 1825 provide for the indemnification of aristocrats who had lost their lands in the revolution. The existing land settlement was confirmed. However, by lowering the interest rates on government bonds, the Chamber created a fund from which the survivors of the *émigrés* who had forfeited land would be paid an annual sum of money. The middle-class bondholders, who lost income, naturally resented this measure. Another measure restored the rule of primogeniture, whereby only the eldest son of an aristocrat inherited the family domains. Charles X supported the Roman Catholic Church by a law punishing sacrilege with sentences of imprisonment or death. Liberals disapproved of all of these measures.

The results of the elections of 1827 compelled Charles X to appease the liberals, who in conjunction with more moderate royalists could muster a majority in the Chamber of Deputies. He appointed a less conservative ministry. Laws directed

Street fighting in the Rue Saint-Antoine in Paris during the July Revolution of 1830. The overthrow of Charles X led to the establishment of a moderate "bourgeois monarchy" under Louis Philippe. [Bildarchiv Preussischer Kulturbesitz.]

against the press and those allowing the government to dominate education were eased. Yet the liberals, who wanted a genuinely constitutional regime, remained unsatisfied. In 1829 the king decided that his policy of accommodation had failed. He dismissed his ministers and in their place appointed an ultraroyalist ministry headed by the Prince de Polignac (1780–1847). The opposition was now forced to the desperate action of opening negotiations with the liberal Orléanist branch of the royal family.

In 1830 Charles X called for new elections, in which the liberals scored a stunning victory. He might have relented and tried to accommodate the new Chamber of Deputies. Instead the king and his ministers decided to attempt a royalist seizure of power. In June and July 1830 Polignac had sent a naval expedition against Algeria. On July 9 reports of its victory reached Paris. The foundation of a French empire in North Africa had been laid. On July 25, 1830, under the euphoria of this for-

eign diversion, Charles X issued the Four Ordinances, which amounted to a royal *coup d'état*. The ordinances restricted freedom of the press, dissolved the recently elected Chamber of Deputies, restricted the franchise to the wealthiest people in the country, and called for new elections under the new royalist franchise.

The Four Ordinances provoked swift and decisive popular political reactions. Liberal newspapers called on the nation to reject the monarch's actions. The laboring populace of Paris, burdened since 1827 by an economic downturn, took to the streets and erected barricades. The king called out troops, and over eighteen hundred people died during the ensuing battles in the city. On August 2 Charles X abdicated and left France for exile in England. The liberals in the Chamber of Deputies named a new ministry composed of constitutional monarchists. They proclaimed Louis Philippe (1830–1848), the duke of Orléans, the new monarch. The July Days had brought to a final close the rule of the Bourbon dynasty in France.

In the Revolution of 1830 the liberals of the Chamber of Deputies filled a power vacuum created by the popular Paris uprising and the failure of effective royal action. Had Charles X provided himself with sufficient troops in Paris, the outcome could have been quite different. Moreover, had the liberals, who favored constitutional monarchy, not acted quickly, the workers and shopkeepers of Paris might have formed a republic. By seizing the moment, the middle class, the bureaucrats, and the moderate aristocratic liberals overthrew the restoration monarchy and still avoided a republic. These liberals feared a new popular revolution such as had swept France in 1792 on the overthrow of the old monarchy. They had no desire for another sans-culotte republic. Consequently a fundamental political and social tension marked the new monarchy as the hard-pressed laborers and the prosperous middle-class people whose temporary alliance had achieved the revolution realized that their basic goals had been quite different.

Politically the July Monarchy, as it was called, was more liberal than the restoration government. Louis Philippe was called the king of the French rather than of France. The tricolor flag of the revolution replaced the white flag of the Bourbons. The Charter was regarded as a right of the people rather than a concession of the monarch. Catholicism became the religion of the majority of the people rather than the official religion. Censorship

728

LES POIRES,

Faites à la cour d'assises de Paris par le directeur de la CARICATURE.

Vendues pour payer les 6,000 fr. d'amende du journal le *Charivari*.

(CHEZ AUBERT, GALERIÉ VERO-DODAT)

Si, pour reconnaître le monarque dans une caricature, vous n'attendez pas qu'il soit designé autrement que par la ressemblance, vous tomberez dans l'absurde. Voyez ces croquis informes, auxquels j'aurais peut-être dû borner ma defense :

Ce croquis ressemble à Louis-Philippe, vous condamnerez donc ? Alors il faudra condamner celui-ci, qui ressemble au premier.

Puis condamner cet autre, qui ressemble au second

Et enfin, si vous êtes consequens, vous ne sauriez absoudre cette poire, qui ressemble aux croquis précédens.

Ainsi, pour une poire, pour une brioche, et pour toutes les têtes grotesques dans lesquelles le hasard ou la malice aura placé cette triste ressemblance, vous pourrez infliger à l'auteur cinq ans de prison et cinq mille francs d'amende!! Avouez, Messieurs, que c'est là une singulière liberté de la presse!!

Political cartoonists found a superb subject in Louis Philippe. In this series of caricatures he is shown being transformed by progressive stages into a pear. The surrounding text and this group of drawings are primarily a satire on the so-called freedom of the press under which publishers were still in danger of heavy fines and the individual cartoonists liable to imprisonment for up to five years for lack of respect to the king. [The Granger Collection.]

❧ Guizot Fits the July Monarchy into the Context of French History ══

François Guizot (1787–1874) was a liberal French historian who became the most important minister of Louis Philippe during the July Monarchy. In this speech of 1831 to the French Chamber of Deputies Guizot defined the goal of the new government as establishing both liberty and order. He argued that previous regimes had attained only one or the other. As the years passed, both Guizot and Louis Philippe would become more concerned about order than about liberty.

Each epoch has its special task. The Revolution of 1789 was under obligation to destroy the ancien régime; it accomplished this with principles and powers which were adequate for the job, but when it tried to establish its own government with these principles and these powers to something else, when it tried to establish its own government with these principles and powers which had just destroyed the ancien régime, it was able to give us nothing but tyranny mixed with anarchy. We had this combination in two forms, powerful under the Convention, weak under the Directory. . . .

The Empire [of Napoleon] arose to re-establish order, order of an exterior, material sort which was the basis of the civil society as the Revolution had founded it. The Empire spread this idea throughout all of Europe; this was its mission and it succeeded at

it. It was incapable, however, of establishing a lasting political government; the necessary conditions were lacking. The Empire fell in its turn, to be succeeded by the Restoration.

What did the Restoration promise? It promised to resolve the problem, to reconcile order with liberty. . . . It was unable to solve the problem. It died in the process, overwhelmed by the burden.

It is on us, on the Revolution of July, that this job has been imposed; it is our duty and responsibility to establish definitively, not order alone, not liberty alone, but order and liberty at the same time. There is no way of escaping this double duty. Yes, gentlemen, our duty is twofold. We are commissioned to establish at the same moment the principle and the institutions of order, the principle and the institutions of liberty: there is the promise of the Revolution of July.

Cited in Thomas C. Mendenhall, Basil D. Henning, and Archibald S. Foord, *The Quest for a Principle of Authority in Europe, 1715–Present* (New York: Henry Holt, 1948), p. 144.

Louis Philippe became King of the French by the Revolution of 1830 and was deposed by the Revolution of 1848. [*The Granger Collection.*]

was abolished. The franchise became somewhat wider but remained on the whole restricted. The king had to cooperate with the Chamber of Deputies; he could not dispense with laws on his own authority.

Socially, however, the Revolution of 1830 proved quite conservative. The hereditary peerage was abolished in 1831, but the everyday economic, political, and social influence of the landed oligarchy continued. Money was the path to power and influence in the government. There was much corruption. Most importantly, the liberal monarchy displayed little or no sympathy for the lower and working classes. The Paris workers in 1830 had called for the protection of jobs, better wages, and the preservation of the traditional crafts rather than for the usual goals of political liberalism. The government of Louis Philippe ignored their de-

CENTERS OF REVOLUTION,
1820–1830

MAP 24.1 *Conservative governments and cooperation among repressive great powers in post-Napoleonic Europe were challenged by uprisings and revolutions, beginning in 1820–1821 in Spain, Naples, and Greece and appearing in Russia, France, and Belgium later in the decade.*

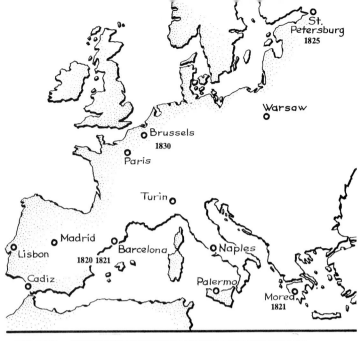

This famous French painting, Liberty Leading the People, by Delacroix, symbolized in the minds of many the militant spirit in which the liberals of 1830 confronted the forces of political reaction. [Bettmann Archive.]

mands and their plight. The laboring classes of Paris and the provincial cities seemed just one more possible source of disorder. In late 1831 troops suppressed a workers' revolt in the city of Lyons. In July 1832 an uprising occurred in Paris during the funeral of a popular Napoleonic general. Again the government called out troops and over eight hundred people were killed or wounded. In 1834 a very large strike of silkworkers in Lyons was crushed. Such discontent might be smothered for a time, but without attention to the social and economic conditions creating that tension new turmoil would eventually erupt.

Belgium Becomes Independent (1830)

The July Days in Paris sent sparks to other political tinder on the Continent. The revolutionary fires first lighted in neighboring Belgium. The former Austrian Netherlands had in 1815 been merged with the kingdom of Holland. The upper classes of Belgium had never reconciled themselves to rule by a country with a different language, religion, and economic life. On August 25, 1830, disturbances broke out in Brussels following the performance of an opera that portrayed a rebellion of Naples against Spanish rule. To put an end to the rioting, the municipal authorities and persons from the propertied classes formed a provisional national government. When compromise between the Belgians and the Dutch failed, William of Holland sent troops and ships against Belgium. By November 10, 1830, the Dutch had been defeated. A national congress then wrote a liberal Belgian constitution, which was promulgated in 1831.

The major powers saw the revolution in Belgium as upsetting the boundaries established by the Congress of Vienna. Russia could not intervene because of the Polish revolt. Prussia and the other German states were suppressing small risings in their own domains. The Austrians were busy putting down disturbances in Italy. France under Louis Philippe favored an independent Belgium and hoped to dominate it. Britain felt that it could tolerate a liberal Belgium as long as it was free of foreign domination. In December 1830 Lord Palmerston (1784–1865), the British foreign minister, gathered representatives of the powers in London. Through skillful negotiations he persuaded them to recognize Belgium as an independent and neutral state. In July 1831 Leopold of Saxe-Coburg (1831–1865) became king of the Belgians.

By the Convention of 1839 the great powers guaranteed the neutrality of Belgium. For almost a century Belgian neutrality remained one of the articles of faith in European international relations. In 1914 it was German violation of the neutrality convention that technically brought Great Britain into World War I.

The Great Reform Bill in Britain (1832)

The revolutionary year of 1830 saw in Great Britain the election of a House of Commons that debated the first major bill to reform Parliament. The death of George IV (1820–1830) and the accession of William IV (1830–1837) required the calling of an election. It was once believed that the July revolution in France had influenced the British elections in the summer of 1830. This theory has been shown to be incorrect through a close analysis of the time and character of the individual county and borough elections. The passage of the Great Reform Bill, which became law in 1832, was the result of a series of events very different from those that occurred on the Continent. In Britain the forces of conservatism and reform made accommodations with each other.

Several factors made this situation possible and meant that Great Britain would become "the chief laboratory of liberal thought during the century."[4] First, there was a larger commercial and industrial class in Britain than in other countries. No matter what group might control the government, British prosperity required attention to those economic interests. Second, there existed in Britain the long tradition of liberal Whig aristocrats, who regarded themselves as the protectors of constitutional liberty. They saw their role as that of making moderate political changes that would render revolutionary changes unnecessary. Their early sympathy for the French Revolution had lessened their influence. However, after 1815 they reentered the political arena and waited to be recalled to power. Finally, there also existed in British law, tradition, and public opinion a strong respect for civil liberties.

In 1820, the year after the passage of the notorious Six Acts, Lord Liverpool shrewdly moved to change his Cabinet. New faces began to appear.

---

[4] George L. Mosse, *The Culture of Western Europe: The Nineteenth and Twentieth Centuries* (New York: Rand McNally, 1965), p. 97.

They included George Canning, Robert Peel (1788–1850), and William Huskisson (1770–1830). These men, sometimes called liberal Tories, favored conservative politics but also knew that the nation and the government must accommodate themselves to the new economic and political forces of the day. Canning introduced the more liberal foreign policy that led to the recognition of the Latin American republics. Peel set about reforming the criminal law and reducing the number of capital offenses. Huskisson was an economic liberal who began a slow process of lowering tariffs for the benefit of the commercial classes. In 1824 the Combination Acts were repealed, and labor organization became possible.

Economic considerations had generally led to these moderate reforms. English determination to maintain the union with Ireland brought about another key reform. England's relationship to Ireland was not unlike that of Russia's to Poland or Austria's to its several national groups. In 1800,

Daniel O'Connell was the most dynamic and effective Irish nationalist leader in the first half of the nineteenth century. His portrait is by George Hayter and was made in 1834 when O'Connell was 59. [The Granger Collection.]

fearful that Irish nationalists might again rebel as they had in 1798 and perhaps turn Ireland into a base for a French invasion, William Pitt the Younger had persuaded Parliament to enact the Act of Union between England and Ireland. Ireland now sent one hundred members to the House of Commons. However, because of the religious scruples of King George III, Pitt was unable to secure the passage of a law to permit Roman Catholics to sit in the House of Commons. Consequently only Protestant Irishmen, who usually had close ties to England, could be elected to represent overwhelmingly Catholic Ireland.

During the 1820s, under the leadership of Daniel O'Connell (1775–1847), Irish nationalists organized the Catholic Association to agitate for Catholic emancipation. In 1828 O'Connell secured his own election to Parliament, where he could not legally take his seat. The British ministry of the duke of Wellington realized that henceforth an entirely Catholic delegation might be elected from Ireland. If they were not seated, civil war might erupt across the Irish Sea. Consequently, in 1829 Wellington and Robert Peel steered the Catholic Emancipation Act through Parliament. Roman Catholics could now become Members of Parliament. This measure, together with the repeal in 1828 of restrictions against Protestant nonconformists, meant that the Anglican monopoly on British political life was over.

Catholic emancipation was a liberal measure that was passed for the conservative purpose of preserving order in Ireland. It included a provision raising the franchise in Ireland so that only the wealthier Irish could vote. Nonetheless this measure alienated many of Wellington's Anglican Tory supporters in the House of Commons. In the election of 1830 a large number of supporters of parliamentary reform were returned to Parliament. Even some Tories believed that parliamentary reform was necessary because they had concluded that Catholic emancipation could have been passed only by a corrupt House of Commons. The Wellington ministry soon fell. The Tories were badly divided. Consequently King William IV turned to the Whigs under the leadership of Earl Grey (1764–1845) to form a government.

The Whig ministry soon presented the House of Commons with a major reform bill that had two broad goals. The first was to abolish "rotten" boroughs, which had small numbers of voters, and to replace them with representatives for the previ-

A painting by B. R. Haydon of a mass meeting in Manchester to support the first Reform Bill. Before the Bill became law in 1832, many large British cities did not elect their own member to the House of Commons. [City of Birmingham Museum and Art Gallery.]

The first meeting of the reformed House of Commons in 1833, painted by G. Hayter. Most seats were still filled by the gentry and members of the wealthy middle classes. But the elimination of rotten boroughs and the election of members from the new urban centers began the transformation of the House of Commons into a more nearly representative national body. [National Portrait Gallery, London.]

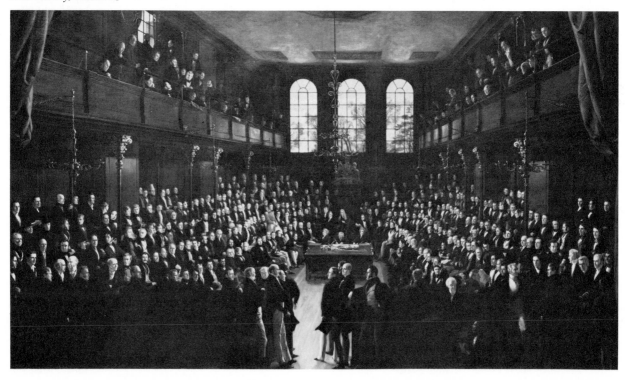

❧ Thomas Babington Macaulay Defends the Great Reform Bill

Macaulay (1800–1859) was a member of the House of Commons that passed the Great Reform Bill in 1831 only to have it rejected by the House of Lords before another measure was successfully enacted in 1832. His speeches in support of the bill derived from his views on the need for Parliament to give balanced representation to major elements in the population. Specifically, he supported the Great Reform Bill because, without creating a democratic government, it allowed the middle class to obtain political influence. He saw the reform of Parliament as a way to prevent political revolution in England. His argument had wide appeal.

[The principle of the ministers] is plain, rational, and consistent. It is this,—to admit the middle class to a large and direct share in the Representation, without any violent shock to the institutions of our country. . . . I hold it to be clearly expedient, that in a country like this, the right of suffrage should depend on a pecuniary qualification. Every argument . . . which would induce me to oppose Universal Suffrage, induces me to support the measure which is now before us. I oppose Universal Suffrage, because I think that it would produce a destructive revolution. I support this measure, because I am sure that it is our best security against a revolution. . . . I . . . do entertain great apprehension for the fate of my country. I do in my conscience believe, that unless this measure, or some similar measure, be speedily adopted, great and terrible calamities will befall us. Entertaining this opinion, I think myself bound to state it, not as a threat, but as a reason. I support this measure as a measure of Reform: but I support it still more as a measure of conservation. That we may exclude those whom it is necessary to exclude, we must admit those whom it may be safe to admit. . . . All history is full of revolutions, produced by causes similar to those which are now operating in England. A portion of the community which had been of no account, expands and becomes strong. It demands a place in the system, suited, not to its former weakness, but to its present power. If this is granted, all is well. If this is refused, then comes the struggle between the young energy of one class, and the ancient privileges of another. . . . Such . . . is the struggle which the middle classes in England are maintaining against an aristocracy of mere locality. . . .

Hansard's Parliamentary Debates, 3rd series, Vol. 2, pp. 1191–1197.

---

ously unrepresented manufacturing districts and cities. Second, the number of voters in England and Wales was increased by about 50 per cent through a series of new franchises. In 1831 the House of Commons narrowly defeated the bill. Grey called for a new election, in which a majority in favor of the bill was returned. The House of Commons passed the reform bill, but the House of Lords rejected it. Mass meetings were held throughout the country. Riots broke out in several cities. Finally, William IV agreed to create enough new peers to give a third reform bill a majority in the House of Lords. Under this pressure the House of Lords yielded, and in 1832 the measure became law.

The Great Reform Bill expanded the size of the English electorate, but it was not a democratic measure. The number of voters was increased by over 200,000 persons, or by almost 50 percent. However, the basis of voting remained a property qualification. Some working-class voters actually were disenfranchised because of the abolition of certain old franchise rights. New urban boroughs were created to allow the growing cities to have a voice in the House of Commons. Yet the passage of the reform act did not, as it was once thought, constitute the triumph of the middle-class interest in England. For every new urban electoral district, a new rural district was also drawn. It was expected that the aristocracy would dominate the rural elections.

The success of the reform bill was its reconcilia-

When King William IV (1830–1837) agreed to create enough new peers to pass the Reform Bill, the House of Lords at last accepted the measure. His portrait is by an unknown artist. [The Granger Collection.]

Chippenham

Festival and Diversions,

IN CELEBRATION OF THE PASSING OF THE

Reform Bill,

On Wednesday August 22nd, 1832.

The Reform Bill having now become the law of the land, whatever might have been the political feelings and opinions of individuals on the expediency of the measure, it is now the imperative duty of all to yield obedience to its provisions. The Committee of Management sincerely hope that ALL PARTIES will meet in one common bond of "UNITY AND LOYALTY," and endeavor to make this the happiest day that Chippenham ever knew.

ORDER OF THE DAY.

The Morning will be ushered in by the Ringing of Bells, and Music; and to render greater joy to the occasion, the more wealthy Inhabitants of Chippenham are invited to close their shops, and attend their poorer neighbours.

AT TWO O'CLOCK,

An Old English DINNER, of Roast Beef, Plum Pudding, and Strong Beer, will be provided in the Market-place for Two Thousand Persons, who are previously to attend the Committee to receive Tickets, and it is desired that all persons take their seats at half-past One o'clock precisely.

AT FOUR O'CLOCK, *(by permission of the Bailiff.)*

The following SPORTS will take place in WESTMEAD, and as the Committee of Management have exerted themselves for the amusement of the Public, a strict attention to peaceable conduct and good order must be preserved, and on the sound of the Bugle all Persons must retire outside the Ropes.

A DONKEY RACE, for all ages, sizes, and sexes, the best of heats, three to start or no race, for One Sovereign.

A SACK RACE, six men or no race, the winner to receive Ten Shillings, the second—Five Shillings, and the third—Half-a-Crown. The Runners to find their own sacks.

A WELCH COCK FIGHT for Ten Shillings, six men or no match. A stick will be placed behind the knees under which the arms must be passed, and the hands tied in front.

A RACE for PONIES not exceeding 13½ hands, of all ages, to carry feather weights, best of heats, three to start or no race. The winner to receive Two Sovereigns, the second—A Sovereign.

A RACE BETWEEN MEN, best of heats, Eight to start or no race. The winner to receive Twelve Shillings and Sixpence, the second—Five Shillings, and the third—Half-a-Crown.

A JINGLING MATCH by Twelve men blindfolded, who will try to catch a man with a bell fastened around him. The winner to receive Ten Shillings.

GOWN PIECES, &c. will be provided for a race by Ladies, and WAISTCOATS & HATS for Boys.

THE FIREWORKS

Will be exhibited in the Market-place at Eight o'Clock in the Evening, and all persons are requested to refrain from firing Squibs and Crackers until after Nine o'Clock.

All Classes are respectfully enjoined to preserve peace and good order throughout the day, that the amusements which have been provided for the Public may be rendered worthy of the occasion on which they are given.

The Committee will attend at the Town-Hall on Tuesday Evening, at Seven o'Clock, to enter the Ponies and Donkeys, and the names of the candidates for the various prizes.

While less clamorous than the vigorous earlier demands for the Reform Bill, the celebrations after its passage in 1832 were none the less lively. These contemporary posters announce the different manners in which two English towns decided to mark the event. At Woodbridge the sobersided inhabitants elected to give a dinner to the poor. At Chippenham, however, they decided to give a vast "Old English Dinner" for two thousand of themselves, the menu for which they proudly announce, the dinner to be followed by a fine program of various sports and, finally, fireworks. [Courtesy Charles Farrell.]

AT A MEETING OF THE

INHABITANTS

OF

WOODBRIDGE,

HELD AT THE

TOWN HALL,

On the 14th. June, 1832,

For the purpose of deciding in what way to celebrate the passing of the

Reform Bill,

MR. THOMAS GRIMWOOD IN THE CHAIR.

Resolved unanimously,—That this Meeting feels anxious to celebrate the passing of the Reform Bill, in such a manner as may evince a high approval of the Measure, be of a public benefit, and at the same time not hurt the feelings of those who may differ in opinion. And that this Meeting conceives a Dinner given to the Poor, will be the best mode of celebrating so beneficial an event, and be far preferable to an Illumination, or other measure liable to abuse.

That a Dinner be accordingly given, and that a Committee be appointed to arrange all details.

That the Committee be open, and that any Inhabitant be at liberty to attend the Meetings of the Committee, and that five members be empowered to act.

That the thanks of this Meeting be given to the Magistrates for the use of the Hall, and to the Churchwardens for their kind and prompt compliance with the Requisitions of this Meeting.

That these Resolutions be printed.

THOMAS GRIMWOOD, Chairman.

The Chairman having left the Chair, the thanks of this Meeting was unanimously voted to the Chairman for his able and impartial conduct in the Chair.

At the close of the Meeting it was resolved to have a Public Dinner of the Inhabitants of the Town and Neighbourhood, on the Town Hall.

Tickets, 5s.—Dinner and a Pint of Wine included.

tion of previously unrepresented property owners and economic interests to the existing political institutions of the country. The act created a political situation in which further reforms of the church, the municipal government, and commercial policy could be achieved in an orderly fashion. Revolution in Britain was unnecessary because the people who sought change had been admitted to the political forum that could legislate those changes. In this manner the historic institutions of Great Britain were maintained while the persons and groups who influenced them became more diverse.

Suggested Readings

F. B. ARTZ, *Reaction and Revolution, 1814–1832* (1934). A useful though dated introduction.

D. BEALES, *From Castlereagh to Gladstone, 1815–1885* (1969). A survey to be read in conjunction with Briggs below.

R. J. BEZUCHA, *The Lyon Uprising of 1834: Social and Political Conflict in the Early July Monarchy* (1974). An excellent discussion of the tensions in France after the Revolution of 1830.

A. BRIGGS, *The Making of Modern England* (1959). The best survey of English history during the first half of the nineteenth century.

M. BROCK, *The Great Reform Act* (1974). The standard work.

G. A. CRAIG, *The Politics of the Prussian Army, 1640–1945* (1955). A splendid study of the conservative political influence of the army on Prussian development.

D. DAKIN, *The Struggle for Greek Independence* (1973). An excellent explanation of the intricacies of the Greek independence question.

G. DE BERTIER DE SAUVIGNY, *The Bourbon Restoration* (trans., 1966), and *Metternich and His Times* (1962). Sympathetic, but not uncritical, studies of the forces of political conservatism.

G. DE RUGGIERO, *The History of European Liberalism* (1927). The major treatment of the subject.

J. DROZ, *Europe Between Revolutions, 1815–1848* (1967).

An examination of Europe as created by the Vienna settlement.

E. HALÉVY, *England in 1815* (1913). One of the most important and influential books written on nineteenth-century Britain.

C. J. HAYES, *Essays on Nationalism* (1926). Pioneering, but still useful studies.

E. J. HOBSBAWM, *The Age of Revolution, 1789–1848* (1962). A very comprehensive survey emphasizing the social ramifications of the liberal democratic and industrial revolutions.

H. KOHN, *The Idea of Nationalism: A Study in Its Origin and Background* (1944). An examination of the roots of nationalism in Western culture.

L. KRIEGER, *The German Idea of Freedom* (1957). A far-ranging examination of the problems and ideology of German liberalism.

W. B. LINCOLN, *Nicholas I: Emperor and Autocrat of All the Russians* (1978). A serious scholarly treatment.

P. MANSEL, *Louis XVIII* (1981). A recent biography that captures much of the tone of life among *émigrés* and royalists.

J. MERRIMAN (Ed.), *1830 in France* (1976). A collection of important essays on the Revolution of 1830.

A. PALMER, *Alexander I: Tsar of War and Peace* (1974). An interesting biography that captures much of the rather mysterious personality of this ruler.

D. H. PINKNEY, *The French Revolution of 1830* (1972). The best account in English.

M. RAEFF, *The Decembrist Movement* (1966). An examination of the unsuccessful uprising, with documents.

N. V. RIASANOVSKY, *Nicholas I and Official Nationality in Russia, 1825–1855* (1959). A lucid discussion of the conservative ideology that made Russia the major opponent of liberalism.

D. THOMSON, *Europe Since Napoleon* (1962). A survey of political developments during the past century and a half.

A. B. ULAM, *Russia's Failed Revolutionaries* (1981). Contains a useful discussion of the Decembrists as a background for other nineteenth-century Russian revolutionary activity.

M. WALKER, *Metternich's Europe* (1968). A useful collection of documents.

P. S. WANDYCZ, *The Lands of Partitioned Poland, 1795–1918* (1974). The best study of Poland during the nineteenth century.

738

25 Economic Advance and Social Unrest (1830-1850)

By 1830 Europe was headed toward an industrial society. Only Great Britain had already attained that status, but the pounding of new machinery and the grinding of railway engines soon began to echo across the entire continent. Further urbanization, the disintegration of traditional social bonds and work habits, and eventually class conflict accompanied the economic development. However, what characterized the second quarter of the century was not the triumph of industrialism but the final gasps of those economic groups who opposed it. Intellectually the period saw the formulation of the major creeds supporting and criticizing the new society. These were years of uncertainty for almost everyone. Even the most confident businessman knew that the trade cycle might bankrupt him in a matter of weeks. For the industrial workers and the artisans unemployment

Child mill laborers. The early use of child labor in English factories followed the pattern of the old family economy, since until about the 1830s most children in factories worked for their parents. [The Mansell Collection.]

became a haunting and recurring problem. For the peasants the question was sufficiency of food. It was a period of self-conscious transition that culminated in 1848 with a continentwide outbreak of revolution. People knew that one mode of life was passing, but they were uncertain what would replace it.

Toward an Industrial Society

Population and Migration

The Industrial Revolution had begun in eighteenth-century Great Britain with the advances in textile production described in Chapter 19. Natural resources, adequate capital, native technological skills, a growing food supply, a social structure that allowed considerable mobility, and strong foreign and domestic demands for goods had given Britain an edge in achieving a vast new capacity for production in manufacturing. Its factories and recently invented machines allowed British produc-

739

ers to furnish customers with more products and better products at lower prices than any competitors. The wars of the French Revolution and of Napolean brought about the final collapse of the French Atlantic trade. The same conflicts had destroyed capital, led to inflated currencies, and killed off much of the labor supply in the continental countries. Consequently Britain's initial lead became further extended, so that in 1850 the nation still remained a generation ahead of its future continental competitors.

Despite the economic lag the continental nations were beginning to make material progress. By the 1830s in Belgium, France, and Germany the number of steam engines in use was growing steadily. Exploitation of the coalfields of the Ruhr and the Saar basins had begun. Coke was replacing charcoal in iron and steel production.

Industrial areas were generally less concentrated than in Britain, and large manufacturing districts, such as the British Midlands, did not yet exist across the English Channel. There were major pockets of production in western Europe, such as the cities of Lyons, Rouen, Liège, and Lille,

❧ Parliament Hears About German Imitation of English Machinery

In 1841 a committee of the British Parliament heard evidence on the exportation of English machinery. In the passage below, a Mr. Charles Noyes informed the committee of the activities supported by the Prussian government to imitate English textile machines. His testimony reveals the contemporary recognition of English technological superiority and the attempts of other European nations to compete with England. Despite efforts such as those described, Britain continued to maintain its domination in textile production even as manufacturers on the Continent began to adopt English methods.

I found at Berlin the most enterprising and systematic exertions made on the part of the Government to obtain a command of the manufacture of machinery; I found no expense spared for that purpose; and the exertions quite astonished me. There is one very important [training] institution at Berlin, called the "Gerwerbe Institut" [Trade Institute], which is a large establishment for practical education, combining design with almost every branch of manufactures into which science and mechanics enter. . . . In going through the rooms of this institution with the professor, Mr. Wedding, I saw suites of apartments completely filled with models of English machines: the professor informed me that they had in it models of every machine in use in Great Britain for the manufacture of cotton, flax, silk, and wool, and likewise a number from America and [elsewhere in] Germany; that by these means they were not only enabled to have our recent improvements, but, what was a matter of importance which we cannot command, that they were enabled frequently to combine in the

same machine two distinct patents. The system he told me was, that this machinery, as soon as produced in England, was immediately imported at the expense of the [Prussian] Government, and set up at the Gerwerbe Institut; that it was proved [tested]; that a working model was immediately made from it, to be deposited in the institution, and that the original was presented as an honorary prize by the Government to some manufacturer in Prussia, who had distinguished himself in the peculiar branch to which it was applicable. In the Institut, likewise, the pupils were taught to make the machinery themselves; they were supplied with the tools, and they were permitted to carry away the machines which they themselves had constructed; I cannot but look upon the whole of this system as the most surprising effort made on the part of the [Prussian] Government to obtain a command of the manufacture of machinery, which is at the present moment so important a feature in English manufactures.

From "Minutes of Evidence taken before the Select Committee . . . [on] The Exportation of Machinery" (1841), as cited in S. Pollard and C. Holmes (Eds.), *Documents of European Economic History*, Vol. 1 (London: Edward Arnold, 1968), p. 429.

The Clifton Bridge, a great iron suspension bridge over the Avon River gorge near Bristol, England, was one of the many spectacular engineering accomplishments of the early nineteenth century. It was designed in 1831 by Isambard Kingdom Brunel (1806–1859), possibly the greatest engineer of his era. Construction began in 1836, and the bridge was completed in 1864. It is still in use. The bridge epitomizes the modern breakthrough in building such structures, as well as railways, subways, massive ships, and others—all dependent on new technologies. [British Tourist Authority, New York.]

but most continental manufacturing still took place in the countryside. New machines were integrated into the existing domestic system. The extreme slowness of continental imitation of the British example meant that at mid-century peasants and urban artisans remained more important politically than industrial factory workers.

While the process of industrialization spread, the population of Europe continued to grow on the base of the eighteenth-century population explosion. The number of people in France rose from 32.5 million in 1831 to 35.8 million in 1851. The population of Germany rose from 26.5 million to 33.5 million during approximately the same period. That of Britain grew from 16.3 million to 20.8 million. More and more of the people of Europe lived in cities. By mid-century one half of the

population of England and Wales had become town dwellers; the proportion for France and Germany was about one quarter. The sheer numbers of human beings put considerable pressure on the physical resources of the cities. Migration from the countryside meant that existing housing, water, sewers, food supplies, and lighting were completely inadequate. Slums with indescribable filth grew, and disease, especially cholera, ravaged the population. Crime increased and became a way of life for those who could make a living in no other manner. Human misery and degradation in numerous early nineteenth-century cities seemed to have no bounds.

The situation in the countryside was little or no better. During the first half of the century the productive use of the land still remained the over-

"Washerwomen" by the French artist Jean-Francois Millet (1814–1875). A peasant by birth himself, Millet often portrayed the grim hard work that continued to characterize the lives of the rural poor in nineteenth-century Europe. [Museum of Fine Arts, Boston. Gift of Mrs. Martin Brimmer.]

whelming fact of life for the majority of Europeans. The enclosures of the late eighteenth century, the land redistribution of the French Revolution, and the emancipation of serfs in Prussia and later in central Europe (Austria, 1848; Russia, 1861) commercialized landholding. Liberal reformers had hoped that the legal revolution in ownership would transform peasants into progressive, industrious farmers. Most of them had instead become very conservative landholders who possessed too little soil to innovate or, in many cases, even to support themselves. The specter of poor harvests still haunted Europe. The worst such experience of the century was the Irish famine of 1845–1847. Perhaps as many as half a million Irish peasants with no land or small plots simply starved when disease blighted the potato crop. Hundreds of thousands emigrated. By mid-century the revolution in landholding had led not only to greater agricultural production but also to a vast uprooting of people from the countryside into cities and from Europe into the rest of the world.

Railways

Industrial advance itself had also contributed to this migration. The decades of the 1830s and 1840s were the great age of railway building. The Stockton and Darlington Line opened in England in 1825. By 1830 another major line had been built between Manchester and Liverpool and had several hundred daily passengers. Belgium had undertaken railway construction by 1835. The first French line opened in 1832, but serious construction came only in the 1840s. Germany entered the railway age in 1835. At mid-century Britain had 9,797 kilometers of railway; France, 2,915; and Germany, 5,856. The railroads, plus canals and improved regular roads, meant that people could leave the place of their birth more easily than ever before. The improvement in transportation also allowed cheaper and more rapid passage of raw materials and finished products.

Railways epitomized the character of the industrial economy during the second quarter of the century. They represented investment in capital goods rather than in consumer goods. There was consequently somewhat of a shortage of consumer goods at cheap prices. This favoring of capital over consumer production was one reason that the working class often found itself able to purchase so little for its wages. The railways in and of themselves also brought about still more industrialization. They created a sharply increased demand for

Railroads literally cut into the cities of Europe. Here in Camden Town in London retaining walls are being built in a deep cut on either side of the newly laid tracks. The picture was made in 1838 by John G. Bourne.

iron and steel and then for a more skilled labor force. The new iron and steel capacity soon permitted the construction of ironclad ships and iron rather than wooden machinery. These great capital industries led to the formation of vast industrial fortunes that would be invested in still newer enterprises. Industrialism had begun to grow on itself.

The Middle Classes

It was the age of the career open to talent. The middle class of businessmen, traders, shippers, factory owners, doctors, lawyers, shopkeepers, and schoolteachers benefited most from the economic and material progress. Their incomes, unlike those of laborers, allowed them to buy consumer goods. Their skills and education permitted them to rise socially. They often had sufficient savings to make either large or small investments in the railroads and other heavy industries. Many of them were able to rise well above the social status of their birth.

The middle *classes*—for the group was very diverse—believed that merit and competition should replace good birth and patronage as avenues to social position and political influence. In place of the former aristocratic value of leisure, they raised the values of thrift and hard work. They tended to measure success and respectability

in terms of money. This attitude made them very unsympathetic toward the plight of the poor. They believed that the poor experienced poverty from either lack of ability or laziness. The middle classes were the people whom the English novelist Charles Dickens (1812–1870) pilloried in *Hard Times* and other novels and whose amoral existence the French novelist Honoré de Balzac (1799–1850) dissected in his fiction. But the confidence of the middle classes was a reflection of the new economic order that their members had created. They were also arrogant because they had learned from the aristocracy that pride and self-confidence were the marks of socially superior people.

Yet for all their economic success and apparent self-confidence, in several countries the middle classes at mid-century still generally lacked effective political power. They were best off in Britain, where aristocratic leaders did listen to them and where they were being absorbed into the political process, as the careers of prime ministers Robert Peel and William Gladstone demonstrated.

In France, by contrast, a very small group of extremely wealthy persons affected politics. During the July Monarchy only about 250,000 persons had the right to vote. In the states of Germany, the Hapsburg Empire, and Russia the small middle classes were relatively powerless. Throughout Europe these people were coming increasingly to resent a lack of political influence equal to their

743

Charles Dickens (1812–1870) sought in his novels to awaken the conscience of the English middle classes to the harsh effects of the industrial revolution on the poor. [New York Public Library Picture Collection.]

wealth and ability. Their enemies were the aristocracy and inefficient royal administrations. Through philosophical and scientific societies, chambers of commerce, and where possible newspapers, they were by the late 1840s voicing their complaints and ambitions.

Some writers from the early nineteenth-century middle class, however, were critical of the social conditions arising from industrialism. During the second quarter of the century numerous physicians who had to enter working-class districts to treat disease wrote books describing the suffering of the poor. Novelists, such as Elizabeth Gaskell (1810–1865) in *Mary Barton,* Frances Trollope (1780–1863) in *Michael Armstrong,* and Benjamin Disraeli (1804–1881, a notable political figure and later a prime minister) in *Sybil,* featured the plight of the British working class. Social commen-

tators, such as Thomas Carlyle (1795–1881) in *Past and Present,* denounced the sacrifice of social welfare to the naked profit motive. Henry Mayhew (1812–1887), a reporter for the London *Morning Chronicle,* wrote a long series of articles in 1849–1850 about the life of the laboring poor in the city. He revealed a world of which middle-class readers had neither knowledge nor experience. Edwin Chadwick (1800–1890), a pioneer of sanitary reform, presented government reports on the degradation of urban and industrial life in Britain. Various parliamentary commissions also published papers describing the harsh realities of the conditions of the working class. All of these materials provided Karl Marx (1818–1883) with some of the most important sources for his denunciation of capitalism.

The Labor Force

The composition and experience of the early nineteenth-century labor force was quite varied. No single description could include all of the factory workers, urban artisans, domestic system craftsmen, household servants, countryside peddlers, farm workers, or railroad navvies. The work force was composed of some persons who were reasonably well off, enjoying steady employment and decent wages. It also numbered the "laboring poor," who held jobs but whose wages allowed them little more than subsistence. The condition of any particular working-class family depended on the skills of its members, the nature of the local labor market, and the trade cycle. But all of these working people faced possible unemployment, with little or no provision for their security. They confronted over the course of their lives the dissolution of many of the traditional social ties of custom and community. Most of the economic relationships in their lives became those of the marketplace, or as Thomas Carlyle said of the "cash nexus."

Within the variety of workers there were two broad categories about whom some general statements can be made: factory workers and artisans. The former were on the side of the future; the latter tried to hold onto the past. During the second quarter of the century the skilled artisans were more likely than the factory workers to be vocally discontent about their situation.

FACTORY WORKERS. Throughout the period there was a relative shortage of factory labor. Most of the new industries paid their workers higher wages than they would have received elsewhere. Moreover, contrary to opinions once held, the factory did not destroy the working-class family. For some time spinners and weavers working in factories were able to employ their own children as helpers. In this manner, to a certain extent, the old family economy was transported into the mills. Only later on, when a laboring family became prosperous enough to send its own children to school, did workers employ children outside their own family to tend the machines, thus splitting up a less prosperous family. There were also some factory owners who really cared about the lives and welfare of their employees.

Nonetheless there were many factories that were dangerous and unhealthy. Women and children were frequently employed for long hours at wages lower than those paid to adult male workers. Factory laws were passed in Great Britain, France, and Prussia, but for many years they had only a marginal impact.

The harshest aspect of factory life, with the exception of the long hours, was the discipline of the machinery itself. Workers could no longer, as in the domestic system, set their own hours or speed of production. All work became determined by the machine. The closing of factory gates to late workers, the fines for such lateness, the dismissals for drunkenness, and the public scolding of faulty laborers constituted attempts to create human discipline and regularity that would match the demands of the cables, wheels, and pistons. To this psychological hardship in the plant must be added the haunting specter of unemployment.

URBAN ARTISANS. The plight of the urban artisans was different. They were attempting to maintain a traditional mode of life rather than adjusting to a new one. At mid-century there were still many more artisans working in small shops with fewer than ten employees than there were factory laborers. Often the introduction of new power machinery, such as the power loom, occurred so slowly that artisans believed that they could still maintain their livelihood. By the time the true situation dawned on them, it was often too late for them to change skills.

The migration of rural domestic craftsmen into the cities created excessive hardship for urban arti-

An engraving of Ackroyd's loom shed at Halifax, a nineteenth-century English textile mill. By the 1850s, more than 1,000,000 workers were employed in the English textile industry. [The Mansell Collection.]

Machinery in early mechanized cotton mills was often tended by women and children, as shown in this 1835 picture. If this picture is reasonably accurate, this mill, with its windows and the wide aisles between the machines, would have been considered a fairly good place to work. However, note that there are few safety devices on the machines to prevent injury to workers. [Bettmann Archive.]

sans, such as weavers, metalworkers, and construction laborers. The urban artisan already felt endangered by machines, and the new city dwellers increased the competition. Where possible, the guilds became more exclusive. Apprentices had difficulty becoming journeymen, and the latter found the ranks of the masters increasingly closed. The old framework of government control of wages and quality had been undermined by the economics of the middle class. With their skills

The drabness of the exterior of the factory and the filth of the smoke from its stacks symbolized to many social critics the dark side of the industrial revolution. Nevertheless, factories, like this one in Manchester, England, also symbolized the vast new productive potential of European society. [E. Bains, History of the Cotton Manufacture in Great Britain. *Courtesy Frank Cass & Co., London.]*

threatened by machinery and with the old economic and social protections gone, these hardpressed artisans, whose social forebears had been the revolutionary sans-culottes, became the most politically radical element in European society.

Early in the century the workers in traditional industries had attempted to protect their position by destroying the machines. These attacks on property failed, and swift repression often followed. By the 1820s artisans and a few less-skilled workers were turning to unions. These efforts were only marginally successful during the first half of the century. In Germany liberal reformers had attempted to break up the guilds. They succeeded in several states but not in Prussia, where the guilds remained effective until the mid-1840s. In France the revolutionary legislation against workers' organizations remained on the books.

Workers' organizations again became legal in Great Britain after 1824. They made considerable headway until the early 1830s. They then collapsed because they lacked sufficient funds to support long strikes. Equally important, the Whig government that had passed the Great Reform Act was most unsympathetic to organized labor. In 1833 that ministry mercilessly suppressed a revolt of farm workers called the Captain Swing uprising. In 1834 it transported to Australia four poor laborers, known as the Tolpuddle Martyrs, for attempting some vague kind of labor organization.

CHARTISM IN GREAT BRITAIN. By the late 1830s the British working class had turned to direct political activity. They linked the solution of their economic plight to a program of political reform known as *Chartism*. In 1836 William Lovett (1800–1877) and other London radical artisans formed the London Working Men's Association. In 1838 the group issued the Charter, demanding six specific reforms. The Six Points of the Charter included universal manhood suffrage, annual election of the House of Commons, the secret ballot, equal electoral districts, abolition of property qualifications for Members of Parliament, and payment of members. For over ten years the Chartists, who were never tightly organized, agitated for their reforms. On three occasions the Charter was presented to Parliament, which refused to pass it. Mass petitions were presented to the House of Commons with millions of signatures. Strikes were called. A Chartist newspaper called *The Northern Star* was published. Feargus O'Connor (1794–1855), the most important Chartist leader,

For a time it appeared that Chartism would become a violent political movement. However, riots, such as this one at Newport in 1839, eventually gave way to more peaceful demonstrations and mass petitions to Parliament to enact the Six Points of the Charter. [The Granger Collection.]

made speeches up and down the island. Despite this vast activity Chartism as a national movement failed. Its ranks were split between those who favored violence and those who wanted to use peaceful tactics. However, locally the Chartists scored several successes and controlled the city councils in Leeds and Sheffield.

The economic foundation of Chartism had been the depression of the late 1830s and early 1840s. As prosperity returned, many working people abandoned the movement. Chartism came to a close in March 1848. A mass march on Parliament planned for that month fizzled. The reviving economy took care of the rest of the problem. Nevertheless the Chartist movement constituted the first large-scale working-class political movement. It had specific goals and largely working-class leadership. Eventually several of the Six Points were enacted into law. Continental working-class observers saw in Chartism the kind of mass movement that workers must eventually adopt if they were to improve their situation.

Intellectual Responses to Industrial Society

Classical Economics

Economists whose thought largely derived from Adam Smith's *Wealth of Nations* (1776) dominated private and public discussions of industrial and commercial policy. Their ideas are generally associated with the phrase *laissez-faire.* Although they thought that the government should perform many important functions, the classical economists favored economic growth through competitive free enterprise. The economists conceived of society as consisting of atomistic individuals from whose competitive efforts the demands of the consumers in the marketplace were met. Most economic decisions should be made through the mechanism of the marketplace. They distrusted government action, believing it to be mischievous and corrupt. The government should maintain a sound currency, enforce contracts, protect property, impose low tariffs and taxes, and leave the remainder of economic life to private initiative. The economists naturally assumed that the state would maintain sufficient armed forces and naval power to protect the economic structure and foreign trade of the nation.

The classical economists suggested complicated and very pessimistic ideas about the working class. Thomas Malthus (1766–1834) and David Ricardo (1772–1823), probably the most influential of all these writers, suggested in effect that the condition of the working class could not be improved. In 1798 Malthus published the first edition of his *Essay on Population.* His ideas have haunted the world ever since. He contended that population must eventually outstrip the food supply. Although the human population grows geometrically, the food supply can expand only arithmetically. There was little hope of averting the disaster,

Harriet Martineau (1802–1876) was one of the most important popularizers of the ideas of the British classical economists. She illustrated their principles through moral tales. [The Granger Collection.]

in Malthus's opinion except through late marriage, chastity, and contraception, the last of which he considered a vice. It took three quarters of a century before contraception became a socially acceptable method of containing the population explosion.

Malthus contended that the immediate plight of the working class could only become worse. If wages were raised, the workers would simply produce more children, who would in turn consume both the extra wages and more food. Later in his life Malthus suggested in a more optimistic vein that if the working class could be persuaded to adopt a higher standard of living, their increased wages might be spent on consumer goods rather than on more children.

In the *Principles of Political Economy* (1817) David Ricardo transformed the concepts of Malthus into the Iron Law of Wages. If wages were raised, more children would be produced. They in turn would enter the labor market, thus expanding the number of workers and lowering wages. As wages fell, working people would produce fewer children. Wages would then rise, and the process would start all over again. Consequently, in the long run wages would always tend toward a minimum level. These arguments simply confirmed employers in their natural hesitancy to raise wages. These concepts also provided strong theoretical support for opposition to labor unions. The ideas of the economists were spread to the public during the 1830s through journals, newspapers, and even short stories, such as Harriet Martineau's series of *Illustrations of Political Economy.*

748

The working class of France and Great Britain, needless to say, resented these attitudes, but the governments embraced them. Louis Philippe and his minister François Guizot told Frenchmen to go forth and enrich themselves. People who simply displayed sufficient energy need not be poor. A goodly number of the French middle class did just that. The July Monarchy saw the construction of major social overhead capital, such as roads, canals, and railways. Little was done about the poverty in the cities and the countryside.

In Germany the middle classes made less headway. However, the Prussian reformers after the Napoleonic wars had seen the desirability of abolishing internal tariffs that impeded economic growth. In 1834 all the major German states, with the exception of Austria, formed the *Zollverein,* or free trading union. Classical economics had somewhat less influence in Germany because of the tradition dating from enlightened absolutism of state direction of economic development. The German economist Friedrich List (1789–1846) argued for this approach to economic growth during the second quarter of the century.

Britain was the home of the major classical economists, and their policies were widely accepted. In 1834 the reformed House of Commons passed a new Poor Law. This measure established a Poor Law Commission, which set out to make poverty the most undesirable of all social situations. Government poor relief was to be disbursed only in workhouses. Life in the workhouse was consciously designed to be more unpleasant than life outside. Husbands and wives were separated; the food was bad; and the work assigned in the house was distasteful. The social stigma of the workhouse was even worse. The law and its administration presupposed that people would not work because they were lazy. The laboring class, not unjustly, regarded the workhouses as new "bastilles."

The second British monument to applied classical economics was the repeal of the Corn Laws in 1846. The Anti-Corn Law League, organized by manufacturers, had sought this goal for over six years. The league wanted the tariffs protecting the domestic price of grain to be abolished. That change would lead to lower food prices, which would then allow lower wages at no real cost to the workers. In turn the prices on British manufactured goods could be lowered to allow a stronger competitive position in the world market. The actual reason for Robert Peel's repeal of the Corn Laws in 1846 was the Irish famine. He had to open British ports to foreign grain to feed the starving Irish. He realized that the Corn Laws could not be reimposed. Peel accompanied the abolition measure with a program for government aid to modernize British agriculture and to make it more efficient. The repeal of the Corn Laws was the culmination of the lowering of British tariffs that had begun during the 1820s. The repeal marked the opening of an era of free trade that continued until late in the century.

UTILITARIANISM. Closely related to the classical economists were the British utilitarians. Their major figures included Jeremy Bentham (1748–1832), James Mill (1773–1836), John Stuart Mill (1806–1873), and Sir Edwin Chadwick (1800–1890). They were a set of radical political reformers who urged that the principle of utility—the greatest good for the greatest number—should constitute the guiding principle of public policy. They lacked all reverence for tradition. They felt that political, economic, and social problems should be addressed rationally and without reference to special interests or privileged groups. They have frequently been considered spokesmen for the middle class, but it would be more correct to see them as forerunners of an efficient bureaucracy. The utilitarians and their disciples were often civil servants, and they frequently worked on governmental commissions. They were the actual authors of much reform legislation, such as the Factory Act of 1833, the Poor Law of 1834, and the Sanitation Act of 1848.

The utilitarians have achieved a bad reputation for lacking emotion and an understanding of humanity. Some of this reputation is deserved. However, their most distinguished spokesman, John Stuart Mill, was anything but doctrinaire. As a young man he revolted against the rigid Benthamite education imposed on him by his father, James Mill. In his *Principles of Political Economy* (1848) John Stuart Mill advocated the education of the working class as a means of raising their standard of living. He believed workers capable of as high a moral existence as any other social group. He urged the formation of labor cooperatives. In 1859 Mill published *On Liberty* to plead for freedom of thought and expression and for the protection of the individual against the intrusion of the state. In 1869 he took up the cause of women's rights in a pioneering essay on *The Subjection of Women.* If utilitarianism had been narrow in its origins, by the close of Mill's life in 1873 the creed had proved itself capable of considerable moderation.

Socialism

Today the socialist movement, in the form of either communist or social democratic political parties, constitutes one of the major political forces in Europe. Less than 150 years ago the advocates of socialism lacked any meaningful political following. Their doctrines were blurred and often seemed silly to their contemporaries. The confusion in early socialist thought reflected its pioneering nature. The social and economic conditions being analyzed were new, and the exact problems to be solved still had to be defined. The early socialists generally applauded the new productive capacity of industrialism, but they denied that the free market could adequately produce and distribute goods in the fashion claimed by the classical economists. The socialists saw primarily mismanagement, low wages, maldistribution of goods, and suffering arising from the unregulated industrial system. Moreover the socialists thought that human society should be organized as a community rather than merely as a conglomerate of atomistic, selfish individuals.

UTOPIAN SOCIALISM. Among the earliest people to define the social question were a group of writers called the *utopian socialists* by their later critics. They were considered utopian because their ideas were often visionary and because they frequently advocated the creation of ideal communities. They were called *socialists* because they questioned the structures and values of the existing capitalistic framework. In some cases they actually deserved neither description.

Claude Henri, Count of Saint-Simon (1760–1825), was the earliest of the socialist pioneers. As a young liberal French aristocrat he had fought in the American Revolution. Later he welcomed the French Revolution, during which he made and lost a fortune. By the time of Napoleon's ascendancy he had turned to a career of writing and social criticism. Saint-Simon believed that history oscillated between organic and critical periods. During organic periods, such as the Middle Ages, order, harmony, and shared values prevailed. During critical periods, such as the Reformation, the structures, values, and customs of a society underwent severe criticism and disintegration. He saw the late eighteenth and early nineteenth centuries as a critical

age. He hoped to set forth a body of ideas and to organize a group of disciples that could project a social blueprint for the inevitable new organic period.

Above all else Saint-Simon believed that modern society would require rational management. Private wealth, property, and enterprise should be subject to an administration other than that of its owners. His ideal government would have consisted of a large board of directors organizing and coordinating the activity of individuals and groups to achieve social harmony. In a sense he was the ideological father of technocracy. Not the redistribution of wealth but its management by experts would alleviate the poverty and social dislocation of

Robert Owen hoped to organize industrial society into a series of small communities such as that pictured on the cover of his publication. He thought such communities would lead people to live by cooperation rather than by competition. [Bettmann Archive.]

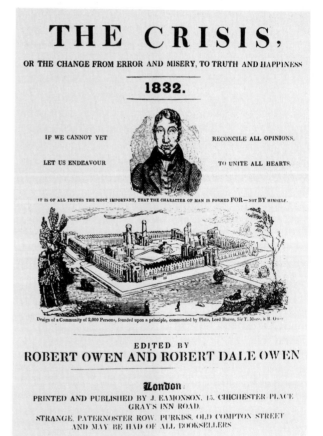

Tunic-clad students in a dance recital at Robert Owen's factory school in New Lanark. Owen's model industrial community included free schooling for the children of his workers. [The Mansell Collection.]

the age. His faith in experts was similar to the Enlightenment *philosophes'* advocacy of political absolutism. Like his eighteenth-century forebears Saint-Simon had little sympathy with democracy. The order and harmony of the new organic age was to come from the genius of great thinkers such as himself. When Saint-Simon died in 1825, he had persuaded only a handful of people that his ideas were correct. Interestingly enough several of those disciples later became leaders in the French railway industry during the 1850s.

The major British contributor to the early socialist tradition was Robert Owen (1771–1858), a self-made cotton manufacturer. In his early twenties Owen became a partner in one of the largest cotton factories in Britain at New Lanark, Scotland. Owen was a firm believer in the environmentalist psychology of the Enlightenment. If human beings were placed in the correct surroundings, they and their character could be improved. Moreover Owen saw no incompatibility between creating a humane industrial environment and making a good profit. At

New Lanark he put his ideas into practice. Workers were provided with good quarters. Recreational possibilities abounded, and the children received an education. There were several churches, although Owen himself was a notorious freethinker on matters of religion and sex. In the factory itself various rewards were given for good work. His plant made a fine profit. Visitors flocked from all over Europe to see what Owen had accomplished through enlightened management.

In numerous articles and pamphlets, as well as in letters to influential people, Owen pleaded for a reorganization of industry based on his own successful model. He envisioned a series of communities shaped like parallelograms in which factory and farm workers might live together and produce their goods in cooperation. During the 1820s Owen sold his New Lanark factory and then went to the United States, where he established the community of New Harmony, Indiana. When quarrels among the members led to the community's failure, he refused to give up his reformist causes. He returned to Britain, where he became the moving force behind the organization of the Grand National Union. This was an attempt to draw all British trade unions into a single body. It collapsed with other labor organizations during the early 1830s. Owen possessed an exaggerated sense of his own importance and was a difficult person. His version of socialism amounted to little more than old-fashioned paternalism transported to the industrial setting. However, he contributed to the socialist tradition a strong belief in the practicality of cooperative production and proof that industrial production and humane working conditions were compatible.

Charles Fourier (1772–1837) was the French intellectual counterpart of Owen. He was a commercial salesman who never succeeded in attracting the same kind of public attention as Owen. He wrote his books and articles and waited at home each day at noon, hoping to meet a patron who would undertake his program. No one ever arrived to meet him. Fourier believed that the industrial order ignored the passionate side of human nature. Social discipline ignored all the pleasures that human beings naturally seek. Fourier advocated the construction of communities, called *phalanxes*, in which

liberated living would replace the boredom and dullness of industrial existence. Agrarian rather than industrial production would predominate in these communities. Sexual activity would be relatively free, and marriage was to be reserved only for later life. Fourier also urged that no person be required to perform the same kind of work for the entire day. People would be both happier and more productive if they moved from one task to another. Through his emphasis on the problem of boredom Fourier isolated one of the key difficulties of modern economic life.

Saint-Simon, Owen, and Fourier expected some existing government to carry out their ideas. They failed to confront the political difficulties of their envisioned social transformations. Other figures paid more attention to the politics of the situation. In 1839 Louis Blanc (1811–1882) published *The Organization of Labor*. Like other socialist writers this Frenchman demanded an end to competition, but he did not seek a wholly new society. He called for political reform that would give the vote to the working class. Once so empowered, workers could use the vote to turn the political processes to their own economic advantage. A state controlled by a working-class electorate would finance workshops

A model for one of Fourier's phalansteries, in which the inhabitants would both live and work, is illustrated in this contemporary German print. [The Granger Collection.]

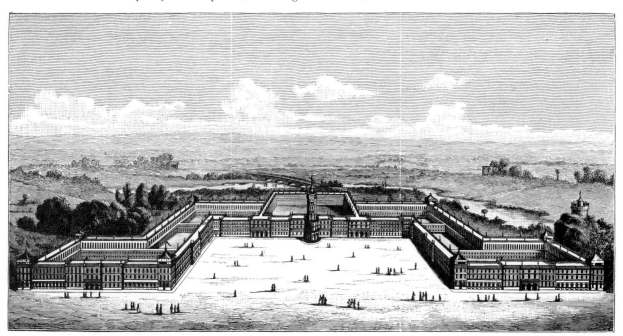

Pierre Joseph Proudhon, here portrayed with his children by the French realist painter Gustave Courbet (1819–1877), was the most important French contributor to anarchist thought. [The Granger Collection.]

to employ the poor. In time such workshops might replace private enterprise, and industry would be organized to ensure jobs. Blanc recognized the power of the state to improve life and the conditions of labor. The state itself could become the great employer of labor.

ANARCHISTS. Other writers and activists of the 1840s, however, rejected both industry and the dominance of government. These were the anarchists. They are usually included in the socialist tradition although they do not exactly fit. Some favored programs of violence; others were peaceful. Auguste Blanqui (1805–1881) was a major spokesman for terror and was one of Europe's earliest professional revolutionaries. He spent most of his adult life in jail. Blanqui urged the development of a professional revolutionary vanguard to attack capitalist society. He sought the abolition of both capitalism and the state. His ideas for the new society were quite vague, but in his call for professional revolutionaries he foreshadowed Lenin.

Pierre Joseph Proudhon (1809–1865) represented the other strain of anarchism. In his most famous work, *What Is Property?* (1840), Proudhon attacked the banking system, which so rarely extended credit to small property owners or the poor. He wanted credit expanded to allow such people to engage in economic enterprise. Society should be organized on the basis of mutualism, which amounted to a system of small businesses.

There would be peaceful cooperation and exchange of goods among these groups. With such a social system the state as it then existed would be unnecessary. His ideas later influenced the French labor movement, which generally avoided political activity.

These various strains of early socialist thought provided the background and the context for the emergence of Marxist socialism. But they did more than that. They influenced the ideas and activities of European socialists and trade unions well into the third quarter of the century. Too often the history of socialism is regarded as a linear development leading naturally or necessarily to the triumph of Marxism. Nothing could be further from the truth. Marxism did eventually triumph over much, though not all, of Europe, but only through competition with other socialist formulas. At mid-century the ideas of Karl Marx were simply one more contribution to a heady mixture of concepts and programs criticizing the emerging industrial capitalist society. Marxist ideology differed from its competitors in the brilliance of its author, its claim to rigorous scientific accuracy, and its message of the inevitable collapse of the capitalistic order.

Marxism

Karl Marx was born in 1818 in the Rhineland. His Jewish middle-class parents sent him to the

some less-extensive rearrangement of society. The *Manifesto* itself was a work of less than fifty pages. It would become the most influential political document of modern European history, but that development lay in the future. At the time it was simply one more political tract. Moreover neither Marx nor his thought had any effect on the revolutionary events of 1848.

The major ideas of the *Manifesto* and of Marx's later work, including *Capital* (Vol. I, 1867), were derived from German Hegelianism, French socialism, and British classical economics. Marx applied

The title page of the Manifesto of the Communist Party *(February 1848), by Marx and Engels, called for the proletariat of all lands to unite. Although written in German, the* Manifesto, *was printed in London where there was no political censorship.* [Culver Pictures.]

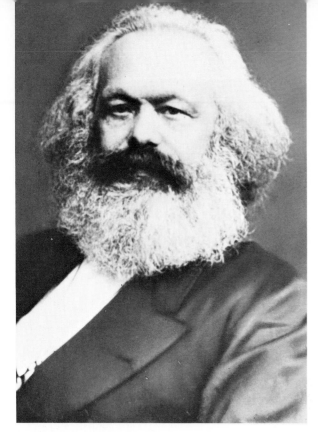

The socialist philosophy of Karl Marx eventually triumphed over most alternative versions of socialism in Europe—even though varying interpretations, criticisms, and revisions of his monumental work continue to today. [Bettmann Archive.]

University of Berlin, where he became deeply involved with Hegelian philosophy and radical politics. During 1842 and 1843 he edited the radical *Rhineland Gazette (Rheinische Zeitung)*. Soon the German authorities drove him from his native land. He lived as an exile in Paris, then in Brussels, and finally, after 1849, in London.

In 1844 Marx met Friedrich Engels (1820–1895), another young middle-class German, whose father owned a textile factory in Manchester, England. The next year Engels published *The Condition of the Working Class in England,* which presented a devastating picture of industrial life. The two men became fast friends. Late in 1847 they were asked to write a pamphlet for a newly organized and ultimately short-lived secret Communist League. *The Communist Manifesto,* published in German, appeared early in 1848. Marx, Engels, and the league had adopted the name *communist* because the term was much more self-consciously radical than *socialist.* Communism implied the outright abolition of private property rather than

❧ Friedrich Engels Describes the Plight of English Workers

As the most industrially advanced country, England offered a vast object lesson for study by social critics like Karl Marx and Friedrich Engels. Engels had visited England, where his father owned a factory. At age twenty-five he already believed that the major difficulty confronting industrial workers was the almost total lack of security in their lives. They seemed to be the victims of chance and of the economic interests of the middle class.

Insecurity is even more demoralising than poverty. English wage-earners live from hand to mouth, and this is the distinguishing mark of their proletarian status. The lower ranks of the German peasantry are largely filled with men who are also poor, and often suffer want, but they are less subject to that sort of distress which is due solely to chance. They do at least enjoy some measure of security. But the proletarian is in quite a different position. He possesses nothing but his two hands and he consumes to-day what he earned yesterday. His future is at the mercy of chance. He has not the slightest guarantee that his skill will in the future enable him to earn even the bare necessities of life. Every commercial crisis, every whim of his master, can throw him out of work. He is placed in the most revolting and inhuman position imaginable. A slave is at least assured of his daily bread by the self-interest of his master. . . . Slaves and serfs are both guaranteed a basic minimum exist-

ence. The proletarian on the other hand is thrown wholly upon his own resources, and yet at the same time is placed in such a position that he cannot be sure that he can always use those resources to gain a livelihood for himself and his family. Everything that the factory worker can do to try and improve his position vanishes like a drop in the bucket in face of the flood of chance occurrences to which he is exposed and over which he has not the slightest control. He is the passive sufferer from every possible combination of mishaps, and can regard himself as fortunate if he keeps his head above water even for a short time. . . . He may fight for survival in this whirlpool; he may try to maintain his dignity as a human being. This he can do only by fighting the middle classes, who exploit him so ruthlessly and then condemn him to a fate which drives him to live in a way unworthy of a human being.

Friedrich Engels, *The Condition of the Working Class in England,* trans. by W. O. Henderson and W. H. Chaloner (Stanford, Calif.: Stanford University Press, 1970), p. 131.

---

to social and economic development Hegel's concept that thought develops from the clash of thesis and antithesis into a new intellectual synthesis. For Marx the conflict between dominant and lesser social groups generated conditions that led to the emergence of a new dominant social group. These new social relationships, in turn, generated new discontent, conflict, and development.

The French socialists provided Marx with a portrayal of the evils of capitalist society and had raised the issue of property redistribution. Both Hegel and Saint-Simon had led Marx to see society and economic conditions as developing through historical stages. The classical economists had produced the analytical tools for an empirical, scientific examination of industrial capitalist society. Marx later explained to a friend:

What I did that was new was to prove: (1) that the *existence of classes* is bound up with *particular historical phases in the development of production;* (2) that the class struggle necessarily leads to the *dictatorship of the proletariat;* (3) that this dictatorship itself only constitutes the transition to the *abolition of all classes and to a classless society.*[1]

In *The Communist Manifesto* Marx and Engels contended that human history must be understood rationally and as a whole. It is the record of humankind's coming to grips with physical nature to produce the goods necessary for survival. That

[1] Albert Fried and Ronald Sanders (Eds.), *Socialist Thought: A Documentary History* (Garden City, N.Y.: Anchor Doubleday, 1964), p. 295.

basic productive process determines the structures, values, and ideas of a society. Historically, the organization of the means of production have always involved conflict between the classes who owned and controlled the means of production and those classes who worked for them. That necessary conflict has provided the engine for historical development; it is not an accidental by-product of mismanagement or bad intentions. Consequently piecemeal reforms cannot eliminate the social and economic evils that are inherent in the very structures of production. What is required is a radical social transformation. Such a revolution will occur as the inevitable outcome of the development of capitalism.

In Marx's and Engels's eyes, during the nineteenth century the class conflict that had characterized previous Western history had become simplified into a struggle between the bourgeoisie and the proletariat, or between the middle class and the workers. The character of capitalism ensured the sharpening of the struggle. Capitalist production and competition would steadily increase the size of the unpropertied proletariat. Large-scale mechanical production crushed both traditional and smaller industrial producers into the ranks of the proletariat. As the business structures grew larger and larger, smaller middle-class units would be squeezed out by the competitive pressures. Competition among the few remaining giant concerns would lead to more intense suffering on the part of the proletariat. As the workers suffered increasingly from the competition among the ever-enlarging firms, they would eventually begin to foment revolution and finally overthrow the few remaining owners of the means of production. For a time the workers would organize the means of production through a dictatorship of the proletariat, which would eventually give way to a propertyless and classless communist society.

This proletarian revolution was inevitable, according to Marx and Engels. The structure of capitalism required competition and consolidation of enterprise. Although the class conflict involved in the contemporary process resembled that of the past, it differed in one major respect. The struggle between the capitalistic bourgeoisie and the industrial proletariat would culminate in a wholly new society that would be free of class conflict. The victorious proletariat by its very nature could not be a new oppressor class: "The proletarian movement is the self-conscious, independent movement of the immense majority, in the interest of the immense majority."[2] The result of the proletarian victory would be "an association, in which the free development of each is the condition for the free development of all."[3] The victory of the proletariat over the bourgeoisie represented the culmination of human history. For the first time in human history one group of people would not be oppressing another.

Marx's analysis was conditioned by his own economic environment. The 1840s had been a period of much unemployment and deprivation. However, capitalism did not collapse as he predicted, nor did the middle class during the rest of the century become proletarianized. Rather, more and more people came to benefit from the industrial system. Nonetheless, within a generation Marxism had captured the imagination of many socialists and large segments of the working class. The doctrines were based on the empirical evidence of hard economic fact. This scientific aspect of Marxism helped the ideology as science became more influential during the second half of the century. Marx had made the ultimate victory of socialism seem certain. His writings had also portrayed for the first time the actual magnitude of the revolutionary transformation. His works also suggested that the path to socialism lay with revolution rather than with reform. The days of the utopians were over.

Conservative Paternalism Reasserted

The socialists were not alone in their criticism of the liberal, capitalistic order. Many conservative Europeans also hated the atomistic view of society set forth by the classical economists and the liberal politicians. These conservatives saw that philosophy as undermining the influence of the aristocracy and the landowning classes. The middle-class concept of the poor was also at odds with the traditional Christian view of charity. These conservatives had much paternalistic sympathy for the working class. The writers who upheld this position were generally less brilliant than the liberals and the socialists. Their view of society had developed during the Romantic movement and harkened back to an idealized view of the Middle Ages. In many ways it was an obsolete view of social prob-

[2]Robert C. Tucker (Ed.), *The Marx–Engels Reader* (New York: W.W. Norton, 1972), p. 353.
[3]Ibid., p. 353.

lems. However, their opinions permitted a temporary political alliance to be forged for a time between workers caught in the pressures of the labor market and advocates of political reaction.

England again provides important examples of this attitude. The movement to enact the first meaningful and enforceable factory legislation was led by Richard Oastler (1789–1861), Michael Sadler (1780–1835), and Lord Shaftesbury (1801–1885). These figures were conservative politically and upheld the position of the church and the aristocracy. After attaining the Factory Act of 1833, Oastler led the Anti-Poor Law movement, which protested the stark utilitarian measures for the relief of the unemployed. In 1843 Lord Shaftesbury fought for the passage of the Mines Act, which removed women and children from appalling labor conditions beneath the earth. In 1847 Shaftesbury and Oastler were again active in the campaign for the Ten Hours Act, which limited the length of the workday.

Continental conservatives often adopted similar attitudes. In 1846 Joseph Maria von Radowitz (1797–1853) published *Contemporary Talks on State and Church,* in which he attacked competition. Conservatives used paternalistic social arguments against the demands of liberals for free trade and industrial development. The conservatives could pose as the protectors of the poor and the industrial classes. They favored the preservation of guilds, the regulation of industry, and the paternalistic relief of poverty. The price of such protection, however, was nonparticipation in politics by the industrial and rural working classes. For some time the working classes were willing to accept that political cost because political liberals repeatedly ignored the social question.

1848: Year of Revolutions

In 1848 a series of liberal and nationalistic revolutions spread across the Continent. No single factor caused this general revolutionary ground swell; rather, a number of similar conditions existed in several countries. Severe food shortages had prevailed since 1846. The harvests of grain and potatoes had been very poor. The famine in Ireland was simply the worst example of a more widespread situation. The commercial and industrial economy was also in a period of downturn. Unemployment was very widespread. All systems of poor relief were overburdened. These difficulties, added to the wretched living conditions in the cities, heightened the sense of frustration and discontent of the urban artisan and laboring classes.

However, the dynamic force for change in 1848 originated not with the working classes but with the political liberals, who were generally drawn from the middle classes. Throughout the Continent liberals were pushing for their program of more representative government, civil liberty, and unregulated economic life. The repeal of the English Corn Laws and the example of peaceful agitation by the Anti-Corn Law League encouraged them. The liberals on the Continent wanted to pursue similar peaceful tactics. However, to put additional pressure on their governments, they began to appeal for the support of the urban working classes. The goals of the latter were improved working and economic conditions rather than a liberal framework of government. Moreover the tactics of the working classes were frequently violent rather than peaceful. The temporary alliance of liberals and workers in several states overthrew or severely shook the old order; then the allies commenced to fight each other.

Finally, outside France nationalism was an important common factor in the uprisings. Germans, Hungarians, Italians, and smaller national groups in eastern Europe sought to create national states that would reorganize or replace existing political entities. The Austrian Empire, as usual, was the state most profoundly endangered by nationalism. The nationalists were also frequently liberal and sometimes benefited from lower- and working-class economic discontent in the major cities.

The immediate results of the 1848 revolutions were quite stunning. The French monarchy fell, and many of the others were badly shaken. Never in a single year had Europe known so many major uprisings. Yet the revolutions proved a false spring for progressive Europeans. Without exception they failed to establish genuinely liberal or national states. The conservative order proved stronger and more resilient than anyone had expected. Moreover the liberal middle-class political malcontents in each country discovered that they could no longer push for political reform without at the same time raising the social question. The liberals refused to follow political revolution with social reform and thus isolated themselves from the working classes. Once separated from potential

THE REVOLUTIONARY CRISIS OF 1848–1851

1848

February 22–24	Revolution in Paris forces the abdication of Louis Philippe
February 26	National workshops established in Paris
March 3	Kossuth attacks the Hapsburg domination of Hungary
March 13	Revolution in Vienna
March 15	The Hapsburg emperor accepts the Hungarian March Laws
	Revolution in Berlin
March 18	Frederick William IV of Prussia promises a constitution
	Revolution in Milan
March 19	Frederick William IV is forced to salute the corpses of slain revolutionaries in Berlin
March 22	Piedmont declares war on Austria
April 23	Election of the French National Assembly
May 15	Worker protests in Paris lead the National Assembly to close the national workshops
May 17	Hapsburg Emperor Ferdinand flees from Vienna to Innsbruck
May 18	The Frankfurt Assembly gathers to prepare a German constitution
June 17	A Czech revolution in Prague is suppressed
June 23–26	A workers' insurrection in Paris is suppressed by the troops of the National Assembly
July 24	Austria defeats Piedmont
September 17	General Jellachich invades Hungary
October 31	Vienna falls to the bombardment of General Windischgrätz
November 15	Papal minister Rossi is assassinated in Rome

November 16	Revolution in Rome
November 25	Pope Pius IX flees Rome
December 2	Hapsburg Emperor Ferdinand abdicates and Franz Joseph becomes emperor
December 10	Louis Napoleon is elected president of the Second French Republic

1849

January 5	General Windischgrätz occupies Budapest
February 2	The Roman Republic is proclaimed
March 12	War is resumed between Piedmont and Austria
March 23	Piedmont is defeated, and Charles Albert abdicates the crown of Piedmont in favor of Victor Emmanuel II
March 27	The Frankfurt Parliament completes a constitution for Germany
March 28	The Frankfurt Parliament elects Frederick William IV of Prussia to be emperor of Germany
April 21	Frederick William IV of Prussia rejects the crown offered by the Frankfurt Parliament
June 18	The remaining members of the Frankfurt Parliament are dispersed by troops
July 3	Collapse of the Roman Republic after invasion by French troops
August 9–13	The Hungarian forces are defeated by Austria aided by the troops of Russia

1850

November 29	The Punctation of Olmütz

1851

December 2	*Coup d'état* of Louis Napoleon

mass support, the liberal revolutions became an easy prey to the armies of the reactionary classes.

France: The Second Republic and Louis Napoleon

As twice before, the revolutionary tinder first blazed in Paris. The liberal political opponents of the corrupt regime of Louis Philippe and his minister Guizot had organized a series of political banquets. These occasions were used to criticize the government and to demand further middle-class admission to the political process. The poor harvests of 1846 and 1847 and the resulting high food prices and unemployment brought working-class support to the liberal campaign. On February 21, 1848, the government forbade further banquets. A very large one had been scheduled for the next

day. On February 22 disgruntled Parisian workers paraded through the streets demanding reform and Guizot's ouster. The next morning the crowds grew, and by afternoon Guizot had resigned. The crowds had erected barricades, and numerous clashes had occurred between the citizenry and the municipal guard. On February 24, 1848, Louis Philippe abdicated and fled to England.

The liberal opposition, led by the poet Alphonse de Lamartine (1790–1869), organized a provisional government. They intended to call an election for an assembly that would write a republican constitution. The various working-class groups in Paris had other ideas; they wanted a social as well as a political revolution. Led by Louis Blanc, they demanded representation in the Cabinet. Blanc and two other radical leaders were made ministers. Under their pressure the provisional government

A painting by Gabé of the capture of the Pantheon in Paris by government troops during the June days in 1848. The rebellion of the Parisian workers and unemployed against the conservative National Assembly was brutally suppressed. [Bulloz.]

Paris Workers Complain About the Actions of their Government

In the late spring of 1848 the government of the recently formed French Republic abolished the national workshops that it had created a few weeks earlier to provide aid for the unemployed. The first selection below illustrates the anger caused by the abolition of the workshops and the sense of betrayal felt by the workers. The second document describes the experience of a cabinetmaker who had for a time enrolled in one of the workshops.

TO THE FINANCE MINISTER OF THE REPUBLIC

Are you really the man who was the first finance minister of the Republic, of the Republic won at the cost of blood thanks to the workers' courage, of this Republic whose first vow was to provide bread every day for all its children by proclaiming the universal right to work. Work, who will give it to us if not the state at a time when industry has everywhere closed its workshops, shops and factories? Yesterday martyrs for the Republic out on the barricades, today its defenders in the ranks of the national guard, the workers might consider it owed them something. . . .

Why do the national workshops so rouse your reprobation . . . ? You are not asking for their reform, but for their total abolition. But what is to be done with this mass of 110,000 workers who are waiting each day for their modest pay, for the means of existence for themselves and their families? Are they to be left a prey to the evil influences of hunger and of the excesses that follow in the wake of despair?

A LETTER TO A NEWSPAPER EDITOR

I live in the fauborg [working class neighborhood]; by trade I am a cabinet-maker and I am enrolled in the national workshops, waiting for trade to pick up again.

I went into the workshops when I could no longer find bread elsewhere. Since then people have said we were given charity there. But when I went in I did not think that I was becoming a beggar. I believed that my brothers who were rich were giving me a little of what they had to spare simply because I was their brother.

I admit that I have not worked very hard in the national workshops, but then I have done what I could. I am too old now to change my trade easily — that is one explanation. But there is another: the fact is that, in the national workshops, there is absolutely nothing to do.

Roger Price (Ed. and Trans.), 1848 *in France* (Ithaca, N.Y.: Cornell University Press, 1975), pp. 103–104.

organized national workshops to provide work and relief for thousands of unemployed workers.

On Sunday, April 23, an election based on universal manhood suffrage chose the new National Assembly. The result was a legislature dominated by moderates and conservatives. In the French provinces there had been much resentment against the Paris radicals. The church and the local notables still exercised considerable influence. Small landowning peasants feared possible confiscation of their holdings by Parisian socialists. The new conservative National Assembly had little sympathy for the very expensive national workshops, which they incorrectly perceived to be socialistic. Throughout May government troops and the Pari-

sian crowd of unemployed workers and artisans clashed. As a result the assembly closed the workshops to new entrants and planned the removal of many enrolled workers. By the latter part of June barricades again appeared in Paris. On June 24, under orders from the government, General Cavaignac, with troops drawn largely from the conservative countryside, moved to destroy the barricades and to quell potential disturbances. During the next two days over four hundred people were killed. Thereafter troops hunted down another three thousand persons in street-to-street fighting. The drive for social revolution had come to an end.

The so-called June Days confirmed the political

"The Uprising" by the French painter Honore Daumier captures the passionate anger which much of the French working class felt against the bourgeois regimes in 1848. [The Phillips Collection, Washington.]

predominance of conservative property holders in French life. They wanted a republic, but a republic safe for small property. This search for social order received further confirmation late in 1848. The victor in the presidential election was Louis Napoleon Bonaparte (1808–1873), a nephew of the great emperor. For most of his life he had been an adventurer living outside France. Twice he had unsuccessfully attempted to lead a *coup* against the July Monarchy. The disorder of 1848 provided him a new opportunity to enter the French political scene. After the corruption of Louis Philippe and the turmoil of the early months of the Second Republic, the voters turned to the name of Bonaparte as a source of stability and greatness.

The election of the "Little Napoleon" doomed the Second Republic. Louis Napoleon was dedicated to his own fame rather than to republican institutions. He was the first of the modern dictators who by playing on unstable politics and social insecurity have so changed European life. He constantly quarreled with the National Assembly and claimed that he rather than they represented the will of the nation. In 1851 the assembly refused to amend the constitution to allow the president to succeed himself. Consequently, on December 2, 1851, the anniversary of the great Napoleon's vic-

tory at Austerlitz, Louis Napoleon seized personal power. Troops dispersed the assembly, and the president called for new elections. Over 200 people died resisting the *coup,* and over 26,000 persons were arrested throughout the country. Almost 10,000 persons who opposed the *coup* were transported to Algeria. Yet in the plebiscite of December 21, 1851, over 7.5 million voters supported the actions of Louis Napoleon and approved a new constitution that consolidated his power. Only about 600,000 citizens dared to vote against him. A year later, in December 1852, an Empire was proclaimed, and Louis Napoleon became Emperor Louis Napoleon. Again a plebiscite approved the action. For the second time in just over fifty years France had turned from republicanism to caesarism.

The Hapsburg Empire: Nationalism Resisted

The events of February 1848 in Paris immediately reverberated throughout the Hapsburg domains. The empire was susceptible to revolutionary challenge on every score. Its government rejected liberal institutions. Its geographical borders ignored the principle of nationalism. Its society per-

De Tocqueville Analyzes the June Revolution in Paris

Alexis de Tocqueville (1805–1859) was a French liberal politician, historian, political scientist and also a keen social observer. By the time of the 1848 uprising in Paris he had lived two years in the United States in the 1830s; *Democracy in America* is still an important analysis of our early institutions. In this passage from his memoirs he described the manner in which the conflict of the June Days of 1848 in Paris differed from earlier political upheavals in France. He understood that what had occurred was a mode of class warfare and that it might characterize European political life for many decades to come.

I come at last to the insurrection of June. . . .

What distinguished it also, among all the events of this kind which have succeeded one another in France for sixty years, is that it did not aim at changing the form of government, but at altering the order of society. . . . It was not, strictly speaking, a political struggle, in the sense which until then we have given to the word, but a combat of class against class, a sort of Servile War. It represented the facts of the Revolution of February in the same manner as the theories of Socialism represented its ideas; or rather it issued naturally from these ideas, as a son does from his mother. We beheld in it nothing more than a blind and rude, but powerful, effort on the part of the workmen to escape from the necessities of their condition, which had been depicted to them as one of unlawful oppression, and to open up by main force a road towards that imaginary comfort with which they had been deluded. It was this mixture of greed and false theory which first gave birth to the insurrection and then made it so formidable. These poor people had been told that the wealth of the rich was in some way the produce of a theft practised upon themselves. They had been assured that the inequality of fortunes was as opposed to morality and the welfare of society as it was to nature. Prompted by their needs and their passions, many had believed this obscure and erroneous notion of right, which, mingled with brute force, imparted to the latter an energy, a tenacity and a power which it would never have possessed unaided.

It must be observed that this formidable insurrection was not the enterprise of a certain number of conspirators, but the revolt of one whole section of the population against another.

Alexis de Tocqueville, *Recollections,* trans. by A. T. de Mattos (New York: Macmillan, 1896), pp. 187–188.

petuated serfdom. During the 1840s even Metternich had urged reform, but none was forthcoming. In 1848 the regime confronted major rebellions in Vienna, Prague, Hungary, and Italy. It was also intimately involved in the disturbances that broke out in Germany.

The Hapsburg troubles commenced on March 3, 1848, when Louis Kossuth (1802–1894), a Magyar nationalist, attacked Austrian domination of Hungary. He called for the independence of Hungary and a responsible ministry under the crown of Hapsburg. Ten days later, inspired by Kossuth's demands, students led a series of major disturbances in Vienna. The army failed to restore order. Metternich resigned and fled the country. The feeble-minded Emperor Ferdinand (1835–1848) promised a moderately liberal constitution. Unsatisfied, the radical students then

Louis Kossuth, A Hungarian nationalist, helped to lead the revolution of 1848 in Budapest. The portrait was made the following year. [*The Granger Collection.*]

The Public Funeral of Victims of the March Revolution of 1848, by Adolph Menzel. The March riots in Vienna sparked by the news of the overthrow of Louis Philippe in Paris had forced the Emperor to dismiss Metternich and to promise a liberal constitution. [Hamburger Kunsthalle.]

formed democratic clubs to press the revolution further. On May 17 the emperor and the imperial court fled to Innsbruck. The government of Vienna at this point lay in the hands of a committee of over two hundred persons primarily concerned with alleviating the economic plight of Viennese workers.

What the Hapsburg government most feared was not the urban rebellions but rather a potential uprising of the serfs. Already there had been isolated instances of serfs invading manor houses and burning records. Almost immediately after the Vienna uprising the imperial government had emancipated the serfs in large areas of Austria. The Hungarian Diet also abolished serfdom in March 1848. These actions smothered the most serious potential threat to order in the empire. The

emancipated serfs now had little reason to support the revolutionary movement in the cities.

The Vienna revolt had further encouraged the Hungarians. The leaders of the Hungarian March revolution were primarily liberal Magyars supported by Magyar nobles who wanted their aristocratic liberties guaranteed against the central government in Vienna. The Hungarian Diet passed a series of March Laws that ensured equality of religion, jury trials, the election of a lower chamber, a relatively free press, and payment of taxes by the nobility. Emperor Ferdinand approved these measures because in the spring of 1848 he was in a position to do little else.

The Magyars also hoped to establish a separate Hungarian state within the Hapsburg domains. They would retain considerable local autonomy while Ferdinand remained their emperor. As part of this scheme for a partially independent state, the Hungarians attempted to annex Transylvania, Croatia, and other territories on the eastern border of the Hapsburg Empire. That policy of annexation would bring Romanians, Croatians, and Serbs under Magyar government. These national groups resisted the drive toward Magyarization. They believed that they had a better chance of maintaining their national or ethnic identity and self-interest under Hapsburg control. Consequently they turned against Hungary. In late March the Vienna government sent Baron Joseph Jellachich to aid the national groups who were rebelling against the rebellious Hungarians. By early September 1848 he was leading an invasion force against Hungary.

In the middle of March 1848, with Vienna and Budapest in revolt, Czech nationalists had demanded that Bohemia and Moravia be permitted to constitute an autonomous Slavic state within the empire similar to that just constituted in Hungary. Conflict immediately developed, however, between the Czechs and the Germans living in these areas. The Czechs summoned a congress of the Slavs, which met in Prague during early June. On June 12, the day the congress closed, a radical insurrection broke out in the city. General Alfred von Windischgrätz, whose wife had been killed by a stray bullet, moved his troops to repress the uprising. The local middle class was happy to see the radicals suppressed as they were by June 17. The Germans in the area approved the smothering of Czech nationalism. The policy of divide and conquer had succeeded.

While confronting the Hungarian and Czech bids for autonomy, the Hapsburg government also faced war in northern Italy. A revolution against Hapsburg domination commenced in Milan on March 18. Five days later the Austrian commander General Joseph Wenzel Radetzky retreated from the city. King Charles Albert of Piedmont (1831–1849), who wanted to expand the influence of his kingdom in the area, aided the rebels in Lombardy (the state of which Milan is the capital). The Austrian force fared badly until July, when Radetzky, reenforced by new troops, defeated Piedmont and suppressed the revolution. For the time being, Austria had held its position in northern Italy.

Vienna and Hungary remained to be recaptured. In midsummer the emperor returned to the capital. A newly elected assembly was attempting to write a constitution. However, within the city the radicals continued to press for further concessions. The imperial government decided to reassert its control. When a new insurrection occurred in October, the imperial army bombarded Vienna and crushed the revolt. On December 2 Emperor Ferdinand, now clearly too feeble to govern, abdicated in favor of his young nephew Francis Joseph (1848–1916). Real power now lay with Prince Felix Schwarzenberg (1800–1852), who intended to use the army with full force. On January 5, 1849, troops occupied Budapest. By March the triumphant Austrian forces had imposed military rule over Hungary, and the new emperor repudiated the recent constitution. The Magyar nobles attempted one last revolt. It was crushed in August by Austrian troops reenforced by 200,000 soldiers happily furnished by Czar Nicholas I of Russia. The imperial Hapsburg government had survived its gravest internal challenge because of the divisions among its enemies and its own willingness to use military force with a vengeance.

Italy: Republicanism Defeated

The brief Piedmont–Austrian war of 1848 marked only the first stage of the Italian revolution. Many Italians hoped that Piedmont would drive Austria from the peninsula and thus prepare the way for Italian unification. The defeat of Piedmont was a sharp disappointment. Liberal and nationalist hopes then shifted to the pope. Pius IX (1846–1878) had a liberal reputation. He had reformed the administration of the Papal States. Nationalists believed that some form of a united Italian state might emerge under the leadership of this pontiff.

In Rome, however, as in other cities, political radicalism was on the rise. On November 15, 1848, a democratic radical assassinated Count Pelligrino Rossi, the liberal minister of the Papal States. The next day popular demonstrations forced the pope to appoint a radical ministry. Shortly thereafter Pius IX fled to Naples for refuge. In February 1849 the radicals proclaimed the Roman Republic. Republican nationalists from all over Italy, including Giuseppe Mazzini (1805–1872) and Giuseppe Garibaldi (1807–1882), two of the most prominent, flocked to Rome. They hoped to use the new republic as a base of operations to unite the rest of the peninsula under a republican government.

In March 1849 radicals in Piedmont forced

In this Dutch lithograph Pope Pius IX (1846–1878) is pictured as a vicious reactionary hiding behind the mask of the suffering Jesus. After 1848 the pope, who had once been thought liberal, followed a strongly reactionary policy in Italy and the Roman Catholic Church. [John R. Freeman.]

Charles Albert to renew the patriotic war against Austria. The almost immediate defeat of Piedmont at the battle of Novara gave the king an opportunity to abdicate in favor of his son, Victor Emmanuel II (1849–1878). The defeat meant that the Roman Republic must defend itself alone. The troops that attacked Rome and restored the pope came from France. The French wanted to prevent the rise of a strong, unified state on their southern border. Moreover protection of the pope was good domestic politics for the French Republic and its president, Louis Napoleon. In early June 1849 ten thousand French soldiers laid siege to the Eternal City. By the end of the month the Roman Republic had dissolved. Garibaldi attempted to lead an army

north against Austria but was defeated. On July 3 Rome fell to the French forces, which continued to occupy it as protection for the pope until 1870. Pius IX returned, having renounced his previous liberalism. He became one of the archconservatives of the next quarter century. Leadership toward Italian unification would have to come from another direction.

Germany: Liberalism Frustrated

The revolutionary contagion had also spread rapidly through numerous states of Germany. Württemberg, Saxony, Hanover, and Bavaria all experienced insurrections calling for liberal government and greater German unity. The major revolution, however, occurred in Prussia. By March 15, 1848, large popular disturbances had erupted in Berlin. Frederick William IV (1840–1861), believing that the trouble stemmed from foreign conspirators, refused to turn his troops on the Berliners. He even announced certain limited reforms. Nevertheless, on March 18, several citizens were killed when troops cleared a square near the palace. The monarch was still hesitant to use his troops forcefully, and there was much confusion in the government. The king also called for a Prussian constituent assembly to write a constitution. The next day, as angry Berliners crowded around the palace, Frederick William IV appeared on the balcony to salute the corpses of his slain subjects. He made further concessions and implied that henceforth Prussia would aid the movement toward German unification. For all practical purposes the Prussian monarchy had capitulated.

Frederick William IV appointed a cabinet headed by David Hansemann (1790–1864), a widely respected moderate liberal. However, the Prussian constituent assembly proved to be radical and democratic. As time passed, the king and his conservative supporters decided that they would ignore the assembly. The liberal ministry resigned and was replaced by a conservative one. In April 1849 the assembly was dissolved, and the monarch proclaimed his own constitution. One of its key elements was a system of three-class voting. All adult males were allowed to vote. However, they voted according to three classes arranged by ability to pay taxes. Thus the largest taxpayers, who constituted only about 5 percent of the population, elected one third of the Prussian Parliament. This system prevailed in Prussia until 1918. In the finally revised Prussian constitution of 1850, the ministry was responsible to the king alone. Moreover, the Prussian army and officer corps swore loyalty directly to the monarch.

While Prussia was moving from revolution to reaction, other events were unfolding in Germany as a whole. On May 18, 1848, representatives from all the German states gathered in Saint Paul's Church in Frankfurt to revise the organization of the German Confederation. The Frankfurt Parliament intended to write a moderately liberal constitution for a united Germany. The liberal character of the Frankfurt Parliament alienated both German conservatives and the German working class.

The offense to the conservatives was simply the challenge to the existing political order. The Frankfurt Parliament lost the support of the industrial workers and artisans by refusing to restore the protection once afforded by the guilds. The liberals were too much attached to the concept of a free labor market to offer meaningful legislation to workers. This failure marked the beginning of a profound split between German liberals and the German working class. For the rest of the century Germany conservatives would be able to play on that division.

As if to demonstrate its disaffection from workers, in September 1848, the Frankfurt Parliament called in troops of the German Confederation to

The Frankfurt Parliament met in a church in that city in September 1848. Its deputies wanted to create a liberal, united Germany. However, as their debates dragged out, the forces of reaction regained strength and the parliament failed. [Bettmann Archive.]

❧ The King of Prussia Declines the Crown Offered by the Frankfurt Parliament

In the spring of 1849 the Frankfurt Parliament completed the writing of a constitution for a united Germany that would exclude Austria. The Parliament offered the crown of a constitutional German monarchy to Frederick William IV of Prussia. He declined the offer. In this letter of May 15, 1849, addressed to the people of Prussia, the monarch explained his reasons and attacked the liberal political thought of the Parliament and the revolutionary events that had allowed it to be called in the first place.

Taking as a pretense the interests of Germany, the enemies of the fatherland have raised the standard of revolt, first in neighboring Saxony, then in several districts of south Germany. To my deep chagrin, even in parts of our own land some have permitted themselves to be seduced into following this standard and attempting, in open rebellion against the legal government, to overturn the order of things established by both divine and human sanction. In so serious and dangerous a crisis I am moved publicly to address a word to my people.

I was not able to return a favorable reply to the offer of a crown on the part of the German National Assembly [the Frankfurt Parliament], because the Assembly has not the right, without the consent of the German governments, to bestow the crown which they tendered me, and moreover, because they offered the crown upon condition that I would accept a constitution which could not be reconciled with the rights and safety of the German states.

I have exhausted every means to reach an understanding with the German National Assembly. . . . Now the Assembly has broken with Prussia. The majority of its members are no longer those men upon whom Germany looked with pride and confidence. The greater part of the deputies voluntarily left the Assembly when they saw that it was on the road to ruin, and yesterday I ordered all the Prussian deputies who had not already withdrawn to be recalled. The other governments [of the several German states] will do the same.

A party now dominates the Assembly which is in league with the terrorists. While they urge the unity of Germany as a pretense, they are really fighting the battle of godlessness, perjury, and robbery, and kindling a war against monarchy; but if monarchy were overthrown, it would carry with it the blessings of law, liberty, and property. . . .

James Harvey Robinson (Ed.), *Readings in European History* (Boston: Ginn & Co., 1906), pp. 571–572.

suppress a radical insurrection in the city. The liberals in the parliament wanted nothing to do with workers who erected barricades and threatened the safety of property.

The Frankfurt Parliament floundered on the issue of unification as well as on the social question. Members differed over the inclusion of Austria in the projected united Germany. The large German (*grossdeutsch*) solution favored inclusion, whereas the small German (*kleindeutsch*) solution advocated exclusion. The latter formula prevailed because Austria rejected the whole notion of German unification. It raised too many other nationality problems within the Hapsburg domains. Consequently the Frankfurt Parliament looked to Prussian leadership. On March 27, 1849, the parliament produced its constitution. Shortly thereafter its delegates offered the crown of a united Germany to Federick William IV of Prussia. He rejected the offer, asserting that kings ruled by the grace of God rather than by the wisdom of man-made constitutions. On his refusal the Frankfurt Parliament began to dissolve. Not long afterwards troops drove off the remaining members.

German liberals never fully recovered from this defeat. The Frankfurt Parliament had alienated the artisans and the working class without gaining any compensating support from the conservatives. The liberals had proved themselves to be awkward, hesitant, unrealistic, and ultimately dependent on the armies of the monarchies. They had failed to unite Germany or to confront effectively the realities of political power in the German states. What was achieved through the various revolutions was an extension of the franchise in some of the German states and the establishment of conservative constitutions. The gains were not negligible, but they were a far cry from the hopes of March 1848.

The events of 1848 and 1849 had one important footnote for Frederick William IV. He gave much more thought to possible German unification under Prussia. In 1850 he attempted to create a German federation, which would have been a union of princes headed by the king of Prussia and excluding Austria. The Austrian Empire firmly rejected the proposal, which would have diminished Hapsburg influence in Germany. In November 1850, in what is known as the Punctation of Olmütz, the Prussian monarch renounced his scheme at the demand of Austria. Prussian historians later called this event the Humiliation of Olmütz.

The turmoil of 1848 through 1850 brought to a close the era of liberal revolution that had begun in 1789. Liberals and nationalists had discovered that rational argument and small insurrections would not achieve their goals. The political initiative passed for a time to the conservative political groups. Nationalists henceforth were less romantic and more hardheaded. Railways, commerce, guns, soldiers, and devious diplomacy rather than language and cultural heritage became the weapons of national unification. The working class also adopted new tactics and organization. The era of the riot and urban insurrection was coming to a close. In the future, workers would turn to trade unions and political parties to achieve their political and social goals. Perhaps most importantly, after 1848 the European middle class ceased to be revolutionary. It became increasingly concerned about the protection of its property against radical political and social movements. The middle class remained politically liberal only as long as liberalism seemed to promise economic stability and social security for its own style of life.

Suggested Readings

S. AVINERI, *The Social and Political Thought of Karl Marx* (1969). An advanced treatment.

I. BERLIN, *Karl Marx: His Life and Environment* (1948). An excellent introduction.

A. BRIGGS (Ed.), *Chartist Studies* (1959). An anthology of significant essays.

S. G. CHECKLAND, *The Rise of Industrial Society in England, 1815–1885* (1964). Strong on economic institutions.

G. D. H. COLE, *A History of Socialist Thought*, 5 vols. (1953–1960). An essential work that spans the entire nineteenth century.

I. DEAK, *The Lawful Revolution: Louis Kossuth and the Hungarians, 1848–1849* (1979). The most significant study of the topic in English.

G. DUVEAU, *The Making of a Revolution* (trans., 1968). A lively book that explores the attitudes of the various French social classes.

E. HALÉVY, *The Growth of Philosophic Radicalism* (1928). The basic discussion of utilitarianism.

T. HAMEROW, *Restoration, Revolution, and Reaction: Economics and Politics in Germany, 1815–1871* (1958). Traces the forces that worked toward the failure of revolution in Germany.

J. F. C. HARRISON, *Quest for the New Moral World: Robert Owen and the Owenites in Britain and America* (1969).

R. HEILBRONER, *The Wordly Philosophers*, rev. ed. (1972). A useful, elementary introduction to nineteenth-century economic thought.

W. O. HENDERSON, *The Industrialization of Europe, 1780–1914* (1969). Emphasizes the Continent.

K. KOLAKOWSKI, *Main Currents of Marxism: Its Rise, Growth, and Dissolution*, 3 vols. (1978). A very important and comprehensive survey.

D. LANDES, *The Unbound Prometheus: Technological Change and Industrial Development in Western Europe from 1750 to the Present* (1969). The best one-volume treatment of technological development in a broad social and economic context.

W. L. LANGER, *Political and Social Upheaval, 1832–1852* (1969). A remarkably thorough survey strong in both social and intellectual history as well as political narrative.

F. MANUEL, *The Prophets of Paris* (1962). A stimulating treatment of French utopian socialism and social reform.

J. M. MERRIMAN, *The Agony of the Republic: The Repression of the Left in Revolutionary France, 1848–1851* (1978). A major study of the manner in which the Second French Republic and popular support for it were suppressed.

J. M. MERRIMAN (Ed.), *Consciousness and Class Experience in Nineteenth-Century Europe* (1979). A collection of important revisionist essays in social and intellectual history covering topics across the Continent.

H. PERKIN, *The Origins of Modern English Society, 1780–1880* (1969). A provocative attempt to look at the society as a whole.

D. ROBERTS, *Paternalism in Early Victorian England* (1979). An interesting study of the paternalistic response to early nineteenth-century social problems.

P. ROBERTSON, *Revolutions of 1848: A Social History* (1952). Covers the developments in each nation.

P. STEARNS, *Eighteen Forty Eight: the Tide of Revolution in Europe* (1974). A good discussion of the social background.

A. J. TAYLOR (Ed.), *The Standard of Living in Britain in the Industrial Revolution* (1975). A collection of major articles on the impact of industrialism.

E. P. THOMPSON, *The Making of the English Working Class* (1964). An important, influential, and controversial work.

C. WOODHAM-SMITH, *The Great Hunger: Ireland, 1845–1849* (1962). A moving account of one of the great social tragedies of the nineteenth century.

770

26 The Age of Nation States

The revolutions of 1848 collapsed in defeat for both liberalism and nationalism. Throughout the early 1850s authoritarian regimes entrenched themselves across the Continent. Yet only a quarter century later many of the major goals of early nineteenth-century liberals and nationalists stood accomplished. Italy and Germany were each at long last united under constitutional monarchies. The Hapsburg emperor had accepted constitutional government; the Hungarian Magyars had attained recognition of their liberties. In Russia the serfs had been emancipated. France was again a republic. Liberalism and even democracy flourished in Great Britain.

Paradoxically most of these developments occurred under the direction and leadership of conservative statesmen. Events within European international affairs compelled some of them to pursue new policies at home as well as abroad. They had to find novel methods of maintaining the loyalty of their subjects. In some cases conservative leaders preferred to carry out a popular policy on their own terms so that they rather than the liberals would receive credit. Finally, some political leaders moved as they did because they had no choice.

The Crimean War (1854-1856)

As has so often been true in modern European history, the impetus for change originated in war. The Crimean War (1854–1856) was rooted in the long-standing rivalry between Russia and the Ottoman Empire. There were two disputes that led to the conflict. First, the Ottoman Empire had recently granted Catholic France rather than Orthodox Russia the oversight of the Christian shrines in the Holy Land. Second, Russia wanted to extend its control over the Ottoman provinces of Moldavia and Walachia (now in Romania). The czar's duty to

After his appointment as prime minister in 1862, Bismarck used the conservative political institutions of Prussia to forge a united German state, the policies of which he dominated for two decades. "Bismarck Towers" such as this one in Hamburg, monuments to Bismarck's accomplishment and leadership, were erected at various sites in Germany. [Bildarchiv Preussischer Kulturbesitz.]

771

protect Orthodox Christians in the Ottoman Empire furnished the pretext for the Russian aggression. Russia occupied the two provinces in the summer of 1853. The Ottoman Empire declared war on Russia in the autumn of that year. The other great powers soon became involved, and a war among major European states resulted. Both France and Great Britain opposed Russian expansion in the eastern Mediterranean where they had extensive naval and commercial interests. Napoleon III also thought that an activist foreign policy would shore up domestic support for his regime. On March 28, 1854, France and Britain declared war on Russia. Much to the disappointment of Czar Nicholas I, Austria and Prussia remained neutral. The Austrians had their own ambitions in the Balkans, and after the Humiliation of Olmütz Prussia followed Austrian leadership for some time.

Florence Nightingale (1820–1910) was a strong-willed English nurse who organized hospitals for English troops during the Crimean War and left an indelible influence on nursing as a profession. [The Granger Collection.]

British infantry storming the Heights of Alma in the Crimean War. Although Britain and France managed to defeat the Russian forces in the Crimea, the allied troops, and especially the British, suffered terribly from disease and inadequate medical care. [Vincent Virga Collection.]

The war was ineptly waged on both sides. The ill-equipped and poorly commanded armies became bogged down along the Crimean coast of the Black Sea. In September 1855, after a long siege, the Russian fortress of Sevastopol finally fell. In March 1856 a conference in Paris concluded the Treaty of Paris, which was highly unfavorable to Russia. It was required to surrender territory near the mouth of the Danube River, to recognize the neutrality of the Black Sea, and to renounce claims of protection over Christians in the Ottoman Empire. Even before the conference Austria had forced Russia to withdraw from Moldavia and Walachia. The image of an invincible Russia that had prevailed across Europe since the close of the Napoleonic wars was totally shattered.

Also shattered was the Concert of Europe (see Chapter 24) as a means of dealing with international relations on the Continent. There was much less fear of revolution than in the early part of the century and consequently much less reverence for the Vienna settlement. As Gordon Craig has commented, "After 1856 there were no more powers willing to fight to overthrow the existing order than there were to take up arms to defend it."[1]

[1]*The New Cambridge Modern History*, Vol. 10 (Cambridge: Cambridge University Press, 1967), p. 273.

Louis Napoleon had little respect for the Congress of Vienna and favored redrawing the map along lines of nationality. The Austrians hoped to compensate for the poor figure they had cut in remaining neutral during the conflict by asserting more influence within the German Confederation. Prussia became increasingly discontented with a role in Germany subordinate to Austria's. Russia, which had been among the chief defenders of the Vienna settlement, now sought to overcome the disgrace of the 1856 Treaty of Paris. The mediocre display of British military prowess led that nation to hesitate about future continental involvement.

Consequently, for about twenty-five years after the Crimean War instability prevailed in European affairs, allowing a largely unchecked adventurism in foreign policy. Without the restraining influence of the Concert of Europe, each nation believed that only the limits of its military power and its diplomatic influence should act as constraints on its international ambitions. Moreover foreign policy increasingly became an instrument of domestic policy. The two most significant achievements to result from this new international situation were the unifications of Italy and of Germany. Those events in turn generated further pressures on neighboring countries.

Italian Unification

Nationalists had long wanted the small, absolutist principalities of the Italian peninsula united into a single state. However, during the first half of the century there had existed broad differences of opinion about the manner and goals of unification.

One approach to the issue had been that of romantic republicans. After the Congress of Vienna numerous secret republican societies were founded, the most famous of which was the *Carbonari* ("charcoal burners"). They were singularly ineffective.

Following the failure of nationalist uprisings in 1831, the leadership of romantic republican nationalism passed to Giuseppe Mazzini (1805–1872). He became the most important nationalist leader in all Europe and brought to the cause of nationalism new emotional fervor. He once declared, "Nationality is the role assigned by God to a people in the work of humanity. It is its mission, its task on earth, to the end that God's thought may be realized in

Giuseppe Mazzini supported the cause of Italian unification with both pen and sword. His books and articles were widely read in nationalist circles. He also led guerilla bands of Italian nationalists against the petty princes of the Italian peninsula before unification. [The Granger Collection.]

the world."[2] In 1831 he founded the Young Italy Society for the purposes of driving Austria from the peninsula and establishing an Italian republic. During the 1830s and 1840s Mazzini and fellow republican Giuseppe Garibaldi (1807–1882) led insurrections. Both were deeply involved in the ill-fated Roman Republic of 1849. Throughout the next decade they continued to conduct what amounted to guerrilla warfare. Because both men spent much time in exile, they became well known across the Continent and in the United States.

Republican nationalism frightened the more moderate Italians, who wanted to rid themselves of Austrian domination but not at the cost of establishing a republic. For a time these people had looked to the pope as a possible vehicle for unification. That solution became impossible after the experience of Pius IX with the Roman Republic in 1849. Consequently, at mid-century "Italy" remained a geographical expression rather than a political entity. However, between 1852 and 1860 the area was transformed into a national state. The process was carried out not by romantic republican nationalists but by Count Camillo Cavour (1810–1861), the moderately liberal prime minister of Piedmont. The method of unification was

[2] Quoted in William L. Langer, *Political and Social Upheaval, 1832–1852* (New York: Harper Torchbook, 1969), p. 115.

Garibaldi represented the popular forces of romantic Italian nationalism more than did anyone else. The landing of his Redshirts on Sicily and their subsequent invasion of southern Italy in 1860 forced Cavour to unite the entire peninsula sooner than he had intended. [Culver Pictures.]

no respect for Mazzini's ideals. A strong monarchist, Cavour rejected republicanism. It was economic and material progress rather than romantic ideals that required a large, unified state on the Italian peninsula.

Cavour believed that if Italians proved themselves to be efficient and economically progressive, the great powers might decide that Italy could govern itself. He joined the Piedmontese Cabinet in 1850 and became premier two years later. He worked for free trade, railway construction, credit expansion, and agricultural improvement. He felt that such material and economic bonds, rather than fuzzy romantic yearnings, must unite the Italians. However, Cavour also recognized the need to capture the loyalties of the Italians who possessed other varieties of nationalistic feelings. To that end

Cavour was the moderately liberal prime minister of the Kingdom of Piedmont. He was determined to make the idea of a united Italy respectable and acceptable to the rest of Europe. [Culver Pictures.]

that of force of arms tied to secret diplomacy. The spirit of Machiavelli must have smiled over the enterprise.

Cavour's Policy

Piedmont (officially styled the Kingdom of Sardinia), in northwestern Italy, was the most independent state on the peninsula. The Congress of Vienna had restored the kingdom as a buffer between French and Austrian ambitions in the area. As we have seen, during 1848 and 1849 King Charles Albert, after having promulgated a conservative constitution, twice unsuccessfully fought Austria. Following the second defeat, he abdicated in favor of his son, Victor Emmanuel II. In 1852 the new monarch chose as his prime minister Count Camillo Cavour. This cunning statesman had begun political life as a strong conservative but had gradually moved toward a moderately liberal position. He made a personal fortune by investing in railroads, reforming agricultural methods on his own estates, and editing a newspaper. He was deeply embued with the ideas of the Enlightenment, classical economics, and utilitarianism. Cavour was a nationalist of a new breed who had

❧ *Cavour Explains Why Piedmont Should Enter the Crimean War*

> As prime minister of Piedmont, Cavour attempted to prove that the Italians were capable of progressive government. In 1855 he urged entry into the Crimean War so that the other Europeans would consider Piedmont a military power. Earlier politics in Italy had been characterized by petty absolute princes and romantic nationalist conspiracies, both of which Cavour scorned. He understood that in the nineteenth century a nation must possess good government, economic prosperity, and a strong army.

The experience of recent years and previous centuries has proved (at least in my opinion) how little Italy has benefited by conspiracies, revolutions and disorderly uprisings. Far from helping her, they have been a tremendous calamity for this beautiful part of Europe. And not only, gentlemen, because individual people so often suffered from them, not only because revolutions became the cause or pretext for repression, but above all because continual conspiracies, repeated revolutions and disorderly uprisings damaged the esteem and, up to a certain point, the sympathy that other European peoples cherished for Italy.

Now, gentlemen, I believe that the principal condition for the improvement of Italy's fate, the condition that stands out above all others, is to lift up her reputation once more, so to act that all the peoples of the world, those governing and those governed, may do justice to her qualities. And for this two things are

necessary: first, to prove to Europe that Italy has sufficient civic sense to govern herself freely and according to law, and that she is in a condition to adopt the very best forms of government; second, to prove that her military valor is as great as that of her ancestors.

You [the Parliament of Piedmont] have done Italy one service by your conduct over the last seven years. You have shown Europe in the most luminous way that Italians are capable of governing themselves with wisdom, prudence, and trustworthiness. But it still remains for you to do Italy an equal, if not a greater, service; it is our country's task to prove that Italy's sons can fight valiantly on battlefields where glory is to be won. And I am sure, gentlemen, that the laurels that our soldiers will win in Eastern Europe will help the future state of Italy more than all that has been done by those people who hoped to regenerate her by rhetorical speeches and writings.

Denis Mack Smith (Ed. and Trans.), *The Making of Italy,* 1796–1870 (New York: Walker and Company, 1968), pp. 199–200.

he fostered the Nationalist Society, which established chapters in other Italian states to press for unification under the leadership of Piedmont. Finally, the prime minister believed that Italy could be unified only with the aid of France. The recent accession of Napoleon III in France seemed to open the way for such aid at some time in the future.

Cavour used the outbreak of the Crimean War to enter the larger European picture. In 1855 Piedmont joined the conflict on the side of France and Britain and sent ten thousand troops to the front. This small but significant participation in the war allowed Cavour to raise the Italian question at the Paris conference. He left Paris with no diplomatic reward, but he had impressed everyone with his

intelligence and political capacity. Cavour also gained the sympathy of Napoleon III. During the rest of the decade Cavour achieved further international respectability for Piedmont by opposing various plots of Mazzini, who was still attempting to lead nationalist uprisings. By the close of the decade Cavour represented a moderate liberal alternative to both republicanism and reactionary absolutism in Italy.

The Piedmontese prime minister continued to bide his time. Then in January 1858 an Italian named Orsini attempted to assassinate Napoleon III. The incident made the French emperor, who had once belonged to a nationalist group, newly aware of the Italian issue. He began to fancy himself as continuing his more famous uncle's liberation of the peninsula. He also saw Piedmont as a potential ally against Austria. In July 1858 Cavour and Napoleon III met at Plombières. Riding alone in a carriage, with the emperor at the reins, the two men plotted to provoke a war in Italy that would permit their two nations to intervene against Austria. A formal treaty in December 1858 confirmed the agreement. France was to receive Nice and Savoy for its aid.

During the winter and spring of 1859 tension grew between Austria and Piedmont as the latter country mobilized its army. On April 22 Austria presented Piedmont with an ultimatum ordering a halt to mobilization. That demand provided sufficient grounds to claim that Austria was provoking a war. France intervened to aid its ally. On June 4 the Austrians were defeated at Magenta and on June 24 at Solferino. In the meantime revolutions had broken out in Tuscany, Modena, Parma, and Romagna. With the Austrians in retreat and the new revolutionary states calling for union with Piedmont, Napoleon III feared too extensive a Piedmontese victory. On July 11 he independently concluded a peace with Austria at Villafranca. Piedmont received Lombardy, but Venetia remained under Austrian control. Cavour felt betrayed by France, but nonetheless the war had driven Austria from most of northern Italy. Later that summer Parma, Modena, Tuscany, and Romagna voted to unify with Piedmont.

At this point the forces of romantic republican nationalism entered the picture and compelled Cavour to pursue the complete unification of northern and southern Italy. In May 1860 Garibaldi landed in Sicily with more than a thousand troops, who had been outfitted in the north. He captured Palermo and prepared to attack the mainland. By September the city and kingdom of Naples, probably the most corrupt example of Italian absolutism, lay under Garibaldi's control. The popular leader had for over two decades hoped to form a republican Italy, but Cavour moved to forestall that possibility. He rushed Piedmontese troops south to confront Garibaldi. On the way they conquered the Papal States except for the area around Rome, which remained under the direct control of the pope. Garibaldi's nationalism won out over his republicanism, and he unhappily accepted the Piedmontese domination. In late 1860 the southern Italian states joined the northern union forged by Piedmont.

The New Italian State

In March 1861 Victor Emmanuel II was proclaimed king of Italy. Three months later Cavour died. The new state more than ever needed his skills because Italy had in effect been more nearly conquered than united by Piedmont. The republicans resented the treatment of Garibaldi. The clericals resented the conquest of the Papal States. In the south armed resistance continued until 1866 against the intrusion of Piedmontese administration. The economies of the two areas were incompatible. The south was rural, poor, and backward. In the north industrialism was under way. The social structures reflected those differences, with landholding groups being dominant in the south and an urban working class emerging in the north.

The political framework of the united Italy did little to help overcome the problems. The constitution, which was that promulgated for Piedmont in 1848, provided for a rather conservative constitutional monarchy. The Senate was appointed, and the Chamber of Deputies was elected on a very narrow franchise. Ministers were responsible to the monarch. These arrangements did not foster a vigorous parliamentary life. The major problems of the nation were often simply avoided by the political leaders. In place of efficient, progressive government such as Cavour had brought to Piedmont, a system of *transformismo* developed. This process meant that transformation of political opponents into government supporters through bribery and favors or inclusion in cabinet coalitions. Italian politics became a byword for corruption.

There also remained territories that many Italians believed should be added to their nation. The most important of these were Venetia and Rome. The former was gained in 1866 as one result of the Austro-Prussian War. Rome and the papacy continued to be guarded by French troops, first sent there in 1849, until the Franco-Prussian War of 1870 forced the withdrawal of the garrison. The Italian state then annexed Rome and transferred the capital there from Florence. The papacy remained confined to the Vatican, and its relations with the Italian state remained hostile until the Lateran Accord of 1929. By 1870 only the small territories of Trent and Trieste remained outside the state. In and of themselves these areas were not important, but they served to fuel the continued hostility of Italian patriots toward Austria. The

THE UNIFICATION OF ITALY

MAP 26.1 *Beginning with the association of Sardinia and Piedmont by the Congress of Vienna in 1815, unification was achieved through the expansion of Piedmont between 1859 and 1870. Both Cavour's statesmanship and the campaigns of ardent nationalists played large roles.*

desire to bring *Italia Irredenta* or "Unredeemed Italy" into the nation was one reason for the Italian support of the Allies against Austria and Germany in 1915.

German Unification

The construction of a united German nation was the single most important political development in Europe between 1848 and 1914. It transformed the balance of economic, military, and interna-

tional power. Moreover the character of the united German state was largely determined by the method of its creation. Germany was united by the conservative army, monarchy, and prime minister of Prussia, among whose chief motives was the outflanking of Prussian liberals. The goal of a unified Germany, sought for two generations by German

1854   Crimean War opens
1855   Cavour leads Piedmont into the war on the side of France and England
1856   Treaty of Paris concludes Crimean War
1858   January 14 Attempt to assassinate Louis Napoleon
        July 20 Secret conference between Louis Napoleon and Cavour at Plombières
1859   War of Piedmont and France against Austria
1860   Garibaldi lands his forces in Sicily and invades southern Italy
1861   March 17 Proclamation of the Kingdom of Italy
        June 6 Death of Cavour
1862   Bismarck becomes prime minister of Prussia
1864   Danish-Prussian War
1865   Convention of Gastein
1866   Austro-Prussian War
        Venetia ceded to Italy
1867   North German Confederation formed
1870   June 19–July 12 Crisis over Hohenzollern candidacy for the Spanish throne
        July 13 Bismarck publishes the Ems dispatch
        July 19 France declares war on Prussia
        September 1 France defeated at Sedan and Napoleon III captured
        September 4 French Republic proclaimed
        October 2 Italian state annexes Rome
1871   January 18 Proclamation of the German Empire at Versailles
        March 18–May 28 Paris Commune
        May 1 Treaty of Frankfurt between France and Prussia

Bismarck was the most influential German and European statesman of the last half of the nineteenth century. [Culver Pictures.]

mode of closer union that might lessen its influence. Liberal nationalists had not recovered from the humiliating experiences of 1848 and 1849. What modified this situation rather quickly was a series of domestic political changes and problems within Prussia.

In 1858 Frederick William IV was adjudged insane, and his brother William assumed the regency. William I (1861–1888), who became king in his own right in 1861, was less of an idealist than his brother and rather more of a Prussian patriot. In the usual tradition of the Hohenzollern dynasty his first concern was for the strength of the Prussian army. In 1860 his war minister and chief of staff proposed to enlarge the army, to increase the number of officers, and to extend the period of conscription from two to three years. The Prussian Parliament, created by the Constitution of 1850, refused to approve the taxes necessary for the military expansion. The liberals, who dominated the body, did not wish to place so much additional power in the hands of the monarchy. A deadlock continued for two years between the monarch and the Parliament.

Bismarck

In September 1862 William I turned for help to the person who more than any other single individual shaped the next thirty years of European his-

liberals, was actually achieved for the most illiberal of reasons.

During the 1850s German unification still seemed very far away. The major states continued to trade with each other through the *Zollverein,* and railways linked the various economic regions. However, Frederick William IV of Prussia had given up his short-lived thoughts of unification under Prussian leadership. Austria continued to oppose any

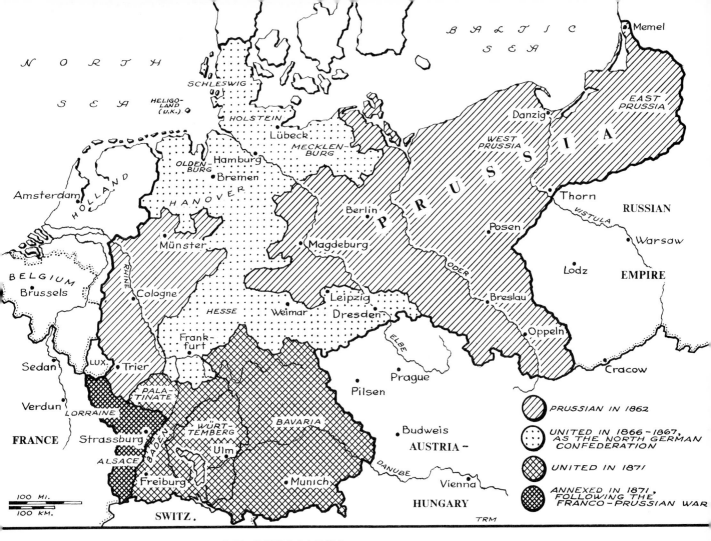

THE UNIFICATION OF GERMANY

MAP 26.2 *Under Bismarck's leadership, and with the strong support of its royal house, Prussia used most of the available diplomatic and military means, on both the German and international stages, to force the unification of German states into a strong national entity.*

tory: Otto von Bismarck (1815–1898). Bismarck came from *Junker* stock. He attended the university, joined a *Burschenschaft*, and for a time displayed an interest in German unification. Then he retired to his father's estate. During the 1840s he was elected to the local provincial diet. At the time of the revolutions of 1848 his stand was so reactionary as to disturb even the king and the leading state ministers. Yet he had made his mark. From 1851 to 1859 Bismarck was the Prussian minister to the Frankfurt Diet of the German Confederation. Later he served as Prussian ambassador to Saint Petersburg. Just before William I called him to be-

come prime minister of Prussia, Bismarck had been transferred to the post of ambassador to Paris.

Although Bismarck had entered public life as a reactionary, he had mellowed into a conservative. He opposed parliamentary government but not a constitutionalism that provided a strong monarch. His origins were those of a *Junker*, but he understood that Prussia—and later, Germany—must have a strong industrial base. He was a fervent Prussian patriot. His years in Frankfurt arguing with his Austrian counterpart had only hardened that patriotism. In politics he was a pragmatist who put more trust in power and action than in ideas. As he declared in his first speech as prime minister, "Germany is not looking to Prussia's liberalism but to her power. . . . The great questions of the day will not be decided by speeches and majority decisions—that was the mistake of 1848–1849—

but by iron and blood."[3] Yet this same minister, after having led Prussia into three wars, spent the next nineteen years seeking to ensure peace.

After being appointed prime minister in 1862, Bismarck immediately moved against the liberal Parliament. He contended that in the absence of new levies the Prussian constitution permitted the government to carry out its functions on the basis of previously granted taxes. Therefore taxes could be collected and spent despite the parliamentary refusal to vote them. The army and most of the bureaucracy supported this interpretation of the constitution. However, in 1863 new elections sustained the liberal majority in the Parliament. Bismarck had to find some way to attract popular support away from the liberals and toward the monarchy and the army. To that end Bismarck set about uniting Germany through the conservative institutions of Prussia. The tactic amounted to diverting public attention from domestic matters to foreign affairs.

THE DANISH WAR (1864). Bismarck pursued a *kleindeutsch*, or small German, solution to the question of unification. Austria was to be ultimately excluded from German affairs when an opportunity presented itself. This maneuver required highly complex diplomacy. The Schleswig-Holstein problem provided the handle for Bismarck's policy. These two duchies had long been administered by Denmark without being incorporated into that kingdom. Their populations were a mixture of Germans and Danes. Holstein, where Germans predominated, belonged to the German Confederation. In 1863 the Danes moved to annex both duchies. The smaller states of the German Confederation proposed an all-German war to halt the annexation. Bismarck wanted Prussia to act alone or only in cooperation with Austria. Together the two large states defeated Denmark in a short war in 1864. They took over the joint administration of the two provinces in question.

The Danish defeat gave Bismarck new personal prestige. The joint holding of the duchies allowed him to prod Austria into war with Prussia. In August 1865 the two powers negotiated the Convention of Gastein, which put Austria in charge of Holstein and Prussia in charge of Schleswig. Bismarck

---

[3] Quoted in Otto Pflanze, *Bismarck and the Development of Germany: The Period of Unification: 1815–1871* (Princeton, N.J.: Princeton University Press 1963), p. 177.

then moved to mend other diplomatic fences. He had gained Russian sympathy by supporting the 1863 suppression of the Polish revolt. Conversations with Napoleon III achieved promises of neutrality in case of an Austro-Prussian conflict. In April 1866 Bismarck concluded a treaty with Italy that stated that Italy would annex Venetia in exchange for support of Prussia should war break out with Austria. Now the issue became the provocation of hostilities.

THE AUSTRO-PRUSSIAN WAR (1866). There had been constant Austro-Prussian tension over the administration of Schleswig and Holstein. Bismarck ordered the Prussian forces to do whatever was necessary to be obnoxious to the Austrians. On June 1, 1866, Austria appealed to the German Confederation to intervene in the dispute. Bismarck claimed that the request violated the terms of the 1864 alliance and the Convention of Gastein. The Seven Weeks' War of the summer of 1866 led to the decisive defeat of Austria at Königgrätz. However, the Treaty of Prague, which ended the conflict on August 23, was quite lenient toward Austria. It lost no territory except Venetia, which was ceded to Napoleon III, who in turn ceded it to Italy. The exchange could not be direct because Austria had actually defeated Italy when the latter honored its commitment to Prussia. The Prussian defeat of Austria and the treaty permanently excluded the Hapsburgs from German affairs. Prussia had become the only major power among the German states.

THE NORTH GERMAN CONFEDERATION. In 1867 the states of Hanover, Hesse, and Nassau, and the city of Frankfurt, which had supported Austria during the war, were incorporated into Prussia, and their ruling dynasties were deposed. Prussia and these newly incorporated territories plus Schleswig and Holstein and the rest of the German states north of the Main River constituted the North German Confederation. The constitution of this body provided for a federation under Prussian leadership. Each state retained its own local government, but the military forces were under federal control. The president of the federation was the king of Prussia, represented by his chancellor. There was a federal council, or *Bundesrat*, composed of nominated members. The lower house, or *Reichstag*, was chosen by universal manhood suffrage. Bismarck had little fear of this broad franchise because he sensed that the peasants would tend to vote conservatively. Moreover the *Reichstag* had little real power because the ministers were responsible only to the monarch. Even legislation did not originate in the *Reichstag*. The legislature did have the right to approve military budgets, but these were usually submitted to cover several years at a time. The constitution of the confederation, which after 1871 became the governing document of the German Empire, possessed some of the appearances but none of the substance of liberalism. Germany was in effect a military monarchy.

The spectacular success of Bismarck's policy overwhelmed the liberal opposition in the Prussian Parliament. The liberals were split between those who prized liberalism and those who supported unification. In the end nationalism proved more attractive than liberalism. In 1866 the Prussian Parliament passed an indemnity measure that retroactively approved the earlier military budget. Bismarck had crushed the Prussian liberals by making the monarchy and the army the most popular institutions in the country. The drive toward unification had achieved Bismarck's domestic political goal.

The Franco-Prussian War and the German Empire (1870–1871)

Bismarck now awaited an opportunity to complete unification by bringing the states of southern Germany into the confederation. Events in Spain provided the excuse. In 1868 a revolution led by conservatives deposed the corrupt Bourbon queen of Spain. In searching for a new monarch, the Spaniards chose Prince Leopold of Hohenzollern-Sigmaringen, a cousin of William I of Prussia. On June 19, 1870, Leopold accepted the Spanish crown with Prussian blessings. Bismarck knew that France would react strongly against the idea of a second bordering state ruled by a Hohenzollern. On July 2 the Spanish publicized Leopold's acceptance, and the French reacted as expected. France sent Count Vincent Benedetti (1817–1900) to consult with William I, who was vacationing at Bad Ems. They discussed the matter at several meetings. On July 12 Leopold's father renounced his son's candidacy for the Spanish throne, fearing that the issue would cause war between Prussia and France. William I seems to have been relieved that conflict had been avoided and that he had not been required to order Leopold to renounce his claim to the Spanish title.

There the matter might have rested had it not been for the impetuosity of the French and the guile of Bismarck. On July 13 the French government instructed Benedetti to ask William I for assurances that he would tolerate no future Spanish candidacy for Leopold. The king refused but said that he might take the question under further consideration. Later that day he sent Bismarck, who was in Berlin, a telegram reporting the substance of the meeting. The chancellor, who desperately wanted a war with France to complete unification, had been disappointed by the peaceful resolution of the Spanish candidacy question. The telegram provided a new opportunity. Bismarck released an edited version of the dispatch. The revised Ems telegram made it appear that William I had insulted the French ambassador. The idea was to goad France into a declaration of war.

The French government of Napoleon III quickly fell for Bismarck's bait, and on July 19 the French declared war. The French emperor had been almost as eager for war as Bismarck because he believed that victory over the North German Confederation would give his regime a new and stronger popular base of support. Once the conflict erupted, the south German states honored treaties signed with Prussia in 1866 and eagerly joined the northern cause against France, whose defeat was not long in coming. On September 1 at the Battle of Sedan the Germans not only beat the French army but also captured the French emperor. By late September Paris stood besieged; it finally capitulated on January 28, 1871. Ten days earlier, in the Hall of Mirrors at the Palace of Versailles, the German Empire had been declared. During the war the states of south Germany had joined the North German Confederation, and their princes had requested William I to accept the imperial title. The princes of the southern states retained their positions as heads of their respective states within the new federation. From the peace settlement with France, Germany received the additional territory of Alsace and part of Lorraine.

Both the fact and manner of German unification produced long-range effects in Europe. A powerful new state had been created in north central Europe. It was rich in natural resources and talented citizens. Militarily and economically the German

Bismarck Edits the Ems Dispatch

On July 13, 1870, William I of Prussia sent Bismarck a telegram reporting his meeting with Benedetti, the French Ambassador, at Ems, a watering place in northwest Germany. The telegram also included a comment by the king's private secretary on later events of the day. Before releasing the dispatch to the press, Bismarck edited it so that the telegram appeared to report that the king of Prussia had treated the French ambassador in a brusque and insulting fashion. Bismarck thus hoped to goad France into a declaration of war. In the text of both telegrams "His Majesty" is William I, and "the Prince" is Charles Anthony, the father of Prince Leopold, the candidate for the Spanish throne. Throughout the negotiations Charles Anthony had spoken on behalf of his son.

THE ORIGINAL MESSAGE SENT BY WILLIAM I TO BISMARCK

"M. Benedetti intercepted me on the Promenade in order to demand of me most insistently that I should authorize him to telegraph immediately to Paris that I shall obligate myself for all future time never again to give my approval to the candidacy of the Hohenzollerns should it be renewed. I refused to agree to this, the last time somewhat severely, informing him that one dare not and cannot assume such obligations à tout jamais [forever]. Naturally, I informed him that I had received no news as yet, and since he had been informed earlier than I by way of Paris and Madrid, he could easily understand why my government was once again out of the matter."

Since then His Majesty has received a dispatch from the Prince. As His Majesty has informed Count Benedetti that he was expecting news from the Prince, His Majesty himself, in view of the above-mentioned demand and in consonance with the advice of Count Eulenburg and myself, decided not to receive the French envoy again but to inform him through an adjutant that His Majesty had now re-ceived from the Prince confirmation of the news which Benedetti had already received from Paris, and that he had nothing further to say to the Ambassador. His Majesty leaves it to the judgement of Your Excellency whether or not to communicate at once the new demand by Benedetti and its rejection to our ambassadors and to the press.

BISMARCK'S EDITED VERSION RELEASED TO THE PRESS

After the reports of the renunciation by the Hereditary Prince of Hohenzollern had been officially transmitted by the Royal Government of Spain to the Imperial Government of France, the French Ambassador presented to His Majesty the King at Ems the demand to authorize him to telegraph to Paris that His Majesty the King would obligate himself for all future time never again to give his approval to the candidacy of the Hohenzollerns should it be renewed.

His Majesty the King thereupon refused to receive the French envoy again and informed him through an adjutant that His Majesty had nothing further to say to the Ambassador.

Louis L. Snyder (Ed. and Trans.), *Documents of German History* (New Brunswick, N.J.: Rutgers University Press, 1958), pp. 215–216.

Empire would be stronger than Prussia had been alone. The unification of Germany was also a blow to European liberalism because the new state was a conservative creation. Conservative politics was now backed not by a weak Austria or an economically retrograde Russia but by the strongest state on the Continent. The two nations most immedi-ately affected by German and also Italian unification were France and Austria. The emergence of the two new unified states revealed the weakness of both France and the Hapsburg Empire. Change had to come in each: France returned to republican government, and the Hapsburgs organized a dual monarchy.

France: From Liberal Empire to the Third Republic

The reign of Emperor Napoleon III (1851–1870) is traditionally divided into the years of the authoritarian empire and those of the liberal empire. The point of division is 1860. Initially, after the *coup* in December 1851, Napoleon III had kept a close rein on the legislature, had strictly controlled the press, and had made life difficult for political dissidents. His support came from property owners, the French Catholic church, and businessmen. They approved the security he brought to property, his protection of the pope, and his aid to commerce and railroad construction. The French victory in the Crimean War had further confirmed the emperor's popularity.

From the late 1850s onward Napoleon III began to modify his policy. In 1860 he concluded a free trade treaty with Britain and permitted the legislature to discuss matters of state more freely. By the late 1860s he had relaxed the press laws and had permitted labor unions. In 1870 he allowed the leaders of the moderates in the legislature to form a ministry. That same year Napoleon III agreed to a liberal constitution that made the ministers responsible to the legislature. All of these liberal moves were closely related to problems in foreign policy. He had lost control of the diplomacy of Italian unification. Between 1861 and 1867 he had supported a military expedition against Mexico led by Archduke Maximilian of Austria. The venture ended in defeat and the execution of the archduke. In 1866 Napoleon III and France rather sat on the sidelines while Bismarck and Prussia reorganized German affairs. The liberal concessions on domestic matters were attempts to compensate for an increasingly unsuccessful foreign policy. The war of 1870 against Germany was simply Napoleon III's last and most disastrous attempt to shore up French foreign policy and to secure domestic popularity.

Whether Napoleon III would have succeeded in sustaining liberal government or his own position became a moot point. The Second Empire, but not the war, came to an inglorious end with the Battle of Sedan in September 1870. The emperor was captured, imprisoned, and then allowed to go to England, where he died in 1873. Shortly after news of the Sedan disaster reached Paris, a republic was

Emperor Napoleon III of France is here pictured with his wife and son. [Culver Pictures.]

proclaimed and a Government of National Defense was established. Paris itself was soon under Prussian siege. During the siege of Paris the French government was transferred to Bordeaux. Paris finally surrendered in January 1871, but the rest of France had been ready to sue for peace long before the capital surrendered.

The Paris Commune

The division between the provinces and Paris became even more decided after the fighting stopped. Monarchists dominated the new National Assembly elected in February. For the time being, executive power was turned over to Adolphe Thiers (1797–1877), who had been active in French politics since 1830. He negotiated a settlement with Prussia (the Treaty of Frankfurt) whereby France was charged with a large indemnity, remained occupied by Prussian troops until the indemnity had been paid, and surrendered territories in Alsace and Lorraine. The city of Paris, which had suffered much during the siege, resented what it regarded as a betrayal by the monarchist National Assembly sitting at Versailles.

The siege of Paris during the Franco-Prussian War led to extreme food shortages. Animals in the zoo were slaughtered, and domestic dogs and cats were butchered, to feed the hungry citizens. The sketches made early in 1871 were published in London newspapers after being sent from Paris by balloon post. [The Granger Collection.]

~ The Paris Commune Is Proclaimed

In September 1870 the French Republic was proclaimed, and shortly thereafter a National Assembly was elected. The city of Paris, which had held out against Prussia longer than any other part of France, was hostile to the National Assembly. On March 18, 1871, a revolt against the assembly occurred in Paris. The National Guard of Paris sought to organize the city as a separate part of France. Below is an excerpt of the proclamation of March 28 of the separation of Paris into an autonomous commune. The rebellious Parisians wanted all of France to be organized into a federation of politically autonomous communes. This communal concept was directly opposed to that of the large national state. Two months after this proclamation the troops of the assembly crushed the commune.

By its revolution of the 18th March, and the spontaneous and courageous efforts of the National Guard, Paris has regained its autonomy. . . . On the eve of the sanguinary and disastrous defeat suffered by France as the punishment it has to undergo for the seventy years of the Empire, and the monarchical, clerical, parliamentary, legal and conciliatory reaction, our country again rises, revives, begins a new life, and retakes the tradition of the Communes of old and of the French Revolution. This tradition, which gave victory to France, and earned the respect and sympathy of past generations, will bring independence, wealth, peaceful glory and brotherly love among nations in the future.

Never was there so solemn an hour. The Revolution which our fathers commenced and we are finishing . . . is going on without bloodshed, by the might of the popular will. . . . To secure the triumph of the Communal idea . . . it is necessary to determine its general principles, and to draw up . . . the programme to be realized. . . .

The Commune is the foundation of all political states, exactly as the family is the embryo of human society. It must have autonomy; that is to say, self-administration and self-government, agreeing with its particular genius, traditions, and wants; preserving, in its political, moral, national, and special groups its entire liberty, its own character, and its complete sovereignty, like a citizen of a free town.

To secure the greatest economic development, the national and territorial independence, and security, association is indispensable; that is to say, a federation of all communes, constituting a united nation.

The autonomy of the Commune guarantees liberty to its citizens; and the federation of all the communes increases, by the reciprocity, power, wealth, markets, and resources of each member, the profit of all.

It was the Communal idea . . . which triumphed on the 18th of March, 1871. It implies, as a political form, the Republic, which is alone compatible with liberty and popular sovereignty.

G. A. Kertesz (Ed.), *Documents in the Political History of the European Continent, 1815–1939* (Oxford: Clarendon Press, 1968), pp. 312–313.

Thiers, familiar with a half-century of Parisian political turmoil, ordered the disarmament of the Paris National Guard on March 17. The attempt on the next day to seize the guard's cannon was bungled. Paris then regarded the National Assembly as its new enemy.

On March 26, 1871, the Parisians elected a new municipal government, called the *Paris Commune*. It was formally proclaimed on March 28. Its goal was to administer the city separately from the rest of the country. Political radicals and socialists of all stripes participated in the Paris Commune at one

In October 1870 Gambetta, who was then chief of the new French government, and his secretary escaped by balloons from beseiged Paris. The city was surrounded by Prussian troops who attempted unsuccessfully to shoot down the balloons, the second of which was said to carry three wealthy Americans also fleeing the city. Gambetta eventually established a governmental headquarters in Tours and prepared to negotiate terms of surrender with Prussia. The drawing was made by an eye-witness, J. C. Palmuri, for the American periodical, Leslie's Weekly. [*Culver Pictures.*]

Fierce fighting marked the suppression of the Paris Commune by the forces of the National Assembly in May 1871. The nineteenth-century engraving shows government troops attacking communards barricaded in the Palais Royal in the center of Paris. [New York Public Library Picture Collection.]

time or another. The National Assembly moved rapidly against the commune. By early April Paris was again a besieged city, but this time it stood surrounded by a French army. On May 8 the army bombarded Paris. On May 21, the day on which the formal treaty with Prussia was signed, the National Assembly forces broke through the city's defenses. During the next seven days the troops restored order to Paris and in the process killed about twenty thousand inhabitants. The communards claimed their own victims as well.

The short-lived Paris Commune very quickly became a legend throughout France and Europe. Marxists regarded it as a genuine proletarian government which the troops of the French bourgeoisie had suppressed. This interpretation is largely mistaken. The commune, though of shifting composition, was dominated by petty bourgeois members. The socialism that was a part of the commune

had its roots in Blanqui and Proudhon rather than in Marx. The goal of the commune was not a workers' republic but a nation composed of relatively independent, radically democratic enclaves. The suppression of the commune consequently represented not only the protection of property but also the triumph of the centralized nation-state over an alternative mode of political organization. Just as the armies of Piedmont and Prussia had united the small states of Italy and Germany, the army of the French National Assembly destroyed the particularistic political tendencies of Paris and by implication those of any other French community.

The Third Republic

The National Assembly put down the Commune directly, but it backed into a republican form of government indirectly and much against its will.

The monarchists, who constituted its majority, were divided in loyalty between the House of Bourbon and the House of Orléans. They could have surmounted this problem because the Bourbon claimant had no children. He could have become king on the condition that the Orléanist heir would follow him to the throne. However, the Bourbon count of Chambord refused to become king if the nation retained the revolutionary tricolor flag. Even the conservative monarchists would not return to the white flag of the Bourbons, which symbolized extreme political reaction.

While the monarchists quarreled over the proper heir, and the heir over the proper flag, time passed and events marched on. By September 1873 the indemnity had been paid and the Prussian occupation troops had withdrawn. Thiers was ousted from office because he had displayed clear republican sentiments. The monarchists wanted a person more sympathetic with their goals to be executive. They elected as president Marshal MacMahon (1808–1893), who was conservative and who was expected to prepare for an eventual monarchist restoration. In 1875 the National Assembly, still monarchist in sentiment but unable to find a candidate for the throne, decided to regularize the political system. It adopted a law that provided for a Chamber of Deputies elected by universal manhood suffrage, a Senate chosen indirectly, and a president elected by the two legislative houses. This relatively simple republican system had resulted from the bickering and frustration of the monarchists.

MacMahon remained as president. He would have liked to transform that office into a much stronger position. After numerous quarrels with the Chamber of Deputies, he resigned in 1879. His departure meant that people dedicated to a republic generally controlled the national government. But France remained an uncertain and unconfident republic. A considerable body of public opinion within the army, the church, and the wealthy families still favored government by a single strong figure. During the late 1880s they looked to General Georges Boulanger (1837–1891) as such a leader. In 1886 and 1887 he had been a popular minister of war who initiated a number of military reforms. When a financial scandal touched several major political figures, Boulanger became all the more appealing for his honesty and integrity. He was elected to the Chamber of Deputies from numerous districts, though afterwards he sat for only one. In 1889 there was much talk and expectation of his carrying out a *coup d'état*. Nothing came of these speculations. The good general had talked with too many different political groups to be trusted by any. He also lacked real drive and political ambition. In the end he left France for life with his Belgian mistress and in 1891 committed suicide on her grave in Brussels.

The political structure of the Third Republic proved much stronger than many citizens suspected at the time. It was able to survive a series of major scandals. In the late 1880s the son of the president was discovered to be selling positions in the Legion of Honor. Early in the next decade a number of ministers and deputies were implicated in the Panama affair. Ferdinand De Lesseps, who had constructed the Suez Canal, organized a company to build a canal in Panama. Various people in authority in France accepted bribes for their public support of the venture. These two *causes célèbres* made the republic look rather sleazy in the eyes of its conservative enemies. But the institutions of the republic allowed new ministers to replace those whose corruption was exposed.

THE DREYFUS AFFAIR. The greatest trauma of the republic occurred over the Dreyfus affair. On December 22, 1894, a French military court found Captain Alfred Dreyfus (1859–1935) guilty of

Captain Alfred Dreyfus was falsely accused of passing French military secrets to Germany. His several trials during the 1890s became the occasion for major clashes, with strong anti-Semitic overtones, between the political left and right in the Third French Republic. [Culver Pictures.]

passing secret information to the German army. The evidence supporting his guilt was at best flimsy and was later revealed to have been forged. Someone in the officer corps had been passing documents to the Germans, and it suited the army investigators to accuse Dreyfus, who was Jewish. However, after Dreyfus had been sent to Devil's Island, secrets continued to flow to the German army. In 1896 a new head of French counterintelligence reexamined the Dreyfus file and found evidence of forgery. A different officer was implicated, but a military court quickly acquitted him of all charges. The officer who had discovered the forgeries was transferred to a distant post.

By then the matter had become one of widespread and sometimes near-hysterical public debate. The army, the French Catholic church, political conservatives, and vehemently anti-Semitic newspapers repeatedly contended that Dreyfus was guilty. Such anti-Dreyfus opinion was quite powerful at the beginning of the affair. In 1898, however, the novelist Émile Zola published a newspaper article entitled *"J'accuse"* ("I Accuse") in which he contended that the army had consciously denied due process to Dreyfus and had plotted to suppress evidence and to forge other evidence. Zola was convicted of libel and received a one-year prison sentence which he avoided only by leaving France for exile in England.

Zola was only one of numerous liberals, radicals, and socialists who had begun to demand a new trial for Dreyfus. Although these forces of the political left had come to Dreyfus's support rather slowly, they soon realized that his cause could aid their own public image. They portrayed the conservative institutions of the nation as having denied Dreyfus the rights belonging to any citizen of the republic. They also claimed, and quite properly so, that Dreyfus had been singled out so that the guilty persons, who were still in the army, could be protected. In August 1898 further evidence of forged material came to light. The officer responsible for those forgeries committed suicide in jail. A new military trial took place, but Dreyfus was again found guilty by officers who refused to admit the original mistake. The president of France immediately pardoned the captain, and eventually, in 1906, a civilian court set aside the results of both previous military trials.

The Dreyfus case divided France as no issue had done since the Paris Commune. By its conclusion the conservative political forces of the nation stood on the defensive. They had for a number of years allowed themselves to persecute an innocent person and to manufacture false evidence against him to protect themselves from disclosure. They had also embraced a strongly anti-Semitic posture. On the political left, radicals, republicans, and socialists developed an informal alliance that outlived the fight over the Dreyfus case itself. These groups realized that republican institutions must be preserved in a conscious fashion if the political left were to achieve any of its goals. Outside political circles ever larger numbers of French citizens understood that their rights and liberties were safer under a republic than under some alternative mode of conservative government. The divisions, suspicions, and hopes growing out of the Dreyfus affair would continue to mark and to divide the Third French Republic until its defeat by Germany in 1940.

The Hapsburg Empire: Formation of the Dual Monarchy

After 1848 the Hapsburg Empire remained a problem both to itself and to the rest of Europe. An ungenerous critic remarked that the empire was supported by a standing army of soldiers, a kneeling army of priests, and a crawling army of informers. In the age of national states, liberal institutions, and industrialism, the Hapsburg domains remained primarily dynastic, absolutist, and agrarian. The response to the revolts at the end of the 1840s has been the reassertion of absolutism. Francis Joseph, who became emperor in 1848 and ruled until 1916, was honest, hard-working, and unimaginative. He reacted to events but rarely commanded them.

During the 1850s his ministers attempted to impose a centralized administration on the empire. The system amounted to a military and bureaucratic government dominated by German-speaking Austrians. The Vienna government abolished all internal tariffs in the empire. It divided Hungary, which had been so revolutionary in 1848, into military districts. The Roman Catholic Church received control of education. Although these actions stirred much domestic resentment and opposition, this system of neoabsolutism actually floundered

The coronation of Francis Joseph as King of Hungary in 1867. The so-called Ausgleich, or Compromise, of 1867 transformed the Hapsburg Empire into a dual monarchy in which Austria and Hungary became almost separate states except for defense and foeign affairs. [Bildarchiv der Osterreichischen Nationalbibliothek, Vienna.]

because of a series of major setbacks in Hapsburg foreign policy. Austrian refusal to support Russia during the Crimean War meant that the new czar would not in the future help to preserve Hapsburg rule in Hungary as Nicholas I had done in 1849. An important external support of Hapsburg power for the past half-century thus disappeared. The Austrian defeat in 1859 at the hands of France and Piedmont and the subsequent loss of territory in Italy confirmed the necessity for new structures of domestic government. For seven years the emperor, the civil servants, the aristocrats, and the politicians attempted to construct a viable system of government.

In 1860 Francis Joseph issued the October Diploma, which created a federation among the states and provinces of the empire. There were to be local diets dominated by the landed classes and a single imperial parliament. The Magyar nobility of Hungary rejected the plan. Consequently, in 1861 the emperor promulgated the February Patent. Technically it interpreted the Diploma, but in point of fact it constituted an entirely different form of government. It established a bicameral imperial parliament, or *Reichsrat,* with an appointed upper chamber and an indirectly elected lower chamber. Again the Magyars refused to cooperate in a system designed to permit German-speaking Austrian domination of the empire. The Hungarians sent no delegates to the legislature. Nevertheless, for six years, the February Patent governed the empire, and it prevailed in Austria proper until World War I. There was no ministerial responsibility to the *Reichsrat.* Few genuine guarantees existed for civil liberties. Armies could be levied and taxes raised without parliamentary consent. When the

The Austrian Prime Minister Explains the Dual Monarchy

The multinational character of the Austrian Empire had long been a source of internal weakness and political discontent. After the defeat of Austria by Prussia in 1866, the Austrian government attempted to regain the loyalty of the Hungarians by making Hungary a separate kingdom within a dual monarchy known thereafter as Austria–Hungary.

The dangers which Austria has to face are of a two-fold nature. The first is presented by the tendency of her liberal-minded German population to gravitate toward that larger portion of the German-speaking people . . . the second is the diversity of language and race in the empire. Of Austria's large Slav population, the Poles have a natural craving for independence after having enjoyed and heroically fought for it for centuries; while the other nationalities are likely at a moment of dangerous crisis to develop pro-Russian tendencies.

Now my object is to carry out a bloodless revolution—to show the various elements of this great empire that it is to the benefit of each of them to act in harmony with its neighbor. . . . But to this I have made one exception. Hungary is an ancient monarchy, more ancient as such than Austria proper. . . . I have endeavoured to give Hungary not a new

position with regard to the Austrian empire, but to secure her in the one which she has occupied. The Emperor of Austria is King of Hungary; my idea was that he should revive in his person the Constitution of which he and his ancestors have been the heads. The leading principles of my plan are . . . the resuscitation of an old monarchy and an old Constitution; not the separation of one part of the empire from the other, but the drawing together of the two component parts by the recognition of their joint positions, the maintenance of their mutual obligations, their community in questions affecting the entire empire, and their proportional pecuniary responsibility for the liabilities of the whole State. It is no plan of separation that I have carried out: on the contrary, it is one of closer union, not by the creation of a new power, but by the recognition of an old one. . . .

Memoirs of Friedrich Ferdinand Count von Beust, Vol. 1, ed. by Baron Henry de Worms (London: Remington, 1887), pp. xx–xxvi.

Reichsrat was not in session, the emperor could simply promulgate laws on his own authority.

Meanwhile negotiations continued between the emperor and the Magyars. These produced no concrete result until the defeat of Austria by Prussia in the summer of 1866 and the consequent exclusion of Austria from German affairs. The military disaster compelled Francis Joseph to come to terms with the Magyars. The subsequent *Ausgleich,* or Compromise, of 1867 transformed the Hapsburg Empire into a dual monarchy. Francis Joseph was separately crowned king of Hungary in Budapest. Except for the common monarch, Austria and Hungary became almost wholly separate states. They shared ministers of foreign affairs, defense, and finance, but the other ministers were different for each state. There were also separate parliaments. Each year sixty parliamentary delegates from each state were to meet to discuss matters of mutual interest. Every ten years Austria and Hungary were to renegotiate their trade relationship. By this cumbersome machinery, unique in all European history, the Hungarian Magyars were reconciled to Hapsburg rule. They had achieved the free hand they had long wanted in local Hungarian matters.

Many of the other national groups within the empire—including the Czechs, the Ruthenians, the Romanians, and the Serbo-Croatians—opposed the Compromise of 1867. The dual monarchy, in effect, permitted the German-speaking Austrians and the Hungarian Magyars to dominate all other nationalities in their respective states. The most vocal critics were the Czechs of Bohemia. They favored a policy of trialism or triple monarchy. In 1871 Francis Joseph was willing to accept this con-

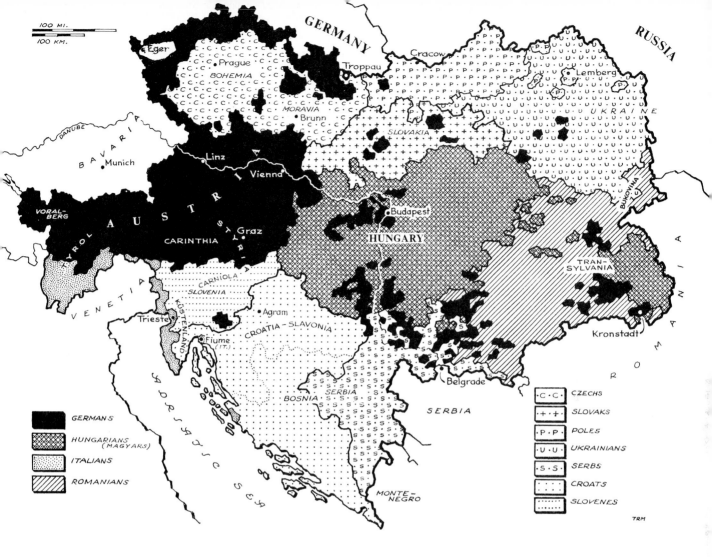

NATIONALITIES WITHIN THE HAPSBURG EMPIRE

MAP 26.3 *The patchwork appearance reflects the unusual problem of the numerous ethnic groups that the Hapsburgs could not, of course, meld into a modern national state. Only the Magyars were recognized in 1867, leaving nationalist Czechs, Slovaks, and the others chronically dissatisfied.*

cept. However, the Hungarian Magyars vetoed the proposal for fear that they might have to make similar concessions to their own subject nationalities.

For over twenty years the Czechs were conciliated by an extension of generous Austrian patronage and admission to the Austrian bureaucracy. By the 1890s Czech nationalism had again become more vocal. In 1897, through a series of ordinances, Francis Joseph gave the Czechs and the

Germans equality of language in various localities. The Germans in the Austrian *Reichsrat* set out on a course of parliamentary disruption to oppose these measures. The Czechs replied in kind. By the turn of the century this obstructionist activity, which included the playing of musical instruments in the parliament chamber, had paralyzed parliamentary life. The emperor ruled by imperial decree with the support of the bureaucracy. In 1907 universal manhood suffrage was introduced into Austria, but it did not change the situation in the *Reichsrat*. In effect, by 1914 constitutionalism was a dead letter in Austria. It flourished in Hungary, but only because the Magyars relentlessly exercised political supremacy over all other competing national groups.

Russia: Emancipation and Revolutionary Stirrings

Reforms of Alexander II

The defeat in the Crimean War and the humiliation of the Treaty of Paris compelled the Russian government to reconsider its domestic situation. Nicholas I had died in 1855 during the conflict. Because of extensive travel in Russia and an early introduction to government procedures, Nicholas's son Alexander II (1855–1881) was quite familiar with the chief difficulties facing the nation. The debacle of the war had created a situation in which reform was both necessary and possible. Alexander II took advantage of this turn of events to institute the most extensive restructuring of Russian society and administration since Peter the Great. Like Peter, Alexander imposed his reforms from the top.

In every area of economic and public life a profound cultural gap existed between Russia and the rest of Europe. Nowhere was this fact more true than in the matter of serfdom. Everywhere else on the Continent it had been abandoned. In Russia the institution had changed very little since the eighteenth century. Landowners had a very free hand with their serfs, and the serfs had little recourse against the lords. In March 1856, at the

Czar Alexander II of Russia emancipated the serfs in 1861 and began numerous other major reforms of the Russian government and army. He was assassinated by radicals who sought even more fundamental reforms of Russian life. [Culver Pictures.]

The harsh treatment of Russian serfs by their landlords prior to emancipation was frequently criticized in the rest of Europe. This French cartoon of 1854 portrays Russian landlords using bundles of their serfs as stakes for a card game. [The Granger Collection.]

Even after emancipation, the life of Russian peasants was difficult. They attempted to secure a livelihood partly from farming and partly from small handcraft industries, such as those seen in this picture of a Russian village in the late nineteenth century. [Culver Pictures.]

army had performed poorly in the Crimean conflict; and the moral opinion of the day had come increasingly to condemn serfdom. Only Russia and certain portions of the United States among the Western nations still retained such forms of involuntary servitude. For over five years government commissions wrestled over the way to implement the czar's desire. Finally, in February 1861, against much opposition from the nobility and the landlords, Alexander II promulgated the long statute ending serfdom in Russia.

The technicalities of the emancipation statute meant that freedom was often more theoretical than practical. The procedures were so complicated and the results so limited that many serfs believed that real emancipation was still to come. Serfs immediately received the personal rights to marry without their landlord's permission as well as to purchase and sell property freely, engage in court actions, and pursue trades. What they did not receive immediately was free title to their land. They were required to pay for frequently insufficient allotments of land over a period of forty-nine

conclusion of the Crimean War, Alexander II announced his intention to abolish serfdom. He had decided that only abolition of the institution would permit Russia to organize its human and natural resources so as to maintain its status as a great power. Serfdom had become economically inefficient; the threat of large or small revolts of serfs was always present; the serfs recruited into the

❧ Alexander II Decides to Emancipate the Serfs

Shortly after becoming czar, Alexander II reached the decision that the Russian serfs should eventually be emancipated. On March 30, 1856, he announced his decision to a group of Moscow nobles. He told them that the serfs would be freed and then asked them to help him to devise the best way to carry out the emancipation, which did not occur for another five years. Note the czar's emphasis on the wisdom of freeing the serfs by a deliberate decision rather than being forced to that action by a revolt.

I have learned, gentlemen, that rumors have spread among you of my intention to abolish serfdom. To refute any groundless gossip on so important a subject I consider it necessary to inform you that I have no intention of doing so immediately. But, of course, and you yourselves realize it, the existing system of

serf owning cannot remain unchanged. It is better to begin abolishing serfdom from above than to wait for it to begin to abolish itself from below. I ask you, gentlemen, to think of ways of doing this. Pass on my words to the nobles for consideration.

George Vernadsky (Ed.), *A Source Book for Russian History from Earliest Times to* 1917, Vol. 3 (New Haven, Conn.: Yale University Press, 1972), p. 589.

years. They were also charged interest during this period. The serfs made the payments to the government, which had already reimbursed the landlords for their losses. The serfs did not receive title to the land until the debt was paid. The redemption payments led to almost unending difficulty. Poor harvests caused the debts to fall into arrears, and the situation was not remedied until 1906. With widespread revolutionary unrest following the Japanese defeat of Russia in 1905, the government grudgingly completed the process of emancipation by canceling the remaining debts.

The abolition of serfdom required the reorganization of local government and the judicial system. The authority of village communes replaced that of the landlord over the peasant. The village elders settled family quarrels, imposed fines, issued internal passports, and collected taxes. In many cases also, the emancipated serfs owned land communally rather than individually. The nobility were permitted a larger role in local administration through a system of provincial and county *zemstvos*, or councils, organized in 1864. These councils were to oversee local matters such as bridge and road repair, education, and agricultural improvement. However, because the councils received inadequate funds, local government never became vigorous.

The flagrant inequities and abuses of the pre-emancipation judicial system could not continue. In 1864 Alexander II promulgated a new statute on the judiciary. For the first time principles of western European legal systems were introduced into Russia. These included equality before the law, impartial hearings, uniform procedures, judicial independence, and trial by jury. The new system was far from perfect. The judges were not genuinely independent, and the czar could increase as well as reduce sentences. For certain offenses, such as those involving the press, jury trials were not held. Nonetheless the system was an improvement both in its efficiency and in its relative lack of the old corruption.

Reforms were also instituted in the army. Russia possessed the largest military establishment on the Continent, but it had floundered badly in the Crimean War. The usual period of recruitment was twenty-five years. Villages had to provide quotas of serfs. Often the recruiters had come to the villages and simply seized serfs from their families. Once in the army, the recruits rarely saw their homes again. Life in the army was exceedingly harsh, even by the usually brutal standards of most mid-century armies. In the 1860s the army lowered the period of recruitment to fifteen years and slightly relaxed disciplinary procedures. In 1874 the enlistment period was lowered to six years of active duty, followed by nine years in the reserves. All males were subject to military service after the age of twenty.

Alexander's reformist departures became more measured shortly after the Polish Rebellion of 1863. As in 1830, Polish nationalists attempted to overthrow Russian dominance. Once again the Russian army suppressed the rebellion. Alexander II then moved to "russify" Poland. In 1864 he emancipated the Polish serfs as a move against the politically restive Polish nobility. Russian law, language, and administration were imposed on all areas of Polish life. Henceforth, until the close of World War I, Poland was treated merely as one other Russian province.

As revealed by the Polish suppression, Alexander II was a reformer only within the limits of his own autocracy. His changes in Russian life failed to create new loyalty or gratitude among his subjects. The serfs felt that their emancipation had been inadequate. The nobles and the wealthier educated segments of Russian society resented the czar's persistent refusal to allow them a meaningful role in government and policy making. Consequently, although Alexander II became known as the Czar Liberator, he was never a popular ruler. He could be very indecisive and was rarely open to new ideas. These characteristics became more pronounced after 1866, when an attempt was made on his life. Thereafter Russia increasingly became a police state. This new repression fueled the activity of radical groups within Russia. Their actions, in turn, made the autocracy more reactionary.

Revolutionaries

The czarist regime had long had its critics. One of the most prominent was Alexander Herzen (1812–1870), who lived in exile. From London he published a newspaper called *The Bell* in which he set forth reformist positions. The initial reforms of Alexander II had raised great hopes among Russian students and intellectuals, but they soon became discontented with the limited character of the restructuring. Drawing on the ideas of Herzen and other radicals, these students formed a revolutionary movement known as *Populism*. They sought a social revolution based on the communal life of the Russian peasants. The chief radical society was called *Land and Freedom*. In the early 1870s hundreds of young Russians, including both men and

women, took their revolutionary message into the countryside. They intended to live with the peasants, to gain their trust, and to teach them about the peasant role in the coming revolution. The bewildered and distrustful peasants turned most of the youths over to the police. In the winter of 1877–1878 almost two hundred students were tried. Most were acquitted or given very light sentences, because they had been held for months in preventive detention and because the court believed that a display of mercy might lessen public sympathy for the young revolutionaries. The court even suggested that the czar might wish to pardon those students given heavier sentences. The czar refused and let it become known that he favored heavy penalties for all persons involved in revolutionary activity.

Thereafter the revolutionaries decided that the czarist regime must be attacked directly. They

Alexander III (1881–1894) attempted to reimpose arbitrary rule after the reforms of Alexander II. The future Czar Nicholas II (1894–1917) is standing directly behind his father. [The Granger Collection.]

The new reactionary policies of Czar Alexander III included use of police against political opponents. This English newspaper engraving of 1887 presents the Russian policy in St. Petersburg discovering a printing press run by political radicals. [The Granger Collection.]

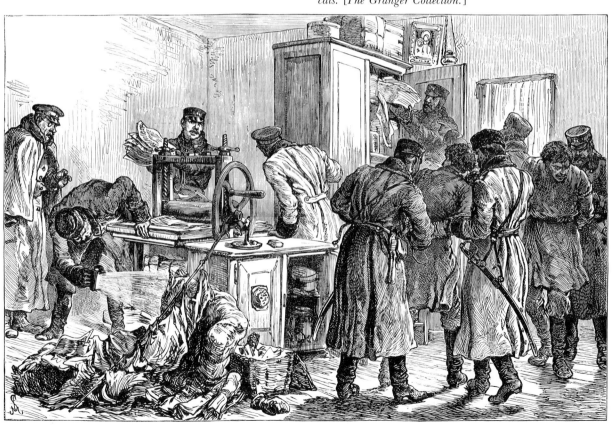

adopted a policy of terrorism. In January 1878 Vera Zasulich attempted to assassinate the military governor of Saint Petersburg. At her trial the jury acquitted her because the governor she had shot had a special reputation for brutality and because some people at the time believed that Zasulich had a personal rather than a political grievance against her victim. Nonetheless the verdict further encouraged the terrorists.

In 1879 Land and Freedom split into two groups. One held to the idea of educating the peasants, and it soon dissolved. The other, known as *People's Will,* was dedicated to the overthrow of the autocracy. Its members decided to assassinate the czar himself. Several assassination attempts failed, but on March 1, 1881, a bomb hurled by a member of People's Will killed Czar Alexander II. Four men and two women were sentenced to death for the deed. All of them had been willing to die for

their cause. The emergence of such dedicated revolutionary opposition constituted as much a part of the reign of Alexander II as did his reforms, for the limited character of those reforms convinced many people from various walks of life that the autocracy could never truly redirect Russian society.

Alexander III, whose reign (1881–1894) further underscored that pessimistic conviction, possessed all the autocratic and repressive characteristics of his grandfather Nicholas I and none of the better qualities of his father. Some slight attention was directed toward the improvement of life in the Russian factories, but primarily Alexander III sought to roll back the reforms of the third quarter of the century. He favored centralized bureaucracy over the new limited modes of self-government. He strengthened the secret police and increased press censorship. In effect, he confirmed

❧ George Kennan Describes Siberian Exile in Alexander III's Russia

Under Alexander III the police-state character of the Russian monarchy intensified. Exile was the most extreme form of punishment short of death. In effect, it robbed the person exiled not only of legal rights but almost of his or her identity, as pointed out in this account by a noted American observer who spent long periods in Siberia in the 1860s and 1880s. It should be noted that he was not the person of the same name who has been an important spokesman in mid-twentieth-century American foreign policy.

Exile by administrative process means the banishment of an obnoxious person from one part of the empire to another without the observance of any of the legal formalities that, in most civilized countries, precede the deprivation of rights and the restriction of personal liberty. The obnoxious person may not be guilty of any crime, and may not have rendered himself unamenable in any way to the laws of the state, but if, in the opinion of the local authorities, his presence in a particular place is "prejudicial to public order," or "incompatible with public tranquillity," he may be arrested without a warrant, may be held from two weeks to two years in prison, and may then be removed by force to any other place within the limits of the empire and there be put under police surveillance for a period of from one year to ten years. He may or

may not be informed of the reasons for this summary proceeding, but in either case he is perfectly helpless. He cannot examine the witnesses upon whose testimony his presence is declared to be "prejudicial to public order." He cannot summon friends to prove his loyalty and good character, without great risk of bringing upon them the same calamity that has befallen him. He has no right to demand a trial, or even a hearing. He cannot sue out a writ of habeas corpus. He cannot appeal to his fellow-citizens through the press. His communications with the world are so suddenly severed that sometimes even his own relatives do not know what has happened to him. He is literally and absolutely without any means whatever of self-defense.

George Kennan, *Siberia and the Exile System,* Vol. 1 (London: Century Co., 1891), pp. 242–243.

all the evils that the revolutionaries saw inherent in autocratic government. His son, Nicholas II, who became czar in 1894, would discover that autocracy could not survive the pressures of the twentieth century.

Great Britain: Toward Democracy

While the continental nations became unified and struggled toward internal political restructuring, Great Britain continued to symbolize the confident liberal state. Britain was not without its difficulties and domestic conflicts, but it seemed able to deal with these through existing political institutions. The general prosperity of the third quarter of the century took the edge off the class hostility of the 1840s. A large body of shared ideas emphasizing competition and individualism was accepted by the members of all classes. Even the leaders of trade unions during these years asked for little more than to receive a portion of the fruits of prosperity and to prove their own social respectability. Parliament itself continued to provide an institution that permitted the absorption of new groups and interests into the existing political processes. In short, the British did not have to create new liberal institutions and then learn how to live within them.

The major political figure of mid-century was Henry John Temple, Lord Palmerston (1784–1865). He became prime minister early in 1855 as the nation became weary of blunders in the con-

Prince Albert and Queen Victoria (1837–1901) of Great Britain successfully accommodated the British monarchy to new liberal democratic political structures. Prince Albert died in 1861. The photograph, by Roger Fenton, is from 1854. [The Mansell Collection.]

duct of the Crimean War. Except for a seventeen-month interlude in 1858 and 1859, he governed until late 1865. Palmerston was a liberal Whig whose chief interest was foreign policy. He generally championed free trade and the right of European nationalities to determine their own political destinies. His bombastic patriotism made him very popular with voters; he rarely hesitated to parade British naval power before the world. Yet Palmerston was a person of the past. He had little sympathy with those political and working-class figures who wanted to extend the franchise beyond the limits of the Great Reform Act of 1832. By the time of his death Palmerston had become the chief obstacle to further political and social reform.

The Second Reform Act (1867)

By the early 1860s it had become clear to most observers that in one way or another the franchise

William Ewart Gladstone (1809–1889) was prime minister of Britain four times between 1868 and 1894. Gladstone was the personification of nineteenth-century British liberalism. His combination of pragmatism with deep moral conviction had great appeal for the Victorian middle class. [New York Public Library Picture Collection.]

Benjamin Disraeli caricatured by John Tenniel in 1864 in Punch as a self-admiring angel. In 1867, as the Conservative leader in the House of Commons, Disraeli sponsored the Second Reform Act, which for the first time enfranchised large numbers of the working class. [New York Public Library Picture Collection.]

would again have to be expanded. The prosperity and the social respectability of the working class convinced many politicians that the workers truly deserved the vote. Organizations such as the Reform League, led by John Bright (1811–1889), were agitating for parliamentary action. In 1866 Lord John Russell's Liberal ministry introduced a reform bill that was defeated by a coalition of traditional Conservatives and antidemocratic liberals. Russell resigned, and the Tory Lord Derby replaced him. What then occurred surprised everyone.

The Conservative ministry, led in the House of Commons by Benjamin Disraeli (1804–1881), introduced its own reform bill in 1867. As the debate proceeded, Disraeli accepted one amendment after another and expanded the electorate well beyond the limits earlier proposed by the Liberals. When the final measure was passed, the number of voters had been increased from approximately 1,430,000 to 2,470,000. Britain had taken a major step toward democracy. Large numbers of working-class voters had been admitted to the electorate. Disraeli hoped that by sponsoring the measure, the Conservatives would receive the gratitude of the new voters. Because reform was bound to come, it was best for the Conservatives to enjoy the credit. Disraeli thought that eventually significant portions of the working class would support Conservative candidates who proved themselves responsive to social issues. He also thought that the growing suburban middle class would become more conservative. In the long run, his intuition proved correct, for in the past century the Conservative Party has dominated British politics.

The immediate election of 1868, however, dashed Disraeli's hopes. William Gladstone (1809–1898) became the new prime minister. Gladstone had begun political life in 1833 as a strong Tory, but over the next thirty-five years he moved steadily toward liberalism. He had supported Robert Peel, free trade, repeal of the Corn Laws, and efficient administration. As chancellor of the exchequer during the 1850s and early

1860s he had lowered taxes and government expenditure. He had also championed Italian nationalism. For many years he continued to oppose a new reform bill. Yet by the early 1860s he had also modified his position on that issue. In 1866 he had been Russell's spokesman in the House of Commons for the unsuccessful liberal reform bill.

Gladstone's Great Ministry (1868–1874)

Gladstone's ministry of 1868–1874 witnessed the culmination of classical British liberalism. Those institutions that still remained the preserve of the aristocracy and the Anglican church were opened to people from other classes and religious denominations. By an Order in Council of 1870 competitive examinations replaced patronage as a means of entering the civil service. In 1871 the purchase of officers' commissions in the army was abolished. The same year saw the removal of Anglican religious requirements for the faculties of Oxford and Cambridge universities. The Ballot Act of 1872 introduced voting by secret ballot. The most momentous measure of Gladstone's first ministry was the

---

❧ Gladstone Praises the Education Act of 1870

The British Education Act of 1870 marked the creation of the first national system of schools in Britain. Prime Minister Gladstone and others admired the measure because it still permitted private religious schools, because it was relatively inexpensive, and because it depended largely on the initiative of local government. In other words, it permitted the liberty and the low taxes that liberals prized.

The great object of all was to make education universal and effective. This was to be done, and doing it we sought, and I think reason and common sense required us to seek, to turn to account for that purpose the vast machinery of education already existing in the country, which had been devised and mainly provided by the Christian philanthropy and the voluntary action of the people. That was the second condition under which the Act was framed. The third was, and I think it was not less wise than the two former, that we should endeavour to separate the action of the State in the matter of education, and the application of State funds, in which I include funds raised by rate [taxes], from all subjects on which, unhappily, religious differences prevail. Those, I

may say, were three of the principles of the measure; and the fourth principle, not less important than the others, was this: that we should trust for the attainment of these great objects, as little as possible to the central Government, and as much as possible to the local authorities and the self-governing power of the people. And let me say in passing, that in my opinion if there be one portion of our institutions more precious in my view than another, it is that portion in which the people are locally organized for the purposes of acquiring the habits and instincts of political action, and applying their own free consciences and free understandings to dealing with the affairs of the community.

A. T. Bassett (Ed.), *Gladstone's Speeches* (London: Methuen, 1916), pp. 412–413.

A photograph, perhaps a montage, of Disraeli's Cabinet in 1876. Disraeli is at the extreme right. His government gave new protection to British trade unions and made a start toward improving the health and housing of the poor. [The Mansell Collection.]

Education Act of 1870. For the first time in British history the government assumed the responsibility for establishing and running elementary schools. Previously British education had been a task relegated to the religious denominations, which received small amounts of state support for the purpose.

All of these reforms were typically liberal. They sought to remove long-standing abuses without destroying existing institutions and to permit all able citizens to compete on the grounds of ability and merit. They attempted to avoid the potential danger to a democratic state of an illiterate citizenry. These reforms also constituted a mode of state building because they created new bonds of loyalty to the nation by abolishing many sources of present and future discontent.

Disraeli in Office (1874–1880)

The liberal policy of creating popular support for the nation through the extension of political liberty and the reform of abuses had its conservative counterpart in concern about social reform. Disraeli succeeded Gladstone as prime minister in 1874 when the election produced sharp divisions among Liberal Party voters over matters of liquor regulation, religion, and education. The two men had stood on different sides of most issues for over a quarter-century. Whereas Gladstone looked to individualism, free trade, and competition to solve social problems, Disraeli had believed that the ruling classes of the country must confront those matters through paternalistic legislation. Disraeli believed in state action to protect weak groups of citizens. In his view such paternalistic legislation would alleviate class antagonism.

Disraeli personally talked a better line than he produced. He had very few specific programs or ideas. The significant social legislation of his ministry stemmed primarily from the efforts of his Home Secretary Richard Cross. The Public Health Act of 1875 consolidated previous sanitary legislation and reaffirmed the duty of the state to interfere with private property on matters of health and physical well-being. Through the Artisans Dwelling Act of 1875 the government became actively involved in providing housing for the working class. The same year, in an important symbolic gesture, the Conservative majority in Parliament passed a law that gave new protection to British trade unions and allowed them to raise picket lines. The Gladstone ministry, although recognizing the legality of unions, had refused such extensive protection.

Charles Stewart Parnell, shown here in an 1880 Vanity Fair drawing by Theobald Chartran, was the leader of the Irish members of Parliament during the Home Rule crisis of the 1880s. [The Granger Collection.]

The Irish Question

In 1880 a second Gladstone ministry took office as an agricultural depression and unpopular foreign policy undermined Disraeli's popularity. In 1884, with Conservative cooperation, a third reform act was passed extending the vote to most male farm workers. However, the major issue of the decade was Ireland. From the late 1860s onward Irish nationalists had sought to achieve home rule for Ireland, by which they meant more Irish control of local government. During his first ministry Gladstone had addressed the Irish question through two major pieces of legislation. In 1869 he carried a measure to disestablish the Church of Ireland, which was the Irish branch of the Anglican church. Henceforth Irish Roman Catholics would not pay taxes to support the hated Protestant church, to which only a small fraction of the population belonged. Second, in 1870 the Liberal ministry sponsored a land act that provided compensation to evicted Irish tenants and loans for tenants who wished to purchase their land.

Throughout the 1870s the Irish question continued to fester. Land remained the center of the agitation. Today the matter of Irish economic development seems more complicated and who owned the land seems less important than the methods of management and cultivation. Nevertheless the organization of the Irish Land League in the late

1870s brought a period of intense agitation and intimidation against the landlords, who were often English. The leader of the Irish movement for a just land settlement and for home rule was Charles Stewart Parnell (1846–1891). In 1881 the second Gladstone ministry passed another Irish land act, which provided further guarantees of tenant rights. This measure only partly satisfied Irish opinion because it was accompanied by a Coercion Act intended to restore law and order to Ireland.

By 1885 Parnell had organized eighty-five Irish members of the House of Commons into a tightly disciplined party that often voted as a bloc. They pursued disruptive tactics to gain attention for the cause of home rule. They bargained with the two English political parties. In the election of 1885 the Irish Party emerged with the balance of power between the English Liberals and Conservatives. The Irish could decide which party would take office. In December 1885 Gladstone announced support of home rule for Ireland. Parnell gave his votes to the formation of a Liberal ministry. However, the issue split the Liberal Party. In 1886 a group of Liberals known as the Liberal Unionists joined with the Conservatives to defeat Gladstone's Home Rule Bill. Gladstone called for a new election, in which the Liberals were defeated. They remained a permanently divided party.

The new Conservative ministry of Lord Salisbury (1830–1903) attempted to reconcile the Irish to English government through public works and administrative reform. The policy, which was tied to further coercion, had only marginal success. In 1892 Gladstone returned to power. A second Home Rule Bill passed the House of Commons but was defeated in the House of Lords. There the Irish question stood until after the turn of the century. The Conservatives sponsored a land act in 1903 that carried out the final transfer of land to tenant ownership. Ireland became a country of small farms. In 1912 a Liberal ministry passed the third Home Rule Bill. Under the provisions of the House of Lords Act of 1911, which curbed the power of that body, the bill had to pass the Commons three times over a Lords veto to become law. The third passage occurred in the summer of 1914, and the implementation of the Home Rule provisions of the bill was suspended for the duration of World War I.

The Irish question affected British politics in a manner not unlike that of the Austrian nationalities problem. Normal British domestic issues could not be adequately addressed because of the political divisions created by Ireland. The split of the Liberal Party proved especially harmful to the cause of further social and political reform. The people who could agree on matters of reform could not agree on Ireland, and the latter problem seemed more important. As the two traditional parties failed to deal with the social questions, by the turn of the century a newly organized Labor Party began to fill the vacuum.

The European Political Scene: 1850–1875

Between 1850 and 1875 the major contours of the political systems that would dominate Europe until World War I had been drawn. Those systems and political arrangements solved, so far as such matters can be solved, many of the political questions and problems that had troubled the Europeans during the first half of the nineteenth century. The concept of the nation-state had on the whole triumphed. Support for governments no longer stemmed from loyalty to dynasties but from various degrees of citizen participation. Moreover the unity of nations was no longer based on dynastic links but on ethnic, cultural, linguistic, and historical bonds. The parliamentary governments of western Europe and the autocracies of eastern

Europe were quite different, but both political systems had been compelled to recognize the force of nationalism and the larger role of citizens in political affairs. Only Russia failed to make such concessions, but the emancipation of the serfs had constituted a concession to a mode of popular opinion. The major sources of future discontent would arise from the demands of labor to enter the political processes and the still unsatisfied aspirations of subject nationalities. Those two areas of unrest would trouble Europe for the next forty years and would eventually undermine the political structures created during the third quarter of the nineteenth century.

Suggested Readings

G. F. A. BEST, *Mid-Victorian Britain* (1972). A good book on the social structure.

R. C. BINKLEY, *Realism and Nationalism, 1852–1871* (1935). A useful, though somewhat dated survey.

R. BLAKE, *Disraeli* (1967). The best recent biography.

J. BLUM, *Lord and Peasant in Russia from the Ninth to the Nineteenth Century* (1961). A clear discussion of emancipation in the later chapters.

W. L. BURN, *The Age of Equipoise* (1964). A thoughtful and convincing discussion of Victorian social stability.

G. CHAPMAN, *The Dreyfus Affair: A Reassessment* (1955). A detached treatment of a subject that still provokes strong feelings.

G. CRAIG, *Germany, 1866–1945* (1978). An excellent new survey.

S. EDWARDS, *The Paris Commune of 1871* (1971). A useful examination of a complex subject.

R. A. KANN, *The Multinational Empire*, 2 vols. (1950). The basic treatment of the nationality problem of Austria–Hungary.

G. KITSON CLARK, *The Making of Victorian England* (1962). The best introduction.

R. R. LOCKE, *French Legitimists and the Politics of Moral Order in the Early Third Republic* (1974). An excellent study of the social and intellectual roots of monarchist support.

P. MAGNUS, *Gladstone: A Biography* (1955). A readable biography.

A. J. MAY, *The Hapsburg Monarchy, 1867–1914* (1951). Narrates in considerable detail and with much sympathy the fate of the dual monarchy.

W. N. MEDLICOTT, *Bismarck and Modern Germany* (1965). An excellent brief biography.

W. E. MOSSE, *Alexander II and the Modernization of Russia* (1958). A brief biography.

C. C. O'BRIEN, *Parnell and His Party* (1957). An excellent treatment of the Irish question.

O. PFLANZE, *Bismarck and the Development of Germany*

(1963). Carries the story through the achievement of unification.

N. RICH, *The Age of Nationalism and Reform*, rev. ed. (1976). A sound volume based on recent research.

D. M. SMITH, *Cavour and Garibaldi in 1860: A Study in Political Conflict* (1954). Explores the two key personalities in Italian unification.

D. M. SMITH, *The Making of Italy, 1796–1870* (1968). A narrative that incorporates the major documents.

A. J. P. TAYLOR, *The Hapsburg Monarchy, 1809–1918* (1941). An opinionated but highly readable work.

D. THOMPSON, *Democracy in France Since 1870*, rev. ed. (1969). A clear guide to a complex problem.

J. M. THOMSON, *Louis Napoleon and the Second Empire* (1954). A straightforward account.

A. B. ULAM, *Russia's Failed Revolutionaries* (1981). A recent study of revolutionary societies and activities prior to the Revolution of 1917.

F. VENTURI, *The Roots of Revolution* (trans., 1960). A major treatment of late nineteenth-century revolutionary movement.

H. S. WATSON, *The Russian Empire, 1801–1917* (1967). A far-ranging narrative.

A. J. WHYTE, *The Evolution of Modern Italy* (1965). An interesting survey of the Italian problem in nineteenth-century diplomacy.

R. WILLIAMS, *The World of Napoleon III*, rev. ed. (1965). Examines the cultural setting.

C. B. WOODHAM-SMITH, *The Reason Why* (1953). A lively account of the Crimean War and the charge of the Light Brigade.

T. ZELDIN, *The Political System of Napoleon III* (1958). An examination of the local sources of political support for Louis Napoleon.

T. ZELDIN, *France: 1848–1945*, 2 vols. (1973, 1977). Emphasizes the social developments.

R. E. ZELNICK, *Labor and Society in Tsarist Russia: The Factory Workers of St. Petersburg, 1855–1870* (1971). An important volume that considers the early stages of the Russian industrial labor force in the era of serf emancipation.

804

27 The Building of European Supremacy: Society and Politics to World War I

Between 1860 and 1914 European political, economic, and social life assumed many of the features characteristic of our world today. Nation-states with large electorates, political parties, centralized bureaucracies, and universal military service emerged. Business adopted large-scale corporate structures, and the labor force organized itself into trade unions. Large numbers of white-collar workers appeared. Urban life came to predominate throughout western Europe. Socialism became a major ingredient in the political life of all nations. The foundations of the welfare state and of vast military establishments were laid. Taxation increased accordingly.

During this half-century the extensive spread of industrialism created an unparalleled productive capacity in Europe. The age of the automobile, the airplane, the bicycle, the refrigerated ship, the tele-phone, the radio, the typewriter, and the electric light bulb dawned. The world's economies, based on the gold standard, became increasingly interdependent. European goods flowed into markets all over the globe. In turn, foreign products, raw materials, and foodstuffs were imported. Europe had also quietly become dependent on the resources and markets of the rest of the world. Changes in the weather conditions in Kansas, Argentina, or New Zealand might now affect the European economy. However, prior to World War I the dependence was concealed by Europe's industrial, military, and financial supremacy. At the time people rather assumed that such supremacy was a natural situation, but the twentieth century would reveal it to have been quite temporary. Nevertheless, while that condition prevailed, Europeans were able to dominate most of the other peoples of the earth and to display the most extreme self-confidence.

Karl Benz at the wheel of one of the first automobiles in 1887. Developed by engineers like Benz in the 1880s, the automobile was a luxury that only the rich could afford in pre-1914 Europe. [Deutsches Museum, Munich.]

Population Trends

There seem to have been more Europeans proportionally about 1900 than ever before or since.

After the street fighting of the revolutions of 1848, the old wall fortifications of Vienna were torn down. In their place were built broad boulevards lined with fine buildings. The new streets were more beautiful—and were also better suited for rapid movement of troops against possible insurrection. This is an early photograph of a portion of the Ringstrasse, the street replacing the walls. [Austrian Information Service, New York.]

A fashionable Paris boulevard in the late nineteenth century. Note the various kinds of horsedrawn carriages and the doubledecked horsedrawn bus. [French Cultural Services, New York.]

Europe then contained just under one quarter of the estimated world population. The demographic expansion to which so much attention has already been paid continued through the second half of the century. The number of Europeans rose from approximately 266 million in 1850 to 401 million in 1900 and 447 million in 1910. However, the rate of European growth began to slow, whereas the population expansion elsewhere did not recede. Depending on the country in Europe, the birth rate either fell or remained stationary. The death rate did likewise. In the long run that ratio meant a more slowly growing population. This situation also meant that the grave demographic differential between the developed and the undeveloped world—which is so much a part of the present food and resource crisis—had been established.

During the second half of the nineteenth century the small family of two or three children became "normal." Knowledge about and means of contraception became more fully dispersed and its practice more widespread. The desire to maintain a high standard of living, the greater likelihood of

The building of sewers for the disposal of urban waste was one of the great accomplishments of nineteenth-century sanitary engineering. This picture was made inside one of the sewers of Paris. [French Cultural Services, New York.]

development of the European economy and the economies of North America, Latin America, and Australia meant better wages and cheap land, which enticed people to move. Within Europe the movement continued toward the cities. By about 1900 in all the major west European nations approximately 50 percent of the people lived in urban areas. These city populations were largely uprooted from traditional social ties. They often confronted poor housing, social anonymity, and potential unemployment. The migrants to cities in the last half of the century rarely possessed the artisan skills of the urban immigrants of fifty years earlier. Their problems and their social setting made them ripe for new kinds of political and economic organization. The failure of people to mix socially and the competition for too few jobs generated new varieties of urban discontent, such as were experienced by the thousands of Russian Jews who migrated to western Europe. Much of the political anti-Semitism of the latter part of the century had its social roots in these problems of urban migration.

Europeans also migrated away from their continent in record numbers. Between 1846 and 1932

infant survival, the cost of rearing children, the smaller number of children in the work force, and the desire of women to limit the number of births contributed to the stabilization of population. It seems that more and more couples decided that they wanted to spend their income on consumer goods rather than on children. Moreover children brought fewer economic advantages to their parents than in the past. Further improvements in sanitation, housing, food processing, and medicine tended to lower the death rate at the same time. This vast but stabilizing European population provided a large consumer market and an increasingly healthy work force.

Europe's peoples were on the move in the last half of the century as never before. Legal movement and migration became easier as the role of the landlords lessened. Railways, steamships, and better roads allowed greater physical mobility. The

Pollution was one of the earliest results of industrialization and the resulting rapid population growth, and it became a major problem for nineteenth-century governments, as it has remained for those of today. This English cartoon of 1858 was published near the time of the passage by Parliament of an act to clean the River Thames. [The Granger Collection.]

THE "SILENT HIGHWAY"-MAN.
"YOUR MONEY OR YOUR LIFE!"

The first subway in the world was built in London between 1860 and 1863 and, although pow-ered with steam-driven locomotives, was a success. However, subways did not become truly prac-ticable until electricity was available as the source of power, and the great age of subway build-ing began with the second London subway, opened in 1890. Within the next thirty years many of the great cities of Europe and America had subway systems in operation. This print shows construction work on the London Underground. The Houses of Parliament are in the back-ground. [Mary Evans Picture Library.]

GROWTH OF MAJOR EUROPEAN CITIES
(FIGURES IN THOUSANDS)

	1850	1880	1910
Berlin	419	1,122	2,071
Birmingham	233	437	840
Frankfurt	65	137	415
London	2,685	4,470	7,256
Madrid	281	398	600
Paris	1,053	2,269	2,888
Vienna	444	1,104	2,031

over fifty million Europeans left their homelands. The major areas to benefit from this movement were the United States, Canada, Australia, South Africa, Brazil, and Argentina. At mid-century most of the emigrants were from Great Britain (and es-pecially Ireland), Germany, and Scandinavia. After 1885 the migration drew its numbers from south-ern and eastern Europe. This exodus helped to relieve the social and population pressures on the Continent. The outward movement of peoples in conjunction with Europe's economic and techno-logical superiority contributed heavily to the Euro-peanization of the world. Not since the sixteenth century had European civilization produced such an impact on other cultures.

The Second Industrial Revolution

As David Landes has suggested, "The period from 1850 to 1873 was the Continental industry's coming-of-age."[1] The gap that had existed for half a century between British and continental economic development was closed. The basic heavy industries of Belgium, France, and Germany underwent major expansion. French development was relatively slow, but steady. The rate of growth became more rapid after the Franco-Prussian War. The expansion of German industry was stunning. Coal mining, iron and steel production, and the chemical industry made rapid progress. German steel production surpassed that of Britain in 1893 and had almost doubled the British effort by the outbreak of World War I. This emergence of an industrial Germany was the major fact of European economic and political life at the turn of the century.

The systematic spread of railways continued to made a key contribution to economic development during the third quarter of the century. Railways cheapened transport costs and made wider regional and continental marketing possible. Railway building by Europeans in other parts of the globe created new overseas markets. The money spent on railways created demand elsewhere in the economy. Rail transportation, besides fostering capital industry and investment, put new pressure on European agriculture. Trains running into the great plains of the United States and steamships crossing the oceans sharply lowered the cost of grain and other foodstuffs imported into Europe. Continental farmers facing this foreign competition received lower prices for their produce.

Factors other than continued railway construction also accounted for the prosperity that followed hard on the heels of the economic troubles of the 1840s. From the 1850s to the early 1870s numerous countries negotiated treaties lowering tariffs, so that goods could flow more easily and cheaply from one nation to another. New laws permitting the formation of joint stock companies and easier business incorporation allowed the garnering of vast capital funds for investment. Such legal reforms favoring capital expansion were enacted in Britain in 1856, in France in 1863, and in Prussia in 1870. The gold standard, whereby any major currency could be exchanged for gold, brought new confidence to international trade. Throughout Europe the various national currencies became more uniform. Currency rationalization was a major achievement of German unification. Finally, large banks, such as the French Crédit Mobilier and the German Darmstädter Bank, channeled funds into capital investment rather than commerce. Finance capitalism had the power to determine to a large extent what enterprises would and would not be undertaken. Banks rather than individual entrepreneurs now seemed to guide the economy.

New Industries

Initially the economic expansion of the third quarter of the century involved the spread of industries similar to those pioneered earlier in Great Britain. Thereafter, however, wholly new industries emerged. It is this latter development that is usually termed the *Second Industrial Revolution*. The first Industrial Revolution was associated with textiles, steam, and iron; the second with steel, chemicals, electricity, and oil. Steel began to replace iron in manufacture and construction. It was stronger, more flexible, and more adaptable. Its uses seemed infinite. In the 1850s Henry Bessemer (1830–1898), an English engineer, discovered a new process, named after him, for manufacturing steel cheaply in large quantities. Bessemer had air injected directly into molten iron. The subsequent process of rapid oxidation allowed steel to be produced from the iron in larger quantities over the same period of time. In 1860 Great Britain, Belgium, France, and Germany had produced 125,000 tons of steel. By 1913 the figure had risen to 32,020,000 tons. Tied to the increased production were new processes for rolling and forming the molten metal for use in shipbuilding, machinery, and automobiles.

The chemical industry also came of age during this period. The Solway process of alkali production replaced the older Leblanc process. The new process allowed more chemical by-products to be recovered. More sulfuric acid could be produced and so could more laundry soap. New dyestuffs and plastics were also developed. The chemical industry, which has been so fundamental to the

---

[1] David S. Landes, *The Unbound Prometheus: Technological Change and Industrial Development in Western Europe from 1750 to the Present* (Cambridge, England: Cambridge University Press, 1969), p. 193.

The Second Industrial Revolution was a period of innovation and experimentation. These early experimental engines were used at Owens Colle Engineering in Manchester, England, at about the turn of the century. [Bettmann Archive.]

Inflating Tube.

In the 1890s bicycles rapidly became a popular and low-cost means of transportation. They have remained so among the working class in Europe to the present day. Here women workers are inflating the rubber tubes. Since rubber does not grow in Europe, the rubber for the tires often came from colonial holdings. [Bettmann Archive.]

quality of life in the twentieth century, represented the earliest example of a combination of scientific and industrial development. Formal scientific research had played only the most minimal role in early industrial development. Trial-and-error amateurism was then the order of the day. By late in the second half of the century chemists and physicists were increasingly called on to solve the problems of industry. This alliance of science, technology, and industry proved to be fundamental to economic development from the 1890s onward. As in so many other fields of the second Industrial Revolution, Germany led the way in fostering scientific research and education.

The most significant change for industry and eventually for everyday life was the application of electrical energy to production. Electricity was the most versatile and transportable source of power ever discovered. It could be employed to run either large or small machines and to make factory construction more efficient. Electricity was a mode of energy that could be taken to the machinery. The first major public power plant was constructed in Great Britain in 1881. Soon electric poles, lines, and generating stations dotted the European landscape. Electric lights were beginning to be used in homes. Streetcar and subway systems were electrified. The industries powered by electricity, in turn, produced more and more products that were run by electricity, so that the electrical industry grew rapidly on itself. Probably no single late-nineteenth-century development has so influenced the material lifestyle of this century.

The turn of the century also saw the emergence of the first large European demand for petroleum. The internal combustion engine was invented in 1876. When the German engineer Gottlieb Daimler (1834–1900) put it on four wheels and obtained a French patent in 1885, the automobile was born. France initially took the lead in auto manufacture, but for many years the car remained a novelty item that only the wealthy could afford. It was the American Henry Ford (1863–1947) who later made the automobile accessible to large numbers of people. The automobile and the new industrial and chemical uses for oil greatly expanded the demand for petroleum. Before the 1890s petroleum had been used primarily for lighting; soon it became the basis for transportation and much of the new chemical industry. Europe, then as now, was almost wholly dependent on imported oil. The major supplying companies were Standard Oil of the United States, British Shell Oil, and Royal Dutch.

The second Industrial Revolution witnessed a shift in the European economic balance of power. In almost all areas of the new industrial expansion Great Britain, which had pioneered the first Industrial Revolution, fell behind the Continent and especially Germany. Britain ceased to be a leader and became simply one more competitor. There was no lack of invention on the part of individual British citizens, but the early industrial lead meant that the nation's industries were often locked into existing production processes and could not easily incorporate new techniques. The British did too little to encourage scientific and technical education. Its managers put too much faith in the inventive amateur, who had so brilliantly fostered the early Industrial Revolution. British investors put too little capital into new industry. Management was immensely complacent. There was too much dependence on old marketing techniques. Attempts to improve the situation came only after the lead had been lost. All of these factors meant that by 1900, while still a great industrial power, Britain was falling behind German competition. This situation had much to do with the international political rivalry of the two powers.

Wider Economic Trends

Business Difficulties

The second half of the century was not a period of uninterrupted or smooth economic growth. The years from 1850 to 1873 saw a general boom in both industry and agriculture. The last quarter of the century witnessed economic advance but of a much slower nature. Bad weather and foreign competition put grave pressures on European agriculture. Grain producers suffered the most. In Britain thousands of acres of land went out of tillage. In eastern Europe the landlords demanded new protective tariffs. There were moves to specialize farming. Denmark, for example, at this time changed to dairy production. Other countries adopted more scientific and mechanized modes of agriculture. Farmers used fertilizers more frequently and took steam engines into the fields to aid in plowing. These techniques made farming more costly, and farms became larger. From the consumers' standpoint these developments meant

A Danish cooperative dairy. In the late nineteenth century, European agriculture was forced increasingly to specialize and to mechanize to meet the competition of cheap food imported from North and South America and from Russia. Denmark, for example, shifted from small-scale grain production to dairy farming in which many farmers often pooled their resources to cut costs. [Mon Museum, Stege, Denmark]

The first telephone exchange in Berlin exhibits the role of both communication and electricity in the second industrial revolution. In this picture men are attending the switchboard; soon, however, women took over these jobs. Telephone companies eventually opened a large area of employment for women. [Bettmann Archive.]

lower food prices. Nevertheless the difficulties of the agricultural sector put a drag on the general economy.

During 1873 a number of major banks failed, and the rate of capital investment slowed. The major railway systems had been built. During the next two decades stagnation occurred in several industries. Prices and profits fell. Wages also became lower, but the simultaneous fall in prices meant that real wages generally held firm and in some countries even improved. There were pockets of unemployment. (In fact the word *unemployment* was coined during this period.) Despite the stagnation, the general standard of living in the industrialized nations improved, although many workers still lived and labored in abysmal conditions. What made this depression less cruel and disruptive than the turmoil of the 1840s was the greater availability of consumer goods and the assurance of a food supply. By the turn of the century the demand for consumer goods and the development of new employing industries made possible by the second Industrial Revolution had lifted Europe from its economic doldrums.

What brought the economy out of this period of stagnation, which contemporaries regarded as a

The Crystal Palace, erected to house the Great Exhibition of 1851, was a fabulous structure of glass and iron designed by the horticulturist and architect Sir Joseph Paxton (1801–1865) and modeled after his greenhouses for the Duke of Devonshire. It originally stood in Hyde Park, London, but after the exhibition it was dismantled and re-erected at Sydenham, the location shown here. It was destroyed by fire in 1936. The Great Exhibition itself was an abundant display of the vast material accomplishments of the industrial revolution and liberal society. [Library of Congress.]

❧ Paris Department Stores Expand their Business

The department store in Europe and the United States became a major institution of retailing in the last half of the nineteenth century. It was one of the reasons for the expansion in late-century consumer demand. This description, written by the Frenchman E. Levasseur in 1907, follows the growth of such stores in Paris and explains why they exerted such considerable economic power. The reader will notice how many of their techniques of retailing are still used today.

It was in the reign of Louis-Philippe [1830–1848] that department stores for fashion goods and dresses . . . began to be distinguished. The type was already one of the notable developments of the Second Empire; it became one of the most important ones of the Third Republic. These stores have increased in number and several of them have become extremely large. Combining in their different departments all articles of clothing, toilet articles, furniture and many other ranges of goods, it is their special object so to combine all commodities as to attract and satisfy customers who will find conveniently together an assortment of a mass of articles corresponding to all their various needs. They attract customers by permanent display, by free entry into the shops, by periodic exhibitions, by special sales, by fixed prices, and by their ability to deliver the goods purchased to customers' homes, in Paris and to the provinces. Turning themselves into direct intermediaries between the producer and the consumer, even producing sometimes some of their articles in their own workshops, buying at lowest prices because of their large orders and because they are in a position to profit from bargains, working with large sums, and selling to most of their customers for cash only, they can transmit these benefits in lowered selling prices. They can even decide to sell at a loss, as an advertisement or to get rid of out-of-date fashions. . . .

The success of these department stores is only possible thanks to the volume of their business, and this volume needs considerable capital and a very large turnover. Now capital, having become abundant, is freely combined nowadays in large enterprises. . . . [T]he large urban agglomerations, the ease with which goods can be transported by the railways, the diffusion of some comforts to strata below the middle classes, have all favoured these developments. . . .

According to the tax records of 1891, these stores in Paris, numbering 12, employed 1,708 persons and rated their site values at 2,159,000 francs; the largest had then 542 employees. These same stores had, in 1901, 9,784 employees; one of them over 2,000 and another over 1,600; their site value was doubled.

Sidney Pollard and Colin Holmes, *Documents of European Economic History* (London: Edwin Arnold, 1972), vol. 3, pp. 95–96.

---

depression, was a new expansion of consumer demand. The lower food prices eventually allowed all classes to spend a marginally larger amount of their income on consumer goods. Urbanization in and of itself created a larger market. People living in cities simply saw more things they wanted to buy than they would have in the countryside. The new industries of the late century were largely directed toward consumer goods. Retailing techniques changed. Department stores, retail chains, new packaging, mail-order catalogs, and advertising were developed. Marketing itself was creating new demand. The foundations of a consumer economy were being laid. Furthermore the overseas imperialism of this period also opened new markets for European consumer goods.

Drift Away from Competition and Free Trade

The economic pressures of the last quarter of the century brought about a shift from economic competition to business consolidation. Big business firms and corporations were organized. They had no desire to compete because they had far too much to lose. Cartels and trade associations, which were the European version of the American trusts, were organized. They attempted to divide markets and to fix prices so as not to drive each other out of business. The great examples were the German General Electric Company, the German Siemens Electric Company, and the British Glass Manufacturers' Association. Other industries, such as the Krupp armaments company, organized vertically in order to control the sources of raw materials and product marketing as well as manufacturing. These new forms of business organization tended to stabilize industries, to make jobs more secure, and to increase consumer demand by creating more steady wages. They did not, however, necessarily produce the lowest consumer prices.

The mid-century ideal of free trade also came under increasing attack as both farming and manufacturing interests sought to ensure a monopoly in their national markets. Governments across the Continent raised new protective tariff barriers.

Austria and Russia turned to this device in 1874 and in 1877, respectively. In 1879 Bismarck imposed a tariff to protect German industry and the *Junker* landlords. Italy moved to protection in 1887, and the Third French Republic passed the Méline Tariff in 1892. Each of these measures was passed to bring new domestic political support to the various governments. Great Britain remained true to free trade. Yet even there, after the turn of the century Joseph Chamberlain (1836–1914) led a campaign for tariff reform. The drive for tariffs meant that business was seeking the kind of government aid that it had largely spurned half a century earlier.

Europeans also looked outside their continent for markets. The late-century age of imperialism was closely related to internal economic problems. European bankers invested large amounts of money in the rest of the world, with the largest portion going to the development of the United

The Krupp works at Essen, Germany, was one of the largest military manufacturing establishments in Europe. This late nineteenth-century photograph is taken in the gun shop. The massive production of such arms meant that in the early twentieth century Europeans would be able to turn on themselves more sheer physically destructive force than at any previous time in history. [Culver Pictures.]

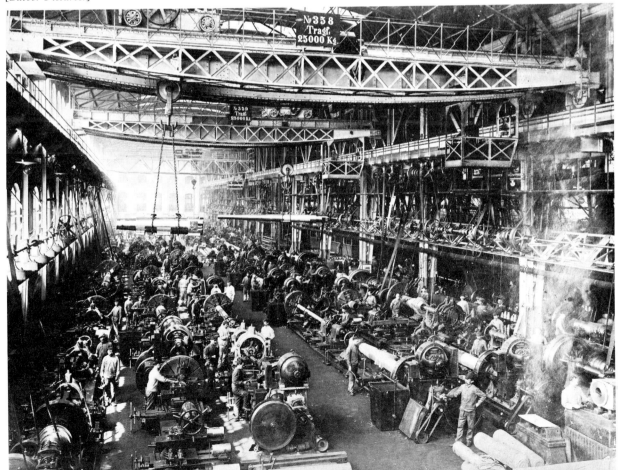

States. But traders and investors also hoped to reap profits from Latin America, Asia, and Africa. The early British textile industry had depended to a great extent on foreign markets. Britain's emulators in the latter part of the century also believed they must penetrate those areas. They needed both raw materials and new outlets for finished goods.

It was once argued that Europeans carved out their colonies in order to create those needed markets. The process is now considered more complicated. In establishing sources for raw materials and in creating markets for finished goods, the Europeans undermined the existing governments and the traditional societies in the underdeveloped portions of the globe. The result was political instability in those areas. It was after such turmoil had been created that the European governments moved in to protect the already-existing commercial presence of their nationals. The foreign markets never proved to be as profitable as their promoters hoped. Right up to World War I Europe itself remained the single largest market for its own goods.

At the close of the nineteenth century Europe clearly predominated in the world economy. It had the most capital, and its industries provided it with the military might to control other areas. However, within Europe two distinct economic zones had come into existence. One consisted of the advanced industrial states, including Britain, Belgium, France, Germany, northern Italy, and the western part of Austria. These areas enjoyed a relatively high standard of living, good transport systems, and healthy, educated populations. The second area consisted of Ireland, the Iberian Peninsula, southern Italy, the Balkans, most of Austria–Hungary, and Russia. There agricultural production dominated, and education was backward. These areas exported grain and foodstuffs to the industrialized sector. This European economic division, which came into being in the late nineteenth century, was not overcome until after World War II, and even then only partially.

Social Ramifications of the Second Industrial Revolution

The Middle Classes

The sixty years prior to World War I were definitively the age of the middle classes. The Great Ex-

hibition of 1851 held in the Crystal Palace in London had displayed the products and the new material life they had forged. Thereafter the middle classes became the arbiter of much consumer taste and the defender of the status quo. After the revolutions of 1848 the middle classes ceased to be a revolutionary group. Most of their political goals had been attained, even if imperfectly. Once the question of social· equality had been raised, large and small property owners across the Continent moved to protect what they possessed. In the late-century drive toward protective tariffs, new business organization, militarism, and empire, the upper levels of the middle class often joined political forces with the aristocracy and other groups such as the church and landowners from traditionally conservative social and political backgrounds.

DIVISIONS WITHIN THE MIDDLE CLASSES. The middle classes, which had never been perfectly homogeneous, now became even more diverse. Their most prosperous members were the owners and managers of great businesses and banks. They lived in a splendor that rivaled and sometimes excelled that of the aristocracy. Some, such as W. H. Smith, the owner of railway newsstands in England, were made members of the House of Lords. The Krupp family of Germany were pillars of the state and received visits from the German emperor and his court. Only a few hundred families acquired such wealth. Beneath them were the comfortable small entrepreneurs and professional people, whose incomes permitted private homes, large quantities of furniture, pianos, pictures, books, journals, education for their children, and vacations. There were also the shopkeepers, the schoolteachers, the librarians, and others who had either a bit of property or a skill derived from education that provided respectable, nonmanual employment. Finally, there was a wholly new element among the white-collar workers. These included secretaries, retail clerks, and lower-level bureaucrats in business and government. The white-collar labor force was often working class in its origins and might even belong to unions, but its aspirations for lifestyle were middle class. This lower-middle-class or petty-bourgeois element in society consciously sought to set itself off from the lifestyle of the working class. People from the lower middle class actively pursued educational opportunities and chances for even the slightest career advancement for themselves and their children. They also tended to spend a considerable portion of their disposable income on consumer goods, such as stylish clothing and furniture, that were distinctively middle-class in appearance.

Significant tensions began to exist among the various strata of middle-class society during the latter part of the century. The small businessmen and shopkeepers, whose numbers rose steadily until shortly after 1900, often resented the power of the great capitalists. The little people of the middle class feared being edged out of the marketplace by large companies, with whom they could not hope to compete. The shopkeeping class always had to work very hard simply to maintain their lifestyle and were often dependent on banks for commercial credit. Department stores and mail-order catalogs endangered their livelihood. There is also good reason to believe that the learned professions were becoming overcrowded. To be a professional person no longer ensured a sound income. The new white-collar work force had just attained respectability and a non-working-class status. They profoundly feared slipping back to their social origins.

Prior to World War I these social groups were reasonably secure but remained quite apprehensive: they feared that the business cycle might turn against them; that their small supplementary incomes from stocks, bonds, or interest from savings might disappear; that somehow the socialists might confiscate their property. After World War I many of those fears were realized. The profound insecurity that the middle classes then experienced became one of the most significant factors of twentieth-century political life.

THE MIDDLE-CLASS FAMILY AND WOMEN. During the late nineteenth century the lifestyle of the middle classes set the tone of the day. Machine-made clothes allowed them to dress well and alike. Machine-made furniture and wallpaper allowed their homes to appear similar. The productive processes they directed allowed the world of everyday life to assume a regularity and a conformity never before quite so possible. At the center of their lives was the family. Although equality and independence were the keynotes of their politics, the opposite qualities predominated in their homes. The bourgeois father presided over his household as a patriarch. Throughout the Continent he controlled most of his wife's property. He could still generally determine whom his daughter married. His son depended on his allowance. He and his sons maintained a double standard of sexual morality, demanding chastity from their sisters

and fidelity from their wives while perhaps frequenting brothels themselves. Women in the family setting were supposed to remain what the English poet Coventry Patmore termed "the angel of the house." Perhaps the middle-class male needed that firm structure of home life and domestic values because he knew that the business world in which he worked might collapse with the next trade cycle or bank panic.

Whatever the hypocrisy involved in this domestic situation, the nineteenth-century middle-class family, by providing a point of departure for social criticism, has proved a powerful force in forging the conscience of the modern world. There was little or no role in that family and home for an active, articulate, thinking woman. By allowing men to provide sufficient income for the entire family, the new industry and its related enterprises gave women only the most minimal economic role. Smaller families lessened child-rearing duties. The more idle the wife or daughter, the greater the evidence of the success of the husband and father. Yet both the ideology and the structures of liberal society generated a weakening of that situation.

Liberal society and its values neither automatically nor inevitably improved the lot of women. Those who pioneered female entry into the professions, activity on government commissions and school boards, or dispersal of birth control information faced grave social obstacles, personal humiliation, and often outright bigotry. However, the intellectual and political tools for their social critique were present in the society itself.

The rationalism and penchant for self-criticism that have characterized modern Western society manifested themselves in the movement to emancipate women. As early as 1792 in Britain Mary Wollstonecraft (1759–1797), in *The Vindication of the Rights of Woman*, had applied the revolutionary doctrines of the rights of man to the predicament of members of her own sex. John Stuart Mill (1806–1873), in conjunction with the thought of his wife, Harriet Taylor, had applied the logic of liberal freedom to the position of women in *The Subjection of Women* (1869). The arguments for utility and efficiency so dear to middle-class liberals could be used to expose the human and social waste implicit in the inferior role assigned to women. That waste was becoming increasingly demonstrated as women successfully pursued jobs in the professions, schoolteaching, social work, and other employment that had formerly been the preserves of men. New areas of female employment

Mary Wollstonecraft (1759–1797) was one of the first writers to call for equal rights for women. Shortly before her early death she was married to William Godwin, the English political writer and novelist. Their child was the future Mary Shelley, author of Frankenstein *and wife of the Romantic poet. The portrait by John Opie is in the National Portrait Gallery, London. [The Granger Collection.]*

In 1911 Mrs. Emmeline Pankhurst led major demonstrations of British suffragettes in favor of the vote for women. Several ended in violence. Here Mrs. Pankhurst is literally being carried off to jail. [Culver Pictures.]

❧ J. S. Mill Analyzes the Causes of the Subjection of Women

John Stuart Mill (1806–1873) was one of the key nineteenth-century advocates of women's rights. In this 1869 essay he was concerned that society benefit from the various talents and capacities that women could bring to the social, political, and intellectual problems of the day. He attempted to explain how custom, public opinion, and traditional education not only denied women their rightful place in society but also cunningly convinced them in numerous subtle ways that they could not achieve such a place.

Men do not want solely the obedience of women, they want their sentiments. . . . They have therefore put everything in practice to enslave their minds. . . . The masters of women wanted more than simple obedience, and they turned the whole force of education to effect their purpose. All women are brought up from the very earliest years in the belief that their ideal of character is the very opposite to that of men; not self-will, and government by self-control, but submission, and yielding to the control of others. All the moralities tell them that it is the duty of women, and all the current sentimentalities that it is their nature, to live for others; to make complete abnegation of themselves, and to have no life but in their affections. And by their affections are meant the only ones they are allowed to have—those to the men with whom they are connected, or to the children who constitute an additional and indefeasible tie between them and a man. When we put together three things—first, the natural attraction between opposite sexes; secondly, the wife's entire dependence on the husband, every privilege or pleasure she has being either his gift, or depending on his will; and lastly, that the principal object of human pursuit, consideration, and all objects of social ambition, can in general be sought or obtained by her only through him—it would be a miracle if the object of being attractive to men had not become the polar star of feminine education and formation of character. And, this great means of influence over the minds of women having been acquired, an instinct of selfishness made men avail themselves of it to the utmost as a means of holding women in subjection, by representing to them meekness, submissiveness, and resignation of all individual will into the hands of a man, as an essential part of sexual attractiveness.

John Stuart Mill, *On Liberty, Representative Government, The Subjection of Women* (London: Oxford University Press, 1960), pp. 443–444.

---

were also opened in clerical jobs. The growing consumer orientation of the economy also gave women new indirect power while they were still in the home. Moreover the socialist critique of capitalist society included a harsh indictment of the social and economic position to which women had been relegated.

Much of the discussion of the social position of women remained merely theory and talk. Some women did gain meaningful employment, but their numbers were small. Women did not rise rapidly through the work force. However, to some extent theory was transformed into practice, or at least protest, so far as political life was concerned. The political tactics used by men to expand the electoral franchise and to influence the governing processes could be and were employed by women toward the same end. The claims to political participation set forth by the respectable, prosperous, and educated working class applied equally well to women.

The most important prewar example of such activity was the British women's suffrage movement led by Mrs. Emmeline Pankhurst (1858–1928). Her husband, who died near the close of the century, had been active in labor and Irish nationalist politics. In 1903 Mrs. Pankhurst and her daughters, Christabel and Sylvia, founded the Women's Social and Political Union. For several years they and their followers, known derisively as *suffragettes*, lobbied publicly and privately for the extension of the vote to women. By 1910, having failed to move the government, they turned to the violent tactics of arson, window breaking, and sabotage of postal boxes. They marched en masse on Parliament. The Liberal government of Henry Asquith imprisoned many of the women and force-fed those who went on hunger strikes in jail. The government refused to extend the franchise. Only in 1918 did some British women receive the vote as a result of their contribution to the war effort. Prior to the war women could vote on national issues only in Norway and Finland. It required the social and emotional upheaval of World War I to bring women in significant numbers to a place of prominence and acceptance in European political life.

The Working Classes

The late-century industrial expansion wrought further changes in the life of the labor force. In all industrializing continental countries the numbers of the urban proletariat rose. Proportionally there were many fewer artisans and highly skilled workers. For the first time factory wage-earners came to predominate. The increasingly mechanized factories often required less highly technical skills from its operatives. There also occurred considerable growth in the very unskilled work associated with shipping, transportation, and building. Work assumed a more impersonal character. Factories were located in cities, and almost all links between factory or day-labor employment and home life dissolved. Large corporate enterprise meant less personal contact between employers and their workers.

On the whole, the standard of living improved throughout the second half of the century. However, that improvement was often more statistical than real. There still existed widespread poverty, poor housing, sweatshop working conditions, and the haunting fears of accident, disability, unemployment, and old age. Between 1900 and World War I, industrial labor discontent was distinctly on the rise as wages failed to keep up with rising prices. During the latter years of the nineteenth century a few big businesses attempted to provide some security for their employees through company housing and pension plans. Although these efforts were in a few cases pioneering, they could not prove adequate for the mass of the labor force.

TRADE UNIONISM. Workers still had to look to themselves for the improvement of their situation. However, after 1848 European workers ceased taking to the streets to voice their grievances in the form of riots. They also stopped trying to revive the paternal guilds and similar institutions of the past. After mid-century the labor force accepted the fact of modern industrial production and its general downgrading of skills and attempted to receive more benefits from that system. Workers turned to new institutions and ideologies.

Women working in the Cadbury candy factory in England. In the late nineteenth century, although most working women continued to be domestic servants, for the first time large numbers of women began to work in factories and retail stores. [Cadbury Limited, Bournville, England.]

This print by Gustave Doré from the third quarter of the nineteenth century portrays an institution in London where homeless persons might spend the night. The gentleman in the middle is reading the Bible to the derelicts who have come in off the street. Many such charitable institutions were closely connected to Christian churches.

Chief among these were trade unions, democratic political parties, and socialism.

Trade unionism came of age as legal protections were extended to unions throughout the second half of the century. Unions became fully legal in Great Britain in 1871 and were allowed to picket in 1875. In France Napoleon III had first used troops against strikes, but as his political power waned, he allowed weak labor associations in 1868. The Third French Republic fully legalized unions in 1884. After 1890 they could function in Germany with little disturbance. Initially most trade unions entered the political process in a rather marginal fashion. As long as the representatives of the tradi-

French glass workers strike at Carmaux in 1896. The right to strike was fiercely opposed by European industrialists and strikes were often long and bitter. This strike at Carmaux, for instance, lasted eighteen months. [Musee Jaures, Castres, France.]

Although the standard of living improved overall during the second half of the nineteenth century, poverty was by no means eradicated. In this drawing by the French artist Theophile Steinlen, indignant members of the middle class attack an obviously poor and hungry man who has stolen a loaf of bread. [New York Public Library Picture Collection.]

tional governing classes looked after labor interests, members of the working class rarely sought office themselves.

The mid-century organizational efforts of the unions were directed toward skilled workers. The goal was the immediate improvement of wages and working conditions. By the close of the century, industrial unions for unskilled workers were being organized. They were very large and included thousands of workers. They confronted extensive opposition from employers, and long strikes were frequently required to bring about employer acceptance. In the prewar decade there were an exceedingly large number of strikes throughout Europe as the unions attempted to raise wages to keep up with inflation. However, despite the advances of unions and the growth of their memberships in 1910 to approximately 3 million in Britain, 2 million in Germany, and 977,000 in France, they never included a majority of the industrial labor force. What the unions did represent was a new collective fashion in which workers could associate to confront the economic difficulties of their lives and to attain better security.

DEMOCRACY AND POLITICAL PARTIES. The democratic franchise provided workers with direct political influence, which meant that they could no longer be ignored. With the exception of Russia all the major European states adopted broad-based, if not perfectly democratic, electoral systems. Great Britain passed its second voting-reform act in 1867 and its third in 1884. Bismarck brought universal manhood suffrage to the German Empire in 1871. The French Chamber of Deputies was democratically elected. Universal manhood suffrage was adopted in Switzerland in 1879, in Spain in 1890, in Belgium in 1893, in the Netherlands in 1896, and in Norway in 1898. Italy finally fell into line in 1912. Democracy brought new modes of popular pressure to bear on all governments. It meant that discontented groups could now voice their grievances and advocate their programs within the institutions of government rather than from the outside.

The advent of democracy witnessed the formation for the first time in Europe of organized mass political parties, which had existed throughout the nineteenth century in the United States. In the liberal European states with narrow electoral bases most voters had been people of property who knew what they had at stake in politics. Organization had been minimal. The new expansion of the electorate brought into the political processes many people whose level of political consciousness, awareness, and interest was quite low. This electorate had to be organized and taught the nature of power and influence in the liberal democratic state. The organized political party—with its workers, newspapers, offices, social life, and discipline—was the vehicle that mobilized the new voters. The largest single group in these mass electorates was the working class. The democratization of politics presented the socialists with opportunities and required the traditional ruling classes to vie with the socialists for the support of the new voters.

Labor, Socialism, and Politics to World War I

Along with new opportunities, the trade unions and the democratic electorates created ideological and practical problems for European socialists. Both the economic dislocation of early industrialization and the exclusion of the workers from poli-

---

MAJOR DATES IN DEVELOPMENT OF SOCIALISM

1864	International Working Men's Association (the First International) founded
1875	German Social Democratic Party founded
1876	First International dissolved
1878	German antisocialist laws passed
1884	British Fabian Society founded
1889	Second International founded
1891	German antisocialist laws permitted to expire
	German Social Democratic Party's Erfurt Program
1895	French Confédération Générale du Travail founded
1899	Eduard Bernstein's *Evolutionary Socialism*
1902	Formation of the British Labor Party
	Lenin's *What Is to Be Done?*
1903	Bolshevik–Menshevik split
1904	"Opportunism" debated at the Amsterdam Congress of the Second International

---

tics had conditioned early socialist doctrines. Socialists of various kinds had called for major social changes, often involving violent revolution. However, unions, democracy, and rising standards of living meant that the ends of socialism might be attained within the existing political framework and without violent revolution. Moreover, as the labor force began to receive direct benefits from the expanding economy, they were less likely to desire its destruction. It was while working out these ideological and tactical problems that the European socialists entered the mainstream of European politics. The internal socialist conflicts of these years have continued to influence the movement in Europe and elsewhere to the present day.

Marx and the First International

Karl Marx himself made considerable accommodation to the new practical realities that developed during the third quarter of the century. He did not abandon the revolutionary doctrines of *The Communist Manifesto,* and in *Capital* (Vol. 1, 1867) he continued to predict the disintegration of capitalism. His private thoughts as revealed in his letters also remained quite revolutionary, but his practical, public political activity reflected a somewhat different approach.

In 1864 a group of British and French trade unionists founded the International Working Men's Association. Known as the First International, it encompassed in its membership a vast array of radical political types, including socialists, anarchists, and Polish nationalists. The First International allowed Marx, who was by then quite active in the London radical community, to write its inaugural address. In it he urged radical social change and the economic emancipation of the working class, but he also supported and approved efforts by workers and trade unions to reform the conditions of labor within the existing political and economic processes. He urged revolution but tempered the means. Privately he often criticized such reformist activity, but those writings were not made public until near the end of the century, and after his death.

During the late 1860s the First International gathered statistics, kept labor groups informed of mutual problems, provided a forum for the debate of socialist doctrine, and extravagantly proclaimed its own size and influence. From these debates and activities Marxism emerged as the single most important strand of socialism. In 1872 Marx and his supporters drove the anarchists out of the First International. Marx was determined to preserve the role of the state against the anarchist attack on authority and large political organizations. Through the meetings and discussions of the First International, German socialists became deeply impressed by Marx's thought. Because, as will be seen, they became the most important socialist party in Europe, they became the chief channel for the preservation and development of Marxist thought.

The First International proved to be a very fragile structure. The events surrounding the Paris Commune presented the final blow to its existence. Few socialists and only one real Marxist were involved in the commune. However, Marx, in a major pamphlet, glorified the commune as a genuine proletarian uprising. British trade unionists, who in 1871 were finally receiving new legal protection, wanted no connection with the crimes of the Parisians. The French authorities used the uprising to suppress socialist activity. Throughout Europe the events in Paris cast a pall over socialism. The First International held its last European congress in 1873. Its offices were then transferred to the United States, where it was dissolved in 1876. Thereafter the fate of socialism and the labor movement depended largely on the economic and political conditions of the individual European countries.

Great Britain: Fabianism and Early Welfare Programs

Neither Marxism nor any other form of socialism made significant progress in Great Britain, the most advanced industrial society of the day. There trade unions grew steadily and the members normally supported Liberal Party candidates. The "new unionism" of the late 1880s and the 1890s organized the dock workers, the gas workers, and similar unskilled groups. Employer resistance to unions heightened class antagonism. In 1892 Keir Hardie became the first independent working man to be elected to Parliament. The next year the small, socialist Independent Labor Party was founded, but it remained ineffective.

Until 1901 general political activity on the part of labor remained quite limited. The Taff Vale decision in that year by the House of Lords, however, removed the legal protection previously accorded union funds. The Trades Union Congress responded by launching the Labor Party. In the election of 1906 the fledgling party sent twenty-nine members to Parliament. Their goals as trade unionists did not yet encompass socialism. Along with this new political departure the British labor movement became more militant. There were scores of strikes before the war, as workers fought for wages to meet the rising cost of living. The government took a larger role than ever before in mediating these strikes, which in 1911 and 1912 involved the railways, the docks, and the mines.

British socialism itself remained primarily the preserve of intellectuals. H. M. Hyndman (1842–1921), a wealthy graduate of Eton, and William Morris (1834–1896), the poet and designer, read Marx's works avidly, but their Social Democratic Federation, founded in 1881, never had more than a handful of members. The socialists who exerted the most influence were the Fabian Society, founded in 1884. The society took its name from Q. Fabius Maximus, the Roman general who defeated Hannibal by waiting a very long time before attacking. Through its name the society intended to indicate a gradual approach to major social reform. Its leading members were Sydney

George Bernard Shaw was the most important British play-wright of the last three centuries. He was also an active Fabian Socialist and a key figure in the interpretation to the British of the Norwegian Henrik Ibsen's forward-looking plays and the German Richard Wagner's music. [Radio Times Hulton Picture Library.]

(1859–1947) and Beatrice (1858–1943) Webb, H. G. Wells (1866–1946), Graham Wallas (1858–1932), and George Bernard Shaw (1856–1950). Many of the Fabians were civil servants who believed that the problems of industry, the expansion of ownership, and the state direction of production could be achieved gradually, peacefully, and democratically. They sought to educate the country to the rational wisdom of socialism. They were particularly interested in modes of collective ownership on the municipal level, the so-called gas-and-water socialism.

The British government and the major political parties responded slowly to these various pressures. In 1903 Joseph Chamberlain launched his unsuccessful tariff-reform campaign to match foreign tariffs and to finance social reform through higher import duties. The campaign badly split the Conservative Party. After 1906 the Liberal Party, led by Henry Campbell-Bannerman (1836–1908) and after 1908 by Herbert Asquith (1852–1928), pursued a two-pronged policy. Fearful of losing seats in Parliament to the new Labor Party, they restored the former protection of the unions. Then, after 1909, with Chancellor of the Exchequer David Lloyd George (1863–1945) as the guiding light, the Liberal ministry undertook a broad program of social legislation. This included the establishment of labor exchanges, the regulation of the sweated labor trades, such as tailoring and lacemaking, and the National Insurance Act of 1911 to provide unemployment benefits and health care. The financing of these programs brought the House of Commons into conflict with

Beatrice and Sidney Webb, a photograph from the late 1920s. These most influential British Fabian Socialists wrote many books on governmental and economic matters, served on special parliamentary commissions, and agitated for the enactment of socialist policies. [Radio Times Hulton Picture Library.]

❧ Sidney Webb Relates Socialism to Democracy

> Members of the Fabian Society represented a major force in British socialism. They believed that through democracy the great social questions of the day could be addressed. They hoped to replace individualism by state action. In their view the goals of socialism could be achieved without revolution. Sidney Webb, whose views follow, and his wife, Beatrice, were frequent voices for the Fabians.

The main stream which has borne European society towards Socialism during the past 100 years is the irresistible progress of Democracy. . . .

In the present Socialist movement these two streams are united: advocates of social reconstruction have learnt the lesson of Democracy, and know that it is through the slow and gradual turning of the popular mind to new principles that social reorganization bit by bit comes. All students of society who are abreast of their time, Socialists as well as Individualists, realize that important organic changes can only be (1) democratic, and thus acceptable to a majority of the people, and prepared for in the minds of all; (2) gradual, and thus causing no dislocation, however rapid may be the rate of progress; (3) not regarded as immoral by the mass of the people, and thus
not subjectively demoralizing to them; and (4) in this country at any rate, constitutional and peaceful. Socialists may therefore be quite one with Radicals in their political methods. Radicals, on the other hand, are perforce realizing that mere political levelling is insufficient to save a State from anarchy and despair. Both sections have been driven to recognize that the root of the difficulty is economic; and there is every day a wider consensus that the inevitable outcome of Democracy is the control by the people themselves, not only of their own political organization, but, through that, also of the main instruments of wealth production; the gradual substitution of organized cooperation for the anarchy of the competitive struggle. . . . The economic side of the democratic ideal is, in fact, Socialism itself.

Sidney Webb, *Fabian Essays in Socialism* (Gloucester, Mass.: Peter Smith, 1967, originally published 1889), pp. 50–52.

---

the Conservative-dominated House of Lords. The result was the Parliament Act of 1911, which allowed the Commons to override the legislative veto of the upper chamber. The new taxes and social programs meant that in Britain, the home of nineteenth-century liberalism, the state was taking on an expanded role in the life of its citizens. The early welfare legislation was only marginally satisfactory to labor, many of whose members still thought they could gain more from the direct action of strikes.

France: "Opportunism" Rejected

French socialism gradually revived after the suppression of the Paris Commune. The institutions of the Third Republic provided a framework for legal activity. The major problem for French socialists was their own internal division rather than government opposition. There were no fewer than five separate parties, plus other independent socialists.

They managed to elect approximately forty members to the Chamber of Deputies by the early 1890s. Despite the lack of a common policy, the socialist presence aided the passage of measures to relieve workers from carrying identity cards and to provide for factory safety inspection and limited working hours and health care. In 1910 the republic inaugurated a scheme for voluntary pensions. However, the most important developments of French labor and socialism were not legislative.

At the turn of the century the two major factions of French socialism were led by Jean Jaurès (1859–1914) and Jules Guesde (1845–1922). Jaurès believed that socialists should cooperate with radical middle-class ministries to ensure the enactment of needed social legislation. Guesde opposed this policy, arguing that socialists could not with integrity support a bourgeois cabinet that they were theoretically dedicated to overthrow. The quarrel came to a head as a by-product of the Dreyfus affair. In 1899, as a means of uniting all supporters of Dreyfus, Prime Minister René Waldeck-Rousseau (1846–1904) appointed the socialist Allexander Millerand to the Cabinet. By 1904 the issue of "opportunism," as such cabinet participation by socialists was termed, came to be debated at the Amsterdam Congress of the Second International. This organization had been founded in 1889 in a new effort to unify the various national socialist parties and trade unions. The Amsterdam Congress condemned "opportunism" in France and ordered the French socialists to form a single party. Jaurès, believing socialist unity the most important issue in France, accepted the decision. French socialists began to work together, and by 1914 the recently united Socialist Party was the second largest group in the Chamber of Deputies. Socialist Party members would not again serve in a French Cabinet until the Popular Front Government of 1936.

The French labor movement, with deep roots in the Proudhonian doctrines of anarchism, was uninterested in both politics and socialism. French workers tended to vote socialist, but the unions avoided active political participation. The Confédération Générale du Travail was founded in 1895 and regarded itself as a rival to the socialist parties. Its leaders sought to improve the workers' conditions through direct action. They embraced the doctrines of syndicalism, which were most persuasively expounded by Georges Sorel (1847–1922) in *Reflections on Violence* (1908). This book enshrined the idea of the general strike as a means of generating worker unity and power. The strike tactic was quite different from the socialist idea of aiding the situation of labor through the action of the state. Strike action on the part of unions flourished between 1905 and 1914, and the Radical ministry on more than one occasion used troops against the strikers. Consequently, in France the forces of labor were suppressed by the liberal state, and the Socialist Party was locked into a doctrine of nonparticipation in the Cabinet, which effectively undermined its potential political influence.

Germany: Social Democrats and Revisionism

The judgment rendered by the Second International against French socialist participation in bourgeois ministries reflected a policy of permanent hostility to nonsocialist governments previously adopted by the German Social Democratic Party,

or SPD. The organizational success of this party more than any other single factor kept Marxist socialism alive into the latter part of the century. The party was founded in 1875. Its origins lay in the labor agitation of Ferdinand Lasalle (1825–1864), who wanted worker participation in German politics. His followers were joined by Wilhelm Liebknecht (1826–1900) and August Bebel (1840–

Under a Dutch banner calling for the proletariat of all lands to unite, a congress of the Second Socialist International meets in Amsterdam in 1904 to debate ideology and practical tactics. [Internationaal Instituut voor Sociale Geschiedenis, Amsterdam.]

A German cartoon from 1884 mocking the failure of Bismarck's anti-socialist legislation of 1878 to stem the growth of the German Social Democratic Party. In 1877 the party had received 500,000 votes and won 12 seats in the Reichstag. By 1890 its share had risen to 1.4 million votes and 35 seats. [Ullstein Bilderdienst, Berlin.]

1913), who were Marxists. Consequently the party was divided from its founding between those who wanted reformist political activity and those who advocated revolution.

The forging experience of the SPD was twelve years of persecution by Bismarck. The so-called Iron Chancellor believed that socialism would undermine German politics and society. Shortly after its founding, he moved against the young SPD. In 1878 there was an attempt to assassinate William I. Although the socialists were not involved, Bismarck used the opportunity to steer a number of antisocialist laws through the *Reichstag*. The measures suppressed the organization, meetings, newspapers, and other public activities of the SPD. To remain a socialist meant to remove oneself from the mainstream of respectable German life and possibly to lose one's job. The antisocialist legislation proved politically counterproductive. From the early 1880s onward the SPD steadily polled more and more votes in elections to the *Reichstag*.

As simple repression failed to separate German workers from socialist loyalties, Bismarck undertook a program of social welfare legislation. In 1883 the German Empire adopted a health insurance measure. The next year saw the enactment of accident insurance legislation. Finally, in 1889, Bismarck sponsored a plan for old age and disability pensions. These programs, to which both workers and employers contributed, represented a paternalistic, conservative alternative to socialism. The state itself would organize a system of social security that did not require any change in the system of property holding or politics. Germany became the first major industrial nation to enjoy this kind of welfare program.

In 1890, after forcing Bismarck's resignation, Emperor William II (1888–1918) allowed the antisocialist legislation to expire the next year in hopes of thus building new support for the monarchy among the working class. Even under the repressive laws members of the SPD could sit in the *Reichstag*. Now, however, the question became what attitude the recently legalized party should assume toward the German Empire. The answer came in the Erfurt Program of 1891, formulated under the political guidance of Bebel and the ideological tutelage of Karl Kautsky (1854–1938). In good Marxist fashion the program declared the imminent doom of capitalism and the necessity of socialist ownership of the means of production. However, these goals were to be achieved by legal political participation rather than by revolutionary activity. Because by its very nature capitalism must fall, the immediate task of socialists was to work for the improvement of workers' lives rather than for the revolution, which was inevitable. In theory the SPD was vehemently hostile to the German Empire, but in practice the party functioned within its institutions. The SPD members of the *Reichstag* maintained clear consciences by refusing to enter the Cabinet, to which they were not invited anyway, and by refraining for many years from voting for the military budget.

The situation of the SPD, however, generated the most important internal socialist challenge to the orthodox Marxist analysis of capitalism and the socialist revolution. Eduard Bernstein (1850–1932) was the author of this socialist heresy. He had spent over a decade of his life in Great Britain and was quite familiar with the Fabians. Bernstein questioned whether Marx and his later orthodox followers, such as Kautsky, had been correct in their pessimistic appraisal of capitalism and the necessity of revolution. In *Evolutionary Socialism* (1899) Bernstein pointed to the rising standard of living in Europe. Ownership of capitalist industry was becoming more widespread through stockholding.

❧ The German Empire Legislates Against the Socialists

Through these 1878 laws Bismarck hoped to destroy the young Social Democratic Party. The measures were intended to make it difficult for the SPD to hold meetings, publish newspapers and pamphlets, and collect money to support its activities. The antisocialist laws remained in effect until 1891.

1. *Associations which aim, by Social Democratic, Socialistic, or Communistic endeavours, at the destruction of the existing order in State or society, are to be forbidden. . . .*

. . . .

9. *Meetings in which Social Democratic, Socialistic, or Communistic tendencies, directed to the destruction of the existing order in State or society, make their appearance, are to be dissolved.*

Meetings, of which facts justify the assumption that they are destined to further such tendencies, are to be forbidden.

Public festivities and processions are placed under the same restrictions.

. . . .

11. *Printed matter, in which Social Democratic, Socialistic, or Communistic tendencies, directed to the destruction of the existing order in State and society in a manner dangerous to the peace, and, in particular, to the harmony between different classes of the population, make their appearance, is to be forbidden.*

In the case of periodical literature, the prohibition can be extended to any further issue, as soon as a single number has been forbidden under this law.

. . . .

16. *The collection of contributions for the furthering of Social Democratic, Socialistic, or Communistic endeavours, directed toward the destruction of the existing order in State or society, as also the public instigation to the furnishing of such contributions, are [sic] to be forbidden by the police.*

. . . .

28. *For districts or localities which are threatened, by the above-mentioned endeavours, with danger to the public safety, the following provisions can be made, for the space of a year at most, by the central police of the state in question, and subject to the permission of the* Bundesrath *[the upper chamber of the Parliament].*

(1) *That meetings may only take place with the previous permission of the police; this prohibition does not extend to meetings for an election to the* Reichstag *or the Diet.*

(2) *That the distribution of printed matter may not take place in public roads, streets, or places, or other public localities.*

(3) *That residence in such districts or localities can be forbidden to all persons from whom danger to the public safety or order is to be feared.*

(4) *That the possession, import, or sale of weapons is forbidden, limited, or confined by certain conditions.*

Bertrand Russell, *German Social Democracy* (London: Longmans, Green, 1896), pp. 100–102.

Eduard Bernstein, here shown late in life, was the father of democratic socialism in Europe. His revisionist theories sharply divided the German socialist camp at the turn of the century. [The Granger Collection.]

Rosa Luxemburg (1870–1919) was a German radical who strongly supported the revolutionary concept of socialism. She was assassinated while in prison. [The Granger Collection.]

The middle class was not falling into the ranks of the proletariat and was not identifying its problems with those of the workers. The inner contradictions of capitalism as expounded by Marx had simply not developed. Moreover the opening of the franchise to the working class meant that revolutionary change might be achieved through parliamentary methods. What was required to realize a humane socialist society was not revolution but more democracy and social reform.

Bernstein's doctrines, known as *revisionism,* were widely debated among German socialists and were finally condemned as theory. His critics argued that evolution toward social democracy might be possible in liberal, parliamentary Britain, but not in authoritarian, militaristic Germany, with its basically powerless *Reichstag.* The critics were probably

correct about the German political scene. Nonetheless, while still calling for revolution, the SPD pursued a course of action similar to that advocated by Bernstein. Its trade union members, prospering within the German economy, did not want revolution. Its grass-roots members wanted to consider themselves patriotic Germans as well as good socialists. Its leaders feared any actions that might renew the persecution that they had experienced under Bismarck. Consequently the party worked at elections, membership expansion, and short-term political and social reform. It prospered and became one of the most important institutions of imperial Germany. Even some middle-class Germans voted for it as a means of opposing the illiberal institutions of the empire. And in August 1914, after long debate among themselves, the

SPD members of the *Reichstag* abandoned their former stance and unanimously voted for the war credits that would finance World War I.

Russia: Industrial Development and the Birth of Bolshevism

During the last decade of the nineteenth century Russia entered the industrial age and confronted many of the problems that the more advanced nations of the Continent had experienced fifty or seventy-five years earlier. Unlike those other countries Russia had to deal with major political discontent and economic development simultaneously. Russian socialism reflected that peculiar situation.

WITTE'S PROGRAM FOR INDUSTRIAL GROWTH. The emancipation of the serfs in 1861 had brought little agricultural progress. The peasants remained burdened with redemption payments, local taxes, excessive national taxes, and falling grain prices. There were few attempts to educate the peasantry in the more advanced techniques of farming. Most of the land held by free peasants was owned communally through the *mir*, or village. This system of ownership was extremely inefficient and employed strip farming and the farming of small plots. Between 1860 and 1914 the population of European Russia rose from approximately 50 million to approximately 103 million people. Land hunger spread among the peasants. There was intense agrarian discontent. Peasants with too little land still had to work on larger noble estates or for more prosperous peasant farmers known as *kulaks*. Uprisings in the countryside were a frequent problem. The agricultural sector benefited little from the late-century industrialism.

Alexander III and, after him, Nicholas II were determined that Russia should become an industrial power. Only by this means could the country maintain its military position and its diplomatic role in Europe. The person who led Russia into the industrial age was Sergei Witte (1849–1915). After a career in railways and other private business, he was appointed finance minister in 1892. Witte epitomized the nineteenth-century modernizer who pursued a policy of planned economic development, protective tariffs, high taxes, the gold standard, and efficiency. He established a strong financial link with the French money market, which led to later diplomatic cooperation between Russia and France.

Witte favored heavy industries. Between 1890 and 1904 the Russian railway system grew from 30,596 kilometers to 59,616 kilometers. The 5,000-mile Trans-Siberian Railroad was almost completed. Coal output more than tripled during the same period. There was a vast increase in pig-iron production, from 928,000 tons in 1890 to 4,641,000 tons in 1913. During the same period steel production rose from 378,000 tons to 4,918,000 tons. Textile manufacturing continued to expand and still constituted the single largest industry. The factory system began to be used more extensively throughout the country.

Industrialism brought considerable social discontent to Russia, as it had elsewhere. Landowners felt that foreign capitalists were earning too much of the profits. The peasants saw their grain exports and tax payments finance development that did not measurably improve their lives. A small but significant industrial proletariat arose. At the turn of the century there were approximately three mil-

Count Sergei Witte was the major planner of industrialism in late nineteenth-century Russia. [The Granger Collection.]

lion factory workers in Russia. Their working and living conditions were very bad by any standard. They enjoyed little state protection, and trade unions were illegal. In 1897 Witte did enact a measure providing for an 11½-hour workday. But needless to say, discontent and strikes continued.

New political departures accompanied the economic development. In 1901 the Social Revolutionary Party was founded. Its members and intellectual roots went back to the Populists of the 1870s. The party opposed industrialism and looked to the communal life of rural Russia as a model for the economic future. In 1903 the Constitutional Democratic Party, or Cadets, was formed. They were liberal in outlook and were drawn from people who participated in the local *zemstvos*. They wanted a parliamentary regime with responsible ministries, civil liberties, and economic progress. The Cadets hoped to model themselves on the liberal parties of western Europe.

LENIN'S EARLY THOUGHT AND CAREER. The situation for Russian socialists differed radically from that in other major European countries. Russia had no representative institutions and only a small working class. The compromises and accommodations achieved elsewhere were meaningless in Russia, where socialism in both theory and practice had to be revolutionary. The Russian Social Democratic Party had been established in 1898, but the repressive policies of the czarist regime meant that the party had to function in exile. It was Marxist, and its members greatly admired the German Social Democratic Party.

The leading late nineteenth-century Russian Marxist was Gregory Plekhanov (1857–1918), who wrote from his exile in Switzerland. At the turn of the century his chief disciple was Vladimir Illich Ulyanov (1870–1924), who later took the name of Lenin. The future leader of the Communist Revolution had been born in 1870 as the son of a high bureaucrat. His older brother, while a student in Saint Petersburg, had become involved in radical politics. He was arrested for participating in a plot against Alexander III and was executed in 1887. In 1893 Lenin moved to Saint Petersburg, where he studied to become a lawyer. Soon he, too, was drawn to the revolutionary groups among the factory workers. He was arrested in 1895 and exiled to Siberia. In 1900, after his release, Lenin left Russia for the West. He spent most of the next seventeen years in Switzerland.

Once in Switzerland Lenin became deeply in-volved in the organizational and policy disputes of the exiled Russian Social Democrats. They all considered themselves Marxists, but they held differing positions on the proper nature of a Marxist revolution in primarily rural Russia and on the structure of their own party. Unlike the backward-looking Social Revolutionaries, the Social Democrats were modernizers who favored further industrial development. The majority believed that Russia must develop a large proletariat before the revolution could come. This same majority hoped to mold a mass political party like the German SPD.

Lenin dissented from both positions. In *What Is to Be Done?* (1902) he condemned any accommodations, such as those practiced by the German SPD. He also criticized a trade unionism that settled for short-term gains rather than true revolutionary change for the working class. Lenin further rejected the concept of a mass party composed of workers. Revolutionary consciousness would not arise spontaneously from the working class. It must be carried to them by "people who make revolutionary activity their profession."[2] Only a small elite party would possess the proper dedication to revolution and be able to resist penetration by police spies. The guiding principle of that party should be "the strictest secrecy, the strictest selection of members, and the training of professional revolutionaries."[3]

In 1903, at the London Congress of the Russian Social Democratic Party, Lenin forced a split in the party ranks. During much of the congress Lenin and his followers lost votes on various questions put before the body. But near the close Lenin's group mustered a very slim majority. Thereafter Lenin's faction assumed the name *Bolsheviks*, meaning "majority," and the other, more moderate, democratic revolutionary faction became known as the *Mensheviks*, or "minority." There was, of course, a considerable public relations advantage to the name *Bolshevik*. (In 1912 the Bolsheviks organized separately.) In 1905 Lenin complemented his organizational theory with a program for revolution in Russia. *Two Tactics of Social Democracy in the Bourgeois-Democratic Revolution* urged that the socialist revolution unite the proletariat and the peasants. Lenin grasped better than any other revolu-

[2] Quoted in Albert Fried and Ronald Sanders (Eds.), *Socialist Thought: A Documentary History* (Garden City, N.Y.: Anchor Doubleday, 1964), p. 459.
[3] Ibid., p. 468.

❧ Lenin Argues for the Necessity of a Secret and Elite Party of Professional Revolutionaries

Social democratic parties in Western Europe had mass memberships and generally democratic structures of organization. In this passage from *What Is To Be Done?* (1902) Lenin explained why the autocratic political conditions of Russia demanded a different kind of organization for the Russian Social Democratic Party. Lenin's ideas became the guiding principles of Bolshevik organization.

I assert that it is far more difficult [for government police] to unearth a dozen wise men than a hundred fools. This position I will defend, no matter how much you instigate the masses against me for my "anti-democratic" views, etc. As I have stated repeatedly, by "wise men," in connection with organisation, I mean professional revolutionaries, irrespective of whether they have developed from among students or working men. I assert: (1) that no revolutionary movement can endure without a stable organisation of leaders maintaining continuity; (2) that the broader the popular mass drawn spontaneously into the struggle, which forms the basis of the movement and participates in it, the more urgent the need for such an organisation, and the more solid this organisation must be . . . ; (3) that such an organisation must consist chiefly of people professionally engaged in revolutionary activity; (4) that in an autocratic state [such as Russia], the more we confine the membership of such an organisation to people who are professionally engaged in revolutionary activity and who have been professionally trained in the art of combating the political police, the more difficult will it be to unearth the organisation; and (5) the greater will be the number of people from the working class and from other social classes who will be able to join the movement and perform active work in it. . . .

The only serious organisation principle for the active workers of our movement should be the strictest secrecy, the strictest selection of members, and the training of professional revolutionaries.

Albert Fried and Ronald Sanders (Eds.), *Socialist Thought: A Documentary History* (Garden City, N.Y.: Anchor Doubleday, 1964), pp. 460, 468.

tionary the profound discontent in the Russian countryside. He knew that an alliance of workers and peasants in rebellion probably could not be suppressed. Lenin's two principles of an elite party and a dual social revolution allowed the Bolsheviks, in late 1917, to capture leadership of the Russian Revolution and to transform the political face of the modern world.

THE REVOLUTION OF 1905 AND ITS AFTERMATH. The quarrels among the Russian socialists and Lenin's doctrines had no immediate influence on events in their country itself. Industrialization proceeded and continued to stir resentment in many sectors. In 1903 Nicholas II dismissed Witte, hoping to quell the criticism. The next year Russia went to war with Japan, partly in expectation that public opinion would rally to the czar. However, the result was Russian defeat and political crisis. The Japanese captured Port Arthur early in 1905.

A few days later, on January 22, a priest named Father Gapon led several hundred workers to present a petition to the czar for the improvement of industrial life. As the petitioners approached the Winter Palace in Saint Petersburg, the czar's troops opened fire. About one hundred people were shot down in cold blood, and many more were wounded. Never again after this event, known as Bloody Sunday, would the Russian people see the czar as their protector and "little father."

During the next ten months revolutionary disturbances spread throughout Russia: sailors mutinied; peasant revolts erupted; and property was attacked. The uncle of Nicholas II was assassinated. Liberal Constitutional Democrat leaders from the *zemstvos* demanded political reform. Student strikes occurred in the universities. Social Revolutionaries and Social Democrats were active

On "Bloody Sunday," January 22, 1905, troops of Czar Nicholas II fired on a peaceful procession of workers who sought to present a petition at the Winter Palace in St. Petersburg. After this day there was little chance that the Russian working class could be reconciled with the existing government. [Soviet Life *from Sovfoto.*]

among urban working groups. In early October 1905 strikes broke out in Saint Petersburg, and for all practical purposes worker groups, called *soviets*, controlled the city. Nicholas II recalled Witte and issued the October Manifesto, which promised Russia constitutional government.

Early in 1906 Nicholas II announced the election of a Duma with two chambers. However, he reserved to himself ministerial appointments, financial policy, military matters, and foreign affairs. The April elections returned a very radical group of representatives. The czar dismissed Witte and replaced him with P. A. Stolypin (1862–1911), who had little sympathy for parliamentary government. Within four months Stolypin persuaded Nicholas

to dissolve the Duma. A second assembly was elected in February 1907. Again cooperation proved impossible, and dissolution of that Duma came in June of that year. The czar then changed the franchise to ensure a conservative parliament. The third Duma, elected on the new basis in late 1907, proved sufficiently pliable for the czar and his minister. Thus within two years of the 1905 Revolution, Nicholas II had recaptured much of the ground he had conceded.

Stolypin set about repressing rebellion, removing some causes of the revolt, and rallying property owners behind the czarist regime. Early in 1907 special field courts-martial tried rebellious peasants, with almost seven hundred executions resulting. Before turning to this repression, the minister had canceled any redemptive payments that the peasants still owed to the government from the emancipation of the serfs in 1861. This step, undertaken in November 1906, was part of a more general policy to eradicate communal land ownership. The peasants were encouraged to assume individual proprietorship of their land holdings and to abandon to communal system associated with the *mirs*. Stolypin believed that farmers working for themselves would be more productive. Agriculture did improve through this policy and through instruction of the peasants in better farming methods. The very small peasant proprietors who sold their land increased the size of the industrial labor force.

Russian moderate liberals who sat in the Duma approved of the new land measures. They liked the idea of competition and individual property ownership. The Constitutional Democrats wanted a more genuinely parliamentary mode of government, but they compromised out of fear of new revolutionary disturbances. There still existed widespread hatred of Stolypin among the older conservative groups in the country. The industrial workers were antagonistic to the czar. In 1911 Stolypin was shot by a Social Revolutionary, who may have been a police agent in the pay of conservatives. Nicholas II found no worthy successor. His government simply continued to muddle along. At court the monk Grigori Efimovich Rasputin (1871?–1916) came into ascendancy because of his alleged power to heal the czar's hemophilic son, the heir to the throne. The undue influence of this

❧ Russian Workers Attempt to Present a Petition to the Czar

Growing unrest in Russia led to, among other things, the organization in 1903 of the Assembly of Russian Factory and Mill Workers of Saint Petersburg under a priest, Father Gapon. On January 22, 1905, the assembly was able to muster a large crowd of workers to converge on Czar Nicholas II's Winter Palace in the hope of peacefully presenting a petition detailing urban grievances and outlining a program of widespread industrial, political, and economic reform. Rather than allow access to the czar, security forces, commanded by the czar's uncle, fired on the crowd. This is the petition's preamble.

We, working men and inhabitants of St. Petersburg of various classes, our wives and our children and our helpless old parents, come to Thee, Sire, to seek for truth and defence. We have become beggars; we have been oppressed; we are burdened by toil beyond our powers; we are scoffed at; we are not recognized as human beings; we are treated as slaves who must suffer their bitter fate and who must keep silence. We suffered, but we are pushed farther into the den of beggary, lawlessness, and ignorance. We are choked by despotism and irresponsibility, and we are breathless. . . . The first request which we made was that our masters should discuss our needs with us; but this they refused, on the ground that no right to make this request is recognized by law. They also declared to be illegal our requests to diminish the working hours to eight hours daily, to agree with us about the prices for our work, to consider our misunderstandings with the *inferior administration of the mills, to increase the wages for the labour of women and of general labourers, so that the minimum daily wage should be one ruble per day, to abolish overtime work, to give us medical attention without insulting us, to arrange the workshops so that it might be possible to work there, and not find in them death from awful draughts and from rain and snow. All these requests appeared to be, in the opinion of our masters and of the factory and mill administrations, illegal. Everyone of our requests was a crime, and the desire to improve our condition was regarded by them as impertinence, and as offensive to them.*

. . . In reality in us, as in all Russian people, there is not recognized any human right, not even the right of speaking, thinking, meeting, discussing our needs, taking measures for the improvement of our condition.

James Mavor, *An Economic History of Russia* (London: J. M. Dent, 1914), pp. 469–470.

Grigori Rasputin was the sinister Russian monk who claimed the power to heal the ill son of Czar Nicholas II and acquired great influence at court. His presence alienated many politically important persons from support of Nicholas. Rasputin was finally assassinated by a group of Russian noblemen. [The Granger Collection.]

strange and uncouth man, the continued social discontent, and the conservative resistance to any further liberal reforms rendered the position and policy of the czar uncertain after 1911. Once again, as in 1904, he and his ministers thought that some bold move on the diplomatic front might bring the regime the broad popular support that it so desperately needed.

The domestic political situation in Russia was only the most extreme version of a pattern that appeared in several of the major European states. Potential or actual political and social unrest existed in Great Britain, France, Germany, Austria, and Russia. It was not at all certain that moderate political concessions could quiet the unrest of the working classes. Conservative governments were looking for some means whereby they might overcome social divisions and avoid further social change and revolution. From the French Revolution onward, war had been the one vehicle that had overcome the social and political cleavages in nations. It would be incorrect to say that this desire for national unity led the European governments to adopt war policies in 1914, but those anxieties may have made them less eager to turn back from the wider conflict. In other words, the domestic social problems experienced by the major governments of Europe were closely related to their diplomatic policy.

Suggested Readings

A. ASHWORTH, *A Short History of the International Economy Since 1850*, rev. ed. (1967). An introductory survey.

J. A. BANKS, *Prosperity and Parenthood: A Study of Family Planning among the Victorian Middle Classes* (1954). Probably the most sensitive and sensible study of the subject.

R. E. CAMERON, *France and the Industrial Development of Europe, 1800–1914*, rev. ed. (1968). The best treatment of the subject.

C. M. CIPOLLA, *The Economic History of World Population* (1962). A basic introduction.

P. GAY, *The Dilemma of Democratic Socialism: Eduard Bernstein's Challenge to Marx* (1952). A clear presentation of the problems raised by Bernstein's revisionism.

H. GOLDBERG, *A Life of Jean Jaurés* (1962). A splendid biography that explains the problems of the French socialists.

O. J. HALE, *The Great Illusion, 1901–1914* (1971). An excellent treatment based on the most recent scholarship.

S. HARCAVE, *First Blood: The Russian Revolution of 1905* (1964). A useful introduction.

C. J. H. HAYES, *A Generation of Materialism, 1871–1900* (1941). A classic account of the close of the century.

W. HENDERSON, *The Rise of German Industrial Power* (1976). A straightforward account.

E. J. HOBSBAWM, *The Age of Capital* (1975). Explores the consolidation of middle-class life after 1850.

L. JENKS, *The Migration of British Capital to 1875* (1927). The basic discussion of a key topic in European economic history.

J. JOLL, *The Second International* (1954). A straightforward treatment of the divisions among socialists before World War I.

K. KOLAKOWSKI, *Main Currents of Marxism: Its Rise, Growth, and Dissolution*, 3 vols. (1978). The relevant sections on the last years of the nineteenth century and the early years of the twentieth are especially good.

D. Landes, *The Unbound Prometheus: Technological Change and Industrial Development in Western Europe from 1750 to the Present* (1969). Includes excellent discussions of late-century development.

G. Lichtheim, *Marxism: An Historical and Critical Study* (1961). Perhaps the clearest one-volume discussion of the development of Marxist thought.

A. J. Mayer, *The Persistence of the Old Regime in Europe to the Great War* (1981). An interesting and very controversial book that argues that less political and social change occurred in the nineteenth century than has usually been thought.

A. H. McBriar, *Fabian Socialism and English Politics, 1884–1918* (1962). The standard discussion.

H. Moller (Ed.), *Population Movements in Modern European History* (1964). A collection of helpful and important articles.

H. Pelling, *The Origins of the Labour Party, 1880–1900* (1965). Examines the sources of the party in the activities of British socialists and trade unionists.

D. L. Russel (Ed.), *The Family in Imperial Russia* (1978). A collection of essays on a little investigated subject.

C. E. Schorske, *German Social Democracy, 1905–1917* (1955). A brilliant study of the difficulties of the Social Democrats under the empire.

J. Scott, *The Glassworkers of Carmaux: French Craftsmen and Political Action in a Nineteenth-Century City* (1974). A classic analysis of the manner in which highly skilled craftsmen confronted and were eventually defeated by the mechanization of their industry.

C., R., and L. Tilly, *The Rebellious Century, 1830–1930* (1975). A pioneering study of the nature of collective violence in European society.

A. B. Ulam, *The Bolsheviks: The Intellectual and Political History of the Triumph of Communism in Russia* (1965). Early chapters discuss prewar developments and the formation of Lenin's doctrines.

M. Vicinus, *Suffer and Be Still: Women in the Victorian Age* (1972). A series of excellent essays on Victorian women.

T. H. Von Laue, *Sergei Witte and the Industrialization of Russia* (1963). A useful account of the last great minister of czarist Russia.

E. Weber, *Peasants into Frenchmen: The Modernization of Rural France, 1870–1914* (1976). An important and fascinating work on the transformation of French peasants into self-conscious citizens of the nation state.

28 The Birth of Contemporary European Thought

DuﾟURING the same period that the modern nation-state developed and the second Industrial Revolution laid the foundations for the modern material lifestyle, the ideas and concepts that have marked European thought for much of the present century took shape. Like previous intellectual changes, these arose from earlier patterns of thought. The Enlightenment provided late nineteenth-century Europeans with a heritage of rationalism, toleration, cosmopolitanism, and appreciation of science. Romanticism led them to value feelings, imagination, national identity, and the autonomy of the artistic experience. By 1900 these strands of thought had become woven into a new fabric. Many of the traditional intellectual signposts were disappearing. The death of God had been proclaimed. Christianity had undergone the most severe attack in its history. The picture of the

The main reading room of the Bibliotheque Nationale in Paris, designed by H. P. F. Larouste in 1862. The development of widespread literacy in Western Europe in the nineteenth century led to an increased demand for reading matter and libraries. [Graphic Photo.]

physical world that had dominated since Newton had undergone major modification. The work of Darwin and Freud had challenged the special place that Western thinkers had assigned to humankind. The value long ascribed to rationality was being questioned. The political and humanitarian ideals of liberalism and socialism gave way for a time to new, aggressive nationalism. At the turn of the century European intellectuals were more daring than ever before, but they were also probably less certain and less optimistic.

The New Reading Public

The social context of intellectual life changed in the last half of the nineteenth century. For the first time in Europe a mass reading public came into existence. In 1850 approximately half the population of western Europe and a much higher proportion of Russians were illiterate. Even those people who might technically be capable of reading and writing did so very poorly. The literacy of the Continent improved steadily, as from the 1860s on-

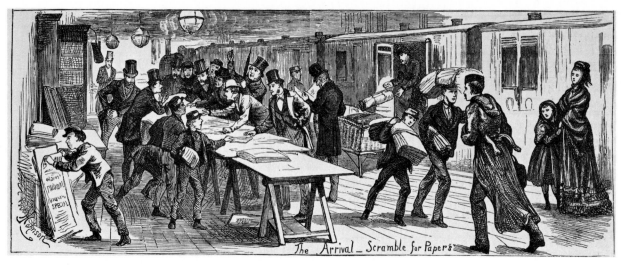

Travelers at an English railway station rushing to buy newspapers in 1875. The late nineteenth century was the heyday of the cheap, mass-circulation newspaper. The enormous new reading public had an insatiable appetite for news. [New York Public Library Picture Collection.]

ward one government after another undertook state-financed education. Hungary provided elementary education in 1868; Britain, in 1870; Switzerland, in 1874; Italy, in 1877; and France, between 1878 and 1881. The already advanced education system of Prussia was extended in various ways throughout the German Empire after 1871. The attack on illiteracy proved most successful in Britain, France, Belgium, the Netherlands, Germany, and Scandinavia, where by 1900 approximately 85 per cent or more of the people could read. Italy, Spain, Russia, Austria-Hungary, and the Balkans lagged well behind, with illiteracy rates of between 30 and 60 per cent.

The new primary education in the basic skills of reading and writing and elementary arithmetic reflected and generated social change. Both liberals and conservatives regarded such minimal training as necessary for orderly political behavior on the part of the newly enfranchised voters. There was also hope that literacy might help the poor to help themselves and might create a better, more productive labor force. This side of the educational crusade embodied the rationalist faith that right knowledge will lead to right action. However, literacy and its extension soon became forces in their own right. The schoolteaching profession grew rapidly in numbers and prestige. Those people who learned to read the little they were taught could continue to read much more on their own.

They soon discovered that the education that led to better jobs and political influence was still open only to those who could afford it. Having created systems of primary education, the major nations had to give further attention to secondary education by the time of World War I. In yet another generation the question would become one of democratic university instruction.

The expanding literate population created a vast market for new reading material. There was nothing less than an explosion of printed matter. Advances in printing and paper technology lowered production costs. The number of newspapers, books, and libraries grew rapidly. Cheap mass-circulation newspapers, such as *Le Petit Journal* of Paris and the *Daily Mail* and *Daily Express* of London, enjoyed their first heyday. Newspapers with very specialized political or religious viewpoints were also published. The number of monthly and quarterly journals for families, women, and free-thinking intellectuals increased. Probably more people with more different kinds of ideas could get into print in the late nineteenth century than ever before in European history. And more people could read their ideas than ever before.

The quantity of readers and reading material did not ensure quality. The cheap newspapers prospered on stories of sensational crimes and political scandal and on pages of advertising. Religious journals depended on denominational ri-

Matthew Arnold Contemplates the Loss of Intellectual Certainties

In this poem, written in 1867, Matthew Arnold (1822–1888) portrayed a man and a woman looking across the waters of the English Channel on a moonlit night. The speaker in the poem notes that Sophocles, the ancient Greek dramatist, had drawn lessons about the misery of life from the ebb and flow of the Aegean Sea. The speaker then compares the movement of the sea to the withdrawal of the Christian faith from the lives of nineteenth-century men and women. Finally, he says that the world that seems so beautiful is really a place where there can be no certainty, love, light, or peace. This pessimism reflects the state of mind of many writers who were no longer sure of the truth of the Christian faith.

DOVER BEACH

The sea is calm to-night.
The tide is full, the moon lies fair
Upon the Straits;—on the French coast the light
Gleams and is gone; the cliffs of England stand,
Glimmering and vast, out in the tranquil bay,
Come to the window, sweet is the night air!
Only, from the long time of spray
Where the sea meets the moon-blanch'd land,
Listen! you hear the grating roar
Of pebbles which the waves draw back, and fling,
At their return, up the high strand,
Begin, and cease, and then again begin,
With tremulous cadence slow, and bring
The eternal note of sadness in.

Sophocles long ago
Heard it on the Aegean, and it brought
Into his mind the turbid ebb and flow
Of human misery; we

Find also in the sound a thought,
Hearing it by this distant northern sea.

The Sea of Faith
Was once, too, at the full, and round earth's shore
Lay like the folds of a bright girdle furl'd.
But now I only hear
Its melancholy, long, withdrawing roar,
Retreating, to the breath
Of the night-wind, down the vast edges drear
And naked shingles of the world.

Ah, love, let us be true
To one another! for the world, which seems
To lie before us like a land of dreams,
So various, so beautiful, so new,
Hath really neither joy, nor love, nor light,
Nor certitude, nor peace, nor help for pain;
And we are here as on a darkling plain
Swept with confused alarms of struggle and flight,
Where ignorant armies clash by night.

In Donald J. Gray and G. B. Tennyson, *Victorian Literature: Poetry* (New York: Macmillan, 1976), pp. 479–480.

valry. A brisk market existed for pornography. There was much cutthroat journalism, as portrayed in George Gissing's (1857–1903) novel *New Grub Street* (1892). Newspapers became major factors in the emerging mass politics. The news could be managed, but in central Europe more often by the government censor than by the publisher. Editorials appeared on the front page.

The mass audience and the new literary world created problems for the literary artist. Much of the contempt for democracy and for the "people" found in late-nineteenth-century literature arose in

reaction to the recently established conditions for publication. The new sense of distance between the artist and the public was in part a result of the changed character of the literate public. As publishers sought to make profits, they often feared offending the sensibilities of their potential readership. Some writers accepted this situation and happily wrote harmless verbiage that supported current moral and political opinion. Others, such as Matthew Arnold (1822–1888), worked to raise the level of popular taste. Still others, such as the French novelist Émile Zola (1840–1902), deliberately offended the complaisant bourgeois values of their readers. These anxieties and tensions were closely related to some writers' criticism of democracy. Artists and their middle-class audience became the subjects of novels, such as James Joyce's (1882–1941) *Portrait of the Artist As a Young Man* (1914).

Because many of the new readers were only marginally literate and still quite ignorant on many scores, the books and journals catering to them seemed and often were thoroughly mediocre. Social and artistic critics were correct in pointing out this low level of public taste. Nevertheless the new education, the new readers, and the hundreds of new books and journals permitted a monumental popularization of knowledge that has become a hallmark of the contemporary world. The new literacy was the intellectual equivalent of the railroad and the steamship. People could leave their original intellectual surroundings.

Literacy is not an end in itself. It leads to other skills and the acquisition of other knowledge. People who can read may not necessarily change their world for the better, but they have a better chance to do so than those who remain illiterate.

Science at Mid-Century

In about 1850 Voltaire would still have felt at home in a general discussion of scientific concepts. The basic Newtonian picture of physical nature that he had popularized still prevailed. Scientists continued to believe that nature operated as a vast machine according to mechanical principles. During the first half of the century scientists had extended mechanistic explanation into several important areas. John Dalton (1766–1844) had formulated the modern theory of chemical composition. However, at mid-century and long thereafter atoms and molecules were thought to resemble billiard balls. During the 1840s several independent researchers had arrived at the concept of the conservation of energy, according to which energy is never lost in the universe but is simply transformed from one form to another. The principles of mechanism had been extended to geology through the work of Charles Lyell (1797–1875), whose *Principles of Geology* (1830) postulated that various changes in geological formation were the result of the mechanistic operation of natural causes over great spans of time.

At mid-century the physical world was thus regarded as rational, mechanical, and dependable. Its laws could be ascertained objectively through experiment and observation. Scientific theory purportedly described physical nature as it really existed. Moreover almost all scientists also believed like Newton and the deists of the eighteenth century that their knowledge of nature demonstrated the existence of a God or a Supreme Being.

Darwin

In 1859 Charles Darwin (1809–1882) published *The Origin of Species,* which carried the mechanical interpretation of physical nature into the world of living things. The book proved to be one of the seminal works of Western thought and earned Darwin the honor of being regarded as the Newton of biology. Both Darwin and his book have been much misunderstood. He did not originate the concept of evolution, which had been discussed widely before he wrote. What he and Alfred Russel Wallace (1823–1913) did, working independently,

Darwin's theories provoked ridicule as well as serious debate. The publication of Darwin's The Descent of Man *in 1871 inspired this cartoon in* Punch *showing Darwin himself (the old man in the upper left) as the culmination of human evolution. [New York Public Library Picture Collection.]*

was to formulate the principle of natural selection, which explained how species had changed or evolved over time. Earlier writers had believed that evolution might occur; Darwin and Wallace explained how it could occur.

Drawing on Malthus, the two scientists contended that more seeds and living organisms come into existence than can survive in their environment. Those organisms possessing some marginal advantage in the struggle for existence live long enough to propagate their kind. This principle of survival of the fittest Darwin called *natural selection*. The principle was naturalistic and mechanistic. Its operation required no guiding mind behind the development and change in organic nature. What neither Darwin nor anyone else in his day could explain was the origin of those chance variations that provided some living things with the marginal

Alfred Russel Wallace, here photographed in his later years, also came upon the principle of evolution by natural selection while working independently from Darwin. [The Granger Collection.]

❧ Darwin Defends a Mechanistic View of Nature

In the closing paragraphs of *The Origin of Species* (1859) Charles Darwin contrasted the view of nature he championed with that of his opponents. He argued that interpreting the development of organic nature through mechanistic laws actually suggested a nobler concept of nature than interpreting its development in terms of some form of divine creation.

Authors of the highest eminence seem to be fully satisfied with the view that each species has been independently created. To my mind it accords better with what we know of the laws impressed on matter by the Creator, that the production and extinction of the past and present inhabitants of the world should have been due to secondary causes, like those determining the birth and death of the individual. When I view all beings not as special creations, but as the lineal descendants of some few beings which lived long before the first bed of the Cambrian [geological] system was deposited, they seem to me to become ennobled. . . .

It is interesting to contemplate a tangled bank, clothed with many plants of many kinds, with birds singing on the bushes, with various insects flitting about, and with worms crawling through the damp earth, and to reflect that these elaborately constructed forms, so different from each other, and dependent upon each other in so complex a manner, have all

been produced by laws acting around us. These laws, taken in the largest sense, being Growth with Reproduction; Inheritance which is almost implied by reproduction; Variability from the indirect and direct action of the conditions of life, and from use and disuse: a Ration of Increase so high as to lead to a Struggle for Life, and as a consequence to Natural Selection, entailing Divergence of Character and the Extinction of less-improved forms. Thus, from the war of nature, from famine and death, the most exalted object which we are capable of conceiving, namely the production of the higher animals, directly follows. There is grandeur in this view of life, with its several powers, having been originally breathed by the Creator into a few forms or into one; and that, whilst this planet has gone cycling on according to the fixed law of gravity, from so simple a beginning endless forms most beautiful and most wonderful have been, and are being evolved.

Charles Darwin, *The Origin of Species and The Descent of Man* (New York: Modern Library, n.d.), pp. 373–374.

chance for survival. Only when the work on heredity of the Austrian monk Gregor Mendel (1822–1884) received public attention after 1900, several years following his death, did the mystery of those variations begin to be unraveled.

Darwin's and Wallace's theory represented the triumph of naturalistic explanation, which removed the idea of purpose from organic nature. Eyes were not made for seeing according to the rational wisdom and purpose of God but had developed mechanistically over the course of time. In this manner the theory of evolution through natural selection not only contradicted the biblical narrative of the Creation but also undermined the deistic argument for the existence of God from the design of the universe. Moreover Darwin's work undermined the whole concept of fixity in nature or the universe at large. The world was a realm of flux and change. The fact that physical and organic nature might be constantly changing allowed people in the late nineteenth century to believe that society, values, customs, and beliefs should also change.

In 1871 Darwin carried his work a step further. In *The Descent of Man* he applied the principle of evolution by natural selection to human beings. Darwin was hardly the first person to treat human beings as animals, but his arguments brought greater plausibility to that point of view. He contended that humankind's moral nature and religious sentiments, as well as its physical frame, had developed naturalistically in response largely to the requirements of survival. Neither the origin nor the character of humankind on earth required the existence of a God for their explanation. Not since Copernicus had removed the earth from the center of the universe had the pride of Western human beings received so sharp a blow.

The Prestige of Science

Darwin's ideas remained highly controversial. They were widely debated in popular and scientific journals. He changed some of them in the course of his writings. However, at issue was not only the correctness of the theory and the place of humankind in nature but also the role of science and scientists in society. The prestige of Darwin's achievement, progress in medicine, and the links of science to the technology of the second Industrial Revolution made the general European public aware of science as never before. The British Fabian Socialist Beatrice Webb recalled from her youth:

Who will deny that the men of science were the leading British intellectuals of that period; that it was they who stood out as men of genius with international reputations; that it was they who were the self-confident militants of the period; that it was they who were routing the theologians, confounding the mystics, imposing their theories on philosophers, their inventions on capitalists, and their discoveries on medical men; whilst they were at the same time snubbing the artists, ignoring the poets, and even casting doubts on the capacity of the politicians?[1]

Contemporaries spoke of a religion of science that would explain all without resort to supernaturalism. Popularizers, such as Thomas Henry Huxley (1825–1895) and John Tyndall (1820–1893) in Britain and Ernst Haeckel (1834–1919) in Germany, wrote and lectured widely on scientific topics. They argued that science held the answer to the major questions of life. They worked for government support of scientific research and for inclusion of science in the schools and universities.

Scientific knowledge and theories became models for thought in other fields even before the impact of Darwinian thought. The French philosopher Auguste Comte (1798–1857), a late child of the Enlightenment and a onetime follower of Saint-Simon, developed a philosophy of human intellectual development that culminated in science. In *The Positive Philosophy* (1830–1842) Comte argued that human thought had gone through three stages of development. In the theological stage, physical nature was explained in terms of the action of divinities or spirits. In the second or metaphysical stage, abstract principles became regarded as the operative agencies of nature. In the final or positive stage, explanations of nature became matters of exact description of phenomena, without recourse to an unobservable operative principle. Physical science had, in Comte's view, entered the positive stage, and similar thinking should penetrate other areas of analysis. In particular Comte thought that positive laws of social behavior could

---

[1] Beatrice Webb, *My Apprenticeship* (London: Longmans, Green, 1926), pp. 130–131.

be discovered in the same fashion as laws of physical nature. For this reason he is generally regarded as the father of sociology. Works like Comte's helped to convince learned Europeans that genuine knowledge in any area must resemble scientific knowledge. This belief had its roots in the Enlightenment and continues to permeate Western thought to the present day.

Theories of ethics were modeled on science during the last half of the century. The concept of the struggle for survival was widely applied to human social relationships. The phrase "survival of the fittest" predated Darwin and reflected the competitive outlook of classical economics. Darwin's use of the phrase gave it the prestige associated with advanced science.

The most famous advocate of evolutionary ethics was Herbert Spencer (1820–1903), the British philosopher. Spencer, a strong individualist, believed that human society progressed through competition. If the weak received too much protection, the rest of humankind was the loser. In Spencer's work, struggle against one's fellow human beings became a kind of ethical imperative. The concept could be applied to justify the avoidance of aiding the poor and the working class or to justify the domination of colonial peoples or to urge aggressively competitive relationships among nations. Evolutionary ethics and similar concepts, all of which are usually termed *social Darwinsim,* often came very close to saying that might makes right.

Interestingly enough, one of the chief opponents of such thinking was Thomas Henry Huxley, the great defender of Darwin. In 1893 Huxley declared that the physical cosmic process of evolution was at odds with the process of human ethical development. The struggle in nature held no ethical implications except to demonstrate how human beings should not behave.

Scientific thought even affected the way in which authors wrote novels. The movement to literary realism, which is considered more fully later in this chapter, was a product of the influence of science. Certain writers wanted to portray the world as they observed it. In France, Gustave Flaubert's (1821–1880) *Madame Bovary* (1857); in England, George Eliot's (1819–1880) *Adam Bede* (1859); and in Russia, Ivan Turgenev's (1818–1883) *A Sportsman's Sketches* (1852) paid new attention to minute physical and natural details. Émile Zola

Auguste Comte was the founder of Positivism. He urged that all knowledge be modeled on the empirical knowledge of science. Because he wanted the understanding of human society to assume a scientific character, he is often regarded as the founder of sociology. [French Cultural Services, New York.]

(1840–1902) found artistic inspiration in Claude Bernard's (1813–1878) *An Introduction to the Study of Experimental Medicine* (1865). Zola, a French novelist, believed that he could write an experimental novel in which the characters and their actions would be observed and reported on as the scientist might relate events within a laboratory experiment. Zola and others believed that absolute physical (and psychological) determinism ruled human events, just as in the physical world determinism prevailed.

Scientists and their admirers enjoyed a supreme confidence during the last half of the century. They genuinely believed that they had, for all intents and purposes, discovered all that might be discovered. The issues for science in the future would be the extension of acknowledged principles and the refinement of measurement. However, the turn of the century held a much more brilliant future for science. That confident, self-satisfied world of late-nineteenth-century science and scientism vanished. A much more complicated picture of nature developed. Before examining those new departures, we must see how the cult of science affected religious thought and practice.

Christianity and the Church Under Siege

The nineteenth century was one of the most difficult periods in the history of the organized Christian churches. Many European intellectuals left the faith. The secular, liberal nation states attacked the political and social influence of the church. The expansion of population and the growth of cities challenged its organizational capacity to meet the modern age. Yet during all of this turmoil the Protestant and Catholic churches still made considerable headway at the popular level.

The intellectual attack on Christianity arose on the grounds of its historical credibility, its scientific accuracy, and its pronounced morality. The *philosophes* of the Enlightenment had delighted in pointing out contradictions in the Bible. The historical scholarship of the nineteenth century brought new issues to the fore.

In 1835 David Friederich Strauss (1808–1874) published a *Life of Jesus* in which he questioned whether the Bible provided any genuine historical evidence about Jesus. Strauss contended that the story of Jesus was a myth that had arisen from the particular social and intellectual conditions of first-century Palestine. Jesus' character and life represented the aspirations of the people of that time and place rather than events that had occurred. Other skeptical lives of Jesus were written and published elsewhere.

During the second half of the century scholars such as Julius Wellhausen (1844–1918) in Germany, Ernst Renan (1823–1892) in France, and William Robertson Smith (1847–1894) in Great Britain contended that the books of the Bible had been written and revised with the problems of Jewish society and politics in the minds of human authors. They were not inspired books but had, like the Homeric epics, been written by normal human beings in a primitive society. This questioning of the historical validity of the Bible caused more literate men and women to lose faith in Christianity than any other single cause.

The march of science also undermined Christianity. This blow was particularly cruel because eighteenth-century deists had led Christians to believe that the scientific examination of nature provided a strong buttress for their faith. William Paley's (1743–1805) *Natural Theology* (1802) and books by numerous scientists had enshrined this belief. The geology of Charles Lyell (1797–1875) suggested that the earth was much older than the biblical records contended. By appealing to natural causes to explain floods, mountains, and valleys, Lyell removed the miraculous hand of God from the physical development of the earth. Darwin's theory cast doubt on the doctrine of the Creation. His ideas and those of other writers suggested that the moral nature of humankind could be explained without appeal to the role of God. Finally, anthropologists, psychologists, and sociologists suggested that religion itself and religious sentiments were just one more set of natural phenomena.

Other intellectuals questioned the morality of Christianity. The old issue of immoral biblical stories was again raised. Much more important, the moral character of the Old Testament God came under fire. His cruelty and unpredictability did not fit well with the progressive, tolerant, rational values of liberals. They also wondered about the morality of the New Testament God, who would sacrifice for his own satisfaction the only perfect being ever to walk the earth. Many of the clergy began to ask themselves if they could honestly preach doctrines they felt to be immoral.

During the last quarter of the century this moral attack on Christianity came from another direction. Writers like Friederich Nietzsche (1844–1900) in Germany portrayed Christianity as a religion of sheep that glorified weakness rather than the strength that life required. Christianity demanded a useless and debilitating sacrifice of the flesh and spirit rather than full-blooded heroic living and daring. Nietzsche once observed, "War and courage have accomplished more great things than love of neighbor."[2]

These widespread skeptical intellectual currents seem to have directly influenced only the upper levels of educated society. Yet they created a climate in which Christianity lost much of its intellectual respectability. Fewer educated people joined the clergy. More and more people found that they could lead their lives with little or no reference to Christianity. The secularism of everyday life proved as harmful to the faith as the direct attacks. This situation especially prevailed in the cities,

[2] Walter Kaufmann (Ed. and Trans.), *The Portable Nietzsche* (New York, Vikings, 1967), p. 159.

which were growing faster than the capacity of the churches to meet the challenge. There was not even enough room in urban churches for the potential worshipers to sit. Whole generations of the urban poor grew up with little or no experience of the church as an institution or of Christianity as a religious faith.

Conflict of Church and State

The secular state of the nineteenth century clashed with both the Protestant and the Roman Catholic churches. Liberals generally disliked the dogma and the political privileges of the established churches. National states were often suspicious of the supranational character of the Roman Catholic Church. However, the primary area of conflict between the state and the churches was the expanding systems of education. The churches feared that future generations would emerge from the schools without the rudiments of religious teaching. The advocates of secular education feared the production of future generations more loyal to religion or the church than to the nation. From 1870 through the turn of the century the issue of religious education was heatedly debated in every major country.

GREAT BRITAIN. In Great Britain the Education Act of 1870 provided for the construction of state-supported school-board schools, whereas earlier the government had given small grants to religious schools. The new schools were to be built in areas where the religious denominations failed to provide satisfactory education. There was rivalry not only between the Anglican church and the state but also between the Anglican church and the Nonconformist denominations, that is, those Christian denominations that were not part of the Church of England. There was intense local hostility among all these groups. The churches of all denominations had to oppose improvements in education because these increased the costs of their own schools. In the Education Act of 1902 the government decided to provide state support for both religious and nonreligious schools but imposed the same educational standards on each.

FRANCE. The British conflict was relatively calm compared with that in France, where there existed a dual system of Catholic and public schools. Under the Falloux Law of 1850 the local priest provided religious education in the public schools.

The very conservative French Catholic church and the Third French Republic were mutually hostile to each other. Between 1878 and 1886 the government passed a series of educational laws sponsored by Jules Ferry (1832–1893). The Ferry Laws replaced religious instruction in the public schools with civic training. Members of religious orders were no longer permitted to teach in the public schools, the number of which was to be expanded. After the Dreyfus affair the French Catholic church again paid a price for its reactionary politics. The Radical government of Waldeck-Rousseau, drawn from pro-Dreyfus groups, suppressed the religious orders. In 1905 the Napoleonic Concordat was terminated, and Church and State were totally separated.

GERMANY AND THE *KULTURKAMPF*. The most extreme example of Church–State conflict occurred in Germany during the 1870s. At the time of unification the German Catholic hierarchy had wanted freedom for the churches guaranteed in the constitution. Bismarck left the matter to the discretion of each federal state, but he soon felt the activity of the Roman Catholic Church and the Catholic Center Party to be a threat to the political unity of the new state. Through administrative orders in 1870 and 1871 Bismarck removed both Catholic and Protestant clergy from overseeing local education and set education under state direction. The secularization of education was merely the beginning of a concerted attack on the independence of the Catholic church in Germany.

The "May Laws" of 1873 which applied to Prussia and not the entire German Empire, required priests to be educated in German schools and universities and to pass state-administered examinations. The state could veto the appointments of priests. The disciplinary power of the pope and the church over the clergy was abolished and transferred to the state. When the bishops and many of the clergy refused to obey these laws, Bismarck used the police against them. In 1876 he had either arrested or driven from Prussia all the Catholic bishops. In the end Bismarck's *Kulturkampf* ("cultural struggle") against the Catholic church failed. Not for the first time Christian martyrs aided resistance to persecution. By the close of the decade the chancellor had abandoned his attack. He had gained state control of education and civil laws governing marriage only at the price of lingering Catholic resentment against the German state.

The *Kulturkampf* was probably the greatest blunder of Bismarck's career.

AREAS OF RELIGIOUS REVIVAL. The successful German Catholic resistance to the intrusions of the secular state illustrates the continuing vitality of Christianity during this period of intellectual and political hardship. In Great Britain both the Angli-can church and the Nonconformist denominations experienced considerable growth in membership. Vast sums of money were raised for new churches and schools. In Ireland the 1870s saw a widespread Catholic devotional revival. Priests in France after the defeat by Prussia organized special pilgrimages by train for thousands of penitents who believed

The Basilica of the Sacred Heart in Paris is a monument to the late nineteenth-century Roman Catholic revival in France. Its construction was begun in 1876 as part of an effort to atone for national sins that were considered by many to be the cause of French defeat in the Franco-Prussian War. [*French Government Tourist Office, New York.*]

The Kulturkampf ("Struggle for culture"), Bismarck's attack on the independence of the German Catholic Church, was the worst failure of his career. Catholics, who formed more than a third of the German population, resisted by organizing the Center Party, which captured a substantial bloc of seats in the Reichstag. By the 1880s Bismarck was forced to halt his campaign against the Church. This cartoon portrays the struggle as a chess game between Bismarck and the pope. Bismarck's pieces are the press, "Germania," and antimonastic legislation. The pope's pieces are encyclicals, interdicts, and the Syllabus of Errors. [Bildarchiv Preussischer Kulturbesitz.]

that France had lost because of their sins. The cult of the miracle of Lourdes originated during these years. There were efforts by churches of all denominations to give more attention to the urban poor.

In effect the last half of the nineteenth century witnessed the final great effort to Christianize Europe. It was well organized, well led, and well financed. It failed not from want of effort but because the population had simply outstripped the resources of the churches. This persistent liveliness of the church accounts in part for the intense hostility of its enemies.

The Roman Catholic Church and the Modern World

Perhaps the most striking feature of this religious revival amidst turmoil and persecution was

the resilience of the papacy. The brief hope for a liberal pontificate from Pope Pius IX (1846–1878) vanished on the night in 1848 when he fled the turmoil in Rome. In the 1860s Pius IX, embittered by the mode of Italian unification, launched a counteroffensive against liberalism in thought and deed. In 1864 he issued the *Syllabus of Errors*, which condemned all the major tenets of political liberalism and modern thought. He set the Roman Catholic Church squarely against the worlds of contemporary science, philosophy, and politics. In 1869 the pope called into session the First Vatican Council. The next year, through the political manipulations of the pontiff and against much opposition from numerous members, the council promulgated the dogma of the infallibility of the pope when speaking officially on matters of faith and morals. No earlier pope had gone so far. The First Vatican Council came to a close in 1870, when Ital-

849

The First Vatican Council met in 1869–1870 and proclaimed the dogma of the pope's infallibility when speaking in his official position on matters of faith and morals. This event marked the high water mark of papal influence in the Roman Catholic Church. The council was the first general one of the church since that at Trent in the sixteenth century. As shown in this painting from the Vatican, its main sessions took place in one of the transepts of Saint Peter's in Rome, with Pope Pius IX presiding. [Archivio Fotografico, Musei Vaticani.]

Pope Leo XIII led the Roman Catholic Church toward a limited recognition of the social and political problems brought on by industrial democracy. His encyclical Rerum Novarum *was the major statement of the Church on the issues of social justice and class conflict. [Culver Pictures.]*

ian troops invaded Rome at the outbreak of the Franco-Prussian War.

Pius IX died in 1878 and was succeeded by Leo XIII (1878–1903). The new pope, who was sixty-eight years old at the time of his election, sought to make accommodation with the modern age and to address the great social questions. He looked to the philosophical tradition of Thomas Aquinas to reconcile the claims of faith and reason. His encyclicals of 1885 and 1890 permitted Catholics to participate in the politics of liberal states.

Leo XIII's most important pronouncement on public issues was the encyclical *Rerum Novarum* (1891). In that document Leo XIII defended private property, religious education, and religious control of the marriage laws, and he condemned socialism and Marxism. However, he also declared that employers should treat their employees justly, pay them proper wages, and permit them to organize labor unions. He supported laws and regulations to protect the conditions of labor. The pope urged that modern society be organized according to corporate groups, including people from various classes, which might cooperate according to Christian principles. The corporate society, derivative of medieval social organization, was to be an

🙵 Leo XIII *Considers the Social Question in European Politics*

In his 1891 encyclical *Rerum Novarum* Pope Leo XIII addressed the social question in European politics. It was the answer of the Catholic church to secular calls for social reforms. The pope denied the socialist claim that class conflict was the natural state of affairs. He urged employers to seek just and peaceful relations with workers.

The great mistake that is made in the matter now under consideration is to possess oneself of the idea that class is naturally hostile to class; that rich and poor are intended by Nature to live at war with one another. So irrational and so false is this view that the exact contrary is the truth. . . . Each requires the other; capital cannot do without labour, nor labour without capital. Mutual agreement results in pleasantness and good order; perpetual conflict necessarily produces confusion and outrage. Now, in preventing such strife as this, and in making it impossible, the efficacy of Christianity is marvellous and manifold. . . . Religion teaches the labouring man and the workman to carry out honestly and well all equitable agreements freely made; never to injure capital, or to outrage the person of an employer; never to employ violence in representing his own cause, or to engage in riot or disorder; and to have nothing to do with men of evil principles, who work upon the people with artful promises and raise foolish hopes which usually end in disaster and in repent-

ance when too late. Religion teaches the rich man and the employer that their work people are not their slaves; that they must respect in every man his dignity as a man and as a Christian; that labour is nothing to be ashamed of, if we listen to right reason and to Christian philosophy, but is an honourable employment, enabling a man to sustain his life in an upright and creditable way; and that it is shameful and inhuman to treat men like chattels to make money by, or to look upon them merely as so much muscle or physical power. Thus, again, Religion teaches that, as among the workman's concerns are Religion herself and things spiritual and mental, the employer is bound to see that he has time for the duties of piety; that he be not exposed to corrupting influences and dangerous occasions; and that he be not led away to neglect his home and family or to squander his wages. Then, again, the employer must never tax his work people beyond their strength, nor employ them in work unsuited to their sex or age. His great and principal obligation is to give every one that which is just.

F. S. Nitti, *Catholic Socialism*, trans. by Mary Mackintosh (London: S. Sonnenschein, 1895), p. 409.

alternative to both socialism and competitive capitalism. On the basis of Leo XIII's pronouncements democratic Catholic parties and Catholic trade unions were founded throughout Europe.

The emphasis of Pius X, who reigned from 1903 to 1914 and who has been proclaimed a saint, was intellectually reactionary. He hoped to restore traditional devotional life. Between 1903 and 1907 he condemned Catholic Modernism, a movement of modern biblical criticism within the church, and in 1910 he required an anti-Modernist oath from all priests. By these actions Pius X set the church squarely against the intellectual currents of the day, and the struggle between Catholicism and modern thought continued. Although Pius X did not strongly support the social policy of Leo XIII, the Catholic church continued to permit its mem-

bers active participation in social and political movements.

Toward a Twentieth-Century Frame of Mind

World War I is often regarded as the point of departure into the contemporary world. Although this view is possibly true of political and social developments, it is an incorrect assessment of intellectual history. The last quarter of the nineteenth century and the first decade of the twentieth century constituted the crucible of contemporary Western and European thought. During this period the kind of fundamental reassessment that Darwin's

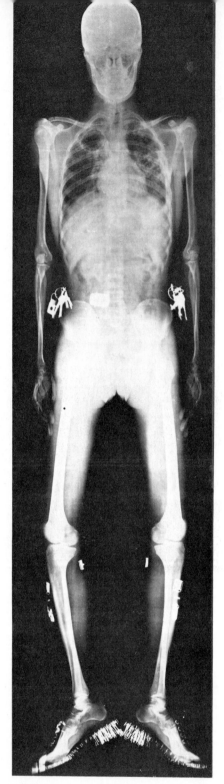

In an early demonstration Roentgen took an X ray of the entire body of a male subject. Note the buckle of his belt, the keys he had attached to the belt, and tacks in the soles and heels of his shoes. [Deutsches Museum, Munich.]

work had previously made necessary in biology and in understanding the place of human beings in nature became writ large in other areas of thinking. Philosophers, scientists, psychologists, and artists began to portray physical reality, human nature, and human society in ways quite different from those of the past. Their new concepts challenged the major presuppositions of mid-nineteenth-century science, rationalism, liberalism, and bourgeois morality.

Science: The Revolution in Physics

The modifications in the scientific world view originated within the scientific community itself. By the late 1870s considerable discontent existed over the excessive realism of mid-century science. It was thought that many scientists believed that their mechanistic models, solid atoms, and absolute time and space actually described the real universe. In 1883 Ernst Mach (1838–1916) published *The Science of Mechanics*, in which he urged that the con-

A watercolor by Harriet Moore of the English chemist and physicist Michael Faraday (1791–1867) in his laboratory. Faraday, who made the first dynamo, was the originator of the concepts that underlie the modern theory of electromagnetics. [The Royal Institution, London.]

cepts of science be considered descriptive not of the physical world but of the sensations experienced by the scientific observer. Science could describe only the sensations, not the physical world that underlay the sensations. In line with Mach, the French scientist and mathematician Henri Poincaré (1854–1912) urged that the concepts and theories of scientists be regarded as hypothetical constructs of the human mind rather than as descriptions of the true state of nature. In 1911 Hans Vaihinger (1852–1933) suggested that the concepts of science be considered "as if" descriptions of the physical world. By World War I few scientists believed any longer that they could portray the "truth" about physical reality. Rather, they

saw themselves as recording the observations of instruments and as setting forth useful hypothetical or symbolic models of nature.

New discoveries in the laboratory paralleled the philosophical challenge to nineteenth-century science. With those discoveries the comfortable world of supposedly "complete" nineteenth-century physics vanished forever. In December 1895 Wilhelm Roentgen (1845–1923) published a paper on his discovery of X rays, a form of energy that penetrated various opaque materials. The publication of his paper was followed within a matter of months by major steps in the exploration of radioactivity. In 1896 Henri Becquerel (1852–1908), through a series of experiments following on

The British scientist Ernest Rutherford was one of the first persons to explore the internal structure of the atom. The portrait is a 1932 painting by Oswald Birley. [Culver Pictures.]

atomic particles is a matter of statistical probability rather than of exactly determinable cause and effect. So much that only fifty years earlier had seemed certain and unquestionable about the physical universe had now once again become problematical.

Nineteenth-century popularizers of science had urged its importance as a path to rational living and decision making. By the early twentieth century the developments in the scientific world itself had dashed such optimistic hopes. The mathematical complexity of twentieth-century physics meant that despite valiant efforts science would rarely again be successfully popularized. However, at the same time, through applied technology and further research in physics and medicine, science af-

Marie Curie (1867–1934), who was born in Poland but worked most of her life in France, was one of the leading figures in the turn-of-the-century advance of physics and chemistry. She is credited with the discovery of radium. [The Granger Collection.]

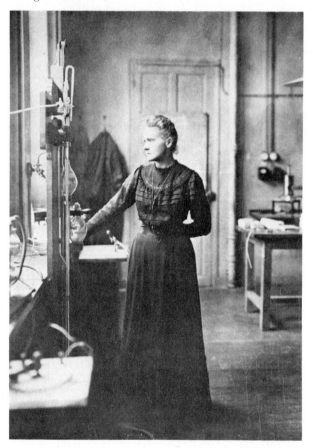

Roentgen's work, found that uranium emitted a similar form of energy. The next year J. J. Thomson (1856–1940), working in the Cavendish Laboratory of Cambridge University, formulated the theory of the electron. The interior world of the atom had become a new area for human exploration. In 1902 Ernest Rutherford (1871–1937), who had been Thomson's assistant, explained the cause of radiation through the disintegration of the atoms of radioactive materials. Shortly thereafter he speculated on the immense store of energy present in the atom.

The discovery of radioactivity and discontent with the existing mechanical models led to revolutionary theories in physics. In 1900 Max Planck (1858–1947) pioneered the articulation of the quantum theory of energy, according to which energy is a series of discrete quantities or packets rather than a continuous stream. In 1905 Albert Einstein (1879–1955) published his first epoch-making papers on relativity. He contended that time and space exist not separately but rather as a combined continuum. Moreover the measurement of space and time depend on the observer as well as on the entities being measured. In 1927 Werner Heisenberg (b. 1901) set forth the uncertainty principle, according to which the behavior of sub-

The German physicist Albert Einstein (1879–1955). Einstein's theory of relativity, published in 1905, set the fundamental theory of physics in a new direction. [Brundy Library.]

fected daily living more than ever before in human history. Consequently nonscientists in legal, business, and public life have been called upon to make decisions involving technological matters that they rarely can or do understand in depth or detail. By the middle of this century some writers—such as the English essayist, novelist, and physicist, C. P. Snow (1905–1980)—spoke of the emergence of "two cultures," one of the scientists and one of literary persons. The problem was establishing ways in which they could communicate meaningfully with each other to address the major problems of human life.

Literature: Realism and Naturalism

Between 1850 and 1914 the moral certainties of learned and middle-class Europeans underwent modifications no less radical than their concepts of the physical universe. The realist movement in literature portrayed the hypocrisy, the physical and psychic brutality, and the dullness that underlay bourgeois life and society. By bringing scientific objectivity and observation to their work, the realist or naturalist writers used the mid-century cult of science so vital to the middle class to confront those same people with the harsh realities of life around them. Realism was a rejection of the Romantic idealization of nature, the poor, love, and polite society. Realist novelists portrayed the dark, degraded, and dirty side of life almost, so some people thought, for its own sake.

An earlier generation of writers, including Charles Dickens (1812–1870) and Honoré de Balzac (1799–1850), had portrayed the cruelty of industrial life and of a society based wholly on money. Other authors, such as George Eliot (1819–1880), had paid close attention to the details of the scenes and the characters portrayed. However, there had always been room in their works for the play of the imagination, fancy, and artistry. They had felt a better moral world possible. The major figures of late-century realism–Émile Zola (1840–1902), Gustave Flaubert (1821–1880), Ivan Turgenev (1818–1883), Anton Chekhov (1860–1904), Maksim Gorki (1868–1936), Henrik Ibsen (1828–1906), Arnold Bennett (1867–1931), and George Moore (1852–1933)—examined the dreary and unseemly side of life without being cer-

George Eliot was the pen name of Mary Ann Evans (1819–1880). She was an important English novelist who portrayed the life of the English countryside with much realistic detail. She was also a significant English religious and ethical thinker. [The Granger Collection.]

Émile Zola of France was the master of the realistic novel. Although his depiction of the harsh details of working class and peasant life shocked many of his readers, his novels sold well. Near the close of his life, he became one of the strongest supporters of Captain Alfred Dreyfus and demanded that the President of France seek justice for the military officer. His splendid portrait is by the photographer Nadar. [Bettmann Archive.]

tain whether a better life was possible. In good Darwinian fashion they regarded and portrayed human beings as animals, subject to the passions, materialistic determinism, and the pressures of environment like any other animals. However, most of them also saw society itself as perpetuating evil.

Flaubert's *Madame Bovary* (1856), with its story of colorless provincial life and a woman's hapless search for love inside and out of marriage, is often considered the first genuinely realistic novel. It portrayed life without heroism, purpose, or even simple civility.

Nevertheless the author who turned realism into a movement was Émile Zola. As noted earlier, he saw himself as creating human experiments in his novels. He once declared, "I have simply done on living bodies the work of analysis which surgeons perform on corpses."[3] Between 1871 and 1893 Zola published twenty volumes of novels exploring subjects normally untouched by writers. In *L'Assommoir* (1877) he discussed the problem of alcoholism, and in *Nana* (1880) he followed the life of a prostitute. Others of his works considered the defeat of the French army and the social strife arising from attempts at labor organization. Zola refused to turn his pen or his readers' thoughts from the most ugly aspects of life. Nothing in his purview received the light of hope or the aura of romance. Although polite critics faulted his taste and middle-class moralists his subject matter, Zola enjoyed a wide following in France and elsewhere. As noted

[3] Quoted in George J. Becker, *Documents of Modern Literary Realism* (Princeton, N.J.: Princeton University Press, 1963), p. 159.

in the previous chapter, he took a leading role in the public defense of Captain Dreyfus.

The Norwegian playwright Henrik Ibsen carried realism into the dramatic presentation of domestic life. He sought to achieve new modes of social awareness and to strip away the illusory mask of middle-class morality. His most famous play is *A Doll's House* (1879). Its chief character, Nora, is the spouse of a narrow-minded middle-class husband who cannot tolerate any independence of character or thought on her part. When for the first time she fully confronts this situation, the play ends as she leaves him, slamming the door behind her. In *Ghosts* (1881) a respectable middle-class woman must deal with a son suffering from syphilis inherited from her husband. In *The Master Builder* (1892) an aging architect kills himself while trying to impress a young woman who perhaps loves him. Ibsen's works were extremely controversial. He had dared to strike at sentimentality in life, the female "angel of the house," and the cloak of respectability that hung so insecurely over the middle-class family.

One of Ibsen's greatest champions was the Irish writer George Bernard Shaw (1856–1950), who spent most of his life in England. During the late 1880s he had vigorously defended Ibsen's work. He went on to make his own realistic onslaught against Romanticism and false respectability. In *Mrs. Warren's Profession* (1893), a play long censored in England, he explored the matter of prostitution. In *Arms and the Man* (1894) and *Man and*

Henrik Ibsen (1828–1906) used his considerable skill as a playwright to probe the hypocrisy of middle class morality and its attitude toward women. [The Granger Collection.]

Virginia Woolf (1882–1941), shown here at age twenty-one, was one of the major voices urging the pursuit of literary and artistic modernism in Great Britain. Her novels constitute one of the monuments of twentieth-century British literature. [The Granger Collection.]

Superman (1903) he heaped scorn on the Romantic ideals of love and war, and in *Androcles and the Lion* (1913) he pilloried Christianity. Shaw added to the impact of his plays by writing long critical prefaces, in which he drove home the point of his social criticism.

Realism struck the public ego in another fashion besides presenting unseemly social situations. The realists tended to see humankind as subject, and often helplessly so, to great physical or historical forces of determinism. Throughout *War and Peace* (1869) Leo Tolstoy (1828–1910) pictured his characters as being tossed on the seas of historical change. The characters of Thomas Hardy's (1840–1928) novels are repeatedly challenged by curious turns of fate. These writers felt that human beings in such settings could not control their lives and lacked the freedom to make conscious, meaningful moral choices. Their characters possess little or no nobility because the artists who created them had ceased to believe that human beings stood just a little lower than the angels or were creatures fully capable of rational behavior.

These writers and many others believed it the duty of the artist to portray reality and the commonplace. In dissecting what they considered the "real" world, they helped to change the moral perception of the good life. They refused to let existing public opinion dictate the subjects about which they wrote or the manner in which they treated them. By presenting their audiences with unmen-

Realism in sculpture, as well as rising awareness of the condition of working people, is represented by the huge Belgian monument to labor by Constantin Émile Meunier (1831–1905). This is a portion of the work dedicated to miners. [Copyright by A. C. L., Brussels.]

tionable subjects, they sought to remove the veneer of hypocrisy that had previously forbade such discussion. They hoped to destroy social and moral illusions and to compel the public to confront reality. That change in itself seemed good. However, few of the realist writers who raised the problems had solutions. They often left their readers unable to sustain old values and uncertain about the sources of new ones.

Philosophy: Revolt Against Reason

Within philosophical circles the adequacy of rational thinking to address the human situation was being questioned. No late-nineteenth-century writer better exemplified this new attitude than the German philosopher Friedrich Nietzsche (1844–1900), who had been educated as a classical philologist rather than as an academic philosopher. His books remained unpopular until late in his life, when his brilliance had deteriorated into an almost totally silent insanity. He was a person wholly at odds with the predominant values of the age. At one time or another he attacked Christianity, democracy, nationalism, rationality, science, and progress. He sought less to change values than to probe the very sources of values in the human mind and character. He wanted not only to tear away the masks of respectable life but also to explore the ways in which human beings made such masks.

His first important work was *The Birth of Tragedy* (1872), in which he urged that the nonrational aspects of human nature were as important and noble as the rational characteristics. Here and elsewhere he insisted on the positive function of instinct and ecstasy in human life. To limit human activity to strictly rational behavior was to impoverish human life and experience. In this work Nietzsche regarded Socrates as one of the major contributors to Western decadence because of the Greek philosopher's appeal for rationality in human affairs. In Nietzsche's view the strength for the heroic life and the highest artistic achievement arose from sources beyond rationality.

858

Friedrich Nietzsche became the most influential German philosopher of the late nineteenth century. His books challenged existing morality and demanded a revaluation of values themselves. He has exerted a vast influence on twentieth-century literature and philosophy in both Europe and North America. [New York Public Library Picture Collection.]

good and what is evil but the social and psychological sources of the judgment of good and evil. He declared, "There are no moral phenomena at all, but only a moral interpretation of phenomena."[4] He dared to raise the question of whether morality itself was valuable: "We need a critique of moral values; the value of these values themselves must first be called in question."[5] In Nietzsche's view morality was a human convention that had no independent existence apart from humankind. For Nietzsche this discovery did not condemn morality but liberated human beings to create life-affirming instead of life-denying values. Christianity, utilitarianism, and middle-class respectability could, in good conscience, be abandoned, and human beings could, if they so willed, create a new moral order for themselves that would glorify pride, assertiveness, and strength rather than meekness, humility, and weakness.

What Nietzsche said about morality was indicative of what other philosophers were saying about similar subjects. There was a growing tendency to see all conceptual categories as useful creations rather than exact descriptions.

The American philosopher William James (1842–1910) was one of the most influential figures to question the adequacy of nineteenth-century rationalism and science. He and his philosophy of pragmatism were very influential in Europe. James suggested that the truth of an idea or a description depended primarily on how well it worked. Knowledge was less an instrument for knowing than for acting.

The most important European philosopher to pursue such lines of thought was the Frenchman Henri Bergson (1859–1941). His most significant works were *Time and Free Will* (1889), *Creative Evolution* (1907), and *Two Sources of Morality and Religion* (1932). Bergson glorified instinct, will, and subjectivism. He regarded human beings as dwell-

In later works, such as the prose poem *Thus Spake Zarathustra* (1883), Nietzsche criticized democracy and Christianity. Both would lead only to the mediocrity of sheepish masses. He announced the death of God and proclaimed the coming of the Overman (*Übermensch*), who would embody heroism and greatness. This latter term was frequently interpreted as some mode of superman or super race, but such was not Nietzsche's intention. He was highly critical of contemporary racism and anti-Semitism. What he sought was a return to the heroism that he associated with Greek life in the Homeric age. He thought that the values of Christianity and of bourgeois morality prevented humankind from achieving life on a heroic level. Those moralities forbade too much of human nature from fulfilling and expressing itself.

Two of Nietzsche's most profound works were *Beyond Good and Evil* (1886) and *The Genealogy of Morals* (1887). Both are difficult books. Much of the former was written in brief, ambiguous aphorisms. Nietzsche sought to discover not what is

[4] Walter Kaufmann (Ed. and Trans.), *The Basic Writings of Nietzsche* (New York: The Modern Library, 1968), p. 275.

[5] Ibid., p. 456.

ing in a world of becoming, where the only certain thing was their sense of themselves. The world was permeated with a great vital force in which all things participated to a greater or lesser degree. The evolutionary nature of the universe meant that both the knower and the object of knowledge were constantly changing. What Bergson did was to set down much of the thought of earlier mystics in the language of evolutionary science.

In their appeal to the feelings and the emotions and in their questioning of the adequacy of rationalism, these writers drew on the romantic tradition. The kind of creative impulse earlier Romantics had considered the gift of artists, these later writers saw as the burden of all humans beings. The character of the human situation that these philosophers urged on their contemporaries was that of an ever-changing flux in which little or nothing but change itself was permanent. Human beings had to forge from their own inner will and determination the truth and values that were to exist in the world. In their impact on twentieth-century developments these philosophies threw into doubt not only the rigid domestic and religious morality of the nineteenth century but also the values of toleration, cosmopolitanism, and benevolence that had been championed during the Enlightenment.

The Birth of Psychoanalysis

A determination to probe beneath surface or public appearances united the major figures of late-nineteenth-century science, art, and philosophy. They sought to discern the various undercurrents, tensions, and complexities that lay beneath the smooth, calm surfaces of hard atoms, respectable families, rationality, and social relationships. Their theories and discoveries meant that articulate, educated Europeans could never again view the surface of life with smugness or complacency or even much confidence. No single intellectual development more clearly and stunningly exemplified this trend than the emergence of psychoanalysis through the work of Sigmund Freud.

Freud was born in 1856 into an Austrian Jewish family that shortly thereafter settled in Vienna. He originally planned to become a lawyer but soon moved to the study of physiology and then to medicine. In 1886 he opened his medical practice in Vienna, where he continued to live until driven out by the Nazis in 1938, a year before his death. All of

The Viennese physician Sigmund Freud (1856–1939) revolutionized the concept of human nature in the Western world. After his books, European thinkers have had to see rationality as only one aspect of human nature. [Bettmann Archive.]

Freud's research and writing was done from the base of his medical practice. His earliest medical interests had been psychic disorders, to which he sought to apply the critical method of science. In late 1885 he had studied for a few months in Paris with Jean-Martin Charcot, who used hypnosis to treat cases of hysteria. In Vienna he collaborated with another physician, Josef Breuer (1842–1925), and in 1895 they published *Studies in Hysteria*.

In the mid-1890s Freud changed the technique of his investigations. He abandoned hypnosis and allowed his patients to talk freely and spontaneously about themselves. Repeatedly he found that they associated their particular neurotic symptoms with experiences related to earlier experiences, going back to childhood. He also noticed that sexual matters were significant in his patients' problems. For a time he thought that perhaps some sexual incident during childhood accounted for the illness of his patients. However, by 1897 he had privately rejected this theory. In its place he formulated a theory of infantile sexuality, according to which sexual drives and energy exist in infants and do not simply emerge at puberty. In Freud's view human beings are creatures of sexuality from birth through adulthood. He thus questioned in the most radical manner the concept of childhood innocence. He also portrayed the little-discussed or little-acknowledged matter of sex as one of the bases of mental order and disorder.

The title page from Freud's landmark work, The Interpretation of Dreams. [*New York Public Library Picture Collection.*]

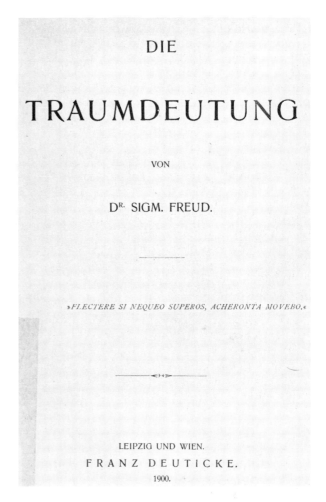

DIE

TRAUMDEUTUNG

VON

DR. SIGM. FREUD.

»*FLECTERE SI NEQUEO SUPEROS, ACHERONTA MOVEBO.*«

LEIPZIG UND WIEN.

FRANZ DEUTICKE.

1900.

During the same decade Freud was also examining the psychic phenomena of dreams. Romantic writers had taken dreams very seriously, but most psychologists had not examined dreams scientifically. As a good rationalist Freud believed that there must exist a reasonable, scientific explanation for the irrational contents of dreams. That examination led him to a reconsideration of the general nature of the human mind. He came to the conclusion that during dreams unconscious wishes, desires, and drives that were excluded from everyday conscious life and experience enjoyed relatively free play in the mind. He argued, "The dream is the (disguised) fulfillment of a (suppressed, repressed) wish."[6] During the waking hours the mind repressed or censored those wishes, which were as important to one's psychological makeup as conscious thought. In fact, those unconscious drives and desires contributed to conscious behavior. Freud developed these concepts and related them to his idea of infantile sexuality in *The Interpretation of Dreams,* published in 1900. It was his most important book.

In later books and essays Freud continued to urge the significance of the role played by the human unconscious. He portrayed a new internal organization of the mind. That inner realm was the arena for struggle and conflict among entities that he termed the *id,* the *ego,* and the *superego.* The first of these consisted of amoral, irrational, driving instincts for sexual gratification, aggression, and general physical and sensual pleasure. The superego constituted the external moral imperatives and expectations imposed on the personality by its society and culture. The ego stood as the mediator between the impulses of the id and the asceticism of the superego. The ego allowed the personality to cope with the inner and outer demands of its existence. Consequently everyday behavior displayed the activity of the personality as its inner drives were partially repressed through the ego's coping with the external moral expectations as interpreted by the superego. It has been a grave misreading of Freud to see him as urging human-

kind to thrust off all repression. He believed that excessive repression could lead to mental disorder but that a certain degree of repression of sexuality and aggression was necessary for civilized living and the survival of humankind.

Freud's work led to nothing less than a revolution in the understanding of human nature. As his views gained adherents just before and after World War I, new dimensions of human life became widely recognized. Human beings were seen as attaining rationality rather than merely exercising it. Civilization itself came to be regarded as a product of repressed or sublimated aggressions and sexual drive.

In Freud's appreciation of the role of instinct, will, dreams, and sexuality, his thought pertained to the Romantic tradition of the nineteenth century. However, Freud must stand as a son of the

---

[6]*The Basic Writings of Sigmund Freud,* trans. by A. A. Brill (New York: The Modern Library, 1938), p. 235.

❧ Freud Explains an Obstacle to the Acceptance of Psychoanalysis

In addition to spawning numerous divergent views, the radical nature of Freud's theories caused them to be heard with misunderstanding, scorn, and opposition. In this 1915 passage, Freud was at pains to give a rational explanation for the nonrational popular reaction to his work. He contended that civilization had been built largely through channeling sexual energies into nonsexual activity. For him, psychoanalysis revealed this important role of the sexual impulses. By so revealing them, psychoanalysis tended to make people uncomfortable. Consequently public opinion played down the discoveries of psychoanalysis by claiming it was either dangerous or immoral.

We believe that civilization has been built up, under the pressure of the struggle for existence, by sacrifices in gratification of the primitive impulses, and that it is to a great extent for ever being recreated, as each individual, successively joining the community, repeats the sacrifice of his instinctive pleasures for the common good. The sexual are among the most important of the instinctive forces thus utilized: they are in this way sublimated, that is to say, their energy is turned aside from its sexual goal and diverted towards other ends, no longer sexual and socially more valuable. But the structure thus built up is insecure, for the sexual impulses are with difficulty controlled; in each individual who takes up his part in the work of civilization there is a danger that a rebellion of the sexual impulses may occur, against this diversion of their energy. Society can conceive of no more power-ful menace to its culture than would arise from the liberation of the sexual impulses and a return of them to their original goal. Therefore society dislikes this sensitive place in its development being touched upon; that the power of the sexual instinct should be recognized, and the significance of the individual's sexual life revealed, is very far from its interests; with a view to discipline it has rather taken the course of diverting attention away from this whole field. For this reason, the revelations of psychoanalysis are not tolerated by it, and it would greatly prefer to brand them as aesthetically offensive, morally reprehensible, or dangerous. . . . It is characteristic of human nature to be inclined to regard anything which is disagreeable as untrue, and then without much difficulty to find arguments against it.

Sigmund Freud, *A General Introduction to Psychoanalysis*, trans. by J. Riviere (Garden City, N.Y.: Garden City Publishing Company, 1943), pp. 23–24.

❧

Enlightenment. Like the *philosophes* he was a realist who wanted human beings to live free of fear and illusions by rationally understanding themselves and their world. He saw the personalities of human beings as being determined by finite physical and mental forces in a finite world. He was hostile to religion and spoke of it as an illusion. Freud, like the writers of the eighteenth century, wished to see civilization and humane behavior prevail. However, more fully than those predecessors, he understood the immense sacrifice of instinctual drives required for civilized behavior. He understood how many previously unsuspected obstacles lay in the way of rationality. Freud believed that the sacrifice and struggle were worthwhile, but he was pessimistic about the future of civilization in the West.

Freud's work marked the beginning of the psychoanalytic movement. By 1910 he had gathered around him a small but highly able group of disciples. Several of his early followers soon moved toward theories of which the master disapproved. The most important of these dissenters was Carl Jung (1875–1961). He was a Swiss whom for many years Freud regarded as his most distinguished and promising student. Before World War I the two men had, however, come to a parting of the ways. Jung had begun to question the primacy of sexual drives in forming human personality and in contributing to mental disorder. He also put much less faith in the guiding light of reason. Jung believed that the human subconscious contained inherited memories from previous generations of human beings. These collective memories, as well as the personal experience of a person, constituted his or her soul. Jung regarded human beings in the twentieth century as alienated from these useful collective memories. One of his more famous books is entitled *Modern Man in Search of a Soul* (1933). Here and elsewhere Jung's thought tended toward mysticism and toward ascribing positive values to religion. Freud was highly critical of most of Jung's work. If Freud's thought derived primarily from the Enlightenment, Jung's was more dependent on Romanticism.

By the 1920s psychoanalysis had become even more fragmented as a movement. Nonetheless, in its several varieties, the movement touched not only psychology but also sociology, anthropology, religious studies, and literary theory. It has been probably the single most important set of ideas whereby men and women in the twentieth century have come to understand themselves and their civilization.

Retreat from Rationalism in Politics

Both nineteenth-century liberals and nineteenth-century socialists agreed that society and politics could be guided according to rational principles. Rational analysis could discern the problems of society and prepare solutions. They generally felt that once given the vote, individuals would behave in their rational political self-interest. Improvement of society and the human condition was

Georges Sorel was the French author of Reflections on Violence, *which portrayed the general strike as the strongest weapon for social change. [Photo Harlingue-Viollet.]*

Max Weber was one of the most influential writers contributing to sociology and economics in the late nineteenth and twentieth centuries. [The Granger Collection.]

possible through education. By the close of the century these views were under attack in both theory and practice. Political scientists and sociologists painted politics as frequently irrational. Racial theorists questioned whether rationality and education could affect human society at all.

During this period, however, one major social theorist stood profoundly impressed by the role of reason in human society. The German sociologist Max Weber (1864–1920) regarded the emergence of rationalization throughout society as the major development of human history. Such rationalization displayed itself in both the development of scientific knowledge and the rise of bureaucratic organization. Weber saw bureaucratization as the most fundamental feature of modern social life. He used this view to oppose Marx's concept of the development of capitalism as the driving force in modern society. Bureaucratization involved the extreme division of labor as each individual person began to fit himself or herself into a particular small role in much larger organizations. Furthermore Weber believed that in modern society people derived their own self-images and sense of personal worth from their position in these organizations. Weber also contended again, in contrast to Marx, that noneconomic factors might account for major developments in human history. For example, in his most famous essay, *The Protestant Ethic and the Spirit of Capitalism* (1905), Weber traced much of the rational character of capitalist enterprise to the ascetic religious doctrines of Puritanism. The Puritans, in his opinion, had accumulated wealth and worked for worldly success less for its own sake than to furnish themselves the assurance that they stood among the elect of God.

In his emphasis on the individual and on the dominant role of rationality, Weber differed from many contemporary social scientists, such as Gustave LeBon, Émile Durkheim, and Georges Sorel in France; Vilfredo Pareto in Italy; and Graham Wallas in England. LeBon (1841–1931) was a psychologist who explored the activity of crowds and mobs. He believed that in crowd situations rational behavior was abandoned. Sorel (1847–1922) argued in *Reflections on Violence* (1908) that people did not pursue rationally perceived goals but were led to action by collectively shared ideals. Durkheim (1858–1917) and Wallas (1858–1932) became deeply interested in the necessity of shared values and activities in a society. These elements rather than a logical analysis of the social situation bound human beings together. Instinct, habit, and affections instead of reason directed human social behavior. Besides playing down the function of reason in society, all of these theorists emphasized the role of collective groups in politics rather than that of the individual formerly championed by liberals.

The same tendencies to question or even to deny the constructive activity of reason in human affairs and to sacrifice the individual to the group manifested themselves in theories of race. Racial thinking had long existed in Europe. Renaissance explorers had displayed considerable prejudice against nonwhite peoples. Since at least the eighteenth century biologists and anthropologists had classified human beings according to the color of their skin, their language, and their stage of civilization. Late-eighteenth-century linguistic scholars had observed similarities between many of the European languages and Sanskrit. They then postulated the existence of an ancient race called the *Aryans,* who had spoken the original language from which the rest derived. During the Romantic period writers had called the different cultures of Europe races. The debates over slavery in the European colonies and the United States had given further opportunity for the development of racial theory. However, in the late nineteenth century the concept of race emerged as a single dominant explanation of the history and the character of large groups of people.

Arthur de Gobineau (1816–1882), a reactionary French diplomat, enunciated the first important theory of race as the major determinant of human history. In his four-volume *Essay on the Inequality of the Human Races* (1853–1854) Gobineau portrayed the troubles of Western civilization as being the result of the long degeneration of the original white Aryan race. It had unwisely intermarried with the inferior yellow and black races, thus diluting the qualities of greatness and ability that originally existed in its blood. Gobineau was deeply pessimistic because he saw no way to reverse the degeneration that had taken place.

Gobineau's essay remained relatively obscure for many years. In the meantime a growing literature by anthropologists and explorers helped to spread racial thinking. In the wake of Darwin's theory, the concept of survival of the fittest was applied to races and nations. The recognition of the animal nature of humankind made the racial idea all the more persuasive. At the close of the century Houston Stewart Chamberlain (1855–1927), an Englishman who settled in Germany, drew together these strands of racial thought into the two volumes of his *Foundations of the Nineteenth Century* (1899). He championed the concept of biological determinism through race, but he was somewhat more optimistic than Gobineau. Chamberlain believed that through genetics the human race could be improved and even that a superior race could be developed. Chamberlain added another element. He pointed to the Jews as the major enemy of European racial regeneration. Chamberlain's book and the lesser works on which it drew aided the spread of anti-Semitism in European political life. Also in Germany the writings of Paul de Lagarde and Julius Langbehn emphasized the supposed racial and cultural dangers posed by the Jews to traditional German national life.

Political and racial anti-Semitism, which have cast such dark shadows across the twentieth century, emerged in part from this atmosphere of racial thought and the retreat from rationality in politics. Religious anti-Semitism dated from at least the Middle Ages. Since the French Revolution west European Jews had gradually gained entry into the civil life of Britain, France, and Germany. Popular anti-Semitism continued to exist as the Jewish community was identified with money and banking interests. During the last third of the century, as finance capitalism changed the economic structure of Europe, people pressured by the changes became hostile toward the Jewish community. This was especially true of the socially and economically

❧ H. S. *Chamberlain* Exalts the Role of Race

Houston Stewart Chamberlain's *Foundations of the Nineteenth Century* (1899) was one of the most influential works of the day to argue for the primary role of race in history. Chamberlain believed that most people in the world were racially mixed and that this mixture weakened those human characteristics most needed for physical and moral strength. However, as demonstrated in the passage below, he also believed that those persons who were assured of their racial purity could act with the most extreme self-confidence and arrogance. Chamberlain's views had a major influence on the Nazi Party in Germany and on others who wished to prove their alleged racial superiority for political purposes.

Nothing is so convincing as the consciousness of the possession of Race. The man who belongs to a distinct, pure race, never loses the sense of it. The guardian angel of his lineage is ever at his side, supporting him where he loses his foothold, warning him like the Socratic Daemon where he is in danger of going astray, compelling obedience, and forcing him to undertakings which, deeming them impossible, he would never have dared to attempt. Weak and erring like all that is human, a man of this stamp recognises himself, as others recognise him, by the sureness of his character, and by the fact that his actions are marked by a certain simple and peculiar greatness, which finds its explanation in his distinctly typical and super-personal qualities. Race lifts a man above himself; it endows him with extraordinary—I might almost say supernatural—powers, so entirely does it distinguish him from the individual who springs from the chaotic jumble of peoples drawn from all parts of the world: and should this man of pure origin be perchance gifted above his fellows, then the fact of Race strengthens and elevates him on every hand, and he becomes a genius towering over the rest of mankind, not because he has been thrown upon the earth like a flaming meteor by a freak of nature, but because he soars heavenward like some strong and stately tree, nourished by thousands and thousands of roots—no solitary individual, but the living sum of untold souls striving for the same goal.

Houston Stewart Chamberlain, *Foundations of the Nineteenth Century*, John Lees, tr. (London: John Lane Limited, 1912), Vol. 1, p. 269.

---

insecure middle class. In Vienna Mayor Karl Lueger (1844–1910) used such anti-Semitism as a major attraction to his successful Christian Socialist Party. In Germany the ultraconservative Lutheran chaplain Adolf Stoecker (1835–1909) revived anti-Semitism. The Dreyfus affair in France allowed a new flowering of hatred toward the Jews.

To this already ugly atmosphere, racial thought contributed the belief that no matter to what extent Jews assimilated themselves and their families into the culture of their country, their Jewishness, and thus their alleged danger to the society, would remain. The problem of race was not in the character but in the blood of the Jew. An important Jewish response to this new, rabid outbreak of anti-Semitism was the launching in 1896 of the Zionist movement to found a separate Jewish state. Its founder was the Austro-Hungarian Theodor

Herzl (1860–1904). The conviction in 1894 of Captain Dreyfus in France and the election of Karl Lueger in 1895 as mayor of Vienna, as well as his personal experiences of discrimination, convinced Herzl that liberal politics and the institutions of the liberal state could not protect the Jews in Europe or assure that they would be treated justly. In 1896 Herzl published *The Jewish State*, in which he called for the organization of a separate state in which the Jews of the world might be assured of those rights and liberties they should be enjoying in the liberal states of Europe. Furthermore Herzl followed the tactics of late-century mass democratic politics by particularly directing his appeal to the economically poor Jews who lived in the ghettos of eastern Europe and the slums of western Europe. The original call to Zionism thus combined a rejection of the anti-Semitism of Europe and a desire to establish some of the ideals of both liberalism and socialism in a state outside Europe.

Racial thinking and revived anti-Semitism were part of a wider late-century movement toward more aggressive nationalism. Previously nationalism had been a movement among European literary figures and liberals. The former had sought to develop what they regarded as the historically distinct qualities of particular national or ethnic literatures. The liberal nationalists had hoped to redraw the map of Europe to reflect ethnic boundaries. The drive for the unification of Italy and Germany had been major causes, as had been the liberation of Poland from foreign domination. The various national groups of the Hapsburg Empire had also sought emancipation from Austrian domination. From the 1870s onward, however, nationalism became a movement with mass support, well-financed organizations, and political parties. Nationalists tended to redefine nationality in terms of race and blood. The new nationalism opposed the internationalism of both liberalism and socialism. The ideal of nationality was used to overcome the pluralism of class, religion, and geography. The nation and its duties replaced religion in the lives of many secularized people. It sometimes became a secular religion in the hands of state schoolteachers, who were replacing the clergy as the instructors of youth. Nationalism of this aggressive, racist variety would prove to be the most powerful ideology of the early twentieth century.

Suggested Readings

J. L. ALTHOLZ, *The Churches in the Nineteenth Century* (1967). A useful overview.

R. ARON, *Main Currents in Sociological Thought*, 2 vols. (1965, 1967). A useful introduction to the founders of the science.

S. BARROWS, *Distorting Mirrors: Visions of the Crowd in Late Nineteenth-Century France* (1981). An important and imaginative examination of crowd psychology as it related to social tension in France.

F. L. BAUMER, *Modern European Thought: Continuity and Change in Ideas, 1600–1950* (1977). The best work on the subject for this period.

F. L. BAUMER, *Religion and the Rise of Scepticism* (1960). Traces the development of religious doubt from the seventeenth to the twentieth centuries.

M. D. BIDDIS, *Father of Racist Ideology: The Social and Political Thought of Count Gobineau* (1970). Sets the subject in the more general context of nineteenth-century thought.

J. W. BURROW, *Evolution and Society: A Study in Victorian Social Theory* (1966). An important study of evolutionary sociology.

O. CHADWICK, *The Secularization of the European Mind in the Nineteenth Century* (1975). The best treatment available.

D. G. CHARLTON, *Positivist Thought in France During the Second Empire, 1852–1870* (1959), and *Secular Religions in France, 1815–1870* (1963). Two clear introductions to important subjects.

C. M. CIPOLLA, *Literacy and Development in the West* (1969). Traces the explosion of literacy in the past two centuries.

A. DANTO, *Nietzsche as Philosopher* (1965). A very helpful and well-organized introduction.

P. GAY, *Freud, Jews, and Other Germans: Masters and Victims in Modernist Culture* (1978). A collection of wide-ranging essays on German intellectual and cultural life.

C. C. GILLISPIE, *Genesis and Geology* (1951). An excellent discussion of the impact of modern geological theory during the early nineteenth century.

C. C. GILLISPIE, *The Edge of Objectivity* (1960). One of the best one-volume treatments of modern scientific ideas.

J. C. GREENE, *The Death of Adam: Evolution and Its Impact on Western Thought* (1959). Emphasizes pre-Darwinian thought.

H. S. HUGHES, *Consciousness and Society: The Reorientation of European Social Thought, 1890–1930* (1958). A wide-ranging discussion of the revolt against positivism.

W. IRVINE, *Apes, Angels, and Victorians* (1955). A lively and sound account of Darwin and Huxley.

W. A. KAUFMANN, *Nietzsche: Philosopher, Psychologist, Antichrist*, rev. ed. (1968). An exposition of Nietzsche's thought and its sources.

J. McMANNERS, *Church and State in France, 1870–1914* (1972). The standard treatment.

J. T. MERZ, *A History of European Thought in the Nineteenth Century*, 4 vols. (1897–1914). Still a useful mine of information.

J. MOORE, *The Post-Darwinian Controversies: A Study of the Protestant Struggle to Come to Terms with Darwin in Great Britain and America, 1870–1900* (1979). A major examination of the impact of Darwinian thought on both science and religion.

R. PASCAL, *From Naturalism to Expressionism: German Literature and Society, 1880–1918* (1973). A helpful survey.

L. POLIAKOV, *The Aryan Myth: A History of Racist and Nationalist Ideas in Europe* (1971). The best introduction to the problem.

P. G. J. PULZER, *The Rise of Political Anti-Semitism in Germany and Austria* (1964). A sound discussion of anti-Semitism in the world of central European politics.

P. RIEF, *Freud: The Mind of the Moralist* (1959). Probably the best one-volume treatment.

C. E. SCHORSKE, *Fin de Siècle Vienna: Politics and Culture* (1980). Major essays on the explosively creative intellectual climate of Vienna.

F. STERN, *The Politics of Cultural Despair: A Study in the Rise of the German Ideology* (1965). An important examination of antimodern and anti-Semitic thought in imperial Germany.

F. M. TURNER, *The Greek Heritage in Victorian Britain* (1981). An examination of the role of Greek antiquity in Victorian thought.

A. VIDLER, *The Church in an Age of Revolution* (1961). A sound account of the problems of Church and State in the nineteenth century.

R. WILLIAMS, *The Long Revolution* (1961). Explores the impact of literacy and popular publishing on English culture.

R. WOLLHEIM, *Sigmund Freud* (1971). An excellent introduction to Freud's intellectual development and his major concepts.

On les aura !

2ᴱ EMPRUNT
DE
LA DÉFENSE NATIONALE
Souscrivez

DEVAMBEZ Imp PARIS

29 Imperialism, Alliances, and War

Expansion of European Power and the "New Imperialism"

During the second half of the nineteenth century, and especially after 1870, European influence and control over the rest of the world grew to an unprecedented degree. North and South America, as well as Australia and New Zealand, became almost integral parts of the European world as the great streams of European immigrants populated them. Until the nineteenth century Asia (with the significant exception of India) and most of Africa had gone their own ways, having little contact with Europe. But the latter part of that century brought the partition of Africa among a number of European nations and the establishment of European economic and political power from the eastern to the western borders of Asia. By the next century this growth of European dominance had brought every part of the globe into a single world economy and had made events in any corner of the world significant thousands of miles away.

The explosive developments in nineteenth-century science, technology, industry, agriculture, transportation, communication, and military weapons provided the chief sources of European power. They made it possible for a small number of Europeans (or Americans) to impose their will on other peoples many times their number by force or by the threat of force. Institutional as well as material advantages allowed Westerners to have their way. The growth of national states that commanded the loyalty, service, and resources of their inhabitants to a degree previously unknown was a Western phenomenon, and it permitted the European nations to deploy their resources in the most effective way. The Europeans also possessed another, less

A patriotic poster for French war bonds. The eager soldier is saying, roughly translated, "We'll get 'em!" The skillful massive propaganda effort undertaken by all governments in World War I reflected the tremendous demands made by total war on all nations. To meet this pressure, governments had to enlist the participation of the entire civilian populace in the war effort. [Vincent Virga Collection.]

tangible weapon: a sense of the superiority of their civilization and way of life. This gave them a confidence that often took the form of an unpleasant arrogance and that fostered the expansionist mood.

The expansion of European influence was not anything new. Spain, Portugal, France, and Britain had controlled territories overseas for centuries, but by the mid-nineteenth century only Great Britain retained extensive holdings. The first half of the century was generally a period of hostility to colonial expansion. Even the British had been sobered by their loss of the American colonies. The French acquired Algeria and part of Indochina, and the British made some additional gains in territories adjacent to their holdings in Canada, India, Australia, and New Zealand. For the most part, however, the doctrine of free trade was dominant, and it opposed the idea of political interference in other lands.

Because Britain ruled the waves and had great commercial advantages as a result of being first in the Industrial Revolution, the British were usually content to let commerce go forward without annexations. Yet they were quite prepared to interfere forcefully if some "backward" country placed barriers in the way of their trade. Still, at mid-century, in Britain as elsewhere, opinion stood predominantly against further political or military involvement overseas.

In the last third of the century, however, the European states swiftly spread their control over perhaps 10 million square miles and 150 million people, about a fifth of the world's land area and a tenth of its population. The movement has been called the *New Imperialism*.

The New Imperialism

Imperialism is a word that has come to be used so loosely as almost to be deprived of meaning. It may be useful to offer a definition that might be widely accepted: "The policy of extending a nation's authority by territorial acquisition or by the establishment of economic and political hegemony over other nations."[1] That definition seems to apply equally well to human actions as far back as ancient Egypt and Mesopotamia and to the performance of European nations in the late nineteenth century. But there were some new elements in the latter

case. Previous imperialisms had either taken the form of seizing land and settling it with the conqueror's people or of establishing trading centers to exploit the resources of the dominated area. The New Imperialism did not completely abandon these devices, but it introduced new ones.

The usual pattern of the New Imperialism was for the European nation to invest capital in the "backward" country, to build productive enterprises and improved means of transportation, to employ great numbers of natives in the process, and thereby to transform the entire economy and culture of the dominated area. To guarantee their investments, the European states would make favorable arrangements with the local government either by enriching the rulers or by threatening them. If these arrangements proved inadequate, the dominant power established different degrees of political control, ranging from full annexation as a colony to protectorate status (whereby the local ruler was controlled by the dominant European state and maintained by its military power), to "spheres-of-influence" status (whereby the European state received special commercial and legal privileges without direct political involvement). Other novelties included the great speed with which European expansion went forward and the way in which participation in this expansion came to be regarded as necessary to retaining status as a great power.

Motives for the New Imperialism: The Economic Interpretation

There has been considerable debate about the motives for the New Imperialism, and after more than a century there is still no agreement. The most widespread interpretation has been economic, most typically in the form given by the English radical economist J. A. Hobson and later adapted by Lenin. As Lenin put it, "Imperialism is the monopoly stage of capitalism,"[2] the last stage of a dying capitalist system. According to this interpretation, competition inevitably leads to the elimination of inefficient capitalists and, therefore, to monopoly. Powerful industrial and financial capitalists soon run out of profitable areas of investment in their own countries and persuade their governments to gain colonies in "backward" countries, where they can find higher profits from their

[1] *American Heritage Dictionary of the English Language* (New York: Houghton Mifflin Co., 1969), p. 660.

[2] V. I. Lenin, *Imperialism, the Highest Stage of Capitalism* (New York: International Publishers, 1939), p. 88.

investments, new markets for their products, and safe sources of the needed raw materials.

The facts of the matter do not support this viewpoint. The European powers did export considerable amounts of capital in the form of investments abroad, but not in such a manner as to fit the model of Hobson and Lenin. Britain, for example, made heavier investments abroad before 1875 than during the next two decades. Only a very small percentage of British and European investments overseas, moreover, went to the new colonial areas. Most went into Europe itself or into older, well-established areas like the United States, Canada, Australia, and New Zealand. Even when investments were made in the new areas, they were not necessarily put into colonies held by the investing country.

The facts are equally discouraging for those who emphasize the need for markets and raw materials. Colonies were not usually important markets for the great imperial nations, and all were forced to rely on areas that they did not control as sources of vital raw materials. It is not even clear that control of the new colonies was particularly profitable. Britain, to be sure, benefited greatly from its rule of India. It is also true that some European businessmen and politicians hoped to find a cure for the great depression of 1873–1896 in colonial expansion. Nevertheless, as one of the leading students of the subject has said, "No one can determine whether the accounts of empire ultimately closed with a favorable cash balance."[3] That is true of the European imperial nations collectively, but it is certain that for some of them, like Italy and Germany, empire was a losing proposition. Some individuals and companies, of course, were able to make great profits from particular colonial ventures, but such people were able to influence national policy only occasionally. Economic motives certainly played a part, but a full understanding of the New Imperialism requires a search for further motives as well.

Cultural, Religious, and Social Interpretations

Advocates of imperialism put forth various justifications. Some argued that it was the responsibility of the advanced European nations to bring the benefits of their higher culture and superior civili-

[3] D. K. Fieldhouse, *The Colonial Empires* (New York: Delacorte, 1966), p. 393.

zation to the people of "backward" lands, but few people were influenced by such arrogant arguments, though many shared the intellectual assumptions. Religious groups argued for the responsibility of Western nations to bring the benefits of Christianity to the heathen with more extensive efforts and aid from their governments. Some politicians and diplomats argued for imperialism as a tool of social policy. In Germany, for instance, some people suggested that imperial expansion might serve to deflect public interest away from domestic politics and social reform. But Germany acquired only a few colonies, and such considerations played little if any role.

In Britain such arguments were made, as was their opposite. The statesman Joseph Chamberlain argued for the empire as a source of profit and economic security that would finance a great program of domestic reform and welfare. To the extent that they had any influence, these arguments were not important as motives for imperialism because they were made well after the British had acquired most of their empire. Another common and apparently plausible justification was that colonies would provide a good place to settle surplus population. In fact, most European emigrants went to areas not controlled by their countries, chiefly to North and South America and Australia.

The Scramble for Africa: Strategic and Political Interpretations

Strategic and political considerations seem to have been more important in bringing on the New Imperialism. The scramble for Africa in the 1880s is one example. Britain was the only great power with extensive overseas holdings on the eve of the scramble. The completion of the Suez Canal in 1869 made Egypt an area of vital interest to the British because it sat astride the shortest route to India. Under Disraeli Britain purchased a major, but not a controlling, interest in the canal in 1875. When Egypt's stability was threatened by internal troubles in the 1880s, the British moved in and established a protectorate. Then, to protect Egypt, they advanced into the Sudan.

France became involved in Africa in 1830 by sending a naval expedition to Algeria to attack the pirates based there. Before long French settlers arrived and established a colony. By 1882 France

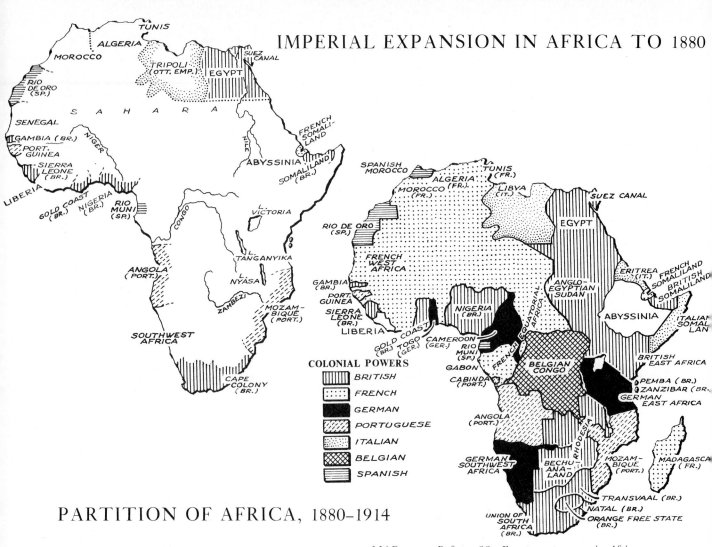

PARTITION OF AFRICA, 1880–1914

COLONIAL POWERS

- BRITISH
- FRENCH
- GERMAN
- PORTUGUESE
- ITALIAN
- BELGIAN
- SPANISH

MAP 29.1 *Before 1880 European presence in Africa was largely the remains of early exploration by old imperialists and did not penetrate the heart of the continent. By 1914 the occupying powers included most large European states; only Liberia and Abyssinia remained independent.*

was in full control of Algeria, and at about the same time, to prevent Tunisia from falling into Italy's hands, France took over that area of North Africa also. Soon lesser states like Belgium, Portugal, Spain, and Italy were scrambling for African colonies. By the 1890s their intervention had compelled Britain to expand northward from the Cape of Good Hope into what is now Zimbabwe. Britain may have had significant strategic reasons for protecting the Suez and Cape routes to India, but France and the smaller European nations did not have such reasons. Their motives were political as well as economic, for they equated status as a great power (Britain stood as the chief model) with the possession of colonies. They therefore sought colonies as evidence of their own importance.

Bismarck appears to have pursued an imperial policy, however brief, from coldly political motives. In 1884 and 1885 Germany declared protectorates over Southwest Africa, Togoland, the Cameroons, and East Africa. None of these places was particularly valuable or of intrinsic strategic importance. Bismarck himself had no interest in overseas colonies and once compared them to fine furs worn by impoverished Polish noblemen who had no shirts underneath. His concern lay in Germany's exposed position in Europe. On one occasion he said, "My map of Africa lies in Europe. Here is Russia, and there is France, and here in the middle are we.

In this picture based on his own sketch, Henry M. Stanley (1841–1904), the explorer-adventurer sent in 1871 by the New York Herald *to what was then called "darkest Africa" to find the supposedly lost missionary, David Livingston arrives at an African village. The travels of these two men in Africa exemplify the diversity of motives that led westerners to explore the interior of the continent in the last half of the nineteenth century. [Radio Times Hulton Picture Library.]*

Cecil Rhodes (1835–1902), shown here resting in an African meadow, on the African plain, was the leading advocate of British interests in South Africa. Rhodes's dream, never realized, was for a railway from Capetown to Cairo running throughout the entire length of Africa on British-controlled territory. [Bettmann Archive.]

873

❧ Bismarck Reminisces About His Foreign Policy

The following is Bismarck's own account of his foreign policy written during the years of his retirement, 1890–1898.

*The triple alliance which I originally sought to conclude after the peace of Frankfurt, and about which I had already sounded Vienna and St. Petersburg, from Meaux, in September 1870, was an alliance of the three emperors with the further idea of bringing into it monarchical Italy. It was designed for the struggle which, as I feared, was before us; between the two European tendencies which Napoleon called Republican and Cossack, and which I, according to our present ideas, should designate on the one side as the system of order on a monarchical basis, and on the other as the social republic to the level of which the antimonarchical development is wont to sink, either slowly or by leaps and bounds, until the conditions thus created become intolerable, and the disappointed populace are ready for a violent return to monarchical institutions in a Cæsarean form. I consider that the task of escaping from this circulus vitiosus, or, if possible, of sparing the present gener-*ation *and their children an entrance into it, ought to be more closely incumbent on the strong existing monarchies, those monarchies which still have a vigorous life, than any rivalry over the fragments of nations which people the Balkan peninsula. If the monarchical governments have no understanding of the necessity for holding together in the interests of political and social order, but make themselves subservient to the chauvinistic impulses of their subjects, I fear that the international revolutionary and social struggles which will have to be fought out will be all the more dangerous, and take such a form that the victory on the part of monarchical order will be more difficult. Since 1871 I have sought for the most certain assurance against those struggles in the alliance of the three emperors, and also in the effort to impart to the monarchical principle in Italy a firm support in that alliance.*

Otto von Bismarck, *Reflections and Reminiscences,* ed. by Theodore S. Hamerow (New York: Harper Torchbooks, 1968), pp. 236–237.

That is my map of Africa."[4] He acquired colonies chiefly to improve Germany's diplomatic position in Europe. He tried to turn France from hostility against Germany by diverting the French toward colonial interests. At the same time German colonies in Africa could be used as a subtle weapon with which to persuade the British to be reasonable.

The Irrational Element

Germany's annexations started a wild scramble by the other European powers to establish claims on what was left of Africa. By 1890 almost all of the continent was parceled out. Great powers and small expanded into areas neither profitable nor strategic for reasons less calculating and rational than Bismarck's. "Empire in the modern period," D. K. Fieldhouse has observed, "was the product of European power: its reward was power or the sense of power."[5]

Such motives were not new. They had been well understood by the Athenian spokesman at Melos in 416 B.C., whose words are reported by Thucydides: "Of the gods we believe and of men we know clearly that by a necessity of their nature where they have the power they rule."[6]

IMPERIALISM IN THE PACIFIC. By the early years of the twentieth century the islands of the Pacific were also apportioned among the Western powers. Southeast Asia was divided among Britain in Burma, Malaya, and North Borneo; France in Indochina; and the Netherlands in the East Indies. China was able to maintain its territory and sovereignty in spite of European interference, in part

[4] Quoted by J. Remak in *The Origins of World War I, 1871–1914* (New York: Holt, Rinehart & Winston, 1967), p. 5.

[5] Fieldhouse, p. 393.

[6] Thucydides, *The Peloponnesian War,* 5.105.2.

because its central government continued to function, but chiefly because of rivalry among the great powers. Still the powers established spheres of influence, opportunities for trade and investment immune from Chinese courts, and even military and naval bases. In addition to imperial nations of fairly long standing, China was of interest to two powers new on the international scene, Japan and the United States. Japan had been brought forcibly into contact with the Western world by the arrival in Tokyo Bay of an American naval force under Commodore Matthew Perry (1794–1858) in 1853.

THE AWAKENING OF JAPAN. The trampling of Japanese pride by Westerners in the succeeding years led to discontent with the existing government, the shogunate. Ever since 1603 the Togugawa clan had controlled the office of shogun, or military chief. The shoguns ruled in the name of the emperor but kept the real power for themselves. When the last shogun showed himself unable to protect Japanese honor against the foreigners from the West, rebellious nobles pressed for his abdication in 1867. The successful rebels were determined to gain parity with the West by adopting such Western ways as were necessary. They instituted reforms that swiftly abolished the remains of Japanese feudalism and began to move Japan into the modern world. In 1868 a new emperor, Mutsuhito, came to the throne. The imperial office was restored to its earlier importance, if only in theory. The new reign and the era it introduced were given the name *Meiji*. The constitutional and political reforms introduced in the Meiji era (1868–1912), as well as the rapid military and technological advance that accompanied it, swiftly made Japan a modern nation. Soon the Japanese adopted Western imperialism as well. In 1895 they defeated the Chinese in a one-sided war, took Formosa and the Liaotung Peninsula, and informally dominated the newly independent Korea.

The emergence of Japan frightened the other powers interested in China. The Russians were building a railroad across Siberia to Vladivostok and were afraid of any power that might threaten Manchuria. Together with France and Germany they applied diplomatic pressure that forced Japan out of the Liaotung Peninsula and its harbor, Port Arthur, and all pressed feverishly for concessions in China. Fearing that China, its markets, and its investment opportunities would soon be closed to its citizens, the United States in 1899 proposed the "Open Door Policy," which opposed foreign an-

The classical columns on the former British Viceroy's House in New Delhi, India, built in 1912, and now the residence of the President of India, illustrate the manner in which Western taste and design were imposed on much of the rest of the world during the age of imperialism. [Government of India Tourist Office, New York.]

nexations in China and allowed businessmen of all nations to trade there on equal terms. The support of Britain helped win acceptance of the policy by all the powers except Russia.

The United States had only recently emerged as a force in international affairs. After freeing itself of British rule and consolidating its independence during the Napoleonic Wars, the Americans had busied themselves with westward expansion on the North American continent until the end of the nineteenth century. The Monroe Doctrine of 1823 had, in effect, made the entire Western Hemisphere an American protectorate. Cuba's attempt to gain independence from Spain was the spark for the new United States involvement in international affairs. Sympathy for the Cuban cause, American investments on the island, the desire for Cuban sugar, and concern over the island's strategic importance in the Caribbean all helped win the Americans over to the idea of a war with Spain.

Victory in the Spanish–American War of 1898 brought the United States an informal protectorate over Cuba and the annexation of Puerto Rico and drove Spain completely out of the Western Hemisphere. The Americans also purchased the Philippine Islands and Guam, and Germany acquired the other Spanish islands in the Pacific. The Americans and the Germans also divided Samoa between them. What was left of the Pacific islands was

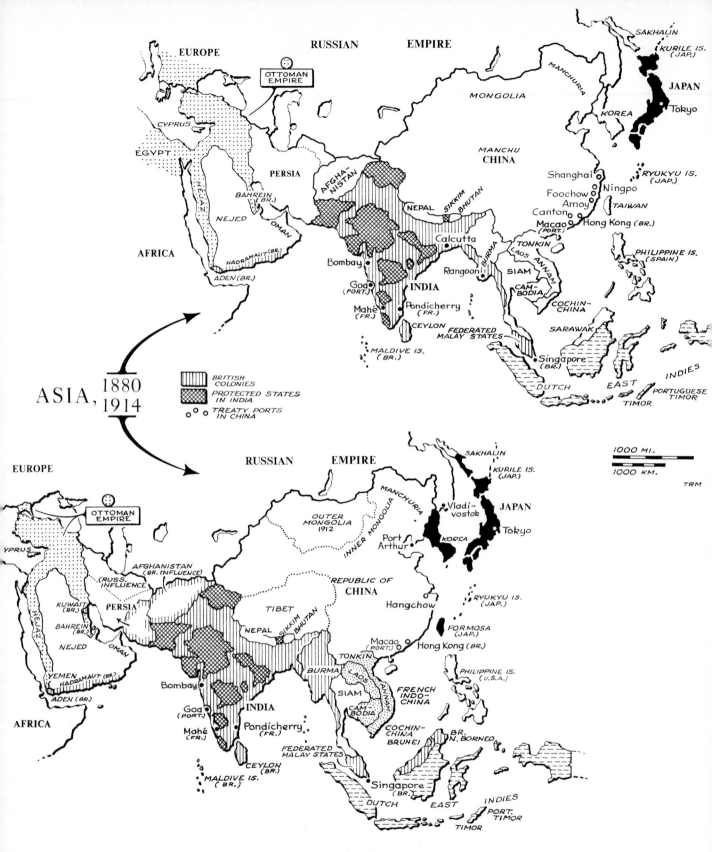

ASIA, 1880 1914

BRITISH COLONIES

PROTECTED STATES IN INDIA

TREATY PORTS IN CHINA

Top map:

EUROPE

RUSSIAN EMPIRE

OTTOMAN EMPIRE

CYPRUS

EGYPT

AFRICA

PERSIA

BAHREIN (BR.)

NEJED

HADRAMAUT (BR.)

ADEN (BR.)

OMAN

HEJAZ

AFGHA-NISTAN

MONGOLIA

MANCHURIA

MANCHU CHINA

SAKHALIN

KURILE IS. (JAP.)

JAPAN

Tokyo

KOREA

RYUKYU IS. (JAP.)

Shanghai

Foochow Ningpo

Amoy

Canton TAIWAN

Macao (PORT.) Hong Kong (BR.)

NEPAL SIKKIM BHUTAN

Calcutta

Bombay

Goa (PORT.)

INDIA

Mahé (FR.)

Pondicherry (FR.)

CEYLON

Rangoon

BURMA

TONKIN

LAOS ANNAM

SIAM

CAM-BODIA

COCHIN-CHINA

PHILIPPINE IS. (SPAIN)

SARAWAK

MALDIVE IS. (BR.)

FEDERATED MALAY STATES

Singapore (BR.)

DUTCH EAST INDIES

TIMOR PORTUGUESE TIMOR

Bottom map:

EUROPE

RUSSIAN EMPIRE

OTTOMAN EMPIRE

CYPRUS

HEJAZ

KUWAIT (BR.)

BAHREIN (BR.)

NEJED

OMAN

YEMEN

HADRAMAUT (BR.)

ADEN (BR.)

AFRICA

AFGHANISTAN (BR. INFLUENCE)

(RUSS. INFLUENCE)

PERSIA

OUTER MONGOLIA 1912

INNER MONGOLIA

MANCHURIA

TIBET

REPUBLIC OF CHINA

SAKHALIN

KURILE IS. (JAP.)

Vladi-vostok

JAPAN

Port Arthur

KOREA

Tokyo

1000 MI.

1000 KM.

TRM

Hangchow

RYUKYU IS. (JAP.)

FORMOSA (JAP.)

Macao (PORT.) Hong Kong (BR.)

NEPAL SIKKIM BHUTAN

Bombay

Goa (PORT.)

INDIA

Mahé (FR.)

Pondicherry (FR.)

CEYLON (BR.)

MALDIVE IS. (BR.)

FEDERATED MALAY STATES

BURMA

SIAM

TONKIN

LAOS ANNAM

CAM-BODIA

COCHIN-CHINA

FRENCH INDO-CHINA

PHILIPPINE IS. (U.S.A.)

BR. N. BORNEO

BRUNEI

Singapore (BR.)

DUTCH EAST INDIES

PORT. TIMOR

TIMOR

876

Kipling Advises the Americans: The Responsibility for Empire

THE WHITE MAN'S BURDEN
1899
(The United States and the Philippine Islands)

Take up the White Man's burden—
  Send forth the best ye breed—
Go bind your sons to exile
  To serve your captives' need;
To wait in heavy harness
  On fluttered folk and wild—
Your new-caught, sullen peoples,
  Half devil and half child.

Take up the White Man's burden—
  The savage wars of peace—
Fill full the mouth of Famine
  And bid the sickness cease;
And when your goal is nearest
  The end for others sought,
Watch Sloth and heathen Folly
  Bring all your hope to nought.

Take up the White Man's burden—
  And reap his old reward:
The blame of those ye better,
  The hate of those ye guard—
The cry of hosts ye humour
  (Ah, slowly!) toward the light:—
"Why brought ye us from bondage,
  "Our loved Egyptian night?"

Take up the White Man's burden—
  In patience to abide,
To veil the threat of terror
  And check the show of pride;
By open speech and simple,
  An hundred times made plain,
To seek another's profit,
  And work another's gain.

Take up the White Man's burden—
  No tawdry rule of kings,
But toil of serf and sweeper—
  The tale of common things.
The ports ye shall not enter,
  The roads ye shall not tread,
Go make them with your living,
  And mark them with your dead!

Take up the White Man's burden—
  Ye dare not stoop to less—
Nor call too loud on Freedom
  To cloak your weariness;
By all ye cry or whisper,
  By all ye leave or do,
The silent, sullen peoples
  Shall weigh your Gods and you.

Take up the White Man's burden—
  Have done with childish days—
The lightly proffered laurel,
  The easy, ungrudged praise.
Comes now, to search your manhood
  Through all the thankless years,
Cold-edged with dear-bought wisdom,
  The judgment of your peers!

"The White Man's Burden (1899)," from *Rudyard Kipling's Verse: Definitive Edition* (New York: Doubleday, 1940) pp. 321–323.

OPPOSITE: MAP 29.2 *As in Africa, the decades before World War I saw imperialism spread widely and rapidly in Asia. Two new powers, Japan and the United States joined the British, French, and Dutch in extending control both to islands and to mainland and in exploiting an enfeebled China.*

soon taken by France and England. Hawaii had been under American influence for some time and had been asking for annexation, which was accomplished in 1898. This outburst of activity after the Spanish war made the United States an imperial and Pacific power. Soon after the turn of the century most of the world had come under the control of the industrialized Western nations. The one remaining area of great vulnerability was the Ottoman Empire, but its fate was closely tied up with European developments and must be treated in that context.

Emergence of the German Empire and the Alliance Systems (1873–1890)

Prussia's victories over Austria and France and its creation of a large, powerful German Empire in 1871 revolutionized European diplomacy. The sudden appearance of a vast new political unit that brought together the majority of the German people to form a nation of great and growing population, wealth, industrial capacity, and military power posed new problems. The balance of power created at the Congress of Vienna was altered radically. Britain retained its position and so did Russia, even though somewhat weakened by the Crimean War. Austria, however, had fallen quite a distance, and its position was destined to deteriorate further as the forces of nationalism threatened to disintegrate the Austro-Hungarian Empire. French power and prestige were badly damaged by the Franco-Prussian War and the German annexation of Alsace–Lorraine. The weakened French were both afraid of their powerful new neighbor and at the same time resentful of the defeat, the loss of territory and population, and the loss of their traditional position of dominance in western Europe.

Until 1890 Bismarck continued to guide German policy. He insisted after 1871 that Germany was a satisfied power and wanted no further territorial gains, and he meant it. He only wanted to consolidate the new international situation by avoiding a new war that might undo his achievement. Aware of French resentment, he tried to assuage it by friendly relations and by supporting French colonial aspirations in order to turn French attention away from European discontents. At the same time he prepared for the worst. If France could not be conciliated, it must be isolated. The kernel of Bis-

"*Colonies for Germany, Too.*" *This German cartoon of 1884 attacks Bismarck for neglecting imperial expansion overseas. He is shown attending to domestic social reform while the southern hemisphere is carved up by other nations. The caption to the cartoon read, "The Pacific Ocean is the Mediterranean of the future." [Thames and Hudson Ltd.]*

marck's policy was to prevent an alliance between France and any other European power—especially Austria or Russia—that would threaten Germany with a war on two fronts.

WAR IN THE BALKANS. His first move was to establish the Three Emperors' League in 1873. It brought together the three great conservative empires of Germany, Austria, and Russia. The league soon collapsed as a result of the Russo-Turkish War, which broke out in 1875 because of

OPPOSITE: *This is a satirical German cartoon of 1896 poking fun at German efficiency as applied to colonial adventures. In the upper picture is the deplorably idyllic jungle; in the bottom, the new and satisfactory tidiness brought about by German imperialism. [The Granger Collection.]*

an uprising in the Ottoman Balkan provinces of Bosnia and Herzegovina. The tottering Ottoman Empire was held together chiefly by the competing aims of those powers who awaited its demise. The weakness of the Ottoman Empire encouraged Serbia and Montenegro to come to the aid of their fellow Slavs. Soon the rebellion spread to Bulgaria. Then Russia entered the fray and turned it into a major international crisis. The Russians hoped to pursue their traditional policy of expansion at Ottoman expense and especially hoped to achieve their most cherished goal: control of Constantinople and the Dardanelles. The Russian intervention also reflected the influence of the Pan-Slavic movement, which sought to bring together all the Slavic peoples, even those under Austrian or Ottoman rule, under the protection of Holy Mother Russia.

The Ottoman Empire was weak, and before long it was forced to ask for peace. The Treaty of San Stefano of March 1878 was a Russian triumph. The Slavic states in the Balkans were freed of Ottoman rule, and Russia itself obtained territorial gains and a heavy monetary indemnity. But the Russian victory was not lasting. The other great powers were alarmed by the terms of the settlement. Austria feared that the great Slavic victory and the powerful increase in Russian influence in the Balkans would cause dangerous shock waves in its own Balkan provinces. The British were alarmed by the damage the Russian victory would do to the European balance of power and especially by the thought of possible Russian control of the Dardanelles. Disraeli was determined to resist, and British public opinion supported him. A music-hall song that became popular gave the language a new word for superpatriotism: *jingoism*.

> We don't want to fight,
> But by jingo if we do,
> We've got the men,
> We've got the ships,
> We've got the money too!

THE CONGRESS OF BERLIN. Even before the Treaty of San Stefano, Disraeli sent a fleet to Constantinople. After the magnitude of Russia's appetite was known, Britain and Austria forced Russia to agree to an international conference at which the provisions of the treaty would be reviewed by the other great powers. The resulting Congress of Berlin met in June and July of 1878 under the presidency of Bismarck. The choice of site and presiding officer was a clear recognition of Germany's new importance and of its chancellor's claim that his policy called for no further territorial gains and aimed at preserving the peace. Bismarck referred to himself as an "honest broker," and the title seems justified. He agreed to the congress simply because he wanted to avoid a war between Russia and Austria into which he feared Germany would be drawn with nothing to gain and much to lose. From the collapsing Ottoman Empire he wanted nothing. "The Eastern Question," he said, "is not worth the healthy bones of a single Pomeranian musketeer."[7]

The decisions of the congress were a blow to Russian ambitions. Bulgaria was reduced in size by two thirds and was deprived of access to the Aegean Sea. Austria–Hungary was given Bosnia and Herzegovina to "occupy and administer," although those provinces remained formally under Ottoman rule. Britain received Cyprus, and France gained permission to expand into Tunisia. These privileges were compensation for the gains that Russia was permitted to keep. Germany asked for nothing but got little credit from Russian for its restraint. The Russians believed that they had saved Prussia in 1807 from complete dismemberment by Napoleon and had expected a show of German gratitude. They were bitterly disappointed, and the Three Emperors' League was dead.

All of the Balkan states were also annoyed by the Berlin settlement. Romania wanted Bessarabia; Bulgaria wanted a return to the borders of the Treaty of San Stefano; and Greece wanted a part of the Ottoman spoils. The major trouble spot, however, was in the south Slavic states of Serbia and Montenegro. They deeply resented the Austrian occupation of Bosnia and Herzegovina, as did many of the natives of those provinces. The south Slavic question, no less than the estrangement between Russia and Germany, was a threat to the peace of Europe.

GERMAN ALLIANCES WITH RUSSIA AND AUSTRIA. For the moment Bismarck could ignore the Balkans, but he could not ignore the breach in his eastern alliance system. With Russia alienated, he turned to Austria and concluded a secret treaty in 1879. The resulting Dual Alliance provided that if either Germany or Austria were attacked by Russia the ally would help the attacked party. If the

---

[7]Quoted by Hajo Holborn, *A History of Modern Germany*, 1840–1945 (New York: Knopf, 1969), p. 239.

signatory countries were attacked by someone else, each promised at least to maintain neutrality. The treaty was for five years and was renewed regularly until 1918. As the central point in German policy, it was criticized at the time, and some have judged it mistaken in retrospect. It appeared to tie the German fortunes to those of the troubled Austro-Hungarian Empire and in that way to borrow trouble. At the same time, by isolating the Russians, it pushed them in the direction of seeking alliances in the West.

Bismarck was fully aware of these dangers but discounted them with good reason. At no time did he allow his Austrian alliance to drag Germany into Austria's Balkan quarrels. As he put it himself, in any alliance there is a horse and a rider, and in this one Bismarck meant Germany to be the rider. He made it clear to the Austrians that the alliance was purely defensive and that Germany would never be a party to an attack on Russia. "For us, " he said, "Balkan questions can never be a motive for war."[8]

Bismarck believed that monarchical, reactionary Russia would not seek an alliance either with republican, revolutionary France or with increasingly democratic Britain. In fact, he expected the news of the Austro-German negotiations to frighten Russia into seeking closer relations with Germany, and he was right. Russian diplomats soon approached him, and by 1881 he had concluded a renewal of the Three Emperors' League on a firmer basis. The three powers promised to maintain friendly neutrality in case either of the others was attacked by a fourth power. Other clauses included the right of Austria to annex Bosnia–Herzegovina whenever it wished and closed the Dardanelles to all nations in case of war. The agreement allayed German fears of a Russian–French alliance and Russian fears of a combination of Austria and Britain against it, of Britain's fleet sailing into the Black Sea, and of a hostile combination of Germany and Austria. Most importantly, the agreement aimed at a resolution of the conflicts in the Balkans between Austria and Russia. Though it did not put an end to such conflicts, it was a significant step toward peace.

THE TRIPLE ALLIANCE. In 1882 Italy, ambitious for colonial expansion and annoyed by the French preemption of Tunisia, asked to join the Dual Alliance. The provisions of its entry were defensive and were directed against France. At this

point Bismarck's policy was a complete success. He was allied with three of the great powers and friendly with the other, Great Britain, which held aloof from all alliances. France was isolated and no threat. Bismarck's diplomacy was a great achievement, but an even greater challenge was to maintain this complicated system of secret alliances in the face of the continuing rivalries among Germany's allies. In spite of another Balkan war that broke out in 1885 and again estranged Austria and Russia, he succeeded. Although the Three Emperors' League lapsed, the Triple Alliance (Germany, Austria and Italy) was renewed for another five years. To restore German relations with Russia, he negotiated the Reinsurance Treaty of 1887, in which both powers promised to remain neutral if either was attacked. All seemed smooth, but a change in the German monarchy soon overturned everything.

In 1888 William II (1888–1918) came to the German throne. He was twenty-nine years old, ambitious and impetuous. He was imperious by temperament and believed in monarchy by divine right. He had suffered an injury at birth that left him with a withered arm, and he compensated for this disability by means of vigorous exercise, by a military bearing and outlook, and sometimes by an embarrassingly loud and bombastic rhetoric.

Like many Germans of his generation, William II was filled with a sense of Germany's destiny as the leading power of Europe. He wanted to achieve recognition at least of equality from Britain, the land of his mother and of his grandmother, Queen Victoria. To achieve a "place in the sun," he and his contemporaries wanted a navy and colonies like Britain's. These aims, of course, ran counter to Bismarck's limited continental policy. When William argued for a navy as a defense against a British landing in north Germany, Bismarck replied, "If the British should land on our soil, I should have them arrested." This was only one example of the great distance between the young emperor, or Kaiser, and his chancellor. In 1890 William used a disagreement over domestic policy to dismiss Bismarck.

As long as Bismarck held power, Germany was secure, and there was peace among the great European powers. Although he made mistakes and was not always successful, there was much to admire in his understanding and management of international relations in the hard world of reality. He had a clear and limited idea of his nation's goals. He

[8]Quoted by J. Remak, p. 14.

resisted pressures for further expansion with few and insignificant exceptions. He understood and used the full range of diplomatic weapons: appeasement and deterrence, threats and promises, secrecy and openness. He understood the needs and hopes of other countries and, where possible, tried to help to accomplish them or used them to his own advantage. His system of alliances created a stalemate in the Balkans at the same time that it ensured German security.

During Bismarck's time Germany was a force for European peace and was increasingly understood to be so. This position would not, of course, have been possible without its great military power, but it also required the leadership of a statesman who was willing and able to exercise restraint and who could make a realistic estimate of what his country needed and what was possible.

Forging of the Triple Entente (1890–1907)

FRANCO-RUSSIAN ALLIANCE. Almost immediately after Bismarck's retirement his system of alliances collapsed. His successor was General Leo von Caprivi (1831–1899), who had once asked, "What kind of jackass will dare to be Bismarck's successor?" Caprivi refused the Russian request to renew the Reinsurance Treaty, in part because he felt in-competent to continue Bismarck's complicated policy and in part because he wished to draw Germany closer to Britain. The results were unfortunate, as Britain remained aloof and Russia was alienated. Even Bismarck had assumed that ideological differences were too great to permit a Franco-Russian alliance, but political isolation and the need for foreign capital unexpectedly drove the Russians toward France. The French, who were even more isolated, were glad to encourage their investors to pour capital into Russia if it would help produce an alliance and security against Germany. In 1894 the Franco-Russian alliance against Germany was signed.

BRITAIN AND GERMANY. Britain now became the key to the international situation. Colonial rivalries pitted the British against the Russians in Central Asia and against the French in Africa. Traditionally Britain had also opposed Russian control of Constantinople and the Dardanelles and French control of the Low Countries. There was no reason to think that Britain would soon become friendly with its traditional rivals or abandon its accustomed friendliness toward the Germans. Yet within a decade of William II's accession Germany had become the enemy in the minds of the British. Before the turn of the century popular British thrillers about imaginary wars portrayed the French as the invader; after the turn of the century the enemy was

"War," an 1895 lithograph by the French painter Henri Rousseau. This drawing was commissioned by a left-wing French journal. Many observers feared that the arms race and the growth of international tension were making another war increasingly likely by the turn of the century. [Collection, The Museum of Modern Art.]

always German. This remarkable transformation has often been attributed to the economic rivalry of Germany and Britain, in which Germany made vast strides to challenge and even overtake British production in various materials and markets. There can be no doubt that Germany made such gains and that many Britons resented them, but the problem was not a serious cause of hostility and waned as the first decade of the century wore on. The real problem lay in the foreign and naval policies of the German emperor and his ministers.

William II's attitude toward Britain was respectful and admiring, especially with regard to its colonial empire and its mighty fleet. At first Germany tried to win the British over to the Triple Alliance, but when Britain clung to its policy of "splendid isolation," German policy took a different tack. The idea was to demonstrate Germany's worthiness as an ally by withdrawing support and even making trouble for Britain. This odd manner of gaining an ally reflected the Kaiser's confused feelings toward Britain, which consisted of dislike and jealousy mixed with admiration. These feelings reflected those of many Germans, especially in the intellectual community, who like William were eager for Germany to pursue a "World Policy" rather than Bismarck's limited one that confined German interests to Europe. They, too, saw England as the barrier to German ambitions, and their influence in the schools, the universities, and the press guaranteed popular approval of actions and statements hostile to Britain.

The Germans began to exert pressure against Britain in Africa by barring British attempts to build a railroad from Capetown to Cairo. They also openly sympathized with the Boers of South Africa in their resistance to British expansion. In 1896 William insulted the British by sending a congratulatory telegram to Paul Kruger (1825–1904), president of the Transvaal, for repulsing a British raid "without having to appeal to friendly powers for assistance."

In 1898 William's dream of a German navy began to achieve reality with the passage of a naval law providing for nineteen battleships. In 1900 a second law doubled that figure. The architect of the new navy was Admiral Alfred von Tirpitz (1849–1930), who openly proclaimed that Germany's naval policy was aimed at Britain. His "risk" theory argued that Germany could build a fleet strong enough, not to defeat the British, but to do sufficient damage to make the British navy inferior to other powers like France or the United States. The theory was, in fact, absurd because as Germany's fleet became menacing, the British would certainly build ships to maintain their advantage, and British financial resources were greater than Germany's. The naval policy, therefore, was doomed to failure. Over time its main achievements were to waste German resources and to begin a great naval race with Britain. It is not too much to say, moreover, that the threat posed by the German navy did more to antagonize British opinion than anything else. As the German navy grew and German policies seemed to become more threatening, the British were alarmed enough to abandon their traditional attitudes and policies.

At first, however, Britain was not unduly concerned. The British were embarrassed by the general hostility of world opinion during the Boer War (1899–1902) and were suddenly alarmed that their isolation no longer seemed so splendid. The Germans had acted with restraint during the war. Between 1898 and 1901 Joseph Chamberlain, the colonial secretary, made several attempts to conclude an alliance with Germany. The Germans, confident that a British alliance with France or Russia was impossible, refused and expected the British to make greater concessions in the future.

THE ENTENTE CORDIALE. The first breach in Britain's isolation came in 1902, when an alliance was concluded with Japan to relieve the pressure of defending British interests in the Far East against Russia. Next Britain abandoned its traditional antagonism toward France and in 1904 concluded a series of agreements with the French, collectively called the *Entente Cordiale*. It was not a formal treaty and had no military provisions, but it settled all outstanding colonial differences between the two nations. The Entente Cordiale was a long step toward aligning the British with Germany's great potential enemy.

Britain's new relationship with France was surprising, but in 1904 hardly anyone believed that the British whale and the Russian bear would ever come together. The Russo-Japanese war of 1904–1905 made such a development seem even less likely because Britain was allied with Russia's enemy. But Britain had behaved with restraint, and the Russians were chastened by their unexpected and humiliating defeat. The defeat had also led to the Russian Revolution of 1905. Although the revolution was put down, it left Russia weak and reduced British apprehensions in that direc-

William II Tries to Pacify British Public Opinion: The Daily Telegraph Interview

In 1908 relations between Germany and Great Britain had become tense for a variety of reasons, but chiefly because of Germany's decision to build a battle fleet and challenge British supremacy at sea. The German Emperor William II decided to try to smooth things over by means of an interview planted in a London newspaper, the *Daily Telegraph*. The article appeared on October 28, 1908, and immediately caused an uproar in Germany as well as in Britain. Some Germans were so incensed by its indiscretions that they called for the emperor's abdication. The British, far from being pacified, were outraged. The following selections from the interview make both reactions understandable. The British interviewer reported:

As I have said, his Majesty honoured me with a long conversation and spoke with impulsive and unusual frankness. "You English," he said, "are mad, mad, mad as March hares. What has come over you that you are so completely given over to suspicions quite unworthy of a great nation? What more can I do than I have done? I declared with all the emphasis at my command, in my speech at Guildhall, that my heart is set upon peace, and that it is one of my dearest wishes to live on the best of terms with England. Have I ever been false to my word? Falsehood and prevarication are alien to my nature. My actions ought to speak for themselves, but you listen not to them but to those who misinterpret and distort them. That is a personal insult which I feel and resent. To be forever misjudged, to have my repeated offers of friendship weighed and scrutinized with jealous, mistrustful eyes, taxes my patience severely. I have said time after time that I am a friend of England, and your Press—or, at least, a considerable section of it—bids the people of England refuse my proffered hand, and insinuates that the other holds a dagger. How can I convince a nation against its will?

"I repeat," continued his Majesty, "that I am the friend of England, but you make things difficult for me. My task is not of the easiest. The prevailing sentiment among large sections of the middle and lower classes of my own people is not friendly to England. I am, therefore, so to speak, in a minority in my own land, but it is a minority of the best elements as it is in England with respect to Germany. That is another reason why I resent your refusal to accept my pledged word that I am the friend of England. I strive without ceasing to improve relations, and you retort that I am your arch-enemy. You make it hard for me. Why is it?"

. . . .

His Majesty then reverted to the subject uppermost in his mind—his proved friendship for England. "I have referred," he said, "to the speeches in which I have done all that a Sovereign can to proclaim my good will. But, as actions speak louder than words, let me also refer to my acts. It is commonly believed in England that throughout the South African War Germany was hostile to her. German opinion undoubtedly was hostile—bitterly hostile. But what of official Germany? Let my critics ask themselves what brought to a sudden stop, and indeed, to absolute collapse, the European tour of the Boer delegates, who were striving to obtain European intervention? They were feted in Holland, France gave them a rapturous welcome. They wished to come to Berlin, where the German people would have crowned them with flowers. But when they asked me to receive them—I refused. The agitation immediately died away, and the delegation returned empty-handed. Was that, I ask, the action of a secret enemy?

"Nor was that all. Just at the time of your Black Week, in the December of 1899, when disasters followed one another in rapid succession, I received a letter from Queen Victoria, my revered grandmother, written in sorrow and affliction, and bearing manifest traces of the anxieties which were preying upon her mind and health. I at once returned a sympathetic reply. Nay, I did more. I bade one of my officers procure for me as exact an account as he could obtain of the number of combatants in South Africa on both sides, and of the actual position of the opposing forces. With the figures before me, I worked out what I considered to be the best plan of campaign under the circumstances, and submitted it to my General Staff for their criticism. Then I dispatched it to England, and that document, likewise, is among the State papers at Windsor Castle, awaiting the severely im-

partial verdict of history. And, as a matter of curious coincidence, let me add that the plan which I formulated ran very much on the same lines as that which was actually adopted by Lord Roberts, [British commander in the Boer War] and carried by him into successful operation. Was that, I repeat, the act of one who wished England ill? Let Englishmen be just and say!

"But, you will say, what of the German Navy? Surely, that is a menace to England! Against whom but England are my squadrons being prepared? If England is not in the minds of those Germans who are bent on creating a powerful fleet, why is Germany asked to consent to such new and heavy burdens of taxation? My answer is clear. Germany is a young and growing Empire. She has a world-wide commerce, which is rapidly expanding, and to which the legitimate ambition of patriotic Germans refuses to assign any bounds. Germany must have a powerful fleet to protect that commerce, and her manifold

interests in even the most distant seas. She expects those interests to go on growing, and she must be able to champion them manfully in any quarter of the globe. Germany looks ahead. Her horizons stretch far away. She must be prepared for any eventualities in the Far East. Who can foresee what may take place in the Pacific in the days to come, days not so distant as some believe, but days, at any rate, for which all European Powers with Far Eastern interests ought steadily to prepare? Look at the accomplished rise of Japan; think of the possible national awakening of China; and then judge of the vast problems of the Pacific. Only those Powers which have great navies will be listened to with respect, when the future of the Pacific comes to be solved; and, if for that reason only, Germany must have a powerful fleet. It may even be that England herself will be glad that Germany has a fleet when they speak together on the same side in the great debates of the future."

Daily Telegraph, London, October 28, 1908.

---

tion. At the same time the British were concerned that Russia might again drift into the German orbit.

THE FIRST MOROCCAN CRISIS. At this point Germany decided to test the new understanding between Britain and France and to press for colonial gains. In March 1905 Emperor William II landed at Tangier, challenged the French protectorate there in a speech in favor of Moroccan independence, and by implication asserted Germany's right to participate in Morocco's destiny. Germany's chancellor, Prince Bernhard von Bülow (1849–1929), intended to show France how weak it was and how little it could expect from Britain and at the same time to gain significant colonial concessions.

The Germans might well have achieved their aims and driven a wedge between France and Britain, but they pushed too far and demanded an international conference to show their power more dramatically. The conference met in 1906 at Algeciras in Spain. Austria sided with its German ally, but Spain, Italy, and the United States voted with Britain and France. The Germans had overplayed their hand, receiving trivial concessions, and the

French were confirmed in their position in Morocco. German bullying had, moreover, driven Britain and France closer together. In the face of the threat of a German attack on France, Sir Edward Grey, the British foreign secretary, without making a firm commitment, authorized conversations between the British and the French general staffs. Their agreements became morally binding as the years passed. By 1914 French and British military and naval plans were so mutually dependent that they were effectively, if not formally, allies.

BRITISH AGREEMENT WITH RUSSIA. Britain's fear of Germany's growing naval power, its concern over German ambitions in the Near East as represented by the German-sponsored plan to build a railroad from Berlin to Baghdad, and its closer relations with France made it desirable for Britain to become more friendly with France's ally, Russia. With French support the British made overtures to the Russians and in 1907 concluded an agreement with them much like the Entente Cordiale with France. It settled Russo-British quarrels in central Asia and opened the door for wider cooperation. The Triple Entente, an informal, but powerful association of Britain, France, and Russia, was now ranged against the Triple Alliance. Because Italy was unreliable, Germany and Austria–Hungary stood surrounded by two great land powers and Great Britain.

William II and his ministers had turned Bismarck's nightmare of the prospect of a two-front war with France and Russia into a reality and had made it more horrible by adding Britain to the hostile coalition. The equilibrium that Bismarck had worked so hard to achieve was destroyed. Britain could no longer support Austria in restraining Russian ambitions in the Balkans. Germany, increasingly terrified by a sense of encirclement, was less willing to restrain the Austrians for fear of alienating them. In the Dual Alliance of Germany and Austria it had become less clear who was the horse and who was the rider. Bismarck's alliance system had been intended to maintain peace, but the new one increased the risk of war and made the Balkans a likely spot for it to break out. Bismarck's diplomacy had left France isolated and impotent; the new arrangement found France associated with the two greatest powers in Europe apart from Germany. The Germans could rely only on Austria, and such was the condition of that troubled empire that it was less likely to provide aid than to need it.

The Road to War

Growing Tensions (1908–1914)

The situation in the Balkans in the first decade of this century was exceedingly complicated. The weak Ottoman Empire controlled the central strip running west from Constantinople to the Adriatic. North and south of it were the independent states of Romania, Serbia, and Greece, as well as Bulgaria, technically still part of the empire but legally autonomous and practically independent. The Austro-Hungarian Empire included Croatia and Slovenia and since 1878 had "occupied and administered" Bosnia and Herzegovina.

With the exception of the Greeks and the Romanians most of the inhabitants of the Balkans spoke variants of the same Slavic language and felt a cultural and historical kinship with one another. For centuries they had been ruled by Austrians, Hungarians, or Turks, and the growing nationalism that characterized late-nineteenth-century Europe made many of them eager for liberty. The more radical among them longed for a union of the south Slavic, or Yugoslav, peoples in a single nation. They looked to independent Serbia as the

H.M.S. Dreadnought *was completed by the British navy in* 1906. *It initiated a whole new class of battleships and gave rise to a new arms race in the decade before World War I.* [*The Granger Collection.*]

center of the new nation and hoped to detach all the Slavic provinces (especially Bosnia, which bordered on Serbia) from Austria. In this regard Serbia was to unite the Slavs at the expense of Austria, as Piedmont had united the Italians and Prussia the Germans.

In 1908 a group of modernizing reformers called the *Young Turks* brought about a revolution in the Ottoman Empire. Their actions threatened to revive the life of the empire and to interfere with the plans of the European jackals preparing to pounce on the Ottoman corpse. These events brought on the first of a series of Balkan crises that would eventually lead to war.

THE BOSNIAN CRISIS. In 1908 the Austrian and Russian governments decided to act quickly before Turkey became strong enough to resist. They struck a bargain in which it was agreed that they would call an international conference where each of them would support the other's demands. Russia would agree to the Austrian annexation of Bosnia and Herzegovina, and Austria would support Russia's request to open the Dardanelles to Russian warships.

Austria, however, declared the annexation before any conference was called. The British, ever concerned about their own position in the Mediterranean, refused to agree to the Russian demand. The Russians felt betrayed by the British, humiliated, and furious. Their "little brothers," the Serbs, were frustrated and angry at the loss of Bosnia, which they hoped one day to include in an independent south Slavic nation led by Serbia. The Russians were too weak to do anything but accept the new situation. The Germans had not been warned in advance of Austria's plans and were unhappy because the action threatened their relations with Russia. But Germany felt so dependent on the Dual Alliance that it assured Austria of its support. Austria had been given a free hand, and to an extent German policy was being made in Vienna. It was a dangerous precedent. At the same time, the failure of Britain and France to support Russia strained the Triple Entente and made it harder for them to oppose Russian interests again in the future if they were to retain Russian friendship.

THE SECOND MOROCCAN CRISIS. The second Moroccan crisis, in 1911, emphasized the French and British need for mutual support. When France sent in an army to put down a rebellion, Germany took the opportunity to "protect German interests"

"The Mailed Fist of the Kaiser Strikes Agadir." This cartoon refers to the landing of the German gunboat Panther at Agadir in Morocco in 1911. William II's purpose was to press the French to make colonial concessions to Germany in Africa and, perhaps, to break up the Entente between the French and the British. The result, instead, was the second Moroccan crisis, which drew the Entente closer together and helped bring on World War I.

in Morocco as a means of extorting colonial concessions in the French Congo. To add force to their demands, the Germans sent the gunboat *Panther* to the port of Agadir, allegedly to protect German citizens there. Once again, as in 1905, the Germans went too far. The *Panther*'s visit to Agadir provoked a strong reaction in Britain. For some time Anglo-German relations had been growing worse, chiefly because of the intensification of the naval race. In 1907 Germany had built its first new battleship of the dreadnought class, which Britain had developed in 1906. In 1908 Germany had passed still another naval law, which accelerated the schedule of production to challenge British naval supremacy. These actions frightened and angered the British because of the clear threat to the secu-

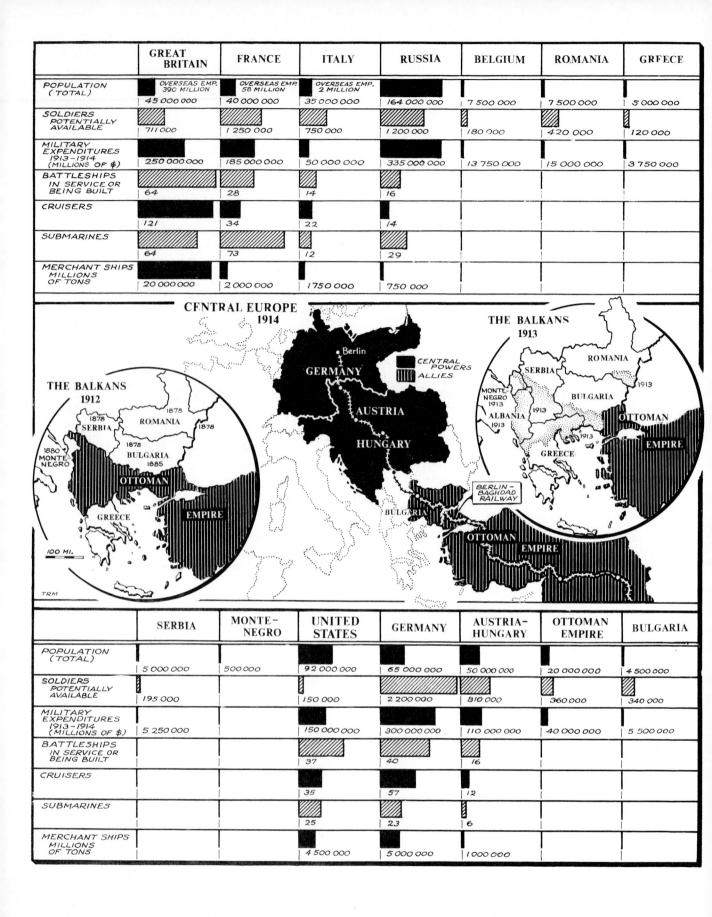

	GREAT BRITAIN	FRANCE	ITALY	RUSSIA	BELGIUM	ROMANIA	GRFECE
POPULATION (TOTAL)	OVERSEAS EMP. 390 MILLION — 45 000 000	OVERSEAS EMP. 58 MILLION — 40 000 000	OVERSEAS EMP. 2 MILLION — 35 000 000	164 000 000	7 500 000	7 500 000	5 000 000
SOLDIERS POTENTIALLY AVAILABLE	711 000	1 250 000	750 000	1 200 000	180 000	420 000	120 000
MILITARY EXPENDITURES 1913–1914 (MILLIONS OF $)	250 000 000	185 000 000	50 000 000	335 000 000	13 750 000	15 000 000	3 750 000
BATTLESHIPS IN SERVICE OR BEING BUILT	64	28	14	16			
CRUISERS	121	34	22	14			
SUBMARINES	64	73	12	29			
MERCHANT SHIPS MILLIONS OF TONS	20 000 000	2 000 000	1 750 000	750 000			

THE BALKANS 1912

SERBIA 1878
ROMANIA 1878
1878
1878
MONTE-NEGRO 1880
BULGARIA 1885
OTTOMAN EMPIRE
GREECE
100 MI.
TRM

CENTRAL EUROPE 1914

GERMANY
Berlin
AUSTRIA
HUNGARY
CENTRAL POWERS
ALLIES
BULGARIA
OTTOMAN EMPIRE
BERLIN–BAGHDAD RAILWAY

THE BALKANS 1913

ROMANIA
SERBIA
MONTE-NEGRO 1913
ALBANIA 1913
1913
BULGARIA
1913
GREECE
OTTOMAN EMPIRE
1913

	SERBIA	MONTE-NEGRO	UNITED STATES	GERMANY	AUSTRIA-HUNGARY	OTTOMAN EMPIRE	BULGARIA
POPULATION (TOTAL)	5 000 000	500 000	92 000 000	65 000 000	50 000 000	20 000 000	4 500 000
SOLDIERS POTENTIALLY AVAILABLE	195 000		150 000	2 200 000	810 000	360 000	340 000
MILITARY EXPENDITURES 1913–1914 (MILLIONS OF $)	5 250 000		150 000 000	300 000 000	110 000 000	40 000 000	5 500 000
BATTLESHIPS IN SERVICE OR BEING BUILT			37	40	16		
CRUISERS			35	57	12		
SUBMARINES			25	23	6		
MERCHANT SHIPS MILLIONS OF TONS			4 500 000	5 000 000	1 000 000		

OPPOSITE: MAP 29.3 *Two maps show the Balkans before and after the two Balkan wars; note the Ottoman retreat. In the center we see the geographical relationship of the Central Powers and their Bulgarian and Turkish allies. Tables give relative strength of World War 1 combatants.*

rity of the island kingdom and its empire. The German actions also forced Britain to increase taxes to pay for new armaments just when the Liberal government was launching its expensive program of social legislation. Negotiations failed to persuade William II and Tirpitz to slow down naval construction.

In this atmosphere the British heard of the *Panther*'s arrival in Morocco. They wrongly believed that the Germans meant to turn Agadir into a naval base on the Atlantic. The crisis passed when France yielded some insignificant bits of the Congo and Germany withdrew from Morocco. The main result was to increase British fear and hostility and to draw the Britons closer to France. Specific military plans were formulated for a British expeditionary force to defend France in case of German attack, and the British and French navies agreed to cooperate. Without any formal treaty the German naval construction and the Agadir crisis had turned the Entente Cordiale into an alliance that could not have been more binding. If France were attacked by Germany, Britain must defend the French, for its own security was inextricably tied up with that of France.

WAR IN THE BALKANS. The second Moroccan crisis also provoked another crisis in the Balkans. Italy sought to gain colonies and to take its place among the great powers. It wanted Libya, which though worth little at the time was at least available. Italy feared that the recognition of the French protectorate in Morocco would encourage France to move into Libya. Consequently, in 1911, Italy attacked the Ottoman Empire to anticipate the French, defeated the faltering Turks, and obtained Libya and the Dodecanese Islands. The Italian victory encouraged the Balkan states to try their luck. In 1912 Bulgaria, Greece, Montenegro, and Serbia joined an attack on the Ottoman Empire and won easily. After this First Balkan War the victors fell out among themselves. The Serbs and the Bulgarians quarreled about the division of Macedonia, and in 1913 a Second Balkan War erupted. This time Turkey and Romania joined the other states against Bulgaria and stripped away much of what the Bulgarians had gained since 1878.

"The European Poker Game" by the German artist Edward Thony depicts the Balkan states in 1912 as cards played by the Great Powers in contest among themselves. [New York Public Library Picture Collection.]

After the First Balkan War the alarmed Austrians were determined to limit Serbian gains and especially to prevent the Serbs from gaining a port on the Adriatic. This policy meant keeping Serbia out of Albania, but the Russians backed the Serbs, and tensions mounted. An international conference sponsored by Britain in early 1913 resolved the matter in Austria's favor and called for an independent kingdom of Albania. But Austria felt humiliated by the public airing of Serbian demands. Then for some time the Serbs defied the powers and continued to occupy parts of Albania. Under Austrian pressure they withdrew, but in September 1913, after the Second Balkan War, the Serbs reoccupied sections of Albania. In mid-October Austria unilaterally issued an ultimatum to Serbia, and the latter country again withdrew its forces from Albania. During this crisis many people in Austria had wanted an all-out attack on Serbia to remove its threat once and for all from the empire. Those demands had been resisted by Emperor Francis Joseph and the heir to the throne, Archduke Francis Ferdinand. At the same time Pan-Slavic sentiment in Russia pressed Czar Nicholas II to take a firm stand, but Russia once again let Austria have its way in its confrontation with Serbia. Throughout the crisis Britain, France, and Germany restrained their respective allies, although each worried about seeming too reluctant to help its friends.

The lessons learned from this crisis of 1913 profoundly influenced behavior in the final crisis, the crisis of 1914. The Russians had once again, as in 1908, been embarrassed by their passivity, and their allies were more reluctant to restrain them again. The Austrians were embarrassed by what had resulted from accepting an international conference and were determined not to repeat the experience. They had seen that better results might be obtained from a threat of direct force; they and their German allies did not miss the lesson.

Sarajevo and the Outbreak of War (June–August 1914)

THE ASSASSINATION. On June 28, 1914, a young Bosnian nationalist shot and killed the Austrian Archduke Francis Ferdinand, heir to the throne, and his wife as they drove in an open car through the Bosnian capital of Sarajevo. The assassin was a member of a conspiracy hatched by a political terrorist society called *Union or Death,* better known as the *Black Hand.* A major participant in the planning and preparation of the crime was the chief of intelligence of the Serbian army's general staff. Even though his role was not actually known at the time, it was generally believed that Serbian officials were involved. The glee of the Serbian press lent support to that belief. The archduke was not a popular person in his own land, and his funeral evoked few signs of grief. He had been known to favor a form of federal government that would have given a higher status to the Slavs in the empire. This position alienated the conservatives and the Hungarians. It also alarmed radical Yugoslav nationalists, who feared that reform might end their dream of an independent south Slav state.

GERMANY AND AUSTRIA'S RESPONSE. News of the assassination produced outrage and condem-nation everywhere. To those Austrians who had long favored an attack on Serbia as a solution to the empire's Slavic problem, the opportunity seemed irresistible. But it was never easy for the Dual Monarchy to make a decision. Conrad von Hötzendorf, chief of the Austrian general staff, urged an attack as he had often done before. Count Stefan Tisza, speaking for Hungary, resisted. Leopold Berchtold, the Austro-Hungarian foreign minister, felt the need for strong action, but he knew that German support would be required in the likely event that Russia should decide to intervene to protect Serbia. He also knew that nothing could be done

THE COMING OF WORLD WAR I

1871	The end of the Franco-Prussian war; creation of the German Empire; German annexation of Alsace–Lorraine
1873	The Three Emperors' League (Germany, Russia, and Austria-Hungary)
1875	The Russo-Turkish War
1878	The Congress of Berlin
1879	The Dual Alliance between Germany and Austria
1881	The Three Emperors' League is renewed
1882	Italy joins Germany and Austria in the Triple Alliance
1888	William II becomes the German emperor
1890	Bismarck is dismissed
1894	The Franco-Russian alliance
1898	Germany begins to build a battleship navy
1902	The British alliance with Japan
1904	The Entente Cordiale between Britain and France
1904–1905	The Russo-Japanese War
1905	The first Moroccan crisis
1907	The British agreement with Russia
1908–1909	The Bosnian crisis
1911	The second Moroccan crisis Italy attacks Turkey
1912–1913	The First and Second Balkan Wars
1914	Outbreak of World War I

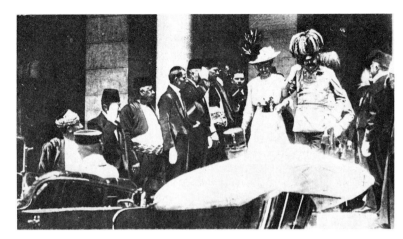

The Austrian Archduke Franz Ferdinand and his wife at Sarajevo, June 28, 1914. Later in the day the royal couple were assassinated by young Slavic revolutionaries trained and supplied in Serbia. The murders set off the crisis that led to World War I. [Popperfoto.]

Moments after the assassination of Archduke Ferdinand and his wife the Bosnian police captured one of the assassins in Sarajevo. [The Granger Collection.]

without Tisza's approval and that only German support could persuade the Hungarians to accept the policy of war. The question of peace or war, therefore, had to be answered in Berlin.

William II and Chancellor Theobald von Bethmann-Hollweg (1856–1921) readily promised German support for an attack on Serbia. It has often been said that they gave the Austrians a "blank check," but their message was firmer than that. They urged the Austrians to move swiftly while the other powers were still angry at Serbia, and they made the Austrians feel that a failure to act would be taken as evidence of Austria–Hungary's weakness and uselessness as an ally. Therefore the Austrians never wavered in their determination to make war on Serbia. They hoped, with the protection of Germany, to fight a limited war that would not bring on a general European conflict, but they were prepared to risk even the latter. The Germans also knew that they risked a general war, but they hoped to "localize" the fight between Austria and Serbia.

Some scholars believe that Germany had long been plotting war, and some even think that a specific plan for war in 1914 was set in motion as early as 1912. The vast body of evidence on the crisis of 1914 gives no support to such notions. The German leaders plainly reacted to a crisis that they had not foreseen and just as plainly made decisions in response to events. The fundamental decision to support Austria, which made it very difficult if not impossible to avoid war, was made by the emperor and the chancellor without significant consultation with either their military or their diplomatic advisers.

William II appears to have reacted violently to the assassination. He was moved by his friendship for the archduke and by outrage at an attack on royalty. It is doubtful that a different provocation would have moved him so much. Bethmann-Hollweg was less emotional but under severe pressure. To resist the decision would have meant flatly to oppose the emperor. The chancellor, moreover, was suspected of being "soft" in the powerful military circles favored by his master. A conciliatory position would have been difficult. Beyond these considerations Bethmann-Hollweg, like many other Germans, viewed the future with apprehension. Russia was recovering its strength and would reach a military peak in 1917. The Triple Entente was growing more powerful, and Germany's only reliable ally was Austria. The chancellor recog-

❧ The Austrian Ambassador Gets a "Blank Check" from the Kaiser

It was at a meeting at Potsdam on July 5, 1914, that the Austrian ambassador received from the Kaiser assurance that Germany would support Austria in the Balkans, even at the risk of war.

After lunch, when I [the Austro-Hungarian Ambassador] again called attention to the seriousness of the situation, the Kaiser authorised me to inform our gracious Majesty that we might in this case, as in all others, rely upon Germany's full support. He must, as he said before, first hear what the Imperial Chancellor has to say, but he did not doubt in the least that Herr von Bethmann Hollweg would agree with him. Especially as far as our action against Serbia was concerned. But it was his (Kaiser Wilhelm's) opinion that this action must not be delayed. Russia's attitude will no doubt be hostile, but for this he had been for years prepared, and should a war between Austria–

Hungary and Russia be unavoidable, we might be convinced that Germany, our old faithful ally, would stand at our side. Russia at the present time was in no way prepared for war, and would think twice before it appealed to arms. But it will certainly set other powers on to the Triple Alliance and add fuel to the fire in the Balkans. He understands perfectly well that His Apostolic Majesty [Francis Joseph] in his well-known love of peace would be reluctant to march into Serbia; but if we had really recognised the necessity of warlike action against Serbia, he (Kaiser Wilhelm) would regret if we did not make use of the present moment, which is all in our favour.

Outbreak of the World War: German Documents Collected by Karl Kautsky, ed. by Max Montgelas and Walther Schücking (New York: Carnegie Endowment for International Peace, 1924), p. 76.

nized the danger of support for Austria, but he believed it to be even more dangerous to withhold that support. If Austria did not crush Serbia, the empire would soon collapse before the onslaught of Slavic nationalism defended by Russia. If Germany did not defend its ally, the Austrians might look elsewhere for help. His policy was one of "calculated risk."

The calculations proved to be incorrect. Bethmann-Hollweg hoped that the Austrians would strike swiftly and present the powers with a *fait accompli* while the outrage of the assassination was still fresh, and that German support would deter Russian involvement. Failing that, he was prepared for a continental war that would bring rapid victory over France and allow a full-scale attack on the Russians, who were always slow to bring their strength into action. All of this policy depended on British neutrality, and the German chancellor convinced himself that the British could be persuaded to stand aloof.

However, the Austrians were slow to act, as always and did not even deliver their deliberately unacceptable ultimatum to Serbia until July 24, when the general hostility toward Serbia had begun to subside. Serbia further embarrassed the Austrians by returning so soft and conciliatory an answer that the mercurial German emperor thought it removed all reason for war. But the Austrians were determined not to turn back, and on July 28 the Austrians declared war on Serbia even though they could not put an army into the field until mid-August.

THE TRIPLE ENTENTE'S RESPONSE. The Russians, previously so often forced to back off, angrily responded to the Austrian demands on Serbia. The most conservative elements of the Russian government opposed war, fearing that it would bring on revolution as it had in 1905. But nationalists, Pan-Slavs, and most of the politically conscious classes in general demanded action. The government responded by ordering partial mobilization, against Austria only. This policy was militarily impossible, but its intention was the diplomatic one of putting pressure on Austria to hold back its attack on Serbia. Mobilization of any kind, however, was a dangerous political weapon because it was generally understood to be equivalent to an act of war. It was especially alarming to General Helmuth von Moltke (1848–1916), head of the German general staff. The possibility that the Russians might start mobilization before the Germans could move would upset the delicate timing of Germany's only battle plan, the Schlieffen Plan, which required an attack on France first, and put Germany in great danger. From this point on, Moltke pressed for German mobilization and war, and the pressure of military necessity mounted until it became irresistible.

The western European powers were not eager for war. France's president and prime minister were on their way back from a visit to Russia when the crisis flared up again on July 24. The Austrians had, in fact, timed their ultimatum precisely so that these two men would be at sea at the crucial moment. Had they been at their desks, they might have attempted to restrain the Russians, but the French ambassador to Russia gave the Russians the same assurances that Germany had given its ally. The British worked hard to avoid trouble by traditional means: a conference of the powers. Austria, still smarting from its humiliation after the London Conference of 1913, would not hear of it. The Germans privately supported the Austrians but publicly took on a conciliatory tone in the hope of keeping the British neutral. Soon, however, Bethmann-Hollweg came to realize what he should have known from the first: if Germany attacked France, Britain must fight. Until July 30 his public appeals to Austria for restraint were a sham. Thereafter he sincerely tried to persuade the Austrians to negotiate and to avoid a general war, but it was too late. While Bethmann-Hollweg was urging restraint on the Austrians, Moltke was pressing them to act. The Austrians wondered who was in charge in Berlin, but they could not turn back without losing their own self-respect and the respect of the Germans.

On July 30 Austria ordered mobilization against Russia. Bethmann-Hollweg resisted the enormous pressure to mobilize, not because he had any further hope of avoiding war but because he wanted Russia to mobilize against Germany first and appear to be the aggressor. Only in that way could he win the support of the German nation for war, especially the pacifistic Social Democrats. His luck was good for a change. The news of Russian general mobilization came only minutes before Germany would have mobilized in any case. The Schlieffen Plan went into effect. The Germans invaded Luxembourg on August 1 and Belgium on August 3. The latter invasion violated the treaty of 1839 in which the British had guaranteed Belgian neutrality. This factor undermined the considerable sentiment in Britain for neutrality and united the nation against Germany. Germany then invaded France, and on August 4 Britain declared war on Germany. The Great War had begun. As Lord Grey put it, the lights were going out all over Europe. They would come on again, but Europe would never be the same.

World War I (1914-1918)

Throughout Europe jubilation greeted the outbreak of war. No general war had been fought since Napoleon, and the horrors of modern warfare were not yet understood. The dominant memory was of Bismarck's swift and decisive campaigns, in which costs and casualties were light and the rewards great. After the repeated crises of recent years and the fears and resentments they had created, war came as a release of tension. The popular press had increased public awareness of and interest in foreign affairs and had fanned the flames of patriotism. The prospect of war moved even a rational man of science like Sigmund Freud to say, "My whole libido goes out to Austria–Hungary."[9]

Strategies and Stalemate: 1914–1917

The strategies of both sides rested on Karl von Clausewitz's (1780–1831) interpretation of the Napoleonic mode of war, which constituted the dominant military theory of the day. Both sides expected to take the offensive, force a battle on favorable ground, and win a quick victory. The Triple Entente powers—or the Allies, as they came to be called—held superiority in numbers and financial resources as well as command of the sea. Germany and Austria, the Central Powers, had the advantages of internal lines of communication and of having launched their attack first.

After 1905 Germany's only war plan was the one developed by Count Alfred von Schlieffen (1833–1913), chief of the German general staff from 1891 to 1906. It aimed at going around the French defenses by sweeping through Belgium to the channel, then wheeling to the south and east to envelop the French and to crush them against the German fortresses in Lorraine. The secret of success lay in making the right wing of the advancing German army immensely strong and deliberately

[9]Quoted in J. Remak, p. 134.

THE SCHLIEFFEN PLAN OF 1905

MAP 29.4 *Germany's grand strategy for quickly winning the war against France in 1914 is shown by the wheeling arrows on the map. The crushing blows at France were, in the original plan, to be followed by the release of troops for use against Russia on Germany's Eastern front. But the plan was not adequately implemented, and the war on the Western front became a long contest in place.*

weakening the left opposite the French frontier. The weakness of the left was meant to draw the French into the wrong place while the war was decided on the German right. As one keen military analyst has explained, "It would be like a revolving door—if a man pressed heavily on one side, the other side would spring round and strike him in the back. Here lay the real subtlety of the plan, not in the mere geographical detour."[10] In the east the Germans planned to stand on the defensive against Russia until France had been crushed, a task they thought would take only six weeks.

The apparent risk, besides the violation of Belgian neutrality and the consequent alienation of Britain, lay in weakening the German defenses against a direct attack across the frontier. The strength of German fortresses and the superior firepower of German howitzers made that risk

[10]B. H. Liddell Hart, *The Real War, 1914–1918* (Boston: Little, Brown, 1964; first published in 1930), p. 47.

A British poster designed to help civilians distinguish British from German aircraft. World War I was the first conflict in which civilian population was subject to air attack. [Library of Congress.]

serves and set too much store by the importance of the courage and spirit of their troops. These proved insufficient against modern weapons, especially the machine gun. The French offensive on Germany's western frontier failed totally. In a sense this defeat was better than a partial success because it released troops for use against the main German army. As a result the French and the British were able to stop the Germans at the Battle of the Marne in September 1914.

Thereafter the nature of the war in the west changed completely and became one of position instead of movement. Both sides dug in behind a wall of trenches protected by barbed wire that stretched from the North Sea to Switzerland. Strategically placed machine-gun nests made assaults difficult and dangerous. Both sides, nonetheless, attempted massive attacks prepared for by artillery barrages of unprecedented and horrible force and

A British recruitment poster. For the first two years of the war, the British army was composed solely of volunteers, with conscription being introduced only in 1916, after very sharp political debate. [National Archives.]

more apparent than real. The true danger was that the German striking force on the right through Belgium would not be powerful enough to make the swift progress vital to success. Schlieffen is said to have uttered the dying words, "It must come to a fight. Only make the right wing strong." The execution of his plan, however, was left to Helmuth von Moltke, the nephew of Bismarck's most effective general. The younger Moltke was a gloomy and nervous man who lacked the talent of his illustrious uncle and the theoretical daring of Schlieffen. He added divisions to the left wing and even weakened the Russian front for the same purpose. The consequence of this hesitant strategy was the failure of the Schlieffen Plan by a narrow margin.

THE WAR IN THE WEST. The French had also put their faith in the offensive, but with less reason than the Germans. They badly underestimated the numbers and the effectiveness of the German re-

WORLD WAR I IN EUROPE

T.R.MILLER

Map labels (Central Powers region, dark shading):

GERMAN EMPIRE
AUSTRIA-HUNGARY

Legend:

- TRIPLE ENTENTE
- ALLIES OF THE TRIPLE ENTENTE
- CENTRAL POWERS
- ALLIES OF THE CENTRAL POWERS

Country and region labels:

NORWAY, SWEDEN, DENMARK, UNITED KINGDOM, NETH., BELG., LUX., FRANCE, SWITZ., ITALY, RUSSIA, ESTONIA, LATVIA, LITHUANIA, E. PRUSSIA, SILESIA, BOHEMIA, MORAVIA, SLOVAKIA, GALICIA, TRANSYLVANIA, TYROL, CROATIA, BOSNIA, SERBIA, MONTENEGRO, ALBANIA, ROMANIA, BULGARIA, GREECE

Seas:

NORTH SEA, BALTIC SEA, ADRIATIC SEA

Cities and places:

Aberdeen, Edinburgh, Hull, Yarmouth, London, Dover, Le Havre, Ypres, Arras, Compiègne, Versailles, Paris, Verdun, Toul, Belfort, Clermont, Geneva, Lyons, Berne, Turin, Milan, Genoa, Marseilles, Rome, Naples, Taranto

Stockholm, Göteborg, Copenhagen, Amsterdam, Brussels, Liége, Sedan, Metz, Strassburg, Mainz, Frankfurt, Koblenz, Cologne, Essen, Bremen, Hamburg, Berlin, Leipzig, Dresden, Nuremberg, Munich, Prague, Vienna, Klagenfurt, Caporetto, Trieste, Venice, Fiume, Agram, Budapest, Debrecen, Hermannstadt, Sarajevo, Belgrade, Nish, Uskub, Strumitza, Bucharest

Petrograd, ST. PETERSBURG, Reval, Memel, Danzig, Kaunas, Vilna, Suwalki, Minsk, Warsaw, Brest-Litovsk, Pinsk, Cracow, Breslau, Lemberg, Gorlice, Sofia

Other map annotations:

HELIGOLAND
KIEL CANAL
ELBE, ODER, RHINE, DANUBE, PO, RHONE, VISTULA
ALSACE, LORRAINE
TANNENBERG
SILESIA

WESTERN FRONT — SEE INSET
ITALIAN FRONT
BALKAN FRONT

FARTHEST RUSSIAN ADVANCE 1914
BATTLELINE DEC., 1917
BATTLELINE MAY, 1915
BRUSILOV'S OFFENSIVE AUG., 1916

AUG. 1917
MAR. 1918
FEB. 1915
MAY 1915
1914
1916
1915
1917-18
DEC. 1917

DARDANELLES
GALLIPOLI 1915-16

250 KM.

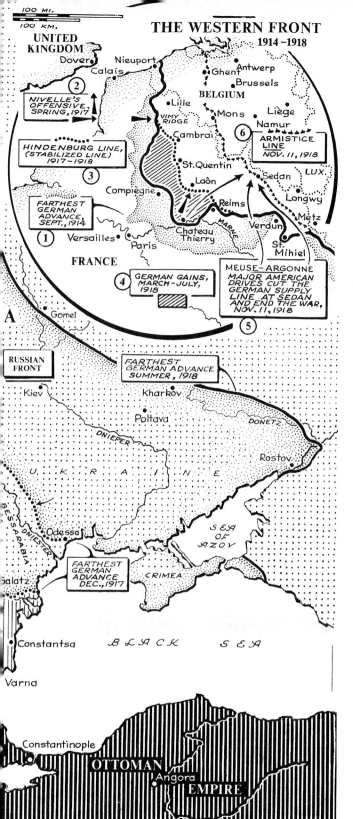

THE WESTERN FRONT
1914-1918

MAP 29.5 *Despite the importance of military action in the Far East, in the Arab world, and at sea, the main theaters of activity in World War I were in the European areas shown here. The crucial Western front is seen in somewhat greater detail in the inset map.*

duration. Still the defense was always able to recover and to bring up reserves fast enough to prevent a breakthrough. Sometimes assaults that cost hundreds of thousands of lives produced advances that could be measured in hundreds of yards. The introduction of poison gas as a solution to the problem proved ineffective. In 1916 the British introduced the tank, which proved to be the answer to the machine gun, but throughout the war defense was supreme. For three years after its establishment the western front moved only a few miles in either direction.

THE WAR IN THE EAST. In the east the war began auspiciously for the Allies. The Russians advanced into Austrian territory and inflicted heavy casualties, but Russian incompetence and German energy soon reversed the situation. A junior German officer, Erich Ludendorff (1865–1937), under the command of the elderly General Paul von Hindenburg (1847–1934), destroyed or captured an entire army at the Battle of Tannenberg and defeated the Russians at the Masurian Lakes. In 1915 the Central Powers pressed their advantage in the east and drove into the Baltic states and western Russia, inflicting over two million casualties in a single year. Russian confidence was badly shaken, but the Russian army stayed in the field.

As the battle lines hardened, both sides sought new allies. Turkey (because of its hostility to Russia) and Bulgaria (the enemy of Serbia) joined the Central Powers.

Italy seemed an especially valuable prize, and both sides bid for Italian support with promises of a division of the spoils of victory. Because what the Italians wanted most was held by Austria, the Allies were able to make the more attractive promises. In a secret treaty of 1915 the Allies agreed to deliver to Italy most of *Italia Irredenta* (i.e., the Trentino, the South Tyrol, Trieste, and some of the Dalmatian Islands) after victory. By the spring of 1915 Italy was engaging Austrian armies. Although the Italian campaign drained the strength of the Central Powers to a degree, the alliance with Italy gen-

This scene of trench warfare on the western front in World War I characterizes the twentieth century's first great international conflict. The trenches were defended by barbed wire and machine guns, the devices that gave the defense the advantage in this war. The masks worn by the French soldiers in this picture were the response to the German attempts to break a deadlock by using poison gas. [Collection Viollet.]

erally proved a disappointment to the Allies and never produced significant results.

Romania joined the Allies in 1916 but was quickly defeated and driven from the war.

In the Far East Japan honored its alliance with Britain and entered the war. The Japanese quickly overran the German colonies in China and the Pacific and used the opportuniy to improve their own position against China.

Both sides also tried the tactic of subversion by appealing to nationalist sentiment in areas held by the enemy. The Germans supported nationalist movements among the Irish, the Flemings in Bel-

gium, and the Poles and the Ukrainians under Russian rule. They even tried to persuade the Turks to lead a Muslim uprising against the British and the French in North Africa.

The Allies also used the device of subversion, with greater success. They sponsored movements of national autonomy for the Czechs, the Slovaks, the south Slavs, and the Poles that were under Austrian rule. They also favored a movement of Arab independence from Turkey. Guided by Colonel T. E. Lawrence (1888–1935), this last scheme proved especially successful in the later years of the war.

In 1915 the Allies undertook to break the deadlock in the fighting by going around it. The idea came chiefly from Winston Churchill (1874–1965), First Lord of the British Admiralty. He proposed an attack on the Dardanelles and the swift capture of Constantinople. This policy would knock Turkey from the war, bring help to the Balkan front, and ease communication with Russia. The plan was daring but promising and, in its original form, presented little risk. British naval superiority and the element of surprise would allow the forcing of the straits and the capture of Constantinople by purely naval action. Even if the scheme failed, the fleet could escape with little loss. Success depended on timing, speed, and daring leadership, but all of these were lacking. The execution of the attack was inept and overly cautious. Troops were landed, and as resistance continued, the Allied commitment increased. Before the campaign was abandoned, the Allies lost almost 150,000 men and diverted three times that number from more useful occupation.

RETURN TO THE WEST. Both sides turned back to the west in 1916. General Erich von Falkenhayn (1861–1922), who had succeeded Moltke in September 1914, sought success by an attack on the French stronghold of Verdun. His plan was not to take the fortress or to break through the line but to inflict enormously heavy casualties on the French, who must defend it against superior firepower coming from several directions. He, too, underestimated the superiority of the defense, and the French were able to hold Verdun with comparatively few men and to inflict almost as many casualties as they suffered. The commander of Verdun, Henri Pétain (1856–1951), became a national hero, and "They shall not pass" became a slogan of national defiance. The Allies tried to end the impasse by launching a major offensive along the

River Somme in July. Aided by a Russian attack in the east that drew off some German strength and by an enormous artillery barrage, they hoped at last to break through. Once again the superiority of the defense was demonstrated. Enormous casualties on both sides brought no result. On all fronts the losses were great and the results meager. The war on land dragged on with no end in sight.

THE WAR AT SEA. As the war continued, control of the sea became more important. The British ignored the distinction between war supplies (which were contraband according to international law) and food or other peaceful cargo, which was not subject to seizure. They imposed a strict blockade meant to starve out the enemy, regardless of international law. The Germans responded with submarine warfare meant to destroy British shipping and to starve the British. They declared the waters around the British Isles a war zone, where even neutral ships would not be safe. Both policies were unwelcome to neutrals, and especially to the United States, which conducted extensive trade in the Atlantic, but the sinking of neutral ships by German submarines was both more dramatic and

The military tank made its first appearance during World War I. It had the military advantages of giving its personnel armored protection, being able to cross many natural and manmade obstacles, and permitting a commander to advance fire power with some impunity closer to an enemy force than was possible by the traditional infantry charge. This photograph shows a light tank crossing an obstacle at a World War I British military experiment station. [Bettmann Archive.]

Verdun, 1916. The battle at Verdun was the longest battle of all time. For ten months millions of shells rained down on the city and the surrounding battlefield, as the French and the Germans stayed locked in the most terrible endurance test of the war. [United Press International Photo.]

more offensive. In 1915 the British liner *Lusitania* was torpedoed by a German submarine. Among the 1,200 drowned were 118 Americans. President Woodrow Wilson (1856–1924) warned Germany that a repetition would not be accepted, and the Germans desisted for the time being rather than further anger the United States. This development gave the Allies a considerable advantage. The German fleet that had cost so much money and had caused so much trouble played no significant part in the war. They only battle it fought was at Jutland in the spring of 1916. The battle resulted in a standoff and confirmed British domination of the surface of the sea.

AMERICA ENTERS THE WAR. In December 1916 President Woodrow Wilson of the United States intervened in an attempt to bring about a negotiated peace, but neither side was willing to renounce war aims that its opponent found unacceptable. The war seemed likely to continue until one or both sides reached exhaustion. Two events early in 1917 changed the situation radically. On February 1 the Germans announced the resumption of unrestricted submarine warfare, which led the United States to break off diplomatic relations. On April 6 the United States declared war on the Central Powers. One of the deterrents to an earlier American intervention had been the presence of autocratic czarist Russia among the Allies. Wilson could conceive of the war only as an idealistic crusade "to make the world safe for democracy." That

problem was resolved in March of 1917 by a revolution in Russia that overthrew the czarist government.

The Russian Revolution

The March Revolution in Russia was neither planned nor led by any political faction. It was the result of the collapse of the monarchy's ability to govern. Although public opinion had strongly supported Russian entry into the war, the conflict put far too great demands on the resources of the country and the efficiency of the czarist government. Nicholas II was weak and incompetent and was suspected of being under the domination of his German wife and the insidious monk Rasputin, who was assassinated by a group of Russian noblemen in 1916. Military and domestic failures produced massive casualties, widespread hunger, strikes by workers, and disorganization in the army. The peasant discontent that had plagued the countryside before 1914 did not subside during the conflict. In 1916 the czar adjourned the Duma and proceeded to rule alone. All political factions were in one way or another discontented.

In early March 1917 strikes and worker demonstrations erupted in Petrograd, as Saint Petersburg had been renamed. The ill-disciplined troops in the city refused to fire on the demonstrators, and the czar abdicated on March 15. The government

British troops during the Third Battle of Ypres (July to November 1917). The battle, which was actually a five-month campaign, cost the British about 400,000 casualties and gained them about five miles of territory. [Imperial War Museum, London.]

American soldiers in France. In 1918 the American army arrived in France in sufficient numbers to make a significant contribution. Here American forces take over a section in the Argonne forest, relieving tired Allied troops. [Radio Times Hulton Picture Library.]

of Russia fell into the hands of members of the reconvened Duma, who soon constructed a provisional government composed chiefly of Constitutional Democrats with Western sympathies. At the same time the various socialists, including both Social Revolutionaries and Social Democrats of the Menshevik wing, began to organize the workers into soviets. Initially they allowed the provisional government to function without actually supporting it. As relatively orthodox Marxists, the Mensheviks believed that a bourgeois stage of development must come to Russia before the revolution of the proletariat could be achieved. They were willing to work temporarily with the Constitutional Democrats (Cadets) in a liberal regime, but they became

estranged as the Cadets failed to control the army or to purge "reactionaries" from the government.

In this climate the provisional government made the important decision to remain loyal to the existing Russian alliances and to continue the war against Germany. In this regard the provisional government was accepting the czarist foreign policy and was associating itself with the source of much domestic suffering and discontent. The fate of the provisional government was sealed by the collapse of the new offensive in the summer of 1917. Disillusionment with the war, shortages of food and other necessities at home, and the growing demand by the peasants for land reform undermined the government, even after its leader-

Field guns, under a red banner, in place in Petrograd (formerly St. Petersburg) during the Russian Revolution in March 1917. [The Granger Collection.]

ship had been taken over by the moderate socialist Aleksandr Kerenski (1881–1970). Moreover discipline in the army had badly disintegrated.

Ever since April the Bolshevik wing of the Social Democratic Party had been working against the provisional government. The Germans, in their most successful attempt at subversion, had rushed the brilliant Bolshevik leader V. I. Lenin in a sealed train from his exile in Switzerland across Germany to Petrograd in the hope that he would cause trouble for the revolutionary government.

Lenin saw the opportunity to achieve the political alliance of workers and peasants that he had discussed theoretically before the war. In speech after speech he hammered away on the theme of peace, bread, and land. The Bolsheviks soon gained control of the soviets, or councils of workers and soldiers. They demanded that all political power go to the soviets. The failure of the summer offensive encouraged them to attempt a *coup,* but the effort was premature and a failure. Lenin fled to Finland, and his chief collaborator, Leon Trotsky (1877–1940), was imprisoned.

The failure of a right-wing counter *coup* gave the Bolsheviks another chance. Trotsky, released from

prison, led the powerful Petrograd Soviet. Lenin returned in October, insisted to his doubting colleagues that the time was ripe to take power, and by the extraordinary force of his personality persuaded them to act. Trotsky organized the *coup* that took place on November 6 and that concluded with an armed assault on the provisional government. The Bolsheviks, almost as much to their own astonishment as to that of the rest of the world, had come to rule Russia.

The victors moved to fulfill their promises and to assure their own security. The provisional government had decreed an election for late November to select a Constituent Assembly. The Social Revolutionaries won a large majority over the Bolsheviks. When the assembly gathered in January, it met for only a day before the Red Army, controlled by the Bolsheviks, dispersed it. All other political parties also ceased to function in any meaningful fashion. In November and January the Bolshevik government promulgated decrees that nationalized the land and turned it over to its peasant proprietors. Factory workers were put in charge of their plants. Banks were taken from their owners and seized for the state, and the debt of the czarist government

902

John Reed Celebrates Lenin's Role in the Bolsheviks' Seizure of Power

John Reed was an American newspaperman who was in Russia during the Revolution of 1917, an enthusiastic convert to Communism, a supporter of the Bolsheviks, and an ardent admirer of Lenin. In the following selections from his account of the Bolshevik revolution he described Lenin's qualities and the part Lenin played in overthrowing the Provisional Government.

Thursday, Oct. 26/Nov. 8

The Congress was to meet at one o'clock, and long since the great meeting-hall had filled, but by seven there was yet no sign of the presidium. . . . The Bolshevik and Left Social Revolutionary factions were in session in their own rooms. All the livelong afternoon Lenin and Trotzky had fought against compromise. A considerable part of the Bolsheviki were in favour of giving way so far as to create a joint all-Socialist government. "We can't hold on!" they cried. "Too much is against us. We haven't got the men. We will be isolated, and the whole thing will fall." So Kameniev, Riazanov and others.

But Lenin, with Trotzky beside him, stood firm as a rock. "Let the compromisers accept our programme and they can come in! We won't give way an inch. If there are comrades here who haven't the courage and the will to dare what we dare, let him leave with the rest of the cowards and conciliators! Backed by the workers and soldiers we shall go on."

At five minutes past seven came word from the left Socialist Revolutionaries to say that they would remain in the Military Revolutionary Committee. "See!" said Lenin, "They are following." . . .

It was just 8:40 when a thundering wave of cheers announced the entrance of the presidium with Lenin—great Lenin—among them. A short, stocky figure, with a big head set down in his shoulders, bald and bulging. Little eyes, a snubbish nose, wide, generous mouth, and heavy chin; clean-shaven now, but already beginning to bristle with the well-known beard of his past and future. Dressed in shabby clothes, his trousers much too long for him. Unimpressive, to be the idol of a mob, loved and revered as perhaps few leaders in history have been. A strange popular leader—a leader purely by virtue of intellect; colourless, humourless, uncompromising and detached, without picturesque idiosyncrasies—but with the power of explaining profound ideas in simple terms, of analysing a concrete situation. And combined with shrewdness, the greatest intellectual audacity.

. . . .

Other speakers followed, apparently without any order. A delegate of the coal-miners of the Don Basin called upon the Congress to take measures against Kaledin, who might cut off coal and food from the capital. Several soldiers just arrived from the Front brought the enthusiastic greetings of their regiments. . . . Now Lenin, gripping the edge of the reading stand, letting his little winking eyes travel over the crowd as he stood there waiting, apparently oblivious to the long-rolling ovation, which lasted several minutes. When it finished, he said simply, "We shall now proceed to construct the Socialist order!" Again that overwhelming human roar.

"The first thing is the adoption of practical measures to realise peace. . . . We shall offer peace to the peoples of all the belligerent countries upon the basis of the Soviet terms—no annexations, no indemnities, and the right of self-determination of peoples. At the same time, according to our promise, we shall publish and repudiate the secret treaties. . . . The question of War and Peace is so clear that I think that I may, without preamble, read the project of a Proclamation to the Peoples of All the Belligerent Countries. . . ."

His great mouth, seeming to smile, opened wide as he spoke; his voice was hoarse—not unpleasantly so, but as if it had hardened that way after years and years of speaking—and went on monotonously, with the effect of being able to go on forever. . . . For emphasis he bent forward slightly. No gestures. And before him, a thousand simple faces looking up in intent adoration. . . .

It was exactly 10:35 when Kameniev asked all in favour of the proclamation to hold up their cards. One delegate dared to raise his hand against, but the sudden sharp outburst around him brought it swiftly down. . . . Unanimous.

. . . .

At two o'clock the Land Decree was put to vote, with only one against and the peasant delegates wild with joy. . . . So plunged the Bolsheviki ahead, irresistible, over-riding hesitation and opposition—the only people in Russia who had a definite programme of action while the others talked for eight long months. . . .

John Reed, *Ten Days That Shook the World* (New York: Boni and Liveright, 1919), pp. 123–129.

November 6, 1917: Bolshevik soldiers attacking the Winter Palace in Petrograd, headquarters of the Provisional Government. This was the only fighting that marked the overthrow of the Provisional Government. Kerensky fled the next day, and the Bolsheviks took control of Russia. [United Press International Photo.]

was repudiated. Property of the church reverted to the state.

The Bolshevik government also took Russia out of the war, which they believed benefited only capitalism. They signed an armistice with Germany in December 1917. On March 3, 1918, they accepted the Treaty of Brest-Litovsk, by which Russia yielded Poland, the Baltic states, and the Ukraine. Some territory in the Transcaucasus region went to Turkey. In addition the Bolsheviks agreed to pay a heavy war indemnity. These terms were a terribly high price to pay for peace, but Lenin had no choice. Russia was incapable of renewing the war effort, and the Bolsheviks needed time to impose their rule on a devastated and chaotic Russia. Moreover Lenin believed that communist revolutions might soon sweep across other nations in Europe as a result of the war and the Russian example.

Alexander Kerensky headed the shortlived provisional government in Russia after the Revolution of March 1917 and before the Bolshevik victory later that year. The photograph was made during his summer of authority. [The Granger Collection.]

❧ Lenin Establishes His Dictatorship

After the Bolshevik *coup* in October, elections for the Constituent Assembly were held in November. The results gave a majority to the Social Revolutionary Party and embarrassed the Bolsheviks. Using his control of the Red Army, Lenin closed the Constituent Assembly in January 1918, after it had met for only one day, and established the rule of a revolutionary elite and his own dictatorship. Here is the crucial Bolshevik decree.

. . . The Constituent Assembly, elected on the basis of lists drawn up prior to the October Revolution, was an expression of the old relation of political forces which existed when power was held by the compromisers and the Cadets. When the people at that time voted for the candidates of the Socialist-Revolutionary Party, they were not in a position to choose between the Right Socialist-Revolutionaries, the supporters of the bourgeoisie, and the Left Social-ist-Revolutionaries, the supporters of Socialism. Thus the Constituent Assembly, which was to have been the crown of the bourgeois parliamentary republic, could not but become an obstacle in the path of the October Revolution and the Soviet power.

The October Revolution, by giving the power to the Soviets, and through the Soviets to the toiling and exploited classes, aroused the desperate resistance of the exploiters, and in the crushing of this resistance it *fully revealed itself as the beginning of the socialist revolution . . . the majority in the Constituent Assembly which met on January 5 was secured by the party of the Right Socialist-Revolutionaries, the party of Kerensky, Avksentyev and Chernov. Naturally, this party refused to discuss the absolutely clear, precise and unambiguous proposal of the supreme organ of Soviet power, the Central Executive Committee of the Soviets, to recognize the program of the Soviet power, to recognize the "Declaration of Rights of the Toiling and Exploited People," to recognize the October Revolution and the Soviet power. . . .*

The Right Socialist-Revolutionary and Menshevik parties are in fact waging outside the walls of the Constituent Assembly a most desperate struggle against the Soviet power. . . .

Accordingly, the Central Executive Committee resolves: The Constituent Assembly is hereby dissolved.

R. V. Daniels (Ed.); *A Documentary History of Communism*, Vol. 1 (New York: Random House, 1960), pp. 133–135.

Until 1921 the new Bolshevik government confronted major domestic resistance. A civil war erupted between the "Red" Russians supporting the revolution and the "White" Russians, who opposed the Bolshevik triumph. In the summer of 1918 the czar and his family were murdered. Loyal army officers contined to fight the revolution and eventually received aid from the Allied armies. However, under the leadership of Trotsky the Red Army eventually overcame the domestic opposition. By 1921 Lenin and his supporters were in firm control.

The End of World War I

The internal collapse of Russia and the later Treaty of Brest-Litovsk brought Germany to the peak of its success. The Germans controlled east-ern Europe and its resources, especially food, and by 1918 they were free to concentrate their forces on the western front. This turn of events would probably have been decisive had it not been balanced by American intervention. Still American troops would not arrive in significant numbers for about a year, and both sides tried to win the war in 1917. An Allied attempt to break through in the west failed disastrously, bringing heavy losses to the British and the French and causing a mutiny in the French army. The Austrians, supported by the Germans, defeated the Italians at Caporetto and threatened to overrun Italy, but they were checked with the aid of Allied troops. The deadlock continued, but time was running out for the Central Powers.

In 1918 the Germans—persuaded chiefly by Ludendorff, by then Quartermaster-General, sec-

Former members of the Russian nobility working in the streets of Petrograd during the winter of 1917–1918. The Russian Revolution completely swept away the old Russian ruling classes. [United Press International Photo.]

ond in command to Hindenburg, but the real leader of the army—decided to gamble everything on one last offensive. The German army pushed forward and even reached the Marne again but got no farther. They had no more reserves, and the entire nation was exhausted. The Allies, on the other hand, were bolstered by the arrival of American troops in ever-increasing numbers. They were able to launch a counteroffensive that proved to be irresistible. As the Austrian fronts in the Balkans and Italy collapsed, the German high command knew that the end was imminent.

Ludendorff was determined that peace should be made before the German army could be thoroughly defeated in the field and that the responsibility should fall on civilians. For some time he had been the effective ruler of Germany under the aegis of the emperor. He now allowed a new government to be established on democratic principles and to seek peace immediately. The new government, under Prince Max of Baden, asked for peace on the basis of the Fourteen Points that President Wilson had declared as the American war aims. These were idealistic principles, including self-determination for nationalities, open diplomacy, freedom of the seas, disarmament, and establishment of a league of nations to keep the peace. Wilson insisted that he would deal only with a democratic German government because he wanted to be sure that he was dealing with the German people and not merely their rulers.

The disintegration of the German army forced William II to abdicate on November 9, 1918. The majority branch of the Social Democratic Party proclaimed a republic to prevent the establishment of a soviet government under the control of their radical, Leninist wing, which had earlier broken away as the Independent Socialist Party. Two days later this republican, socialist-led government signed the armistice that ended the war by accepting German defeat. At the time of the armistice the German people were, in general, unaware that their army had been defeated in the field and was crumbling. No foreign soldier stood on German soil. It appeared to many Germans that they could expect a negotiated and mild settlement. The real peace was quite different and embittered the German people, many of whom came to believe that Germany had not been defeated but had been tricked by the enemy and betrayed—even stabbed in the back—by republicans and socialists at home.

The victors rejoiced, but they also had much to mourn. The casualties on all sides came to about ten million dead and twice as many wounded. The economic and financial resources of the European states were badly strained. The victorious Allies, formerly creditors to the world, became debtors to the new American colossus, itself barely touched by the calamities of war.

The old international order, moreover, was dead. Russia was ruled by a Bolshevik dictatorship that preached world revolution and the overthrow of capitalism everywhere. Germany was in chaos, and Austria–Hungary had disintegrated into a swarm of small national states competing for the remains of the ancient empire. These kinds of change stirred the colonial territories ruled by the European powers, and overseas empires would never again be as secure as they had seemed before the war. Europe was no longer the center of the world, free to interfere when it wished or to ignore the outer regions if it chose. Its easy confidence in material and moral progress was shattered by the brutal reality of four years of horrible war. The memory of that war lived on to shake the nerve of the victorious Western powers as they confronted the new conditions of the postwar world.

The Settlement at Paris

The representatives of the victorious states gathered at Versailles and other Parisian suburbs in the first half of 1919. Wilson speaking for the United States, David Lloyd George (1863–1945) for Britain, Georges Clemenceau (1841–1929) for France, and Vittorio Emanuele Orlando (1860–1952) for Italy made up the Big Four. Japan, now recognized for the first time as a great power, also had an important part in the discussions. The diplomats who met in Paris had a far more difficult task than the one facing those who had sat at Vienna a century earlier. Both groups attempted to restore order to the world after long and costly wars, but Metternich and his associates could confine their thoughts to Europe. France had acknowledged defeat and was willing to take part in and uphold the Vienna settlement. The diplomats at Vienna were not much affected by public opinion, and they could draw the new map of Europe along practical lines determined by the realities of power and softened by compromise.

The Peacemakers

The negotiators at Paris in 1919 were not so fortunate. They represented constitutional, generally democratic governments, and public opinion had become a mighty force. Though there were secret sessions, the conference often worked in the full glare of publicity. Nationalism had become almost a secular religion, and Europe's many ethnic groups could not be relied on to remain quiet while they were distributed on the map at the whim of the great powers. World War I, moreover, had

been transformed by propaganda and especially by the intervention of Woodrow Wilson into a moral crusade to achieve a peace that would be just as well as secure. The Fourteen Points set forth the right of nationalities to self-determination as an absolute value, in spite of the fact that there was no way to draw the map of Europe to match ethnic groups perfectly with their homelands. All these elements made compromise difficult.

Wilson's idealism, moreover, came into conflict with the more practical war aims of the victorious powers and with many of the secret treaties that had been made before and during the war. The British and French people had been told that Germany would be made to pay for the war. Russia had been promised control of Constantinople in return for recognition of the French claim to Alsace–Lorraine and British control of Egypt. Romania had been promised Transylvania at the expense of Hungary. Some of the agreements contradicted others: Italy and Serbia had competing claims to the islands and shore of the Adriatic. During the war the British had encouraged Arab hopes of an independent Arab state carved out of the Ottoman Empire, but those plans conflicted with the Balfour Declaration (1917), in which the British seemed to accept Zionist ideology and to promise the Jews a national home in Palestine.

In 1919 President Woodrow Wilson left the United States on board the George Washington *to take part in the peace negotiations being held at Versailles in France. [Culver Pictures.]*

Both of these plans stood in conflict with an Anglo-French agreement to divide the Near East between the two Western powers.

The continuing national goals of the victors presented further obstacles to an idealistic "peace without victors." France, keenly conscious of its numerical inferiority to Germany and of the low birth rate that would keep it inferior, was naturally eager to achieve a settlement that would permanently weaken Germany and preserve French superiority. Italy continued to seek the acquisition of *Italia Irredenta;* Britain continued to look to its imperial interests; Japan pursued its own advantage in Asia; and the United States insisted on freedom of the seas, which favored American commerce, and on its right to maintain the Monroe Doctrine.

Finally, the peacemakers of 1919 faced a world still in turmoil. The greatest immediate threat appeared to be posed by the spread of Bolshevism. While Lenin and his colleagues were distracted by civil war, the Allies landed small armies at several places in Russia in the hope of overthrowing the Bolshevik regime. The revolution seemed likely to spread as Communist governments were established in Bavaria and Hungary, and Berlin experienced a dangerous Communist uprising led by the "Spartacus group." The Allies were sufficiently worried by these developments to allow and to support suppression of these Communist movements by right-wing military forces, and they even allowed an army of German volunteers to operate against the Bolsheviks in the Baltic states. The fear of the spread of Communism played a part in the thinking of the diplomats at Versailles, but it was far from dominant. The Germans kept playing on such fears as a way of getting better terms, but the Allies, and especially the French, would not hear of it. Fear of Germany remained the chief concern for France, whereas attention to interests that were more traditional and more immediate governed the policies of the other Allies.

The Peace

The Paris settlement consisted of five separate treaties between the victors and the defeated powers. Formal sessions began on January 18, 1919, and the last treaty was signed on August 10, 1920. Wilson arrived in Europe to unprecedented acclaim. Liberals and idealists expected a new kind of international order achieved in a new and better way, but they were soon disillusioned. "Open cove-

The Big Three at Versailles. Georges Clemenceau, French Prime Minister (left), American President Woodrow Wilson (center), and British Prime Minister David Lloyd George (right) tip their hats to the crowd after signing the Treaty of Versailles on June 28, 1919. [Culver Pictures.]

nants openly arrived at" soon gave way to closed sessions in which Wilson, Clemenceau, and Lloyd George made arrangements that seemed cynical to outsiders. The notion of "a peace without victors" became a mockery when the Soviet Union (as Russia was now called) and Germany were excluded from the peace conference. The Germans were simply presented with a treaty and compelled to accept it in a manner that fully justified their complaint that the treaty had not been negotiated but dictated. The principle of national self-determination was violated many times, as was unavoidable, but the diplomats of the small nations were angered by their exclusion from decisions. The undeserved adulation accorded Wilson on his arrival gradually turned into equally undeserved scorn. He had not abandoned his ideals lightly but had merely given way to the irresistible force of reality.

THE LEAGUE OF NATIONS. Wilson was able to make unpalatable concessions without abandoning his ideals because he put great faith in a new instrument for peace and justice, the League of Nations. Its convenant was an essential part of the peace treaty. The league was not intended as an international government but as a body of sovereign states who agreed to pursue some common practices and to consult in the common interest, especially when war threatened. In that case the members promised to submit the matter to arbitration or to an international court or to the League Council. Refusal to abide by this agreement would justify league intervention in the form of economic and even military sanctions. But the league was unlikely to be effective because it had no armed forces at its disposal, and any action required the unanimous consent of its council, consisting of Britain, France, Italy, the United States, and Japan, as well as four other states that had temporary seats. The Covenant of the League bound its members to "respect and preserve" the territorial integrity of all its members, and this was generally seen as a device to ensure the security of the victorious powers. The exclusion from the League Assembly of Germany and the Soviet Union further undermined the league's claim to evenhandedness.

COLONIES. Another provision of the covenant dealt with colonial areas. These were to be placed under the "tutelage" of one of the great powers under league supervision and encouraged to advance toward independence. Because there were no teeth in this provision, very little advance was made. Provisions for disarmament were doomed to be equally ineffective. Members of the league remained fully sovereign and continued to pursue their own national interests. Only Wilson seems to have put much faith in its future ability to produce peace and justice, and this belief allowed him to approve territorial settlements that violated his own principles.

GERMANY. In the west the main territorial issue was the fate of Germany. Although a united Germany was less than fifty years old, no one seems to have thought of undoing Bismarck's work and dividing it into its component parts. The French would have liked to detach the Rhineland and set it up as a separate buffer state, but Lloyd George and Wilson would not permit that. Still, they could not ignore France's need for protection against a resurgent Germany. France received Alsace–Lorraine and the right to work the coal mines of the Saar for fifteen years. Germany west of the Rhine and fifty kilometers east of it was to be a demilitarized zone, and Allied troops on the west bank could stay there for fifteen years. In addition to this physical barrier to a new German attack, the treaty provided that Britain and the United States would guarantee to aid France if it were attacked by Germany. Such an attack was made more unlikely by the permanent disarmament of Germany. Its army was limited to 100,000 men on long-term service; its fleet was all but eliminated; and it was forbidden to have war planes, submarines, tanks, heavy artillery, or poison gas. As long as these provisions were observed, France would be safe.

THE EAST. The settlement in the east ratified the collapse of the great defeated empires that had ruled it for centuries. Germany's frontier was moved far to the west, excluding much of Silesia and most of Prussia. What was left of East Prussia was cut off from the rest of Germany by a corridor carved out to give the revived state of Poland access to the sea. The Austro-Hungarian Empire disappeared entirely, giving way to many smaller successor states. Most of its German-speaking people were gathered in the small Republic of Austria, cut off from the Germans of Bohemia and forbidden to unite themselves with Germany. The Magyars occupied the much-reduced Kingdom of Hungary. The Czechs of Bohemia and Moravia joined with the Slovaks and Ruthenians to the east to form Czechoslovakia, and this new state included several million unhappy Germans. The southern Slavs were united in the Kingdom of Serbs, Croats, and Slovenes, or Yugoslavia. Italy gained the Trentino and Trieste. Romania was enlarged by receiving Transylvania from Hungary and Bessarabia from

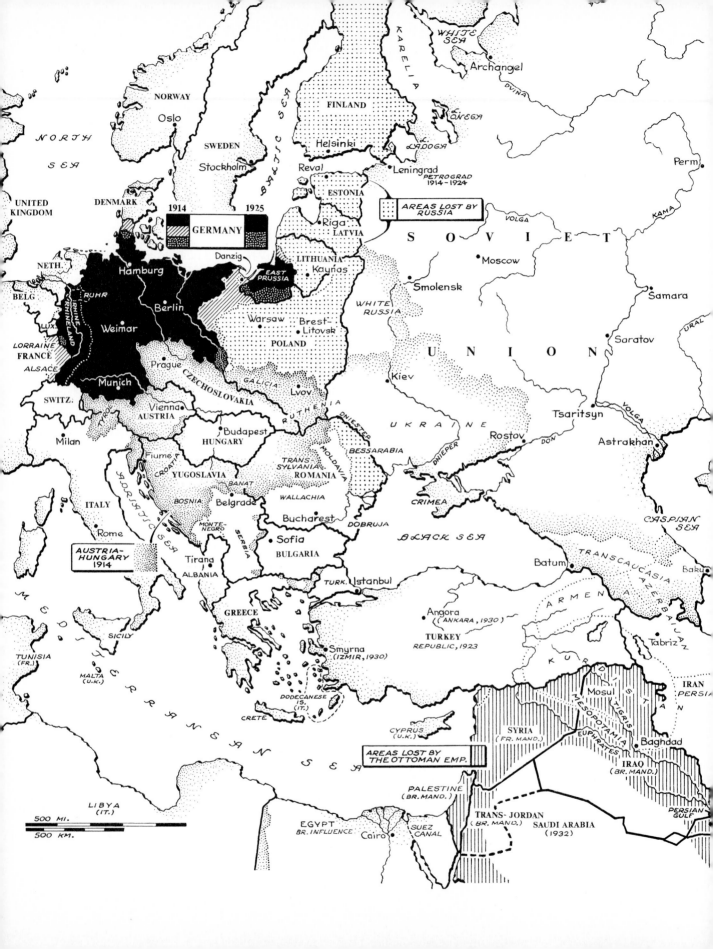

WORLD WAR I PEACE SETTLEMENT IN EUROPE AND THE MIDDLE EAST

OPPOSITE: MAP 29.6 *The map of central and Eastern Europe, as well as that of the Middle East, underwent drastic revision after World War I. The enormous geographical losses suffered by Germany, Austria-Hungary, the Ottoman Empire, Bulgaria, and Russia were the other side of the coin represented by gains for France, Italy, Greece, and Romania and the appearance, or reappearance, of at least eight new independent states from Finland in the north to Yugoslavia in the south. The mandate system for former Ottoman territories outside Turkey proper laid foundations for several new, mostly Arab, states in the Middle East.*

Russia. Bulgaria was diminished by the loss of territory to Greece and Yugoslavia. Russia lost vast territories in the west. Finland, Estonia, Latvia, and Lithuania became independent states, and a good part of Poland was carved out of formerly Russian soil. The old Ottoman Empire disappeared. The new republic of Turkey was limited to little more than Constantinople and Asia Minor, while the former Ottoman territories of Palestine and Iraq came under British control and Syria and Lebanon under French control as mandates of the League of Nations. Germany's former colonies in Africa were divided among Britain, France, and South Africa, and the German Pacific possessions went to Australia, New Zealand, and Japan.

REPARATIONS. Perhaps the most debated part of the peace settlement dealt with reparations for the damage done by Germany during the war. Before the armistice the Germans promised to pay compensation "for all damages done to the civilian population of the Allies and their property." The Americans judged that the amount would be between $15 billion and $25 billion and that Germany would be able to pay that amount. However, France and Britain, worried about repaying their war debts to the United States, were eager to have Germany pay the full cost of the war, including pensions to survivors and dependents. There was general agreement that Germany could not afford to pay such a sum, whatever it might be, and no sum was fixed at the conference. In the meantime Germany was to pay $5 billion annually until 1921. At that time a final figure would be set, which Germany would have to pay in thirty years. The French did not regret the outcome. Either Germany would pay and be bled into impotence, or she would refuse to pay and justify French intervention.

To justify these huge reparations payments, the Allies inserted the notorious Clause 231 into the treaty:

The Allied and Associated Governments affirm, and Germany accepts, the responsibility of Germany and her allies for causing all the loss and damage to which the Allied and Associated Governments and their nationals

This British cartoon points out the devastating effect on postwar Germany of the heavy reparations payments demanded by the Allies. The caption reads: "Perhaps it would gee-up better if we let it touch earth." [New York Public Library Picture Collection.]

have been subjected as a consequence of the war imposed upon them by aggression of Germany and her allies.

The Germans, of course, did not believe that they were solely responsible for the war and bitterly resented the charge. They had suffered the loss of vast territories containing millions of Germans and great quantities of badly needed natural resources; they were presented with an astronomical and apparently unlimited reparations bill. To add insult to injury, they were required to admit to a war guilt that they did not feel. Finally, to heap insult on insult, they were required to accept the entire treaty as it was written by the victors, without any opportunity for negotiation. Germany's Prime Minister Philipp Scheidemann (1865–1939) spoke of the treaty as the imprisonment of the German people and asked, "What hand would not wither that binds itself and us in these fetters?" But there was no choice. The Social Democrats and the Catholic Center Party formed a new government, and their representatives signed the treaty. These were the parties that formed the backbone of the Weimar government that ruled Germany until 1933, and they never overcame the stigma of accepting the Treaty of Versailles.

Evaluation of the Peace

Few peace settlements have undergone more severe attacks than the one negotiated in Paris in 1919. It is natural that the defeated powers should object to it, but the peace soon came under bitter criticism in the victorious countries as well. Many of the French thought that it failed to provide adequate security for France, because it tied that security to promises of aid from the unreliable Anglo-Saxon countries. In England and the United States a wave of bitter criticism arose in liberal quarters because the treaty seemed to violate the idealistic and liberal aims and principles that the Western leaders had professed. It was not a peace without victors, did not put an end to imperialism, attempted to promote the national interests of the winning nations, and violated the principles of national self-determination by leaving significant pockets of minorities outside the borders of their national homelands.

The most influential critic was John Maynard Keynes (1883–1946), a brilliant British economist who took part in the peace conference. He re-

signed in disgust when he saw the direction it was taking and wrote a book called *The Economic Consequences of the Peace* (1920). It was a scathing attack, especially on reparations and the other economic aspects of the peace. It was also a skillful assault on the negotiators and particularly on Wilson, who was depicted as a fool and a hypocrite. Keynes argued that the Treaty of Versailles was both immoral and unworkable. He called it a Carthaginian peace, referring to the utter destruction of Carthage by Rome after the Third Punic War. He argued that such a peace would bring economic ruin and war to Europe unless it were repudiated. Keynes had a great effect on the British, who were already suspicious of France and glad of an excuse to withdraw from continental affairs. The decent and respectable position came to be one that aimed at revision of the treaty in favor of Germany. Even more important was the book's influence in the United States. It fed the traditional tendency toward isolationism and gave powerful weapons to Wilson's enemies. Wilson's own political mistakes helped prevent American ratification of the treaty. Consequently America was out of the League of Nations and not bound to defend France. Britain, therefore, was also free from its obligation to France. France was left to protect itself without adequate means to do so for long.

Many of the attacks on the Treaty of Versailles are unjustified. It was not a Carthaginian peace. Germany was neither dismembered nor ruined. Reparations could be and were scaled down, and until the great world depression of the 1930s, the Germans recovered a high level of prosperity. Complaints against the peace should also be measured against the peace that the victorious Germans imposed on Russia at Brest-Litovsk and the plans they had made for a European settlement in case of victory. Both were far more severe than anything enacted at Versailles. The attempt at achieving self-determination for nationalities was less than perfect, but it was the best solution Europe had ever accomplished in that direction.

The peace, nevertheless, was unsatisfactory in important ways. The elimination of the Austro-Hungarian Empire, however inevitable that might seem, created a number of serious problems. Economically it was disastrous, for it separated raw materials from manufacturing areas and producers from their markets by new boundaries and tariff walls. In hard times this separation created friction and hostility that aggravated other quarrels also created by the peace treaties. Poland contained unhappy German minorities, and Czechoslovakia was a collection of nationalities that did not find it easy to live together as a nation. Disputes over territories in eastern Europe promoted further tension. The peace was inadequate on another level, as well. It rested on a victory that Germany did not admit. The Germans believed that they had been cheated rather than defeated. At the same time the high moral principles proclaimed by the Allies undercut the validity of the peace, for it plainly fell far short of those principles.

Finally, the great weakness of the peace was its failure to accept reality. Germany and Russia must inevitably play an important part in European affairs, yet they were excluded from the settlement and from the League of Nations. Given the many discontented parties, the peace was not self-enforcing; yet no satisfactory machinery for enforcing it was established. The league was never a serious force for this purpose. It was left to France, with no guarantee of support from Britain and no hope of help from the United States, to defend the new arrangements. Finland, the Baltic states, Poland, Romania, Czechoslovakia, and Yugoslavia were created as a barrier to the expansion westward of Russian Communism and as a threat in the rear to deter German revival. Most of these states, however, would have to rely on France in case of danger, and France was simply not strong enough for the task if Germany should rearm. The tragedy of the Treaty of Versailles was that it was neither conciliatory enough to remove the desire for change, even at the cost of war, nor harsh enough to make another war impossible. The only hope for a lasting peace required the enforcement of the disarmament of Germany while the more obnoxious clauses of the peace treaty were revised. Such a policy required continued attention to the problem, unity among the victors, and far-sighted leadership; but none of these was present in adequate supply during the next two decades.

Suggested Readings

L. ALBERTINI, *The Origins of the War of 1914*, 3 vols. (1952, 1957). Discursive but invaluable.

M. BALFOUR, *The Kaiser and His Times* (1972). A fine biography of William II.

V. R. BERGHAHN, *Germany and the Approach of War in 1914* (1973). A work similar in spirit to Fischer's but stressing the importance of Germany's naval program.

V. DEDIJER, *The Road to Sarajevo* (1967). A detailed study of the assassination of the Archduke Francis Ferdinand and its background.

S. B. FAY, *The Origins of the World War*, 2 vols. (1928). The best and most influential of the revisionist accounts.

D. K. FIELDHOUSE, *The Colonial Experience: A Comparative Study from the Eighteenth Century* (1966). An excellent recent study.

F. FISCHER, *Germany's Aims in the First World War* (1967). An influential interpretation that stirred a great controversy in Germany and around the world by emphasizing Germany's role in bringing on the war.

F. FISCHER, *War of Illusions* (1975). A long and diffuse book that tries to connect German responsibility for the war with internal social, economic, and political developments.

I. GEISS, *July 1914* (1967). A valuable collection of documents by a student of Fritz Fischer's. The emphasis is on German documents and responsibility.

O. J. HALE, *The Great Illusion 1900–1914* (1971). A fine survey of the period especially good on public opinion.

P. KENNEDY, *The Rise of the Anglo-German Antagonism 1860–1914* (1980). An unusual and thorough analysis of the political, economic and cultural roots of important diplomatic developments.

J. M. KEYNES, *The Economic Consequences of the Peace* (1920). The famous and influential attack on the Versailles Treaty.

L. LAFORE, *The Long Fuse* (1965). A readable account of the origins of World War I that focuses on the problem of Austria–Hungary.

W. L. LANGER, *European Alliances and Alignments*, 2nd ed. (1966). A splendid diplomatic history of the years 1871–1890.

W. L. LANGER, *The Diplomacy of Imperialism* (1935). A continuation of the previous study for the years 1890–1902.

W. LAQUEUR AND G. L. MOSSE (Eds.), *1914; The Coming of the First World War* (1966). A collection of valuable essays.

B. H. LIDDELL HART, *The Real War 1914–1918* (1964). A fine short account by an outstanding military historian.

E. MANTOUX, *The Carthaginian Peace* (1952). A vigorous attack on Keynes's view.

J. STEINBERG, *Yesterday's Deterrent* (1965). An excellent study of Germany's naval policy and its consequences.

Z. STEINER, *Britain and the Origins of the First World War* (1977). A perceptive and informed account of the way British foreign policy was made in the years before the war.

A. J. P. TAYLOR, *The Struggle for Mastery in Europe, 1848–1918* (1954). Clever but controversial.

L. C. F. TURNER, *Origins of the First World War* (1970). Especially good on the significance of Russia and its military plans.

914

30 Political Experiments of the 1920s

P URSUIT of experimentation in politics and of normality in economic life marked the decade following the conclusion of the Paris settlement. Many of the experiments failed, and the normality proved quite elusive. By the close of the decade the political path had been paved for the nightmares of brutally authoritarian governments and international aggression. Yet many of the people who had survived the Great War had hoped and worked for a better outcome. Authoritarianism and aggression were not the inescapable destiny of Europe. Their emergence was the result of failures in securing alternative modes of political life and international relations.

Lenin broadcasting from the radio room in the Kremlin. Without Lenin's masterful leadership, the Bolsheviks might never have been able to win control of Russia. The Bolsheviks conducted the most radical political experiment of the 1920s. [United Press International Photo.]

Political and Economic Factors After the Paris Settlement

New Governments

In 1919 experimental political regimes studded the map of Europe. From Ireland to Russia new governments were seeking to gain the active support of their citizens and to solve the grievous economic problems caused by the war. In the Soviet Union the Bolsheviks regarded themselves as forging nothing less than a new kind of civilization. They gave little significant consideration to anything but an authoritarian rule.

It was otherwise elsewhere on the Continent. Democratically elected parliamentary governments appeared where the autocratic, military empires of Germany and Austria–Hungary had previously held sway. Their goals were substantially more modest than those of the Bolsheviks. Yet to pursue parliamentary politics where it had never been meaningfully practiced proved no simple task. The Wilsonian vision of democratic, self-determined nations floundered on the harsh realities of economics, aggressive nationalism, and revived political conservatism. Too often the will for democratic, parliamentary government, as well as experience in its exercise, was absent from the nations on which it had been bestowed. Moreover, in many of the new democracies important sectors of the citizenry believed that parliamentary politics was by its very nature corrupt or unequal to great nationalistic enterprise.

Demands for Revision of Versailles

Several other Europe-wide problems haunted the early interwar period and directly affected the decisions and actions of individual nations. The Paris settlement fostered both resentment and discontent in numerous countries. Germany had been humiliated. The arrangements for reparations led to seemingly endless haggling over payments. Various national groups in the successor states of eastern Europe felt that injustice had been done in their particular case of self-determination. There were demands for further border adjustments. On the other side the victorious powers, and especially France, often believed that the provisions of the treaty were being inadequately enforced. Consequently, throughout the 1920s, calls either to revise or to enforce the Paris treaties contributed to domestic political turmoil across the Continent. All too many political figures were willing to fish in these troubled international waters for a large catch of domestic votes.

Postwar Economic Problems

Simultaneous with the move toward political experiment and demands for revision of the recently established international order was a widespread desire to return to the economic prosperity of the prewar years. However, after 1918 it was impossible to restore what American President Warren Harding would shortly term "normalcy." During the conflict Europeans had turned against themselves and their civilization the vast physical power that they had created in the previous century. More than 750,000 British soldiers had per-

ished. The combat deaths for France and Germany were 1,385,000 and 1,808,000, respectively. Russia had lost no fewer than 1,700,000 troops. Scores of thousands more from other belligerent nations had also been killed. Still more millions had been wounded. These casualties meant not only the waste of human life and talent but also the loss of producers and consumers. There had also been widespread destruction of transport facilities, mines, and industry.

Another casualty of the conflict was the financial dominance and independence of Europe. At the opening of hostilities Europe had been the financial and credit center of the world. At the close of the fighting Europeans stood deeply in debt to each other and to the United States. The Bolsheviks had repudiated the debt of the czarist government, much of which was owed to French creditors. Other nations could not pursue this revolutionary course. The Paris settlement had imposed heavy financial obligations on Germany and its allies. The United States refused to ask reparations from Germany but firmly demanded repayment of war debts from its own allies. On the one hand, the reparation and debt structure meant that no nation was fully in control of its own economic life. On the other hand, the absence of international economic cooperation meant that more than ever individual nations felt compelled to pursue or to attempt to pursue selfish, nationalistic economic aims. It was perhaps the worst of all possible international economic worlds.

The market and trade conditions that had prevailed before 1914 had also changed radically. Russia, in large measure, withdrew from the European economic order. The political reconstruction of eastern and central Europe into the multitude of small successor states broke up the trade region formerly encompassed by Germany and Austria–Hungary. Most of those new states had weak economies hardly capable of competing in modern economic life. The new boundaries separated raw materials from the factories using them. Railway systems on which finished and unfinished products traveled might now lie under the control of two or more nations. Political and economic nationalism went together. New customs barriers were raised.

International trade also followed new patterns. The United States became less dependent on European production and assumed the status of a major competitor. During the war the belligerents had been forced to sell many of their holdings on other continents to finance the conflict. As a consequence Europeans exercised less dominance over the world economy. Postwar economic growth within colonies or former colonies lowered the demand for European goods. The United States and Japan began to penetrate markets in Latin America and Asia previously dominated by European producers and traders.

New Roles for Government and Labor

The war effort in all countries occasioned new dimensions of state interference and direction in the economy. Large government bureaucracies had been organized to plan the course of production and the distribution of goods. Prices had been controlled, raw materials stockpiled, consumer goods rationed, and economic priorities set by government technocrats. The mechanism of the freely operating market so dear to nineteenth-century liberals had been rejected as a vehicle for economic decision-making. The economic planning skills learned during the war could be transferred to peacetime operations. Moreover governments had learned about the immense productive and employment power of an economy placed under state control.

Labor had achieved new prominence within the wartime economic setting. The unions had actively supported the war effort of their nations. They had ensured labor peace for production. In turn, their members had received better wages, and their leaders had been admitted to high political councils. This wartime cooperation of unions and labor leaders with the various national governments destroyed the internationalism of the prewar labor movement, but it also meant that henceforth the demands of labor could not be ignored by governments. Although in peacetime wages might be lowered, they could very rarely be reduced to prewar levels. European workers intended to receive their just share of the fruits of their labor. Collective bargaining and union recognition brought on by the war also could not be abandoned. This improvement in both the status and the effective influence of labor was one of the most significant social and political changes to flow from World War I.

The social condition of the work force seemed to be improving while that of the middle class seemed to be stagnating or declining. Throughout the 1920s people from the various segments of the middle class remained very suspicious of the new role of labor and of socialist political parties. This suspicion and fear of potential loss of property on the part of the middle classes led them to seek to perpetuate the status quo and to fend off further social and economic advances of the working classes. In this regard, the European middle classes, once the vanguard of the liberal revolution, had become a thoroughly conservative political force.

The war and the peace settlement wrought one other major change that affected the course of political and economic life. The turn to liberal democracy and the extension of the franchise to women and previously disenfranchised males meant that for the first time in European history the governments handling economic matters were responsible to mass electorates. Economics and politics had become more intimately connected than ever before. The economic and social anxieties of the electorate could and eventually did overcome its political scruples. Whereas previously economic discontent had been articulated through riots and later through unions, it could now be voiced through the ballot box.

Joyless Victors

France and Great Britain, with the aid of the United States, had won the war. France became the strongest military power on the Continent. Britain had escaped with almost no physical damage. Both nations, however, had lost vast numbers of young men in the conflict. Their economies were weak, and their overseas wealth and power stood much diminished. Compared with contemporary events in Germany, Italy, and Russia, the interwar political development of the two major democracies seems rather tame. Neither experienced a revolution or a shift to authoritarian government. Yet this surface calm was largely illusory. Both were troubled democracies. To neither did victory in war bring the good life in peace.

France: The Search for Security

At the close of World War I, as after Waterloo, the revolution of 1848, and the defeat of 1871, the French voters elected a doggedly conservative Chamber of Deputies. The preponderance of military officers among its members led to the nickname of the "Horizon Blue Chamber." The overwhelmingly conservative character of the chamber was registered in 1920 by its defeat of Georges Clemenceau's bid for the presidency. The crucial factor had been, of all things, the alleged leniency of the Paris treaties and the failure to establish a separate Rhineland state. The deputies wanted to achieve future security against Germany and Russian Communism. They intended to make as few concessions to domestic social reform as possible. The 1920s were marked by fluctuations in ministries and a drift in domestic policy. The political turnstile remained ever active. Between the end of the war and January 1933, France was governed by no fewer than twenty-seven different cabinets.

NEW ALLIANCES. During the first five years after the Treaty of Versailles France accepted its role as the leading European power. The French plan was to enforce strictly the clauses of the treaty that were meant to keep Germany weak and, at the same time, to build a system of eastern alliances to replace the lost prewar alliance with Russia. In 1920 and 1921 three eastern states that had much to lose from revision of the treaty—Czechoslovakia, Romania, and Yugoslavia—formed the Little Entente. Before long France made military alliances with these states as well as with Poland. A dispute with Czechoslovakia over the control of Teschen prevented the Poles from joining the Little Entente, but the independent existence of Poland depended on the maintenance of the Versailles settlement. This new system of eastern alliances was the best France could do, but it was far weaker than the old Franco-Russian alliance. The new states combined were no match for the former power of imperial Russia, and they were neither united nor reliable. Poland and Romania were more concerned about Russia than about Germany, and the main target of the Little Entente was Hungary. If one of the eastern states were threatened by a resurgent Germany, there was considerable doubt that the others would be eager to come to its aid.

The formation of this new alliance system heightened the sense of danger and isolation felt by the two excluded powers, Germany and the Soviet Union. In 1922, while the European states were holding an economic conference at Genoa, the Russians and the Germans met at Rapallo nearby and signed a treaty of their own. It established diplomatic and economic relations that proved useful to both sides. Although the treaty contained no secret political or military clauses, such arrangements were suspected to exist. And it is now known that the Germans helped train the Russian army and gave their own army valuable experience in the use of tanks and planes in the Soviet Union. The news of Rapallo confirmed the French in their growing belief that Germany was unwilling to live up to the terms of the Versailles Treaty and helped move them to strong action.

QUEST FOR REPARATIONS. In early 1923 the Allies, and France in particular, declared Germany to be in technical default of its reparations payments. Raymond Poincaré (1860–1934), France's powerfully nationalistic prime minister, took the opportunity to teach the Germans a lesson and force them to comply. On January 11, to ensure receipt of the hard-won reparations, the French government ordered its troops to occupy the Ruhr mining and manufacturing district. The response of the Weimar Republic was to order passive resistance. This policy amounted to calling a general strike in the largest industrial region of the nation. Confronted with this tactic, Poincaré sent French civilians to run the German mines and railroads. France got its way. The Germans paid, but France confronted a great price for its victory. The English were alienated by the French heavy-handedness and took no part in the occupation. They became more suspicious of France and more sympathetic to Germany. The cost of the Ruhr occupation, moreover, vastly increased French as well as German inflation and damaged the French economy. As one scholar has explained: the French "threatened to choke Germany to death; the Germans threatened to die. Neither side dared carry its threat to extremity."[1] From the French viewpoint, consequently, victory in the war and the achievement of considerable military power seemed to have brought the nation little of the prestige and effective influence it sought.

In 1924 the conservative ministry gave way to a coalition of leftist parties, the so-called *Cartel des Gauches*, led by Edouard Herriot (1872–1957). The chief policy changes of the new Cabinet were recognition of the Soviet Union and a more conciliatory policy toward Germany. Leadership on this score came from Aristide Briand (1862–1932), who was foreign minister for the remainder of the decade. He championed the League of Nations

[1]A. J. P. Taylor, *The Origins of the Second World War* (New York: Fawcett, 1961), p. 33.

and attempted to persuade his nation that its military power did not give it unlimited influence on the foreign affairs of Europe. Under the leftist coalition a mild inflation also occurred. It had begun under the conservatives but picked up intensity in 1925. When the value of the franc fell sharply on the international money market in 1926, Poincaré returned to office as head of a national govenment composed of several parties. The value of the franc recovered somewhat, and inflation cooled. For the rest of the 1920s the conservatives remained in power. The country enjoyed a general prosperity that lasted until 1931, longer than in any other nation.

Great Britain

World War I profoundly changed British politics if not the political system. In 1918 Parliament expanded the electorate to include all men aged twenty-one and women aged thirty. (In 1928 the age for women voters was also lowered to twenty-one.) The prewar structure of parties and leadership also shifted. A coalition Cabinet composed of Liberal, Conservative, and Labor ministers had directed the war effort. The wartime ministerial participation of the Labor Party did much to dispel its radical image. For the Liberal Party, however, the conflict brought unexpected division. Until 1916 Liberal Prime Minister Herbert Asquith had presided over the Cabinet. As disagreements over war management developed, he was ousted by fellow Liberal David Lloyd George. The party then became sharply split between followers of the two men. In 1918, against the wishes of both the Labor Party and the Asquith Liberals, Lloyd George decided to maintain the coalition through the tasks of the peace conference and the domestic reconstruction. The wartime coalition, now minus its Labor members, won a stunning victory at the polls. However, Lloyd George could thereafter remain prime minister only as long as his dominant Conservative partners wished to keep him.

During the 1918 election campaign there had been much talk about creating "a land fit for heroes to live in." It did not happen. Except for the three years immediately after the war the British economy was depressed throughout the 1920s. Genuine postwar recovery simply did not get under way. Unemployment never dipped below 10 per cent and often hovered near 11 per cent. There were never fewer than a million workers

unemployed. Government insurance programs to cover unemployed workers, widows, and orphans were expanded. But there was no similar meaningful expansion in the number of jobs available. From 1922 onward accepting the "dole" with little expectation of future employment became a wretched and degrading way of life for scores of thousands of poor British families.

THE FIRST LABOR GOVERNMENT. In October 1922 the Conservatives dropped Lloyd George and replaced him with Bonar Law (1858–1923), one of their own. A Liberal would never again be prime minister. Stanley Baldwin (1867–1947) soon replaced Law, who fell victim to throat cancer. Baldwin decided to attempt to cure Britain's economic plight by abandoning free trade and imposing protective tariffs. The voters rejected the proposed policy in 1923. At the election the Conservative Party lost its majority in the House of Commons, but only votes from both Liberal and Labor party members could provide an alternative majority. Labor had elected the second largest group of members to the Commons. Consequently, in December 1923, King George V (1910–1936) asked Ramsay MacDonald (1866–1937) to form the first Labor ministry in British history. The Liberal Party did not serve in the Cabinet but provided the necessary votes in the House of Commons to give the Labor ministry a working majority.

The Labor Party was socialistic in its platform, but not revolutionary. The party had expanded beyond its early trade union base. MacDonald himself had opposed World War I and for a time had also broken with the party. His own version of socialism owed little, if anything, to Marx. His program consisted of plans for extensive social reform rather than for the nationalization or public seizure of industry. A sensitive politician, if not a great leader, MacDonald understood that the most important task facing the ministry was proving to the nation that the Labor Party was both respectable and responsible. His nine months in office achieved just that goal if little else of major importance. The establishment of Labor as a viable governing party signaled the permanent demise of the Liberal Party. It has continued to exist, but the bulk of its voters have drifted into either the Conservative or the Labor ranks.

THE GENERAL STRIKE OF 1926. The Labor government fell in the autumn of 1924 over charges of inadequate prosecution of a communist

Stanley Baldwin was the Conservative Party Prime Minister during the general strike of 1926. His solid, calm appearance seemed to many voters to suggest the qualities most needed in their government. [Bettmann Archive.]

During the British general strike of May 1926, middle class workers devised various ways to continue about their business. Here they are using a truck as a bus to carry them to work. [The Granger Collection.]

writer. Stanley Baldwin returned to office, where he remained until 1929. The problem of the stagnant economy remained uppermost in the public mind. Business and political leaders continued to believe that all would be well if they could restore the prewar conditions of trade. A major element in those conditions had been the gold standard as the basis for international trade. In 1925 the Conservative government returned to the gold standard, abandoned during the war, in hopes of re-creating the former monetary stability. However, the government set the conversion rate for the pound against other currencies too high and thus in effect raised the price of British goods to foreign customers.

In order to make their products competitive on the world market, British management attempted to lower prices by cutting wages. The coal industry was the sector most directly affected by the wage cuts. It was inefficient and poorly managed and had been in trouble ever since the end of the war.

❧ Stanley Baldwin Reflects on the British General Strike

After halting much economic activity for more than a week in 1926, the British general strike came to a peaceful conclusion. Baldwin, who was the Conservative prime minister at the time, thought the outcome spoke well for British character and British freedom. In examining the impact of the strike, he was particularly concerned to present British institutions in a favorable light, as contrasted with the new social order then emerging in the Soviet Union. He hoped that communist doctrines would not come to influence the British labor movement.

It may have been a magnificent demonstration of the solidarity of labour, but it was at the same time a most pathetic evidence of the failure of all of us to live and work together for the good of all. . . .But if that strike showed solidarity, sympathy with the miners—whatever you like—it showed something else far greater. It proved the stability of the whole fabric of our own country, and to the amazement of the world not a shot was fired. We were saved by common sense and the good temper of our own people. We have been called a stupid people; but the moment the public grasped that what was at stake was not the solidarity of labour nor the fate of the miners, but the life of the State, then there was a response to the country's need deep and irresistible. And mark this: in my view there was that feeling in the country because the leaders of the strike and the men who were on strike felt it in their innermost hearts, too. They felt a conflict of loyalties. They knew that same conflict was raging in the breasts of thousands of men who had fought for their country ten years ago. Many of the strikers were uneasy in their minds and their consciences, because the British workman, as I know him, does not like breaking contracts, as so many of them did. I do not think many of them like stopping food supplies and shutting down the Press. I sometimes amuse myself with wondering what their language would have been like if these things had been done by the Government. And, after all, when all has been said about England, about the mistakes we make, and about our stupidity, and about how much better they do things in Russia, yet how many of those men or any of us, would prefer to have been born and brought up in any country in the world but this, or to send our children to be brought up there. In these postwar years, in spite of all the depression, in spite of all our troubles, never before has the wealth of this country, through the taxes and the rates, been so distributed to those less fortunate and for the provision of those thrown out of work. . . .

I want to see our British Labour movement free from alien and foreign heresy. I want to see it pursued and developed on English lines, led by English men. The temptations that beset the growth of these vast organizations [the labor unions], in many respects as they are today outside the law, controlling multitudes of men and large sums of money—the temptation to set such a machine in motion and make people follow it is great indeed.

Stanley Baldwin, *Our Inheritance* (London: Hodder and Stoughton, 1928), pp. 222–224.

Labor relations in the coal industry had been unruly for some time. In 1926, after cuts in wages and a breakdown in negotiations, the coal miners went out on strike. Soon thereafter, in May 1926, sympathetic workers in other industries engaged in a general strike lasting nine days. There was much tension but little violence. In the end the miners and the other unions capitulated. With such high levels of unemployment organized labor was in a relatively weak position. After the general strike the Baldwin government attempted to reconcile labor primarily through an expansion of housing and reforms in the poor laws. Despite the economic difficulties of these years the actual standard of living of most British workers, including those receiving government insurance payments, actually improved somewhat.

EMPIRE. World War I also modified Britain's imperial position. The aid given by the dominions, such as Canada and Australia, demonstrated a new independence on their part. Empire was a two-way proposition. The idea of self-determination as applied to Europe could not be prevented from filtering into imperial relationships. In India the Congress Party, led by Mohandas Gandhi (1869–1948), was beginning to attract widespread support. The British started to talk more about eventual self-government for the nation. Moreover, during the 1920s the Indian government achieved the right to impose tariffs for the protection of its own industry rather than for the advantage of British manufacturers. The British textile producers no longer had totally free access to the vast Indian market.

IRELAND. A new chapter was written in the unhappy relations between Britain and Ireland during and after the war. In 1914 the Irish Home Rule Bill had passed Parliament, but its implementation was postponed for the duration of the conflict. As the war dragged on, Irish nationalists became determined to wait no longer. On Easter Monday 1916 a nationalist uprising occurred in Dublin. It was the only rebellion of a national group to occur against any government engaged in the war. The British suppressed it in less than a week but then made a grave tactical blunder. They executed the Irish nationalist leaders who had been responsible for the uprising. Overnight those rebels became national martyrs. Leadership of the nationalist cause quickly shifted from the Irish Party in Parliament to the extremist Sinn Fein ("Ourselves Alone") movement.

In the election of 1918 the Sinn Fein Party won all but four of the Irish parliamentary seats outside Ulster. They refused to go to the Parliament at Westminster. Instead they constituted themselves into a Dail Eireann, or Irish Parliament. On January 21, 1919, they declared Irish independence. The military wing of Sinn Fein became the Irish Republican Army (IRA). The first president was Eamon De Valera (1882–1975), who had been born in the United States. Very quickly what amounted to a guerrilla war broke out between the IRA and the British army supported by auxiliaries known as the Black and Tans. There was unusually intense bitterness and hatred on both sides.

In late 1921 secret negotiations commenced between the two governments. In the treaty concluded in December 1921 the Irish Free State took its place beside the earlier dominions in the British Commonwealth: Canada, Australia, New Zealand, and South Africa. The six counties of Ulster, or Northern Ireland, were permitted to remain part of what was now called the United Kingdom of Great Britain and Northern Ireland, with provisions for home rule. No sooner had the treaty been signed than a new Irish civil war broke out between Irish moderates and diehards. The moderates supported the treaty; the diehards wanted the oath to the British monarch abolished and a totally independent republic established. The second civil war continued until 1923. De Valera, who supported the diehards, resigned the presidency and organized resistance to the treaty. In 1932 he was again elected president. The next year the Dail Eireann abolished the oath of allegiance to the monarch.

During World War II Ireland remained neutral. In 1949 it declared itself the wholly independent republic of Eire.

Trials of the New Democracies

Both France and Great Britain had prewar experience in liberal democratic government. Their primary challenges lay in responding to economic pressures and allowing new groups, such as the Labor Party, to share political power. In Germany, Poland, Austria, Czechoslovakia, and the other successor states the issue for the 1920s was to make new parliamentary governments function in a satisfactory and stable manner. Prior to the war both Germany and Austria–Hungary had possessed elected parliaments, but those bodies had not exercised genuine political power. The question after the war became whether those groups who had previously sat powerless in parliaments could assume both power and responsibility. Another question was how long conservative institutions, such as the armies and the conservative political groups, would tolerate or cooperate with the liberal experiments. At the same time all of these newly organized states confronted immense postwar economic difficulties.

Successor States in Eastern Europe

Only the barest outline can be given of the dreary political story of the successor states. It had been an article of faith among nineteenth-century liberals that only good could flow from the demise of Austria–Hungary. The new states in eastern Europe were to symbolize the principle of national self-determination and to provide a buffer against the westward spread of Bolshevism. However, they were in trouble from the beginning. They were poor and overwhelmingly rural nations dwelling in an industrialized world. Nationality problems continued to exist. The major social and political groups were generally unwilling to make compromises. With the exception of Czechoslovakia, all of these states succumbed to some form of authoritarian government.

In Hungary during 1919 the Bolsheviks had erected a socialist government led by Béla Kun (1885–1937). The Allies quickly authorized an invasion by Romanian troops to remove the Communist danger. They then established Admiral Miklós Horthy (1858–1957) as regent, a position he held until 1944. During the 1920s the effective ruler of Hungary was Count Stephen Bethlen (1874–1947). He presided over a government that was parliamentary in form but aristocratic in character. In 1932 he was succeeded by General Julius Gömbös (1886–1936), who pursued policies of anti-Semitism and rigged elections. No matter how the popular vote turned out, the Gömbös party controlled the Parliament. There was also deep resentment in Hungary over the territory it had lost to other nations through the Paris settlement.

The situation in Austria was little better. The new Austria consisted of a capital city surrounded by some other territory. A quarter of the eight million Austrians lived in Vienna. Viable economic life was almost impossible, and union with Germany was forbidden by the Paris settlement. Throughout the 1920s the leftist Social Democrats and the conservative Christian Socialists contended for power. Unwilling to use only normal political methods, both groups employed small armies to terrorize their opponents and to impress their followers. In 1933 the Christian Socialist Engelbert Dollfuss (1892–1934) became chancellor. He tried to steer a course between both the Austrian Social Democrats and the German Nazis, who had begun to penetrate Austria. In 1934 he outlawed all political parties except the Christian Socialists, the agrarians, and the paramilitary groups, which composed his own Fatherland Front. He used government troops against the Social Democrats. During an unsuccessful Nazi *coup* in 1934, Dollfuss was shot. His successor, Kurt von Schuschnigg (b. 1897) presided over Austria until Hitler annexed it in 1938.

In southeastern Europe revision of the Versailles Treaty arrangements was somewhat less an issue. Parliamentary government floundered nevertheless. In Yugoslavia (known as the Kingdom of the Serbs, Croats, and Slovenes until 1929), the clash of nationalities eventually led to the imposition of royal dictatorship in 1929 under King Alexander I (1921–1934), himself a Serb. His dictatorship saw the outlawing of political parties and the jailing of popular politicians. Alexander I was assassinated in 1934, but the authoritarian government continued under the regency for his son. Other royal dictatorships were imposed, in Romania by King Carol II (1930–1940) and in Bulgaria by King Boris III (1918–1943). They regarded their own illiberal regimes as countering even more extreme antiparliamentary movements and as quieting the discontent of the varied nationalities within their borders. In Greece a parliamentary monarchy floundered amidst military *coups* and calls for a republic. In 1936 General John Metaxas (1871–1941) instituted a dictatorship that for the time being ended parliamentary life in Greece.

The nation whose postwar fortunes probably most disappointed liberal Europeans was Poland. For over a hundred years the country had been erased from the map. Restoration of an independent Poland had been one of Woodrow Wilson's Fourteen Points. When the country was finally reconstructed in 1919, nationalism proved an insufficient bond to overcome political disagreements stemming from class, diverse economic interests, and regionalism. The new Parliament was plagued with a vast number of small political parties. The constitution assigned too little power to the executive. In 1926 General Josef Pilsudski (1857–1935) carried out a military *coup*. He ruled personally until the close of the decade, when the government passed into the hands of a group of military leaders.

Only one central European successor state escaped the fate of self-imposed authoritarian government. Czechoslovakia possessed a strong industrial base, a substantial middle class, and a tradition of liberal values. During the war Czechs and Slovaks had cooperated to aid the Allies. They had learned to work together and to trust each other. After the war the new government had carried out agrarian reform and had broken up large estates in favor of small peasant holdings. In the person of Thomas Masaryk (1850–1937) the nation possessed a gifted leader of immense integrity and fairness. The country had a real chance of constructing a viable modern nation state. However, it was plagued with discontent among its smaller national groups, including the German population of the Sudetenland assigned to Czechoslovakia by the Paris settlement. The parliamentary regime might very well have been able to deal with this problem, but extreme German nationalists looked to Hitler for aid. For his part, the German dictator wished to expand into eastern Europe. In 1938 at Munich the great powers divided liberal Czechoslovakia to appease the aggressive instincts of Hitler.

The fate of the successor states proved most disappointing to those who had hoped for political liberty to result from the dissolution of the Hapsburg Empire and other border adjustments in east-

Thomas Masaryk (1850–1937) was the widely respected president of the democracy of Czechoslovakia after World War I. [The Granger Collection.]

MAJOR POLITICAL EVENTS OF THE 1920s

1919	August Constitution of the Weimar Republic promulgated
1920	Kapp *Putsch* in Berlin
1921	March Kronstadt mutiny leads Lenin to initiate his New Economic Policy
	December Treaty between Great Britain and the Irish Free State
1922	April Treaty of Rapallo between Germany and the Soviet Union
	October Fascist March on Rome leads to Mussolini's assumption of power
1923	January France invades the Ruhr
	November Hitler's Beer Hall *Putsch*
	December First Labor Party government in Britain
1924	Death of Lenin
1925	Locarno Agreements
1926	General strike in Britain
1928	Kellogg–Briand Pact
1929	January Trotsky expelled from the Soviet Union
	February Lateran Accord between the Vatican and the Italian state
	November Bukharin expelled from his offices in the Soviet Union; Stalin's central position thus affirmed

---

ern Europe. By the early 1930s in most of those states the authoritarianism of the Hapsburgs had been replaced by that of other rulers. However, the most momentous democratic experiment between the wars was conducted in Germany. There, after a century of frustration and disappointment, a liberal state had been constructed. It was in Germany that parliamentary democracy and its future in Western civilization faced its major trial.

The Weimar Republic

The German Weimar Republic was born from the defeat of the imperial army, the revolution of

1918 against the Hohenzollerns, and the hopes of German Liberals and Social Democrats. Its name derived from the city in which its constitution was written and promulgated in August 1919. While the constitution was being debated, the republic, headed by the Social Democrats, accepted the humiliating terms of the Versailles Treaty. Although its officials had signed only under the threat of an Allied invasion, the republic was nevertheless permanently associated with the national disgrace and the economic burdens of the treaty. Throughout the 1920s the government of the republic was required to fulfill the economic and military provisions imposed by the Paris settlement. It became all too easy for nationalists and military figures whose policies had brought on the tragedy and defeat of the war to blame the young republic and the socialists for the results of the conflict. In Germany, more than in other countries, the desire to revise the treaty was closely related to a desire to change the mode of domestic government.

The Weimar Constitution was a highly enlightened document. It guaranteed civil liberties and provided for direct election, by universal suffrage, of the *Reichstag* and the president. However, it also contained certain crucial structural flaws that allowed the eventual overthrow of its institutions. Within the *Reichstag* a complicated system of proportional representation was adopted. This system made it relatively easy for very small political parties to gain seats in the *Reichstag* and resulted in shifting party combinations that led to considerable instability. Ministers were technically responsible to the *Reichstag,* but the president appointed and removed the chancellor. Perhaps most importantly, Article 48 allowed the president, in times of emergency, to rule by decree. In this manner the constitution permitted the possibility of presidential dictatorship.

Beyond the burden of the Versailles Treaty and the potential constitutional pitfalls, the Weimar Republic suffered from a lack of sympathy and a lack of loyalty on the part of many Germans. A social revolution had not accompanied the changes in political structure. Many important political figures actually favored a constitutional monarchy. The schoolteachers, civil servants, and judicial officials of the republic were generally the same people who had previously served the Kaiser and the empire. Prior to the war they had distrusted or even hated the Social Democratic Party, which figured so prominently in the establishment and the politics of the republic. The officer corps was deeply suspicious of the government and profoundly resentful of the military provisions of the peace settlement. They and other nationalistic Germans perpetuated the myth that the German army had surrendered on foreign soil only because it had been stabbed in the back by civilians at home. In other words, large numbers of Germans in significant social and political positions wanted both to revise the peace treaty and to modify the system of government. The early years of the republic only solidified those sentiments.

A number of major and minor humiliations as well as considerable economic instability impinged on the new government. In March 1920 the right-wing Kapp *Putsch* or armed insurrection erupted in Berlin. Led by a conservative civil servant and supported by army officers, the attempted *coup* failed. But the collapse occurred only after government officials had fled the city and German workers had carried out a general strike. The same month a series of strikes took place in the Ruhr mining district. The government sent in troops. Such extremism from both the left and the right would haunt the republic for all its days. In May 1921 the Allies presented a reparations bill for 132 billion gold marks. The German republican government accepted this preposterous demand only after new Allied threats of occupation. Throughout the early 1920s there were numerous assassinations or attempted assassinations of important republican leaders. Violence was the hallmark of the first five years of the republic.

INVASION OF THE RUHR AND INFLATION. Inflation brought the major crisis of this period. The financing of the war and the continued postwar deficit spending generated an immense rise in prices. Consequently the value of German currency fell. By early 1921 the German mark traded against the American dollar at a ratio of 64 to 1, compared with a ratio of 4.2 to 1 in 1914. The German financial community contended that the value of the currency could not be stabilized until the reparations issue had been solved. In the meantime the printing presses kept pouring forth paper money, which was used to redeem government bonds as they fell due.

The French invasion of the Ruhr in January 1923 and the German response of economic passive resistance produced cataclysmic inflation. The Weimar government paid subsidies to the Ruhr labor force, who had laid down their tools. Unemployment soon spread from the Ruhr to other parts of the country, creating a new drain on the

In 1923 German inflation became so extreme that eventually money was not worth the paper on which it was printed. In these photographs from that time, [LEFT] a German housewife finds it cheaper to use the inflated currency to light her stove than to spend it on kindling wood, while [RIGHT] poor citizens sell tin cans to raise money. [LEFT: *United Press International Photo;* RIGHT: *The Granger Collection.*]

In January 1923 French troops occupied the Ruhr region of Germany because of alleged defaults in the delivery of reparations to France. [*The Granger Collection.*]

❧ Lilo Linke Recalls the Mad Days of the German Inflation

> In 1923 the presses that were printing paper currency in Germany could hardly keep up with the rising prices. This memoir recounts the difficulties of those days and the resentments that arose as money because worth less than the paper on which it was printed.

The whole population had suddenly turned into maniacs. Everyone was buying, selling, speculating, bargaining, and dollar, dollar, dollar was the magic word which dominated every conversation, every newspaper, every poster in Germany. Nobody understood what was happening. There seemed to be no sense, no rules in the mad game, but one had to take part in it if one did not want to be trampled underfoot at once. Only a few people were able to carry through to the end and gain by the inflation. The majority lost everything and broke down, impoverished and bewildered.

The middle class was hurt more than any other, the savings of a lifetime and their small fortunes melted into a few coppers. They had to sell their most precious belongings for ten milliard inflated marks to buy a bit of food or an absolutely necessary coat, and their pride and dignity were bleeding out of many wounds. Bitterness remained for ever in their hearts. Full of hatred, they accused the international financiers, the Jews and Socialists—their old enemies—of having exploited their distress. They never forgot and never forgave and were the first to lend a willing ear to Hitler's fervent preaching.

In the shop, notices announced that we should receive our salaries in weekly parts, after a while we queued up at the cashier's desk every evening, and before long we were paid twice daily and ran out during the lunch hour to buy a few things, because as soon as the new rate of exchange became known in the early afternoon our money had again lost half its value.

Lilo Linke, *Restless Days* (New York: Knopf, 1935), pp. 131–132.

---

treasury and also reducing tax revenues. The printing presses by this point had difficulty providing enough paper currency to keep up with the daily rise in prices. In November 1923 an American dollar was worth more than 800 million German marks. Money was literally not worth the paper it was printed on. Stores were unwilling to exchange goods for the worthless currency, and farmers withheld produce from the market. The moral and social values of thrift and prudence were thoroughly undermined. The security of middle-class savings, pensions, and insurance policies was wiped out, as were investments in government bonds. Simultaneously debts and mortgages could be paid off. Speculators in land, real estate, and industry made great fortunes. Union contracts generally allowed workers to keep up with rising prices. Inflation thus was not a disaster to everyone. However, to the middle class and the lower middle class the inflation was still one more traumatic experience coming hard on the heels of the military defeat and the peace treaty. Only when the

social and economic upheaval of these months is grasped can the later German desire for order and security at almost any cost be comprehended.

HITLER'S EARLY CAREER. Late in 1923 Adolf Hitler (1889–1945) made his first major appearance on the German political scene. In 1889 he had been born the son of a minor Austrian customs official: By 1907 he had gone to Vienna, where his hopes of becoming an artist were soon dashed. He lived off money sent by his widowed mother and later off his Austrian orphan's allowance. He also painted postcards for further income and later found work as a day laborer. In Vienna he became acquainted with Mayor Karl Lueger's Christian Social Party, which prospered on an ideology of anti-Semitism and from the social anxieties of the lower middle class. Hitler's own relatively precarious situation and his own social observations taught him how desperately the lower middle class feared slipping into a working-class condition. He also absorbed the rabid German nationalism and extreme anti-Semitism that flour-

OCCUPIED BY THE ALLIES AND
THE UNITED STATES TO 1923:
• ALL OF THE RHINELAND.
• THE RUHR.
• BRIDGEHEAD AREAS, EAST OF
  THE RHINE, EACH WITH A
  RADIUS OF 18 MILES, AND
  BORDERED BY A NEUTRAL
  ZONE, 6 MILES WIDE.
• OCCUPIED CITIES:
  –FOR 15 YEARS, COLOGNE,
   KOBLENZ AND MAINZ.
  –PUNITIVELY: RUHRORT,
   DÜSSELDORF, AND
   DUISBURG IN 1921,
   AND ESSEN IN 1923.

DEMILITARIZED
AREAS:
• A 30-MILE-WIDE
  STRIP ALONG THE
  EAST BANK OF
  THE RHINE.

EUPEN AND
MALMEDY, TO
BELGIUM BY
PLEBISCITE,
1920.

SAAR BASIN
UNDER THE
LEAGUE OF
NATIONS, TO
GERMANY BY
PLEBISCITE,
1935.

MAGINOT
LINE

FRENCH-GERMAN
BOUNDARY, 1914

50 MI.
50 KM.

GERMANY'S WESTERN FRONTIER

MAP 30.1   *The sensitive French-Belgian-German border
area between the two world wars. In spite of efforts to restrain tension in the twenty-year period, there were persistent
difficulties related to the Ruhr, Rhineland, Saar, and
Eupen-Malmédy regions that necessitated strong defenses.*

ished in Vienna. He came to hate Marxism, which he associated with Jews. During World War I Hitler fought in the German army, was wounded, was promoted to the rank of corporal, and was awarded the Iron Cross for bravery. The war gave him his first sense of purpose.

After the conflict Hitler settled in Munich. In the new surroundings he became associated with a small nationalistic, anti-Semitic political party that in 1920 adopted the name of National Socialist German Workers Party better known simply as the Nazis. The same year the group began to parade under a red banner with a black swastika. It issued a platform, or program, of Twenty-five Points. Among other things these called for the repudiation of the Versailles Treaty, the unification of Austria and Germany, the exclusion of Jews from German citizenship, agrarian reform, the prohibition of land speculation, the confiscation of war profits, state administration of the giant cartels, and the replacement of department stores with small retail shops. Originally the Nazis had called for a broad program of nationalization of industry in an attempt to compete directly with the Marxist political parties for the vote of the workers. As the tactic failed, the Nazis redefined the meaning of the word *socialist* in the party name so that it suggested a *nationalistic* outlook. In 1922 Hitler said:

"Whoever is prepared to make the national cause his own to such an extent that he knows no higher ideal than the welfare of his nation; whoever has understood our great national anthem, *Deutschland, Deutschland, über Alles* ["Germany, Germany, over All"], to mean that nothing in the wide world surpasses in his eyes this Germany, people and land, land and people—that man is a Socialist."[2]

This definition, of course, had nothing to do with traditional German socialism. The "socialism" that Hitler and the Nazis had in mind was not state ownership of the means of production but the subordination of all economic enterprise to the welfare of the nation. It often implied protection for very small economic enterprise. Increasingly over the years the Nazis discovered that their social appeal was to the lower middle class, which found itself squeezed between well-organized big business and socialist labor unions or political parties. The Nazis

[2] Alan Bullock, *Hitler: A Study in Tyranny*, rev. ed. (New York: Harper & Row, 1962), p. 76.

This picture of Adolf Hitler was made in May 1927. At the time he was not yet a major political figure, and the Nazi movement was relatively small. [United Press International Photo.]

tailored their message to this very troubled economic group.

Soon after the promulgation of the Twenty-five Points, the Stormtroopers, or SA *(Sturm Abteilung)*, were organized under the leadership of Captain Ernst Roehm. It was a paramilitary organization that initially provided its members with food and uniforms and later in the decade with wages. In the mid-1920s the SA adopted its famous brownshirted uniform. The Stormtroopers were the chief Nazi instrument for terror and intimidation before the party came into control of the government. They were a law unto themselves. The organization constituted a means of preserving military discipline and values outside the small army permitted by the Paris settlement. The existence of such a private party army was a sign of the potential for violence in the Weimar Republic and the widespread contempt for the law and the institutions of the republic.

The social and economic turmoil following the French occupation of the Ruhr and the German inflation provided the fledgling party with an opportunity for direct action against the Weimar Republic, which at that point seemed incapable of providing military or economic security to the nation. By this time, because of his immense oratorical skills and organizational abilities, Hitler personally dominated the Nazi Party. On November 9, 1923, Hitler and a band of followers, accompanied by General Ludendorff, attempted an unsuccessful *Putsch* at a beer hall in Munich. When the local authorities crushed the rising, sixteen Nazis were killed. Hitler and Ludendorff were arrested and tried for treason. The general was acquitted. Hitler employed the trial to make himself into a national figure. In his defense he condemned the republic, the Versailles Treaty, the Jews, and the weakened condition of his adopted country. He was convicted and sentenced to five years in prison. He actually spent only a few months in jail before being paroled. During this time he wrote *Mein Kampf* ("My Struggle"). Another result of the brief imprisonment was a decision on Hitler's part that in the fu-

929

❧ The National Socialist German Workers Party Issues a Platform

These statements from the Nazi Party's Twenty-five Points of 1920 illustrate the calls for nationalism, territorial expansion, anti-Semitic public policy, and aid for the poor and lower middle class that in time attracted broad support throughout Germany.

1. *We demand the union of all Germans to form a Great Germany on the basis of self-determination enjoyed by nations.*

2. *We demand equality of rights for the German people in its dealings with other nations, and abolition of the peace treaties of Versailles and Saint-Germain.*

3. *We demand land and territory (colonies) for the nourishment of our people and for settling our excess population.*

4. *None but members of the nation may be citizens of the state. None but those of German blood, whatever their creed, may be members of the nation. No Jew, therefore, may be a member of the nation.*

5. *Anyone who is not a citizen of the state may live in Germany only as a guest and must be regarded as being subject to foreign laws.*

. . . .

7. *We demand that the state shall make it its first duty to promote the industry and livelihood of citizens of the state. If it is not possible to nourish the entire population of the state, foreign nationals (non-citizens of the state) must be excluded from the Reich.*

. . . .

10. *It must be the first duty of each citizen of the state to work with his mind or with his body. The activities of the individual may not clash with the interests of the whole, but must proceed within the frame of the community and be for the general good.*

. . . .

15. *We demand extensive development of provision for old age.*

16. *We demand creation and maintenance of a healthy middle class, immediate communalization of wholesale business premises, and their lease at a cheap rate to small traders, and that extreme considerations shall be shown to all small purveyors to the state, district authorities, and smaller localities.*

22. *We demand abolition of a paid army and formation of a national army.*

. . . .

Raymond E. Murphy (Ed.), *National Socialism,* U.S. Department of State, Publication 1864 (Washington, 1943), pp. 222–224.

---

ture he and his party must seek to seize political power by legal methods.

THE STRESEMANN YEARS. Elsewhere the officials of the republic were attempting to repair the damage from the inflation. Gustav Stresemann (1878–1929) was primarily responsible for the reconstruction of the republic and for its achievement of a sense of self-confidence. He served as chancellor only from August to November 1923, but he provided the nation with a new basis for stability. Stresemann abandoned the policy of passive resistance in the Ruhr. The country simply could not afford it. Then, with the aid of banker Hjalmar Schacht, he introduced a new German currency. The rate of exchange was one trillion of the old German marks for one new *Rentenmark.*

Stresemann also moved against challenges from both the left and the right. He supported the crushing of both Hitler's abortive *Putsch* and smaller communist disturbances. In late November 1923 he resigned as chancellor and assumed the position of foreign minister, a post that he held until his death in 1929. In that office he exercised considerable influence over the affairs of the republic.

In 1924 the Weimar Republic and the Allies agreed to a new systematization of the reparation payments. The Dawes Plan, submitted by the American banker Charles Dawes, lowered the annual payments and allowed them to fluctuate according to the fortunes of the German economy. The French were to evacuate the Ruhr, and the last French troops left that region in 1925. The same year Friedrich Ebert (1871–1925), the Social Democratic president of the republic, died. Field Marshal Paul von Hindenburg, a military hero and a conservative monarchist, was elected as his successor. He governed in strict accordance with the constitution, but his election suggested that a new conservative tenor had come to German politics. It looked as if conservative Germans had become reconciled to the republic. This conservatism was in line with the prosperity of the latter part of the decade. The new political and economic stability meant that foreign capital flowed into Germany, and employment, which had been poor throughout most of the postwar years, improved smartly. Giant industrial combines spread. The prosperity helped to establish broader acceptance and appreciation of the republic.

In foreign affairs Stresemann pursued a conciliatory course. He was committed to a policy of fulfilling the provisions of the Versailles Treaty, even as he attempted to revise it by diplomacy. He was willing to accept the settlement in the west but was a determined, if sometimes secret, revisionist in the east. He aimed to recover German territories lost to Poland and Czechoslovakia and possibly to unite with Austria, chiefly by diplomatic means. The first step, however, was to achieve respectability and economic recovery. That goal required a policy of accommodation and "Fulfillment," for the moment at least.

LOCARNO. These developments gave rise to the Locarno Agreements of October 1925. The spirit of conciliation led politicians Austen Chamberlain for Britain and Aristide Briand for France to ac-

The signing of the Locarno Agreements in October of 1925, which brought a new, if temporary, spirit of conciliation and hope to Europe. [*United Press International Photo.*]

❧ A. P. Herbert Casts a Dim Glance at Locarno

In 1925 the Locarno Agreements generally received widespread praise. However, this humorous poem suggests another view. Many people in Britain besides A. P. Herbert thought that the concerns of the overseas empire were more important to British security and national interest than the problems of central and eastern Europe.

The foreigner's an alien,
*   He does not rule the waves;*
Give me the good Australian
*   Who cleans his teeth and shaves.*

Oh, let the hairy Magyar
*   Stew in his horrid juice,*
And scrap the Foreign Office,
*   For it ain't no kind of use!*

Poor old Britannier! Talk about disarm?
It's these here diplomatists that do the greatest harm.
Scrap the Foreign Office! Why d'you want to roam?
Ain't you got enough misfortunes in the home?

The paper's all Croatians
*   And Jugo-Slavs and Czechs,*
In all these bearded nations
*   We're buried to the necks;*
But it takes a flood or earthquake
*   Or other nasty mess*
To get the British Empire
*   Into the British Press!*

Poor old Britannier! Excuse a little sob;
Ain't your far-flung Empire a whole-time job?
Less of this Locarny-blarney! Why d'you want to
*   roam?*
Ain't you got enough misfortunes in the home?

A. P. Herbert, "Foreign Policy, or the Universal Aunt," in *A Book of Ballads* (London: E. Benn, 1931), pp. 406–407.

cept Stresemann's proposal for a fresh start. France and Germany both accepted the western frontier established at Versailles as legitimate. Britain and Italy agreed to intervene against the aggressor if either side violated the frontier or if Germany sent troops into the demilitarized Rhineland. Significantly no such agreement was made about Germany's eastern frontier, but the Germans made treaties of arbitration with Poland and Czechoslovakia, and France strengthened its ties with the Little Entente. France supported German membership in the League of Nations and agreed to withdraw its occupation troops from the Rhineland in 1930, five years earlier than specified at Versailles.

Germany was pleased to have achieved respectability and a guarantee against another Ruhr occupation, as well as the possibility of revision in the east. Britain was pleased to be allowed to play a more evenhanded role. Italy was glad to be recognized as a great power. The French were happy, too, because the Germans voluntarily accepted the permanence of their western frontier, which was

also guaranteed by Britain and Italy, while France maintained its allies in the east. As A. J. P. Taylor has put it, "Any French statesman of 1914 could have been bewildered with delight by such an achievement."[3]

The Locarno Agreements brought a new spirit of hope to Europe. Germany's entry into the League of Nations was greeted with enthusiasm. Chamberlain, Briand, and Stresemann jointly received the Nobel Peace Prize in 1926. The spirit of Locarno was carried even further when the leading European states, Japan, and the United States signed the Kellogg–Briand Pact in 1928, renouncing "war as an instrument of national policy." The joy and optimism were not justified. France had merely recognized its inability to coerce Germany without help. Britain had shown its unwillingness to uphold the settlement in the east. Austen Chamberlain declared that no British government ever would "risk the bones of a British grenadier" for the Polish corridor. Germany was by no means rec-

[3]Taylor, p. 58.

onciled to the eastern settlement. It continued its clandestine military connections with the Soviet Union, which had commenced with the Treaty of Rapallo, and planned to continue to press for revision.

In both France and Germany, moreover, the conciliatory politicians represented only a part of the nation. In Germany, especially, most people continued to reject Versailles and regarded Locarno as only an extension of it. When the Dawes Plan ran out in 1929, it was replaced by the Young Plan, named after the American businessman Owen D. Young, which lowered the reparation payments, put a term on how long they must be made, and removed Germany entirely from outside supervision and control. The intensity of the outcry in Germany against the continuation of any reparations showed how far the Germans were from accepting their situation. In spite of these problems, major war was by no means inevitable. Europe, aided by American loans, was returning to prosperity. German leaders like Stresemann would certainly have continued to press for change, but there is little reason to think that they would have resorted to force, much less to a general war. Continued prosperity and diplomatic success might have won the loyalty of the German people for the Weimar Republic and moderate revisionism, but the Great Depression of the 1930s brought new forces to power.

The Fascist Experiment in Italy

While its wartime allies continued to pursue parliamentary politics and its former enemies set out on the troubled path of democracy, Italy moved toward a new form of authoritarian government. From the Italian Fascist movement of Benito Mussolini (1883–1945) was derived the general term of *fascist*, which has frequently been used to describe the various right-wing dictatorships that arose between the wars.

The exact meaning of *fascism* as a political term remains much disputed among both historians and political scientists. However, a certain consensus does exist. The governments regarded as fascist were antidemocratic, anti-Marxist, antiparliamentary, and frequently anti-Semitic. They hoped to hold back the spread of Bolshevism, which seemed at the time a very real threat. They sought a world safe for the middle class, small businesses, owners of moderate amounts of property, and small farmers. The fascist regimes rejected the political inheritance of the French Revolution and of nineteenth-century liberalism. Their adherents believed that normal parliamentary politics and parties sacrificed national honor and greatness to petty party disputes. They wanted to overcome the class conflict of Marxism and the party conflict of liberalism by consolidating the various groups and classes within the nation for great national purposes. As Mussolini declared in 1931, "The fascist conception of the state is all-embracing, and outside of the state no human or spiritual values can exist, let alone be desirable."[4] The fascist governments were usually single-party dictatorships characterized by terrorism and police surveillance. These dictatorships were rooted in the base of mass political parties.

The Rise of Mussolini

The Italian *Fasci di Combattimento* ("Band of Combat") was founded in 1919 in Milan. Its members came largely from Italian war veterans who felt that the sacrifices of the conflict had been in vain. They resented the failure of Italy to gain the city of Fiume, toward the northern end of the Adriatic Sea, at the Paris conference. They feared socialism and inflation.

Their leader, Benito Mussolini, had been born the son of a blacksmith. For a time he had been a schoolteacher, then a day laborer. He became active in Italian socialist politics and by 1912 had become editor of the socialist newspaper *Avanti*. In 1914 Mussolini broke with the socialists and supported Italian entry into the war on the side of the Allies. His interventionist position lost him the editorship of *Avanti*. He then established his own paper, *Il Popolo d'Italia*. Later he served in the army and was wounded. In 1919, although of some prewar political stature, Mussolini was simply one of many Italian politicians. His *Fasci* organization was for its part simply one of numerous small political groups in a country characterized by such entities. As a politician Mussolini was an opportunist par excellence. He proved capable of changing his ideas and principles to suit every new occasion.

[4]Quoted in Denis Mack Smith, *Italy: A Modern History* (Ann Arbor: University of Michigan Press, 1959), p. 412.

Action for him was always more important than thought or rational justification. His one real rule was that of political survival.

Postwar Italian politics was a muddle. During the conflict the Italian Parliament had for all intents and purposes ceased to function. It had been quite willing to allow ministers to rule by decree. However, the parliamentary system as it then existed had begun to prove quite unsatisfactory to large sectors of the citizenry. Many Italians besides those in Mussolini's band of followers felt that Italy had emerged from the war as less than a victorious nation, had not been treated as a great power at the peace conference, and had not received the territories it deserved. The main spokesman for this discontent was the extreme nationalist poet and novelist Gabriele D'Annunzio (1863–1938). In 1919 he successfully led a force of patriotic Italians in an assault on Fiume. Troops of the Italian parliamentary government eventually drove him out. D'Annunzio had provided the example of the political use of a nongovernmental military force. The action of the government in removing him from Fiume gave the parliamentary ministry a somewhat less than patriotic appearance.

Between 1919 and 1921 Italy also experienced considerable internal social turmoil. Numerous industrial strikes occurred, and workers occupied factories. Peasants seized uncultivated land from large estates. Parliamentary and constitutional government seemed incapable of dealing with this unrest. The Socialist Party had captured a plurality of seats in the Chamber of Deputies during the 1919 election. A new Catholic Popular Party had also done quite well. Both appealed to the working and agrarian classes. However, neither party would cooperate with the other, and parliamentary deadlock resulted. Under these conditions many Italians honestly and still others conveniently believed that there existed the danger of a communist revolution.

Initially Mussolini was uncertain of the direction of the political winds. He first supported the factory occupations and land seizures. However, never one to be concerned with consistency, he soon reversed himself. He had discovered that large numbers of both upper-class and middle-class Italians who were pressured by inflation and who feared property loss had no sympathy for the workers or the peasants. They wanted order rather than some vague social justice that might harm

their own interests. Consequently Mussolini and his Fascists took direct action in the face of the government inaction. They formed local squads of terrorists who disrupted Socialist Party meetings, mugged Socialist leaders, and terrorized Socialist supporters. They attacked strikers and farm workers and protected strikebreakers. Conservative land and factory owners were grateful. The officers and institutions of the law simply ignored the crimes of the Fascist squads. By early 1922 the Fas-

Gabriele D'Annunzio was an Italian poet and fervent nationalist. In 1919 he led a private military raid against Fiume, which he believed had wrongfully been denied to Italy by the Versailles Treaty. The painting is by Romaine Brooks. [The Granger Collection.]

Scenes from the Fascist march on Rome in October 1922. When it was clear the king would not authorize force against them, the marchers, in their characteristic black shirts, posed for the friendly photographer. [*United Press International Photo.*]

cists had turned their intimidation through arson, beatings, and murder against local officials in cities such as Ferrara, Ravenna, and Milan. They controlled the local government in many parts of northern Italy.

In the election of 1921 Mussolini and thirty-four of his followers were sent to the Chamber of Deputies. Their importance grew as the local Fascists gained more direct power. The movement now had hundreds of thousands of supporters. In October 1922 the Fascists, dressed in their characteristic black shirts, began a march on Rome. King Victor Emmanuel III (1900–1946), because of both personal and political fear, refused to sign a decree that would have authorized the use of the army against the marchers. Probably no other single decision so ensured a Fascist seizure of power. The Cabinet resigned in protest. On October 29

the monarch telegraphed Mussolini in Milan and asked him to become prime minister. The next day Mussolini arrived in Rome by sleeping car and greeted his followers as head of the government when they entered the city.

Technically Mussolini had come into office by legal means. The monarch did possess the power to appoint the prime minister. However, Mussolini had no majority or even near majority in the Chamber of Deputies. Behind the legal facade of his assumption of power lay the months of terrorist disruption and intimidation and the threat of the Fascist march itself. The non-Fascist politicians, whose ineptitude had prepared the way for Mussolini, believed that his regime, like others of previous months, would be temporary. They failed to comprehend that he was not a traditional Italian politician.

Benito Mussolini stands surrounded by his followers after receiving his appointment as prime minister from the king. [The Granger Collection.]

The Fascists in Power

Mussolini had not really expected to be appointed prime minister. He moved cautiously to shore up his support and to consolidate his power. His success was the result of the impotence of his rivals, his own effective use of his office, his power over the masses, and his sheer ruthlessness. On November 23, 1922, the king and Parliament granted Mussolini dictatorial authority for one year to bring order to the lower levels of the government. Wherever possible Mussolini appointed Fascists to office. Late in 1924, under Mussolini's guidance, the Parliament changed the election law. Previously parties had been represented in the Chamber of Deputies in proportion to the popular vote cast for them. According to the new election law, the party that gained the largest popular vote (with a minimum of at least 25 per cent) received two thirds of the seats in the chamber. Coalition government, with all its compromises and hesitant policies, would no longer be necessary. In the election of 1924 the Fascists won a great victory and complete control of the Chamber of Deputies. They used that majority to end legitimate parliamentary life. A series of laws passed in 1925 and 1926 permitted Mussolini, in effect, to rule by decree. In 1926 all other political parties were dissolved. By the close of that year Italy had been transformed into a single-party, dictatorial state.

Their growing dominance over the government had not, however, diverted the Fascists from their course of violence and terror. They were put in charge of the police force, and the terrorist squads became institutionalized into government militia. In late 1924 their thugs murdered Giacomo Matteotti (1885–1924), a major non-Communist socialist leader. He had persistently criticized Mussolini and had exposed the criminality of the Fascist movement. In protest against the murder, a number of opposition deputies withdrew from the Chamber of Deputies. That tactic gave the prime minister an even freer hand. The deputies were refused readmission.

The parallel organization of the party and the government sustained support for the regime. For every government institution there existed a corresponding party organization. In this manner the Fascist Party dominated the political structure at every level. When all other political parties were outlawed, the citizens had to look to the Fascists in their community for political favors. They also knew the high price of opposition. By the late 1920s the Grand Council of the party had become an organ of the state. It drew up and presented the list of persons who would stand for election to the Chamber of Deputies. Major policies to be approved by the chamber first passed the Grand Council. And Mussolini himself controlled the council.

The party used propaganda quite effectively. A cult of personality surrounded Mussolini. His skills

Mussolini was a powerful public orator. His gestures, which often appear comic in hindsight, were part of a carefully cultivated public image designed to make him appear at all times a leader. [Culver Pictures.]

❧ Mussolini Heaps Contempt on Political Liberalism

> The political tactics of the Italian Fascists wholly disregarded the liberal belief in the rule of law and the consent of the governed. In 1923 Mussolini explained why the Fascists so hated and repudiated these liberal principles. The reader should note his emphasis on the idea of the twentieth century as a new historical epoch requiring a new kind of politics and his undisguised praise of force in politics.

Liberalism is not the last word, nor does it represent the definitive formula on the subject of the art of government. . . . Liberalism is the product and the technique of the 19th Century. . . . It does not follow that the Liberal scheme of government, good for the 19th century, for a century, that is, dominated by two such phenomena as the growth of capitalism and the strengthening of the sentiment of nationalism, should be adapted to the 20th Century, which announces itself already with characteristics sufficiently different from those that marked the preceding century. . . .

I challenge Liberal gentlemen to tell me if ever in history there has been a government that was based solely on popular consent and that renounced all use of force whatsoever. A government so constructed there has never been and never will be. Consent is an ever-changing thing like the shifting sand on the sea coast. It can never be permanent. It can never be complete. . . . If it be accepted as an axiom that any system of government whatever creates malcontents, how are you going to prevent this discontent from overflowing and constituting a menace to the stability of the State? You will prevent it by force. By the assembling of the greatest force possible. By the inexorable use of this force whenever it is necessary. Take away from any government whatsoever force—and by force is meant physical, armed force—and leave it only its immortal principles, and that government will be at the mercy of the first organized group that decides to overthrow it. Fascism now throws these lifeless theories out to rot. . . . The truth evident now to all who are not warped by [liberal] dogmatism is that men have tired of liberty. They have made an orgy of it. Liberty is today no longer the chaste and austere virgin for whom the generations of the first half of the last century fought and died. For the gallant, restless and bitter youth who face the dawn of a new history there are other words that exercise a far greater fascination, and those words are: order, hierarchy, discipline. . . .

Know then, once and for all, that Fascism knows no idols and worships no fetishes. It has already stepped over, and if it be necessary it will turn tranquilly and step again over, the more or less putrescent corpse of the Goddess of Liberty.

Benito Mussolini, "Force and Consent" (1923), as cited and translated in Jonathan F. Scott and Alexander Baltzly, *Readings in European History Since 1814* (New York: F. S. Crofts, 1931), pp. 680–682.

in oratory and his general intelligence allowed him to hold his own with both large crowds and the leaders of the more respectable portions of the community. The latter tolerated and often admired him in the belief that he had saved them from Bolshevism. The persons who did have the courage to oppose Mussolini were usually driven into exile, and some were murdered.

The Italian dictator made one important domestic departure that brought him significant political dividends. Through the Lateran Accord of February 1929, the Roman Catholic Church and the Italian state made peace with each other. Ever since the armies of Italian unification had seized papal lands in the 1860s, the church had been hostile to the state. The popes had remained virtual prisoners in the Vatican after 1870. The agreement of 1929 recognized the pope as the temporal ruler of Vatican City. The Italian government agreed to pay an indemnity to the papacy for confiscated land. The state also recognized Catholicism as the religion of the nation, exempted church property from taxes, and allowed church law to govern the institution of marriage. The Lateran

Accord brought further respectability to Mussolini's authoritarian regime.

The Beginning of the Soviet Experiment

The political right had no monopoly on authoritarianism between the wars. The consolidation of the Bolshevik Revolution in Russia established the most extensive and durable of all twentieth-century authoritarian governments. However, the dictatorships of the left and the right did differ from each other. Unlike the Italian Fascists or the German National Socialists, the Bolsheviks had seized power illegally through revolution. For several years they confronted effective opposition, and their leaders long felt insecure about their hold on the country. The Communist Party was not a mass party nor a nationalistic one. Its early membership rarely exceeded more than 1 per cent of the Russian population. The Bolsheviks confronted a much less industrialized economy than existed in Italy or Germany. They believed in and practiced the collectivization of economic life attacked by the right-wing dictatorships. The Marxist-Leninist ideology was far more all-encompassing than the nationalism of the Fascists and the racism of the Nazis. Communism was an exportable commodity. The Communists regarded their government and their revolution not as local events in a national history but as an epoch-making event in the history of the world and the development of humanity.

The Third International

The policies of the early Russian Communist Revolution directly and importantly affected the rise of the Fascists and the Nazis in western Eu-

Lenin addressing a May Day demonstration in Moscow in 1918. [Culver Pictures.]

Lenin and Trotsky (saluting) in Red Square in Moscow in 1919, from a documentary film made by Herman Axelbank. Trotsky's organizational skill was largely responsible for the Red Army's victory in the Russian Civil War of 1918–1920. By 1921, as a result of war, revolution, and civil war, the Russian economy had all but collapsed. [United Press International Photo.]

rope. The success of the revolution in Russia had the paradoxical effect of dividing socialist parties and socialist movements in the rest of Europe. In 1919 the Soviet Communists founded the Third International of the European socialist movement. It became better known as the Comintern. A year after its inception the Comintern imposed its Twenty-one Conditions on any other socialist party that wished to become a member. The conditions included acknowledgement of leadership from Moscow, rejection of reformist or revisionist socialism, and repudiation of previous socialist leaders. The Comintern wished to make the Russian model of socialism, as developed by Lenin, the rule for all socialist parties outside the Soviet Union.

The decision whether to join or not to join the Comintern under these conditions split every major socialist party on the Continent. As a result, separate communist parties and social democratic parties emerged. The former modeled themselves after the Soviet party and pursued policies dictated by Moscow. The social democratic parties attempted to pursue both social reform and liberal parliamentary politics. Throughout the 1920s and early 1930s the communists and the social democrats tended to fight each other more intensely than they fought either capitalism or conservative political parties. This division of the European political left meant that right-wing political movements rarely had to confront a united opposition on the political left.

War Communism

Within the Soviet Union the Red Army under the organizational genius of Leon Trotsky had suppressed internal and foreign military opposition to the new government. Within months of the revolution a new secret police, known as *Cheka,* appeared. Throughout the civil war Lenin had declared that the Bolshevik Party, as the vanguard of the revolution, was imposing the dictatorship of the proletariat. Political and economic administration became highly centralized. All major decisions flowed from the top in a nondemocratic manner. Under the economic policy of "War Communism" the revolu-

940

❧ The Third International Issues Conditions of Membership

After the Russian Revolution, the Russian Communist Party organized the Third Communist International. Any communist party outside the Soviet Union was required to accept these Twenty-one Conditions, adopted in 1919, in order to join the International. In effect, this program demanded that all such parties adopt a distinctly revolutionary program and cease operating as legal parties within their various countries. By this means, the Soviet Union sought to achieve leadership of the socialist movement throughout Europe. As non-Russian socialist parties debated whether to join the Third International, they quickly split into social democratic parties that remained independent of Moscow and communist parties that adopted the policy imposed by the Russian Communist Party.

1. *The daily propaganda and agitation must bear a truly communist character and correspond to the program and all the decisions of the Third International. All the organs of the press that are in the hands of the party must be edited by reliable communists who have proved their loyalty to the cause of the proletarian revolution. . . .*

3. *The class struggle in almost all of the countries of Europe and America is entering the phase of civil war. Under such conditions the communists can have no confidence in bourgeois law. They must every-where create a parallel illegal apparatus, which at the decisive moment could assist the party in performing its duty of revolution. . . .*

4. *The obligation to spread communist ideas includes the particular necessity of persistent, systematic propaganda in the army. . . .*

5. *It is necessary to carry on systematic and steady agitation in the rural districts. . . .*

7. *The parties desiring to belong to the Communist International must recognize the necessity of a complete and absolute rupture with reformism . . . , and they must carry on propaganda in favor of this rupture among the broadest circles of the party membership. . . .*

8. *. . . Every party desirous of belonging to the Third International must ruthlessly denounce the methods of "their own" imperialists in the colonies, supporting, not in words, but in deeds, every independence movement in the colonies. . . .*

14. *Every party that desires to belong to the Communist International must give every possible support to the Soviet Republics in their struggle against all counterrevolutionary forces. . . .*

16. *All decisions of the congresses of the Communist International. . . . are binding on all parties affiliated to the Communist International. . . .*

17. *In connection with all this, all parties desiring to join the Communist International must change their names. Every party that wishes to join the Communist International must bear the name:* Communist party *of such-and-such country. This question as to name is not merely a formal one, but a political one of great importance. The Communist International has declared a decisive war against the entire bourgeois world and all the yellow, social democratic parties. Every rank-and-file worker must clearly understand the difference between the communist parties and the old official "social democratic" or "socialist" parties which have betrayed the cause of the working class.*

18. *Members of the party who reject the conditions and thesis of the Communist International, on principle, must be expelled from the party.*

International Communism in the Era of Lenin: A Documentary History, ed. by Helmut Gruber (Garden City, N.Y.: Doubleday, 1972), pp. 241–246.

tionary government confiscated and then operated the banks, the transport facilities, and heavy industry. The state also forcibly requisitioned grain produced by the peasants and shipped it from the countryside to feed the army and the workers in the cities. The fact of the civil war permitted suppression of possible resistance to this economic policy.

"War Communism" aided the victory of the Red Army over its opponents. The revolution had survived and triumphed. However, the policy generated domestic opposition to the Bolsheviks, who in 1920 numbered only about 600,000 members. The alliance of workers and peasants forged by the slogan of "Peace, Bread, and Land" had begun to come apart at the seams. Many Russians were no longer willing to make the sacrifices demanded by the central party bureaucrats. In 1920 and 1921 major strikes occurred in numerous factories. Peasants were discontented and resisted the requisition of grain. In March 1921 the navy mutinied at Kronstadt. The Red Army crushed the rebellion with grave loss of life. Each of these incidents suggested that the proletariat itself was opposing the dictatorship of the proletariat. Also, by late 1920 it had become clear that further revolution would not sweep across the rest of Europe. For the time being the Soviet Union would constitute a vast island of revolutionary socialism in the larger sea of worldwide capitalism.

The New Economic Policy

Under these difficult conditions Lenin made a crucial strategic retreat. In March 1921, following the Kronstadt mutiny, he outlined the New Economic Policy, normally referred to as *NEP*. Apart from what he termed "the commanding heights" of banking, heavy industry, transportation, and international commerce, there was to be considerable private economic enterprise. In particular, peasants were to be permitted to farm for a profit. They would pay taxes like other citizens, but they could sell their surplus grain on the open market. The NEP was in line with Lenin's earlier conviction that the Russian peasantry held the key to the success of revolution in the nation. After 1921 the countryside did become more stable, and a secure

Russian men and women helping to convey newly-arrived lumber to a paper mill. Such cooperative effort was essential if Lenin's New Economic Policy was to succeed. [United Press International Photo.]

Hungry peasants arriving in Moscow in 1921 looking for shelter and food. It is estimated that between 1918 and 1921 perhaps as many as seven million Russians died from hunger and sickness. The famine in the winter of 1920–1921 was particularly severe. [United Press International Photo.]

food supply seemed assured for the cities. Similar free enterprise flourished within light industry and domestic retail trade. By 1927 industrial production had reached its 1913 level. The revolution seemed to have transformed Russia into a land of small family farms and small privately owned shops and businesses.

Stalin Versus Trotsky

The New Economic Policy had caused sharp disputes within the Politburo, the highest governing committee of the Communist Party. The partial return to capitalism seemed to some members nothing less than a betrayal of sound Marxist principles. These frictions increased as Lenin's firm hand disappeared. In 1922 he suffered a stroke that broke his health. He returned to work but never again dominated party affairs. In 1924 Lenin died. As the power vacuum developed, an intense struggle for future leadership of the party commenced. Two factions emerged. One was led by Trotsky; the other by Joseph Stalin (1879–1953), who had become general secretary of

Russian oil workers at Baku on the Caspian Sea in 1927. Lenin's New Economic Policy, in effect from 1921 to 1928, entailed a return to capitalism in agriculture, light industry, and retail trade. [United Press International Photo.]

943

revolutions took place elsewhere in the world. Russia needed the skills and wealth of other nations to build its own economy. As Trotsky's influence within the party began to wane, he also demanded that party members be permitted to criticize the

Leon Trotsky's brilliant organization of the Red Army secured the Bolshevik victory in the Russian Civil War. However, he later lost his power and influence when, following Lenin's death, Stalin outmaneuvered him in the party strife of the late 1920s. [Culver Pictures.]

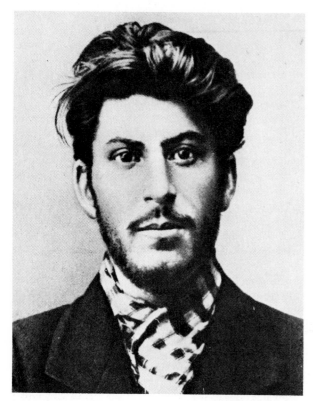

The youthful Stalin, possibly a tsarist police photo. As he worked his way up the Bolshevik political hierarchy he became a master of the details of its bureaucracy, experience that eventually helped him to oust and destroy his opponents, real and fancied, in the politburo. [The Granger Collection.]

the party in 1922. Shortly before his death Lenin had criticized both men. He was especially harsh toward Stalin. However, the general secretary's base of power lay with the party membership and with the daily management of party affairs. Consequently he was able to withstand the posthumous strictures of Lenin.

The issue between the two factions was power within the party, but the struggle was fought out over the question of Russia's path toward industrialization and the future of the communist revolutionary movement. Trotsky, speaking for what became known as the left wing, urged rapid industrialization financed through the expropriation of farm production. Agriculture should be collectivized, and the peasants should be made to pay for industrialization. Trotsky further argued that the revolution in Russia could succeed only if new

policies of the government and the party. However, Trotsky was very much a latecomer to the advocacy of open discussion. When in control of the Red Army, he had been known as an unflinching disciplinarian.

A right-wing faction opposed Trotsky. Its chief ideological voice was that of Nikolai Bukharin (1888–1938), the editor of *Pravda*, the official party paper. Stalin was the major political manipulator. In the mid-1920s this group pressed for the continuation of Lenin's NEP and a policy of relatively slow industrialization. Stalin emerged as the victor in these intraparty rivalries.

Stalin had been born in 1879 into a very poor family. Unlike the other early Bolshevik leaders, he had not spent a long period of exile in western Europe. He was much less an intellectual and internationalist. He was also much more brutal. His handling of various recalcitrant national groups within Russia after the revolution had shocked even Lenin. Stalin's power lay in his command of bureaucratic and administrative methods. He was neither a brilliant writer nor an effective public speaker; however, he mastered the crucial, if dull, details of party structure, including admission and promotion. That mastery meant that he could draw on the support of the lower levels of the party apparatus when he came into conflict with other leaders.

In the middle of the decade Stalin supported Bukharin's position on economic development. In 1924 he also enunciated, in opposition to Trotsky, the doctrine of "socialism in one country." He urged that socialism could be achieved in Russia alone. Russian success did not depend on the fate of the revolution elsewhere. In this manner Stalin nationalized the previously international scope of the Marxist revolution. Stalin cunningly used the apparatus of the party and his control over the Central Committee of the Communist Party to edge out Trotsky and his supporters. By 1927 Trotsky had been removed from all his offices, expelled from the party, and exiled to Siberia. In 1929 he was sent out of Russia and eventually took up residence in Mexico, where he was murdered in 1940, presumably by one of Stalin's agents. With

Lenin and Stalin photographed together in Moscow in the summer of 1922, after Stalin's appointment as General Secretary of the Communist Party. The following December Lenin suffered a paralytic stroke and was unable to check Stalin's increasing dominance of party affairs. Lenin died in January 1924.

the removal of Trotsky from all positions of influence Stalin was firmly in control of the Soviet state. It remained to be seen where he would direct its course and what "socialism in one country" would mean in practice.

Results of the Decade of Experiment

At the close of the 1920s it appeared that Europe had finally emerged from the difficulties of the World War I era. The initial resentments over the peace settlement seemed to have abated. The major powers were cooperating. Democracy was still functioning in Germany. The Labor Party was about to form its second ministry in Britain. France had settled into a less assertive international role. Mussolini's Fascism seemed to have little relevance to the rest of the Continent. The successor states had not fulfilled the democratic hopes of the Paris conference, but their troubles seemed their own. The Soviet Union, though still harboring a communist menace, stood largely withdrawn into its own internal development and power struggles.

The European economy seemed finally to be on an even keel. The frightening inflation was over, and unemployment had eased. American capital was flowing into the Continent. The reparations payments had been systematized by the Young Plan. Yet both this economic and this political stability proved illusory and temporary. What brought them to an end was the deepest economic depression in the modern history of the West. As the governments and electorates responded to the economic collapse, the search for liberty gave way in more than one instance to a search for security. The political experiments of the 1920s gave way to the political tragedies of the 1930s.

Suggested Readings

K. D. BRACHER, *The German Dictatorship* (1970). A comprehensive treatment of both the origins and the functioning of the Nazi movement and government.

A. BULLOCK, *Hitler: A Study in Tyranny*, rev. ed. (1964). The best biography.

E. H. CARR, *A History of Soviet Russia*, 9 vols. (1950–19—). An extensive and important study.

S. F. COHEN, *Bukharin and the Bolshevik Revolution: A Po-litical Biography,* 1888–1938 (1973). An interesting examination of Stalin's chief opponent on the Communist right.

G. D. H. COLE, *A History of the Labour Party from* 1914 (1948). A straightforward account by a sympathetic supporter.

R. DAHRENDORF, *Society and Democracy in Germany* (1967). An important commentary by a leading sociologist.

I. DEUTSCHER, *The Prophet Armed* (1954), *The Prophet Unarmed* (1959), and *The Prophet Outcast* (1963). A major biography of Trotsky.

E. EYCK, *A History of the Weimar Republic*, 2 vols. (trans. 1963). The story as narrated by a liberal.

L. FISCHER, *The Life of Lenin* (1964). A sound biography by an American journalist.

P. FUSSELL, *The Great War and Modern Memory* (1975). A brilliant account of the literature arising from World War I during the 1920s.

P. GAY, *Weimar Culture; The Outsider as Insider* (1968). A sensitive analysis of the intellectual life of Weimar.

H. J. GORDON, *Hitler and the Beer Hall Putsch* (1972). An excellent account of the event and the political situation in the early Weimar Republic.

N. GREENE, *From Versailles to Vichy: The Third Republic,* 1919–1940 (1970). A useful introduction to a difficult subject.

H. GRUBER, *International Communism in the Era of Lenin: A Documentary History* (1967). An excellent collection of otherwise difficult-to-find documents.

C. A. MACARTNEY AND A. W. PALMER, *Independent Eastern Europe: A History* (1962). The best one-volume survey.

C. S. MAIER, *Recasting Bourgeois Europe: Stabilization in France, Germany, and Italy in the Decade after World War I* (1975). An important interpretation written from a comparative standpoint.

A. MARWICK, *The Deluge: British Society and the First World War* (1965). Full of insights into both major and more subtle minor social changes.

E. NOLTE, *Three Faces of Fascism* (1963). An important, influential, and difficult work on France, Italy, and Germany.

R. PIPES, *The Formation of the Soviet Union*, 2nd ed. (1964). A study of internal policy with emphasis on Soviet minorities.

H. ROGGER AND E. WEBER (Eds.), *The European Right: A Historical Profile* (1965). An anthology of articles on right-wing political movements in various European countries.

C. SETON-WATSON, *Italy from Liberalism to Fascism,* 1870–1925 (1967). A useful survey.

H. SETON-WATSON, *Eastern Europe Between the Wars,* 1918–1941 (1946). Somewhat dated but still a useful work.

D. MACK SMITH, *Italy: A Modern History*, rev. ed. (1969). Very good chapters on the Fascists and Mussolini.

R. J. SONTAG, *A Broken World, 1919–1939* (1971). An exceptionally thoughtful and well-organized survey.

A. J. P. TAYLOR, *English History, 1914–1945* (1965). Lively and opinionated.

R. TUCKER, *Stalin as Revolutionary, 1879–1929: A Study in History and Personality* (1973). A useful and readable account of Stalin's rise to power.

H. A. TURNER, JR. (Ed.), *Reappraisals of Fascism* (1975). A collection of very important articles on Fascist movements.

T. WILSON, *The Downfall of the Liberal Party, 1914–1935* (1966). A close examination of the surprising demise of a political party in Britain.

E. WISKEMANN, *Fascism in Italy: Its Development and Influence* (1969). A comprehensive treatment.

R. WOHL, *The Generation of 1914* (1979). An important work that explores the effect of the war on political and social thought.

For works on diplomatic developments, see Chapter 33.

948

31 Europe and the Depression of the 1930s

I̲N EUROPE, unlike the United States, the 1920s had not been "roaring." Economically they had been a decade of much insecurity, of a search for elusive stability, of a short-lived upswing, and then of collapse in finance and production. The Depression that commenced in 1929 was the most severe downturn ever experienced by the capitalist economies. The unemployment, low production levels, financial instability, and contracted trade arrived and would not depart. Marxists thought that the final downfall of capitalism was at hand. Capitalist businesspeople and political leaders despaired over the failure of the market mechanism to save them. Voters looked for new ways out of the doldrums, and politicians sought escapes from the pressures that the Depression had brought on them. One result of the fight for economic security was the establishment of the Nazi dictatorship in Germany. Another was the piecemeal construction

The Nazi party utilized massive political rallies such as this one, held in Berlin in 1937, to make public display of its size and power. [United Press International Photo.]

of what has since become known as the *mixed economy;* that is, governments became directly involved in economic decisions. In both cases most of the political and economic guidelines of nineteenth-century liberalism were abandoned for good. Two other casualties of these years were decency and civility in political life.

Toward the Great Depression

Three factors combined to bring about the intense severity and the extended length of the Depression. There was a financial crisis that stemmed directly from the war and the peace settlement. To this was added a crisis in the production and distribution of goods in the world market. These two problems became intertwined in 1929, and as far as Europe was concerned, they reached the breaking point in 1931. Finally, both of these difficulties became worse than might have been necessary because of the absence of strong economic leadership and responsibility on the part of any major west European country or the United States. Without cooperation or leadership in the Atlantic economic community, the economic collapse in finance and production simply lingered and deepened.

The Financial Tailspin

Most European nations emerged from World War I with inflated currencies. Immediately after the armistice the unleashed demand for consumer and industrial goods continued to drive up prices. The price and wage increases generally subsided after 1921, but the problem of maintaining the value of their currencies still haunted political leaders—and even more after the German financial disaster of 1923. This frightening experience accounted in part for the refusal of most governments to run budget deficits when the Depression struck. They feared inflation as a political danger in the same manner that European governments since World War II have feared unemployment.

The problems of reparation payments and international war-debt settlement further complicated the picture. France and the United States provided the stumbling blocks in these matters. France had paid reparations as a defeated nation after 1815 and 1871. As a victor it now intended to receive reparations and to finance its postwar recovery through them. The 1923 invasion of the Ruhr demonstrated French determination on this question.

The United States was no less determined to receive repayments of the wartime loans extended to its allies. There were also various debts that the European Allies owed to each other. It soon became apparent that German reparations were to provide the means of repaying the American and other Allied debts. Most of the money that the Allies collected from each other also went to the United States.

In 1922 Great Britain announced that it would collect payment on its own debts only to the extent that the United States required payments from Britain. However, the American government would not relent. The reparations and the war debts made normal business, capital investment, and international trade very difficult and expensive for the European nations. Various modes of government controls were exercised over credit, trade, and currency. Speculation in currency drew funds away from capital investment in productive enterprise. The monetary problems served to reinforce the general tendency toward high tariff policies. If a nation imported too many goods from abroad, it might have difficulty meeting those costs and the expenses of debt or reparations payments. The financial and money muddle thus discouraged trade and production and in turn harmed employment.

An unemployed German in Berlin photographed about 1930 wearing a sign declaring "I seek work of any kind!" As his dress indicates, he was from either the upper working class or the lower middle class, and such people had rarely known unemployment during earlier periods of economic hardship in Europe. [Bildarchiv Preussischer Kulturbesitz. Herbert Hoffmann.]

In 1924 the Dawes Plan brought more system to the administration and transfer of reparations. Those procedures, in turn, smoothed the debt repayments to the United States. Thereafter large amounts of private American capital flowed into Europe and especially into Germany. Much of this money, which provided the basis for Europe's brief prosperity after 1925, was in the form of short-term loans. In 1928 this lending began to contract as American money became diverted from European investments into the booming New York stock market. The crash of Wall Street in October 1929—the result of virtually unregulated financial speculation—saw the loss of large amounts of money. United States banks had made very large loans to customers who then invested the money in the stock market. When stock prices fell, the customers could not repay the banks. Consequently, within the United States there occurred a major contraction of all kinds of credit, and numerous banks failed. Thereafter little American capital was available for investment in Europe. Furthermore loans already made to Europeans were not renewed, as American banks used their available funds to cover domestic shortages.

As the credit to Europe began to run out, a major financial crisis struck the continent. In May 1931 the Kreditanstalt, a major bank in Vienna, collapsed. It was a primary lending institution for much of central and eastern Europe. The German banking system came under severe pressure and was saved only through government guarantees. However, it became clear that under this crisis situation Germany would be unable to make its next reparation payment as stipulated in the 1929 Young Plan. As the German difficulties reached such large proportions, American President Herbert Hoover announced in June 1931 a one-year moratorium on all payments of international debts. The Hoover moratorium was a prelude to the end of reparations. Hoover's action was a sharp blow to the French economy, for which reparations had continued to be important. The French agreed to the moratorium most reluctantly but really had little alternative because the German economy was in a state of virtual collapse. The Lausanne Conference of the summer of 1932 in effect brought the era of reparations to a close. The next year the debts owed to the United States were settled either through small token payments or simply through default. Nevertheless the financial politics of the 1920s had done its damage.

Problems in Agricultural Commodities

In addition to the dramatic financial turmoil and collapse there was also a less dramatic, but equally fundamental, downturn in production and trade. The 1920s witnessed a contraction in the market demand for European goods relative to the continent's productive capacity. Part of this problem originated within Europe and part outside. In both instances the difficulty arose from agriculture. Better methods of farming, improved strains of wheat, expanded tillage, and more extensive transport facilities all over the globe vastly increased the quantity of grain produced. World wheat prices fell to record lows. This development was, of course, initially good for consumers. However, it meant lower incomes for European farmers and especially for those of central and eastern Europe. At the same time higher industrial wages raised the cost of the industrial goods used by the farmer or peasant. The farmers could not purchase those products. Moreover farmers began to have difficulty paying off their mortgages and normal annual operation debts. They borrowed money to plant their fields, expecting to pay the debt when the crops were sold. The fall in commodity prices raised problems of repayment.

The difficulties of agricultural finance became especially pressing in eastern Europe. Immediately after the war numerous land-reform programs had been undertaken in this region. The democratic franchise in the successor states had opened the way for considerable redistribution of tillable soil. In Romania and Czechoslovakia large amounts of land changed hands. This occurred to a lesser extent in Hungary and Poland. However, the new relatively small farmers proved to be inefficient and were unable to earn sufficient incomes. Protective tariffs often prevented the export of grain among European countries. The credit and cost squeeze on east European farmers and on their counterparts in Germany played a major role in their disillusionment with liberal politics. For example, in Germany farmers provided the Nazis with a major source of political support.

Outside Europe similar problems affected other producers of agricultural commodities. The prices they received for their products plummeted. Government-held reserves accumulated to record levels. This glut of major world commodities involved the supplies of wheat, sugar, coffee, rubber, wool, and lard. The people who produced these goods in

❧ The League of Nations Reports the Collapse of European Agriculture

A crisis in agriculture was as much a cause of the Depression as was the turmoil in the financial community. The League of Nations reported in 1931 how, in part, the desperate situation in agriculture had developed.

It is the lowness of prices that constitutes the agricultural crisis. It is becoming difficult to sell products, and in many cases prices have reached a level at which they are scarcely, if at all, sufficient to cover the cost of production.

The reason for the crisis and for its continuance is to be found in the fact that agricultural prices are low in comparison with the expenditure which the farmer must meet. . . . Agricultural products cost a lot to produce and then fetch very little in the market. In spite of the great technical progress achieved, operating costs remain implacably higher than selling prices, farmers obtain no longer a fair return on their labour or on their capital. Frequently the returns of agricultural undertakings are not enough to cover the necessary outlay for the purchase of the material or products necessary for continued operation or for the payment of wages and taxes and so forth.

This disproportion between the income and expenditure of agricultural undertakings . . . appears to constitute the dominant and decisive element of the prevailing agricultural depression.

Until 1929, prices were low as compared with prices of industrial products, but were above pre-war prices. The predominating tendency to a fall which was observed was not altogether general nor was it abnormally rapid. The general character of the price movement completely changed in 1930. A fall, sometimes catastrophic, spread with extreme violence to almost all agricultural produce, It was so rapid that at the end of the year, whilst some products reached the pre-war level of prices, others fell as low as one-quarter or one-half below the 1913 level. . . . Farmers throughout the world have suffered from it.

League of Nations, Economic Committee, *The Agricultural Crisis,* Vol. 1 (1931), pp. 7–8, reprinted in S. B. Clough, T. Moodie, and C. G. Moodie, *Economic History of Europe: The Twentieth Century* (New York: Harper & Row, 1968), pp. 216–217.

underdeveloped nations could no longer make enough money to buy finished goods from industrial Europe. As world credit collapsed, the economic position of these commodity producers became all the worse. Commodity production had simply outstripped world demand.

The result of the collapse in the agricultural sector of the world economy and the financial turmoil was stagnation and depression for European industry. Coal, iron, and textiles had depended largely on international markets. Unemployment spread from these industries to those producing finished consumer goods. The persistent unemployment of Great Britain and to a lesser extent of Germany during the 1920s already meant "soft" domestic markets. The policies of reduced government spending with which the governments confronted the Depression further weakened domestic demand. By the early 1930s the Depression was growing on itself.

Areas of Growth Within the Depressed Economies

Despite the Depression some economic growth did take place between the wars. Depression did not mean economic regression. The economic growth was spotty, unsteady, and concentrated in special areas. Three of these industries deserve brief mention. They were radio, automobiles, and synthetic goods. The technological basis for each of them had been developed prior to World War I but their major impact on the economy occurred afterwards.

Ganz Deutschland
hört den Führer

mit dem Volksempfänger

"All Germany listens to the Führer with the people's radio receiver," declares a sales poster in 1936 for a cheap radio. Such instruments were pushed by the Nazis because they quickly came to realize that the efficient exploitation of such a medium of mass electronic communication was of fundamental importance to an authoritarian regime and that the presence of these receivers in nearly every home allowed the Nazi propaganda to penetrate virtually the entire German nation at will. [Bildarchiv Preussischer Kulturbesitz.]

RADIO. Radio and radio technology came of age in the 1920s and 1930s. The wartime requirements for communication had speeded up the development and the production of the wireless. In 1922 broadcasting facilities had been established in Britain. The nationalized British Broadcasting System was organized in 1926. Other radio broadcasting facilities spread across the Continent during the same years. The radio was a consumer gadget of the first order. The expanding electric systems made its use possible. The radio itself was sold and then required other businesses to supply service parts. The radio industry, in turn, expanded the scope and transformed the nature of advertising. By the end of the 1920s millions of radios were in European homes. It was a product bought not by the wealthy, who had various other modes of leisure, but by the relatively poor and middle-class groups of the population. It was the first product of sophisticated electrical technology to capture the mass market. Radio—like its successor, television—transformed European life and tended to produce a more nearly uniform culture. Radio also helped to make the propaganda programs of the authoritarian states possible.

AUTOMOBILES. Automobiles were a second interwar growth industry. Only during those years did the motor car become a product of widespread consumption. In France Louis Renault and André Citroën built cars that the middle class wanted and could afford to buy. The automobile revolutionized European life rather less than it did American life. But the auto did bring new mobility and also possessed obvious military uses. Its production called forth new demand for steel, glass, rubber, petroleum, and highways. The automobile, like the radio, required a sales and service—as well as a production—industry.

SYNTHETICS. During these years the production of synthetic goods began to assume major economic significance. Rayon, invented before World War I, led the way in this area. Its production and consumption for hose and underwear grew rapidly. The product itself was soon much improved through the acetate process. Rayon began to replace cotton as the cheap textile for everyday use. The production of this synthetic fabric proved especially attractive to governments, such as those of Germany and Italy, that sought economic self-sufficiency. The prospect of war in the late 1930s led various governments to encourage the chemical industries to search for other synthetic substances that might replace natural products if foreign sources for the latter were shut off.

Depression and Government Policy

It is important to remember these areas of industrial expansion between the wars. The Depression did not mean absolute economic decline. Nor did it mean that everyone was out of a job. The numbers of employed always well exceeded those without work. What the economic downturn did mean was the spread of actual or potential insecurity. People in practically all walks of life feared that their own economic security and lifestyle might be the next to go. The Depression also brought on a frustration of social and economic expectations. People with jobs frequently improved their standard of living or received promotion much more slowly than they might have under sound economic conditions. Although they were employed, they seemed in their own eyes to be going nowhere. Their anxieties created a major source of social discontent.

The governments of the late 1920s and early 1930s were not particularly well fitted in either structure or ideology to confront these problems. The demand from the electorates was to do something. What the government did in large measure depended on the severity of the Depression in a particular country and the self-confidence of the nation's political system. The Keynesian theory of governments' spending the economy out of Depression was not yet available. John Maynard Keynes's *General Theory of Employment, Interest, and Money* was not published until 1936. The orthodox economic policy of the day called for cuts in government spending so as to avoid inflation. It was then expected that eventually the market mechanism would bring the economy back to prosperity. However, the length and severity of the Depression, plus the possibility of direct democratic political pressure, led governments across Europe to interfere with the economy as never before.

Government participation in economic life was not new. One need only recall the policies of mercantilism and the government encouragement of railway building. But from the early 1930s onward government involvement increased rapidly. Private economic enterprise became subject to new trade, labor, and currency regulations. The political goals of restoration of employment and provision for defense established new state-related economic priorities. Generally speaking, as in the past, the extent of state intervention increased as one moved from west to east across the Continent. These new economic policies in most cases also involved further political experimentation.

Confronting the Depression in the Democracies

The Depression brought to an end the business-as-usual attitude that had marked the political life

of Great Britain and France during the late 1920s. In Britain the emergency led to a new coalition government and the abandonment of economic policies considered almost untouchable for a century. The economic stagnation in France proved to be the occasion for a bold political and economic program sponsored by the parties of the left. The relative success of the British venture gave the nation new confidence in the democratic processes; the new departures in France created social and political hostilities that undermined faith in republican institutions.

Great Britain: The National Government

In 1929 a second minority Labor government, headed by Ramsay MacDonald, assumed office. As the number of British unemployed rose to more than 2.5 million workers in 1931, the ministry became divided over the remedy for the problem. MacDonald believed that the budget should be slashed, government salaries reduced, and the benefits to people on government unemployment insurance lowered. This was a bleak program for a Labor government. MacDonald's strong desire to make the Labor Party respectable led him away from more radical programs. Many of the Cabinet ministers rejected MacDonald's proposals. They would not consent to taking income away from the poor and the unemployed. The prime minister requested the resignations of his Cabinet and arranged for a meeting with King George V.

Everyone assumed that the entire Labor ministry was about to leave office. However, to the surprise of his party and the nation, MacDonald did not resign. At the urging of the king and probably of his own ambition, MacDonald formed a coalition ministry called the *National Government* composed of Labor, Conservative, and Liberal ministers. The bulk of the Labor Party believed that their leader had sold out. In the election of 1931 the National Government received a very comfortable majority. After the election, however, MacDonald, who remained prime minister until 1935, was little more than the tool of the Conservatives. They held a majority in their own right in the House of Commons, but the appearance of a coalition was useful for imposing unpleasant programs.

The National Government took three decisive steps to attack the Depression. To balance the budget, it raised taxes, cut insurance benefits to the unemployed and the elderly, and lowered government salaries. Its leaders argued that the fall in prices that had taken place meant that lowering those benefits and salaries did not appreciably cut real income. In September 1931 the National Government went off the gold standard. The value of the British pound on the international money market fell by about 30 per cent. Exports were somewhat stimulated by this move. In 1932 Parliament passed the Import Duties Bill, which placed a 10 per cent *ad valorum* tariff on all imports except those from the empire. In the context of previous British policy all of these steps were nothing less than extraordinary. Gold and free trade, the hallmarks of almost a century of British commercial policy, stood abandoned.

The policies of the National Government produced significant results. Great Britain avoided the banking crisis that hit other countries. By 1934 industrial production had expanded somewhat beyond the level for 1929. Britain was the first nation to achieve restoration of that level of production. Of course, the mediocre British industrial performance of the 1920s made the British task easier.

The government also encouraged lower interest rates. Those, in turn, led to the largest private housing boom in British history. Industries related to housing and the furnishing of homes prospered. Those people who were employed generally experienced an improvement in their standard of living. Nonetheless the hard core of unemployment remained. In 1937 the number of jobless had fallen to just below 1.5 million. That same year, when George Orwell described the laboring districts of the nation in *The Road to Wigan Pier*, the poverty and the workless days of the people whom he met dominated his picture.

Britain had entered the Depression with a stagnant economy and left the era with a stagnant economy. Yet the political system itself was not fundamentally challenged. There were demonstrations of the unemployed, but social insurance, though hardly generous, did support them. To the employed citizens of the country the National Government seemed to pursue a policy that avoided the extreme wings of both the Labor and the Conservative parties. When MacDonald retired in

✎ George Orwell Observes a Woman in the Slums

Although Great Britain was beginning to emerge from the Great Depression by the late 1930s, much poverty and human degradation remained. This scene, described in 1937 by the social critic and novelist George Orwell (1903–1950), captures a glimpse of the sadness and hopelessness that many British citizens experienced every day of their lives.

The train bore me away, through the monstrous scenery of slag-heaps, chimneys, piled scrap-iron, foul canals, paths of cindery mud criss-crossed by the prints of clogs. . . . As we moved slowly through the outskirts of the town we passed row after row of little grey slum houses running at right angles to the embankment. At the back of one of the houses a young woman was kneeling on the stones, poking a stick up the leaden waste-pipe which ran from the sink inside, and which I suppose was blocked. I had time to see everything about her—her sacking apron, her clumsy clogs, her arms reddened by the cold. . . . She had a round pale face, the usual exhausted face of the slum girl who is twenty-five and looks forty, thanks to miscarriages and drudgery; and it wore, for the second in which I saw it, the most desolate, hopeless expression I have ever seen. It struck me then that we are mistaken when we say that "It isn't the same for them as it would be for us," and that people bred in the slums can imagine nothing but the slums. For what I saw in her face was not the ignorant suffering of an animal. She knew well enough what was happening to her—understood as well as I did how dreadful a destiny it was to be kneeling there in the bitter cold, on the slimy stones of a slum backyard, poking a stick up a foul drain-pipe.*

George Orwell, *The Road to Wigan Pier* (New York: Berkeley Medallion Books, 1967, originally printed in 1937), p. 29.

Oswald Mosley in May 1939 leads a demonstration in London of his British Union of Fascists and National Socialists. [*United Press International Photo.*]

1935, Stanley Baldwin again took office. He was succeeded in 1937 by Neville Chamberlain (1869–1940). The new prime minister is today known for the disaster of the Munich agreement. When he took office, he was known as one of the more progessive thinkers on social issues in the Conservative Party.

Britain did see one movement that flirted with the extreme right-wing politics of the Continent. In 1932 Sir Oswald Mosley (b. 1896) founded the British Union of Fascists. He had held a minor position in the second Labor government and was disappointed in its feeble attack on unemployment. Mosley urged a program of direct action through a new corporate structure for the economy. His group wore black shirts and attempted to hold mass meetings. He gained only a few thousand adherents. Mosley's popularity reached its height in 1934. Thereafter his anti-Semitism began to alienate supporters, and by the close of the decade he had become little more than a political oddity.

France: The Popular Front

The timing of the Depression in France was the reverse of that in Britain. It came later and lasted much longer. Only in 1931 did the economic slide begin to affect the French economy. Even then unemployment did not become the major problem it did elsewhere. Rarely were more than half a million workers without jobs. However, in one industry after another wages were lowered. Tariffs were raised to protect French goods and especially French agriculture. Ever since that time French farmers have enjoyed unusual protection from the government. These measures helped maintain the home market but did little to overcome industrial stagnation. Relations between labor and management were tense.

The first political fallout of the Depression was the election of another Radical coalition government in 1932. Fearful of contributing to inflation as it had after 1924, the Radical government pursued a generally deflationary policy. In the same year that the new ministry took office, reparation payments had stopped. As the economic crisis tightened, normal parliamentary and political life became difficult and confused.

Outside the Chamber of Deputies politics assumed a very ugly face. The old divisions between left and right hardened. Various right-wing groups with authoritarian tendencies became active. These leagues included the *Action Française,* founded prior to World War I in the wake of the Dreyfus affair, and the *Croix de Feu* ("Cross of Fire"), composed of army veterans. The memberships of these and other similar groups numbered somewhat more than two million persons. Some wanted a monarchy; others favored what would have amounted to military rule. They were hostile to the idea of parliamentary government, socialism, and communism. They wanted what they regarded as the greater good and glory of the nation to be set above the petty machinations of political parties. In this regard they resembled the Fascists and the

❧ Motor Cars Become More Popular in France

The Depression came to France later than to other countries. During the late 1920s and early 1930s the motor car industry grew. More French citizens drove cars, and the manufacture of cars became more standardized. This passage from a report on the French economy describes this development and emphasizes the desire of French consumers to have real choices in regard to motor-car styles.

Nearly twelve times as many passenger cars are in use today in France as there were in 1913, *the number of registered or tax-paying passenger cars having grown from* 107,857 *in that year to* 1,279,142 *at the end of* 1932; *since* 1928, *when the number was* 757,668, *the increase has been over half a million.* . . .

In the French motor-car industry noteworthy progress has been made in standardization during the last seven years. The industry is one in which there was particular scope for the introduction of some form of standardization, for owing to the multiplicity of small manufacturers (50 or more of whom produced between them only about 10 *per cent of the total output of the country, each seeking to strike a note of individuality), there was an inevitable tendency towards an unduly large variety of designs and dimensions, even of the most ordinary parts. A normalization bureau was set up in* 1926 *by the association of accessory and spare parts manufacturers, and by* 1928 *standards had been established for* 29 *parts, resulting in price reductions, in some cases, of* 86 *to* 95 *per cent. For instance, the number of different types of caps for radiators and petrol tanks has been reduced from* 88 *to five.* . . .

Government departments and public utility concerns, such as the Ministry of War and the motor transport concession holders working in collaboration with the railways, are lending useful support to the normalization movement by inserting a clause in their specifications requiring suppliers of vehicles to employ only parts conforming to the accepted standards. . . .

The tendency towards standardization was further manifested about 1929, *by a fairly general decision of leading French motor-car manufacturers, whereby each firm concentrated its energies on two or three types of cars, instead of trying to cater for the whole range of motor-car users, private and industrial; the Citroën and Peugeot firms, in particular, being prominent protagonists of the new policy. The individualistic French temperament, however, proved itself too strong for this policy to be followed for long; and at the motor shows of* 1931–1933 *a reversion to the former practice of putting on the markets as many different types of cars as each producer thought he had a chance of selling, was clearly apparent.*

J. R. Cahill, *Economic Conditions in France* (London: 1934), pp. 253, 257–258, as cited in Sidney Pollard and Colin Holmes, *Documents of European Economic History,* Vol. 3 (London: Edward Arnold, 1973), pp. 587–588.

❧ The Right Wing Attacks the Third French Republic

The Stavisky affair provided new opportunity for various French right-wing political groups to criticize the liberal institutions of the Third Republic. In this proclamation of January 7, 1934, one such organization, the *Camelots du Roi*, accused one minister, and by implication all French politicians, of having aided Stavisky in a fraudulent bond scheme. The minister did later resign, but he was not directly implicated in the theft. Also, the reader should note how this proclamation invites the people of Paris to demonstrate against the Chamber of Deputies and to take the law into their own hands. The violence of the night of February 6, 1934, resulted from such invitations to right-wing demonstration.

To the People of Paris.

At a time when the Government and the Parliament of the Republic declare themselves incapable of balancing our budget, and continue to defend the topsy-turvy foundations of their regime; while they refuse to reduce the burden of taxation and are actually inflicting more taxes on the French people a scandal breaks out. This scandal shows that, far from protecting the savings of the people, the Republican Authorities have given free course to the colossal rackets of an alien crook. A Minister, M. Dalimier, by his letters of 25 June and 23 September 1932, deliberately provided an instrument which enabled the thief Stavisky to rob the insurance companies and the Social Insurance Fund of over half a milliard francs. He has been urged to resign; but he has refused to do so. He should be in prison together with his pals Stavisky and Dubarry [another person implicated in the plot]; instead of which, he continues to be a member of the Government whose duty it is to inquire into this affair. Dalimier is not alone; we can see behind him a crowd of other ministers and influential members of Parliament, all of whom have, in one way or another, favoured the adventurer's rackets, especially by instructing the police to leave him alone, and by suspending during many years the legal proceedings that should have been taken against him. There is no law and no justice in a country where magistrates and the police are the accomplices of criminals. The honest people of France who want to protect their own interests, and who care for the cleanliness of public life, are forced to take the law into their own hands.

At the beginning of this week, Parliament will reassemble and we urge the people of Paris to come in large numbers before the Chamber of Deputies, to cry "Down with the Thieves" and to clamour for honesty and justice.

Sidney Pollard and Colin Holmes, *Documents of European Economic History*, Vol. 3 (London: Edward Arnold, 1973), p. 369.

Nazis. Their activities and propaganda aided the dissolution of loyalty to republican government and injected bitterness and vindictiveness into French political life. These leagues also created one moment of extraordinary havoc that produced important long-range political consequences.

The incident grew out of the Stavisky affair, the last of those curious *causes célèbres* that punctuated the political fortunes of the Third Republic. Serge Stavisky was a small-time gangster who appears to have had good connections within the government. In 1933 he became involved in a fraudulent bond scheme. When finally tracked down by the police, he committed suicide in January 1934. The official handling of the matter suggested a political cover-up. It was alleged that people in high places wished to halt the investigation. To the right wing in France the Stavisky incident symbolized all the seaminess, immorality, and corruption of republican politics. On February 6, 1934, a very large demonstration of the right-wing leagues took place in Paris. The exact purpose and circumstances of the rally remain uncertain, but the crowd did attempt to march on the Chamber of Deputies. Violence erupted between right and left political groups and between them and the police. Fourteen

In February 1934 right-wing street riots broke out in Paris as a result of the political handling of the Stavisky Affair. Within a year these riots had given rise to new cooperation among French left-wing parties who feared the threat from the right. [The Granger Collection.]

demonstrators were killed; scores of others were injured. It was the largest disturbance in Paris since the Commune of 1871.

In the wake of the night of February 6, the Radical ministry of Edouard Daladier (1884–1970) resigned and was replaced by a national coalition government composed of all living former premiers. The Chamber of Deputies permitted the ministry to deal with economic matters by decree. However, the major result of the right-wing demonstrations was a political self-reassessment by the parties of the left. Radicals, Socialists, and Communists began to realize that a right-wing *coup* might be possible in France. Consequently, between 1934 and 1936 the French left began to make peace within its own ranks. This was no easy task. French Socialists, led by Léon Blum (1872–1950), had been the major target of the French Communists since the split over joining the Comintern in 1920. Only Stalin's fear of Hitler as a danger to the Soviet Union made this new cooperation possible. In spite of deep suspicions on all sides, the Popular Front had been established by Bastille Day in 1935. Its purpose was to preserve the republic and to press for social reform.

The election of 1936 gave the Popular Front a majority in the Chamber of Deputies. The Socialists were the largest single party for the first time in French history. Consequently they organized the Cabinet as they had long promised they would do when they constituted the majority party of a coalition. Léon Blum assumed the premiership on June 5, 1936. From the early 1920s this Jewish intellectual and humanitarian had opposed the communist version of socialism. Cast as the successor to Jean Jaurès, who had been assassinated in 1914, Blum wanted socialism in the context of democratic, parliamentary government. He hoped to bring France a program akin to the New Deal that President Franklin Roosevelt had carried out in the United States.

During May 1936, before the Popular Front came to power, strikes had begun to spread throughout French industry. Immediately after assuming office on June 6, the Blum government faced further spontaneous work stoppages involving over half a million workers who had occupied factories in sit-down strikes. These were the most extensive labor disturbances in the history of the Third Republic. They aroused new fears in the conservative business community, which had already been frightened by the election of the Popular Front. Blum acted swiftly to bring together representatives of labor and management. On June 8 he announced the conclusion of the Matignon Accord, which reorganized labor–management relations in France. Wages were immediately raised from 7 to 15 per cent, depending on the job involved. Employers were required to recognize unions and to bargain collectively with them. Annual, paid two-week vacations for workers were adopted. The forty-hour week was established throughout French industry. Blum hoped to overcome labor hostility to French society, to establish a foundation for justice in labor–management relations, and to increase the domestic consumer demand of the nation.

Blum followed his labor policy with other bold departures. He raised the salaries of civil servants and instituted a program of public works. Government loans were extended to small industry. Spending on armaments was increased, and some armament industries were nationalized. To aid agriculture, he set up a National Wheat Board to manage the production and sale of grain. Initially he had promised to resist devaluation of the franc. However, by the autumn of 1936 international monetary pressure forced him to devalue. He did so again in the spring of 1937. The devaluations brought little aid to French exports because they came too late. All of these moves enraged the conservative banking and business community. In March 1937 they brought sufficient influence to bear on the ministry to cause Blum to halt the program of reform. It was not taken up again. Blum's Popular Front colleagues considered the pause in reform an unnecessary compromise. In June 1937 Blum resigned. The Popular Front ministry itself held on until April 1938, when it was replaced by a Radical ministry under Daladier.

The Popular Front had brought much hope to labor and to socialists, but it did not lead France out of the Depression. Some of its programs actually harmed production. The business community, because of its apprehensions and hostility, became even less venturesome after the Popular Front reforms. Not until 1939 did French industrial production reach the level of 1929. In a sense the Popular Front had come too late to give either the economy or French political life new vitality. Internal divisions and conservative opposition meant that the Popular Front had enjoyed less than a free hand. By the close of the 1930s citizens from all walks of life had begun to wonder if the republic was worth preserving. The left continued to re-

❧ French Management and Labor Reach an Agreement

When the Popular Front government came to power in France in 1936, it immediately confronted widespread strikes. Premier Léon Blum called together the representatives of labor and management. The result of these negotiations was the Matignon Accord, which gave the unions more secure rights, raised wages, and brought the strikes to an end.

The delegates of the General Confederation of French Production (CGPF) and the General Confederation of Labour (CGT) have met under the chairmanship of the Premier (Léon Blum) and have concluded the following agreement, after arbitration by the Premier:

1. The employer delegation agrees to the immediate conclusion of collective agreements.

2. These agreements must include, in particular, articles 3. . . .

3. All citizens being required to abide by law, the employers recognize the freedom of opinion of workers and their right to freely join and belong to trade unions.

In their decisions on hiring, organization or assignment of work, disciplinary measures or dismissals, employers agree not to take into consideration the fact of membership or nonmembership in a union. . . .

The exercise of trade union rights must not give rise to acts contrary to law.

4. The wages actually paid to all workers as of 25 May 1936 will be raised, as of the resumption of work, by a decreasing percentage ranging from 15 per cent for the lowest rates down to 7 per cent for the highest rates. In no case must the total increase in any establishment exceed 12 per cent. . . .

The negotiations, which are to be launched at once, for the determination by collective agreement of minimum wages by regions and by occupations must take up, in particular, the necessary revision of abnormally low wages. . . .

. . . .

6. The employer delegation promises that there will be no sanctions for strike activities.

7. The CGT delegation will ask the workers on strike to return to work as soon as the managements of establishments have accepted this general agreement and as soon as negotiations for its application have begun between the managements and the personnel of the establishments.

V. R. Lorwin, *The French Labour Movement* (Cambridge, Mass.: Harvard University Press, 1954), pp. 313–315.

A display of unity by leaders of the French Popular Front at a Bastille Day rally in Paris, July 14, 1937. Léon Blum of the Socialist Party is on the left with Mme. Blum, and Maurice Thorez (1900–1964), the Secretary of the French Communist Party, stands beside him on the right. [Photo Trends.]

main divided. Business people found the republic inefficient and, in their opinion, too much subject to socialist pressures. The right wing hated the republic in principle. When the time came in 1940 to defend the republic, there were too many citizens who were less than sure that it was worth defending.

Germany: The Nazi Seizure of Power

Depression and Political Deadlock

The outflow of foreign, and especially American, capital from Germany commencing in 1928 undermined the economic prosperity of the Weimar Republic. The resulting economic crisis brought parliamentary government to an end. In 1928 a coalition of center parties and the Social Democrats governed. All went reasonably well until the Depression struck. Then the coalition

partners differed sharply on economic policy. The Social Democrats wanted no reduction in social and unemployment insurance. The more conservative parties, remembering the inflation of 1923, insisted on a balanced budget. The coalition dissolved in March 1930. To resolve the parliamentary deadlock in the *Reichstag*, President von Hindenburg appointed Heinrich Brüning (1885–1970) as chancellor. Lacking a majority in the *Reichstag*, the new chancellor governed through emergency presidential decrees as authorized by Article 48 of the constitution. The party divisions in the *Reichstag* prevented the overriding of the decrees. In this manner the Weimar Republic was transformed into a presidential dictatorship.

German unemployment rose from 2,258,000 in March 1930 to over 6,000,000 in March 1932. There had been persistent unemployment during the 1920s, but nothing of such magnitude or duration. The economic downturn and the parliamentary deadlock worked to the advantage of the more extreme political parties. In the election of 1928 the Nazis had won only 12 seats in the *Reichstag*,

POLITICAL DEVELOPMENTS OF THE LATE 1920S AND THE 1930S

1928   First Five-Year Plan launched in the Soviet Union

1929   June Second Labor Party government in Britain

October New York stock market crash

1930   March Brüning government begins in Germany

Stalin calls for moderation in his policy of agricultural collectivization because of "dizziness from success"

September Nazis capture 107 seats in German *Reichstag*

1931   August National Government formed in Britain

1932   March 13 Hindenberg defeats Hitler for German presidency

May 31 Franz von Papen forms German Cabinet

July 31 German *Reichstag* election

November 6 German *Reichstag* election

December 2 Kurt von Schleicher forms German Cabinet

1933   January 30 Hitler made German chancellor

February 27 *Reichstag* Fire

March 5 *Reichstag* election

March 23 Enabling Act consolidates Nazi power

1934   February 6 Stavisky affair riots in Paris

June 30 Blood purge of the Nazi Party

August 2 Death of Hindenberg

December 1 Assassination of Kirov leads to the beginning of Stalin's purges

1936   May Popular Front government in France

July–August Most famous of public purge trials in Russia

---

and the Communists had won 54 seats. Two years later, after the election of 1930, the Nazis held 107 seats and the Communists 77.

The power of the Nazis in the streets was also on the rise. The unemployment fed thousands of men into the Stormtroopers, which had 100,000 members in 1930 and almost 1 million in 1933. The SA freely and viciously attacked Communists and Social Democrats. For the Nazis politics meant the capture of power through the instruments of terror and intimidation as well as by legal elections. Anything resembling decency and civility in political life vanished. The Nazis held rallies that resembled secular religious revivals. They paraded through the streets and the countryside. They gained powerful supporters and sympathizers in the business, military, and newspaper communities. Some intellectuals were also sympathetic. The Nazis were able to transform this discipline and enthusiasm born of economic despair and nationalistic frustration into impressive electoral results.

Hitler Comes to Power

For two years Brüning continued to govern through the confidence of Hindenburg. The economy did not improve, and the political situation deteriorated. In 1932 the eighty-three-year-old president stood for reelection. Hitler ran against him and forced a runoff. In the first election the Nazi leader garnered 30.1 per cent of the vote, and he later gained 36.8 per cent in the second. Although Hindenburg was returned to office, the results of the poll convinced him that Brüning no longer commanded sufficient confidence from conservative German voters. On May 30, 1932, he dismissed Brüning and, on the next day he appointed Franz von Papen (1878–1969) in his place. The new chancellor was one of a small group of extremely conservative advisers on whom the aged Hindenburg had become increasingly dependent. Others included the president's son and several military figures. With the continued paralysis in the *Reichstag*, their influence over the president virtually amounted to control of the government. Consequently the crucial decisions of the next several months were made by only a handful of people.

Papen and the circle around the president wanted to find some way to draw the Nazis into cooperation with them without giving any effective power to Hitler. The government needed the mass popular support that only the Nazis seemed able to generate. The Hindenburg circle decided to convince Hitler that the Nazis could not come to power on their own. Papen removed the ban on Nazi meetings that Brüning had imposed and then called a *Reichstag* election for July 1932. The Nazis won 230 seats and polled 37.2 per cent of the vote. As the price for his entry into the Cabinet, Hitler demanded appointment as chancellor. Hindenburg refused. Another election was called in November, partly as a means of wearing down the Nazis' financial resources. It was successful in that regard. The number of Nazi seats fell to 196, and their percentage of the popular vote dipped to 33.1 per cent. The advisers around Hindenburg still refused to appoint Hitler to office.

In early December 1932 Papen resigned, and Kurt von Schleicher (1882–1934) became chancellor. There now existed much fear of civil war between groups on the left and the right. Schleicher decided to attempt the construction of a broad-based coalition of conservative groups and trade unionists. The prospect of such a coalition, including groups from the political left, frightened the Hindenburg circle even more than the prospect of Hitler. They did not trust Schleicher's motives, which have never been very clear. Consequently they persuaded Hindenburg to appoint Hitler as chancellor. To control him and to see that he did little mischief, Papen was named vice-chancellor, and other traditional conservatives were appointed to the Cabinet. On January 30, 1933, Adolf Hitler became the chancellor of Germany.

Hitler's Consolidation of Power

Hitler had come into office by legal means. All of the proper legal forms and procedures had been observed. This fact was very important, for it permitted the civil service, the courts, and the other agencies of the government to support him with good conscience. He had forged a rigidly disciplined party structure and had mastered the techniques of mass politics and propaganda. He understood how to touch the raw social and political nerves of the electorate. His major support came from the lower middle class, the farmers, and the young. Each of these groups had especially suffered from the insecurity of the 1920s and the Depression of the early 1930s. Hitler promised them security against communists and socialists, effective government in place of the petty politics of the other parties, and an uncompromising nationalist vision of a strong, restored Germany.

Much credit was once given to German big business for the rise of Hitler. However, little evidence exists that business money financed the Nazis in a fashion that made any crucial difference to their success or failure. Hitler's supporters were frequently suspicious of business and giant capitalism.

Hitler and President von Hindenburg pictured riding together in an open carriage in 1933 shortly after the aged president had appointed Hitler chancellor. After von Hindenburg's death the next year, Hitler assumed the powers of the presidency as well as those of the chancellorship. [Culver Pictures.]

They wanted a simpler world and one in which small property would be safe from both socialism and large-scale capitalist consolidation. These people looked to Hitler and the Nazis rather than to the Social Democrats because the latter, though concerned with social issues, never appeared sufficiently nationalistic. The Nazis won out over other conservative nationalistic parties because, unlike the latter, they did address themselves to the problem of lower-middle-class social insecurity.

Once in office Hitler moved with almost lightning speed to consolidate his control. This process

963

The Reichstag fire of February 27, 1933 created fear of a Communist revolution in Germany. In this political atmosphere the Nazis completed their seizure of power. [The Granger Collection.]

had three facets: the capture of full legal authority, the crushing of alternative political groups, and the purging of rivals within the Nazi Party itself.

On February 27, 1933, a mentally ill Dutch communist set fire to the *Reichstag* building in Berlin. The Nazis quickly turned the incident to their own advantage by claiming that the fire proved the existence of an immediate Communist threat against the government. To the public it seemed plausible that the Communists might attempt some action against the state now that the Nazis were in power. Under Article 48 Hitler made the Emergency Decree suspending civil liberties and proceeded to arrest Communists or alleged Communists. This decree was not revoked for as long as Hitler ruled Germany.

In early March another *Reichstag* election took place. The Nazis still received only 43.9 per cent of the vote. However, the arrest of the newly elected Communist deputies and the political fear aroused by the fire meant that Hitler could control the *Reichstag*. On March 23, 1933, the *Reichstag* passed an Enabling Act that permitted Hitler to rule by decree. Thereafter there were no legal limits on his exercise of power. The Weimar Constitution was never formally repealed or amended. It had sim-

ply been supplanted by the February Emergency Decree and the March Enabling Act.

Perhaps better than anyone else Hitler understood that he and his party had not inevitably come to power. All of his potential opponents had stood divided between 1929 and 1933. He intended to prevent them from regrouping. In a series of complex moves Hitler outlawed or undermined various German institutions that might have served as rallying points for opposition. In early May 1933 the offices, banks, and newspapers of the free trade unions were seized, and their leaders were arrested. The Nazi Party itself, rather than any government agency, undertook this action. In late June and early July all of the other German political parties were outlawed. By July 14, 1933, the National Socialists were the only legal party in Germany. During the same months the Nazis had moved against the governments of the individual federal states in Germany. By the close of 1933 all major institutions of potential opposition had been eliminated.

The final element in Hitler's consolidation of power involved the Nazi Party itself. By late 1933 the SA, or Stormtroopers, consisted of approximately one million active members and a larger number of reserves. The commander of this party army was Ernst Roehm, a possible rival to Hitler himself. The German army officer corps, on whom Hitler depended to rebuild the national army, were jealous of the SA leadership. Consequently, to protect his own position and to shore up support with the regular army, on June 30, 1934, Hitler personally ordered the murder of key SA officers, including Roehm. Others killed between June 30 and July 2 included the former chancellor General Kurt von Schleicher and his wife. The exact number of victims purged is unknown, but it has been estimated to have exceeded one hundred persons. The German army, which was the only institution in the nation that might have prevented the murders, did nothing. A month later, on August 2, 1934, President Hindenburg died. Thereafter the offices of chancellor and president were combined. Hitler was now the sole ruler of Germany and of the Nazi Party.

The Police State

Terror and intimidation had been a major factor in the Nazi march to office. As Hitler consolidated his power, he oversaw the organization of a police

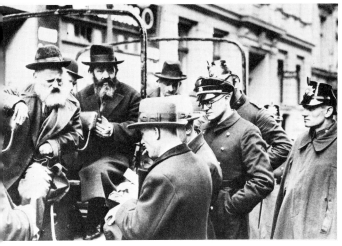

Jews being interrogated in Berlin in 1933. The Nazi accession to power led immediately to the issuance of anti-Jewish laws and to a government-sponsored boycott of Jewish businesses. During the early days of the boycott Jews frequently were interrogated, detained, and even arrested. [Wide World Photos.]

During the night of November 9, 1938, all across Germany the windows of stores owned by Jewish businessmen were smashed in one of the major Nazi pre-war outbursts of anti-Semitism. This photograph was made in Berlin the following day. The Nazis then confiscated the insurance money and refused to allow the Jewish businesses to be compensated for their losses. [The Granger Collection.]

A Jewish couple in Berlin in October 1941 wearing yellow stars of David marked Jude *(Jew). The wearing of the stars was required of all German Jews by a law passed the previous month. The final step in the Nazi's anti-Jewish campaign, the deportation of Jews to concentration camps in Eastern Europe, began in early 1942. [Wide World Photos.]*

state. The chief vehicle of police surveillance was the SS *(Schutzstaffel)*, or security units, commanded by Heinrich Himmler (1900–1945). This group had originated in the mid-1920s as a bodyguard for Hitler and had become a more elite paramilitary organization than the larger SA. In 1933 the SS was composed of approximately fifty-two thousand members. It was the instrument that carried out the blood purges of the party in 1934. By 1936 Himmler had become head of all police matters in Germany and stood second only to Hitler in power and influence.

The police character of the Nazi regime was all-pervasive, but the people who most consistently experienced the terror of the police state were the German Jews. Anti-Semitism had been a key plank of the Nazi program. It was anti-Semitism based on biological racial theories stemming from late-nineteenth-century thought rather than from religious discrimination. Prior to World War II the Nazi attack on the Jews went through three stages of increasing intensity. In 1933, shortly after assuming power, the Nazis excluded Jews from offices in the civil service. For a time they also attempted to enforce boycotts of Jewish shops and businesses. The boycotts won relatively little public support. In 1935 a series of measures known as the *Nuremberg Laws* robbed German Jews of their citizenship. All persons with at least three Jewish grandparents were defined as Jews. The professions and the major occupations were closed to Jews. Marriage and sexual intercourse between Jews and non-Jews were prohibited. Legal exclusion and humiliation of the Jews became the order of the day.

The persecution of the Jews increased again in 1938. Business careers were forbidden. In November 1938, under orders from the Nazi Party, thousands of Jewish stores and synagogues were burned or otherwise destroyed. The Jewish community itself was required to pay for the damage because the government confiscated the insurance money. In all manner of other ways, large and petty, the German Jews were harassed. This persecution allowed the Nazis to inculcate the rest of the population with the concept of a master race of pure German "Aryans" and also to display their own contempt for civil liberties. After the war

❧ The Nazis Pass Their Racial Legislation

Anti-Semitism had been a fundamental tenet of the Nazi Party and became a major policy of the Nazi government. This comprehensive legislation of September 15, 1935, carried anti-Semitism into all areas of public life and into some of the most personal areas of private life as well. It was characteristically titled the Law for the Protection of German Blood and Honor. Hardly any aspect of Nazi thought and action was as shocking to the non-German world as was this policy toward the Jews.

Imbued with the knowledge that the purity of German blood is the necessary prerequisite for the existence of the German nation, and inspired by an inflexible will to maintain the existence of the German nation for all future times, the Reichstag has unanimously adopted the following law, which is now enacted:

Article I: (1) *Any marriages between Jews and citizens of German or kindred blood are herewith forbidden. Marriages entered into despite this law are invalid, even if they are arranged abroad as a means of circumventing this law.*

(2) *Annulment proceedings for marriages may be initiated only by the Public Prosecutor.*

Article II: Extramarital relations between Jews and citizens of German or kindred blood are herewith forbidden.

Article III: Jews are forbidden to employ as servants to their households female subjects of German or kindred blood who are under the age of forty-five years.

Article IV: (1) *Jews are prohibited from displaying the Reich and national flag and from showing the national colors.*

(2) *However, they may display the Jewish colors. The exercise of this right is under state protection.*

Article V: (1) *Anyone who acts contrary to the prohibition noted in Article I renders himself liable to penal servitude.*

(2) *The man who acts contrary to the prohibition of Article II will be punished by sentence to either a jail or penitentiary.*

(3) *Anyone who acts contrary to the provisions of Articles III and IV will be punished with a jail sentence up to a year and with a fine, or with one of these penalties.*

Article VI: The Reich Minister of Interior, in conjunction with the Deputy to the Führer and the Reich Minister of Justice, will issue the required legal and administrative decrees for the implementation and amplification of this law.

Article VII: This law shall go into effect on the day following its promulgation, with the exception of Article III, which shall go into effect on January 1, 1936.

Louis L. Snyder (Ed. and Trans.), *Documents of German History* (New Brunswick, N.J.: Rutgers University Press, 1958), pp. 427–428.

Heinrich Himmler (1900–1945), who was head of the Nazi secret police. [The Granger Collection.]

broke out, Hitler decided in 1942 to destroy the Jews in Europe. It is thought that over six million Jews, mostly from east European nations, died as a result of that staggering decision, unprecedented in its scope and implementation.

Nazi Economic Policy

Besides consolidating power and persecuting allegedly inferior races, Hitler still had to confront the reality of the Depression. German unemployment had been a major factor in his rise to power. The Nazis attacked this problem and achieved a degree of success that astonished and frightened the rest of Europe. By 1936, while the rest of the European economy continued to stagnate, the

specter of unemployment and other difficulties associated with the Depression for all intents and purposes no longer haunted Germany. As far as the economic crisis was concerned, Hitler had become the most effective political leader in Europe. This fact was a most important element in accounting for the internal strength and support of his tyrannical regime. The Nazi success against the Depression provided the regime with considerable contemporary credibility. As might be expected, the cost in terms of liberty and human dignity had been very high.

Hitler reversed the deflationary policy of the cabinets that had preceded him. He instituted what amounted to a massive program of public works

Joseph Goebbels (1897–1945), who headed the Nazi propaganda drive at home and abroad. [The Granger Collection.]

Hermann Göring (1893–1946), Hitler's second in command, is here photographed flanked by other Nazi officers, [United Press International Photo.]

Nazi economic policies maintained private property and private capitalism. However, all significant economic enterprise and decisions became subordinated to the goals of the state. Prices were controlled and investments restricted. Currency regulation interfered with trade. Production that related to the military buildup received top priority and even redirected some industries. For example, in the late 1930s, the German chemical producers diverted a large proportion of their resources toward the manufacture of various synthetics.

With the crushing of the trade unions in 1933, strikes became illegal. There was no genuine collective bargaining. The government handled labor

One of the few structures designed by Speer actually to be completed, the German Chancellory, used by the Nazis until its destruction in World War II. [Ullstein Bilderdienst.]

The architect Albert Speer (born 1905) became a favored member of Hitler's inner circle. He and Hitler developed plans for an entire new design for the city of Berlin. This is a photograph of the model designed by Speer for the new capital of Hitler's Reich. In the center is the Brandenburg Gate, the only major structure planned for preservation from Berlin's past. Beyond the gate is Unter den Linden running up the picture to a vast domed structure on the site of the former royal palace and lined left and right with the massive offices of the government. [Courtesy Albert Speer. Photo Hermann Speer.]

and spending. Many of these projects related directly or indirectly to rearmament. Canals were built, and land was reclaimed. Construction of a large system of highways with clear military uses was begun. Some unemployed workers were sent back to farms if they had originally come from there. Other laborers were frozen in their jobs and were not permitted to change employment. In 1935 renunciation of the military provisions of the Versailles Treaty led to open rearmament and expansion of the army with little opposition, as will be explained in Chapter 32. These measures essentially restored full employment. In 1936 Hitler instructed Hermann Göring (1893–1946), who had headed the air force since 1933, to undertake a Four-Year Plan to prepare the army and the economy for war. The state determined that Germany must be economically self-sufficient. Armaments received top priority. This economic program satisfied both the yearning for social and economic security and the desire for national fulfillment.

disputes through compulsory arbitration. Both workers and employers were required to participate in the Labor Front, the existence of which was intended to prove that class conflict had ended. It sponsored a "Strength Through Joy" program that provided vacations and other forms of recreation for the labor force.

However, behind the direction of both business and labor stood the Nazi terror and police. The Nazi economic experiment proved that with the sacrifice of all political and civil liberty, of a free trade-union movement, of private exercise of capital, and of consumer satisfaction, full employment for the purposes of war and aggression could be achieved.

Fascist Economics In Italy

The Fascists had promised to bring order to the instability of Italian social and economic life. Discipline was a substitute for economic policy and creativity. During the 1920s Mussolini undertook programs of public works, such as draining the Pontine Marshes for settlement. The shipping industry was subsidized, and protective tariffs were introduced. Mussolini desperately sought to make Italy self-sufficient. He embarked on the "battle of wheat" to prevent foreign grain from appearing in products on Italian tables. There was an extraordinary expansion of wheat farming in Italy. However, these policies did not keep the Depression from affecting Italy. Production, exports, and wages fell. Even the increased wheat production backfired. So much poor marginal land that was expensive to cultivate came into production that the domestic price of wheat, and thus of much food, actually rose.

Both before and during the Depression the Fascists sought to steer an economic course between socialism and a liberal *laissez-faire* system. Their policy was known as *Corporatism*. It constituted a planned economy linked to the private ownership of capital and to government arbitration of labor disputes. Major industries were first organized into syndicates representing labor and management. The two groups negotiated labor settlements within this framework and submitted differences to compulsory government arbitration. The Fascists contended that class conflict would be avoided if both labor and management looked to the greater goal of productivity for the nation. It is a matter of considerable dispute whether this arrangement favored workers or managers. What is certain is that from the mid-1920s Italian labor unions lost the right to strike and to pursue their own independent economic goals. In that respect management clearly profited.

After 1930 these industrial syndicates were further organized into entities called *corporations*. These bodies included all industries relating to a major area of production, such as agriculture or metallurgy, from raw materials through finished product and distribution. A total of twenty-two such corporations was established to encompass the whole economy. In 1938 Mussolini abolished the Italian Chamber of Deputies and replaced it with a Chamber of Corporations. This vast organizational framework did not increase production; instead, it led to excessive bureaucracy and corruption. The corporate state allowed the government to direct much of the nation's economic life without a formal change in ownership. Consumers and owners simply no longer could determine what was to be produced. The Fascist government gained further direct economic power through the Institute for Industrial Reconstruction, which extended loans to businesses in financial difficulty. The loans, in effect, established partial state ownership.

How corporatism might have affected the Italian economy in the long run cannot really be calculated. In 1935 Italy invaded Ethiopia. Economic life was put on a formal wartime footing. The League of Nations imposed economic sanctions, urging member nations to refrain from purchasing Italian goods. The sanctions had little effect. Thereafter taxes rose. During 1935 the government imposed a forced loan on the citizenry by requiring property owners to purchase bonds. Wages continued to be depressed. As the international tensions increased during the late 1930s, the Italian state assumed more and more direction over the economy. The order of Fascism in Italy had not proved to be an order of prosperity. It had brought economic dislocation and a falling standard of living.

Stalin's Five-Year Plans and Purges

While the capitalist economies of western Europe floundered in the doldrums of the Depression, the Soviet Union entered on a period of tremendous industrial advance. Like similar eras of past Russian economic progress, the direction and impetus came from the top. Stalin far exceeded his czarist predecessors in the intensity of state coercion and terror he brought to the task. Russia achieved its stunning economic growth during the 1930s only at the cost of literally millions of human lives and the degradation of still other millions. Stalin's economic policy clearly proved that his earlier rivalry with Trotsky had been a matter of political power rather than one of substantial ideological difference.

The Decision for Rapid Industrialization

Through 1928 Lenin's New Economic Policy (NEP), as championed by Bukharin with Stalin's support, had charted the course of Soviet economic development. Private ownership and enterprise were permitted to flourish in the countryside as a means of ensuring an adequate food supply for the workers in the cities. A few farmers, the *kulaks,* had become quite prosperous. They probably numbered less than 5 per cent of the rural population. During 1928 and 1929 these and other farmers withheld grain from the market because of dissatisfaction with prices. Food shortages occurred in the cities and provided a cause of potential unrest against the regime. The goals of the NEP were no longer being fulfilled. Sometime during these troubled months Stalin came to a momentous decision. Russia must industrialize rapidly in order to match the economic and military power of the West. Agriculture must be collectivized to produce sufficient grain for food and export and to free peasant labor for the factories. This program, which basically embraced Trotsky's earlier economic position, unleashed nothing less than a second Russian revolution. The costs and character of "Socialism in One Country" now became clear.

AGRICULTURAL POLICY. In 1929 Stalin ordered party agents into the countryside to confiscate any hoarded wheat. The *kulaks* bore the blame for the grain shortages. As part of the general plan to erase the private ownership of land and to collectivize farming, the government undertook a program to eliminate the *kulaks* as a class. However, the definition of a *kulak* soon embraced anyone who opposed Stalin's policy. In the countryside there was extensive resistance from peasants and farmers at all levels of wealth. The stubborn peasants were determined to keep their land. They wreaked their own vengeance on the policy of col-

lectivization by slaughtering more than 100 million horses and cattle between 1929 and 1933. The situation in the countryside amounted to nothing less than open warfare. The peasant resistance caused Stalin to call a brief halt to the process in March 1930. He justified the slowdown on the grounds of "dizziness from success."

Soon thereafter the drive to collectivize the farms was renewed with vehemence, and the costs remained very high. As many as ten million peasants were killed, and millions of others were sent forcibly to collective farms or labor camps. Initially, because of the turmoil on the land, agricultural production fell. There was famine in 1932 and 1933. Milk and meat remained in short supply because of the livestock slaughter. Yet Stalin persevered. The uprooted peasants were moved to thousand-acre collective farms. The machinery for these units was provided by the state through machine-tractor stations. In this fashion the state retained control over major farm machines. That monopoly was a powerful weapon.

The upheaval of collectivization did change Russian farming in a very dramatic way. In 1928 approximately 98 per cent of Russian farmland consisted of small peasant holdings. Ten years later, despite all the opposition, over 90 per cent of the land had been collectivized, and the quantity of farm produce directly handled by the government had risen by 40 per cent. Those shifts in control meant that the government now had primary direction over the food supply. The farmers and peasants could no longer determine whether there would be stability or unrest in the cities. Stalin and the Communist Party had won the battle of the wheat fields, but they had not solved the problem of producing sufficient quantities of grain. That difficulty has continued to plague the Soviet Union to the present day.

THE FIVE-YEAR PLANS. The revolution in agriculture had been undertaken for the sake of industrialization. The increased grain supply was to feed the labor force and provide exports to finance the imports required for industrial development. The scope of the industrial achievement of the Soviet Union between 1928 and World War II stands as one of the most striking accomplishments of the twentieth century. Russia made a more rapid advance toward economic growth than any other nation in the Western world has ever achieved during any similar period of time. By even the conservative estimates of Western observers, Soviet indus-

❧ Stalin Explains the Problem of Agriculture

> By the late 1920s Stalin had changed his earlier views and had decided that the Soviet Union must industrialize rapidly. This shift meant that the agricultural sector must also be modernized in order to feed industrial workers and to pay for needed imports. Stalin saw the means to improved farming in the large-scale collectivization of agriculture and the introduction of farm machinery. When implemented, this policy led to widespread peasant resistance in the countryside.

The characteristic feature of the present state of our national economy is that we are faced by the fact of an excessive lag in the rate of development of grain farming behind the rate of development of industry, while at the same time the demand for marketable grain on the part of the growing towns and industrial areas is increasing by leaps and bounds. The task then is not to lower the rate of development of industry to the level of the development of grain farming . . . , but to bring the rate of development of grain farming into line with the rate of development of industry and to raise the rate of development of grain farming to a level that will guarantee rapid progress of the entire national economy, both industry and agriculture.

Either we accomplish this task, and thereby solve the grain problem, or we do not accomplish it, and then a rupture between the socialist town and the small-peasant countryside will be inevitable.

. . . .

What ways and means are necessary to accelerate the rate of development of agriculture in general, and of grain farming in particular?

There are three such ways, or channels:

(a) By increasing crop yields and enlarging the area sown by the individual poor and middle peasants.

(b) By further development of collective farms.

(c) By enlarging the old and establishing new state farms.

. . . .

I should like to draw your attention to the collective farms, and especially to the state farms, as levers which facilitate the reconstruction of agriculture on a new technical basis, causing a revolution in the minds of the peasants and helping them to shake off conservatism, routine. The appearance of tractors, large agricultural machines and tractor columns in our grain regions cannot but have its effect on the surrounding peasant farms. Assistance rendered the surrounding peasants in the way of seed, machines and tractors will undoubtedly be appreciated by the peasants and taken as a sign of the power and strength of the Soviet State, which is trying to lead them on to the high road of a substantial improvement of agriculture.

J. Stalin, *Collected Works*, Vol. 2 (Moscow: Foreign Language Publishing House, 1952–1956), pp. 268–269, 272, 279. Originally written in 1928.

trial production rose approximately 400 per cent between 1928 and 1940. Emphasis was placed on the production of iron, steel, coal, electrical power, tractors, combines, railway cars, and other heavy machinery. Few consumer goods were produced. The labor for this development was supplied internally. Capital was raised from the export of grain even at the cost of internal shortage. The technology was generally borrowed from already-industrialized nations.

The organizational vehicle for industrialization was a series of Five-Year Plans first begun in 1928.

The State Planning Commission, or Gosplan, oversaw the program. It set goals of production and organized the economy to meet them. The task of coordinating all facets of production was immensely difficult and complicated. Deliveries of materials from mines or factories had to be assured before the next unit could carry out its part of the plan. There was many a slip between the cup and the lip. The troubles in the countryside were harmful. A vast program of propaganda was undertaken to sell the Five-Year Plans to the Russian people and to elicit cooperation. However, the

Russian collective farmers on their way to work in 1931. Stalin's forced collectivization of Russian agriculture gave the Soviet government control of the food supply, but it also led to the Soviet Union's chronic inability to produce enough grain to feed its citizens. [Wide World Photos.]

industrial labor force soon became subject to regimentation similar to that being imposed on the peasants. By the close of the 1930s the accomplishment of the three Five-Year Plans was truly impressive and probably allowed the Soviet Union to survive the German invasion. Industries that had never existed in Russia now challenged and in some cases, such as tractor production, surpassed their counterparts in the rest of the world. Large, new industrial cities had been built and populated by hundreds of thousands of people.

Many non-Russian contemporaries looked at the Soviet economic experiment quite uncritically. While the capitalist world lay in the throes of the Depression, the Soviet economy had grown at a

A tractor station on a Russian collective farm. One of the aims of Soviet agricultural policy was to increase the productivity of Russian farms by mechanizing agriculture. Mechanization also led to increased state control, since the collectives had to rent all machinery from the state. [Sovfoto.]

pace never realized in the West. The American writer Lincoln Steffens reported after a trip to Russia, "I have seen the future and it works." Beatrice and Sydney Webb, the British Fabian Socialists, spoke of "a new civilization" in the Soviet Union. These and other similar writers ignored the shortages in consumer goods and the poor housing. More importantly, they seem to have had little idea of the social cost of the Soviet achievement. Millions of human beings had been killed and millions more uprooted. The total picture of suffering and human loss during those years will probably never be known; however, the deprivation and sacrifice of Soviet citizens far exceeded anything described by Marx and Engels in relation to nineteenth-century industrialization in western Europe.

The internal difficulties caused by collectivization and industrialization led Stalin to make an important shift in foreign policy. In 1934 he began to fear that the nation might be left isolated against future aggression by Nazi Germany. The Soviet Union was not yet strong enough to withstand such an attack. Consequently that year he ordered the Comintern to permit Communist parties in other countries to cooperate with noncommunist political parties against Nazism and Fascism. This marked a reversal of the Comintern policy established by Lenin as part of the Twenty-one Conditions in 1919. The new Stalinist policy originating from Moscow allowed the formation of the Popular Front government in France. After more than a decade of vicious rivalry between Communists and democratic Socialists, for a few years the two groups would attempt to cooperate against the common right-wing foe.

The Purges

Stalin's decisions to industrialize rapidly, to move against the peasants, and to reverse the Comintern policy did arouse internal political opposition. They were all departures from the policies of Lenin. In 1929 Stalin forced Bukharin, the fervent supporter of the NEP and his own former ally, off the Politburo. Little detailed information is known about further opposition, but it does seem to have existed among lower-level party followers of Bukharin and other previous opponents of rapid industrialization. Sometime in 1933 Stalin began to fear loss of control over the party apparatus and the emergence of possibly effective rivals. These

fears were probably produced as much by his own paranoia as by real plots. Nevertheless they resulted in the Great Purges, one of the most mysterious and horrendous political events of this century. The purges were not understood at the time and have not been fully comprehended either inside or outside the Soviet Union to the present day.

On December 1, 1934, Sergei Kirov (1888–1934), the popular party chief of Leningrad (formerly Saint Petersburg and Petrograd) and a member of the Politburo, was assassinated. In the wake of the shooting thousands of people were arrested, and still larger numbers were expelled from the party and sent to labor camps. At the time it was believed that Kirov had been murdered by opponents of the regime. Direct or indirect complicity in the crime became the normal accusation against the persons whom Stalin attacked. It now seems practically certain that Stalin himself authorized Kirov's assassination in fear of eventual rivalry with the Leningrad leader.

The purges after Kirov's death were just the beginning of a larger process. Between 1936 and 1938 a series of spectacular show trials were held in Moscow. Previous high Soviet leaders, including former members of the Politburo, publicly confessed all manner of political crimes. They were convicted and executed. It is still not certain why they made their palpably false confessions. Still other leaders and lower-level party members were tried in private and shot. Thousands of people received no trial at all. The purges touched persons in all areas of party life. There was apparently little rhyme or reason to why some were executed, others sent to labor camps, and still others left unmolested. After the civilian party members had been purged, the prosecutors turned against the army. Important officers, including heroes of the civil war, were sent to their deaths. Within the party itself hundreds of thousands of members were expelled, and applicants for membership were removed from the rolls. The exact numbers of executions, imprisonments, and expulsions are unknown but certainly ran into the millions.

The trials and purges astonished Western observers. Nothing quite like this phenomenon had been seen before. Political murders and executions were not new, but the absurd confessions were novel. The scale of the political turmoil was also unprecedented. The Russians themselves did not believe or comprehend what was occurring. There existed no national emergency or crisis. There

By the late 1930s the cult of Stalin was an ever-present fact of Soviet life. Even at beach re-sorts his picture was always near. In this 1950 photograph swimmers in the Black Sea carry large pictures of him on small rafts. Notice the war ships in the background. [Sovfoto.]

were only accusations of sympathy for Trotsky or of complicity in Kirov's murder or of other name-less crimes. If a rational explanation is to be sought, it probably must be found in Stalin's concern over his own power. In effect, the purges created a new party structure absolutely loyal to him. The "old Bolsheviks" of the October Revolution were among his earliest targets. They and others active in the first years of the revolution knew how far Stalin had moved from Lenin's policies. New, younger members appeared to replace all of the party members executed or expelled. The newcomers had little knowledge of old Russia or of the ideals of the original Bolsheviks. They had not been loyal to Lenin, to Trotsky, or to any Soviet leader except Stalin himself.

Scope of the Dictatorships

By the middle of the 1930s dictators of the right and the left had established themselves across much of Europe. Political tyranny was hardly new to Europe, but several factors combined to give these rulers unique characteristics. They drew their immediate support from well-organized polit-ical parties. Except for the Bolsheviks, these were mass parties. The roots of support for the dictators lay in nationalism, the social and economic frustra-tion of the Depression, and political ideologies that promised to transform the social and political or-ders. As long as the new rulers seemed successful, they were not lacking in support. They had in the eyes of many citizens brought an end to the pettiness of everyday politics.

After coming to power, these dictators possessed a practical monopoly over mass communications. Through the armies, police forces, and party discipline they also held a monopoly on terror and coercive power. They could propagandize large populations and compel large groups of people to obey them and their followers. Finally, as a result of the second Industrial Revolution, they commanded a vast amount of technology and a capacity for immense destruction. Earlier rulers in Europe may have shared the ruthless ambitions of Hitler, Mussolini, and Stalin, but they had not found at their disposal the ready implements of physical force to impose their wills. Mass political support, monopoly of police and military power, and technological capacity meant that the dictators of the 1930s held more extensive sway over their nations than any other group of rulers who had ever governed on the Continent. Soon the issue would become whether they would be able to maintain peace among themselves and with their democratic neighbors.

Suggested Readings

W. S. ALLEN, *The Nazi Seizure of Power: The Experience of a Single German Town,* 1930–1935 (1965). A classic treatment of Nazism in a microcosmic setting.

N. BRANSON AND M. HEINEMANN, *Britain in the Nineteen Thirties* (1971). Primarily considers the social and economic problems of the day.

J. COLTON, *Léon Blum: Humanist in Politics* (1966). One of the best biographies of any twentieth-century political figure.

R. CONQUEST, *The Great Terror: Stalin's Purges of the Thirties* (1968). The best treatment of the subject to this date.

G. CRAIG, *Germany, 1866–1945* (1978). An important new survey.

I. DEUTSCHER, *Stalin: A Political Biography,* 2nd ed. (1967). The best biography in English.

M. DOBB, *Soviet Economic Development Since 1917,* 6th ed. (1966). A basic introduction.

H. HOLBORN, *A History of Modern Germany: 1840–1945* (1969). A very comprehensive treatment.

C. KINDLEBERGER, *The World in Depression,* 1929–1939 (1973). An account by a leading economist whose analysis is comprehensible to the layperson.

D. LANDES, *The Unbound Prometheus: Technological Change and Industrial Development in Western Europe from 1750 to the Present* (1969). Includes an excellent analysis of both the Great Depression and the few areas of economic growth.

W. LAQUEUR AND G. L. MOSSE (Eds.), *The Great Depression* (1970). A useful collection of articles.

V. R. LORWIN, *The French Labor Movement* (1954). A good introduction.

D. SCHOENBAUM, *Hitler's Social Revolution: Class and Status in Nazi Germany* (1966). A fascinating analysis of Hitler's appeal to various social classes.

D. MACK SMITH, *Mussolini's Roman Empire* (1976). A general description of the Fascist regime in Italy.

A. SOLZHENITSYN, *The Gulag Archipelago,* 3 vols. (1974–1979). A major examination of the labor camps under Stalin by one of the most important of contemporary Russian writers.

Reference should also be made to the works cited in Chapter 30.

976

32 World War II and the Cold War

Again the Road to War (1933 — 1939)

World War I and the Versailles Treaty in and of themselves had only a marginal relationship to the world depression of the 1930s. But in Germany, where the reparations settlement had contributed to the vast inflation of 1923, economic and social discontent focused on the Versailles settlement as the cause of all ills. Throughout the late 1920s Adolf Hitler and the Nazi Party had never ceased denouncing Versailles as the source of all Germany's trouble, and the economic woes of the early 1930s seemed to bear them out. Nationalism and attention to the social question, along with party discipline, had been the sources of Nazi success. They continued to influence Hitler's foreign policy

Nuremburg, 1945. By the end of the war, Nuremburg, which had been the scene of the annual Nazi Party rally and was soon to witness the trial of the leading Nazis as war criminals, lay in ruins. The allied bombings had reduced most of Germany's cities to heaps of rubble. [National Archives.]

after he became chancellor in early 1933. Moreover the Nazi destruction of the Weimar Constitution and of political opposition meant that to an extraordinary degree German foreign policy lay in Hitler's own hands. Consequently it is important to know what his goals were and what plans he had for achieving them.

Hitler's Goals

For almost twenty years after the outbreak of World War II there was general agreement that the war was the outcome of Hitler's expansionist ambitions, which might have been unlimited and which certainly included vast conquests in eastern Europe and dominance of the European continent. A more recent view is that Hitler was not very much different from any other German statesman, wanting only a revision of Germany's eastern boundaries, elimination of the restrictions of the Versailles Treaty, "and then to make Germany the greatest power in Europe by her natural weight."[1]

[1] A. J. P. Taylor, *The Origins of the Second World War* (New York: Atheneum, 1968), p. 70.

977

❧ Hitler Describes His Goals in Foreign Policy

From his early career, Hitler had certain long-term general views and goals. They were set forth in his *Mein Kampf*, which appeared in 1925, and included consolidation of the German *Volk*, provision of more land for the Germans, and contempt for such "races" as Slavs and Jews. Here are some of Hitler's views on land.

The National Socialist movement must strive to eliminate the disproportion between our population and our area—viewing this latter as a source of food as well as a basis for power politics—between our historical past and the hopelessness of our present impotence. . . .

The demand for restoration of the frontiers of 1914 is a political absurdity of such proportions and consequences as to make it seem a crime. Quite aside from the fact that the Reich's frontiers in 1914 were anything but logical. For in reality they were neither complete in the sense of embracing the people of German nationality, nor sensible with regard to geomilitary expediency. . . .

As opposed to this, we National Socialists must hold unflinchingly to our aim in foreign policy, namely, *to secure for the German people the land and soil to which they are entitled on this earth. . . .*

. . . The soil on which some day German generations of peasants can beget powerful sons will sanc-

tion the investment of the sons of today, and will some day acquit the responsible statesmen of blood-guilt and sacrifice of the people, even if they are persecuted by their contemporaries. . . .

Much as all of us today recognize the necessity of a reckoning with France, it would remain ineffectual in the long run if it represented the whole of our aim in foreign policy. It can and will achieve meaning only if it offers the rear cover for an enlargement of our people's living space in Europe. . . .

If we speak of soil in Europe today, we can primarily have in mind only Russia *and her vassal border states. . . .*

. . . See to it that the strength of our nation is founded, not on colonies, but on the soil of our European homeland. Never regard the Reich as secure unless for centuries to come it can give every scion of our people his own parcel of soil. Never forget that the most sacred right on this earth is a man's right to have earth to till with his own hands, and the most sacred sacrifice the blood that a man sheds for this earth.

Adolf Hitler, *Mein Kampf*, trans. by Ralph Manheim (Boston: Houghton, Mifflin, 1943), pp. 646, 649, 652, 653, 656.

The same view asserts that Hitler did not have a consistent plan in foreign policy but was an opportunist who went the way that events and opportunity took him, emphasizing his own statement: "I go the way that Providence dictates with the assurance of a sleepwalker."[2]

The truth appears to be a combination of these apparently contradictory views. From the first expression of his goals in *Mein Kampf* to his last days in the bunker where he died, Hitler's racial theories and goals held the central place in his thought.

[2] Quoted by Alan Bullock in "Hitler and the Origins of the Second World War," in E. M. Robertson (Ed.), *The Origins of the Second World War* (London: Macmillan, 1971), p. 192.

He meant to go far beyond Germany's 1914 boundaries, which were the limit of the vision of his predecessors. He meant to bring the entire German people *(Volk)*, understood as a racial group, together into a single nation. The new Germany would include all the Germanic parts of the old Hapsburg Empire, including Austria. This virile and growing nation would need more space to live *(Lebensraum)*, which would be taken from the Slavs, a lesser race, fit only for servitude. The new Germany would be purified by the removal of the Jews, another inferior race in Nazi theory. The plan always required the conquest of Poland and the Ukraine as the primary areas for the settlement of Germans and for the provision of badly needed food. Neither *Mein Kampf* nor later statements of policy were blueprints for action. Hitler was a brilliant improviser who sought after and made good use of opportunities as they arose, but he never lost sight of his goal, which would almost certainly require a major war.

THE DESTRUCTION OF VERSAILLES. When Hitler came to power, Germany was far too weak to permit the direct approach. The first problem was to shake off the fetters of Versailles and to make Germany a formidable military power. In October of 1933 Germany withdrew from an international disarmament conference and also from the League of Nations. Hitler argued that because the other powers had not disarmed as they had promised, it was wrong to keep Germany helpless. These acts alarmed the French but were merely symbolic. In January of 1934 Germany made a nonaggression pact with Poland that was of greater concern, for it put into question France's chief means of containing the Germans. At last, in March 1935, Hitler formally renounced the disarmament provisions of the Versailles Treaty with the formation of a German air force, and soon he reinstated conscription, which aimed at an army of half a million men.

His path was made easier by growing evidence that the League of Nations was ineffective as a device for keeping the peace and that collective security was a myth. In September 1931 Japan occupied Manchuria, provoking an appeal to the League of Nations by China. The league responded by sending out a commission under the Earl of Lytton. The Lytton Report condemned the Japanese for resorting to force, but the powers were unwilling to impose sanctions. Japan withdrew from the league and kept control of Manchuria.

When Hitler announced his decision to rearm Germany, the league formally condemned that action, but it took no action to prevent Germany's rearming. The response of France and Britain was hostile, but they felt unable to object because they had not carried out their own promises to disarm. Instead, they met wth Mussolini in June 1935 to form the so-called Stresa Front, making an agreement to use force to maintain the status quo in Europe. But Britain, desperate to maintain superiority at sea, even contrary to the Stresa accords and at the expense of French security needs, soon made a separate naval agreement with Hitler, allowing him to rebuild the German fleet to 35 per cent of the

THE COMING OF WORLD WAR II

1919
June	The Versailles Treaty

1923
January	France occupies the Ruhr

1925
October	The Locarno Agreements

1931
Spring	Onset of the Great Depression in Europe

1933
January	Hitler comes to power
October	Germany withdraws from the League of Nations

1935
March	Hitler renounces disarmament, starts an air force, and begins conscription
October	Mussolini attacks Ethiopia

1936
March	Germany reoccupies and remilitarizes the Rhineland
July	Outbreak of the Spanish Civil War
October	Formation of the Rome–Berlin Axis

1938
March	*Anschluss* with Austria
September	The Munich Conference and partition of Czechoslovakia

1939
March	Hitler occupies Prague
	France and Great Britain guarantee Polish independence
August	The Nazi–Soviet pact
September 1	Germany invades Poland
September 3	Britain and France declare war on Germany

British navy, and Italy's expansionist ambitions in Africa soon brought it into conflict with the Western powers. Hitler had taken a major step toward his goal without provoking serious opposition.

Italy Attacks Ethiopia

The Italian attack on Ethiopia made the impotence of the League of Nations and the timidity of the Allies even clearer. Using a border incident as an excuse, Mussolini attacked Ethiopia in October 1935 to avenge a humiliating defeat the Italians had suffered in 1896, to begin the restoration of Roman imperial glory, and, perhaps, to turn the thoughts of Italians away from the corruption of the Fascist regime and their economic misery. France and Britain were eager to appease Mussolini in order to offset the growing power of Germany. They were prepared to allow him the substance of conquest if he would only maintain Ethiopia's formal independence, but for Mussolini the form was more important than the substance. His attack outraged opinion in the West, and the French and British governments were forced at least to appear to resist. The League of Nations condemned Italian aggression and, for the first time, voted economic sanctions. It imposed an arms embargo that limited loans and credits to and imports from Italy. But Britain and France were afraid of alienating Mussolini, so they refused to place an embargo on oil, the one economic sanction that could have prevented Italian victory. Even more importantly, the British fleet did not prevent the movement of Italian troops and munitions through the Suez Canal. The results of this wavering policy were disastrous. The League of Nations and collective security were totally discredited, and Mussolini was alienated as well. He now turned to Germany, and by November 1, 1936, he could speak publicly of a Rome–Berlin "Axis."

Remilitarization of the Rhineland

No less important a result of the Ethiopian affair was its effect on Hitler's evaluation of the strength and determination of the Western powers. On March 7, 1936, he took his greatest risk yet, sending a small armed force into the demilitarized Rhineland. This was a breach not only of the Versailles Treaty but of the Locarno Agreements of 1925 as well, agreements that Germany had made voluntarily. It also removed one of the most important elements of French security. France and Britain had every right to resist, and the French espe-

Striking a typically bombastic pose, Mussolini addressed Italian troops about to embark for the war in Ethiopia in 1935. [United Press International.]

cially had a claim to retain the only element of security left after the failure of the Allies to guarantee her defense, yet neither did anything but make a feeble protest with the League of Nations. British opinion would not permit any support for France. The French themselves were paralyzed by internal division and by military ideas that concentrated on defense and feared taking the offensive. Both countries were further weakened by a growing pacifism.

In retrospect it appears that the Allies lost a great opportunity to stop Hitler before he became a serious menace. The failure of his gamble, taken against the advice of his generals, might have led to his overthrow; at the least it would have made German expansion to the east dangerous if not impossible. Nor is there much reason to doubt that the French army could easily have routed the tiny German force in the Rhineland. As the German General Alfred Jodl said some years later, "The French covering army would have blown us to bits."[3]

A Germany that was rapidly rearming and had a defensible western frontier presented a completely new problem to the Western powers. Their response was the policy of "appeasement." It was based on the assumption that Germany had real grievances, that Hitler's goals were limited and ultimately acceptable, and that the correct policy was to bring about revision by negotiation and conces-

sion before a crisis could arise and lead to war. Behind this approach was the general horror at the thought of another war. Memories of the losses in the last war were still fresh, and the advent of aerial bombardment made the thought of a new war terrifying. A firmer policy, moreover, would have required rapid rearmament, but British leaders especially were reluctant to pursue this path because of the expense and because of the widespread belief that the arms race had been a major cause of the last war. As Germany armed, the French huddled behind their newly constructed defensive wall, the Maginot Line, and the British hoped things would go well.

The Spanish Civil War

The new European alignment that found the Western democracies on one side and the fascist states on the other was made clearer by the Spanish Civil War, which broke out in July 1936. In 1931 the Spaniards had driven out their king and established a democratic republic. The new government followed a program of moderate reform that antagonized landowners, the Catholic church, nationalists, and conservatives without satisfying the demands of peasants, workers, Catalan separatists, or radicals. Elections in February 1936 brought to power a Spanish Popular Front government ranging from republicans of the left to communists and anarchists. The defeated groups, especially the Falangists, the Spanish version of fascists, would not accept defeat at the polls. In

[3] Quoted by W. L. Shirer in *The Collapse of the Third Republic*, (New York: Simon & Schuster, 1969), p. 281.

The Spanish Civil War. Here Loyalist volunteers attack Franco's forces in the medieval Moorish fortress of the Alcazar of Toledo. Although closely besieged for ten weeks, the Alcazar held out until relieved by Franco's army in September 1936. The war itself continued with increasing savagery until Franco's victory in March 1939. [United Press International.]

Pablo Picasso's Guernica is the artist's vision of the terror-bombing in the Spanish Civil War of the Basque town of Guernica in northern Spain on April 26, 1937 by German airplanes aiding Franco—one of the first calculated aerial bombardments of civilians. It was painted by Picasso in May and June 1937. [Prado.]

July General Francisco Franco (1892–1975) led an army from Spanish Morocco in rebellion against the republic.

Thus began a civil war that lasted almost three years, cost hundreds of thousands of lives, and provided a training ground for World War II. Germany and Italy aided Franco with troops, airplanes, and supplies. The Soviet Union sent airplanes, equipment, and advisers to the republicans. Liberals and leftists from Europe and America volunteered to fight in the republican ranks against fascism.

The civil war, fought on blatantly ideological lines, had a profound effect on world politics. It brought Germany and Italy closer together, leading to the Rome–Berlin Axis Pact. The Axis powers were joined in the same year by Japan in the Anti-Comintern Pact, ostensibly against communism but really a new and powerful diplomatic alliance. Western Europe, especially France, had a great interest in preventing Spain from falling into the hands of a fascist regime closely allied with Germany and Italy, but the appeasement mentality reigned. Although international law permitted the sale of weapons and munitions to the legitimate republican government, France and Britain forbade the export of war materials to either side, and

the United States passed new neutrality legislation to the same end. When the city of Barcelona fell to Franco early in 1939, the fascists had won effective control of Spain.

Austria and Czechoslovakia

Hitler made good use of his new friendship with Mussolini. He had always planned to make his native Austria a part of the new Germany. In 1934 the Nazi Party in Austria assassinated the prime minister and tried to seize power. Mussolini, not yet allied with Hitler, and suspicious of German intentions, moved an army to the Brenner Pass in the Alps between Austria and Italy, preventing German intervention and causing the coup to fail. In 1938 the new diplomatic situation encouraged Hitler to try again. He seems to have hoped to achieve his goal by propaganda, bullying, and threats, but the Austrian Premier Kurt Schuschnigg refused to collapse. On March 9 the premier announced a plebiscite on the following Sunday, March 13, in which the Austrian people could decide the question of union with Germany for themselves. Hitler dared not let the plebiscite take place and sent his army into Austria on March 12. To his great relief Mussolini made no objection,

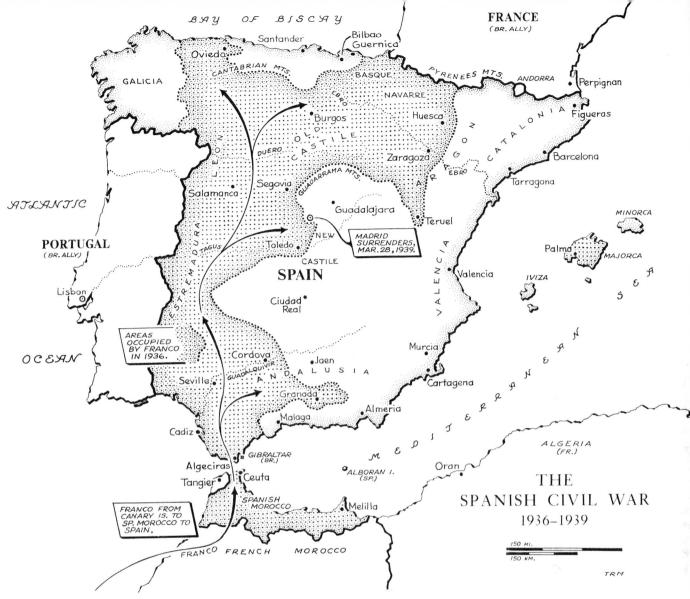

MAP 32.1 *The dotted area on the map shows the large portion of Spain quickly overrun by Franco's insurgent armies during the first year of the war. In the following two years, progress came more slowly for the fascists as the war became a kind of international rehearsal for the coming World War II. Madrid's fall to Franco in the spring of 1939 had been preceded by that of Barcelona a few weeks earlier.*

and Hitler could march into Vienna to the cheers of his Austrian sympathizers. This peaceful outcome was fortunate for the Germans. Their army was far from ready for combat, and a high percentage of German tanks and trucks broke down along the roads of Austria.

The *Anschluss,* or union of Germany and Austria, was another clear violation of Versailles, but the treaty was now a dead letter; the latest violation produced no reaction from the West. It had great strategic significance, however, especially for the position of Czechoslovakia, one of the bulwarks of French security. The union with Austria left the Czechs surrounded by Germany on three sides.

The very existence of Czechoslovakia was an affront to Hitler. It was democratic and pro-Western; it had been created as a check on Germany and was allied both to France and to the Soviet Union. It also contained about 3.5 million Germans who lived in the Sudetenland near the German border. These Germans had been the dominant class in the old Austro-Hungarian Empire and resented their new minority position. Supported by Hitler and led by Konrad Henlein, the chief Nazi in Czechoslovakia, they made ever-increasing demands for privileges and autonomy within the Czech state. The Czechs made many concessions, but Hitler did not want to improve the lot of the Sudeten Germans. He wanted to destroy Czechoslovakia. He told Henlein, "We must always demand so much that we can never be satisfied."[4]

As pressure mounted, the Czechs grew nervous. In May 1938 they received false rumors of an imminent attack by Germany and mobilized their army. The French, British, and Russians all issued warnings that they would support the Czechs. Hitler, who had not planned an attack at that time, was forced to make a public denial of any designs on Czechoslovakia. The public humiliation infuriated him, and from that moment he planned a military attack on the Czechs. The affair stiffened Czech resistance, but it appears to have frightened the French and British. The French, as had become their custom, deferred to British leadership. The British prime minister was Neville Chamberlain, a man thoroughly committed to the policy of appeasement. He was determined not to allow Britain to come close to war again. He put pressure on the Czechs to make further concessions to Germany, but no concession was enough.

On September 12, 1938, Hitler made a provocative speech at the Nuremberg Nazi Party rally. His assertions led to rioting in the Sudetenland and the declaration of martial law by the Czech government. German intervention seemed imminent. Chamberlain, aged sixty-nine, had never flown before, but between September 15 and September 29 he made three flights to Germany in an attempt to appease Hitler at Czech expense and thus to avoid war. At Hitler's mountain retreat, Berchtesgaden, on September 15 Chamberlain accepted the separation of the Sudetenland from Czechoslovakia. And he and the French premier, Daladier, forced the Czechs to agree by threatening to desert them if they did not. A week later Chamberlain flew yet again to Germany only to find that Hitler had raised his demands: he wanted cession of the Sudetenland in three days and immediate occupation by the German army.

[4]Quoted by Alan Bullock in *Hitler, A Study in Tyranny* (New York: Harper & Row, 1962), p. 443.

A Nazi poster of 1939 proclaims: "German women unite! German girls, you belong to us!" [Library of Congress.]

Munich

Chamberlain returned to England thinking that he had failed, and France and Britain prepared for war. Almost at the last moment Mussolini proposed a conference of Germany, Italy, France, and Britain. It met on September 29 at Munich. Hitler received almost everything he had demanded. The Sudetenland, the key to Czech security, became part of Germany, thus depriving the Czechs of any chance of self-defense. In return the powers agreed to spare the rest of Czechoslovakia. Hitler promised, "I have no more territorial demands to make in Europe." Chamberlain returned to England with the Munich agreement and told a cheering crowd that he had brought "peace with honour. I believe it is peace for our time."

Even in the short run the appeasement of Hitler at Munich was a failure. Soon Poland and Hungary tore bits of territory from Czechoslovakia, and the

The Munich Conference, October 1938. The figures in front are, from left to right, Chamberlain of Great Britain, Daladier of France, Hitler of Germany, and Mussolini of Italy. [Imperial War Museum, London.]

Slovaks demanded autonomy. Finally, on March 15, 1939, Hitler broke his promise and occupied Prague, putting an end to Czechoslovakia and to illusions that his only goal was to restore Germans to the Reich. Defenders of the appeasers have argued that their policy was justified because it bought valuable time in which the West could prepare for war. But that argument was not made by the appeasers themselves, who thought that they were achieving peace, nor does the evidence appear to support it.

If the French and the British had been willing to attack Germany from the west while the Czechs fought in their own defense, there is reason to think that their efforts might have been successful. High officers in the German army were opposed to Hitler's risky policies and might have overthrown him. Even failing such developments, a war begun in October 1938 would have forced Hitler to fight without the friendly neutrality and material assistance of the Soviet Union and without the resources of eastern Europe that became available to him as a result of appeasement. If, moreover, the West ever had a chance of alliance with the Soviet Union against Hitler, the exclusion of the Russians from Munich and the appeasement policy helped de-

Italian Fascists giving Hitler their famous dagger salute during his state visit to Italy in May 1938. The visit cemented the alliance between the German and Italian dictators. [United Press International.]

In March 1939 the Germans occupied Prague and extinguished Czech independence [National Archives.]

stroy it. Munich remains an example of short-sighted policy that helped bring on a war in disadvantageous circumstances because of the very fear of war and the failure to prepare for it.

Hitler's occupation of Prague discredited appeasement in the eyes of the British people. In the summer of 1939 a Gallup Poll showed that three quarters of the British public believed it worth a war to stop Hitler. Though Chamberlain himself had not lost all faith in his policy, he felt the need to respond to public opinion, and he responded to excess. It was apparent that Poland was the next target of German expansion. In the spring of 1939 the Germans put pressure on Poland to restore the formerly German city of Danzig and to allow a railroad and a highway through the Polish Corridor to connect East Prussia with the rest of Germany. When the Poles would not yield, the usual propaganda campaign began, and the pressure mounted. On March 31 Chamberlain announced a Franco-British guarantee of Polish independence. Hitler appears to have expected to fight a war with Poland but not with the Western allies, for he did not take their guarantee seriously. He had come to hold their leaders in contempt. He knew that both countries were unprepared for war and that large segments of their populations were opposed to fighting a war to save Poland.

Belief in the Polish guarantee was further undermined by the inability of France and Britain to get effective help to the Poles. An attack on Germany's western front was out of the question for the French, still dominated by the defensive mentality of the Maginot Line. The only way to defend Poland was to bring Russia into the alliance against Hitler, but a Russian alliance posed many problems. Each side was profoundly suspicious of the other. The French and the British were hostile to Russia's communist ideology, and since Stalin's purge of the officer corps of the Red Army, they

❧ Winston Churchill Warns of the Effects of the Munich Agreement

Churchill delivered his speech on the Munich agreement before the House of Commons on October 5, 1938. Following are excerpts from it.

The Chancellor of the Exchequer [Sir John Simon] said it was the first time Herr Hitler had been made to retract—I think that was the word—in any degree. We really must not waste time after all this long Debate upon the difference between the positions reached at Berchtesgaden, at Godesberg and at Munich. They can be very simply epitomized, if the House will permit me to vary the metaphor. One pound was demanded at the pistol's point. When it was given, £2 were demanded at the pistol's point. Finally, the dictator consented to take £1 17s. 6d. and the rest in promises of good will for the future. . . .

.   .   .   .

I do not grudge our loyal, brave people, who were ready to do their duty no matter what the cost, who never flinched under the strain of last week—I do not grudge them the natural, spontaneous outburst of joy and relief when they learned that the hard ordeal would no longer be required of them at the moment; but they should know the truth. They should know that there has been gross neglect and deficiency in our defenses; they should know that we have sustained a defeat without a war, the consequences of which will travel far with us along our road; they should know that we have passed an awful milestone in our history, when the whole equilibrium of Europe has been deranged, and that the terrible words have for the time being been pronounced against the Western democracies: "Thou art weighed in the balance and found wanting." And do not suppose that this is the end. This is only the beginning of the reckoning. This is only the first sip, the first foretaste of a bitter cup which will be proffered to us year by year unless, by a supreme recovery of moral health and martial vigor, we arise again and take our stand for freedom as in the olden time.

Winston S. Churchill, *Blood, Sweat, and Tears* (New York: G. P. Putnam's Sons, 1941), pp. 56, 66.

stood unconvinced of the military value of an alliance with Russia. Besides, the Russians could not help Poland without the right of transit through Romania and the right of entry into Poland. Both nations, suspicious of Russian intentions, and with good reason, refused to grant these rights. As a result Western negotiations with Russia moved forward slowly and cautiously.

Nazi–Soviet Pact

The Russians had at least equally good reason to hesitate. They resented being left out of the Munich agreement. They were annoyed by the low priority the West seemed to give to negotiations with Russia compared with the urgency with which they dealt with Hitler. They feared, quite rightly, that the Western powers meant them to bear the burden of the war against Germany. As a result they opened negotiations with Hitler, and on August 23, 1939, the world was shocked to learn of a Nazi–Soviet nonaggression pact. Its secret provisions, which were easily guessed and soon carried out, divided Poland between the two powers and allowed Russia to take over the Baltic states and to take Bessarabia from Romania. The most bitter ideological enemies had become allies. Communist parties in the West changed their line overnight from the ardent advocacy of resistance to Hitler to a policy of peace and quiet. Ideology gave way to political and military reality. The West offered the

Russians danger without much prospect of gain. Hitler offered Stalin gain without immediate danger. There could be little doubt as to the decision.

The Nazi–Soviet Pact sealed the fate of Poland, and the Franco-British commitment guaranteed a general war. On September 1, 1939, the Germans invaded Poland. Two days later Britain and France declared war on Germany. World War II had begun.

World War II (1939-1945)

World War II has a better claim to its name than its predecessor, for it was truly global. Fighting took place in Europe and Asia, the Atlantic and the Pacific oceans, the Northern and Southern Hemispheres. The demand for the fullest exploitation of material and human resources for increased production, the use of blockades, and the intensive bombing of civilian targets made the war of 1939 even more "total," that is, comprehensive and intense, than that of 1914.

The German Conquest of Europe

The German attack on Poland produced swift success. The new style of "lightning warfare," or *Blitzkrieg*, employed fast-moving, massed armored columns supported by airpower. The Poles were inferior in tanks and planes, and their defense

On the eve of World War II, in August 1939, the Soviet Union and Nazi Germany shocked the rest of the world by signing a non-aggression pact. For years National Socialists and Communists had been the most bitter enemies and regularly hurled insults at each other, but now they came together in a marriage of convenience. This British cartoon by David Low (1891–1963) emphasizes the ironic character of the new relationship.[Cartoon by David Low. By arrangement with the Trustees and the London Evening Standard.]

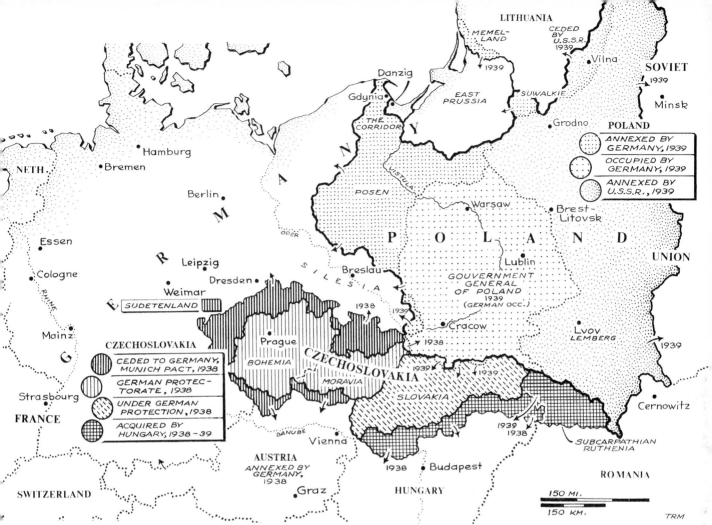

PARTITIONS OF CZECHOSLOVAKIA AND POLAND, 1938–1939

MAP 32.2 *The immediate background of World War II is found in the complex international drama unfolding on Germany's eastern frontier in 1938 and 1939. Germany's expansion inevitably meant the victimization of Austria, Czechoslovakia, and Poland. With the failure of the Western powers' appeasement policy and the signing of a German-Soviet pact, the stage for the war was set.*

soon collapsed. The speed of the German victory astonished everyone, not least the Russians, who hastened to collect their share of the booty before Hitler could deprive them of it. On September 17 they invaded Poland from the east, dividing the country with the Germans. They then forced the encircled Baltic countries to sign treaties with them. By 1940 Estonia, Latvia, and Lithuania were absorbed as constituent republics into the USSR (Union of Soviet Socialist Republics or the Soviet

Union). In November 1940 the Russians invaded Finland, but the Finns put up a surprisingly effective resistance. Although they were finally worn down and compelled to yield territory and bases to Russia, they retained their independence. Russian difficulties in Finland may well have encouraged Hitler to invade the Soviet Union in June 1941, just twenty-two months after the 1939 treaty.

Through the fall of 1939 and the winter of 1939–1940 the western front was quiet. The French huddled behind the Maginot Line while Hitler and Stalin swallowed Poland and the Baltic states. Britain hastily rearmed and organized the traditional naval blockade. Cynics in the West called it the phony war, or "*Sitzkrieg*," but Hitler shattered the stillness in the spring of 1940. In

April, without warning and with swift success, the Germans invaded Denmark and Norway. Hitler's northern front was secure, and he now had both air and naval bases closer to Britain. A month later a combined land and air attack struck Belgium, the Netherlands, and Luxembourg. German airpower and armored divisions were irresistible. The Dutch surrendered in a few days, and the Belgians, though aided by the French and the British, surrendered less than two weeks later. The British and French armies in Belgium were forced to flee to the English Channel to seek escape from the beaches of Dunkerque. By the heroic effort of hundreds of Britons manning small boats, over 200,000 British and 100,000 French soldiers were saved, but casualties were high and much valuable equipment was abandoned.

The Maginot Line ran from Switzerland to the Belgian frontier. Until 1936 the French had ex-pected the Belgians to continue the fortifications along their German border. After Hitler remilitarized the Rhineland without opposition, the Belgians lost faith in their French alliance and returned to neutrality, leaving the Maginot Line exposed on the left flank. Hitler's swift advance through Belgium therefore circumvented France's main line of defense. The French army, poorly and hesitantly led by superannuated generals who lacked a proper understanding of the use of tanks and planes, quickly collapsed. Mussolini, eager to claim the spoils of victory when it was clearly safe to do so, sent an army across the French border on June 10, less than a week before the new French government, under the ancient hero of Verdun, Henri Philippe Pétain, asked for an armistice. In two months Hitler had accomplished what Germany had failed to achieve in four years of bitter fighting in the previous war.

Dunkirk. Late in May 1940 the German army, having broken through the French defenses, reached the coast of the English Channel. The Germans might have destroyed the Allied armies, but their indecision allowed over 200,000 British troops and about two-thirds as many French to escape by sea to England. The British Navy, aided by countless civilian boats, rescued these men from the beach at Dunkirk, France. [Imperial War Museum, London.]

ALL BEHIND YOU, WINSTON

In May 1940 Winston Churchill replaced Neville Chamberlain as Prime Minister of Great Britain. The spirit of appeasement was dead, and David Low's cartoon celebrates the new spirit of determination and resistance Churchill inspired. The recognizable faces in the first three or four rows are those of the then leading British politicians of all parties; in the front row to the right of Churchill, who was a Conservative, are Clement Atlee and Ernest Bevin, the leaders of Labor. Chamberlain is behind Churchill. [Cartoon by David Low. By arrangement with the Trustees and the London Evening Standard.]

The terms of the armistice, signed June 22, 1940, allowed the Germans to occupy more than half of France, including the Atlantic and English Channel coasts. In order to prevent many of the French from fleeing to North Africa to continue the fight, and even more to prevent the French from turning their fleet over to Britain, Hitler left southern France unoccupied. Pétain set up a dictatorial regime at the resort city of Vichy and followed a policy of collaboration with the Germans in order to preserve as much autonomy as possible. Most of the French were too stunned to resist. Many thought that Hitler's victory was certain and saw no alternative to collaboration. A few, most notably General Charles de Gaulle (1890–1969), fled to Britain, where they organized the French National Committee of Liberation, or "Free French." Vichy controlled most of French North Africa and the navy, but the Free French began operating in central Africa and from London beamed messages of hope and defiance to their compatriots in France. As the passage of time dispelled expectations of a quick German victory, a French underground movement arose that organized many forms of resistance.

The Battle of Britain

The fall of France left Britain isolated, and Hitler expected the British to come to terms. He was prepared to allow Britain to retain its empire in return for a free hand for Germany on the Conti-

nent. The British had never been willing to accept such an arrangement and had fought the long and difficult war against Napoleon to prevent the domination of the Continent by a single power. If there was any chance that the British would consider such terms, that chance disappeared when Winston Churchill (1874–1965) replaced Chamberlain as prime minister in May of 1940.

Churchill had been an early and forceful critic of Hitler, the Nazis, and the policy of appeasement. A descendant and biographer of the Duke of Marlborough (1650–1722), who had fought to prevent the domination of Europe by Louis XIV in the seventeenth century, Churchill's sense of history, his feeling for British greatness, and his hatred of tyranny and love of freedom made him reject any thought of compromise. His skill as a speaker and a writer allowed him to infuse the British people with his own courage and determination and to undertake what seemed almost a hopeless fight. Hitler and his allies, including the Soviet Union, controlled all of Europe. Japan was having its way in Asia. The United States was neutral, dominated by isolationist sentiment, and determined to avoid involvement outside the Western Hemisphere.

One of Churchill's greatest achievements was establishing a close relationship with the American President Franklin D. Roosevelt, who found ways to help the British in spite of strong political opposition. In 1940 and 1941, before the United States was at war, America sent military supplies, traded badly needed warships for leases on British naval bases, and even convoyed ships across the Atlantic to help the British survive.

As weeks passed and Britain remained defiant, Hitler was forced to contemplate an invasion, and that required control of the air. The first strikes by the German air force *(Luftwaffe)*, directed against the airfields and fighter planes in southeastern England, began in August 1940. There is reason to think that if these attacks had continued, Germany might soon have gained control of the air and with it the chance of a successful invasion. In early September, however, seeking revenge for some British bombing raids on German cities, the *Luftwaffe* made London its major target. For two months London was bombed every night. Much of the city was destroyed and about fifteen thousand people were killed, but the theories of victory through airpower alone proved vain. Casualties were many times fewer than expected and morale was not shattered. In fact, the bombings brought the Brit-

Women knitting in a bomb shelter in Ramsgate, England. The shelter was cut through a chalk cliff and was sixty feet below the surface. In the late 1930s, as war appeared increasingly likely, the British had made extensive preparations for dealing with air raids. [United Press International.]

ish people together and made them more resolute. At the same time the Royal Air Force (RAF) inflicted heavy losses on the *Luftwaffe*. Aided by the newly developed radar and an excellent system of communications, the Spitfire and Hurricane fighter planes destroyed more than twice as many enemy planes as were lost by the RAF. Hitler had lost the Battle of Britain in the air and was forced to abandon his plans for invasion.

The German Attack on Russia

From the first, the defeat of Russia and the conquest of the Ukraine to provide *Lebensraum* for the German people had been a major goal for Hitler. Even before the assault on Britain he had informed his staff of his intention to attack Russia as soon as conditions were favorable. In December of 1940, even while the bombing of England continued, he ordered his generals to prepare for an invasion of Russia by May 15, 1941. He appears to have thought that a *Blitzkrieg* victory in the east would destroy all hope and bring the British to their senses.

Operation Barbarossa, the code name for the invasion of Russia, was aimed at knocking Russia out of the war before winter could set in. Success depended in part on an early start, but here Hitler's Italian alliance proved costly. Mussolini was jealous of Hitler's success and annoyed by the treatment he had received from the German dictator. Unable to make progress against the French army even while Hitler was crushing the part of it on his own frontier, Mussolini was not allowed any gain at the expense of France or even of French Africa. Instead he launched an attack against the British in Egypt and drove them back some sixty miles. Encouraged by this success, he invaded Greece from his base in Albania (which he had seized in 1939). His purpose was revealed by his remark to his son-in-law, Count Ciano: "Hitler always faces me with a *fait accompli*. This time I am going to pay him back in his own coin. He will find out in the newspapers that I have occupied Greece."[5] But in North Africa the British counterattacked and drove the Italians back into Libya, and the Greeks themselves pushed into Albania. In March 1941 the British sent help to the Greeks, and Hitler was forced to divert his attention to the

[5] Quoted in Gordon Wright, *The Ordeal of Total War, 1939–1945* (New York: Harper & Row, 1968), pp. 35–36.

AXIS EUROPE, 1941

MAP 32.3 *On the eve of the German invasion of the Soviet Union the Germany-Italy Axis bestrode most of Western Europe by annexation, occupation, or alliance—from Norway and Finland in the north to Greece in the south and from Poland to France. Britain, the Soviets, a number of insurgent groups, and, finally, America had before them the long struggle of conquering this Axis "fortress Europe."*

Balkans and to Africa. General Erwin Rommel (1891–1944), later to earn the title "The Desert Fox," went to Africa and soon got the British out of Libya and back into Egypt. In the Balkans the German army swiftly occupied Yugoslavia and crushed

Greek resistance, but the price was a delay of six weeks. The diversion caused by Mussolini's vanity proved to be costly the following winter in the Russian campaign.

Operation Barbarossa was launched against Rus-

Moscow or the Ukraine? Hitler and his generals study a map of the Russian front in August 1941. From left to right are Keitel, Brauchitsch, Warlimont, and Hitler. [Bibliothek für Zeitgeschichte, Stuttgart.]

sia on June 22, 1941, and it came very close to success. In spite of their deep suspicion of Germany and the excuse later offered by apologists for the Soviet Union that the Nazi–Soviet Pact was meant to give Russia time to prepare, the Russians were taken quite by surprise. Stalin appears to have panicked. He had not fortified his frontier, nor had he issued orders for his troops to withdraw when attacked. In the first two days some two thousand planes were destroyed on the ground. By November Hitler had gone further into Russia than Napoleon: the German army stood at the gates of Leningrad, on the outskirts of Moscow, and on the Don River. Of the 4.5 million troops with which the Russians had begun the fighting, they had lost 2.5 million; of their 15,000 tanks only 700 were left. Moscow was in panic, and a German victory seemed imminent.

But the Germans could not deliver the final blow. In August there was a delay in their advance to decide on a course of action. One plan was to drive directly for Moscow and take it before winter. There is some reason to think that such a plan might have worked and brought victory, for unlike the situation in Napoleon's time, Moscow was the hub of the Russian system of transportation. Hitler, however, imposed his own view on his generals and diverted a significant part of his forces to the south. By the time he was ready to return to the offensive near Moscow, it was too late. Winter struck the German army, which was neither dressed nor equipped to face it. Given precious time, Stalin was able to restore order and build defenses for the city. Even more importantly, there

was time for troops to come from Siberia, where they had been placed to check a possible Japanese attack. In November and December the Russians were able to counterattack. The *Blitzkrieg* had turned into a war of attrition, and the Germans began to have visions of Napoleon's retreat.

Hitler's Europe

Hitler often spoke of the "new order" that he meant to impose after he had established his Third Reich throughout Europe. The first two German empires (*Reichs*) were those of Charlemagne in the ninth century and William II in the nineteenth, and Hitler predicted that his own would last for a thousand years. If his organization of Germany before the war is a proper index, he had no single plan of government but relied frequently on intuition and pragmatism. His organization of conquered Europe had the same characteristics of spontaneity and patchwork. Some conquered territory was annexed to Germany; some was administered directly by German officials; some lands were nominally autonomous but were ruled by puppet governments.

The demands and distractions of war and the fact that Hitler's defeat prevented him from fully carrying out his plans make it hard to be sure what his intentions were, but the measures he took before his death provide indications. They give evidence of a regime probably unmatched in history for carefully planned terror and inhumanity. To accomplish his plan of giving *Lebensraum* to the Germans at the expense of people he deemed inferior, Hitler established colonies of Germans in parts of Poland, driving the local people from their land and employing them as cheap labor. He had similar plans on an even higher scale for Russia. The Russians would be driven eastward to central Asia and Siberia; they would be kept in check by frontier colonies of German war veterans, and the more desirable lands of European Russia would be settled by Germans.

Hitler's long-range plans included Germanization as well as colonization. In lands inhabited by people racially akin to the Germans, like the Scandinavian countries, the Netherlands, and Switzerland, the natives would be absorbed into the German nation. Such peoples would be reeducated and purged of dissenting elements, but there would be little or no colonization. He even had plans, only slightly realized, of adopting selected people from the lesser races into the master race.

994

German concentration camps—the dead and the dying as found by Western armies in 1945. The Nazis set up their first concentration camps in Germany to hold the German opponents of their regime, but later, after the war had begun and had moved east into non-German territory, the new camps established in Poland were deliberately planned as part of Hitler's "final solution," the extermination of the Jews, although Jews were not his only victims. Even in those camps not avowedly dedicated to extermination the conditions were brutal in the extreme, and the armies that liberated them in 1945 found in all of them scenes such as those in these photographs. [United Press International Photo.]

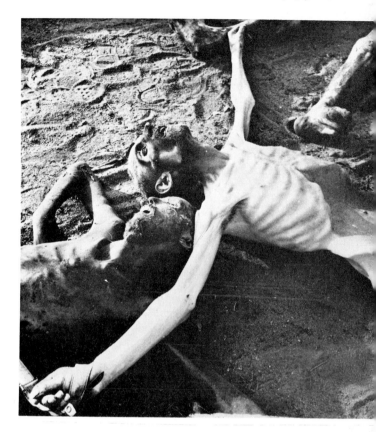

One of these plans involved bringing half a million Ukrainian girls into Germany as servants and finding German husbands for them; about fifteen thousand actually did reach Germany.

In the economic sphere Hitler regarded the conquered lands merely as a source of plunder. From eastern Europe he removed everything useful, including entire industries. In Russia and Poland the Germans simply confiscated the land. In the west the conquered countries were forced to support the occupying army at a rate several times the real cost. The Germans used the profits to buy up everything useful and desirable, stripping the conquered peoples of most necessities. The Nazis were frank about their policies. One of Hitler's high officials said, "Whether nations live in prosperity or starve to death interests me only insofar as we need them as slaves for our culture."[6]

Racism and the Holocaust

The most horrible aspect of the Nazi rule in Europe arose not from military or economic necessity but from the inhumanity and brutality inherent in Hitler's racial doctrines. He considered the Slavs *Untermenschen*, subhuman creatures like beasts who need not be thought of or treated as people. In parts of Poland the upper and professional classes were entirely removed, either jailed, deported, or killed. Schools and churches were closed; marriage was controlled by the Nazis to keep down the Polish birth rate; and harsh living conditions were imposed. In Russia things were even worse. Hitler spoke of his Russian campaign as a war of extermination. Heinrich Himmler, head of Hitler's elite SS guard, planned the elimination of thirty million

[6]Quoted by Gordon Wright, *The Ordeal of Total War, 1939–1945* (New York: Harper & Row, 1968), p. 117.

Slavs to make room for the Germans, and he formed extermination squads for the purpose. The number of Russian prisoners of war and deported civilian workers who died under Nazi rule may have reached six million.

Hitler had special plans for the Jews. He meant to make all Europe *Judenrein* ("free of Jews"). For a time he thought of sending them to the island of Madagascar, but later he arrived at the "final solution of the Jewish problem": extermination. The

An Observer Describes the Mass Murder of Jews in the Ukraine

After World War II some German officers and officials were put on trial at Nuremberg by the victorious powers for crimes they were charged with having committed in the course of the war. The following selections from the testimony of a German construction engineer who witnessed the mass murder of Jews at Dubno in the Ukraine on October 5, 1942, reveal the brutality with which Hitler's attempt at a "final solution of the Jewish problem" was carried out.

On October 5, 1942, when I visited the building office at Dubno, my foreman told me that in the vicinity of the site, Jews from Dubno had been shot in three large pits, each about 30 metres long and 3 metres deep. About 1,500 persons had been killed daily. All the 5,000 Jews who had still been living in Dubno before the pogrom were to be liquidated. As the shooting had taken place in his presence, he was still much upset.

Thereupon, I drove to the site accompanied by my foreman and saw near it great mounds of earth, about 30 metres long and 2 metres high. Several trucks stood in front of the mounds. Armed Ukrainian militia drove the people off the trucks under the supervision of an S.S. man. The militiamen acted as guards on the trucks and drove them to and from the pit. All these people had the regulation yellow patches on the front and back of their clothes, and thus could be recognized as Jews.

My foreman and I went directly to the pits. Nobody bothered us. Now I heard rifle shots in quick succession from behind one of the earth mounds. The people who had got off the trucks—men, women and children of all ages—had to undress upon the orders of an S.S. man, who carried a riding or dog whip. They had to put down their clothes in fixed places, sorted according to shoes, top clothing and underclothing. I saw a heap of shoes of about 800 to 1,000 pairs, great piles of underlinen and clothing.

Without screaming or weeping, these people undressed, stood around in family groups, kissed each other, said farewells, and waited for a sign from an-

other S.S. man, who stood near the pit, also with a whip in his hand. During the fifteen minutes that I stood near I heard no complaint or plea for mercy. I watched a family of about eight persons, a man and a woman both about fifty with their children of about one, eight and ten, and two grown-up daughters of about twenty to twenty-nine. An old woman with snow-white hair was holding the one-year-old child in her arms and singing to it and tickling it. The child was cooing with delight. The couple were looking on with tears in their eyes. The father was holding the hand of a boy about ten years old and speaking to him softly; the boy was fighting his tears. The father pointed to the sky, stroked his head, and seemed to explain something to him.

At that moment the S.S. man at the pit shouted something to his comrade. The latter counted off about twenty persons and instructed them to go behind the earth mound. Among them was the family which I have mentioned. I well remember a girl, slim and with black hair, who, as she passed close to me pointed to herself and said "23." I walked around the mound and found myself confronted by a tremendous grave. People were closely wedged together and lying on top of each other so that only their heads were visible. Nearly all had blood running over their shoulders from their heads. Some of the people shot were still moving. Some were lifting their arms and turning their heads to show that they were still alive. The pit was already two-thirds full. I estimated that it already contained about 1,000 people.

From the *Nuremberg Proceedings*, as quoted in Louis L. Snyder. *Documents of German History*, (New Brunswick: Rutgers University Press, 1958), pp. 462–464.

Nazis built extermination camps in Germany and Poland and used the latest technology to achieve the most efficient means of killing millions of men, women, and children for no other reason than their birth into the designated group. Before the war was over, perhaps six million Jews had died in what has come to be called the *Holocaust.* Only about a million remained alive, those mostly in pitiable condition.

World War II was unmatched in modern times in cruelty. When Stalin's armies conquered Poland and entered Germany, they raped, pillaged, and deported millions to the east. The British and American bombing of Germany killed thousands of civilians, and the dropping of atomic bombs on Japan inflicted terrible harm on civilian popula- tions. The bombings, however, were thought of as acts of war that would help defeat the enemy. Sta- lin's atrocities were not widely known in the West at the time and are not even today. The victorious Western Allies, therefore, were shocked by what they saw when they came on the Nazi extermina- tion camps and their pitiful survivors; little wonder that they were convinced that the effort of resist- ance to the Nazis and all the pain it cost were well worth it.

Japan and America's Entry into the War

The sympathies of the American government were very much on the British side, and the various forms of assistance that Roosevelt gave Britain

Pearl Harbor, December 7, 1941. The successful Japanese attack on the American base at Pearl Harbor in Hawaii, together with simultaneous attacks on other Pacific bases, brought the United States into war against the Axis powers. This picture shows the effects of the Japanese bombing upon the battleships Arizona, Tennessee, *and* West Virginia. *[Official United States Navy Photograph.]*

would have justified a German declaration of war. Hitler, however, held back, and it is not clear that the United States government would have overcome isolationist sentiment and entered the war in the Atlantic if war had not been thrust on America in the Pacific. Since the Japanese conquest of Manchuria in 1931, American policy toward Japan had been suspicious and unfriendly. The outbreak of the war in Europe emboldened the Japanese to move forward more quickly in their drive to dominate Asia. They allied themselves with Germany and Italy, made a treaty of neutrality with the Soviet Union, and penetrated into Indochina at the expense of defeated France. At the same time they continued their war in China and made plans to gain control of Malaya and the East Indies at the expense of beleaguered Britain and the conquered Netherlands. The only barrier to Japanese expansion was the United States.

The Americans had temporized, unwilling to cut off vital supplies of oil and other materials for fear of provoking a Japanese attack on Southeast Asia and Indonesia. The Japanese seizure of Indochina in July 1941 changed that policy, which had already begun to stiffen. The United States froze Japanese assets and cut off oil supplies; the British and Dutch did the same. Japanese plans for expansion could not continue without the conquest of the Indonesian oil fields and Malayan rubber and tin. In October a war faction led by General Hideki Tojo (1885–1948) took power in Japan and decided to risk a war rather than yield. On Sunday morning, December 7, 1941, even while Japanese representatives were discussing a settlement in Washington, Japan launched an air attack on Pearl Harbor, Hawaii, the chief American naval base in the Pacific. The technique was similar to the one Japan had used against the Russian fleet at Port Arthur in 1904, and it caught the Americans equally by surprise. A large part of the American fleet and many airplanes were destroyed, and the American capacity to wage war in the Pacific was destroyed for the time being. The next day the United States and Britain declared war on Japan, and three days later Germany and Italy declared war on the United States.

The Tide Turns

The potential power of the United States was enormous, but right after Pearl Harbor America was ill prepared for war. Though conscription had been introduced in 1940, the army was tiny, inexperienced, and ill supplied. American industry was not ready for war. The Japanese swiftly captured Guam, Wake Island, and the Philippine Islands. At the same time they attacked Hong Kong, Malaya, Burma, and Indonesia. By the spring of 1942 they controlled these places and the southwest Pacific as far as New Guinea. They were poised for an attack on Australia, and it seemed that nothing could stop them.

In the same year the Germans advanced deeper into Russia and almost reached the Caspian Sea in their drive for Russia's oil fields. In Africa, too, Axis fortunes were high. Rommel drove the British back into Egypt toward the Suez Canal and finally was stopped at El Alamein, only seventy miles from Alexandria. Relations between the democracies and their Soviet ally were still far from close; German submarine warfare was threatening British supplies; the Allies were being thrown back on every front; and the future looked bleak.

The first good news for the Allied cause in the Pacific came in the spring of 1942. A naval battle in the Coral Sea sent many Japanese ships to the bottom and gave security to Australia. A month later the United States defeated the Japanese in a fierce air and naval battle off Midway Island, blunting the chance of another assault on Hawaii and doing enough damage to halt the Japanese advance.

Marshal Tito of Yugoslavia (born 1892, and whose original name was Josip Broz), on the right, led his country's partisan resistance against the Nazis during World War II. [The Granger Collection.]

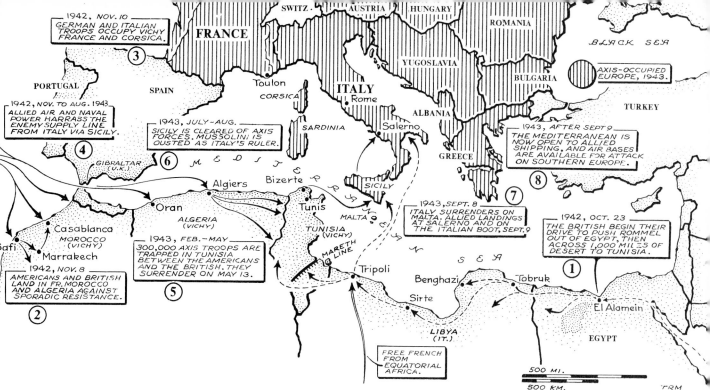

1942, NOV. 10 GERMAN AND ITALIAN TROOPS OCCUPY VICHY FRANCE AND CORSICA. ③

1942, NOV. TO AUG. 1943 ALLIED AIR AND NAVAL POWER HARRASS THE ENEMY SUPPLY LINE FROM ITALY VIA SICILY. ④

1943, JULY–AUG. SICILY IS CLEARED OF AXIS FORCES. MUSSOLINI IS OUSTED AS ITALY'S RULER. ⑥

1943, AFTER SEPT 9 THE MEDITERRANEAN IS NOW OPEN TO ALLIED SHIPPING, AND AIR BASES ARE AVAILABLE FOR ATTACK ON SOUTHERN EUROPE. ⑧

AXIS-OCCUPIED EUROPE, 1943.

1943, FEB.–MAY 300,000 AXIS TROOPS ARE TRAPPED IN TUNISIA BETWEEN THE AMERICANS AND THE BRITISH. THEY SURRENDER ON MAY 13. ⑤

1942, NOV. 8 AMERICANS AND BRITISH LAND IN FR. MOROCCO AND ALGERIA AGAINST SPORADIC RESISTANCE. ②

1943, SEPT. 8 ITALY SURRENDERS ON MALTA. ALLIED LANDINGS AT SALERNO AND ON THE ITALIAN BOOT, SEPT. 9 ⑦

1942, OCT. 23 THE BRITISH BEGIN THEIR DRIVE TO PUSH ROMMEL OUT OF EGYPT, THEN ACROSS 1,000 MILES OF DESERT TO TUNISIA. ①

FREE FRENCH FROM EQUATORIAL AFRICA.

500 MI.
500 KM.

NORTH AFRICAN CAMPAIGNS, 1942–1945

MAP 32.4 *Control of North Africa was important to the Allies in order to have access to Europe from the south. The map diagrams this theater of the war from Morocco to Egypt and the Suez Canal.*

Soon American Marines landed on Guadalcanal in the Solomon Islands and began in a small way to reverse the momentum of the war. The war in the Pacific was far from over, but Japan was checked sufficiently to allow the Allies to concentrate their efforts first in Europe.

The nations opposed to the Axis powers numbered more than twenty and were located all over the world, but the main combatants were Great Britain, the Soviet Union, and the United States. The two Western democracies cooperated in everything to an unprecedented degree, but suspicion between them and their Soviet ally continued. Although the Russians accepted all the aid they could get, they did not trust their allies, complained of inadequate help, and demanded that the democracies open a "second front" on the mainland of Europe. In 1942 American preparation and production were inadequate for an invasion of Europe, and control of the Atlantic by German submarines was such as to prevent safe crossing by the required number of troops. Not until 1944 were conditions right for the invasion, but in the meantime other developments forecast the doom of the Axis.

ALLIED LANDINGS IN AFRICA, SICILY, AND ITALY. In November 1942 an Allied force landed in French North Africa. Even before that landing the British Field Marshal Bernard Montgomery (1887–1976), after stopping Rommel at El Alamein, had begun a drive to the west, and the American General Dwight D. Eisenhower (1890–1969) pushed eastward through Morocco and Algeria. The two armies caught the German army between them in Tunisia and crushed it. The Suez Canal and the Mediterranean were now under Allied control, and southern Europe was exposed. In July and August 1943 the Allies took Sicily. Mussolini was driven from power, and the new government tried to make peace, but the Germans moved into Italy. The Allies landed in Italy, and Marshal Pietro Badoglio (1871–1956), the leader of the new Italian government, went over to their side, declaring war on Germany. Churchill had spoken of Italy as the "soft underbelly" of the Axis, but German resistance was tough and determined. Still the need to defend Italy put a strain on the Germans' energy and resources and left them vulnerable on other fronts.

BATTLE OF STALINGRAD. The Russian campaign became especially demanding. In the summer of 1942 the Germans resumed the offensive

on all fronts but were unable to get very far except in the south. The goal was the oil fields near the Caspian Sea, and they got as far as Stalingrad on the Volga, a key point for the protection of the flank of the German army in the south. Hitler was determined to take the city and Stalin to hold it. The Battle of Stalingrad raged for months with unexampled ferocity. The Russians lost more men than the Americans lost in combat during the entire war, but their heroic defense prevailed. Because Hitler again overruled his generals and would not allow a retreat, an entire German army was lost. Stalingrad marked the turning point of the Russian campaign. Thereafter material help from America and, even more, increased production from their own industry, which had been moved to or built up in the safety of central and eastern Russia, allowed the Russians to gain and

Stalingrad after the battle: Russians returning to the ruined city in February 1943. In this crucial battle the Russians suffered terrible losses but stopped the German advance and cut off and destroyed an entire German army. This battle is generally regarded as the turning point of the war in the East. [Sovfoto.]

Dresden in ruins. In February 1945, with the end of the war in sight, the Allies launched a series of air raids on Dresden in Germany, which was without defense. The raids destroyed the heart of the city and are thought to have caused twice as many casualties as those caused by the first atomic bomb dropped on Hiroshima, Japan, in August of the same year. [Bildarchiv Preussischer Kulturbesitz.]

D-Day, June 6, 1944. The Allied landing in France on the coast of Normandy. [Imperial War Museum, London.]

keep the offensive. As the German military and material resources dwindled, the Russians advanced westward inexorably.

STRATEGIC BOMBING. In 1943 the Allies began to gain ground in production and logistics as well. The industrial might of the United States began to come into full force, and at the same time new technology and tactics made great strides in eliminating the submarine menace. In the same year the American and British air forces began a series of massive bombardments of Germany by night and day. The Americans were more committed to the theory of the "precision bombing" of military and industrial targets vital to the enemy war effort, so they flew the day missions. The British regarded precision bombing as impossible and therefore useless. They preferred indiscriminate "area bombing" aimed at destroying the morale of the German people, and this kind of mission could be done at night. It does not appear that either kind of bombing had much effect on the war until 1944. Then the Americans introduced long-range fighters that could protect the bombers and allow accurate mis-

sions by day. By 1945 the Allies had cleared the skies of German planes and could bomb at will. Concentrated attacks on industrial targets, especially communications centers and oil refineries, did very real damage and helped shorten the war. Terror bombing continued, too, but seems not to have had any useful result. The bombardment of Dresden in February 1945 was especially savage and destructive. It was much debated within the British government and has raised moral questions since, for it seems to have had no military value.

The Defeat of Nazi Germany

On June 6, 1944 ("D-Day"), American, British, and Canadian troops landed in force on the coast of Normandy. The "second front" was opened. General Dwight D. Eisenhower, the commander of the Allied armies, faced a difficult problem. The European coast was heavily fortified. Amphibious assaults, moreover, are especially vulnerable to changes of wind and weather. Success depended on meticulous planning, advance preparation by

1001

DEFEAT OF THE AXIS
IN EUROPE,
1942–1945

THE AXIS

ALLIED WITH THE AXIS

OCCUPIED BY THE AXIS

Jaroslavl

VOLGA

SOVIET

Moscow

Kuibyshev
(WARTIME CAPITAL)

Tula

DEC., 1941
FARTHEST AXIS ADVANCE
NOV. 1942

rel

Voronezh

Kursk

Stalingrad

UNION

VOLGA

Kharkov

Astrakhan

A I N E

DON

Rostov

C A S P I A N   S E A

DNEPER

Elista

Kerch

Maikop

Grozny

CRIMEA

Yalta

T R A N S C A U C A S I A

B L A C K   S E A

Batum

Tiflis

Sinop

Kars

IRAN

Ankara

TURKEY

Mosul

TIGRIS

Adana

EUPHRATES

ntalya

Aleppo

IRAQ

CYPRUS (U.K.)

SYRIA

LEBANON

T R MILLER

heavy bombing, and successful feints to mask the point of attack. The German defense was strong, but the Allies were able to establish a beachhead and then to break out of it. In mid-August the Allies landed in southern France to put more pressure on the enemy. By the beginning of September France had been liberated.

All went smoothly until December, when the Germans launched a counterattack on the Belgian front through the Forest of Ardennes. Because the Germans were able to push forward into the Allied line, this was called the Battle of the Bulge, and it brought heavy losses and considerable alarm to the Allies. That effort, however, was the last gasp for the Germans. The Allies recovered the momentum and pushed eastward. They crossed the Rhine in March of 1945, and German resistance crumbled. This time there could be no doubt that the Germans had lost the war on the battlefield.

In the east the Russians swept forward no less swiftly. By March 1945 they were within reach of Berlin. Because the Allies insisted on unconditional surrender, the Germans fought on until May. Hitler and his intimates committed suicide in an underground hideaway in Berlin on May 1, 1945. The Russians occupied Berlin by agreement with their Western allies. The Third Reich had lasted a dozen years instead of the millennium predicted by Hitler.

Fall of the Japanese Empire

The war in Europe ended on May 8, 1945, and by then victory over Japan was in sight. The original Japanese attack on the United States had been a calculated risk against the odds. The longer the war lasted, the greater was the advantage to the American superiority in industrial production and human resources. Beginning in 1943 the American forces, still relatively small in number, began a campaign of "island hopping." They did not try to recapture every Pacific island held by the Japanese but selected major bases and places strategically located along the enemy supply line. Starting from the Solomons, they moved northeast toward the Japanese homeland. By June of 1944 they had

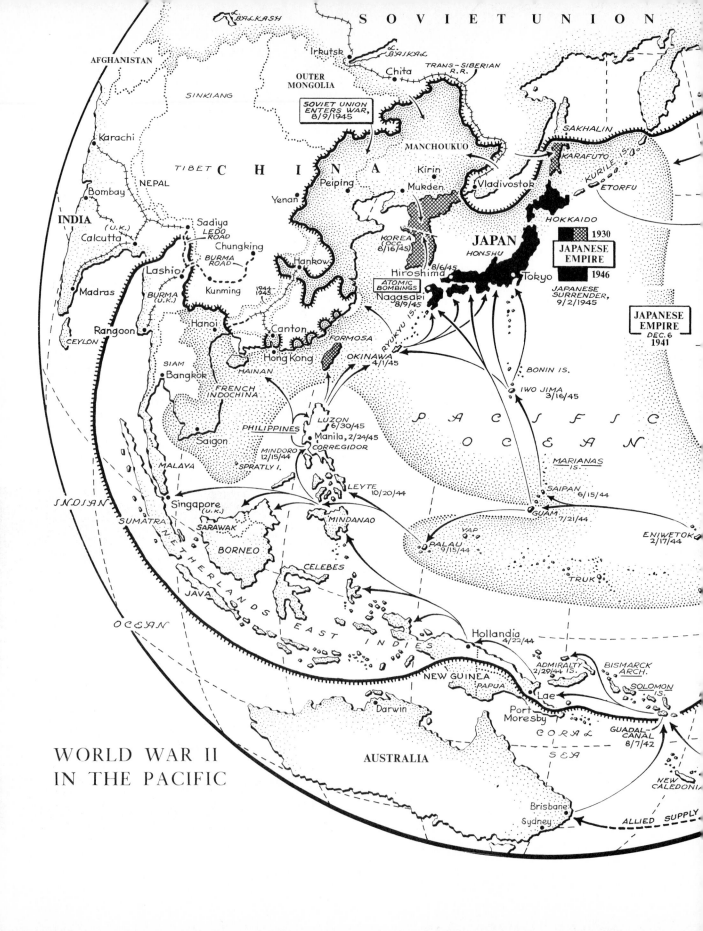

WORLD WAR II
IN THE PACIFIC

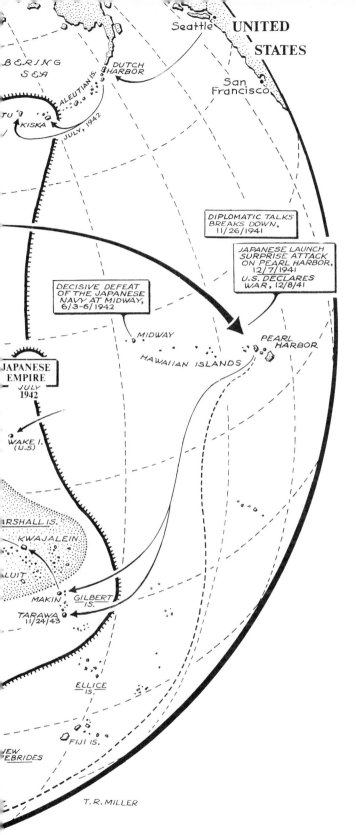

MAP 32.6 *As in Europe, the Pacific war was a problem in Allied recapture of areas that had been quickly taken earlier by the enemy. The enormous area represented by the map shows the initial expansion of Japanese holdings to cover half the Pacific and its islands, as well as huge sections of eastern Asia, and the long struggle to push the Japanese back to their homeland and defeat them by the summer of 1945.*

reached the Mariana Islands, which they could use as bases for bombing the Japanese in the Philippines, in China and in Japan itself. In October of the same year the Americans recaptured most of the Philippines and drove the Japanese fleet back into its home waters. In 1945 Iwo Jima and Okinawa fell, in spite of a determined Japanese resistance that included "kamikaze" attacks, suicide missions in which specially trained pilots deliberately flew their explosive-filled planes into American warships. From these new bases, closer to Japan, the American bombers launched a terrible wave of bombings that destroyed Japanese industry and disabled the Japanese navy, but still the Japanese

The mushroom-shaped cloud of the atomic bomb has come to symbolize the possibility of total human destruction that has haunted the statesmen and peoples of the world since 1945. This photograph shows one of the post-war test explosions held on remote atolls in the Pacific. [Official United States Navy Photograph.]

1005

The ruins of Hiroshima in August 1945. *The atomic blast completely destroyed the city and killed* 70,000 *of its* 200,000 *inhabitants.* [*Wide World Photos.*]

government, dominated by a military clique, refused to surrender.

Confronted with Japan's determination, the Americans made plans for a frontal assault on the Japanese homeland, which, they calculated, might cost a million American casualties and even greater losses for the Japanese. At this point science and technology presented the Americans with another choice. Since early in the war a secret program had been in progress. Its staff, made up in significant part of exiles from Hitler's Europe, was working to use atomic energy for military purposes. On August 6, 1945, an American plane dropped an atomic bomb on the city of Hiroshima. The city was destroyed, and more than 70,000 of its 200,000 residents were killed. Two days later the Soviet Union declared war on Japan and invaded Manchuria. The next day a second atomic bomb fell, this time on Nagasaki. Even then the Japanese did not yield. The Japanese Cabinet was prepared to resist further, to face an invasion rather than give up. It was only the unprecedented intervention of Emperor Hirohito

that convinced the government to surrender on August 14. Even then they made the condition that Japan could keep its emperor. Although the Allies had continued to insist on unconditional surrender, President Harry S Truman (1884–1972), who had come to office on April 12, 1945, on the death of Franklin D. Roosevelt, accepted the condition, and peace was formally signed aboard the *USS Missouri* in Tokyo Bay on September 2, 1945.

Revulsion and horror at the only use of atomic bombs as well as hindsight arising from the Cold War have surrounded with debate the decision to use the bomb against Japanese cities. Some have suggested that the bombings were unnecessary to win the war and that their main purpose was to frighten the Russians into a more cooperative attitude after the war. Others have emphasized the bureaucratic, almost automatic nature of the decision, once it had been decided to develop the bomb. To the decision makers and their contemporaries, however, matters were simpler. The bomb was a way to end the war swiftly without the need of invasion or

TERRITORIAL CHANGES AFTER WORLD WAR II

MAP 32.7 *The map pictures the shifts in territory following the defeat of the Axis. No treaty of peace has formally ended the war with Germany. (See also the map on page 993.)*

an extended period of bombardment, and it would save American lives. The decision to use it was conscious, not automatic, and required no ulterior motive.

The Cost of War

World War II was the most terrible war in history. Military deaths are estimated at some fifteen million, and at least as many civilians were killed. If deaths linked indirectly to the war are included, the figure of victims might reach as high as forty million. Most of Europe and significant parts of Asia were devastated. Yet the end of so terrible a war brought little opportunity for relaxation. The dawn of the Atomic Age and the dramatic end it brought to the war made people conscious that another major war might bring an end to humanity. Everything depended on the conclusion of a stable peace, but even as the fighting came to an end, conflicts among the victors made the prospects of a lasting peace doubtful.

Preparations for Peace and the Onset of the Cold War

The split between the Soviet Union and its wartime allies should cause no surprise. As the self-proclaimed center of world communism, the Soviet Union was openly dedicated to the overthrow of the capitalist nations, though this message was muted when the occasion demanded. On the other side, the Western allies were no less open about their hostility to communism and its chief purveyor, the Soviet Union. Though they had been friendly to the early stages of the Russian Revolution, they had sent troops in hopes of overthrowing the Bolshevik regime. The United States did not grant formal recognition to the Union of Soviet Socialist Republics until 1933. The Western powers' exclusion of the Soviets from the Munich conference and Stalin's pact with Hitler did nothing to improve relations.

1007

President Roosevelt and Prime Minister Churchill meeting on a warship at Placentia Bay, Newfoundland, in August 1941. There they signed the Atlantic Charter, a vague and general statement of liberal aims for the post-war world. [Imperial War Museum, London.]

Though cooperation against a common enemy and strenuous propaganda efforts in the West helped improve Western feeling toward the Soviet ally, Stalin remained suspicious and critical of the Western war effort, and Churchill never ceased planning to contain the Soviet advance into Europe. For some time Roosevelt seems to have been hopeful that the Allies could continue to work together after the war, but even he was losing faith as the war and his life drew to a close. Differences in historical development and ideology, as well as traditional conflicts over political power and influence, soon dashed whatever hopes there were of a mutually satisfactory peace settlement and continued cooperation to uphold it.

The Atlantic Charter

In August 1941, even before the Americans were at war, Roosevelt and Churchill had met on a ship off Newfoundland and agreed to the Atlantic Charter, a broad set of principles in the spirit of Wilson's Fourteen Points, which provided a theoretical basis for the peace they sought. When Russia and the United States joined Britain in the war, the three powers entered a purely military alliance in January 1942, leaving all political questions aside. The first political conference was the meeting of foreign ministers in Moscow in October 1943. The ministers re-affirmed earlier agreements to fight on until the enemy surrendered without condition and to continue cooperating after the war in a united-nations organization.

Tehran

The first meeting of the three leaders of state took place at Tehran, the capital of Iran, in 1943. Western promises to open a second front in France the next summer (1944) and Stalin's agreement to join in the war against Japan when Germany was defeated created an atmosphere of goodwill in which to discuss a postwar settlement. Stalin wanted to retain what he had gained in his pact with Hitler and to dismember Germany. Roosevelt and Churchill were conciliatory, but they made no firm commitments. The most important decision was the one that chose Europe's west coast as the point of attack instead of southern Europe, by the way of the Mediterranean. That meant, in retrospect, that Soviet forces would occupy eastern Europe and control its destiny. At Tehran in 1943 the Western allies did not foresee this clearly, for the Russians were still fighting deep within their own frontiers, and military considerations were paramount everywhere.

By 1944 the situation was different. In August Soviet armies were in sight of Warsaw, which had risen in expectation of liberation. But the Russians halted, allowing the Polish rebels to be annihilated while they turned south into the Balkans. They gained control of Romania and Hungary, advances of which centuries of expansionist czars had only dreamed. Alarmed by these developments, Churchill went to Moscow and met with Stalin in October. They agreed to share power in the Balkans on the basis of Soviet predominance in Romania and Bulgaria, Western predominance in Greece, and equality of influence in Yugoslavia and Hungary. These agreements were not enforceable without American approval, and the Americans were known to be hostile to such un-Wilsonian devices as "spheres of influence."

Yalta

The next meeting of the "Big Three" was at Yalta in the Crimea in February 1945. The Western armies had not yet crossed the Rhine, and the Soviet army was within a hundred miles of Berlin. The war with Japan continued, and no atomic explosion had yet taken place. Roosevelt, faced with an invasion of Japan and prospective heavy losses, was eager to bring the Russians into the Pacific war as soon as possible. As a true Wilsonian he also suspected Churchill's determination to maintain the British Empire and Britain's colonial advantages. The Americans thought that Churchill's plan to set up British spheres of influence in Europe would encourage the Russians to do the same and lead to friction and war. To encourage Russian participation in the war against Japan, Roosevelt and Churchill made extensive concessions to Russia in Sakhalin and the Kurile Islands, in Korea, and in Manchuria. Again in the tradition of Wilson, Roosevelt laid great stress on a united-nations organization: "Through the United Nations, he hoped to achieve a self-enforcing peace settlement that would not require American troops, as well as an open world without spheres of influence in which American enterprise could work freely."[7] Soviet agreement on these points seemed well worth concessions elsewhere.

[7] Robert O. Paxton, *Europe in the Twentieth Century* (New York: Harcourt Brace Jovanovich, 1975), p. 487.

The "Big Three" met at Yalta in February 1945 to plan the final defeat of Germany and Japan and to settle the future of the post-war world. [*United Press International Photo.*]

BATTLELINE AT THE
TIME OF THE YALTA
CONFERENCE, FEB.,'45

Memel
LITHUANIA

Lübeck
Wismar
Hamburg
Bremen
Magdeburg
Kassel
Cologne
Remagen
Frankfurt
Mannheim
Nürnberg
Metz
Strasbourg
Munich
Milan
ITALY
Bologna
Florence
Nice
NETH.
BELG.
LUX.
SWITZ.
FRANCE
Danzig
Berlin
Torgau
Leipzig
Chemnitz
Karlsbad
Breslau
Prague
CZECHOSLOVAKIA
Brünn
Pilsen
Vienna
Linz
AUSTRIA
Graz
Budapest
HUNGARY
Trieste
YUGOSLAVIA

CONQUERED BY
THE RUSSIANS TO
THE TIME OF THE
SURRENDER

POLAND

GERMAN-HELD AREAS
AT THE TIME OF
THE SURRENDER,
MAY 7 & 9, 1945

BRENNER
PASS

200 MI.
200 KM.

MUCH OF YUGOSLAVIA
WAS HELD BY TITO'S
COMMUNIST PARTISANS

TRM

YALTA TO THE SURRENDER

MAP 32.8 *"The Big Three", Roosevelt, Churchill, Stalin, met at YALTA in the Crimea in February of 1945. At the meeting concessions were made to Stalin concerning the settlement of Eastern Europe, as Roosevelt was eager to bring the Russians into the Pacific war as soon as possible. This map shows the positions held at the time of the surrender.*

Agreement on European questions was more difficult. On Germany the three powers easily agreed on its disarmament and denazification and on its division into four zones of occupation by France and the Big Three. Churchill, however, began to balk at Stalin's plan to dismember Germany and objected to his demand for reparations in the amount of $20 billion as well as forced labor from all the zones, with Russia to get half of everything. These matters were left undecided to fester and cause dissension in the future.

The settlement of Eastern Europe was no less a problem. Everyone agreed that the Soviet Union deserved neighboring governments that were friendly, but the West insisted that they also be inde-

pendent, autonomous, and democratic. The Western leaders, and especially Churchill, were not eager to see Eastern Europe fall under Russian domination; they were also, especially Roosevelt, truly committed to democracy and self-determination. But Stalin knew that independent, freely elected governments in Poland and Romania would not be safely friendly to Russia. He had already established a subservient government in Poland at Lublin in competition with the Polish government-in-exile in London. Under pressure from the Western leaders, however, he agreed to reorganize the government and include some Poles friendly to the West. He also signed a Declaration on Liberated Europe promising self-determination and free democratic elections. Stalin may have been eager to avoid conflict before the war with Germany was over—he never was free of the fear that the Allies might still make an arrangement with Germany and betray him—and he probably thought it worth endorsing some meaningless principles as the price of continued harmony. In any case, he wasted little time in violating these agreements.

Potsdam

The Big Three met for the last time in the Berlin suburb of Potsdam in July 1945. Much had changed since the last conference. Germany was defeated, and news of the successful experimental explosion of an atomic weapon reached the American president during the meetings. The cast of characters was also different: President Truman replaced Roosevelt, and Clement Attlee (1883–1967), leader of the Labor Party that had defeated Churchill's Conservatives in a general election, replaced Churchill as Britain's spokesman during the conference. Previous agreements were reaffirmed but progress on undecided questions was slow.

Russia's western frontier was moved far into what had been Poland and included part of German East Prussia. In compensation Poland was allowed "temporary administration" over the rest of East Prussia and Germany east of the Oder–Neisse river line, a condition that became permanent. In effect Poland was moved about a hundred miles west, at the expense of Germany, to accommodate the Soviet Union. The Allies agreed that Germany would be divided into occupation zones until the final peace treaty was signed. As no such treaty has ever been made, Germany remains divided to this day.

Churchill, Truman, and Stalin join in a three-way hand shake on July 23, 1945, at the Pots-
dam Conference. The conference ran from July 17–August 2, 1945. Churchill was voted out of
office on July 26 and was replaced at the meeting by the new British Prime Minister, Clement
Atlee. [United Press International.]

A Council of Foreign Ministers was established to draft peace treaties for Germany's allies. Growing disagreements made the job difficult, and it was not until February 1947 that Italy, Romania, Hungary, Bulgaria, and Finland signed treaties. The Russians were dissatisfied with the treaty that the United States made with Japan in 1951 and signed their own agreements with the Japanese in 1956. These disagreements were foreshadowed at Potsdam.

Causes of the Cold War

Some scholars attribute the hardening of the atmosphere to the advent of Truman in place of the more sympathetic Roosevelt and to the American possession of an effective atomic bomb. The fact is that Truman was trying to carry Roosevelt's policies forward, and there is evidence that Roosevelt himself had become distressed by Soviet actions in Eastern Europe. Nor did Truman use the successful test of the atomic bomb to try to keep Russia out of the Pacific. On the contrary, he worked hard to ensure Russian intervention against Japan. In part the new coldness among the Allies arose from the mutual feeling that each had violated previous agreements. The Russians were plainly asserting permanent control of Poland and Romania under puppet Communist governments. The United States, on the other hand, was taking a harder line on the extent of German reparations to the Soviet Union.

In retrospect, however, it appears unlikely that friendlier styles on either side could have avoided a split that rested on basic differences of ideology and interest. The Soviet Union's attempt to extend its control westward into central Europe and the Balkans and southward into the Middle East was a continuation of the policy of czarist Russia. It had been Britain's traditional role to try to restrain Russian expansion into these areas, and it was not surprising that the United States should inherit that task as Britain's power waned. The alternative was to permit a major change in the balance of power in the world in favor of a huge nation, traditionally hostile, dedicated in its official ideology to overthrow nations like the United States, and governed by an absolute dictator who had already demonstrated many times his capacity for the most amazing deceptions and the most horrible cruelties. Few nations would be likely to take such risks.

Nevertheless the Americans made no attempt to roll back Soviet power where it existed, though American military forces were the greatest in their history, their industrial power was unmatched in the world, and atomic weapons were an American monopoly. In less than a year from the war's end American forces in Europe were reduced from 3.5 million to half a million men. The speed of the withdrawal was the result of pressure to "get the boys home" but was fully in accord with American plans and peacetime goals. These were the traditional ones of support for self-determination, autonomy and democracy in the political area, free trade, freedom of the seas, no barriers to investment, and the Open Door in the economic sphere. These goals agreed with American principles, and they also served American interests well. As the strongest, richest nation in the world, the one with the greatest industrial plant and the strongest currency, the United States would benefit handsomely if such an international order were established.

American hostility to colonial empires created tension with France and Britain, but these were minor. The main conflict came with the Soviet Union. From the Soviet perspective the extension of its frontiers and the domination of formerly independent states in Eastern Europe were necessary for the security of the USSR and a proper compensation for the fearful losses that the Russians had suffered in the war. American resistance

The headquarters of the United Nations in New York City. [*United Nations.*]

to the new state of things could be seen as a threat to the Soviets' security and legitimate aims. American objections over Poland and other states could be seen as attempts to undermine regimes friendly to Russia and to encircle the Soviet Union with hostile neighbors. Such behavior might be seen to justify Russian attempts to overthrow regimes friendly to the United States in Western Europe and elsewhere.

The growth in France and Italy of large Communist parties plainly taking orders from Moscow led the Americans to believe that Stalin was engaged in a great worldwide plot to destroy capitalism and democracy by subversion. In the absence of reliable evidence about Stalin's intentions, certainty is not possible, but most people in the West

❧ Churchill Invents the Iron Curtain; Cold War Declared

Winston Churchill chose an American audience (at Westminster College in Fulton, Missouri) for the March 5, 1946, speech that contributed *iron curtain* to the language and, more importantly, defined the existence of what came to be known as the *Cold War* between the communist and the democratic camps.

A shadow has fallen upon the scenes so lately lighted by the Allied victory. Nobody knows what Soviet Russia and its Communist international organization intends to do in the immediate future, or what are the limits, if any, to their expansive and proselytizing tendencies. . . .

From Stettin in the Baltic to Trieste in the Adriatic, an iron curtain has descended across the Continent. Behind that line lie all the capitals of the ancient states of central and eastern Europe. Warsaw, Berlin, Prague, Vienna, Budapest, Belgrade, Bucharest and Sofia, all these famous cities and the populations around them lie in the Soviet sphere and all are subject in one form or another, not only to Soviet influence but to a very high and increasing measure of control from Moscow. Athens alone, with its immortal glories, is free to decide its future at an election under British, American and French observation. The Russian dominated Polish government has been encouraged to make enormous and wrongful inroads upon Germany, and mass

expulsions of millions of Germans on a scale grievous and undreamed of are now taking place. The Communist parties, which were very small in all these eastern states of Europe, have been raised to preeminence and power far beyond their numbers and are seeking everywhere to obtain totalitarian control. Police governments are prevailing in nearly every case, and so far, except in Czechoslovakia, there is no true democracy. . . .

. . . I do not believe that Soviet Russia desires war. What they desire is the fruits of war and the indefinite expansion of their power and doctrines. . . .

. . . If the western democracies stand together in strict adherence to the principles of the United Nations Charter, their influence for furthering these principles will be immense and no one is likely to molest them. If, however, they become divided or falter in their duty, and if these all-important years are allowed to slip away, then indeed catastrophe may overwhelm us all.

"Winston Churchill's Speech at Fulton," in *Vital Speeches of the Day*, Vol. 12 (March 15, 1946) (New York: City News Publishing Co.), pp. 331–332.

---

thought the suspicions plausible. Rivalry between the Soviet Union and the United States dominated international relations for the next three decades, and in the flawed world of reality it is hard to see how things could have been otherwise. The important question was whether the conflict would take a diplomatic or a military form.

Cold War

Evidence of the new mood of hostility among the former allies was not long in coming. In February 1946 both Stalin and his foreign minister, Vyacheslav Molotov, gave public speeches in which they spoke of the Western democracies as enemies. A

month later Churchill gave a speech in Fulton, Missouri, in which he viewed Russian actions in Eastern Europe with alarm. He spoke of an Iron Curtain that had descended on Europe, dividing a free and democratic West from an East under totalitarian rule. He warned against Communist subversion and urged Western unity and strength as a response to the new menace. In this atmosphere difficulties grew.

The attempt to deal with the problem of atomic energy was an early victim of the Cold War. The Americans put forward a plan to place the manufacture and control of atomic weapons under international control, but the Russians balked at the proposed requirements for on-site inspection and

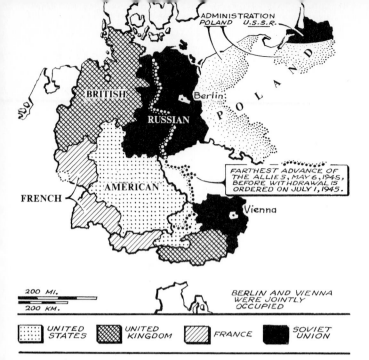

UNITED STATES   UNITED KINGDOM   FRANCE   SOVIET UNION

OCCUPIED GERMANY AND AUSTRIA

MAP 32.9 *At the war's end, defeated Germany, including Austria, was occupied by the victorious Allies in the several zones shown here. Austria, by prompt agreement, was re-erected into an independent, neutral state and no longer occupied. But the German zones have hardened into an "East" Germany (the former Soviet zone) and a "West" Germany (the former British, French, and American zones). The city of Berlin, within the Soviet zone, was similarly divided.*

for limits on the veto power in the United Nations. The plan fell through. The United States continued to develop its own atomic weapons in secrecy, and the Russians did the same. By 1949, with the help of information obtained by Soviet spies in Britain and the United States, the Soviet Union exploded its own atomic bomb, and the race for nuclear weapons was on.

Any hopes that the new United Nations organization, with its headquarters in New York as a symbol of firm American adherence to international responsibility, would resolve the world's conflicts were soon disappointed. Like the League of Nations, it is dependent on voluntary contributions of money and troops. The UN Charter, moreover, forbids interference in the internal affairs of nations, and many of the problems of the 1940s were internal in nature. Finally, the Security Council, which is responsible for maintaining world peace, gives a veto to each of the permanent members. Because the Soviet Union was generally in the minority, it used the veto repeatedly, making it clear that the United Nations was not adequate to resolve existing problems.

Western resistance to what the West increasingly perceived as Soviet intransigence and Communist plans for subversion and expansion took clearer form in 1947. Since 1944 civil war had been raging in Greece between the royalist government restored by Britain and insurgents supported by the communist countries, chiefly Yugoslavia. In 1947 Britain informed the United States that it was financially no longer able to support the Greeks. On March 12 President Truman asked Congress for legislation to support Greece and also Turkey, which was under Soviet pressure to yield control of the Dardanelles. Congress voted funds to aid Greece and Turkey, but the Truman Doctrine, as enunciated in a speech of March 12, had a broader significance. The president advocated a policy of supporting "free people who are resisting attempted subjugation by armed minorities or by outside pressures," by implication anywhere in the world.

American aid to Greece and Turkey took the form of military equipment and advisers, but the threat in Western Europe was the growth of Communist parties fed by postwar poverty and hunger. To deal with this menace, the Americans devised the European Recovery Program, named the Marshall Plan after George C. Marshall, the secretary of state who introduced it. This was a plan for broad economic aid to European states on condition only that they work together for their mutual benefit. The invitation included the Soviet Union and its satellites. Finland and Czechoslovakia were willing to participate, and Poland and Hungary showed interest. The Soviets, fearing that American economic aid would attract many satellites out of their orbits, forbade them to take part. The Marshall Plan was a great success in restoring prosperity to Western Europe and in setting the stage for Europe's unprecedented postwar economic growth. It also led to the waning of Communist strength in the West and to the establishment of solid democratic regimes.

From the Western viewpoint this policy of "containment" was a new and successful response to the Soviet and communist challenge. To Stalin it may have seemed a renewal of the old Western attempt to isolate and encircle the USSR. His answer was to put an end to all multiparty governments behind the Iron Curtain and to replace them with thoroughly Communist regimes completely under his control. He also called a meeting of all Communist parties around the world at Warsaw in the autumn of 1947. There they organized the Communist Information Bureau (Cominform), a revival of the old Comintern, dedicated to spreading revolutionary communism throughout the world. The era of the popular front was officially over. Communist leaders in the West who favored friendship, collaboration, and reform were replaced by hard-liners who attempted to sabotage the new structures.

In February 1948 a more dramatic and brutal display of Stalin's new policy took place in Prague. The Communists expelled the democratic members of what had been a coalition government and murdered Jan Masaryk, the foreign minister and son of the founder of Czechoslovakia, Thomas Masaryk. President Eduard Beneš (1884–1948) was also forced to resign, and Czechoslovakia was brought fully under Soviet rule.

These Soviet actions, especially those in Czechoslovakia, increased American determination to go ahead with its own arrangements in Germany. The wartime Allies had never agreed on the details of a German settlement and kept putting off decisions. At first they all agreed on the dismemberment of Germany but not on the form it should take. By the time of Yalta, Churchill had come to fear Russian control of Eastern and Central Europe and began to oppose dismemberment. There were differences in economic policy, too. The Russians proceeded swiftly to dismantle German industry in the eastern zone, but the Americans acted differently. They concluded that such a policy would require the United States to support Germany for the foreseeable future. It would also cause political chaos and open the way for communism. They preferred, therefore, to try to make Germany self-sufficient, and this meant restoring rather than destroying its industrial capacity. To the Soviets the restoration of a powerful industrial Germany, even in the western zones only, was frightening and unacceptable. The same difference of approach hampered agreement on reparations because the Soviets claimed the right to industrial equipment in all the zones, and the Americans resisted their demands.

Disagreement over Germany produced the most heated of postwar debates. When the Western powers agreed to go forward with a separate constitution for the western sectors of Germany in February 1948, the Soviets walked out of the joint Allied Control Commission. In the summer of that year the Western powers issued a new currency in their zone. Berlin, though well within the Soviet zone, was governed by all four powers. The Soviets feared the new currency circulating in Berlin at better rates than their own and chose to seal the city off by closing all railroads and highways to West Germany. Their purpose was to drive the Western powers out of Berlin. The Western allies responded to the Berlin Blockade with an airlift of supplies to the city that lasted almost a year. In May 1949 the Russians were forced to back down and open access to Berlin, but the incident was decisive. It greatly increased tensions and suspicions between the opponents, and it hastened the lasting separation of Germany into two states. West Germany formally became the German Federated Republic in September 1949, and the eastern region became the German Democratic Republic a month later. Ironically Germany had been dismembered in a way no one had planned or expected.

NATO AND THE WARSAW PACT. Meanwhile the nations of Western Europe had been coming closer together. The Marshall Plan encouraged international cooperation, and in March 1948 Belgium, the Netherlands, Luxembourg, France, and Britain signed the Treaty of Brussels, providing for cooperation in economic and military matters. In April 1949 these nations joined with Italy, Denmark, Norway, Portugal, and Iceland to sign a treaty with Canada and the United States that formed the North Atlantic Treaty Organization (NATO). NATO committed its members to mutual assistance in case any of them was attacked. For the first time in history the United States was committed to defend allies outside the Western Hemisphere. The NATO treaty formed the West into a bloc. A few years later West Germany, Greece, and Turkey joined the alliance.

Soviet relations with the states of Eastern Europe were governed by a series of bilateral treaties providing for close ties and mutual assistance in case of attack. In 1949 the Council of Mutual Assistance (COMECON) was formed to integrate the economies of these states. Unlike the NATO states the

Eastern alliance system was under direct Soviet domination through local Communist parties controlled from Moscow and overawed by the presence of the Red Army. The Warsaw Pact of May 1955, which included Albania, Bulgaria, Czechoslovakia, East Germany, Hungary, Poland, Romania, and the Soviet Union, merely gave formal recognition to a system that already existed. Europe was divided into two unfriendly blocs. The Cold War had taken firm shape in Europe.

Suggested Readings

A. BULLOCK, *Hitler: A Study in Tyranny*, rev. ed. (1964). A brilliant biography.

W. S. CHURCHILL, *The Second World War*, 6 vols. (1948–1954). The memoirs of the great British leader.

H. FEIS, *From Trust to Terror: The Onset of the Cold War, 1945–1950* (1970). The best general account.

H. W. GATZKE, *Stresemann and the Rearmament of Germany* (1954). An important monograph.

H. W. GATZKE (Ed.), *European Diplomacy Between Two Wars* (1972). A collection of important essays.

M. GILBERT, The Roots of Appeasement (1966). A study of diplomacy and opinion in the 1920s.

M. GILBERT AND R. GOTT, *The Appeasers*, rev. ed. (1963). A revealing study of British policy in the 1930s.

B. H. LIDDELL HART, *History of the Second World War*, 2 vols. (1971). A good military history.

K. HILDEBRAND, *The Foreign Policy of the Third Reich* (1970).

G. KOLKO, *The Politics of War* (1968). An interesting example of the new revisionist school that finds the causes of the Cold War in economic considerations and emphasizes American responsibility.

L. LAFORE, *The End of Glory* (1970). A well-written interpretive essay on the origins of World War II.

W. L. LANGER AND S. E. GLEASON, *The Challenge of Isolation* (1952). American foreign policy in the 1930s.

S. MARKS, *The Illusion of Peace* (1976). A good discussion of European international relations in the 1920s and early 1930s.

N. RICH, *Hitler's War Aims*, 2 vols. (1973–1974).

E. M. ROBERTSON (Ed.), *The Origins of the Second World War* (1971). A valuable collection of essays.

M. SHERWIN, *A World Destroyed: The Atomic Bomb and the Grand Alliance* (1975). An analysis of the role of the atomic bomb in the years surrounding the end of World War II.

R. J. SONTAG, *A Broken World* 1919–1939 (1971). An excellent survey.

MAJOR EUROPEAN ALLIANCE SYSTEMS

MAP 32.10 *The North Atlantic Treaty Organization, which includes both Canada and the United States, stretches as far east as Turkey. By contrast, the Warsaw Pact nations are contiguous communist states of eastern Europe, with the Soviet Union, of course, as the dominant member.*

A. J. P. TAYLOR, *The Origins of the Second World War* (1966). A lively, controversial, even perverse study.

C. THORNE, *The Approach of War 1938–1939* (1967). A careful analysis of diplomacy.

J. W. WHEELER-BENNET, *Munich: Prologue to Tragedy* (1966). A fine study of the crisis.

A. WOLFERS, *Britain and France Between Two Wars* (1940). Still a valuable study of the policy of the Western powers.

G. WRIGHT, *The Ordeal of Total War 1939–1945* (1968). An excellent survey.

1018

33 Europe in the Era of the Superpowers

ALMOST forty years have passed since the conclusion of World War II and the onset of the Cold War. In this period of considerably more than a human generation, Europe has remained divided between Communist and non-Communist states and between allies of the United States and those of the Soviet Union. Such division is hardly a new feature of European history. For centuries the continent was separated into Roman and barbarian areas; later into Christian and Islamic spheres; then into Protestant, Catholic, and Orthodox camps; and finally into liberal and conservative states. Each of these divisions left an imprint on the culture of Europe. This seems no less true of the Cold War separation, although the lat-

An antinuclear demonstration in West Germany in 1982. The economic and military superiority of Europe over the rest of the world collapsed after the Second World War. Although post-war Europe has enjoyed an economic boom, by the 1980s many West Europeans felt trapped between the two nuclear superpowers, the United States and the Soviet Union. [Sygma.]

ter may prove less long-lived than the previous divisions.

The four decades of the Cold War and its aftermath have witnessed extraordinary changes in European political and economic life. These in turn have produced significant results for the rest of the world once dominated by Europeans. Leadership in the western part of the continent shifted to the United States and in the eastern part to the Soviet Union. The successor states of the Austria–Hungarian Empire previously coveted by Hitler fell under Soviet domination. Britain, France, Belgium, the Netherlands, and Portugal have conducted what is no doubt a permanent retreat from world empire. They have thus concluded an era of European world dominance that commenced during the Renaissance.

Many of those same nations began to cooperate economically and politically with each other as at no time in previous European experience. Peaceful economic integration and possible political unity became facts of everyday life. During these same years much of the continent experienced the most extensive material prosperity in its history. Even though the relative power of Europe has clearly declined since 1939, the Cold War rivalry, decolonization, the movement toward unity, and economic growth have led to a continuing European influence elsewhere in the world.

Europe and the Soviet-American Rivalry

From approximately 1848 to 1948 the nation-state characterized European political life and rivalry. Generally these countries sought to expand their political influence and economic power at each other's expense. During the same century Europe's economic and technological supremacy allowed certain of its states to rule or administer a vast area of the globe inhabited by non-European peoples. These nation-states have obviously continued to exist, but the economic and political collapse occasioned by World War II led them to become more interrelated and interdependent. The loss of economic and military superiority coincided with and in some cases aided the rise of nationalism throughout the colonial world. The United States and the Soviet Union—with their extensive economic resources, military forces, and nuclear capacities—have filled the power vacuum created by the European collapse.

The new situation of Europe, lying between two superpowers, marked a genuine turning point in the history of the continent. Prior to 1939 Great Britain, France, and Germany had been, in the context of the times, "world" powers. During the 1930s even Italy, through its ventures in Ethiopia, had aspired to that position. By the onset of the 1960s it had become evident that all of these nations had become simply "European" powers and were no longer wholly independent states even in that position. The impact of the Marshall Plan and the nuclear deterrent power of America meant that the United States would exert a relatively permanent influence on Europe. There was to be no return to the isolationism that had characterized American policy after World War I. Europe as a whole, and more particularly Germany, became an arena for continuing confrontation and tension between the United States and the Soviet Union. The kind of direct and indirect power that European nations had once exerted elsewhere in the world was now being exercised over them.

The first round of Cold War confrontations culminated in the formation of NATO (1949) and the intervention of United States and United Nations forces in Korea (1950). In 1953 Stalin died, and later that year an armistice was concluded in Korea. Both events produced hope that international tensions might lessen. In early 1955 Austria agreed to become a neutral state, and Soviet occupation forces left. Later that year the leaders of France, Great Britain, the Soviet Union, and the United States held a summit conference at Geneva. Nuclear weapons and the future of divided Germany were the chief items on the agenda. Although there was much public display of friendliness among the participants, there were few substantial agreements on major problems. Nonetheless the fact that world leaders were discussing problems and issues produced the so-called spirit of Geneva. This atmosphere proved to be short-lived, and the rivalry of power and polemics soon resumed.

The year 1956 was one of considerable significance for both the Cold War and the recognition of the realities of European power in the postwar era. In July President Gamal Abdel Nasser (1918–1970) of Egypt nationalized the Suez Canal. Great Britain and France feared that this action would close the canal to their supplies of oil in the Persian Gulf. In October 1956 war broke out between Egypt and the eight-year-old state of Israel (for a discussion of the formation of Israel, see the section later in this chapter titled "The Arab–Israeli Dispute"). The British and the French seized the opportunity of this conflict to intervene. Publicly they spoke of acting to separate the combatants, but their real motive was to recapture the canal. The Anglo-French military operation was a fiasco of the first order and resulted in a humiliating diplomatic defeat. The United States refused to support the Anglo-French action. The Soviet Union protested in the most severe terms. The Anglo-French forces had to be withdrawn, and control of the canal remained with Egypt. The Suez intervention proved that without the support of the United States the nations of Western Europe could no longer undertake meaningful military operations. They could no longer impose their will on the rest of the world. At the same time it appeared that the United States and the Soviet Union had acted to restrain their allies from undertaking actions that might result in a wider conflict. The fact that neither of the superpowers wanted war

The "spirit of Geneva" is displayed in this picture of the four major leaders who met there in the summer of 1955 for a summit conference. From left to right they are Nikolai Bulganin of the Soviet Union, Dwight Eisenhower of the United States, Edgar Faure of France, and Anthony Eden of Great Britain. [United Press International Photo.]

put limitations on the actions of both Egypt and the Anglo-French forces.

The autumn of 1956 also saw important developments in Eastern Europe. These demonstrated in a similar fashion the limitations on independent action among the Soviet bloc nations. When the prime minister of Poland died, the Polish Communist Party leaders refused to choose as his successor the person selected by Moscow. Considerable tension developed. The Soviet leaders even visited Warsaw to make their opinions known. In the end Wladyslaw Gomulka (b. 1905) emerged as the new Communist leader of Poland. He was the choice of the Poles, and he proved acceptable to the Soviets because he promised continued economic and military cooperation and most particularly continued Polish membership in the Warsaw Pact. Within those limits he moved to halt the collectivization of Polish agriculture and to improve the relationship between the Communist government and the Polish Roman Catholic Church.

Hungary provided the second trouble spot for the Soviet Union. In late October, as the Polish problem was approaching a solution, demonstra-

Budapest, October 1956. Street battles raged for several days until Soviet tanks finally put down the Hungarian revolt. [Raymond Darolle. Sygma.]

tions of sympathy for the Poles occurred in Budapest. The Communist government moved to stop the demonstrations and street fighting erupted. A new ministry headed by former premier Imre Nagy (1896–1958) was installed by the Hungarian Communist Party. Nagy was a Communist who sought a more independent position for Hungary. He went much farther in his demands than had Gomulka in Poland, and Nagy made direct appeals for political support from non-Communist groups in Hungary. Nagy called for the removal of Soviet troops and the ultimate neutralization of Hungary. He even went so far as to call for Hungarian withdrawal from the Warsaw Pact. These demands were wholly unacceptable to the Soviet Union. In early November Soviet troops invaded the country; deposed Nagy, who was later executed; and im-

A woman carrying flowers and followed by a black flag leads a procession of mourners in an anti-Soviet demonstration in Marx Square in Budapest, 1956. [Raymond Darolle. Sygma]

posed Janos Kadar (b. 1912) as premier. The Suez intervention had provided an international diversion that helped to permit free action by the Soviet Union. The Polish and Hungarian disturbances had several results. They demonstrated the limitations of independence within the Soviet bloc, but they did not bring an end to independent action. They also demonstrated that the example of Austrian neutrality would not be imitated elsewhere in Eastern Europe. Finally, the failure of the United States to take any action in the Hungarian uprising proved the hollowness of American political rhetoric about liberating the captive nations of Eastern Europe.

The events of 1956 brought to a close the era of fully autonomous action by the European nation-states. In very different ways and to differing degrees the two superpowers had demonstrated the new political realities. After 1956 the Soviet Union began to talk about "peaceful coexistence" with the United States. In 1958 negotiations commenced between the two countries for limitations on the testing of nuclear weapons. However, that same year the Soviet Union announced that the status of West Berlin must be changed and the Allied occupation forces withdrawn. The demand was refused. In 1959 tensions relaxed sufficiently for several Western leaders to visit Moscow and for Soviet Premier Nikita Khrushchev (1894–1971) to tour the United States. A summit meeting was scheduled for May 1960, and American President Eisenhower was to go to Moscow.

The Paris Summit Conference of 1960 proved anything but a repetition of the friendly days of 1955. Just before the gathering, the Soviet Union shot down an American U-2 aircraft that was flying reconnaissance over Soviet territory. Khrushchev demanded an apology from President Eisenhower for this air surveillance. Eisenhower accepted full responsibility for the policy but refused to issue any apology. Khrushchev then refused to take part in the summit conference just as the participants arrived in the French capital. The conference was thus aborted, and Eisenhower's proposed trip to the Soviet Union never took place.

The Soviet actions to destroy the possibility of the summit conference on the eve of its opening were not simply the result of the American spy flights. The Soviets had long been aware of the American flights but chose to protest at this time for two reasons. Khrushchev had hoped that the leaders of Britain, France, and the United States would be sufficiently divided over the future of Germany so that a united Allied front would be impossible. The divisions did not come about as he had hoped. Consequently the conference would have been of little use to him. Second, by 1960 the communist world itself had become split between the Soviets and the Chinese. The latter were portraying the Russians as lacking sufficient revolutionary zeal. Khrushchev's action was in part a response to those charges and proof of the hard-line attitude of the Soviet Union toward the capitalist world.

The abortive Paris conference opened the most difficult period of the Cold War. In 1961 the new U.S. president, John F. Kennedy (1917–1963), and Premier Khrushchev met in Vienna. The conference was inconclusive, but the American president left wondering if the two nations could avoid war. Throughout 1961 thousands of refugees from East Germany were crossing the border into West Berlin. This outflow was a political embarrassment to East Germany and a detriment to its economic life. In August 1961 the East Germans erected a concrete wall along the border between East and West Berlin. Henceforth it was possible to cross only at designated checkpoints and with proper papers. The United States protested and sent Vice President Lyndon Johnson (1908–1973) to Berlin to reassure its citizens, but the Berlin Wall remained—and does so to the present day. The refugee stream was halted, and the United States' commitment to West Germany was brought into doubt.

A year later the most dangerous days of the Cold War occurred during the Cuban missile crisis. The Soviet Union attempted to place missiles in Cuba, which was a nation friendly to Soviet aims lying less than a hundred miles from the United States. The United States blockaded Cuba, halted the shipment of new missiles, and demanded the removal of existing installations. After a very tense week, with numerous threats and messages between Moscow and Washington, the crisis ended and the Soviets backed down.

The Cuban missile crisis was the last major Cold War confrontation that would have involved Europe directly because there had existed the possibility of the launching of missiles over Europe or from European bases. Thereafter the American–Soviet rivalry shifted to the war in Vietnam and the Arab–Israeli conflict in the Near East. A "hotline" communications system was installed between Moscow and Washington for more rapid and direct exchange of diplomatic messages in times of crisis.

President Kennedy Defines the Cold War Arena

This passage is from President John F. Kennedy's speech at the time of the Berlin Wall crisis of 1961. He called for a democratic challenge to communism throughout the world. The commitment to Southeast Asia would later lead to the major war in Vietnam.

The immediate threat to free men is in West Berlin. But that isolated outpost is not an isolated problem. The threat is worldwide. Our effort must be equally wide and strong, and not be obsessed by any single manufactured crisis. We face a challenge in Berlin, but there is also a challenge in Southeast Asia, where the borders are less guarded, the enemy harder to find, and the dangers of Communism less apparent to those who have so little. We face a challenge in our own hemisphere, and indeed wherever else the freedom of human beings is at stake.

Public Papers of the Presidents of the United States, John F. Kennedy. January 20 to December 31, 1961, ed. by Wayne C. Gover (Washington: U.S. Government Printing Office, 1962), p. 533.

In 1963 the two powers concluded a Nuclear Test Ban Treaty. This agreement marked the beginning of a lessening in the tensions between the United States and the Soviet Union. The German problem somewhat subsided in the late 1960s as West Germany under Premier Willy Brandt (b. 1913) moved to improve its relations with the Soviet Union and Eastern Europe. In 1968 the Soviet Union invaded Czechoslovakia to prevent its emergence into further independence. Although deplored by the United States, this action led to no renewal of tensions. During the presidency of Richard Nixon (1969–1974) the United States embarked on a policy of detente or reduction of tension with the Soviet Union. This policy involved trade agreements and mutual reduction of strategic armaments. In 1975 President Gerald Ford attended a conference in Helsinki, Finland, that in effect recognized the Soviet sphere of influence in Eastern Europe. The Helsinki Accords also committed its signatory powers, including the Soviet Union, to recognize and protect the human rights of their citizens. The foreign policy of President Jimmy Carter (b. 1924) placed much stress on the observance of these human rights clauses. However, the Soviet invasion of Afghanistan in 1979, though not directly affecting Europe, hardened relations between Washington and Moscow. The United States refused to participate in the 1980 Olympic Games held in Moscow and placed an embargo on American grain being shipped to the Soviet Union. The Reagan administration adopted a much tougher policy and rhetoric, although it relaxed the embargo and placed less emphasis on human rights. It sharply slowed arms limitation negotiations and moved to bring about a larger deployment of advanced American weapons in Europe. It carried out economic sanctions during the Polish crisis of 1981–1982.

The late 1960s and early 1970s saw other changes in postwar relations between Europe and the United States. The NATO alliance became somewhat weaker as France moved to oppose United States influence over Europeans. The unpopularity of United States involvement in Vietnam strained its relations with NATO allies. Moreover the apparent genuine possibility for a time of Communist governments in Portugal and Italy after 1974 raised new questions about the strength and unity of NATO. During the late 1970s the influence of the United States over Western Europe remained, but it was clear that the desires of Europeans as well as of Americans would have to be taken into greater account as policy was formulated for the future. During the early 1980s the need for America to defer to the sensibilities of Europeans came to the fore over the issue of the placement of nuclear weapons in Europe and most particularly in Germany. The emergence of a significant peace movement with much popular support aimed at a Europe free of nuclear weapons caused considerable questioning of the military policy of the United States. The peace movement put pressure on the governments of Western Europe and the United States to require more mutual cooperation in military planning.

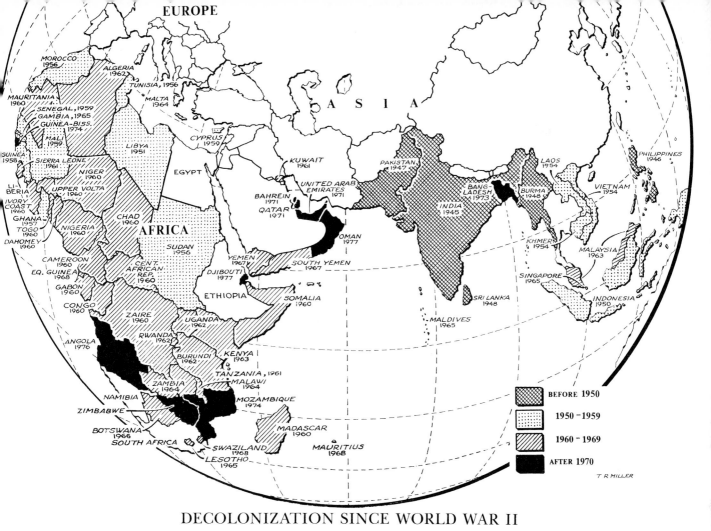

DECOLONIZATION SINCE WORLD WAR II

Decolonization and the Cold War

MAP 33.1 *The extent of the rapid retreat from imperialism on the part of the Western powers after World War II is graphically shown on this outline map covering half the globe—from West Africa to the Southwest Pacific.*

Retreat from Empire

At the onset of World War II many of the nations of Europe were still imperial powers. Great Britain, France, the Netherlands, Belgium, Italy, and Portugal governed millions of non-European peoples. One of the most striking and significant postwar developments has been the decolonization of these imperial holdings and the consequent emergence of the so-called Third World political bloc. The process of retreat from empire involved the colonial powers in three major stages of difficulties. The first was the turmoil created by nationalist movements and revolts in the colonies. The second was the injection of Cold War diplomacy and rivalries into the power vacuums formed by the European withdrawals. Finally, in recent years the control of important natural resources and particularly of oil by the new nations of the Third World has put considerable economic pressure on both Western Europe and the United States. This last condition may well prove one of the most important factors in world politics for the remainder of this century.

The decolonization that has occurred since 1945 has been a direct result of both the war itself and the rise of indigenous nationalist movements within the European colonial world. World War II drew the military forces of the colonial powers back to Europe. The Japanese conquests of Asia helped to turn out the European powers from that area. After the military and political dislocations of

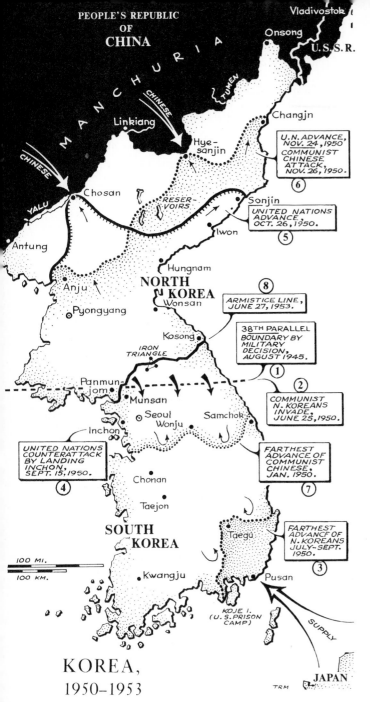

PEOPLE'S REPUBLIC OF CHINA

MANCHURIA

Linkiang

CHINESE

Onsong

Vladivostok

U.S.S.R.

TUMEN

Changjn

U.N. ADVANCE, NOV. 24, 1950. COMMUNIST CHINESE ATTACK, NOV. 26, 1950. (6)

CHINESE

Hye-sanjin

Chosan

RESERVOIRS

Sonjin

YALU

Antung

Iwon

UNITED NATIONS ADVANCE, OCT. 26, 1950. (5)

Hungnam

Anju

NORTH KOREA

Pyongyang

Wonsan

ARMISTICE LINE, JUNE 27, 1953. (8)

Kosong

38TH PARALLEL BOUNDARY BY MILITARY DECISION, AUGUST 1945. (1)

IRON TRIANGLE

Panmun-jom

(2)

COMMUNIST N. KOREANS INVADE, JUNE 25, 1950.

Munsan

Seoul Wonju

Samchok

Inchon

UNITED NATIONS COUNTERATTACK BY LANDING INCHON, SEPT. 15, 1950. (4)

FARTHEST ADVANCE OF COMMUNIST CHINESE, JAN. 1950. (7)

Chonan

Taejon

SOUTH KOREA

Taegu

FARTHEST ADVANCE OF N. KOREANS JULY-SEPT. 1950. (3)

100 MI.

100 KM.

Kwangju

Pusan

KOJE I. (U. S. PRISON CAMP)

SUPPLY

KOREA, 1950–1953

TRM

JAPAN

MAP 33.2 *The North Korean invasion of South Korea in 1950 and the bitter three-year war to repulse the invasion and stabilize a firm boundary near the thirty-eighth parallel are outlined here. The war was a dramatic application of the American policy of "containment" of communism.*

pean empires. Within the colonies there had also arisen nationalist movements of varying strengths. These were often led by gifted persons who had been educated in Europe. The values and political ideologies they had learned in Europe itself helped them to present effective critiques of the colonial situation. Such leadership, as well as the frequently blatant injustice imposed on colonial peoples, paved the way for effective nationalist movements.

There was a wide variety in decolonization. Some cases were relatively systematic; in others the European powers simply beat a hasty retreat. In 1947 Britain left India. The result of internal disputes, including religious differences, was the creation of two states, India and Pakistan. In 1948 Burma and Sri Lanka (formerly Ceylon) became independent. During the 1950s the British attempted to prepare colonies for self-government. Ghana (formerly the Gold Coast) and Nigeria—which became self-governing in 1957 and 1960, respectively—were the major examples of planned decolonization. In other areas, such as Malta and Cyprus, the British withdrawal occurred under the pressure of militant nationalist movements.

The smaller colonial powers had much less choice. The Dutch were forced from Indonesia in 1950. In 1960 the Belgian Congo, now Zaire, became independent in the midst of great turmoil. For a considerable time, as will be seen, France attempted to maintain its position in Southeast Asia but met defeat in 1954. It was similarly driven from North Africa. President De Gaulle carried out a policy of referendums on independence within remaining French colonial possessions. By the late 1960s only Portugal remained a traditional colonial power. In 1975 it finally abandoned its African colony of Angola.

The retreat from empire represents a major turning point in both European and world history. European and Western influences remain active in the former colonial world. Multinational corporations can and do exert considerable power over developing economies. The trade policies of the major Western industrial nations can do likewise. However, it now seems certain that in the future the command over natural resources possessed by

the war came the postwar economic collapse. The latter meant that the colonial powers could no longer afford to maintain their positions abroad.

Finally, the war aims of the Allies undermined colonialism. It was difficult to fight against tyranny in Europe while maintaining colonial dominance abroad. Moreover the postwar policy of the United States generally opposed the continuation of Euro-

some of these new nations will mean a considerable loss of independence by European and Western nations generally. At the end of the nineteenth century the technological power of Europe allowed certain nations to become colonial powers. At the close of the twentieth century the dependence of European industry and technology on the resources of the developing countries may very well mean that the former colonies will exert immense influence over the destiny of Europeans. The oil embargo of 1973 imposed on Europe by the oil-producing countries of the world demonstrated the potential for such powerful influence. The rest of this century will be largely devoted to the working out of this new economic balance. Although the political power of Europe will thus be lessened, the impact of its culture and of the technology originally developed in Europe will continue to expand as nations throughout the world continue to become westernized.

France, the United States, and Vietnam

As far as the general history of the West is concerned, the decolonization policies of France produced the major postwar upheavals. French decolonization became an integral part of the Cold War and led directly to the involvement of the United States in the Southeast Asian country of Vietnam. The problem of decolonization helped to transfer the Cold War rivalry that had developed in Europe to other continents. Nowhere did those rivalries become more intense than in Asia. Moreover, there was a close relationship between events in Asia and in Europe.

KOREA. To elucidate how the United States became so deeply involved in the French attempt to maintain its position in Vietnam, brief attention must first be given to the policy of the United States in regard to the Korean War.

Between 1910 and 1945 Japan as an Asian colonial power in its own right occupied and exploited Korea. By the close of World War II the Japanese had been driven out of the Korean peninsula. At home, under the direction of the United States, the Japanese nation was politically reconstructed into a democracy. The influence of the army and of large business combines was reduced. Women were allowed to vote, and representative institutions were imposed. General Douglas MacArthur (1880–1964) was the representative of the United States during this crucial period. Maintenance of a demo-cratic Japan was to be a cornerstone of postwar United States policy.

The Japanese empire still had to be dealt with. Consequently the United States and the Soviet Union presided over the division of Korea into two parts with the thirty-eighth parallel as the line of separation. It was anticipated that the country would eventually be reunited. However, by 1948 two separate states had been organized: the Democratic People's Republic of Korea under Kim Ilsung in the north and the Republic of Korea under Syngman Rhee in the south. The former was supported by the Soviet Union and the latter by the United States.

Numerous border clashes occurred between the two states. In late June 1950 forces from North Korea invaded across the thirty-eighth parallel. The United States intervened and was soon supported by the mandate of the United Nations. Great Britain, Turkey, and Australia sent token forces. The troops were commanded by General MacArthur. The Korean police action was technically a United Nations venture to halt aggression. (It had been made possible by a boycott by the Soviet ambassador to the United Nations at the time of the key vote.) From the standpoint of the United States the point of the Korean conflict was to contain the spread and to halt the aggression of communism. The United States policymakers tended to conceive of the communist world as a single unit directed from Moscow. The movement of forces into South Korea was in their view simply another example of communist pressure against a noncommunist state similar to that previously confronted in Europe.

General MacArthur's forces had initially repelled the North Koreans. He then pushed them almost to Manchuria. Late in 1950, however, the Chinese, responding to the pressure against their border, sent troops to support North Korea. The American forces had to retreat. The United States policymakers believed that the Chinese, who since 1949 had been under the communist government of Mao Tse-tung (1893–1976), were simply the puppets of Moscow. For over two years the war bogged down. Eventually a border near the thirty-eighth parallel was restored. The war lasted until June 26, 1953, when an armistice was signed. In Korea limited military action had halted and contained the military advance of a communist nation. The lessons of the Cold War learned in Europe appeared to have been successfully applied to Asia.

VIETNAM AND ITS NEIGHBORS

MAP 33.3 *The Southeast Asia scene of the long and complex struggle centered in Vietnam is shown by the map.*

The American government was confirmed in its faith in a policy of containment.

VIETNAM. During the years of the Korean conflict another war was being fought in Asia between France and the Viet Minh nationalist movement in Indochina. France, in its push for empire, had occupied this territory (which contained Laos, Cambodia, and Vietnam) between 1857 and 1883. It had administered the area and invested heavily in it, but the economy of Indochina remained overwhelmingly agrarian. During World War I tens of thousands of Indochinese troops supported France. The French also educated many people from the colony. However, neither the aid during the war nor the achievement of Western education allowed the Vietnamese to escape discrimination from their French colonial rulers.

By 1930 a movement against French colonial rule had been organized by Ho Chi Minh (1892–1969) into the Indochinese Communist Party. Ho had traveled throughout the world and had held jobs in several places in Europe prior to World War I. He and other Indochinese had lobbied at the Versailles Conference in 1919 to have the principle of self-determination applied to their country. In 1920 he was part of the wing of the French Socialist Party that formed the French Communist Party. In 1923 he was sent to Moscow. By 1925 he had formed the Vietnam Revolutionary Youth. After organizing the Indochinese Communist Party, he traveled in Asia and spent considerable time in the Soviet Union. Throughout the 1930s, however, the French succeeded in suppressing most activities by the Communist Party in their colony.

World War II provided new opportunities for Ho Chi Minh and other nationalists. When Japan invaded, it found the pro-Vichy French colonial administration ready to collaborate. Consequently action against the Japanese thereafter meshed quite neatly with action against the French. It was during these wartime circumstances that Ho Chi Minh established his position as a major nationalist leader. He was a Communist to be sure, but he was first and foremost a nationalist. Most importantly, he had achieved his position in Vietnam during the war independent of the support of the Chinese Communist movement.

In September 1945 Ho Chi Minh declared the independence of Vietnam under the Viet Minh. There was considerable internal Vietnamese resistance to this claim of political control. The opposition arose from religious groups and non-Communist nationalists. After the war the French immediately took advantage of these divisions to establish a government favorable to their own interests. The United States, in line with its wartime anticolonialist position, urged the French to make some kind of accommodation with Ho Chi Minh. In 1946 France and the Viet Minh reached an armistice. It proved to be quite temporary, and in 1947 full-fledged war broke out. The next year the

French established a friendly Vietnamese government under Bao Dai. It was to be independent within a loose union with France. This arrangement would have meant very limited independence and was clearly unacceptable to both the Viet Minh and most other nationalists.

Until 1949 the United States had displayed only the most minimal concern for the Indochina War. However, the defeat in China of Chiang Kai-shek (1887–1975) in 1949 and the establishment of the communist People's Republic of China changed that situation dramatically. This turn of events led the United States to regard the French colonial war against Ho Chi Minh as an integral part of the Cold War conflict. The French government, hoping for United States support, worked to maintain that point of view. Early in 1950 the United States recognized the Bao Dai government. At approximately the same time the Soviet Union and the People's Republic of China recognized the government of Ho Chi Minh. Indochina was thus transformed from a colonial battleground into an area of Cold War confrontation.

In May 1950 the United States announced that it would supply financial aid to the French war effort. Between that time and 1954 more than $4 billion flowed from the United States to France. However, the war itself deteriorated for the French. In the spring of 1954 their army was overrun by the Viet Minh forces at the battle of Dien Bien Phu. Psychologically and militarily the French could not muster new energy for the war. Pierre Mendès-France (b. 1907) was elected premier in Paris on the promise of concluding the conflict. At this point the United States government was badly divided, but it decided against military intervention.

During the late spring and early summer of 1954 a conference was held at Geneva to settle the Indochina conflict. All in all it proved a most unsatisfactory gathering. To one degree or another, all of the major powers were involved in the proceedings, but they did not sign the agreements. Technically the agreements existed between the armed forces of France and those of the Viet Minh. The precedents for such arrangements were the surrender of the German army in 1945 and the Korean armistice of 1953. The Geneva conference provided for the division of Vietnam at the seventeenth parallel. This was to be a temporary border. By 1956 elections were to be held to reunify the country. North of the parallel, centered on the city of Hanoi, the

Viet Minh were in charge; below it, the French were in charge, with Saigon the major city. The prospect of elections meant that theoretically both groups could function politically in the territory of the other. In effect, the conference attempted to transform a military conflict into a political one.

The United States was less than happy about the results of the Geneva discussions. Its first major response came in September 1954, with the formation of the Southeast Asia Treaty Organization (SEATO). It was a collective security agreement that in some respects paralleled the European NATO alliance. However, it did not involve the integration of forces achieved in NATO, nor did it include all the major states of the region. Its membership consisted of the United States, Great Britain, France, Australia, New Zealand, Thailand, Pakistan, and the Philippines.

By 1955 American policymakers had begun to think about the Indochina region, and more especially Vietnam, largely in terms of the Korean example. The United States government assumed that the government being established in North Vietnam was, like the government of North Korea, basically a communist puppet state. The same year French troops began to withdraw from the south. As they left, the various Vietnamese political groups began to fight for power. Into the turmoil of the power vacuum stepped the United States with military and economic aid. Among the Vietnamese politicians, it chose to support Ngo Dinh Diem. He was a strong non-Communist nationalist who had not collaborated with the French. The Americans hoped that he would become a leader around whom a non-Communist Vietnamese nationalist movement might rally. However, because the United States had publicly been deeply committed to the French, any government it supported would be, and was, viewed with suspicion by Vietnamese nationalists. In October 1955 Diem established a Republic of Vietnam in the territory for which the Geneva conference had made France responsible. By 1956 the United States was training troops and government officials, paying salaries, and providing military equipment.

In the meantime Diem announced that he and his newly established government were not bound by the Geneva agreements and that elections would not be held in 1956. The American government, which had not signed the Geneva documents, supported his position. Diem undertook an anti-Communist campaign, attacking many citizens who had earlier resisted the French. This was the beginning of a program of political repression that characterized his regime and those that followed. There was a long series of ordinances that gave the government extraordinary power over its citizens. Diem alienated the peasants by restoring rents to landlords and generally strengthening large landowners. He abolished elected village councils and replaced them with his own officials, who had often come from the north. In fact, Diem's major base of political support lay with the more than one million Vietnamese who had migrated to the south after 1954.

Soldiers of the United States equipped with sophisticated weapons examine a Viet Cong guerilla booby trap in Vietnam. One of the great frustrations of the war for the Americans was the ability of relatively simple guerilla tactics of sabotage to slow or even halt altogether technologically advanced American operations. [Official United States Navy Photograph.]

By 1960 Diem's policy had created considerable internal resistance in South Vietnam. In that year the National Liberation Front was founded, with the goals of overthrowing Diem, unifying the country, reforming the economy, and ousting the Americans. It was anticolonial, nationalist, and Communist. Its military arm was called the Viet Cong. Sometime in the very late 1950s the government of North Vietnam began to aid the insurgent forces of the south. The Viet Cong and their supporters carried out a program of widespread terrorism and political disruption. They imposed an informal government through much of the countryside. Many peasants voluntarily supported them; others supported them from fear of reprisals. In addition to the Communist opposition, Diem confronted mounting criticism from non-Communist citizens. The Buddhists agitated against the Roman Catholic president. The army was less than satisfied with him. Diem's response to all of these pressures was further repression and dependence on an ever smaller group of advisers.

The Eisenhower and early Kennedy administrations in America continued to support Diem while demanding reforms. The American military presence grew from somewhat more than six hundred persons in early 1961 to over sixteen thousand troops in late 1963. The political situation in Vietnam became increasingly unstable. On November 1, 1963, Diem was overthrown and murdered in an army coup. The United States was deeply involved in this plot. Its officials hoped that if the Diem regime were eliminated, the path would be opened for the establishment of a new government in South Vietnam capable of generating popular support. Thereafter the political goal of the United States was to find a leader who could fill this need. It finally settled on Nguyen Van Thieu, who governed South Vietnam from 1966 to 1975.

President Kennedy was assassinated on November 22, 1963. His successor, Lyndon Johnson, continued and vastly expanded the commitment to South Vietnam. In August 1964, after an attack on an American ship in the Gulf of Tonkin, the first bombing of North Vietnam was authorized. In February 1965 major bombing attacks began that continued, with only brief pauses, until the early weeks of 1973. The land war grew in extent, with over 500,000 Americans stationed in South Vietnam. In 1969 President Richard Nixon commenced a policy of gradual withdrawal of troops. The program was called *Vietnamization*. From the

After almost five years of negotiations, the United States and South Vietnam signed a cease fire
with the Hanoi regime and the Viet Cong in Paris on January 28, 1973. [Sygma.]

spring of 1968 onward long-drawn-out peace negotiations were conducted in Paris. In January
1973 a cease-fire was finally arranged. The troops
of the United States were pulled back, and prisoners of war held in North Vietnam were returned.
Thereafter violations of the cease-fire occurred on
both sides. In early 1975 an evacuation of South
Vietnamese troops from the northern part of their
country turned into a complete rout as they were
attacked by the troops of North Vietnam. On April
30, 1975, the city of Saigon fell to the troops of the
Viet Cong and North Vietnam. The Second Indochina War had come to an end.

The Second Indochina War, which was in effect
a continuation of the first war, which the French
had lost, was an event of immense controversy and
complexity. It was widely debated throughout the
world at the time and will continue to be debated

for many years. The United States saw the conflict
as part of the Cold War and as a repetition of
Korea. Aggression from the north had to be
halted. There was also hope that the military
power of the United States might buy time so that a
strong nationalist, non-Communist regime could
be established in South Vietnam. However, the
United States misread the situation in Vietnam and
especially its superficial resemblance to what had
taken place in Korea. The United States ignored
the basic colonial character of the Vietnamese political scene. It also overlooked the larger size of
Vietnam, the different topography, the weakness
of the South Vietnamese army, and the corruption
of the government of South Vietnam.

The war grew out of a power vacuum left by
decolonization. It produced a major impact on all
the Western world. For a decade after the Cuban

missile crisis the attention of the United States was largely diverted from Europe. American prestige suffered, and the American commitment to Western Europe came into question. Moreover the blundering of American policy in Southeast Asia made many Europeans wonder about the basic wisdom of the American government. Many young Europeans—and not a few Americans—born after World War II came to regard the United States not as a protector of liberty but as an ambitious, aggressive, and cruel power trying to keep colonialism alive after the end of the colonial era. The American involvement in Vietnam probably proved fundamental to the emergence of a new commitment to unity and economic integration in Europe. That involvement allowed Europeans still living in the shadow of American power and influence to reassert their own independence and to strike out in new directions.

Toward Western European Unification

Since 1945 the nations of Western Europe have taken unprecedented steps toward cooperation and potential unity. The moves toward unification have related primarily to economic integration. These actions have arisen from American encouragement, in response to the Soviet domination of Eastern Europe, and from a sense of lack of effective political power on the part of the states of Western Europe. The process of economic integration has not been steady, nor is it near completion; but it has provided a major new factor in the domestic politics of the states involved.

The movement toward unity could have occurred in at least three ways: politically, militarily, or economically. The economic path was taken largely because the other paths were blocked. In 1949 ten European states organized the Council of Europe, which meets in Strasbourg, France. Its organization involved foreign ministers and a Consultative Assembly elected by the parliaments of the participants. The Council of Europe was and continues to be only an advisory body. It had been hoped by some persons that the council might become a parliament of Europe, but during the early 1950s none of the major states was willing to surrender any of its sovereignty to the newly organized body. The initial failure of the council to bring about significant political cooperation meant that for the time being unity would not come about by political or parliamentary routes.

Between 1950 and 1954 there was some interest in a more thorough integration of the military forces of NATO. When the Korean War broke out, the United States began to urge the rearmament of Germany. The German forces would provide Western Europe with further protection against possible Soviet aggression while the United States was involved in Korea. France continued to fear a German army. In 1951 the French government suggested the creation of a European Defense Community that would constitute a supranational military organization. It would require a permanent British commitment of forces to the Continent to help France, in effect, counter any future German threat. The proposal continued to be considered for some time, but in 1954 the French Parliament itself vetoed the program. In 1955 Germany was permitted to rearm and to enter NATO. Supranational military organization had not been achieved.

Rather than in politics or the military the major moves toward European cooperation and potential unity came in the economic sphere. Unlike the other two possible paths of cooperation, economic activity involved little or no immediate loss of political sovereignty. Moreover the material benefits of combined economic activity would bring new popular support to all of the governments involved.

The Marshall Plan of the United States created the Organization for European Economic Cooperation (OEEC). It was a vehicle set up to require common planning and cooperation among the participating countries and to discourage a return to the prewar economic nationalism. The OEEC and later NATO gave the countries involved new experience in working with each other and demonstrated the productivity, the efficiency, and the simple possibility of cooperative action.[1] Although neither organization provided a means of political or economic integration, the experience was most important.

Among European leaders and civil servants there existed a large body of opinion that only through the abandonment of economic national-

---

[1] The OEEC continued in existence until 1961, when it was reorganized as the Organization for Economic Cooperation and Development (OECD). Both organizations included nations not involved in the more formal moves toward unity. The OECD also included Japan and has been interested in Third World economic development.

Konrad Adenauer of West Germany and Charles De Gaulle of France were the two major West European statesmen of the late 1950s and early 1960s. They pursued policies of reconciliation between their two nations and a policy of a more nearly united Europe based on the Common Market. [United Press International Photo.]

ism could the newly organized democratic states avoid the economic turmoil that had proved such fertile ground for dictatorship. Economic cooperation carried the possibility of greater efficiency, prosperity, and employment. The leading figures holding these opinions were Robert Schuman (1886–1963), the foreign minister of France; Konrad Adenauer (1876–1967), the chancellor of the Federal Republic of Germany; Alcide De Gasperi (1881–1954), the prime minister of Italy; and Paul-Henri Spaak (1899–1972), the prime minister of Belgium. Among major civil servants and bureaucrats, Jean Monnet (1885–1981) of France was the leading spokesman.

In 1950 Schuman proposed that the coal and steel production of Western Europe be undertaken on an integrated, cooperative basis. The next year France, West Germany, Italy, and the "Benelux" countries (Belgium, the Netherlands, and Luxembourg) organized the European Coal and Steel

Community. Its activity was limited to a single part of the economy, but that was a sector that affected almost all other industrial production. An agency called the *High Authority* administered the plan. The authority was genuinely supranational, and its members could not be removed during their appointed terms. The Coal and Steel Community prospered. By 1955 coal production had grown by 23 per cent. Iron and steel production was up by almost 150 per cent. The community both benefited from and contributed to the immense growth of material production in Western Europe during this period. Its success reduced the suspicions of government and business groups about the concept of coordination and economic integration.

It took more than the prosperity of the European Coal and Steel Community to draw European leaders toward further unity. The unsuccessful Suez intervention and the resulting diplomatic isolation of France and Britain persuaded many

The European Economic Community Is Established

The 1957 Treaty of Rome identified the major goals of the European Economic Community (Common Market) for the original six members.

Article 2: It shall be the aim of the Community, by establishing a Common Market and progressively approximating the economic policies of Member States, to promote throughout the Community a harmonious development of economic activities, a continuous and balanced expansion, an increased stability, an accelerated raising of the standard of living and closer relations between its Member States.

Article 3: For the purposes set out in the preceding Article, the activities of the Community shall include, under the conditions and with the timing provided for in this Treaty:

(a) the elimination, as between Member States, of customs duties and of quantitative restrictions in regard to the importation and exportation of goods, as well as of all other measures with equivalent effect;

(b) the establishment of a common customs tariff and a common commercial policy towards third countries;

(c) the abolition, as between Member States, of the obstacles to the free movement of persons, services and capital;

(d) the inauguration of a common agricultural policy;

(e) the inauguration of a common transport policy;

(f) the establishment of a system ensuring that competition shall not be distorted in the Common Market;

(g) the application of procedures which shall make it possible to co-ordinate the economic policies of Member States and to remedy disequilibria in their balances of payments;

(h) the approximation of their respective municipal law to the extent necessary for the functioning of the Common Market;

(i) the creation of a European Social Fund in order to improve the possibilities of employment for workers and to contribute to the raising of their standard of living;

(j) the establishment of a European Investment Bank intended to facilitate the economic expansion of the Community through the creation of new resources; and

(k) the association of overseas countries and territories with the Community with a view to increasing trade and to pursuing jointly their effort towards economic and social development.

Treaty Establishing the European Economic Community (Brussels: Secretariat of the Interim Committee for the Common Market and Euratom, 1957), pp. 17–18.

Europeans that only through unified action could they exert any significant influence on the two superpowers or control their own destinies. Consequently, in 1957, through the Treaty of Rome, the six members of the Coal and Steel Community agreed to form a new organization: the European Economic Community. The *Common Market,* as the EEC soon came to be called, envisioned more than a free-trade union. Its members sought to achieve the eventual elimination of tariffs, a free flow of capital and labor, and similar wage and social benefits in all the participating countries. Its chief institutions were a Council of Foreign Ministers and a High Commission composed of technocrats. The former came to be the dominant body.

The Common Market achieved a stunning degree of success during its early years. By 1968 all tariffs among the six members had been abolished well ahead of the planned schedule. Trade and labor migration among the members grew steadily. Moreover nonmember states began to copy the community and later to seek membership. In 1959 Britain, Denmark, Norway, Sweden, Switzerland, Austria, and Portugal formed the European Free Trade Area. However, by 1961 Great Britain had decided to seek Common Market membership. Twice, in 1963 and 1967, British membership was vetoed by President De Gaulle of France. The French president felt that Britain was too closely related to the United States and its policies to support the European Economic Community whole-heartedly.

The French veto of British membership demonstrated the major difficulty confronting the Common Market during the 1960s. The Council of Ministers, representing the individual national interests of member states, came to have more influence than the High Commission. Political as well as economic factors increasingly entered into decision making. France particularly was unwilling to compromise on any matter that it regarded as pertaining to its sovereignty. On more than one occasion President De Gaulle demanded his own policies and refused French participation under any other conditions. This attitude caused major problems over agricultural policy.

Despite the French actions the Common Market survived and continued to prosper. In 1973 Great Britain, Ireland, and Denmark became members. Discussions continued on further steps toward integration, including a common currency. Throughout the late seventies, however, there and into the eighties seemed to be a loss of momentum. Norway and Sweden with relatively strong economies declined to join. Although in 1982 Spain, Portugal, and Greece applied for membership, there continued to be a sense of stagnation within the Community. The Community will no doubt survive, but a decade of major strain seems to lie ahead.

Internal Political Developments in Western Europe

After the war, with the exceptions of Portugal and Spain, which remained dictatorships until the mid-1970s, the nations of Western Europe continued to pursue the path of liberal democracy. But their leaders realized that the prewar democratic political structures alone had been insufficient to ensure peace, stability, material prosperity, and domestic liberty for their peoples. It had become clear that democracy required a social and economic base as well as a political structure. Economic prosperity and social security in the eyes of most Europeans became a duty of government as a way of staving off the kind of turmoil that had brought on tyranny and war. They also regarded such programs as a means of avoiding communism.

MAJOR DATES IN THE ERA OF THE SUPERPOWERS

1948	Berlin Blockade
1949	Formation of the North Atlantic Treaty Organization
1950	Outbreak of the Korean War
1953	Death of Stalin
1956	July—Egypt seizes the Suez Canal
	October—Anglo-French attack on the Suez Canal
	Hungarian Revolution
1957	Treaty of Rome establishes the European Economic Community
1958	De Gaulle comes to power in France
1960	Paris Summit Conference collapses
1962	Cuban missile crisis
1963	Russian–American Test Ban Treaty
1967	Six Days' War between Israel and Egypt
1968	Russian invasion of Czechoslovakia
1973	Yom Kippur War between Israel and Egypt
1975	Helsinki Accords
1978	Camp David Accords
1979	Russian invasion of Afghanistan
1980	Socialist victory in France
1981	Military crackdown on Solidarity Movement in Poland

Except for the British Labor Party the vehicles of the new postwar politics were not, as might have been expected, the democratic socialist parties. On the whole those parties did not prosper after the onset of the Cold War. They stood opposed by both Communists and groups more conservative than themselves. Rather the new departures were led by various Christian Democratic parties, usually leading coalition governments. These Christian Democratic political parties were a major new feature of postwar politics. They were largely Roman Catholic in leadership and membership. Catholic parties had previously existed in Europe. But from the late nineteenth century through the 1930s they had been very conservative and had tended to protect the social, political, and educational interests of the church. They had traditionally opposed communism but had few positive programs of their own. The postwar Christian Democratic parties of Germany, France, and Italy were progressive.

They accepted democracy and advocated social reform. They welcomed non-Catholics to membership. Democracy, social reform, economic growth, and anticommunism were their hallmarks. Not until the late 1960s were those goals seriously challenged or questioned.

The events of the war years in large measure determined the political leadership of the postwar decade. On the Continent those groups and parties that had been active in the resistance against Nazis and fascism held an initial advantage. Until 1947 those groups frequently included the Communist Party. Thereafter Communists were quite systematically excluded from all Western European governments. This policy was quite naturally favored and encouraged by the United States. The immediate domestic problems after the war included not only those created by the physical damage of the conflict but often those that had existed in 1939.

The war in most cases had not solved those prewar difficulties, but it had often opened new opportunities or possibilities for solution.

Great Britain: Power in Decline

In July 1945 the British electorate overwhelmingly voted for a Labor Party government. For the first time the Labor Party commanded in its own right a majority of the House of Commons. Clement Attlee (1883–1967) replaced Churchill as prime minister. The British had not so much rejected the great wartime leader as they had renounced the Conservative Party, which had, in effect, governed since 1931. In the public mind the Conservatives were associated with the economic problems of the 1930s. For purposes of postwar reconstruction and redirection the Labor Party seemed to have a better program.

❧ The British Labor Party Issues a Cautious Platform

The Labor Party was committed to a program of socialism in 1945. However, its platform of that year made clear that the party would move cautiously in carrying out its policy. Both the commitment to social change and the promise of caution proved attractive to the electorate, with the result that Labor came to power.

By the test of war some industries have shown themselves capable of rising to new heights of efficiency and expansion. Others, including some of our older industries fundamental to our economic structure, have wholly or partly failed. . . .

Each industry must have applied to it the test of national service. If it serves the nation, well and good; if it is inefficient and falls down on its job, the nation must see that things are put right.

These propositions seem indisputable, but for years before the war anti-Labour Governments set them aside, so that British industry over a large field fell into a state of depression, muddle and decay. Millions of working and middle-class people went through the horrors of unemployment and insecurity. It is not enough to sympathise with these victims: we must develop an acute feeling of national shame—and act.

The Labour Party is a Socialist Party, and proud of it. Its ultimate purpose at home is the establishment

of the Socialist Commonwealth of Great Britain—free, democratic, efficient, progressive, public-spirited, its material resources organised in the service of the British people.

But Socialism cannot come overnight, as the product of a week-end revolution. The members of the Labour Party, like the British people, are practical-minded men and women.

There are basic industries ripe and over-ripe for public ownership and management in direct service of the nation. There are many smaller businesses rendering good service which can be left to go on with their useful work.

There are big industries not yet ripe for public ownership which must nevertheless be required by constructive supervision to further the nation's needs and not to prejudice national interests by restrictive anti-social monopoly or cartel agreements—caring for their own capital structures and profits at the cost of a lower standard of living for all.

Let Us Face the Future, cited in J. F. C. Harrison, *Society and Politics in England,* 1780–1960 (New York: Harper & Row, 1965), pp. 450–451.

Attlee's ministry was socialist but clearly non-Marxist. It made a number of bold departures in both economic and social policy. The government assumed ownership of certain major industries, including the Bank of England, the airlines, public transport, coal, electricity, and steel. The ministry also undertook a major housing program. Probably its most popular accomplishment was the establishment of a major program of welfare legislation. This involved further unemployment assistance, old-age pensions, school lunches, and, most importantly, free medical service to all citizens. All of these departures were expensive, and immediate postwar economic recovery was slow. By the close of 1948 the drive toward further social reform had come to a halt. During the next several years the Labor Party itself became badly divided between one wing that advocated more socialism and government services and another that contended that the nation could for the time being afford few or no new programs.

The forward domestic policy of the Labor government was matched by a policy of gradual retreat on the world scene. In 1947 the enunciation of the Truman Doctrine in regard to Greece and Turkey marked Britain's admission that it could not afford to oversee the security of those areas. In the same year Britain recognized the independence of Pakistan and India. In the postwar era Britain would be repeatedly confronted by nationalist movements within the empire and would gradually, and usually gracefully, retreat from those outposts. In 1949 the government devalued the pound sterling from $4.03 to $2.80. The once-strong economy was clearly in trouble; the nation could earn insufficient foreign exchange from its exports to pay for its imports. The military, imperial, and economic power that had once made Britain the foremost of European nations had eroded and would continue to do so for the next three decades.

In 1951 the Conservative Party under Churchill returned to office, and the party remained there until 1964. This was the longest period of continuous government by any party in modern British history. Internal Labor Party divisions contributed to this development, but so did the policies of the Conservatives. Under Churchill and then under his successors, Anthony Eden in 1955–1957, Harold Macmillan in 1957–1963, and Alec Douglas-Home in 1963–1964, the Conservatives attempted to draw a picture of major differences between themselves and the Labor Party. In reality

Wrecked ships were strewn throughout the Suez Canal after the Franco-British attack of 1956. [United Press International Photo.]

the differences were of degree rather than of kind. The Conservative government did return the steel industry to private ownership, but it did not return to a free economy. The program of national welfare and health services continued, and the Conservatives actually undertook a building program larger than that of the Labor Party.

The problem of decline of power and prestige continued. From the mid-1950s onward one part of the empire after another became independent. The Suez intervention of 1956 brought an end to independent British military intervention. Increasingly British policy was made subservient to that of the United States. However, the economy constituted the most persistent difficulty. Throughout

1037

the decade the slogan "Export or die" was heard. Exports did grow rapidly, yet more slowly than imports. Productivity remained discouragingly low. British unions were old-fashioned and less forward-looking than those on the Continent. Management was quite timid. Perhaps most importantly, there was a low rate of capital investment in both privately and nationally owned industries. The trade unions were often more interested in carving up existing wealth than in creating new wealth to be distributed. The government too often favored economic programs that were not aimed at long-term growth.

In 1964 the Labor Party returned to office under Harold Wilson. It promised to right the economic situation, but the economy only worsened. The pound was devalued further. Wilson renewed the attempt to join the Common Market, which Macmillan had begun in 1963. Labor, like the Conservatives, confronted the veto of France. In 1970 the electorate again turned to the Conservative Party, then led by Edward Heath. His major accomplishment was to take Britain into the Common Market in 1973. However, domestically Heath floundered badly in his dealings with the trade unions. The country suffered a crippling coal strike in the winter of 1973–1974.

In 1974 Wilson returned to office, primarily on the grounds that the Labor Party might have better relations with the unions. The Labor government was able to reach some agreements on limitations for pay raises. Still inflation raged and in 1976 the value of the pound sterling dipped below $1.60. The same year Wilson voluntarily resigned and was replaced by James Callaghan. The new prime minister took virtually no new departures, and the problem of a stagnant economy linked to inflation continued. In March of 1979, after a defeat in the House of Commons, Callaghan called for new elections. Labor lost decisively to the Conservative Party, which since 1975 has been led by Margaret Thatcher, the first woman to be the British prime minister.

Within the context of the British Conservative Party Thatcher stood much farther to the right than had Heath. Her Cabinet pursued a policy of very high interest rates, sharp tax cuts, and somewhat reduced government spending. Initially Thatcher also took a very hard line with the trade unions, although she and her ministers later became more cooperative with the unions. The re-

sults of these policies, popularly known as Thatcherism, have been quite mixed. Inflation did come under limited control, but the rate of unemployment in 1981 reached the levels of the Great Depression years. Many members of her own party and representatives of British industry have been quite critical.

The summer of 1981, however, saw an important new problem arise for British society and political leadership. Riots broke out in several of the major cities, including Liverpool and London. The riots were violent and involved extensive property damage and loss of life. Two factors seem to account for these disturbances. First, thousands of British youth were without jobs, and they saw Thatcher's policies as being responsible for that situation. Second, during the past two decades tens of thousands of nonwhite immigrants had come to settle in Britain from the nation's former colonies. The clash of cultures and the competition for scarce employment have led to widespread racism of a very public character. Some of the riots of 1981 involved racial clashes; others involved both white and nonwhite youths jointly attacking the police, who had come to be viewed in some urban areas as symbols of political repression. The Thatcher government took only the most minimal action to address the economic conditions that fostered the riots. Some government funds were appropriated to create new jobs. But in the years ahead both the economic stagnation and the racial animosity promise the possibility of further instability.

The fragmentation in British society and economic life was matched by new factionalism in politics. Thatcher's emergence represented the victory of the right wing of the British Conservative Party over its more moderate center. Throughout the Callaghan ministry and after, the Labor Party experienced even more disunity. The left wing of the Labor Party, led by Anthony Benn, challenged the leadership of Callaghan, who was replaced by Michael Foot in 1980. Thereafter several members of the Labor Party who were former government ministers, including David Owen, Roy Jenkins, and Shirley Williams, resigned from the Labor Party. They joined with a few lesser-known Conservatives to form a new political party in 1980 known as the Social Democratic Party. This new party saw itself as carving out a broad middle position between the Conservative and Labor parties. Public opinion polls show considerable support for the new group, but its fortunes have yet to be tried at a general election.

Any attempt to gauge the probable success of the Social Democrats or the likely direction of British politics in the near future became confused in the spring of 1982. After years of fruitless negotiations over the question of legal ownership, the government of Argentina ordered the invasion of the Falkland Islands, which are located in the South Atlantic off the shore of South America and which have been governed by Great Britain for over a century and a half. The Argentines claimed the dispute involved the recapture of territory held by a colonial power. The British contended that the Argentines had committed an act of international aggression, an opinion in which the government of the United States concurred. The invasion occurred on April 3. Shortly thereafter the British dispatched a very large fleet to the South Atlantic. During the following weeks the largest naval engagements since World War II took place between the British and Argentine navies. Both forces sus-tained major losses before the British emerged the victors. In Britain itself the war over the Falklands generated considerable public support for the Thatcher government. Britain will no doubt find itself required to keep a substantial military force stationed for some time well over eight thousand miles from Europe. This commitment will in all likelihood require some rethinking of the deployment of NATO naval resources. The Falklands crisis illustrates the unpredictability of international politics and, more important, the manner in which political developments outside of Europe can now have very direct affects on the fortunes of the continent.

In addition to the war in the South Atlantic and the gravest economic situation in the Western world, Britain has also had to confront in recent years a major internal disturbance in Northern Ireland. By the treaty of 1921 the Ulster counties remained a part of the United Kingdom while retaining a large measure of self-government. The Protestant majority used its power to discriminate systematically against the Roman Catholic minority

In April 1982, Argentinian troops landed in the Falkland Islands. Here Argentinian tanks are shown in front of a British shipping company. The invasion led to a major armed clash with Britain. By the beginning of June, the large Argentine army on the islands had been forced to surrender. [Sygma.]

in the province. In 1968 a Catholic civil rights movement was launched. Demonstrations and counterdemonstrations resulted. Units of the Provisional Wing of the Irish Republican Army became active in seeking to unite Ulster with the Irish Republic. In turn militant Protestant organizations became mobilized. The British government sent in units of the army to restore order. Soon the army units became the target of both groups of militant Irish. In 1972 the British suspended the Northern Irish Parliament and began to govern the province directly. Thus far the troops remain, and well over thirteen hundred people have been killed in terrorist activity. During 1981 certain Irish Republican Army prisoners held in government prisons

[LEFT] *Bringing peace to Northern Ireland has been a major problem in British political life for over a decade.* [*United Press International Photo.*]

[BELOW] *Children in Belfast stoning British armored cars. An entire generation of Northern Irish children has grown up in an atmosphere of continuous violence.* [*Sygma.*]

took part in hunger strikes to protest the conditions of their imprisonment. No less than ten prisoners starved themselves to death. Riots followed each death, but the British government steadfastly refused to grant the status of political prisoner to persons who it believed had been properly convicted for acts of terrorism. No peaceful solution has yet proved forthcoming in the Irish situation.

West Germany: The Economic Miracle

No country in Europe since the war has so contrasted with Britain as the Federal Republic of Germany. The nation was organized in 1949 from the three Western Allied occupation sectors. Its amazing material progress from the ruins of the conflict

Few sights better illustrate the astounding economic recovery of Europe after 1945 than the contrast between these two views of Berlin. The ghostly picture (BELOW) shows the heavy destruction caused by the intense wartime bombing of the city. The contrasting photograph (RIGHT) shows the rebuilt center of West Berlin that emerged in the following decade. Only the ruins of the Emperor William I Memorial Church were left as they stood to serve as a permanent monument and a reminder of war's destruction. [BELOW: United Press International Photo; RIGHT: German Information Center, New York.]

became known as the economic miracle of postwar Europe. Between 1948 and 1964 West German industrial production grew by 600 per cent. Unemployment became almost unknown. All of this time the country remained the center of Cold War disputes and was occupied by thousands of foreign

troops. In the midst of Cold War tensions the Germans prospered.

The economic growth of the nation stemmed from a number of favorable factors. The Marshall Plan provided a strong impetus to recovery. The government of the republic throughout the 1950s and 1960s pursued a policy of giving private industry a relatively free hand while providing sufficient planning to avoid economic crisis. The goods produced by Germany proved attractive to the customers of other nations. *Volkswagen* became a household word throughout the world. Moreover domestic demand was vigorous, and skilled labor and energetic management were available. Finally, Germany had very few foreign commitments or responsibilities. A relatively small portion of its national income had to be spent on defense. This situation aided capital formation.

In a very real sense postwar West Germany indulged in economic expansion rather than in politics or active international policy. Unlike the Weimar Constitution, the constitution of the Federal Republic did not permit the proliferation of splinter parties. Nor did the president possess extraordinary power. The Federal Republic returned to the arena of nations very slowly. In 1949 it participated in the Marshall Plan and two years later in the European Coal and Steel Community. In 1955 the nation joined NATO, and in 1957 it was one of the charter members of the European Economic Community. The Federal Republic has been perhaps the major champion of European cooperation.

Throughout this period political initiative lay with the Christian Democrats led by Konrad Adenauer. His domestic policies were relatively simple and consistent: West Germany must become genuinely democratic and economically stable and prosperous. His foreign policy was profoundly anti-Communist. Under what was known as the Hallstein Doctrine, the Federal Republic refused to have diplomatic ties with any nation, except the Soviet Union, that extended diplomatic recognition to East Germany. Adenauer's position on East Germany contributed to the Cold War climate, and it may have led the United States to overestimate the threat of Communist aggression in Europe. The Hallstein Doctrine separated the Federal Republic from all the nations of Eastern Europe.

Adenauer remained in office until 1963, when he retired at the age of eighty-seven. The Christian Democrats remained in power, led first by Ludwig

Erhard and later by Kurt Kiesinger. In 1966, however, they were compelled to form a coalition with the Social Democratic Party (SDP). After the war this party had revived but had been unable to capture a parliamentary majority. By the early 1960s the SDP had expanded its base beyond the working class and had become more a party of social and economic reform than a party of socialism. This shift reflected the growing prosperity of the German working class. The major leader of the SDP in the 1960s was Willy Brandt, the mayor of West

In one of the most moving events of Willy Brandt's effort to improve German relations with the states of eastern Europe, the German chancellor knelt at the memorial to Warsaw Jews killed by the Germans during World War II. He was in Poland in December 1970 to sign a treaty that would lead to regular diplomatic relations between the two countries. [United Press International Photo.]

❧ The West German Chancellor Looks Toward the Close of This Century

In January 1982 Helmut Schmidt, the chancellor of West Germany, gave an interview which provided his thoughts on the major issues confronting Europe during the closing years of this century.

I would like to stress that I do not believe in prophecies by politicians. Having said this, . . .

There will not be a world war or another great war between now and the end of the century. I cannot look very far into the next century. But the year 2000 is about the span of my lifetime; I will be 82 in the year 2000, and I think I can look as far as that.

There will be no world war, because the responsibility of governments and the awareness of the danger of war are much greater nowadays than they have ever been in the first three-quarters of the 20th century. And they will get, in the long last, they will have arms reductions and arms control.

Secondly, as in the past also in the future there will be ups and downs in the economic well-being of their governments. After Keynes and after Lord Beveridge, two great Englishmen [who were the economists whose thought was largely responsible for government management of Western economies], they seemed to have learned how to manage their economies only to learn in the last decade that this doesn't hold true under any possible circumstances. But I think we will again learn to overcome our economic, our structural economic deficiences.

This leads me to the third aspect, which might in the end be the prevailing one.

When this century started, we had quite a few less than two billion people on the earth. At the end of the century, the number will have more than tripled to more than six billion people.

It is not industry that has to be blamed for the overexhaustion of natural resources. Of course industry is to be blamed for many things, but generally speaking if you want not only to feed but to give a fair standard of living to four billion people today, try to do this for six billion people within the next 18 years or so. It will necessarily mean additional overexhaustion of natural resources, the so-called natural environment and so on. And what mankind will have to learn during the last 20 years of this century is not only to set the goal for stabilization of global population but also to find the means to achieve that goal.

The New York Times, January 3, 1982, p. 15.

Berlin. In 1966 he became vice-chancellor in the coalition government. In 1969 Brandt and the SDP carried the election in their own right.

The most significant departure of the SDP occurred in the area of foreign policy. While continuing to urge further Western unity through the Common Market, Brandt moved carefully but swiftly to establish better relations with Eastern Europe (a policy called *Ostpolitik*). In 1970 he met with the leadership of East Germany. Later that year he went to Moscow to sign a treaty of cooperation. By November 1970 Brandt had completed a reconciliation treaty with Poland that recognized the Oder–Neisse river line as the Polish western border. A treaty with Czechoslovakia soon followed. In 1973 both the Federal Republic of Germany and the German Democratic Republic were admitted to the United Nations. Brandt's policy of *Ostpolitik* to a large extent regularized the German situation, but that regularity will probably remain only as long as the two superpowers desire it. Brandt's moves were in part a subdevelopment of the policy of detente on the part of the United States and the Soviet Union. In 1974 Brandt resigned. He was succeeded by Helmut Schmidt, who has continued a policy of conversations with the Communist bloc nations and Moscow. Schmidt has also taken a lead in asserting the necessity of close United States consultation with its West European allies on both economic and military matters.

France: Search for Stability and Glory

France experienced the most troubled postwar domestic political scene of any major European nation. The Third Republic had been in very deep difficulty in 1940. It had come to satisfy neither the left nor the right of the political world. More important, the republic had been incapable of staving off military defeat. To these inherited problems was added after the war the fact of wide-scale collaboration with the Nazi conquerors. A few trials, executions, and prison sentences superficially handled the problem of the Vichy collaborators, but much bitterness remained.

After the defeat of 1940 a little-known general named Charles de Gaulle (1890–1970) had organized a Free French government in London. In 1944 De Gaulle presided over the provisional government in liberated France. He was an immensely proud, patriotic person who seemed to regard himself as personally embodying the spirit of France. He had a low regard for traditional liberal democratic politics and hated the machinations of political parties, which he thought unnecessarily divided the nation. In 1946 De Gaulle suddenly resigned from the government, believing that the newly organized Fourth Republic, like the Third, gave far too little power to the executive. The Fourth French Republic thus lost the single strong leader it had possessed. After De Gaulle's departure the republic returned to the rapid turnover of ministries that had characterized the Third Republic during the 1920s and 1930s. Between 1948 and 1958 there were no less than nineteen ministries. The faces of the ministers changed, but the problems remained.

A major source of domestic discontent related to colonial problems in North Africa and Indochina. Between 1947 and 1954 France fought the long, bitter war to retain some measure of control over Indochina. That conflict has been examined more closely earlier in this chapter. By 1954, however, Premier Mendès-France's government admitted defeat and began to preside over a withdrawal from the region. It marked a major defeat for a Western nation by a former colony. The Mendès-France government also granted independence to Tunisia. Morocco was soon moving toward independence. The Suez fiasco of 1956 marked another conspicuous loss of power and prestige for France.

Indochina, Tunisia, and Morocco were regarded as colonial problems by the French. However, in their eyes Algeria, conquered in 1830 and now possessing over a million French citizens, was not a colony but an integral part of France. In 1954 a revolt broke out in Algeria, led by the Algerian Liberation Movement (the FLN). The revolt deeply divided France. The army and right-wing political groups were determined to hold Algeria. Nevertheless the war, which was intensely bitter and brutal, became increasingly unpopular. There were demands for a negotiated settlement. When the civilian government began to make moves in that direction in 1958, an army mutiny occurred in Algeria and unrest soon spread to Corsica. France seemed on the brink of civil war.

At this point the politicians in Paris turned to General De Gaulle, whom the army trusted would uphold their cause. The general accepted office only on the condition that he be given a free hand to govern and to submit a new constitution to the nation. De Gaulle created the Fifth French Republic in which the president possessed extraordinary power. He could appoint and dismiss the premier and dissolve the Chamber of Deputies. De Gaulle submitted the constitution to a popular referendum, in which it was overwhelmingly approved. Having secured his own power, De Gaulle moved to attack the Algerian problem. He believed that France could not win militarily in Algeria and that a continued struggle might bring even more political disruption in France itself. French public opinion had also shifted in favor of making some kind of accommodation that would end the bloodshed. De Gaulle made large concessions to the FLN, and by 1962 Algeria was independent. There was much domestic opposition to De Gaulle's policy. Hundreds of thousands of French citizens in Algeria returned to France, putting new pressures on its economy and resources. However, the president of the republic held the nation behind him. He had become a symbol of stability and nationalism. There always existed the fear in the late 1950s and early 1960s that De Gaulle might again resign and leave the nation subject to possible disruptive forces.

De Gaulle combined the methods of Louis Napoleon with the patriotism of Clemenceau. Throughout the 1960s he pursued a policy of making France the leading nation in a united Europe. Often De Gaulle pursued strictly nationalist goals that frustrated those who favored united action. His nationalism was probably necessary as a

❧ President De Gaulle Insists on Maintaining French Autonomy

De Gaulle was determined to maintain the national independence of France both in Europe and in the Atlantic community. In this 1966 speech he criticized those who would compromise that independence by having France subordinate itself to various international organizations, such as NATO and the United Nations. He particularly resented the influence of the United States in European affairs.

It is true that, among our contemporaries, there are many minds—and often some of the best—who have envisaged that our country renounce its independence under the cover of one or another international grouping. Having thus handed over to foreign bodies the responsibility for our destiny, our leaders would—according to the expression sanctioned by that school of thought—have nothing more to do than "plead France's case."

. . . Thus some—exalting in the dream of the international—wanted to see our country itself, as they placed themselves, under the obedience of Moscow. Thus others—invoking either the supranational myth, or the danger from the East, or the advantage that the Atlantic West could derive from unifying its

economy, or even the imposing utility of world arbitration—maintained that France should allow her policy to be dissolved in a tailor-made Europe, her defense in NATO, her monetary concepts in the Washington Fund, her personality in the United Nations, et cetera.

Certainly, it is a good thing that such institutions exist, and it is only in our interest to belong to them; but if we had listened to their extreme apostles, these organs in which, as everyone knows, the political protection, military protection, economic power and multiform aid of the United States predominate— these organs would have been for us only a cover for our submission to American hegemony, Thus, France would disappear swept away by illusion.

Cited in Ronald C. Monticone, *Charles De Gaulle* (Boston: Twayne Publishers, 1975), pp. 67–68.

---

means of healing the internal wounds to French pride and prestige brought about by the colonial and Algerian defeats. He pursued systematically good relations with Germany but was never friendly with Great Britain. He deeply resented the influence of the United States in Western Europe.

De Gaulle wanted Europe to become a third force in the world between the superpowers. For that reason he pushed for the development of a French nuclear capacity and refused to become a party to the 1963 Nuclear Test Ban Treaty. He took French military forces out of NATO in 1967 and caused its headquarters to be moved from Paris to Brussels, but he did not take France out of the alliance itself. He was highly critical of the American involvement in Vietnam. That American adventure served to convince him even further that Europe under French leadership must prepare to fend for itself.

It is not certain that the rest of the world ever understood De Gaulle or he them. He imposed a kind of presidential dictatorship on France but

permitted civil liberties to be observed and parliamentary politics to function. Yet what was important was what the president and his ministers decided. For ten years he succeeded. Then in 1968 he confronted a domestic unrest in France that was even more widespread than that confronted by Léon Blum in the spring of 1936. The troubles commenced among student groups in Paris, and then they spread to other major sectors of French life. Hundreds of thousands of workers went on strike. Having assured himself of the support of the army, De Gaulle made a brief television speech to rally his followers. Soon they, too, came into the streets to demonstrate for De Gaulle and stability. The strikes ended. Police often moved against the student groups. The government itself quickly moved to improve the wages and benefits to workers. May 1968 had revealed the fragile strength of the Fifth Republic. It had also revealed that the economic progress of France since the war had created a large body of citizens with sufficient stake in the status quo to fear and prevent its disruption.

In 1969 President De Gaulle resigned after some relatively minor constitutional changes were rejected in a referendum. Georges Pompidou (1911–1974), who succeeded to the presidency, was reelected in the next election. He was a strong supporter of De Gaulle and his policies. He and his own successor, Valéry Giscard d'Estaing (b. 1926), set about to improve the economic conditions that had fostered discontent among factory workers in 1968. They also continued to favor a strong policy favoring European unity. In 1973, three years after De Gaulle's death in political retirement, France permitted Great Britain to join the Common Market.

The center-right government of Valéry Giscard d'Estaing was elected in 1974 on a platform of social reform. The new president also spoke of an "opening" to the political left. It seemed that he might be willing to accept the support of the French Socialist Party for his programs. Giscard d'Estaing was essentially a technocrat who wanted to see the traditionally harsh ideological split in France healed. He and others of his persuasion saw such splits as preventing the serious handling of major economic problems. Yet his interest in some mode of alliance with the left remained a matter of rhetoric. Indeed, during the parliamentary elections of 1978 he made major election-eve speeches deploring the possibility of a political victory for the left.

Such a victory had for a time seemed possible, on the one hand, because of disillusionment with Giscard d'Estaing's timid policies and, on the other, because of new cooperation between the French Socialist Party and the French Communist Party. Beginning in the late 1960s François Mitterand had led an impressive drive to reorganize the Socialist Party. Its membership increased, as did its performance at the polls. In 1972 the Socialist Party and the Communist Party led by Georges Marchais formed a Common Front and agreed on a social and economic program that would be enacted if they were elected. The Socialists accepted the alliance because it seemed the only way that a left-wing majority could be achieved. The motives of the Communists were less clear, but it would seem that they thought such an alliance would give them considerable political leverage within left-wing politics. They hoped to become the tail that wagged the dog.

However, after 1972 the strength of the Socialist Party continued to grow and that of the Communist Party did not. It became clear by 1977 that if the proposed coalition won the election, the Communists would be able to exert relatively little pressure within the Cabinet. Consequently, in the middle of 1977, the Communist Party resumed its traditional stance of harshly criticizing the Socialists. In September 1977 the Common Front in effect came to an end. During the parliamentary elections of 1978 the two left-wing parties failed to cooperate. Communists refused to vote for Socialists, and Socialists refused to vote for Communists. The result of the election was a victory for the right and the center.

The presidential election of 1980 witnessed a sharp turnaround in French politics. Mitterand, the Socialist Party candidate, decisively defeated Giscard d'Estaing. A few weeks later the Socialists also captured control of the French Parliament. Both socialist victories were achieved without formal alliance or support from the Communists.

Mitterand became president of France for several reasons. Giscard d'Estaing had become personally unpopular and was regarded as increasingly aloof from the French people. The electorate had also become tired of technocratic politics that tended to impose economic and social solutions from above. Giscard d'Estaing's traditional supporters were divided because groups farther to the right of him failed to give support. These factors, however, should not detract from the very remarkable accomplishment of political rebuilding of the left carried out by Mitterand over the past decade. During those years he slowly but steadily wooed traditional Communist voters away from support of that party and toward support of the Socialists. When a Socialist victory rather than a Communist victory appeared the likely result of turning out the Gaullists, the French voters decided to try the Socialists. For the first time in twenty-three years a genuinely new administration came to power in France.

Mitterand appointed a large Cabinet that included four Communists. They were appointed only after they agreed to support the Socialist Party policies. Opinion was divided over the significance of these appointments. Some observers saw the inclusion of Communists in the Cabinet as a danger to French and NATO security. Others believed that the presence of the Communists meant that Mitterand would have some control over them and that the move was necessary to ensure labor peace, as several of the major French labor unions are controlled by the Communists. In foreign policy Mitterand reasserted support for NATO and was critical of the Soviet Union and particularly of the Soviet invasion of Afghanistan. Domestically Mitterand intended to increase government ownership of several industries.

Instability in the Mediterranean World

For a quarter century after World War II the major Mediterranean states were stable, though for very different reasons. Spain and Portugal remained governed by General Francisco Franco (1892–1975) and Antonio Salazar (1889–1970), respectively. They had established themselves during the turmoil between the wars and continued to preside over illiberal regimes. Italy had attained a course of reasonably steady progress under the leadership of the Christian Democrats. Greece had become stabilized during the 1950s, primarily thanks to American military and economic aid. By the middle of the 1960s each of these nations had begun to experience internal tensions that have since led to considerable turmoil throughout the region. Moreover, at the far southeastern end of the Mediterranean the Arab–Israeli conflict has proved a continuing source of instability.

The unrest in so much of Mediterranean Europe has been a cause of considerable concern for the United States and for many of its NATO allies. The conflict between Greece and Turkey over Cyprus constituted an intra-NATO dispute. The possibility of communist government in Italy led to much rethinking about European defense arrangements. No matter what the political future of Spain may hold, there will be difficulties over agreements about the stationing of United States forces that would not have occurred under Franco. Taken as a whole, the Mediterranean turmoil is the most potent example of the disintegration of the framework of European alliances and political suppositions that have guided postwar Western European international relations. A period of considerable flux no doubt lies ahead.

PORTUGAL. Salazar ruled Portugal with an iron hand until 1968, when a stroke removed him from the political scene. His successor, Marcelo Caetono, continued to pursue authoritarian policies. The government remained determined to hold its possessions in Africa long after other European states had abandoned traditional colonial policies. Both at home and abroad major opposition to the government developed within the army officer corps. In 1974 General Antonio de Spinola led a successful army revolt against Caetono.

Since that time Portugal has indulged itself in the kind of political activity that had been forbidden for almost half a century. There have been large numbers of popular demonstrations, intense political party activity, and broad discussion of economic, social, and political problems. The Portuguese Communist Party proved to be exceedingly well organized. It was able to contribute to the overthrow of the Spinola government. However, in the elections of 1975 the Communists did not do well. The government came under the control of the Socialists, led by Mario Soares. In 1976 a democratic constitution was promulgated. Thereafter considerable political shifting and instability took place. The parliamentary elections of 1980 saw the victory of a more conservative political alliance. Nonetheless, for the moment democracy in Portugal seems secure.

SPAIN. Spain has also entered on a period of considerable uncertainty. As long as he lived, Franco tolerated virtually no political life outside that of his own supporters. The Spanish police were active against any political opposition. Many political activists remained either in exile or in jail. However, opposition continued to grow. A large number of illegal political parties had been organized. Franco died in 1975. As he had provided, his successor was Juan Carlos, from the old Bourbon royal family of Spain, who became king. The new monarch, though trained by Franco, made it clear that he wished Spain to be liberalized both politically and culturally. In December 1976 the Spanish voters approved a more liberal constitution. The question now became whether Juan Carlos could obtain the cooperation and trust of the recently legalized political parties. One event of 1981 would seem to have solidified their working relationship and mutual respect. In February 1981 a small group of military officers attempted a right-wing coup against the legislative assembly. Juan Carlos very quickly made himself the symbol of the ongoing democracy and successfully called for the continuation of the democratic experiment.

GREECE. At the other end of the Mediterranean, Greece has also experienced a decade of upheaval. In 1965 King Constantine II (b. 1940) came into conflict with the political left. During the next several months leftist and liberal Greek politicians hoped to exert new influence on the monarch. In the spring of 1967 conservative army officers, claiming to be saving Greece from a communist takeover, staged a coup. A few months later Constantine failed in his attempt at a counter-coup, and he fled the country. The strongly authoritarian army junta imposed tight control over the population and imprisoned political opponents. In the summer of 1974, however, confrontation between Greece and Turkey over the future of Cyprus led to the collapse of the Greek military government. Turkey had invaded Cyprus under the pretext of protecting the Turkish part of the population. The Greek junta was incapable of dealing with the crisis, and a civilian government, headed by former premier Constantine Karamanlis (b. 1907), took over. In 1975 a referendum by the Greek people decided against restoration of the monarchy. The problem of the future of Cyprus remained a source of friction between Greece and Turkey. In October 1981, the Greek Socialist Party led by Andreas Papandreou won the elections. This event raised new anxiety on the part of the United States government about continued Greek participation in NATO.

ITALY. Instability has threatened Italy from different sources. The transformation from a fascist to a nonfascist government commenced during the war. In 1943 the Grand Fascist Council had ousted Mussolini. He was later summarily executed by Italian partisans. A government friendly to the Allies was installed in southern Italy, and it expanded its control as the Allied armies moved northward. At the close of the conflict the prefascist political parties quickly reemerged. In 1946 the nation voted to abolish the monarchy.

The Christian Democrats governed under the leadership of Alcide de Gasperi. Until 1947 the Italian Communist Party served in the coalition, but it was excluded in that year. Thereafter Italy remained a nation with a single major large political party, the Christian Democrats, who formed coalitions with other smaller parties. Government by bargained coalition became the order of the day. Under this system, which resembled the system of *transformismo* that had prevailed before Mussolini, the Italian economy experienced a period of growth not unlike that of West Germany. Italy became a genuinely modern nation. It manufactured autos, refrigerators, and office equipment. The nation was very active in the drive for European unity.

However, by the late 1960s and early 1970s discontent was stirring against the Christian Democrats. Their methods of government had led to corruption, inefficiency, and political paralysis. Inflation became intense as economic growth stagnated. As a result, the Italian Communist Party, the largest and best organized in Western Europe, began to make significant inroads into political life. It won a considerable number of municipal elections. During 1976 the Communists won over 35 per cent of the popular vote for the Chamber of Deputies. They were refused admission to the Cabinet but were granted several important posts within the Chamber of Deputies.

The architect of the Communist advance within Italian politics was Enrico Berlinguer. He set forth a policy known as the *historic compromise*. The policy represented a major break not only with the previous stand of the Italian Communist Party but also with a Moscow-dominated Communist movement. By the "historic compromise" Berlinguer announced the willingness of the Italian Communist Party to enter a coalition government with the Christian Democrats and other non-Communist parties. In other words, the Italian Communists have for the time being renounced revolution as the path to political power. They have also agreed to participate in a government that they would not dominate or control. The Italian Communist Party has also promised that as a partner in a coalition or as the governing party, should it be elected, it will govern constitutionally and will respect individuals' civil liberties. It has also urged continued Italian participation in NATO and criticized the recent authoritarian policies of the Polish Communist government. To date these promises have not been put to the test. The compromises, however, represent an important example of the strains emerging among Communist parties in Europe.

The Italian Communist success, stemming from its announced willingness to cooperate with middle-class and Christian political parties, has led to a further radicalization of the political left in Italy. The "historic compromise" has made the Italian Communist Party seem quite conservative to the unknown numbers of people who wish to see radical, but so far unclearly defined, political and social change in the nation. These groups have resorted to terrorism to make their power felt and to illustrate how the Communists have now become a pillar of the existing establishment. The best known of the terrorist organizations is the Red Brigades. In the spring of 1978, while several members of

On May 9, 1978, *the body of former Italian premier Aldo Moro was found in the rear of an automobile on a street in Rome. He had been kidnapped on March 16 by an Italian terrorist organization known as the Red Brigades and was murdered when the Italian government refused to negotiate for his release.* [*United Press International Photo.*]

the Red Brigades were on trial for earlier violence, other members kidnapped Aldo Moro, a former premier of Italy and a major leader of the Christian Democratic Party. The government refused to negotiate for his release. After several weeks of captivity Moro was assassinated, and his body was left in a car on a street in Rome. During the crisis both the Christian Democratic Party and the Italian Communist Party condemned terrorism. Since the Moro assassination Italian politics has resumed its familiar pattern. The Christian Democrats rule and have experienced some electoral gains. The Communists govern several major cities but cannot win a national election or gain seats in the Cabinet. Terrorism still continues to be a factor in public life.

THE ARAB–ISRAELI DISPUTE. A final source of instability in the Mediterranean world is the Arab–Israeli conflict. This dispute involves Europe because many of the citizens of Israel are immigrants from Europe and because Europe, like the United States, is highly dependent on oil from Arab countries. Moreover the Middle East also remains an arena for potential problems between the United States and the Soviet Union.

The modern state of Israel was the achievement of the world Zionist movement founded in 1897 by Theodore Herzl and later led by Chaim Weizmann. The British Balfour Declaration of 1917 had favored the establishment of a national home for the Jewish people in Palestine. Between the wars thousands of Jews, mainly from Europe, immigrated into the area, which was then governed by Great Britain under a mandate of the League of Nations. During the interwar period the Yishuv or Jewish community in Palestine developed its own political parties, press, labor unions, and educational system. There were numerous conflicts with the Arabs already living in Palestine, for they considered the Jewish settlers intruders. The British rather unsuccessfully attempted to mediate those clashes.

This situation might have prevailed longer in Palestine except for the outbreak of World War II and the attempt by Hitler to exterminate the Jewish population of Europe. The Nazi persecution united Jews throughout the world behind the Zionist ideal of a Jewish state in Palestine. At the same time the knowledge of Nazi atrocities mobilized the conscience of the United States and the other Western powers. It seemed morally right that something be done for Jewish refugees from Nazi concentration camps. In 1947 the British turned over to the United Nations the whole problem of the relationship of Arabs and Jews in Palestine. That same year the United Nations passed a resolution calling for a division of the territory into a Jewish state and an Arab state.

The Arabs in Palestine and the surrounding area resisted the United Nations resolution. Not unnaturally, they resented the influx of new settlers. Large numbers of Palestinian Arabs were displaced and themselves became refugees. In May 1948 the Yishuv declared the independence of a new Jewish state called Israel. The United States, through President Truman, almost immediately recognized the new nation, whose first prime minister was David Ben-Gurion (1886–1973). During 1948 and 1949 Israel fought its war of independence against the Arabs. In that war Israel expanded its borders beyond the limits originally set forth by the United Nations. By 1949 Israel had, through force of arms, secured its existence and peace, but it had not secured diplomatic recognition by its Arab neighbors—Egypt, Jordan, Syria, and Saudi Arabia, to name those closest. The peace amounted to little more than an armed truce.

ISRAEL AND ITS NEIGHBORS

MEDITERRANEAN SEA

Tripoli

LEBANON
Beirut

Damascus

SYRIA

GOLAN HEIGHTS

Haifa

SEA OF GALILEE

WEST BANK

Tel Aviv
Jaffa

ISRAEL

JORDAN WATER TO THE NEGEV

JORDAN

Amman
Jerusalem

Gaza

GAZA STRIP

Beersheba

DEAD SEA

NILE DELTA

Damietta

Port Said

El 'Arish

El Mansura

Ismailia

SUEZ CANAL

E G Y P T

El Auja

NEGEV

Suez

GIDI PASS

MITLA PASS

Cairo
Helwan

Kuntilla

SINAI PENINSULA

Eilat   Aqaba

SAUDI

GULF OF SUEZ

GULF OF AQABA

MT. SINAI

ARABIA

EL NABQ
SHARM EL SHEIKH

TIRAN I.

RED SEA

100 MI.

100 KM.

MAP 33.4 *The map shows the geography of the difficult problem of Israel and its surrounding Arab neighbors. Syria, Jordan, and Egypt are the states with lands now occupied by Israel. The future of those lands and of earlier Palestinian refugees makes up the major set of problems still unresolved in the area.*

Then in 1952 a group of Egyptian army officers seized power in Egypt. Their leader was Gamal Abdel Nasser. He established himself as a dictator and, more importantly, as a spokesman for militant Arab nationalism. His policy was marked by a clear hatred of all the old imperial powers. In 1956

Nasser nationalized the Suez Canal. That same year, as noted previously, Great Britain and France responded to Nasser's action by attacking the canal. Israel joined with France and Britain. This alliance helped Israel fend off certain Arab guerrilla attacks but associated Israel with the former imperial powers. After 1956 a United Nations peacekeeping force separated the armies of Israel and Egypt. The bases of the UN force were located in Egypt. Still there was no official Arab recognition of the existence of Israel.

An uneasy peace continued until 1967. Meanwhile, the Soviet Union increased its influence in Egypt, and the United States increased its influence in Israel. Both great powers supplied weapons to their friends in the area. In 1967 President Nasser made the calculation, which proved to be quite wrong, that the Arab nations could defeat Israel, which by then was nearly two decades old. He began to mass troops in the Sinai Peninsula, and he attempted to close the Gulf of Aqaba to Israeli shipping. He also demanded the withdrawal of the UN peacekeeping force. Diplomatic activity failed to stem the crisis and the Arab attempt to isolate Israel. On June 5, 1967, the armed forces of Israel, under the direction of Defense Minister Moshe Dayan (1915–1981), attacked Egyptian airfields rather than endure additional provocation by Egypt. Almost immediately Syria and Jordan entered the war on the side of Egypt. Yet by June 11 the Six Days' War was over, and Israel had won a stunning victory. The military forces of Egypt lay in shambles. Moreover Israel occupied the entire Egyptian Sinai Peninsula, as well as the West Bank region along the Jordan River that had previously been part of the state of Jordan. This victory marked the height of Israeli power and prestige.

In 1970 President Nasser died. He was succeeded by Anwar el-Sadat (1918–1981). Sadat had first to shore up his support at home. The existing tensions between Israel and the defeated Egypt, of course, continued, and the Soviet Union still poured weapons into Egypt. However, Sadat deeply distrusted the Russians and in 1972 ordered them to leave the country. He and his advisers also felt that only another war with Israel could return to Egypt the lands lost in 1967. In October 1973, on the Jewish holy day of Yom Kippur, the military forces of Egypt and Syria launched an attack across the Suez Canal into Israeli-held territory. The invasion came as a complete surprise to the Israelis. Initially the Egyptian forces made con-

President Carter was host to Prime Minister Begin of Israel and President Sadat of Egypt in September 1978 at a series of meetings that raised hopes for a peace treaty between the two eastern Mediterranean nations but left many unresolved difficulties between Israel and her neighbors. [United Press International Photo.]

siderable headway. Then the Israeli army thrust back the invasion. In November 1973 a truce was signed between the forces in the Sinai. Although Israel had been successful in repelling the Egyptians, the cost in troops and prestige was very high.

The Yom Kippur War added a major new element to the Middle East problem. In the fall of 1973 when the war broke out, the major Arab oil-producing states shut off the flow of oil to the United States and Europe. This dramatic move was an attempt to force the Western powers to use their influence to moderate the policy of Israel. The threat of the loss of oil was particularly frightening to Europeans, who possess almost no major sources of the oil on which their industry depends. In the future this Arab oil can be expected to play an even more influential part in Middle East developments.

The most recent important development in the troubled area occurred in November 1977. President Sadat of Egypt, in a dramatic personal gesture, flew to Israel, addressed the Israeli Parliament, and held discussions with Prime Minister Menachem Begin (b. 1913), although the two states were still technically at war. In effect, for the first time the head of a major Arab state recognized the existence of Israel. Previously all contacts had taken place either through the United Nations or other third parties. The Sadat initiative, roundly condemned in many Arab quarters, resulted in direct conversations, the most important of which occurred at Camp David in the United States under the direction of President Carter. The Camp David Accords of September 1978 have provided one framework through which negotiations on the Middle East questions have taken place. Since 1978 numerous meetings have occurred between Egyptian and Israeli officials. Other Arab states have not joined these talks, however. The major stumbling block to future agreements is the Palestine refugee problem. The Palestine Liberation Organization (PLO) remains the major spokesman for the refugees. The PLO continues to demand a separate Palestinian state. The government of Israel has steadily refused to recognize the

PLO. Israel also believes that virtually any independent Palestinian state would be a threat to its own independence and ultimate survival.

In early 1981 Prime Minister Begin's coalition was reelected, but in October of that year President Sadat was assassinated by Muslim extremists. The death of the Egyptian president cast doubt on the long-range stability of the Camp David process. Further strains appeared in late December 1981, when the Israeli parliament suddenly annexed the Golan Heights while the attention of most of the Western world was on the crisis in Poland. The general turmoil in the region seems certain to continue for some time.

IRAN. Another indication of the unrest in the Middle East and the difficulty confronted by the superpowers was demonstrated in the Iranian revolution. In 1978 the Shah of Iran, who had long received the strong support of the United States, was overthrown in a revolution led by Muslim fundamentalists. The chief figure in the revolution was Ayatollah Ruholloh Khomeini. The revolutionaries were discontented with the social injustice of the Shah's regime and with the manner in which the modernization of the country had challenged traditional Muslim religious values. In October 1979 the deposed Shah arrived in the United States to receive medical treatment for cancer. On November 4, 1979, a group of Iranian revolutionaries stormed the American embassy in Tehran and took more than fifty military and foreign-serv-

this development has characterized the policy and rhetoric of several Communist parties operating within the democracies of Western Europe. It has been particularly associated with the Communist parties of France, Italy, and Spain. Eurocommunism consists of two basic political policies. The first is the assertion of the independence of the parties involved from the influence of the Communist Party of the Soviet Union. Second, these parties have said publicly that they are willing to function within the existing parliamentary systems. The latter policy has been taken to mean the renunciation of revolution as a path to political power and the acceptance of existing constitutional arrangements; that is, these Communist parties have said that if they lose an election while in office, they will then surrender office to the victorious party. We have already noted these ideas in contemporary Italy.

Eurocommunism has developed primarily since 1968. The Soviet invasion of Czechoslovakia, the well-publicized persecution of Soviet dissidents, and the general absence of human rights in the Soviet Union made the Russian experience a rather unattractive model for young Europeans of the post–World War II generation. The West European Communist parties could hardly expect to win elections as long as they remained intimately aligned with the Soviet Union. Moreover the postwar prosperity of Western Europe that has contrasted so markedly with the life of Eastern Europe also meant that Western Communist parties felt the need to modify their tactics. The "historic compromise" of the Italian Communist Party and the cooperation of the French Communist Party with the French Socialists from 1972 to 1977 were examples of these new tactics. In Spain, under the leadership of Santiago Carillo the Communist Party has even attempted to introduce democratic procedures within the party itself. This latter policy has not been followed in France or Italy.

In 1977 the Soviet Union formally condemned Eurocommunism. The Soviet Union seems to have feared that too much independence on the part of West European Communist parties might lead to further unrest in Eastern Europe.

No European Communist Party advocating the policy of Eurocommunism has come to power.

ice personnel as hostages. The United States found itself unable to rescue them. A military force sent out by President Carter failed in its rescue attempt. The imprisonment of the hostages became a major concern throughout the 1980 American presidential campaign. The hostages were finally released as a result of extensive diplomatic negotiations on January 20, 1981, just minutes after President Reagan took the oath of office.

Eurocommunism in Western Europe

Within West European politics the past decade has witnessed the emergence of what may be a new version of communism. Termed *Eurocommunism,*

1052

European voters, and most particularly the large democratic socialist parties, have remained quite skeptical. There are several reasons for skepticism. First, Communist calls for independence from Moscow are not new. West European Communist parties have always displayed some independence of the Soviet Union and have insisted that the special conditions in their own nations must be taken into account in formulating policy. Second, from time to time in the past, most notably in the Popular Front governments of the 1930s and the immediate postwar cabinets of several countries, the Communists have participated. Neither of those previous developments changed the goal of the Communist parties from the pursuit of a monopoly of power in the state. On the whole European voters have not fully believed the Communist pledge to give up power on the loss of future elections. Europeans of conservative, liberal, and democratic-socialist persuasion have seen the Communist parties change tactics and policies in the past. They remain uncertain about the sincerity and the permanence of the policies of Eurocommunism. They are not certain that once in power or in the cabinets the Communists would not revert to their former goals.

Finally, Europeans, unlike many American observers, have not equated the Eurocommunist call for independence from Moscow with democratic politics. With the exception of the Spanish Communist Party, the West European Communist parties have remained very centrally organized. They have not permitted any significant internal democracy or internal criticism. As long as this rigid organization is retained, European voters may remain wary of the democratic protestations of the Communists.

The Soviet Union and Eastern Europe

The Soviet Union Since the Death of Stalin (1953)

Many Russians had hoped that the end of the war would signal a lessening of Stalinism. No other nation had suffered greater losses or more deprivation than the Soviet Union. Its people anticipated some immediate reward for their sacrifice and heroism. They desired a reduction in the scope of the police state and a redirection of the economy away from heavy industry to consumer products. They were disappointed. Stalin did little or nothing to modify the character of the regime he had created. The police remained ever-present. The cult of personality expanded, and the central bureaucracy continued to grow. Heavy industry was still favored over production for consumers. Agriculture continued to be troubled. Stalin's personal authority over the party and the nation remained unchallenged. In foreign policy Stalin moved to solidify Soviet control over Eastern Europe for the purposes of both communist expansion and Soviet national security. He attempted to impose the Soviet model on those nations. The Cold War stance of the United States simply served to confirm Stalin in his ways.

By late 1952 and early 1953 it appeared that Stalin might be ready to unloose a new series of purges. In January 1953 a group of Jewish physicians was arrested and charged with plotting the deaths of important leaders. Charges of extensive conspiracy appeared in the press. All of these developments were similar to the events that had preceded the purges of the 1930s. Then quite suddenly in the midst of this new furor, on March 6, 1953, Stalin died.

For a time no single leader replaced Stalin. Rather the Presidium (the renamed Politburo) pursued a policy of collective leadership. A considerable amount of reshuffling occurred among the top party leaders. Lavrenti Beria (1899–1953), the dreaded director of the secret police, was removed from his post and eventually executed. Georgi Malenkov (b. 1902) became premier, a position he held for about two years. Gradually, however, power and influence began to devolve on Nikita Khrushchev (1894–1971), who in 1953 had been named party secretary. By 1955 he had edged out Malenkov and had successfully urged the appointment of Nikolai Bulganin (1895–1975) in his place. Three years later Khrushchev himself became premier. His rise constituted the end of collective leadership, but at no time did he enjoy the extraordinary powers of Stalin.

The Khrushchev era, which lasted until the autumn of 1964, witnessed a marked retreat from Stalinism though not from extreme authoritarianism. Indeed, the political repression of Stalin had been so extensive that there was considerable room for relaxation of surveillance within the limits of tyranny. Politically the demise of Stalinism meant

Soviet Premier Nikita Khrushchev attacked the policies of Stalin in a long secret speech before the 1956 Communist Party Congress in Moscow. Subsequently his own adventuresome foreign policy and unsuccessful agricultural policy led to his downfall in 1964. [United Press International Photo.]

shifts in leadership and party structure by means other than purges. In 1956, at the Twentieth Congress of the Communist Party, Khrushchev made a secret speech (later published outside the Soviet Union) in which he denounced Stalin and his crimes against socialist justice during the purges of the 1930s. The speech caused shock and consternation in party circles and opened the way for limited, but genuine, internal criticism of the Soviet government. Gradually the strongest supporters of Stalinist policies were removed from the Presidium. By 1958 all of Stalin's former supporters were gone, but none had been executed.

Under Khrushchev, intellectuals were somewhat more free to express their opinions. This so-called thaw in the cultural life of the country was closely related to the premier's interest in the opinions of experts on problems of industry and agriculture. He often went outside the usual bureaucratic channels in search of information and new ideas. Novels such as Aleksandr Solzhenitsyn's (b. 1918) *One Day in the Life of Ivan Denisovich* (1963) could be published. However, Boris Pasternak (1890–1960), the author of *Dr. Zhivago*, was not permitted to accept the Nobel Prize for literature in 1958. The intellectual liberalization of Soviet life during this period should not be overestimated. It looked favorable only in comparison with what had preceded it and has continued to seem so because of the decline of

such freedom of expression since Khrushchev's fall.

The economic policy also somewhat departed from the strict Stalinist mode. By 1953 the economy had recovered from the strains and destruction of the war, but consumer goods and housing still remained in very short supply. The problem of an adequate food supply also continued. Malenkov had favored improvements in meeting the demand for consumer goods; Khrushchev also favored such a departure. Khrushchev also moved in a moderate fashion to decentralize economic planning and execution. During the late 1950s he often boasted that Soviet production of consumer goods would overtake that of the West. Steel, oil, and electric-power production continued to grow, but the consumer sector improved only marginally. The ever-growing defense budget and the space program that successfully launched the first human-engineered satellite of the earth, *Sputnik*, in 1957 made major demands on the nation's productive resources. Economically Khrushchev was attempting to move the country in too many directions at once.

Khrushchev strongly redirected Stalin's agricultural policy. He recognized that in spite of the collectivization of the 1930s the Soviet Union had not produced an agricultural system capable of feeding its own people. Administratively Khrushchev removed many of the most restrictive regulations on private cultivation. The machine tractor stations were abandoned. Existing collective farms were further amalgamated. The government undertook an extensive "virgin lands" program to extend wheat cultivation by hundreds of thousands of acres. This policy initially increased grain production to new records. However, in a very few years the new lands became subject to erosion. The farming techniques applied had been inappropriate for the soil. The agricultural problem has simply continued to grow. Currently the Soviet Union imports vast quantities of grain from the United States and other countries. United States grain imports have constituted a major facet of the policy of detente.

Adventuresomeness also characterized Khrushchev's foreign policy. In 1956 the Soviet Union adopted the phrase "peaceful coexistence" in regard to its relationship with the United States. The policy implied no less competition with the capitalist world but suggested that war might not be the best way to pursue communist expansion. The pre-

∾ Khrushchev Denounces the Crimes of Stalin: The Secret Speech ▬▬▬

In 1956 Khrushchev denounced Stalin in a secret speech to the Party Congress.
The New York Times published a text smuggled from Russia.

Stalin acted not through persuasion, explanation, and patient cooperation with people, but by imposing his concepts and demanding absolute submission to his opinion. Whoever opposed this concept or tried to prove his viewpoint and the correctness of his position was doomed to removal from the leading collective [group] and to subsequent moral and physical annihilation. . . .

Stalin originated the concept "enemy of the people." This term automatically rendered it unnecessary that the ideological errors of a man or men engaged in a controversy be proved; this term made possible the usage of the most cruel repression violating all norms of revolutionary legality, against anyone who in any way disagreed with Stalin, against those who were only suspected of hostile intent, against those who had bad reputations.

This concept "enemy of the people" actually eliminated the possibility of any kind of ideological fight or the making of one's views known on this or that issue, even those of a practical character. In the main, and in actuality, the only proof of guilt used, against all norms of current legal science, was the "confession" of the accused himself; and, as subsequent probing proved, "confessions" were acquired through physical pressures against the accused. . . .

Lenin used severe methods only in the most necessary cases, when the exploiting classes were still in existence and were vigorously opposing the revolution, when the struggle for survival was decidedly assuming the sharpest forms, even including civil war.

Stalin, on the other hand, used extreme methods and mass repressions at a time when the revolution was already victorious, when the Soviet State was strengthened, when the exploiting classes were already liquidated and Socialist relations were rooted solidly in all phases of national economy, when our party was politically consolidated and had strengthened itself both numerically and ideologically. It is clear that here Stalin showed in a whole series of cases his intolerance, his brutality and his abuse of power. Instead of proving his political correctness and mobilizing the masses, he often chose the path of repression and physical annihilation, not only against actual enemies, but also against individuals who had not committed any crimes against the party and the Soviet Government. . . .

The New York Times, June 5, 1956, pp. 13–16.

---

vious year Khrushchev had participated in the Geneva summit meeting alongside Bulganin. Thereafter followed visits around the world, culminating with one to the United States in 1959. By the early 1960s it had become clear that Khrushchev had made few inroads on Western policy. He was under increasing domestic pressure and also pressure from the Chinese. The militancy of the denunciation of the U-2 flight, the aborting of the Paris summit meeting, the Berlin Wall, and the Cuban missile crisis were all responses to those pressures. The last of these adventures brought a clear Soviet retreat.

By 1964 numerous high Russian leaders and many people lower in the party had concluded that Khrushchev had tried to do too much too soon and had done it too poorly. On October 16, 1964, after defeat in the Central Committee of the Communist Party, Khrushchev resigned. He was replaced by Alexei Kosygin (1904–1980) as premier and Leonid Brezhnev (b. 1906) as party secretary. The latter eventually emerged as the dominant figure. In 1977 the constitution of the Soviet Union was changed to combine the offices of president and party secretary. Brezhnev became president, and thus head of the state as well as of the party. He holds more personal power than any Soviet leader since Stalin.

Domestically the Soviet government has become markedly more repressive since 1964. All intellectuals have enjoyed less and less freedom and little direct access to the government leadership. In

1974 the government expelled Solzhenitsyn. Perhaps most important among recent developments, Jewish citizens of the Soviet Union have become subject to harassment. Major bureaucratic obstacles have been placed in the way of the emigration of Soviet Jews to Israel. These policies suggest a return to the limitations of the Stalinist period.

The internal repression has given rise to a dissident movement. Certain Soviet citizens have dared to criticize the regime in public and to carry out small demonstrations against the government. They have accused the Soviet government of violating the human rights provisions of the 1975 Helsinki Accords. The dissidents have included a number of prominent citizens, such as the Nobel Prize physicist Andrei Sakharov. The response of the Soviet government to the dissident movement has been further repression. Prominent dissidents, such as Anatoly Shcharansky, Aleksandr Ginzburg, and Vladimir Slepak, have been arrested, tried on clearly trumped-up charges, and sentenced to long periods of imprisonment or internal exile in Siberia. The Soviet government obviously feels it cannot tolerate the dissident movement. The questions that now arise and cannot be answered have to do with how much internal opposition to the government exists in the Soviet Union and what, if any, possibility the opposition has of making its thought and will known.

In foreign policy the Brezhnev years have witnessed attempts to reach accommodation with the United States while continuing to press for expanded Soviet influence and further attempts to maintain Soviet leadership of the communist movement. During the Vietnam war the Soviet Union pursued a policy of restrained support for North Vietnam. Under President Richard Nixon the United States pursued a policy of detente based on arms limitation and trade agreements. Nonetheless Soviet spending on defense, and particularly on naval expansion, continued to grow. During the Ford and Carter administrations in the United States, Soviet involvement in African affairs was troubling.

More important in leading to a cooling of relations between the superpowers was the Soviet invasion of Afghanistan in December 1979. A Soviet presence had already existed in that country, but for reasons that still remain unclear the Soviet government felt that it was required to send in troops to ensure its influence in central Asia. As noted earlier, the invasion brought a grain embargo and a boycott on participation in the Moscow Olympic Games from the United States government. The invasion also dashed any hope for U.S. Senate ratification of the arms limitation treaty signed by President Carter and President Brezhnev in 1979. The Reagan administration has continued a similar policy but has stiffened it by postponing arms negotiations. It has, however, relaxed the grain embargo. The Afghanistan invasion also seems to have tied the hands of the Soviet government in its own sphere of influence in Eastern Europe. There seems little doubt that the Soviet hesitation to react

Soviet tanks invaded Kabul, capital of Afghanistan, in January 1980. [*United Press International Photo.*]

more strongly to recent events in Poland, which are discussed in the next section, stems in part from having military resources committed to Afghanistan and from having encountered broad condemnation for the invasion from some West European Communist parties and from the governments of nations not aligned with the West.

Polycentrism in the Communist World

Throughout the Cold War observers in the West have concentrated their attention on the tensions between the Soviet Union and the United States. But beyond its continuing confrontation of and rivalry with America, the Soviet government has also had to deal with growing tension and division within the world communist movement. During most of the Stalin era the Soviet Union was the center of world communism. Stalin hoped to impose his model on other parties. Immediately after the war the Soviets attempted to construct governments in the peoples' democracies of Eastern Europe in the Stalinist mold. Since the late 1940s the unity of world communism, which was always more frail than Cold War rhetoric suggested, became strained and finally shattered. As early as 1948 Yugoslavia began to construct its own model for socialism independent of Moscow. From 1956 onward the governments of eastern Europe began to seek a freer hand in internal affairs. By the late 1950s the monumental split between the Soviet Union and the People's Republic of China had developed. The communist world has come to have many centers—thus the descriptive term *polycentrism*—and the Soviet Union has had to compete for leadership.

There have been three stages in postwar relations between the Soviet Union and Eastern Europe. They were the years of Stalinism, then of revolt, and finally of socialist polycentrism. These stages closely paralleled internal developments in the Soviet Union itself.

Prior to the death of Stalin in 1953 the so-called peoples' democracies were brought steadily into line with Soviet policy. By 1948 single-party communist governments had been established in Bulgaria, Romania, Hungary, Yugoslavia, Albania, Czechoslovakia, Poland, and East Germany. Yugoslavia, headed by Marshal Tito (1892–1980), pursued an independent course of action and was bitterly denounced by Stalin. Elsewhere, however, Soviet troops and Stalinist party leaders prevailed.

The economies of those states were made to conform to the requirements of Soviet economic recovery and growth. The Soviet Union paid low prices for its imports from Eastern Europe and demanded high prices for its exports. In this fashion and through outright reparations it drained the resources of the region for its own uses. The Soviet Union prevented the Eastern European nations from participating in the Marshall Plan and responded with its own Council for Economic Mutual Assistance in 1949. In 1955 it organized the Warsaw Pact to confront NATO.

The Stalinist system of control was bound to generate discontent. This first manifested itself shortly after Stalin's death in 1953, when a brief revolt occurred in East Berlin. It was immediately crushed. Talk in the early Eisenhower administration in America about the "liberation" of Eastern Europe may have contributed to this disturbance by raising hopes of some form of United States support. Khrushchev's speech of 1956 in which he denounced Stalin sent reverberations throughout Eastern Europe as well as the Soviet Union. It was no accident that following the speech came the Polish October Revolution and the Hungarian Revolution of 1956. In the short run the bids for independence had the most limited kind of success; however, in retrospect they can be seen as marking the close of the Stalinist period and as paving the way for the emergence of polycentrism.

During the early years of the Cold War it was common in the West to regard the communist movement as a single monolithic structure. There was a failure to take into account the role of nationalism in Eastern Europe and the potential for division between the Soviet Union and China. The events of 1956 delineated the limits of acceptable independence for the Soviet-dominated successor states. Those nations of Eastern Europe must remain members of the Warsaw Pact, and their leaders had to be willing to consult and cooperate with the Soviet Union. They might trade with Western Europe and the United States and even establish cultural contacts, but their chief political and economic orientation must remain with the Soviet Union.

Since 1956, within these limits considerable diversity has appeared within the communist bloc in Eastern Europe. In Hungary the Janos Kadar government, which was installed by Soviet troops, pursued a program of economic growth and consumer satisfaction. Hungary is now probably the most prosperous and stable country in the region. East Germany and Bulgaria retained the closest relationships with the Soviet Union. After the Berlin Wall crisis of 1961 and the subsequent halt in the outflow of refugees, East Germany experienced very substantial economic growth. Romania has witnessed a resurgence of limited nationalism. Under the leadership of President Nicolae Ceauşescu (b. 1918), it has maintained ties with both the Soviet Union and China. Moreover, it has also cultivated friendly relations with the United States, as witnessed by President Nixon's visit in 1969 and President Ceauşescu's visit to America in 1977. However, in all of these countries the independence achieved is extremely limited and exists within the limits of one-party government, authoritarianism, and absence of the traditional civil liberties. The developments that have occurred in Czechoslovakia and Poland illustrate the character of those very real political confines.

In 1968 the Soviet Union moved to crush an experiment in developing a socialist model independent of Soviet domination. In that year the nations of the Warsaw Pact invaded Czechoslovakia to halt the political experimentation of the Alexander Dubcek government. It was quite clear that the Soviet Union felt that it could not tolerate so liberal a communist regime on its own borders. Dubcek was permitting in Czechoslovakia the very kind of intellectual freedom and discussion that was simultaneously being suppressed within Russia itself. At the time of the invasion Soviet Party Chairman Brezhnev declared the right of the Soviet Union to interfere in the domestic politics of other communist countries. Such direct interference has nevertheless not occurred since 1968. Moreover, at a conference of Communist parties held in East Berlin in 1976 the Soviet Union accepted a declaration stating that there could be several paths to socialism. The main proponents of this policy were the Communist parties of Western Europe. As the Communist Party of Italy in particular, as well as that of France, has seen election to full or shared power as a genuine possibility, it has attempted to put a distance between itself and the Soviet Union. However, to date none of these declarations and acknowledgements of socialist independence from Soviet domination has been put to a meaningful test.

Such a test seems to have occurred in Poland since the summer of 1980. The Soviet Union has a deep strategic interest in that nation because it was across Poland that the armies of both Napoleon and Hitler invaded Russia. After 1956 the Polish Communist Party, led by Wladyslaw Gomulka (b. 1905), made peace with the Roman Catholic Church, halted land collectivization, established trade with the West, and participated in cultural exchange programs with noncommunist nations. However, Poland experienced chronic economic mismanagement and persistent shortages in food and consumer goods. In 1970 food shortages led to a series of strikes, the most famous of which occurred in the shipyards at Gdansk. In December 1970 the Polish authorities broke the strike at the cost of a number of workers' lives. These events led to the departure of Gomulka. His successor was Edward Gierek (b. 1913).

In the decade after 1970 the Polish economy made very little progress. Food and other consumer goods remained in very short supply. The government tried to work its way out of these difficulties through very large loans from banks in the United States and Western Europe. In early July 1980 the Polish government raised meat prices. The result was hundreds of protest strikes across the country. The strikes were directed against the economic situation and against what was regarded as the mismanagement of the nation's affairs by the current leaders of the Polish Communist Party. On August 14 workers occupied the Lenin shipyard at Gdansk. They demanded the reinstatement of certain workers who had led the 1970 strike, the building of a memorial to the workers killed in 1970, a guarantee of no reprisals against the strikers of 1980, family subsidies, and raises in wages. The strike soon spread to other shipyards, transport facilities, and factories connected with the shipbuilding industry. The most important leader to emerge from among the strikers was Lech Walesa (b. 1944). He and the other strike leaders refused to negotiate with the government through any of the traditionally government-controlled unions. The Gdansk strike ended on August 31 with the workers having been promised the right to organize an independent union and the right of access to television and the press on the part of the union (by now called *Solidarity*) and the Polish Roman Catholic Church. Less than a week later, on September 6, Edward Gierek was dismissed as the head of the Polish Communist Party by the Polish Politburo and was replaced by Stanislaw Kania. Later in September the Polish courts recognized Solidarity as an independent union, and the state-

Lech Walesa, leader of the Polish Solidarity Movement, at a moment of triumph in September 1980. For a time, Solidarity seemed capable of gradually inducing the government to liberalize Poland. But in December 1981, under pressure from Moscow the Polish army took control of the country. Solidarity was suspended, and Walesa was held incommunicado. [Sygma.]

controlled radio for the first time in thirty years broadcast a Roman Catholic mass.

The Soviet Union watched these events with growing unease and displeasure. It feared that other Eastern European states might attempt to copy Poland. Throughout 1980 and 1981 Soviet leaders sent warning messages to the Poles and troop maneuvers were carried out on the Polish borders. Despite these pressures the early months of 1981 witnessed still further changes in Poland. Solidarity carried out new strikes demanding a five-day work week. The small independent farmers in the countryside soon organized a rural union known as *Rural Solidarity,* and it too was recognized

by the courts. In the midst of this external and internal pressure the Polish Communist government still had to attempt to redirect economic policy toward greater production and the payment of its massive foreign debts. Food shortages led to rationing. In order to set out on a new course and to give itself a further appearance of legitimacy, the Polish Communist Party called a special party congress for July of 1981. The calling of the congress was in itself extraordinary, but the manner in which it was carried out was even more surprising. For the first time in any European communist state, there were secret elections and real choices were permitted among the candidates. When the

1059

✎ The Premier of Poland Announces the Imposition of Martial Law ═══

On December 13, 1981, General Wojciech Jaruzelski, the premier of Poland and head of the Polish Communist Party, announced the imposition of martial law. The action was taken after months of liberal reform in Poland led by the independent trade union Solidarity. The government turned to military rule out of fear that the political activity of Solidarity would endanger the rule of the Communist Party in Poland. The announced reason for the imposition of martial law was to prevent disorder.

Our country is on the edge of the abyss. Achievements of many generations, raised from the ashes, are collapsing into ruin. State structures no longer function. New blows are struck each day at our flickering economy. Living conditions are burdening people more and more.

Through each place of work, in many Polish people's homes, there is a line of painful division. The atmosphere of unending conflict, misunderstanding and hatred sows mental devastation and damages the tradition of tolerance.

Strikes, strike alerts, protest actions have become standard. Even students are dragged into it. . . .

With our aims, it cannot be said that we [the Communist Party government] did not show good will, moderation, patience, and sometimes there was probably too much of it. It cannot be said the Government did not honor the social agreements [made with Solidarity in 1980 at Gdansk]. We even went further. The initiative of the great national understanding was backed by the millions of Poles. It created a chance, an opportunity to deepen the system of de-

mocracy of people ruling the country, widening reforms. Those hopes failed.

Around the negotiating table there was no leadership from Solidarity. Words said in Radom and in Gdansk [strike calls and political demands from Solidarity] showed the real aims of its leadership. These aims are confirmed by everyday practice, growing aggressiveness of the extremists, clearly aiming to take apart the Polish state system.

How long can one wait for a sobering up? How long can a hand reached for accord meet a fist? I say this with a broken heart, with bitterness. It could have been different in our country. It should have been different. But if the current state had lasted longer, it would have led to a catastrophe, to absolute chaos, to poverty and starvation. . . .

I declare that today the army Council of National Salvation has been constituted, and the Council of State obeying the Polish Constitution declared a state of emergency at midnight on the territory of Poland. . . .

The New York Times, December 14, 1981, p. 16.

---

congress met and elected new members for the Polish Politburo, those congress elections were also secret and allowed real choice. By making these concessions, admitting past mistakes, and erecting a memorial to the 1970 strikers, the Polish Communist Party had clearly sought to make itself more acceptable to the political grassroots of the nation. Poland remained a nation governed by a single party, but for the time being, real debate was permitted within that party. These political changes, which were very considerable, did not lead to the solving of the underlying economic problem. Strikes continued, as did the duel between Solidarity and the government.

In October 1981 Kania was dismissed by the Politburo and was replaced as head of the party by General Wojciech Jaruzelski (b. 1923). This move brought the army to the center of Polish events. Early in December 1981 General Jaruzelski, in a surprise move, declared martial law in Poland. The army suspended civil liberties and moved against Solidarity. Many of the chief leaders of Solidarity were placed under arrest, and many other Poles were also imprisoned. In an attempt to make the action appear evenhanded, the military also arrested a number of former Communist Party leaders suspected of corruption. The imposition of martial law met some resistance from Polish workers, and several miners were killed. The United States reacted to these events by blaming the Soviet Union and placing economic sanctions against the Soviet Union and against Poland. The West European allies of the United States gave little support to the action because they feared disrupting their own economic ties to the Soviet Union. The Polish military leaders succeeded in repressing the Poles, but they were not successful in addressing the major economic problems of the country.

Suggested Readings

S. H. BEER, *British Politics in the Collectivist Age* (1965). The best discussion of twentieth-century political structures in Britain.

C. E. BLACK, *The Dynamics of Modernization: A Study in Comparative History* (1966). A useful study with implications for both European and non-European history.

Z. BRZEZINSKI, *The Soviet Block: Unity and Conflict* (1967). A discussion of Eastern Europe.

L. T. CALDWELL AND W. DIEBOLD, JR., *Soviet American Relations in the 1980's: Superpower Politics and East-West Trade* (1980). An attempt to delineate the major problems in Soviet-American relations during the present decade.

A. W. DE PORTE, *Europe Between the Superpowers: The Enduring Balance* (1979). A very important recent study.

R. EMERSON, *From Empire to Nation: The Rise to Self-assertion of Asian and African Peoples* (1960). An important discussion of the origins of decolonization.

B. B. FALL, *The Two Vietnams: A Political and Military Analysis*, rev. ed. (1967). A discussion by a journalist who spent many years on the scene.

R. HISCOCKS, *The Adenauer Era* (1966). A treatment of postwar German political development.

S. HOFFMAN (Ed.), *In Search of France* (1963). A useful collection of essays on the problems of postwar France.

R. W. HULL, *The Irish Triangle: Conflict in Northern Ireland* (1976). A thoughtful and generally dispassionate treatment of a difficult problem.

N. R. KEDDIE, *Roots of Revolution: An Interpretative History of Modern Iran* (1981). A useful treatment of an important, controversial, and ongoing event.

W. W. KULSKI, *De Gaulle and the World: The Foreign Policy of the Fifth French Republic* (1968). A straightforward treatment of De Gaulle's drive toward French and European autonomy.

W. LAQUEUR, *Europe Since Hitler* (1970). A well-balanced and comprehensive account of postwar developments.

W. LEONHARD, *The Kremlin Since Stalin* (1962). A brief but informative discussion of the post-Stalin power struggles.

W. LEONHARD, *Three Faces of Communism* (1974). An analysis of the ideological divisions within the Communist world.

R. F. LESLIE, *The History of Poland Since 1863* (1981). An excellent collection of essays that provide the background for current tensions in Poland.

D. MacRae, JR., *Parliament, Politics, and Society in France, 1946–1958* (1967). A close analysis of the turmoil of the Fourth Republic.

L. MARTIN (Ed.), *Strategic Thought in the Nuclear Age* (1979). A collection of useful essays on an issue that lies at the core of the American relationship to Western Europe.

R. MAYNE, *The Recovery of Europe, 1945–1973* (1973). A sound treatment emphasizing the movement toward economic integration.

G. MYRDAL, *Asian Drama: An Inquiry into the Poverty of Nations*, 3 vols. (1968). A significant discussion of the economic and social problems of the postcolonial world by a thoughtful economist.

M. M. POSTAN, *An Economic History of Western Europe, 1945–1964* (1967). A basic survey.

R. ROSE, *Governing Without Consensus: An Irish Perspective* (1971). An excellent exploration of the origins and development of the Irish problem.

A. SAMPSON, *The New Anatomy of Britain* (1973). A critical discussion of the British political and economic elite.

L. SCHAPIRO, *The Communist Party of the Soviet Union* (1960). An important analysis of the most important institution of Soviet Russia.

J. J. SERVAN-SCHREIBER, *The American Challenge* (trans., 1968). A French journalist's analysis of American economic influence in France.

R. SHAPLEN, *The Lost Revolution: The U.S. in Vietnam* (1965). A clear analysis of the problems that confronted the United States.

A. ULAM, *Expansion and Coexistence: The History of Soviet Foreign Policy, 1917–1967* (1968). The best one-volume treatment.

H. C. WALLICH, *Mainsprings of the German Revival* (1955). A discussion of the origins of the German economic miracle.

1062

34 Twentieth-Century States of Mind

HE PLURAL form of the word *state* in the title of this chapter is quite intentional. No single characteristic has so marked the thought of the twentieth-century West as the absence of unity and shared values. As discussed in Chapter 28, many of the traditional religious and intellectual certainties dissolved during the fifty years prior to 1914. Already philosophers, theologians, writers, and social thinkers had found themselves compelled to look for new paths of thought and new intellectual signposts. The crises that flowed from the two world wars, the Great Depression, the conflict of political ideologies, and the shadow of nuclear warfare have in turn created problems more rapidly, perhaps, than solutions can be formulated. The pressure of events, as well as the absence of intellectual cer-

Called "Les Quatre Temps" (The Four Seasons), this vast commercial center, which is visited by more than 50,000 a day, is part of a web of new suburbs which the French government has been building around Paris since the 1950s. The vast scale and futuristic architecture of this project are indicative of the prosperity and technical expertise of postwar Western Europe. [Sygma.]

tainty, has caused major thinkers to go in more different directions than ever before in the Western experience. Anxiety, fear, and even desperation have been the chief features of that search for new values.

The intellectual life of this century has taken place amidst the most extreme social and political conditions. The world wars confirmed the power of human beings not simply to do great harm to each other but actually to destroy the species. From the opening months of World War I onward, Westerners have known that they could kill scores of thousands of each other between a single rising and setting of the sun. Since 1945 the entire world has been aware of the devastating potential of nuclear weapons. Within individual nation-states, people have experienced the most extreme forms of political repression in the history of the West, and that repression has occurred under both right-wing and left-wing governments. In sheer magnitude the racial atrocities of the Nazis and the peasant slaughters under Stalin's agricultural policy were unprecedented. The economic unrest of the 1920s and 1930s brought uncertainty and in

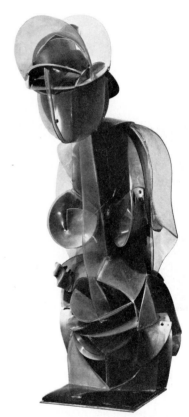

Head, by Amedeo Modigliani (1884–1920), an Italian painter and sculptor of the early twentieth century, displays the impact of nonwestern art on Europe. Its portrayal of a traditional subject of sculpture in a nontraditional manner illustrates the way in which various strains of European thought and art became transformed in the late nineteenth and early twentieth centuries. [The Tate Gallery, London.]

Torso, by Antoine Pevsner (1886–1962), was completed in 1926. By depicting the traditional theme of the human form through use of new materials from the present, it illustrates a sense of disjunction between present and past cultures and of the artist's alienation from contemporary technology. The torso, with few recognizable features, has become what almost amounts to a plastic skeleton. To some, it suggests that technology has too radically reshaped human life. [Construction in plastic and copper: $29\frac{1}{2}''$ x $11\frac{5}{8}''$. Collection, The Museum of Modern Art, New York; Katherine S. Dreier Bequest.]

many cases extreme suffering to millions of people. Throughout the colonial world the onetime subject nations began to rebel and to condemn the major values of Western civilization. The attempts by Western nations to maintain colonial dominance and influence gave rise to widespread internal criticism. During all of these developments the technology that had brought Europe and the West to its pinnacle of world domination seemed to be turning against its creators, first in the destructiveness of war and then as a danger to the environment.

Such a time of turmoil was not entirely new to the Western experience. The third and fourth centuries saw a variety of differing attempts to come to grips with the social and political disintegration of the Roman Empire. The problems of the late empire brought about major political reorganization and the conversion to Christianity. Many twentieth-century intellectuals have regarded themselves as living in no less a tumultuous period.

Extreme social and political conditions have encouraged extreme intellectual solutions. Between the wars distinguished writers and philosophers in considerable numbers supported either fascism or communism. Other writers began to identify with the aspirations of the restive colonial peoples. These intellectuals condemned both colonialism and the civilization that fostered it. A major segment of the intellectual community rejected rationalism, reason, and science as the primary guides to a better and more humane life. Equally significantly, most of the intellectual movements addressing themselves to modern problems have been very short-lived. Whereas one can see the Enlightenment as extending over most of the eighteenth century, the chief intellectual developments of this century have often sustained themselves for only a decade.

Although writers and thinkers have been testing new solutions for the new problems of this century, there has also been considerable continuity with the past. New departures have not meant total separation. For example, although rationalism and the prestige of science have been challenged, science, medicine, and rational business and government practices have touched the realities of everyday life as never before. Through World War II the most extreme modes of nationalism flourished in Europe, but since 1945 the kind of international cooperation that the *philosophes* of the eighteenth century desired has made unprecedented progress. This century has been one of ever-growing secular-

ism, but Christian theologians and religious institutions have demonstrated considerable vitality. Finally, in its very self-criticism the civilization of twentieth-century Europe has displayed its links with the past. For it has been the capacity of the West to nurture internal criticism that has permitted it to adapt itself to new problems and conditions.

The Diffusion of Knowledge and Culture

The twentieth century has witnessed unparalleled changes in the pursuit and diffusion of knowledge. The invention and institutionalization of radio, television, and computers have created an informational revolution. The communications revolution has made the world smaller and has led to a wider uniformity of culture. The daily events of politics are reported instantaneously. Different nations can share the same programming, and the same products can be advertised. Through computer science more information of all kinds can be gathered and stored. There has also been a continuation of the vast explosion of printed matter that began about the middle of the nineteenth century. In the face of radio and television, Europeans have not ceased to read and write books. This century has seen more books of every kind printed than ever before; storage is now a problem for libraries. However, the printed word has become only one mode of public communication. The sheer quantity of information now available on nearly every subject has in itself contributed to the fragmentation of public opinion and intellectual endeavor.

The increase in the quantity of information has been accompanied by a growing number of Europeans' receiving some form of university education. At the turn of the century in every major European country only a few thousand people were enrolled in the universities. By the 1970s that figure had risen to hundreds of thousands. More people from more different kinds of social and economic backgrounds were receiving higher education. Equally importantly, for the first time large numbers of women were receiving such training. This expansion in the student and educated populations has been closely related to the intense self-criticism of Europeans. Millions of citizens have become equipped with those critical intellectual

This enormous antenna, weighing 380 tons, is used by the Bell Systems to guide and communicate with satellites. By the 1970s communications satellites could transmit live broadcasts and telephone conversations around the globe. [A.T.&T. Photo Center.]

skills that in previous centuries were usually the possession of very small literate elites.

The "student experience"—that is, leaving home and settling for several years in a community composed primarily of late adolescents—has come to be widely shared. Previously only a relatively few privileged persons had known this experience. Since World War II it has become one of the major features of European and Western society. One of its most striking results was the student rebellion of the 1960s. Student uprisings began in the early 1960s in the United States and then spread into Europe and other parts of the world. Students at the Sorbonne in Paris were the leading instigators of the events in France, which in May 1968 shook the foundations of the Gaullist government. About the same time German students forced the entire

restructuring of the university system. Students were also in the forefront of the socialist experiment in Czechoslovakia, which was suppressed by the Soviet invasion in 1968. Student disturbances occurred in several of the British universities, and Italian students have been no less active. The growth in the number of students and their political activities has accounted in part for the disunity of intellectual life. As more different kinds of people come to participate in university and intellectual life, there is bound to be less unity.

The expansion in the number of students also meant a general increase in the numbers of university teachers. As a result, there have been more scientists, historians, economists, literary critics, and other professional intellectuals during the last seventy-five years than in all previous human history.

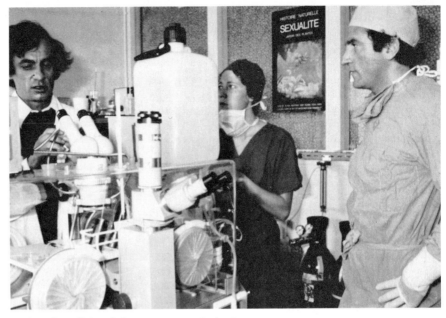

In the late twentieth century, the progress of medical technology has begun to turn the science fiction of previous eras into fact. This hospital near Paris is one of those in which doctors can now conceive human life in a laboratory test tube. An egg taken from the mother is fertilized in a test tube. The fertilized ovocyte is then placed in the mother's womb for the duration of the pregnancy. Such medical and technological breakthroughs have raised many ethical issues. [Sygma.]

In May 1968 riots erupted in Paris against the policies of the government of Charles De Gaulle. The violence of the month can be seen in the barricades made of overturned and burned-out cars. [United Press International Photo.]

Moreover, not since the early years of the Reformation have university intellectuals exerted such widespread influence. The major intellectual developments of the seventeenth, eighteenth, and nineteenth centuries took place primarily, though not entirely, outside the university. In the twentieth century the university has become the most likely home for the intellectual. And the symbol of success on the part of a writer in almost any field has been the inclusion of her or his work in the university curriculum.

All of these factors, in addition to the difficult political and social events of the century, have meant that the former unity of Western thought has become shattered. Some observers have regarded this development as opening the possibility for new creativity. For one highly significant group of twentieth-century writers the disruption of intellectual unity and the disappearance of former spiritual guideposts spawned a situation of extreme anxiety.

Existentialism

The single intellectual movement that perhaps best characterizes the predicament and mood of twentieth-century European culture is existentialism. It is symptomatic that most of the philosophers associated with this movement disagree with each other on major issues. Existentialism, which has been termed the philosophy of Europe in the twentieth century, like the modern Western mind in general, has been badly divided. The movement represents in part a continuation of the revolt against reason that began in the nineteenth century.

Friedrich Nietzsche, whose thought was considered in Chapter 28, was one of the major forerunners of existentialism. Another was the Danish writer Sören Kierkegaard (1813–1855), who wrote during the second quarter of the nineteenth century but received little attention until after World War I. He was a rebel against Hegelian philosophy and Christianity as he found them in Denmark. In works such as *Fear and Trembling* (1843), *Either/Or* (1843), and *Concluding Unscientific Postscript* (1846), he urged that the truth of Christianity could not be contained in creeds, doctrines, and church organizations. It could be grasped only in the living experience of those who faced extreme human situations. This emphasis on lived experience as the

true test of the validity of philosophy and religion has characterized most twentieth-century existential writers. Kierkegaard also criticized Hegelian philosophy and, by implication, all modes of academic rational philosophy. Its failure, he felt, was the attempt to contain all of life and human experience within abstract categories. Kierkegaard spurned this faith in the power of mere reason. "The conclusions of passion," he once declared, "are the only reliable ones."[1]

The intellectual and ethical crisis of World War I brought Kierkegaard's thought to the fore and also created new interest in Nietzsche's critique of reason. The human sacrifice and the destruction of property made many people doubt whether human beings were actually in control of their own destiny. The conflict stood as an affront to the concept of human improvement and the view of human beings as creatures of rationality. The war itself had been fought with the instruments developed through rational technology. The pride in rational human achievement that had characterized much nineteenth-century European civilization lay in ruins. The sunny faith in rational human development and advancement had not been able to withstand the extreme experiences of war.

Existential thought came to thrive in this climate and received further encouragement from the trauma of World War II. The major existential writers included the Germans Martin Heidegger (1889–1976) and Karl Jaspers (1883–1969) and the Frenchmen Jean-Paul Sartre (1905–1980) and Albert Camus (1913–1960). Their books are often very difficult and in some cases simply obscure, and the writers frequently disagreed with each other. Yet all of them in one way or another questioned the primacy of reason and scientific understanding as ways of coming to grips with the human situation. Heidegger went so far as to argue, "Thinking only begins at the point where we have come to know that Reason, glorified for centuries, is the most obstinate adversary of thinking."[2] The tradition of the Enlightenment suggested that analysis or the separation of human experience into its component parts was the proper path to understanding. Existential writers

---

[1]Quoted in Walter Kaufmann (Ed.), *Existentialism from Dostoevsky to Sartre* (Cleveland: The World Publishing Company, 1962), p. 18.

[2]Quoted in William Barrett, *Irrational Man* (Garden City, N.Y.: Doubleday, 1962), p. 20.

❧ Sartre Discusses the Character of His Existentialism

Jean-Paul Sartre, dramatist and philosopher, was the most important French contemporary existentialist. He is widely read in European and American universities. In the first paragraph of this 1946 statement Sartre asserted that all human beings must experience a sense of anguish or the most extreme anxiety when undertaking a major commitment. That anguish arises because consciously or unconsciously they are deciding whether all human beings should make the same decision. In the second paragraph Sartre argued that the existence or nonexistence of God would make no difference in human affairs. What humankind must do is to discover the character of its own situation by itself.

The existentialist frankly states that man is in anguish. His meaning is as follows—When a man commits himself to anything, fully realizing that he is not only choosing what he will be, but is thereby at the same time a legislator deciding for the whole of mankind—in such a moment a man cannot escape from the sense of complete and profound responsibility. There are many, indeed, who show no such anxiety. But we affirm that they are merely disguising their anguish or are in flight from it. Certainly, many people think that in what they are doing they commit no one but themselves to anything: and if you ask them, "What would happen if everyone did so?" they shrug their shoulders and reply, "Everyone does not do so." But in truth, one ought always to ask oneself what would happen if everyone did as one is doing; nor can one escape from that disturbing thought except by a kind of self-deception. The man who lies in self-excuse, by saying "Everyone will not do it" must be ill at ease in his conscience, for the act of lying implies the universal value which it denies. By its very disguise his anguish reveals itself.

. . . .

Existentialism is nothing else but an attempt to draw the full conclusions from a consistently atheistic position. Its intention is not in the least that of plunging men into despair. And if by despair one means—as the Christians do—any attitude of unbelief, the despair of the existentialist is something different. Existentialism is not atheist in the sense that it would exhaust itself in demonstration of the nonexistence of God. It declares, rather, that even if God existed that would make no difference from its point of view. Not that we believe God does exist, but we think that the real problem is not that of His existence; what man needs is to find himself again and to understand that nothing can save him from himself, not even a valid proof of the existence of God. In this sense existentialism is optimistic. It is a doctrine of action, and it is only by self-deception, by confusing their own despair with ours that Christians can describe us as without hope.

Jean-Paul Sartre, *Existentialism and Humanism,* trans. by Philip Mairet (London: Methuen, 1960), in Walter Kaufmann (Ed.), *Existentialism from Dostoevsky to Sartre* (New York: Meridian Books, 1956), pp. 292, 310–311.

rejected this approach. They argued that the human condition was greater than the sum of its parts and must be grasped as a whole.

The Romantic writers of the early nineteenth century had also questioned the primacy of reason, but they did so in a much less radical manner than the existentialists. The Romantics emphasized the imagination and intuition, but the existentialists tended to dwell primarily on the extremes of human experience. Death, dread, fear, and anxiety provided their themes. The titles of their works illustrate their sense of foreboding and alienation: *Being and Time* (1962) by Heidegger; *Nausea* (1938) and *Being and Nothingness* (1943) by Sartre; *The Plague* (1947) and *The Stranger* (1942) by Camus. The touchstone of philosophic truth became the experience of individual human beings under such extreme situations. The existentialists saw human beings as compelled to formulate their own ethical values rather than being able to find ethical guid-

Jean-Paul Sartre and Simone de Beauvoir (born 1908), two leading French intellectuals of the mid-century. His was a major voice of the existentialist movement, and she has written extensively on the social position, experience, and psychology of women, as well as on other social and philosophical issues. [United Press International Photo.]

ance from traditional religion, rational philosophy, intuition, or social customs. This opportunity and necessity to lay down values for oneself became the dreadful freedom of existentialist philosophy.

In large measure the existentialists were protesting against a world in which reason, technology, and the political policies of war and genocide had produced unreasonable results. Their thought reflected the uncertainty of social institutions and ethical values that existed during the era of the two world wars. However, since the 1950s their thought has become the subject of study in universities throughout the world. They will probably continue to be subjects of philosophy and literature classes, but it seems unlikely that they will again achieve their former popularity. In that respect

their somewhat lessening influence reflects the relative prosperity and material comfort achieved by a growing majority of Europeans during the last quarter century. The new generation of Europeans born after World War II has not known the experiences that gave rise to existential philosophy. Existentialism was the philosophy of the political and social crisis of Europe in the first half of the twentieth century. As the perceived crisis passed, so also has the immediate influence of existentialism.

Intellectuals and Politics

After World War I writers, philosophers, critics, and artists throughout Europe believed that a new course had to be set for their culture. Many of them thought that the political values and institutions of liberal democracy had failed. Liberalism had neither prevented the war nor achieved a minimum standard of decent living for the general population. Conservative intellectuals saw liberalism as fostering social and political unrest and undermining national greatness. Consequently considerable numbers of intellectuals during the 1920s and the 1930s felt that they must align themselves with either fascism or communism. Political ideology had become the order of the day. Art, literature, and philosophy were subordinated to political ends.

Hitler and Mussolini attracted numerous intellectuals and university teachers to support their policies. Some of these writers were little more than paid literary hacks, but others were persons of considerable standing in the academic community. However, the most important political movement to attract the allegiance of twentieth-century European intellectuals was communism. It seemed to provide a very direct manner of dealing with the social question and a vehicle for opposing the spread of fascism.

As the liberal democracies floundered in the Depression and as right-wing regimes spread across the continent, communism seemed to many people at the time a way to protect humane values. Throughout Europe students in the universities affiliated with the Communist Party. They and older intellectuals visited the Soviet Union and praised Stalin's achievements. Some of these writers did not know of Stalin's terror; others simply closed their eyes to it, somehow believing that humane ends might come from inhumane methods. During the late 1920s and the 1930s communism became little less than a substitute religion. One group of former Communists, writing after World War II, described their attraction and later disillusionment with communism in a book entitled *The God That Failed* (1949).

The Russian Revolution and its later developments led both to the attraction of intellectuals to communism and eventually to their later rejection of the ideology. In Russia the revolution had seemed to construct a new social order in the name and on the behalf of the proletariat. Under Lenin there had occurred a brief period of literary and artistic experimentation. Later the Soviet Union had also taken a lead in opposing fascism. However, the revolution had also split the ranks of socialists between communists and "democratic" socialists. Many writers and philosophers of left-wing orientation had chosen communism because of its discipline and because of its supposedly proved success in Russia. But as the brutal nature of Stalinism became known, numerous intellectuals attempted to set a distance between themselves and the Soviet experiment.

Four events proved crucial to the disillusionment of the intellectuals. These were the great public purge trials of 1936 and later, the Spanish Civil War (1936–1939), the Nazi–Soviet Pact of 1939, and the Soviet invasion of Hungary in 1956. Arthur Koestler's play *Darkness at Noon* (1940) recorded a former Communist's view of the purges. George Orwell, who had never been a Communist but who had sympathized, presented the disappointment with Stalin's policy in Spain in *Homage to Catalonia* (1938). The Nazi–Soviet Pact removed

OPEC, The Organization of Petroleum Exporting Countries, meets at its world headquarters in Vienna. Composed mostly of nonwestern states, OPEC has been extremely successful in controlling the price of petroleum since the mid-1970s. The high prices charged for oil and the continuing dependence of the industrialized nations on imported fuel has led to an enormous transfer of funds from the West to the oil-producing countries. [Sygma.]

the image of Stalin as an opponent of fascism. Jean-Paul Sartre long put faith in the Soviet Union, but the Hungarian invasion cooled his ardor.

Yet disillusionment with the Soviet Union or with Stalin did not in all cases mean disillusionment with Marxism or with a radical socialist critique of European society. Some writers and social critics looked to the establishment of alternative communist governments based on non-Soviet modes. During the decade after World War II Yugoslavia provided such a different model. Since the late 1950s radical students and intellectuals have looked for inspiration to the Chinese Revolution. Still other groups have hoped for the development of a European Marxist system. Among the more important contributors to this non-Soviet tradition was the Italian Communist Antonio Gramsci (1891–1937) and his work *Letters from Prison* (published posthumously in 1947). The thought of such non-Soviet Communists has become very important to West European Communist parties, such as that of Italy, which hope to gain office democratically.

Another mode of Marxist accommodation within mid-twentieth-century European thought has been a redefinition of the basic message of Marx himself. During the 1930s a considerable body of previously unprinted essays by Marx was published. These books and articles are quite abstract and philosophical and were written by Marx before *The Communist Manifesto* of 1848. They make the "young Marx" appear to belong more nearly to the humanist than to the revolutionary tradition of European thought. Since World War II these works, including *Philosophic Manuscripts of 1844* and *German Ideology,* have been widely read. Today many people are more familiar with them than with the *Manifesto* or *Capital.* The writings of young Marx have allowed many people to consider themselves sympathetic to Marxism without also seeing themselves as revolutionaries or supporters of the Soviet Union.

In effect, by the last quarter of this century Marxism and even communism have become fragmented. Politically their supporters stand divided in loyalty to the differing models of the Soviet Union, China, Yugoslavia, and others in the non-European world. Ideologically there are divisions among Soviet ideologues, Maoists, and the more independent thinkers of Western Europe. Yet in its various forms Marxism still remains probably the single most influential tradition of political thought in Europe today. Even for people who may not wish a communist state, Marxism has come to provide a vehicle for the criticism of contemporary European society. Moreover the impact of various modes of Marxist thought in the non-European world may now constitute the most important Western influence in the postcolonial age.

The Christian Heritage

In most ways Christianity has continued to be hard-pressed during the twentieth century. Material prosperity and political ideologies have replaced religious faith as the dominant factors in many people's lives. However, despite their loss of much popular support and former legal privileges, the Christian churches still exercise considerable social and political influence. In Germany the churches were one of the few major institutions not wholly conquered by the Nazis. Lutheran clergymen, such as Martin Niemöller and Dietrich Bonhoeffer, were leaders of the opposition to Hitler. After the war, in Poland and elsewhere in Eastern Europe the Roman Catholic Church actively opposed the influence of communism. In western Europe religious affiliation provided much of the initial basis for the Christian Democratic parties. Across the continent the churches have raised critical questions about colonialism, nuclear weapons, human rights, and other moral issues. Consequently, in the most secular of all ages the church has affected numerous issues of state.

A theological revival took place during the first half of the century. Nineteenth-century theologians had frequently softened the concept of sin and had tended to portray human nature as not very far removed from the divine. The horror of World War I destroyed that optimistic faith. Many Europeans felt that evil had stalked the continent.

The most important Christian response to this experience was the theology of Karl Barth (1886–1968). In 1919 this Swiss pastor published *A Commentary on the Epistle to the Romans,* which reemphasized the transcendence of God and the dependence of humankind on the divine. Barth portrayed God as wholly other than, and different from, humankind. In a sense Barth was returning to the Reformation theology of Luther, but the work of Kierkegaard had profoundly influenced his reading of the reformer. Barth, like the Danish writer, regarded the lived experience of men and women as the best testimony to the truth of his theology. Those extreme moments of life described by Kierkegaard provided the basis for a real knowl-

Contemporary architecture as demonstrated by the interior of the Church of Notre Dame at Le Raincy near Paris (1922), designed by Auguste Perret (1874–1954). It is a high point in the new technology of architectural use of reinforced concrete. [French Cultural Services.]

edge of humankind's need for God. This view totally challenged much nineteenth-century writing about human nature. Barth's theology, which became known as *neo-orthodoxy,* proved to be very influential throughout the West in the wake of new political disasters and human suffering.

Liberal theology, however, was not swept away by neo-orthodoxy. The German–American Paul Tillich (1886–1965) was the most important liberal theologian. He looked to a theology of culture and tended to regard religion as a human rather than a divine phenomenon. Whereas Barth saw God as dwelling outside humankind, Tillich believed that evidence of the divine had to be sought from within human nature and human culture. Other liberal theologians, such as Rudolf Bultmann

(1884–1976), continued to work out the problems of naturalism and supernaturalism that had plagued earlier writers. Bultmann's major writing took place prior to World War II but was popularized thereafter in Anglican Bishop John Robinson's *Honest to God* (1963). Another liberal Christian writer from Britain, C. S. Lewis (1878–1963), attracted millions of readers during and after World War II. He was a layman and his books were often in the form of letters or short stories. His most famous work is *The Screwtape Letters* (1942).

Perhaps the most significant postwar religious departures occurred within the Roman Catholic Church. Pope John XXIII (1958–1963) undertook the most extensive changes to occur in Catholicism for over a century and some would say since the

The Church of the Holy Family in Barcelona is a major work of Spanish architect Antonio Gaudi (1852–1926). Rounded, growing forms characterize this structure, and it is still far from complete. [Spanish National Tourist Office, New York.]

Pope Paul VI (1963–1978) at the altar of Saint Peter's in Rome presides over a session of the Second Vatican Council. The gathering initiated more changes in the Roman Catholic Church than had any development since the Council of Trent in the sixteenth century. [Archivio Fotografico, Musei Vaticani.]

caused many men and women to leave the priesthood and religious orders, and many of the laity deeply resented the policy on family planning.

Paul VI died in 1978, as did John Paul I, his immediate successor, whose reign lasted only thirty-four days. The second new pope of 1978 was Karl Wojtyla of Poland, the former archbishop of Cracow. John Paul II was the youngest pope to be elected in over a century. The College of Cardinals

John Paul II became pope October 17, 1978 after the brief thirty-four-day reign of John Paul I. In more than one way the choice of the new pope is epoch-making. At 58 he is the youngest pontiff since Pius IX. More important, he is the first non-Italian to hold the position since the sixteenth century; and, being Polish, he brings personal experience with the eastern, communist-dominated areas of Europe to the papacy for the first time. [United Press International Photo.]

Council of Trent in the sixteenth century. In 1959 Pope John summoned the twenty-first ecumenical council of the church to be called since the series started under the emperor Constantine in the fourth century. It was known as Vatican II. He died before it had completed its work; but his successor, Pope Paul VI, continued the council, which met between 1962 and 1965. Among the numerous changes in liturgy, the Mass became celebrated in the vernacular. Free relations were established with other Christian denominations. More power was shared with bishops. Pope Paul also appointed a number of cardinals from nations of the former colonial world. However, after having taken these very liberal moves, the pope firmly upheld the celibacy of priests and maintained the church's prohibition on contraception. The former position

✑ Pope John Paul II Discusses the Role of Women and Work

In the encyclical "On Human Work," issued in 1981, Pope John Paul II examined the character of work and proper labor relations as understood by the Roman Catholic Church. In the context of a plea for the dignity of labor and the necessity for social justice, the pope set forth his views on the issue of women in the work-place. Although recognizing the necessity for many women to work, the pope emphasized the view of the church that women should first and foremost fulfill their roles in the life of the home and family. The double purpose of the encyclical—the plea for social justice and the call for a somewhat traditional role for women—symbolizes the hallmark of this papacy, that is, liberalism in some areas and traditionalism in others.

Experience confirms that there must be a social re-evaluation of the mother's role, of the toil connected with it and of the need that children have for care, love and affection in order that they may develop into responsible, morally and religiously mature and psychologically stable persons. It will redound to the credit of society to make it possible for a mother—without inhibiting her freedom, without psychological or practical discrimination and without penalizing her as compared with other women—to devote herself to taking care of her children and educating them in accordance with their needs, which vary with age.

Having to abandon these tasks in order to take up paid work outside the home is wrong from the point of view of the good of society and of the family when it contradicts or hinders these primary goals of the mission of a mother.

In this context it should be emphasized that, on a more general level, the whole labor process must be organized and adapted in such a way as to respect the requirements of the person and his or her forms of life, above all life in the home, taking into account the individual's age and sex. It is a fact that in many societies women work in nearly every sector of life.

But it is fitting that they should be able to fulfill their tasks in accordance with their own nature, without being discriminated against and without being excluded from jobs for which they are capable, but also without lack of respect for their family aspirations and for their specific role in contributing, together with men, to the good of society. The true advancement of women requires that labor should be structured in such a way that women do not have to pay for that advancement by abandoning what is specific to them and at the expense of the family, in which women as mothers have an irreplaceable role.

The New York Times, September 16, 1981, p. D26

---

clearly anticipated a long reign in which the changes made in the church during the past quarter of a century might be consolidated. John Paul II, who survived an assassination attempt in 1981, has pursued a three-pronged policy. He has reasserted a traditional policy in regard to the priesthood and the nature of family life. He has stressed the authority of the papacy in doctrinal matters and has attempted to limit doctrinal and liturgical experiment on the part of those Catholics regarded as either exceedingly liberal or conservative. Finally, he has encouraged the expansion of the church in the non-Western world. In this last effort he has stressed the need for social justice while at the same time limiting the political activity

of priests. All of these policies have provoked controversy within the church and between the church and the world. These policies have also commanded broad support in the church, largely because of the attractive and charismatic personal qualities of John Paul II.

Toward the Twenty-first Century

A century ago a book like this one might have concluded with a statement of the superiority of Western over all other cultures. In that hundred years the position of Europe in power politics has changed. The century has seen vast destruction

Recumbent Figure, by the English sculptor Henry Moore (born 1898), uses basic shapes and materials in a traditional manner, but it exemplifies the twentieth-century search for new perspectives on human nature and on physical nature. Although the statue is clearly modern, its "eroded" form suggests less separation from past culture than do many contemporary works. [*The Tate Gallery, London.*]

and inhumanity. Consequently this volume must conclude with an affirmation of the continuity of Western culture with its past, its potential for new creativity, and its capacity for new interaction with other cultures.

Europeans have not outgrown their history. Many of the formative influences traced in this volume continue to hold sway. For some observers technology may appear to be an enemy and a threat to the environment, but science touches in a positive manner the lives of more people than might have been imagined even fifty years ago.

And it will be from scientific understanding that the problems of the environment and of resource shortages will be solved. Although many intellectuals have praised the irrational, rationalism in the processes of everyday life has never been more present, and the use of reason still promises the best hope to humankind. Since World War II the problems of constitutional order and human rights have continued to be major concerns of political life and discussion. Within both communist and noncommunist Europe the spirit of criticism still thrives, though in very different ways.

Chariot, by the Italian sculptor Alberto Giacometti (1901–1966), was completed in 1950 and displays the questioning spirit of the years immediately after World War II. It brings man and the machine together but suggests the idea of the diminution of humankind by forces larger than itself in the twentieth century. [Bronze, 57″ x 26⅛″. Collection, The Museum of Modern Art, New York.]

These persistent features of European life have not assured that its civilization, as well as the results flowing from it, will be morally good, but they have meant that it has possessed in itself the possibility of correcting itself and of raising questions about what are the good life and the good society. The possibility of asking those questions is necessary before the desired improvement and reform can be attained. Perhaps the chief carriers of Western culture today are those within its midst who most criticize it and demand that it justify itself.

Suggested Readings

W. M. ABBOTT (Ed.), *The Documents of Vatican II* (1966). A useful way of looking at the changes in contemporary Catholicism.

R. ARON, *The Opium of the Intellectuals* (1957). A critical discussion of Communism and the intellectual community.

B. BARBER, *Science and the Social Order* (1952). A good introduction to the institutional impact of science in this century.

W. BARRETT, *Irrational Man* (1958). A sound treatment of existentialism in its broader intellectual context.

F. L. BAUMER, *Modern European Thought: Continuity and Change in Ideas, 1600–1950* (1977). Excellent chapters on this century.

R. CROSSMAN (Ed.), *The God That Failed* (1949). Essays from former Communist intellectuals.

W. P. DIZARD, *Television: A World Review* (1966). A useful discussion of an important topic.

D. FLEMING AND B. BAILYN (Eds.), *The Intellectual Migration: Europe and America, 1930–1960* (1969). An important collection of essays on the migration of European intellectuals to the United States largely due to the political situation in twentieth-century Europe.

E. FROMM (Ed.), *Socialist Humanism: An International Symposium* (1965). Essays dealing with humanistic approaches to Marxism.

H. S. HUGHES, *The Obstructed Path: French Social Thought in the Years of Desperation, 1930–1960* (1968). A book that well illustrates the fragmentation of twentieth-century thought.

M. JAY, *The Dialectical Imagination* (1973). An important work on the development of Marxist thought among German intellectuals.

W. KAUFMANN (Ed.), *Existentialism from Dostoevsky to Sartre* (1956). An excellent introduction to this movement of thought.

J. PASSMORE, *A Hundred Years of Philosophy* (1968). An exceptionally fine one-volume history.

S. P. SCHILLING, *Contemporary Continental Theologians* (1966). A basic survey of modern theology.

R. N. STROMBERG, *After Everything: Western Intellectual History Since 1945* (1975). A lively and thoughtful account of a very difficult subject.

W. WAGAR (Ed.), *European Intellectual History Since Darwin and Marx* (1966). A collection of high-quality essays.

W. WAGAR (Ed.), *Science, Faith, and Man: European Thought Since 1914* (1968). A collection of documents with good introductions.

J. D. WILKINSON, *The Intellectual Resistance in Europe* (1981). An important treatment of intellectuals who resisted the Nazis.

R. WOHL, *The Generation of 1914* (1979). A major work that considers the impact of World War I on European intellectual life.

Appendix
Some Prominent Emperors, Kings, and Popes

ROMAN EMPIRE

Augustus	27 B.C.–A.D. 14	Trajan	98–117	Severus Alexander	222–235
Tiberius	14– 37	Hadrian	117–138	Philip the Arab	244–249
Caligula	37– 41	Antoninus Pius	138–161	Decius	249–251
Claudius	41– 54	Marcus Aurelius	161–180	Valerian	253–260
Nero	54– 68	Commodus	180–193	Gallienus	260–268
Vespasian	69– 79	Septimius Severus	193–211	Aurelian	270–275
Titus	79– 81	Caracalla	211–217	Diocletian	284–286
Domitian	81– 96	Elagabalus	218–222		

WEST		EAST		WEST		EAST	
Maximian	286–305	Diocletian	284–305	Gratian	375–383		
Constantius	305–306	Galerius	305–311	Valentinian II	383–392		
		Maximius	308–313	Theodosius	394–395	Theodosius	379–395
		Licinius	308–324	Honorius	395–423	Arcadius	393–408
Constantine	308–337	Constantine	324–337			Theodosius II	408–450
Maxentius	307–312			Valentinian III	425–455	Marcian	450–457
Constantine II	337–340					Leo	457–474
Constans	337–350			Romulus	475–476	Zeno	474–491
Constantius II	351–361	Constantius II	337–361			Anastasius	491–518
Julian	360–363	Julian	361–363			Justin	518–527
Jovian	363–364	Jovian	363–364			Justinian	527–565
Valentinian	364–375	Valens	364–378				

i

CAROLINGIAN KINGDOM

Pepin, Mayor of the Palace	680–714	Charlemagne and Carloman, Joint Kings	768–771
Charles Martel, Mayor of the Palace	715–741	Charlemagne, King	771–814
Pepin the Short, Mayor of the Palace	741–751	Charlemagne, Emperor	800–814
Pepin the Short, King	751–768	Louis the Pious, Emperor	814–840

WEST FRANKS

Charles the Bald	840–877
Louis II the Stammerer	877–879
Louis III	879–882
Carloman	879–884

LOTHARINGIA

Lothar	840–855
Louis II	855–875
Charles	855–863
Lothar II	855–869

EAST FRANKS

Louis the German	840–876
Carloman	876–880
Louis	876–882
Charles the Fat	884–887

HOLY ROMAN EMPIRE

SAXONS

Henry the Fowler	919–936
Otto I	962–973
Otto II	973–983
Otto III	983–1002

SALIANS

Conrad II	1024–1039
Henry III	1039–1056
Henry IV	1056–1106
Henry V	1106–1125
Lothar II	1125–1137

HOHENSTAUFENS

Frederick I Barbarossa	1152–1190
Henry IV	1190–1197
Philip of Swabia	1198–1208
Otto IV (*Welf*)	1198–1215
Frederick II	1215–1250
Conrad IV	1250–1254

LUXEMBURG, HAPSBURG, AND OTHER DYNASTIES

Rudolf of Hapsburg	1273–1291
Adolph of Nassau	1292–1298
Albert of Austria	1298–1308
Henry VII of Luxemburg	1308–1313
Ludwig IV of Bavaria	1314–1347
Charles IV	1347–1378
Wenceslas	1378–1400
Rupert	1400–1410
Sigismund	1410–1437

HAPSBURGS

Frederick III	1440–1493
Maximilian I	1493–1519
Charles V	1519–1556
Ferdinand I	1556–1564
Maximilian II	1564–1576
Rudolf II	1576–1612
Matthias	1612–1619
Ferdinand II	1619–1637
Ferdinand III	1637–1657
Leopold I	1658–1705
Joseph I	1705–1711
Charles VI	1711–1740
Charles VII	1742–1745
Francis I	1745–1765
Joseph II	1765–1790
Leopold II	1790–1792
Francis II	1792–1806

THE PAPACY

Leo I	440– 461	Innocent III	1198–1216	Julius II	1503–1513	Pius IX	1846–1878
Gregory I	590– 604	Gregory IX	1227–1241	Leo X	1513–1521	Leo XIII	1878–1903
Nicholas I	858– 867	Boniface VIII	1294–1303	Adrian VI	1522–1523	Pius X	1903–1914
Silvester II	999–1003	John XXII	1316–1334	Clement VII	1523–1534	Benedict XV	1914–1922
Leo IX	1049–1054	Gregory XI	1370–1378	Paul III	1534–1549	Pius XI	1922–1939
Nicholas II	1058–1061	Martin V	1417–1431	Paul IV	1555–1559	Pius XII	1939–1958
Gregory VII	1073–1085	Eugenius IV	1431–1447	Pius V	1566–1572	John XXIII	1958–1963
Urban II	1088–1099	Nicholas V	1447–1455	Gregory XIII	1572–1585	Paul VI	1963–1978
Paschal II	1099–1118	Pius II	1458–1464	Pius VII	1800–1823	John Paul I	1978
Alexander III	1159–1181	Alexander VI	1492–1503	Gregory XVI	1831–1846	John Paul II	1978–

ENGLAND

ANGLO-SAXONS

Alfred the Great	871– 900
Ethelred the Unready	978–1016
Canute (*Danish*)	1016–1035
Harold I	1035–1040
Hardicanute	1040–1042
Edward the Confessor	1042–1066
Harold II	1066

NORMANS

William the Conqueror	1066–1087
William II	1087–1100
Henry I	1100–1135
Stephen	1135–1154

ANGEVINS

Henry II	1154–1189
Richard I	1189–1199
John	1199–1216
Henry III	1216–1272
Edward I	1272–1307
Edward II	1307–1327
Edward III	1327–1377
Richard II	1377–1399

HOUSES OF LANCASTER AND YORK

Henry IV	1399–1413
Henry V	1413–1422
Henry VI	1422–1461
Edward IV	1461–1483
Edward V	1483
Richard III	1483–1485

TUDORS

Henry VII	1485–1509
Henry VIII	1509–1547
Edward VI	1547–1553
Mary I	1553–1558
Elizabeth I	1558–1603

STUARTS

James I	1603–1625
Charles I	1625–1649
Charles II	1660–1685
James II	1685–1688
William III and Mary II	1689–1694
William III alone	1694–1702
Anne	1702–1714

HANOVERIANS (from 1917, WINDSORS)

George I	1714–1727
George II	1727–1760
George III	1760–1820
George IV	1820–1830
William IV	1830–1837
Victoria	1837–1901
Edward VII	1901–1910
George V	1910–1936
Edward VIII	1936
George VI	1936–1952
Elizabeth II	1952–

FRANCE

CAPETIANS

Hugh Capet	987– 996
Robert II the Pious	996–1031
Henry I	1031–1060
Philip I	1060–1108
Louis VI	1108–1137
Louis VII	1137–1180
Philip II Augustus	1180–1223
Louis VIII	1223–1226
Louis IX	1226–1270
Philip III	1270–1285
Philip IV	1285–1314
Louis X	1314–1316
Philip V	1316–1322
Charles IV	1322–1328

VALOIS

Philip VI	1328–1350
John	1350–1364
Charles V	1364–1380
Charles VI	1380–1422
Charles VII	1422–1461
Louis XI	1461–1483
Charles VIII	1483–1498
Louis XII	1498–1515
Francis I	1515–1547
Henry II	1547–1559
Francis II	1559–1560
Charles IX	1560–1574
Henry III	1574–1589

BOURBONS

Henry IV	1589–1610
Louis XIII	1610–1643
Louis XIV	1643–1715
Louis XV	1715–1774
Louis XVI	1774–1792

POST 1792

Napoleon I, Emperor	1804–1814
Louis XVIII (*Bourbon*)	1814–1824
Charles X (*Bourbon*)	1824–1830
Louis Philippe (*Bourbon-Orléans*)	1830–1848
Napoleon III, Emperor	1851–1870

ITALY

Victor Emmanuel II	1861–1878	Victor Emmanuel II	1900–1946
Humbert I	1878–1900	Humbert II	1946

SPAIN

		HAPSBURGS		BOURBONS			
Ferdinand and	1479–1516	Philip I	1504–1506	Philip V	1700–1746	Ferdinand VII (restored)	1814–1833
Isabella	1479–1504	Charles I (Holy Roman Emperor as Charles V) 1506–1556		Ferdinand VI	1746–1759	Isabella II	1833–1868
				Charles III	1759–1788	Amadeo	1870–1873
				Charles IV	1788–1808	Alfonso XII	1874–1885
		Philip II	1556–1598	Ferdinand VII	1808	Alfonso XIII	1886–1931
		Philip III	1598–1621	Joseph Bonaparte		Juan Carlos I	1975–
		Philip IV	1621–1665		1808–1813		
		Charles II	1665–1700				

AUSTRIA AND AUSTRIA-HUNGARY

(Until 1806 all except Maria Theresa were also Holy Roman Emperors.)

Maximilian I, Archduke	1493–1519	Maximilian II	1564–1576	Leopold I	1658–1705	Leopold II	1790–1792
		Rudolf II	1576–1612	Joseph I	1705–1711	Francis II	1792–1835
Charles I (Emperor as Charles V)	1519–1556	Matthias	1612–1619	Charles VI	1711–1740	Ferdinand I	1835–1848
		Ferdinand II	1619–1637	Maria Theresa	1740–1780	Francis Joseph	1848–1916
Ferdinand I	1556–1564	Ferdinand III	1637–1657	Joseph II	1780–1790	Charles I	1916–1918

PRUSSIA AND GERMANY

HOHENZOLLERNS

Frederick William the Great Elector	1640–1688	Frederick II the Great	1740–1786	William I	1861–1888
Frederick I	1701–1713	Frederick William II	1786–1797	Frederick III	1888
Frederick William I	1713–1740	Frederick William III	1797–1840	William II	1888–1918
		Frederick William IV	1840–1861		

RUSSIA

		ROMANOVS			
Ivan III	1462–1505				
Basil III	1505–1533				
Ivan IV the Terrible	1533–1584	Michael	1613–1645	Elizabeth	1741–1762
Theodore I	1584–1598	Alexius	1645–1676	Peter III	1762
Boris Godunov	1598–1605	Theodore III	1676–1682	Catherine II the Great	1762–1796
Theodore II	1605	Ivan IV and Peter I	1682–1689	Paul	1796–1801
Basil IV	1606–1610	Peter I the Great alone 1689–1725		Alexander I	1801–1825
				Nicholas I	1825–1855
		Catherine I	1725–1727	Alexander II	1855–1881
		Peter II	1727–1730	Alexander III	1881–1894
		Anna	1730–1740	Nicholas II	1894–1917
		Ivan VI	1740–1741		

Index